SO-AIY-042

This book may be kept

UNDERSTANDING PUBLIC OPINION

301.154
M 14 u
3 1 2 5 3

March 1954

Copyright 1952 by The Macmillan Company

All rights reserved—no part of this book may be reproduced in any form without permission in writing from the publisher, except by a reviewer who wishes to quote brief passages in connection with a review written for inclusion in magazine or newspaper.

PRINTED IN THE UNITED STATES OF AMERICA

First printing

Carl A. Rudisill Library
LENOIR RHYNE COLLEGE

interpretation of such serious phenomena as increases in racial or other forms of prejudice, waves of religious revivalism, stock-market hysteria, war scares, and red witch hunts. A few points, all to be developed in subsequent chapters, over which it is worth while for the reader to ponder at the outset, include the following:

1. The point already made; namely, that *social phenomena don't just happen.* For every effect there is a cause. Social psychological relationships *do* exist between forms of behavior in different spheres of human activity. The causes of wars, depressions, and social movements of all kinds seem very clear as presented in logical sequence in chapters of a historical work. Differences of opinion, of course, exist, causing some cynics to dismiss history as "bunk" or as "lies mutually agreed upon." There may be no way ever to determine with absolute certainty whose analysis is correct, and journalistic students of public opinion cannot be expected to be more omniscient than philosophers and social scientists. In their reportorial, as well as personal search for truth, however, they are more likely to approximate its discovery if they learn early and never forget that explanations do exist.

2. *Such a tolerant point of view is not tantamount to approval of every heretical or otherwise different point of view.* One can, for instance, understand why the German people accepted the propaganda of Hitler and Goebbels without liking naziism any better. It is not maudlin sentimentalism to recognize the causes of a child's delinquent behavior or of adult criminality; rather, such understanding is the first step toward formation of a realistic approach toward solution. The newsgatherer who does his best to be open-minded, tolerant, and shockproof does not have to abandon his own biases any more than does the psychiatrist who cultivates the same traits. There is, however, a difference between blind bigotry and personal preferences as a result of upbringing, experience, or enlightened self-interest. The smartest people are those with the maximum amount of insight; they are the least likely to "kid" themselves as to the causes of their own likes and dislikes.

3. *The majority is not always right.* History is replete with examples of horrible mistakes which have been made with overwhelming popular approval. In many such cases ignorance was the cause, as when men believed for centuries that the world is flat, or for centuries longer continued to die needlessly until the germ's responsibility for

illness was discovered. Sometimes an event can cause a majority to change its mind almost instantaneously, as was the case with millions of American isolationists Dec. 7, 1941. Even when facts are available, however, what often seems in retrospect to have been inexcusably bad behavior may persist for generations or centuries.

4. Another way of stating virtually the same point is: *rightness or wrongness is no criterion by which to evaluate the popularity of any idea.* People are not stupid on purpose, and even the cruelest and most unjust behavior is motivated. There is not an editor or other so-called moulder of public opinion who has not at some time observed an old idea suddenly "catch on," perhaps an idea of which he was the originator. Why? Because of the way it has been reworded? Because of the prestige of its new advocates? Because public susceptibilities— "the times"—have changed? If the idea is right, it was just as right when first propounded as when it succeeds in winning converts; and the same is true if the idea is wrong. Throughout history every great man was hated by a large number of his contemporaries. Every important new idea was opposed vigorously. Nations time and time again have followed foolish, even disastrous, albeit popular, policies. Majorities have been taken in by quack nostrums, and hysteria has been epidemic many times in every century, possibly every decade. It is a sobering experience to read history and to discover how often great leaders and groups of people have been mistaken. There is no reason to believe that present-day man is any wiser than his ancestors; to scholars of the future much of what we consider advanced enlightenment doubtless will seem almost savage.

5. To repeat and summarize, then, *the proper concern of the student of public opinion should be its "why."* That is the aspect of the subject with which this book is primarily concerned. Some attention will be given to methods of determining the *what* of public opinion, for it is not an infrequent assignment to be asked to survey local opinion on some newsworthy matter. Almost every newsgatherer at some time in his career writes, "Public opinion here today ————." Consideration also will be given propaganda devices as perfected by public relations counsel, pressure groups and other would-be moulders of public opinion. Primary interest, however, is not in the propaganda seed that is sown but in the soil into which it falls. To state the author's intention in another way: if the issue were maintaining American

military forces in X country, the concern would not be with who or how many favor or disfavor the proposal. Neither would it be whether the idea is good or bad. Rather, it would be: why do those who favor the proposal do so? Why do others oppose it? Even the existence of the Deity can be submitted to the same test. It is no explanation to say that people believe in God because there is a God. His existence could be denied; or there could be belief in his existence even though he were nonexistent.

6. A prime asset of a student of public opinion is humility. As a separate branch of social psychology, the study of public opinion is very new. *Public Opinion Quarterly* has been published only since January, 1937. The American Association for Public Opinion Research, whose official publication the *Quarterly* now is, was organized in 1947. The Institute for Propaganda Analysis lasted from October, 1937 to just after Pearl Harbor. The *International Journal of Public Opinion and Attitude Research* began publication in March, 1947. Books and magazine articles are not too abundant in comparison with the "literature" in other fields. Furthermore, altogether too much of what passes as early research in this field has been in the form of panacea-hunting. Too many social scientists have been too eager to get on any bandwagon which might possibly be headed in the direction of something statistically valid. First, propaganda analysis was all the rage, and many who should have known better acted and talked as though all the riddles of collective social behavior would be solved if it became possible to pin the proper labels on every word, spoken or written, intended to influence the thought or behavior of anyone other than its originator. As a result "propaganda" became a bogey word and skepticism became so widespread that every persuasive argument, no matter how valid, was suspect. The emotional disbelief so widespread in America after war broke out in Europe in 1939 was as unrealistic and dangerous as was the gullibility of 1914 to 1917.

After Pearl Harbor caused propaganda analysis to lose favor, there was a scholarly rush to public opinion polling as the clue to what makes people tick and as the way to prove that the social sciences can be as exact as the physical sciences. The results of the election on Nov. 2, 1948 were a tremendous blow to the easy-answer scholars. Undaunted, however, they revised their second semester syllabi to shift the emphasis to the new cult of content analysis. As this book is being written faith in this new "science" is growing among those who formerly worshipped at the shrines of propaganda analysis and public opinion polling. The idea is that if you can count the number of favorable and unfavorable references in any written piece you can predict the total effect upon a reader. To this author it seems as unrealistic to ride this hobby so hard as it did to go "all-out" for its predecessor fads. Propaganda analysis is good; so is polling; so is content analysis, but perfecting any or all of them will not prove the social sciences are exact. Nor will the knowledge of public opinion be complete. In fact, the task of coming to grips with the really important aspects of that subject still will be neglected.

Maybe it never will be possible to apply statistical methods for the ultimate answers in this field. Maybe the working principles always will be hypotheses, as in much of psychiatry. They will be hypotheses, however, capable of empirical testing. Collective social behavior can be studied and *it is utterly fallacious to believe that the study of public opinion can be separated from that of the broader subject of why men behave as human beings.* Similar causes can be observed to be followed by similar effects. There remains a great deal to be done in applying general psychological and sociological knowledge to this important aspect of the field as a whole. Much of the effort which goes into trying to find a magic formula by which to comprehend public opinion might better be spent in testing, through observation and experimentation, the findings of the experimental psychological laboratory, the anthropologist's field notes, and the sociologist's observations. This book is in considerable part an attempt to do so for the benefit of the newspaperman who deals with the superficialities of social behavior and would do a better job if he could see a little deeper beneath the surface, and for the benefit of newspaper readers.

TABLE OF CONTENTS

PART I

DEFINITIONS AND
FUNDAMENTAL PRINCIPLES

CHAPTER ONE

THE NATURE OF PUBLIC OPINION

*The nature of public opinion makes it as difficult for news-
papermen as for pollsters to determine what and/or why it is.*

Straw Votes

After Nov. 2, 1948 there was a tremendous beating of
journalistic as well as pollsters' breasts. In a message to the annual
Sigma Delta Chi convention November 11 at Milwaukee, Roy A.
Roberts, long-time general manager of the Kansas City *Star*, expressed the chastened viewpoint which became prevalent: "We didn't
do the job of old fashioned reporting we should have done." The
reason? To quote Mr. Roberts further:

"Just as Mr. Dewey and his strategy board accepted the early polls
and planned their campaign accordingly, to their sorrow, so, I am
afraid, newspapers complacently accepted the verdict as a certainty
and didn't dig in as they would have done otherwise to keep an accurate line on what the mass mind was thinking and how it was reacting to the campaign. They thought the election was in the bag and
overlooked the hole in the bag."

Similarly, in a widely quoted letter to his editor, James Reston of
the New York *Times,* confessed:

"In a way our failure was not unlike Mr. Dewey's; we overestimated the tangibles and underestimated intangibles; we relied too
much on techniques of reporting which are no longer foolproof; just
as he was too isolated with other politicians, so we were too isolated
with other reporters; and we, too, were far too impressed by the tidy
statistics of the polls."

Reston chided himself and fellow reporters for not "wandering
around talking to the people," of which practice *Life* editorialized in

[3]

its November 15 issue: "Even the few correspondents who got off the campaign trains and talked with the people had mental blinders that prevented them from seeing what was to their right and to their left." Such confessions, and the many others of which they were typical, undoubtedly were good for the collective journalistic soul. Left unchallenged by them, however, was the basic assumption that the outcome of the 1948 presidential election *could* have been forecast correctly—and by political reporters. It was just laziness on their part and what Roberts called "politis" on the part of their superiors which caused the colossal error of prediction.

Among the professional pollsters—Gallup, Roper, Crossley and the others who had convinced themselves after 1936 and 1940 and 1944 that they had mastered the proper forecasting techniques—the alibi was similar. In essence they apologized thusly: we got lazy and stopped counting noses a couple of months before the voting took place, and we incorrectly assumed that the admittedly large number of undecided voters at that time would divide about equally and not affect the outcome materially. Everyone also joined in the paeans of praise for Harry Truman for having conducted a whirlwind campaign which kept winning him votes right up to the time the ballot boxes were closed.

Thus two groups vitally concerned—the newspapermen and the pollsters—bravely took it "on the chin" with implied promises that "next time it will be different." The spirit was well demonstrated by Elmo Roper of *Fortune* on Dec. 6, 1948, in an address before the Economic club of Detroit when he recalled General Stilwell's comments after the American and British defeat in Burma. As Roper remembered it, Stilwell's statement "ran something like this: 'I claim we took a helluva beating. We got run out of Burma and it's humiliating as hell.' " Roper continued, "Now we come to the part that I would like to suggest adding as equally applicable here, and this is, 'I think we ought to find out what caused it and go back and retake it!' That expresses my thought now."

Because of the attention, involving anger, chagrin, amusement and admiration for the "comeback" spirit, directed at the pollsters and journalists, the feelings of a third group with a tremendous interest in the matter generally were overlooked. Comprising that group are thousands of social scientists who for more than a decade before the fatal November 2 had been going "all out" in support of research in polling techniques. The stake of these technicians was to establish with industry and with government administrators that it is possible to measure human thought and behavior with somewhat the same exactness with which experiments are conducted by the physical scientists. To do so would be to prove that the social sciences really are scientific.

To both the pollsters and the scholars, political straw votes have been important primarily because of the opportunity the subsequent elections provided of testing the accuracy of their techniques. If the straws were successful it was concluded that other polls also are reliable as indices to public opinion. There has been nothing modest about polling enthusiasts in the claims they have made for themselves. "This job," George Gallup once said, "almost makes you an evangelist for democracy." By this, according to Volta Torrey in the Oct. 24, 1943, issue of *PM,* he meant that his polls usually showed the public to be ahead of Congress on most important matters. Torrey quoted Gallup as follows: "The will of the people cannot be misread now as it was after the last war. This is because it is now possible to discover opinion on an issue apart from a personality. If there had been a Gallup poll in 1920, it would have shown (a) that Harding would win, but (b) that a majority of the people were for the League of Nations."

In this attitude the professional pollsters have had the backing of a large body of social scientists. Typical of their writings is the following from an article, "Do the Polls Serve Democracy?" by John C. Ranney, assistant professor of government at Smith College, in the Fall, 1946 *Public Opinion Quarterly*:

"The chief advantage of the polls is that, in an age of increasing strain upon traditional democratic procedures, they have made a constructive technical contribution by reflecting sensitively and flexibly the currents of public feeling, by making this information available to political leaders in a way which is neither rigid nor mandatory, and by testing the claims of special interests to represent the desires of the people as a whole. These are services performed by no other agency, and they should not be underestimated."

Both pollsters and professors are fond of quoting James Bryce's lament in *The American Commonwealth* (Macmillan, 1888): "The obvious weakness of government by opinion is the difficulty of ascertaining it." It has been the pollsters' claim that they have eliminated this weakness and have, in fact, established a fifth estate destined to become as important as the older four. With the will of the people always known, some of the pollsters and their friends have come close to suggesting, the only valid role of Congress is to go through the technical motions to make that will into law.

There have, of course, been adverse criticisms of the polls from the start. Some of them have been confined to the researchers' methods, and *Public Opinion Quarterly,* now the official publication of the American Association for Public Opinion Research, has been full of discussions of methods of sampling, how to word questions, how to interview and how to eliminate "bugs" in the polling methodology. The social value of the polls also has been challenged frequently, after every election by some members of Congress. Straw votes have been accused of influencing the outcomes of elections by creating a "bandwagon" effect to the benefit of candidates shown to be leading. Legislators also have been unduly influenced, it is contended, and have voted for measures which, if they had considered them on their merits, they would have opposed.

The bandwagon argument, of course, was disproved, in the pollsters' favor, when Harry Truman won despite the virtually unanimous predictions of the scientists and journalists that he'd be badly beaten. The explanation by the critics that in that instance the bandwagon principle worked in reverse to cause Republicans to be overconfident and remain away from the polls was impossible of proof.

Other criticisms seemed to be substantiated. The supposedly scientific polls *did* fail, all of them; and their failure was as dramatic as that of the unscientific *Literary Digest* poll in 1936. For 12 years the professionals had been inviting the volume of Bronx cheers they received after the Truman victory by insisting that they never could be as wrong as the defunct magazine, because they had learned to obtain correct samples of the voting population as a whole, whereas the *Digest* had confined itself to the upper crust—those whose names appeared in telephone books. Furthermore, the *Digest* had conducted its poll by mail, meaning that only the most interested returned ballots; the professionals interviewed subjects face to face.

The results in 1936, 1940, and 1944 had seemed to confirm the professionals' contention that not the size of the sample but its representativeness was what was important. The *Literary Digest* in 1936 obtained 2,370,523 straw votes and predicted Franklin Delano Roosevelt would obtain 40.9 per cent of the popular vote. Instead, FDR got 60.2 per cent, and the stock of Roper and Gallup went up. Roper, with only about 5,000 ballots, had predicted 61.7 per cent for FDR while Gallup, on the basis of approximately 40,000 ballots, had said 53.8 per cent. In 1940, Gallup predicted Roosevelt would receive 52 per cent of the popular vote; Roper said 55.2 per cent. FDR actually got 54.7 per cent. In 1944 the scientific polls really seemed to have "come of age" when Roosevelt got 53.3 per cent of the popular vote after Gallup had predicted 51.5 per cent and Roper 53.6 per cent.

These uncannily accurate forecasts presumably resulted because the pollsters had succeeded in sampling exactly the right people to get a valid cross section of the electorate which subsequently went to the polls. This they did by obtaining the same proportions of different kinds of voters in their samples as are to be found in the voting population as a whole. For instance, if 20 per cent of all persons to vote are over 60 years of age, 20 per cent of those in the sample must be sexagenarians or better; if 40 per cent of the total votes will be cast by women, 40 per cent of the sample must be women. And the same holds for geographical distribution, economic status and past voting record. Certainly the basic necessity of making the sample representative is indisputable, and the intra-pollster arguments over whether the quota system of finding those to be polled in each category or the pin-point, or area, system is better is of secondary importance. For the record, the quota system is that whereby each interviewer is told merely to find a certain number falling into a certain category. Its weakness is supposed to be because the interviewers are likely to waylay persons who are most easily found or who are more articulate or better informed. The area system results in more of a random sample; when it is used the interviewer is assigned a given geographical area which is known to be typical and is told to rap on every door, or on every other door or in some other way to get a geographical as well as categorical cross section. Thus, whereas the quota interviewer would not worry if he found nobody home, the area interviewer would return until he found the resident in.

What most of those who have engaged in post mortem analyses of the 1948 results have overlooked is the important fact that the elections in which the pollsters presumably proved themselves able to forecast accurately were all ones in which Franklin Delano Roosevelt was a candidate. The pollster organizations got their start between the first and second elections of FDR. Consequently, the real test of whether the polls were as good as they seemed couldn't come until 1948. Unquestionably the factors which the pollsters used in selecting their samples when FDR was running were the correct ones. Possibly, as a matter of fact, straw vote editors might have ignored all but one or two of the categories, namely: "For whom did you vote last time?" and "To what income group do you belong?" In retrospect it seems utterly naive to have believed that the factors used are absolutes and eternal, applicable to all elections at all times. Certainly if polls had existed in 1928 they would have been way off if the pollsters had neglected the factor of religion in getting up their samples. In depression days economic status probably is the most compelling factor determining one's outlook on matters political and governmental. In good days, however, the lack of any strong class consciousness in the United States makes that factor comparatively much less important. Thus, before 1928 the *Literary Digest* could succeed with its telephone books. In order to prepare an adequate sample at any time it is necessary to judge what the significant issues of the campaign are to be: those which will influence voters in making up their minds. Then, one must go deeper to determine the factors, institutional and otherwise, likely to affect voters in making up their minds regarding the issues. Obviously, qualitative as well as quantitative factors enter in because, unless the unlikely situation of a single-issue campaign is to be studied, there is a conflict of interests in the cases of many if not most voters. For instance, one's religious background conceivably might incline one toward one candidate, whereas his economic interests incline him toward another. In the case of Voter A the religious factor may prove stronger; in the case of Voter B the reverse may be true. Pollsters can deal only in statistical averages. They must search for the most important factors in the hope that the qualitative aspects will cancel each other out. If, however, it is possible accurately to determine what these factors are, the straw polling becomes superfluous; all that is needed is analysis of census figures.

The best—in fact, almost the only—study to point up the conflicts of interests which occur as voters make up their minds was that conducted by the Bureau of Applied Social Research of Columbia University in 1940 in Erie County, Ohio. The results are included in *The People's Choice* by Paul F. Lazarsfeld, Bernard Berelson, and Hazel Gaudet (Duell, Sloan & Pearce, 1944). Regarding cross pressures the authors said in part:

"We found the Protestant vote allied to the Republicans and the Catholic votes more strongly Democratic. We found that individuals on the higher SES [Social Economic Status] levels tended to vote Republican and their poorer neighbors to vote Democratic. In other words, a vote decision can be considered the net effect of a variety of pressures.

"Now what if these individual factors work in opposite directions? Suppose an individual is *both* prosperous and Catholic? How will he make up his mind? Or suppose he belongs to the Protestant faith and lives in a poor section of the community? Which of the conflicting influences will win out? People who are subject to contradictory and opposing influences of this kind are said to be under cross-pressures.

"The more evenly balanced these opposing pressures were, the longer the voter delayed in making up his mind."

Unless there can be discovered *absolutes*—factors which are of predominant importance at all times to the exclusion of others—the pollsters always will be on precarious ground in their straw voting.

Suppose, however, for the sake of continuing the argument, that that time does come. Suppose that straw voting can be relied upon, without exceptions, to predict the outcome of elections. Does it then follow that equal reliance must be placed in other kinds of public opinion polling: that done day by day on issues?

Polls On Issues

The most obvious difference between a straw vote and a poll on an issue is that whereas everyone who participates in the former has the opportunity at least of acting in accordance with his opinion—that is, he can vote in an actual election—no similar "follow up" opportunity is vouchsafed those who reply "yes," "no," or "no opinion" to such a query as, "Do you approve this country's policy in regard to Guatemala?"

A further related difference: whereas all but a negligible proportion of those whose votes are solicited in a straw poll have heard of the candidates, only a minority may have as much as a hazy notion of the public issue about which their opinions are sought. This fact has been demonstrated over and over again by the pollsters themselves when they have prefaced their important questions by inquiries regarding the extent of their subjects' information. Some of the results have been astounding as when, a year after the program went into full operation, only 26 per cent knew what the wartime lend-lease program was; when, at the height of congressional debate on the Full Employment Act of 1946, only 8 per cent knew what it provided; when, while the Senate was preparing to debate the Marshall Plan, 51 per cent of those questioned by Gallup pollsters never had heard of the plan.

Of similar examples of widespread public ignorance and/or indifference there is almost no end. In many instances newspapers have devoted pages and pages to presentation of the facts and the pros and cons involved. The cumulative lesson should be sobering to the newspaperman, perhaps a blow to his ego. Pertinent to the present subject, it suggests several questions:

1. When can public opinion be said to exist? When 50 per cent are informed and/or concerned? 25 per cent? 10 per cent?

2. What is the public that is being polled? What publics, in fact, are there? What is a public anyway?

3. And what is an opinion? What makes an opinion public? What is public opinion?

Because the professional pollsters and their social scientist friends never have given satisfactory answers to these and similar questions, they have been subjected to severe criticism by several scholarly skeptics. Prominent among these is Prof. Herbert Blumer, University of Chicago sociologist, who spoke his piece at the annual meeting of the American Sociological Society in New York in December, 1947. Entitled "Public Opinion and Public Opinion Polling," his paper appeared in the October, 1948, *American Sociological Review*. In it he accused the pollsters of making no effort "to try to identify or to isolate public opinion as an object" but of taking "the narrow operationalist position that public opinion consists of what the public opinion polls poll." Said Blumer:

"What I think needs to be noted is that the casting of ballots is distinctly an action of separate individuals wherein a ballot cast by one individual has exactly the same weight as a ballot cast by another individual. In this proper sense, and in the sense of real action, voters constitute a population of disparate individuals, each of whom has equal weight to the others. Consequently, the sampling procedure which is based on a population of disparate individuals is eminently suited to securing a picture of what the voting is likely to be. However, to regard the successful use of polling in this area as proof of its automatic validity when applied to an area where people do not act as equally weighted disparate individuals begs the very question under consideration. I would repeat that the formation and expression of public opinion giving rise to effective public opinion is not an action of a population of disparate individuals having equal weight but is a function of a structured society, differentiated into a network of different kinds of groups and individuals having differential weight and influence and occupying different strategic positions. Accordingly, to my mind, the success attending polling in the prediction of elections gives no validity to the method as a means of studying, recording or measuring public opinion as it forms and functions in our society."

That was strong medicine for the savants, but at least it was stated more politely than Lindsay Rogers, Burgess Professor of Public Law of Columbia University, put virtually the same argument in his book, *The Pollsters* (Knopf, 1949). "To say that 'public opinion' is being 'measured' is to make skimmed milk masquerade as cream," is a typical acidulous Rogers aphorism. What Rogers asks even more poignantly than Blumer is essentially: "What have you got when you've got it?" He wrote: "Some opinions of a majority are not necessarily public. . . . When issues are less general and relate to the pros and cons of separate governmental problems, there is frequently no real public opinion. . . . Large sections of the public do not have sufficient information to justify the formation of opinions, let alone their expression. . . . Most men and women do not study public questions and endeavor to form rational opinions. They have neither the time nor interest."

To determine the cogency of these fundamental attacks on the very effort to poll public opinion at all requires a backtrack to examine some fundamental social psychological concepts.

What Is a Public?

Although the opposite unfortunately still is true regarding many other terms in their lexicon, social scientists are in substantial agreement in their definitions of "public." According to William Albig in *Public Opinion* (McGraw-Hill, 1939), "publics are simply large groups." A bit more expansively, Alfred M. Lee in "Public Opinion in Relation to Culture," in the February, 1945 *Psychiatry,* defined a public as "a group of any size in which the members are more or less conscious of common interests." Similarly, Charles W. Smith, Jr. wrote in *Public Opinion in a Democracy* (Prentice-Hall, 1939), "It will make for clarity if we think of the public simply as composed of all the people capable of thought in a particular area or group."

Distinguishing characteristics of a public, as generally agreed upon by the experts, include the following:

A public is not to be defined or located geographically. It is not contiguity or common living but a mutuality of interest which is the bond between members of a public. Thus a public differs from a *crowd,* which, by definition, means a number of people at the same place at the same time, and from a *community* which is characterized by both locality and a common living.

In one important respect a public and a crowd are similar: each has a common center or object of interest to which all its members attend. In neither case is the relationship between members face-to-face. In a baseball park, for instance, it is the game and not other members of the crowd in the stands that is "the tie that binds." Similarly, members of a public are interested in each other only incidentally. More importantly, they share a common interest in music or sports or politics or whatever the interest may be. All members of the crowd at a particular athletic contest may be part of a sports public, but there are many more members of that public who do not happen to be present on the specific occasion.

Except by rare coincidence in modern times community and public are not coterminous. A community is that geographical area in which it is possible for one to satisfy many aspects of societal living: familial, economic, recreational and so forth. On a frontier an isolated settlement might constitute all that exists of its inhabitants' world. Communication, essential for the existence of publics, being virtually nonexistent, self-sufficiency becomes necessary because imposed by the exigencies of existence.

Today to bound the limits of any community is becoming more and more difficult because to be a "complete" person it is necessary to range far afield from one's dwelling unit, both physically and mentally. "Community," as a sociological term, however, still retains the concept of "relative completeness," and means a group occupying a territorial area where there is common living as well as a common earth. Therefore, the communal bond seems to be not this particular interest or that but a whole complex of interests necessary to the many-sided existence which men lead. Publics may exist within large communities and may transcend the borders of small communities. Some day the entire world may be one community, so interconnected that no provincialism is possible. As long as there are interests, however, there will be different publics. There may come to be an international political public when world government is achieved, but it is unlikely that, before the millennium, all men will share enough major interests with other men to form the basis of world understanding.

Despite the breaking down of the geographical limits of the community, the term still has a strong geographical connotation because the breaking-down process has not progressed too far to render it obsolete. When we say "it's a nice little community," we generally mean "it's a satisfactory place to live where, for all practical purposes, one can earn a living, marry and rear a family with adequate facilities—educational, recreational, cultural and the like—to satisfy his social needs." When we lament, "that town is losing its community spirit" we mean that the "sense of belonging" is disappearing, that persons are looking beyond the geographical confines of what was considered to be the community to find satisfactions which formerly they could find merely by staying at home. Similarly, "neighborliness is gone" means that the feeling of mutual dependence has disappeared from the smaller geographical area within a community—the immediate environs of one's home. It is the spread and growth of publics, as improved means of transportation and communication and commercial relations have made it possible for persons widely separated in space to share interests and experiences, that, in large part, has caused the breakdown of the geographical community as a realistic social force.

There is no such thing as THE public. There are, rather, as many publics as there are interests, and any person can belong simultaneously to several different publics, as a sports public, religious public, political public, scientific public, and so forth. Such obviously is not true of a crowd, community, society, state, or nation—all terms which occasionally are used carelessly as synonyms for public. You can be a member of only one of each of them at a time.

Trying to determine just how many and what publics exist is somewhat of a frustrating experience. One can search for them as a biologist hunts new specimens of plant or animal life. Once found they often are as difficult to classify as are some botanical and zoological discoveries. For instance, is there one all-inclusive sports public or many different kinds of sports publics? If only one, does it include baseball fans who have no interest in hockey, hockey fans who pay no attention to football, football fans who do not care for boxing, and so forth? If you decide there is a separate public for each sport, does the baseball public include those interested in the major leagues as well as those who follow only a Class C team? Does it include softball addicts? Followers of college or high school baseball? Are Cardinal and Giant fans members of the same public or sub-public? Is there a distinct Ted Williams or Jackie Robinson public or sub-public?

It is comparatively easy to resolve the difficulty as regards sports or music or several other fields by recognizing the existence of sub-publics and sub-sub or auxiliary publics. It is more difficult to categorize interest groups in such fields as science, business, and labor. It is most difficult to do so in the field of politics and government. Professional pollsters operate as though there were a single American public. For straw vote purposes it consists of all qualified to vote in a presidential election. The pollsters assume that the same public that can be—in fact, must be—used every four years to predict who will be chosen to inhabit the White House, can be used for a meaningful poll on any issue related to any aspect of public affairs; a change in the labor laws; federal aid to education; unhampered dissemination of birth control information; statehood for Alaska, and so forth.

Accepting the orthodox definition of a public as an interest group, it is apparent that the publics in which any kind of meaningful opinion might be expected to exist on such matters are not the same in a majority of cases. A single American public exists because of the nationalistic interest supporting the United States as a governmental entity to which its citizenry wishes to belong. Unfortunately for those who would like to use that public for polling purposes, that nationalistic interest is broad and general. The "interests" are not the specific ones suggested by a large number of the questions asked in polls on public issues. Writes Smith: "The range of questions on which the public is incapable of forming an intelligent opinion is rapidly increasing. . . . More and more details must be left to experts and not public opinion. . . . In a large society the formation of intelligent opinions on public matters becomes increasingly difficult."

To repeat a previous quotation from Rogers: "Some opinions of a majority are not necessarily public." This means that you can obtain the views of a church congregation on Picasso's art, but because the question does not relate to the "interest" which causes the communicants to have a "sense of belonging," you do not have a "public" opinion, but merely a "majority" opinion of a number of people convenient to poll because they happened to be at the same place at the same time. Because almost every adult is a member of the voting public, you can enter a shop or place of entertainment and conduct a straw vote on a coming election; in such case you are polling your interviewees as members of the voting public, not as members of the economic, religious, sports, or other public to which they also all belong. Such a sampling method, of course, would be subject to grave criticism because of its unrepresentativeness.

Members of a public have a sense of belonging. In this respect publics are similar to crowds, communities, nations, and states. The bond, as stated, is a particular interest of which each member is conscious. The test of whether a public exists is the attitude of the minority or minorities as regards an issue which may arise to divide or split opinion. This is so because a public exists only when its members function together. If they do not do so then not one but two or more publics exist. To put it another way, the members of the public remain members because the common interest is stronger than differences which separate them in other aspects of their living. It is like members of violently different political parties belonging to the same religious denomination. Society as a whole consists of people whose interests cross and crisscross all other phases of their existence. So you find members of a music public in labor unions and manufacturers' associations, among Jews, Protestants, and Catholics, among college graduates and eighth-grade graduates. It is the conflict of these interests (or publics) which makes the evaluation, or even discovery of what is called public opinion difficult.

Properly to understand the concept of public requires an understanding also of what is meant by several other terms—society, nation, state, and association—all in the effort to draw nearer to answers to the questions: What is it the pollsters have been polling? What is it possible to poll? What do you have after you've polled whatever it is you are polling? How do you go about it?

Society exists "wherever there is life," according to R. M. MacIver and Charles H. Page in *Society* (Rinehart, 1949). It is, these authorities write, "a system of usages and procedures, of authority and mutual aid, of many groupings and divisions, of controls of human behavior and of liberties. This ever-changing, complex system we call society. It is the web of social relationships. And it is always changing."

Because he is helpless at birth and could not live unless others took care of him, man cannot escape being a social being. Thus, society is a much broader concept than public. The multitude of publics which exist form a part of the "web of social relationships" which constitutes society. In any society there exists a *diversity* of interests; a public exists because of the *cohesive force* of a particular interest or of related interests. When they stray from questions related definitely to the interests of the presidential voting public, the pollsters really are polling American society, not the American public. Since that society is made up of so many different interests, the present sampling methods are grossly inadequate. The factors of age, sex, economic status, geography and political affiliation are by no means the only, probably not even the major ones which would have to be considered to make society opinion-sampling representative. Put another way, what the pollsters do is ask members of all kinds of publics questions which should properly be asked of particular publics. Carried to the extreme this would mean asking a highly technical engineering question of a miscellaneous collection of people containing only a handful of engineers qualified to answer and calling the result the "public opinion" of the group as a whole. Even though most of the issues about which the pollsters seek answers are ones on which the president and members of Congress presumably can act, it does not follow that everyone eligible to cast a vote for president or congressman is qualified by interest or information to participate in the poll.

State and *nation* often are used incorrectly as synonyms which, except coincidentally, they are not. The former is an artificial agency —a political or governmental association existing for the purpose of taking care of an important phase of life. "The state is one form of social organization, not the whole community in all its aspects," write MacIver and Page. It includes many publics, but a public can exist beyond the borders of any particular state to include members of other states. Mozart's public, for example, is international.

A nationality group is one which seeks political autonomy; if it obtains it there comes into being a nation-state. Thus, the nation grows out of a sense of nationality and not the opposite. The Poles, Czechs, and many other nationality groups existed for centuries without becoming states. MacIver and Page define nationality as "a type of community sentiment, created by historical circumstances and supported by common psychological factors, of such an extent and so strong that those who feel it desire to have a common government peculiarly or exclusively their own." As Edward Hallett Carr pointed out in *Conditions of Peace* (Macmillan, 1942), nationality and self-determination have been identical only in western Europe. The following definitive paragraph is from W. B. Pillsbury's *The Psychology of Nationality and Internationalism* (D. Appleton & Co., 1919):

"By a nation we mean a group of individuals that feels itself one, is ready within limits to sacrifice the individual for the group advantage, that prospers as a whole, each of whom rejoices with the advancement and suffers with the losses of the group. The spirit of nationality may be defined as personification of this unity. As opposed to this the state would be merely the system of government, a unity for the sake of making and enforcing laws. It rests upon a feeling of community in most cases, but frequently the recognized unity extends beyond the bounds of the state and still more often the edicts of the state may be enforced upon individuals who do not feel themselves a part of the national group."

Obviously *race* and *nation* are not synonymous even coincidentally. A nation, as is true of a public, can contain a range of racial types. Not only can, but does. And, of course, a state can be comprised of members of more than one nationality group. So can a crowd and so can a community. As a nationality group the citizens of the United States could be polled on matters related to that nationalism, but the pertinent questions would be strictly limited in number and would concern such matters as secession and civil war. Paradoxically, those who voted to dissolve the union hardly could be considered still to belong to the nation or national public although they still would be members of the American state—that is, subject to the laws of the land.

A public is not a formal organization or association. The bond between members of a public, again to repeat a point already made several times, is mutuality of interest, not locality, nationality, race, or common citizenship in a state. A public does not have membership dues, officers and regular meetings. People with similar interests— that is, members of the same public—however, do form organizations related to those interests to foster and satisfy those interests. To quote MacIver and Page again: "We define an association, then, as a group organized for the pursuit of an interest or group of interests in common."

All members of a public, however, do not join the same association; they may never join any. Leadership within a public usually does come from such associations as exist but, for example, all who call themselves Republicans do not belong to the Republican party. Nor do all teachers belong to educational organizations; nor all workers to labor unions; nor all music lovers to any musical society. Such associations are deliberately formed and kept alive; persons join them on their own volition which, of course, is not true of one's membership in society, or, generally, in community, nation, or state. It would be hazardous to conclude that the opinion of the business world as a whole had been obtained by a poll only of members of Chambers of Commerce or of working people by interviewing only trade unionists.

What might result from such segmental polling, however, would be a clearer picture of the weight likely to be pulled by any part of the business or labor ranks than any poll which included nonmembers as well as members of active associations. As Blumer points out, all members of any public do not exercise equal influence upon government or other persons. In fact, the individual's effectiveness must be gauged qualitatively rather than quantitatively as is possible in the case of an election in which every voter has one vote and no more. And so we are almost back where we started when we turned to an examination of the question, "What is a public?" and are probably as ready as we'll ever be to consider the other word in the important phrase with which this book deals. In other words—

What Is an Opinion?

Not so many centuries ago nobody in the so-called civilized world questioned the "fact" that the world is flat. Then someone said the world is round and was persecuted for his heresy. In time so many others were saying the same thing that persecution gave way to debate. There followed scientific evidence and demonstration by exploration to match the "proof" hitherto found in sacred writings. Today almost nobody denies that the world is round.

Thus, belief gave way to opinion which, in turn, was superseded by new belief. Today the average person who believes the world is round is no more able to prove it than his ancestor living in the twelfth century was able to prove it is flat, if by proof we mean scientific proof, which is what we do mean in modern times. Beliefs are matters of faith, and faith in what one has been told about science can be just as strong—and sometimes just as misplaced—as faith in the scriptures.

Beliefs are not opinions. Beliefs are what we "know" to be true; opinions are what we "think" is true. As defined by Albig: "An opinion is an expression on a controversial point," indicating that whenever one opinion exists, other opinions on the same matter also exist. If that were not so, there would be no controversy. As in the case of the shape of the world, science in recent centuries has destroyed many of man's long-standing beliefs. The modern scientist is trained to question axioms; and the spread of scientific-mindedness, many laboratory experiments have revealed, has made better educated persons less dogmatic than more poorly educated persons. This superior open-mindedness means a greater likelihood of people's changing their minds on the basis of iconoclastic evidence; it does not mean, however, that beliefs rooted in science—while they last—are not just as strong as beliefs rooted in religion or superstition. Outside their special fields, likewise, even the most highly trained can be as narrow-minded as the ignorant.

Pollsters cannot avoid obtaining beliefs as well as opinions in answer to some of their questions, because one man's belief may be another's opinion. Almost everyone has overheard, if he has not himself participated in, a conversation going something like this:

"This measure should be defeated because it is un-American."

"That, my dear sir, is a matter of opinion."

"You are wrong. What I am telling you is the truth for the following reasons. . . ."

The difference between belief and opinion is a qualitative one—a matter of intensity or certainty which the standard polls to date hardly have attempted to measure. Some questions cannot be answered without expressing beliefs, for example, that asked by the *Fortune* poll in December, 1948: "Do you think there is a God who rewards and punishes after death?" In other cases basic beliefs "show through" as the principal conditioning factors determining answers to such questions as "Do you think most people can be trusted?" (National Opinion Research Center, Aug. 1, 1948) and "Do you think Negroes should or should not be required to occupy a separate part of a train or bus when traveling from one state to another?" (American Institute of Public Opinion, July 25, 1948).

Such questions have been very much in the minority as far as professional pollsters are concerned. In addition to the purely informational questions ("Have you heard of the North Atlantic Pact?") which usually preface other questions, pollsters' questions generally fall into four main categories, as follows:

1. Personal habits and preferences: "What sport do you yourself enjoy watching most?" (AIPO, May 15, 1948); "Where do you get most of your daily news about what is going on—from the newspapers or the radio?" (NORC, May 1, 1948); "What other languages, if any, can you speak well enough to make others understand you?" (AIPO, June 5, 1948); "If you were free to do so, would you like to go to settle in another country?" (AIPO, Apr. 7, 1948).

2. Predictions: "Do you think Joe Louis can beat Jersey Joe Walcott when or if they fight again next summer?" (AIPO, Apr. 3, 1948); "Do you think that a serious depression is likely in the United States within the next two years?" (AIPO, Apr. 30, 1948); "Regardless of how you feel, do you think federal income taxes will be increased or decreased this coming year?" (AIPO, Jan. 7, 1949).

3. *Judgments and evaluations:* "Are you satisfied or dissatisfied with the progress that the United Nations has made to date?" (AIPO, May 26, 1948); "Do you approve or disapprove of the way Truman is handling his job as president?" (AIPO, Apr. 23, 1948); "Do you feel the United States is now dealing with Russia in an intelligent manner?" (FOR, June, 1948).

4. *Straw votes on public issues:* "Would you favor or oppose having Hawaii admitted as the forty-ninth state in the union?" (AIPO, Apr. 16, 1948); "Do you think it would be a good idea for President Truman to call an international meeting with Stalin and heads of other nations to work out more effective plans for peace?" (AIPO, May 2, 1948); "Would you approve or disapprove of having the government spend 100 million for research to find the causes and cure of diseases of the heart?" (AIPO, June 26, 1948); "Would you favor or oppose having the United Nations adopt a plan for control of atomic energy which would permit the United Nations to inspect atomic plants in the United States and any other country at any time?" (AIPO, May 28, 1948).

With the exception of those to some of the questions in the "personal habits and preferences" category, the answers to all such questions are expressions of opinion. Since they are mostly of the "yes" or "no" type, however, the results do not show the wide differences which may exist between those who reply similarly. Take, for instance, the question on the Louis-Walcott fight. One interviewee picking Louis might feel, "It's a pushover—knockout for the champion in the first round," whereas another might favor Louis by a very narrow margin on points. This is not too serious because the issue is not too important. Evaluating the record of the United Nations or passing judgment on the proposal to extend statehood to Hawaii is more serious. As in the Louis-Wallcott case, however, the intensity of the opinions of interviewees would not be obtained unless there were further questions seeking to gauge it. Some efforts in this direction have been made, but asking a person whether he holds a particular opinion "strongly," "very strongly," "weakly," or "very weakly" has this grave weakness: these terms cannot mean the same thing to any two interviewees.

A more important weakness of one-shot questions such as these typical ones listed is that they do not reveal anything regarding the reasons for the "yes" and "no" answers. Every person who is dissatisfied with the United Nations, for instance, conceivably could have a different reason for his dissatisfaction. The same, of course, is true of the question regarding Hawaii and all of the other questions, several of which were supplemented by others seeking to obtain reasons.

Opinions are psychological end-products. To understand their nature one must delve further—into the reasons for the reasons. Psychologists, sociologists, and anthropologists have been seeking the answers for some time now, not by considering "how individual opinions are formed" as an isolated object of research but as part of the much larger problem of social behavior as a whole. Observing the undeniable fact that men think and act similarly in many important respects, early scholars generally adopted one of two possible approaches. They either studied man as he participated in groups; or they studied him as much as possible as an isolated individual. The most important "school" of thought to come out of the efforts of those who took the former approach was that which postulated the existence of some kind of *group mind*. At least two important sets of theories, on the other hand, developed from the efforts of those who took the latter approach. They are known as the *rational man* theories and *instincts*. Modern scholars almost without important exception have discarded all three sets of theories, but among laymen considerable belief still lingers on, justifying brief attention here to each in turn.

Although they differed in details and terminology, group-mind advocates (notably Espinas, Durkheim, Lazarus, Le Bon and William McDougall) held in common the belief that there exists something separate and apart from the individual minds composing it, compelling obedience to it. All such theories minimize the importance of the individual, deny that there is much free choice accorded him. They center instead on the idea that most social behavior owes its origin and characteristics to causes external to the individuals comprising society. Today such ideas seem as naive, metaphysical, and unscientific as primitive attempts to explain natural phenomena in terms of spirits, witches, ghosts, and goblins. There continues, however, to be value in the group-mind concepts as they lead to descriptions of some forms of social behavior even though these descriptions do not constitute explanations of that behavior. The group-mind advocates correctly concluded, and amassed a quantity of evidence to show, that man *does* act differently in crowds and other groups, or when he is conscious of their influence, than he does when he is alone.

Those who believe in the rational man—and this theory has many more contemporary followers than either of the others—hold that men think and act similarly, in large part at least, because each man thinks out a problem and makes his own decision, clearly, logically, and in isolation from other men. As a psychological concept this is similar to the religious idea of free will and individual responsibility for one's acts. It was fostered by the seventeenth- and eighteenth-century philosophers who emphasized the importance of the individual and helped rationalize Protestantism, the democratic revolutions, and *laissez-faire* economics. Since Pavlov, Freud, the behaviorists, and a couple of generations of research by social psychologists and cultural anthropologists, belief in such independent thinking has diminished. No matter how hard we try, we cannot escape the habits and attitudes of childhood nor the impact at all times of our personal and cultural environments.

Even more discredited among scholars than either the group-mind or rational-man theories are instincts as the explanation for similarities in human thought and action. Growing out of the theories regarding heredity and evolution of Lamarck, Darwin, and others, the human instincts theories held that men act similarly because of uniform, innate characteristics which are the same for all persons. Instincts were said to be inborn tendencies to act, unlearned mechanisms which mature as the individual does, some coming awake at different times of life. Psychologists of the late nineteenth and early twentieth centuries really "went overboard" as regards instincts. Everyone had his own list and many invented fancy synonyms such as "springs of action," "à priori syntheses," "neural explanations," "prepotent reflexes" and the like. Since it was known that during gestation the human embryo at different times resembles fish, birds, and other animals, it was contended that the "recapitulation of the race" extended to mental as well as physical stages, that human beings went through all of the important stages that their ancestors have passed through all the way back to the Garden of Eden. Laymen were drawn into the discussion of "heredity versus environment" with

the Sunday newspaper magazine sections providing plenty of argu-
mentative material.

The quest for instincts led to virtually every human thought and
action being accredited to them. The lists grew longer and longer and
more and more contradictory and self-eliminating. As "the" explanation, instincts just didn't hold up because they just didn't operate
uniformly. That is, for example, if there were an instinct to hate,
further explanation still would be needed to explain why one man
hates this object and his neighbor another; why one hates many things
and intensely whereas someone else has a small list of hates and never
apparently gets very mad about anything. The same is true of love,
covetousness, generosity, fear, anger, pride, and scores and scores of
other nouns which describe forms of observable behavior. People just
don't go around loving or hating in a vacuum; there always has to be
an object of anger or fear or whatever the emotion might be. Before
the instinct fad died down, however, it had tremendous repercussions
in many fields. Carleton Parker, for instance, built an entire school
of economic thought on instincts; he was the "father" of welfare
capitalism, teaching employers that the best management is that which
satisfies the most basic instincts possessed by employees. All of which
proves that a lot of good can come from unscientific thinking but not
much by way of casting light on why men think and act as they do.

The search for the clue to social behavior has taken another group
of investigators into the laboratory to study personality types. The
results have been important in providing new ways to classify and
describe ways in which people come to think and act in their attempts
to adjust themselves to their social environments. Any social group
puts a premium on certain behavior and penalizes those who behave
differently. Hence, those who possess the traits considered desirable
have a comparatively easy time of it whereas others whose physical
appearances or dispositions are a handicap may have psychological
scars as a result of their attempts to conform. Knowing a person is an
extravert or an introvert (Jung's terms corresponding to William
James' tough- and tender-minded) may help us anticipate what to
expect from him at a cocktail party, but there is no evidence that
these personality traits are inborn rather than the result of conditioning; and certainly, pertinent to our present interest, no evidence to
indicate that one type would be more likely than the other to believe

Hawaii should become the forty-ninth state. The same goes for Kretschmer's three types based on physical build: the athletic (egg-shaped), the pyknic (roly-poly) and asthenic (lean and slender) and for many other similar classifications.

To summarize, the clues as to how individual opinions are formed are not to be found anywhere in the innate psychological or physiological makeup of man. Whatever value theories about group minds, rational man, instincts, or personality types may have in other aspects, it is decidedly limited or worthless here. If any of the theories were valid there would be much greater similarity between men than exists. All members of homogeneous groups would be either satisfied or dissatisfied with the United Nations or the president of the United States or the amount being spent on medical research.

As a matter of fact most members of homogeneous groups *do* think alike as regards such matters, but the explanation is to be found, not by attempting to separate the study of man from that of his environment, but by recognizing the inseparability of the two. In other words, much of what has been called *human nature* must be regarded as human or *social behavior*. That is the modern point of view of what, for want of a better name, is called the *habits and attitudes* school of thought. Its theories and findings to date have stood the tests of scientific checking much better than was true of any of its predecessors, even though the moderns see the problem as much more complicated and do not expect to discover any simple formula by which to analyze or predict human thought and action.

Since most of the rest of this book consists of an elaboration of the main tenets of the habits and attitudes school, only a brief statement will be given in this chapter to indicate how the thinking differs from that of the other schools. A habit, according to the dictionaries, is a "usual way of action," whereas an attitude is a "usual way of thinking, acting, or feeling." The orthodox sociological definitions are substantially the same. Since our interest is public opinion, we are concerned more with attitudes than with habits and so are the social psychologists who really include habits in their generally accepted definition of an attitude as a "tendency to act." An opinion is defined as "a verbalization of an attitude." It derives from an attitude or attitudes which, in turn, are the result of the entire psychological past of a person.

Only when a crisis occurs—that is, when it becomes necessary actually to act—is it possible to tell whether an opinion is a correct verbalization of an attitude, or merely what a person thinks his attitudes are. For instance, one can say that he has no anti-Negro prejudice yet feel exceedingly uncomfortable if required to sit beside a Negro on a street car or bus. Some attitudes, that is, are unconscious and it would take psychiatric or psychoanalytic treatment to reveal them. As in the case of instincts, though, without an object toward which it is directed, an attitude has no meaning. There is no abstract attitude of love any more than there is an instinct to love. One's love must be directed toward a particular person or object. The same for his hates, fears and other attitudes. To be meaningful there must be a "value" or an "interest" toward which an attitude is directed.

Attitudes are not formed by the influence of a group mind or of instincts, or through rational thought, but by conditioning. Similarities in men's thoughts and behavior are due to the fact that in the same cultural environment, the conditioning is similar for all persons reared in that environment. It is impossible to separate the study of the individual from his participation in the group. Without others he never develops into what is called a human being. Isolated, he can form habits but he is not influenced by customs which are group phenomena. The heredity versus environment argument is as erroneous as it would be to dispute which is more important, the bobbing cork or the water. The reality of the situation exists in the interaction, and the same is true of man and society.

Two types of conditioning can be distinguished: personal-social and cultural, although the media by which the individual is affected may be the same. Nevertheless, there is a difference between the type of conditioning which results from a fright or other unusual personal experience early in life and the training which one receives in how to behave in the toilet and at the table so as not to be considered uncouth by others of his social group. No two persons, even identical twins, have exactly the same environment. Pavlov's work on the conditioned reflex demonstrated how personal habits and attitudes can be formed, and Freud demonstrated the lasting effect of infantile and childhood experiences. A cruel father or an over-indulgent grandmother can affect a person's personality and outlook on life; a physical affliction which makes it impossible for one to participate fully in group

activities may be a permanent influence. It all depends on the circumstances, including specific experiences and how one's associates feel
and act toward a cripple or fat boy, however, what the effect may be.
A hunchback may develop a disagreeable personality as a defense
mechanism against sneers and taunts, but his reactions are socially
determined and are not organic. All fat men are not jolly although
some probably developed cheery "fronts" in an effort to win friends
and become exceptions to the rule that "nobody loves a fat man."

Much more important is the cultural conditioning which begins
shortly after birth. To get along, each member of a social group
must learn its rules and must conform to them. These rules are variously called institutions, customs, folkways, and mores which, in turn,
derive from traditions, myths, and legends and are enforced by taboos,
codes, rituals, and conventions. In succeeding chapters all of these
terms will be defined and their effect upon public opinion will be explained and evaluated.

In *Man and His Works* (Knopf, 1948), Melville Herskovits defines culture as "the man-made part of the environment." In another
part of the same book he writes, "The clearest definition of culture
in psychological terms states: culture is the learned portion of human
behavior." And in still another place: "A culture is the way of life of
a people; while a society is the organized aggregate of individuals who
follow a given way of life. In still simpler terms a society is composed
of people; the way they behave is their culture."

Part of the way people behave is the way they think. In large complex societies different persons think differently about virtually every
matter, important or otherwise. The clues as to why this is so are to
be found through examination of the forces at work in the society,
that is, by study of the culture. That, in essence, is what Louis H.
Bean did in *How to Predict Elections* (Knopf, 1948) in which he
concluded, fully six months before the momentous November 2, that
a Democratic victory seemed to be in the cards. He was right and
all of the scientific samplers of public opinion were wrong. By
statistical analysis of past presidential elections Bean determined that
economic conditions are the most important factor in deciding the
balance of power between the two major political parties—the "ins"
and the "outs." Describing predicting elections as "an art and not a
science," Bean advised those who might want to do it as follows:

"There are four steps in the practice of this art: first, marshal the historical facts to discover the general trend or tendency, if any; second, ascertain the major factors that have caused variations in the trend; third, appraise the factors that are responsible for the current or latest development; and, fourth, decide which factors are most likely to prevail in the future and estimate their possible effect. If no new elements appear other than those known to have prevailed in the past, one may forecast election results with confidence, and quite often with gratifying accuracy. There is always something new in politics, however, new faces and new issues, and their influence cannot be determined from a record, but must be inferred on the basis of one's general knowledge and experience. For this reason political forecasts are often based merely on past experience and are always a more or less hazardous undertaking."

When, therefore, we know enough about the habits and attitudes of the social group with which we are concerned—that is, when we understand its culture thoroughly—we shall be able to predict how members of the group will react to new experiences. At present we are a long way from possessing such a body of knowledge and further away from applying it in this way. Within the past century, however, historians have learned to view the successions of wars, revolutions, mass movements, and ideologies which they formerly were able only to chronicle, in this light. The chapters in their books relating the events leading up to an important historical climax enumerate chains of causes and effects. The student comes to understand how new ideas or discoveries in one field affect thought and action in other fields and learns that nothing "just happens." It must, of course, be admitted that in the rush to board the bandwagon of the "new" historians, many have produced questionable products. History, however, is not "bunk," "lies agreed upon," or "merely rationalizations." If the researcher has integrity and the scientific spirit, he can trace the diffusion and influence of new forces to explain the overt incidents with which history traditionally deals. The student of the contemporary scene must learn to do likewise.

What Is Public Opinion?

Until he has done so; that is, until he has learned enough about the social origins of attitudes, their roles in social motivation and the causal relationships between attitudes and opinions, what use is there in trying to study public opinion? Because public opinion, the end product, is the force which directly affects us. And it is now time to try to define what it is. Putting together the orthodox definitions for "public" and "opinion" we have: *public opinion is the expression on a controversial point within an interest group*. The reader may feel perfectly free to tear that apart and conclude that it doesn't mean much. Of course it doesn't, and neither do most of the other definitions to be found in other books on the subject. So difficult to define, in fact, is public opinion that several recent writers haven't even attempted it. Among them are William Albig in *Public Opinion* and Charles W. Smith, Jr., in *Public Opinion In a Democracy*. Those two books are among the best that ever have been written in this field. They contain plenty of statements about public opinion and *how* it operates. They are weak on explanations of the causes—the *why* of public opinion which will be the emphasis in this book. But they skillfully dodge terse all-inclusive definitions for which their readers should be grateful because the many others who have done so have confused more than they have clarified the problem.

By different writers public opinion has been used to mean the following: (1) group mind; (2) collective consciousness; (3) attitudes and opinions in the field of politics only; (4) unanimous opinions; (5) widespread beliefs, consensus, settled convictions; (6) social consciousness; (7) the sum total of all opinions, or mass thought; (8) the opinions of educated persons only; (9) the process of developing opinions rather than the end products, and (10) only opinions reached as a result of rational thought.

Among those taking the last view is Clyde L. King who writes in the "Introduction" to *Readings in Public Opinion* edited by W. Brooke Graves (D. Appleton & Co., 1928), "Public opinion is the social judgment reached upon a question of general or civic import after conscious, rational public discussion. . . . Public opinion is a rational judgment reached after discussion." Those who hold this view contend that public opinion involves conscious departures from customs and traditions. However, such departures are not on a rational basis if what the majority of scholars have come to believe about rational thought is valid. King says that public opinion results from discussion and therefore is rational; but no discussion is possibly entirely rational. If King's definition were to be used it would limit the subject matter to that which is almost if not absolutely non-existent. Thus limited, public opinion cannot be considered what usually is meant when anyone speaks of it. Nobody certainly would be justified in taking the time to write a book about it; instead, he would do better to direct his attention to public emotion.

Consistent with the foregoing definitions and discussions of "public" and "opinion," public opinion can be said to be the state of opinion within a public on certain issues or matters when there are differences as well as agreements. Public opinion is just the opinions of the members of a group plus their differences. Leonard Doob in *Public Opinion and Propaganda* (Holt, 1948), puts it this way: "Public opinion refers to people's attitudes on an issue when they are members of the same social group." As the discussion on publics made clear, for public opinion to exist there must be differences among the members of a public. Something becomes a matter of public opinion when it is a subject of popular concern or controversy. Public opinion is not just the opinion of a number of persons, but the opinions of those persons on matters naturally growing out of the focus of interest which keeps the group together. Public opinion never is static; there is constant interaction within any group or any controversial matter. Public opinion is not essentially rational but is based on attitudes which in turn are based on emotions, prejudices, stereotypes and so forth which are cultural in origin. In "Toward a Science of Public Opinion" in the January, 1937 *Public Opinion Quarterly*, Floyd H. Allport wrote: "The term public opinion is given its meaning with reference to a multi-individual situation in which individuals are expressing themselves, or can be called upon to express themselves, as favoring or supporting (or else disfavoring or opposing) some definite condition, person, or proposal of widespread importance, in such a proportion of numbers, intensity, and constancy as to give rise to the probability of affecting action, directly or indirectly, toward the object concerned."

Although hardly a day passes that the average newspaper does not indicate, in news story or editorial, that it considers public opinion a mighty newsworthy social force, Walter Lippmann excepted, few if any newspapermen ever have attempted to examine philosophically or even to define public opinion. Nevertheless, newspapermen probably have as clear an idea as others who use the term regarding what they mean by it. For instance, when a newspaperman writes—as they frequently do—that "public opinion is in favor of this" or that "public opinion opposes that," what he means is that, in his judgment, if a vote were taken, the result would be as indicated. When he observes, "public opinion is aroused," he means that there would be a heavy turnout at the polls. Conversely, "public opinion has not yet crystallized" means that the vote would be light. Translated, "public opinion is divided" means "it would be close."

Such, at least, is what he ought to mean, as the translations are pretty good meanings. They recognize that for public opinion to exist every member of a public does not necessarily have to be informed or even interested. Thus, they imply that some of those whose individual opinions go to make up the composite public opinion count for more than do others. A danger which a newspaperman must avoid is to consider public opinion as merely synonymous with majority opinion without taking into consideration the size of the articulate group he has in mind and ignoring the qualitative aspects of the different individual opinions involved.

Newspapermen also must be on the alert against promiscuous use of such expressions as "public opinion forced him to act," "fear of public opinion caused him to refrain from acting," "he lost out because he disregarded public opinion," "public opinion caught up with him," and so forth. It is quite possible for public officeholders and others, including newspapermen, to confuse the expression of opinions by some segments of a public with public opinion as a whole. A noisy minority, in other words, can create a bandwagon effect or, as Floyd H. Allport put it, "an illusion of universality." In the article already mentioned Allport calls such "confusions of public opinion with the public presentation of opinion" the *journalistic fallacy*, indicating that it is considered a newspaperman's sin. A related error is to call "public" the pressure an influential person or group may exert. Sometimes the person affected may believe those who "apply the heat" represent large numbers; other times he knows that, though numerically small, his tormentors are financially, politically, or otherwise powerful. To credit or blame public opinion for a great many actions is to divert attention from reality.

Especially must the newspaperman be wary about such expressions as "public opinion here today is—" unless he has conducted a survey sufficient to justify his making the claim. The regrets of the political writers after Nov. 2, 1948 because they had not gotten out among the people to learn the truth seem rather pathetic when the complete picture of what study and analysis of public opinion involves is viewed. In "The Pontifical Press" in the June, 1937 *Esquire*, Fletcher Knebel panned "those young reporters who misguide a gullible public by calling a spade an excavator." Typical extracts from the article follow:

"The big shot reporters and international chroniclers take it for granted that they should let the opinion of some government underling become the thought of the entire nation.

"Recently the Associated Press plunged into an international story with the magnificent observation that 'Britain looked with cold suspicion toward Japan. . . .' Even the most sophisticated of readers could not avoid conjuring up a picture of millions of beefeaters glowering into their tea and muttering about Japan.

"Probably the A.P. talked with one or two sub-officials before cabling the story. But give it the benefit of the doubt and say it talked to half a dozen and read several British newspaper editorial comments. That, presumably, makes it all of Britain. . . .

"Or take this one, a routine method of molding Great Events. It happens to come from a Detroit newspaper—'Lansing today wondered whether C. Donald Kennedy, business manager of the State Highway department, might be slated for budget director in the incoming administration.' And if more than one-twentieth of Lansing gave a whoop on that particular day about the political aspirations of Mr. Kennedy, admirable public servant that he may be, human nature in that precinct was reversing the statistics of the ages.

"The writer actually meant that 'several job-seekers, politicians, busybodies, and friends have wondered recently,' but to write it that way would practically amount to a journalistic strip act." [1]

The whole article, in the same vein, is worth reading—frequently if you are in a newspaper reporter's job, or if, as a newspaper reader, you wish to get your three, four, five or ten cents worth.

[1] Reprinted from June, 1937, *Esquire*. Copyright, 1937, by Esquire, Inc.

CHAPTER TWO

THE NATURE OF MAN

Because man is what he is, the axiom, "Give the people the facts and they will determine the proper action to take," is of questionable validity.

Of the importance of freedom of speech, assembly, and the press few if any believers in democracy have any doubt. Even the most severe critics of the contemporary American newspaper would oppose any attempts at government restraints prior to publication as more likely to decrease than to increase the supply of information required by a people in a democracy if they are to govern themselves wisely.

"Freedom of the press is essential to political liberty," declared the Commission on Freedom of the Press in its highly critical *A Free and Responsible Press* (University of Chicago, 1947). The commission's bill of indictment against the newspapers consisted of charges of alleged failures to live up to the expectations of the Founding Fathers responsible for the Bill of Rights that an uncensored press would function as a foremost "bulwark of democracy."

With the controversy which the commission's report stirred up this book is not concerned. This author shares the commission's fundamental faith in freedom of the press and its distrust of censorship. He also agrees with another leading critic of the newspapers, Morris L. Ernst, who began the foreword to his *The First Freedom* (Macmillan, 1946) with these words: "The peace of the world depends on human understanding and human understanding depends on the free flow, throughout the planet, of movies, radio, and the printed word."

In the light of what was said in the preceding chapter about rational-man theories, however, there is much room for questioning the faith of those who hold that if the people only can obtain the facts

[33]

—the pure, unadulterated, ungarnished facts—they will then almost automatically "find the way," as the phrase goes. Such, in fact, is merely a utopian dream. Serious as many of the imperfections of modern journalism undeniably are, they do not provide the whole answer as to why men are not smarter about recognizing wherein their own best interests lie. Given the most perfect press that the most sanguine idealists could imagine, there still would be the reader—with whom this book is primarily concerned—as a major obstacle to the attainment of social utopia.

Any newspaperman of even limited experience is close enough to the mine run of newspaper readers to know this cardinal fact regarding them: *most of them are ignorant about and indifferent to most of what goes on in the world.* One service which the professional pollsters performed—perhaps their most valuable—was to reveal this fact. No matter how imperfect their samples may have been, it was startling to learn in November, 1944 that it was possible for the American Institute of Public Opinion to find *any* group of voters all of whom said they intended to vote for Franklin D. Roosevelt, which included only 55 per cent who knew that the vice-presidential candidate was Harry S. Truman. In August, 1948 there were 9 per cent of all voters (regardless of how they intended to vote) who did not know President Truman was a candidate to succeed himself, and 51 per cent were unable to name his running mate, Senator Alben W. Barkley. The same poll, also by the AIPO, revealed that 12 per cent could not name the Republican candidate for president and 42 per cent did not know the Republican vice-presidential nominee.

These questions, of course, were asked of the most easily discovered public—the potential presidential election voting public—and since the questions were for information only, it would seem to make little difference how the sample was obtained. As regards issues the results have been even more discouraging to anyone who believes public enlightenment is a prerequisite to good government. Confessed Dr. George Gallup, head of the American Institute of Public Opinion, in an address at Syracuse University in the fall of 1945:

"I am frequently amazed at the lack of information many people reveal. I often wonder how democratic governments can work as well as they do when so many people are so poorly informed. I am talking about the readers of your newspapers. . . .

"Thirty-three million of us don't know what a tariff is. Over 70 million don't know what is meant by a subsidy. Only about half of the voters of the country can correctly identify General deGaulle. Less than half of the adult population knows that the United States was never a member of the League of Nations. . . .

"Of approximately 90 million adults in the United States 27 million didn't know as late as the middle of 1944 that the Japs had taken the Philippines. . . .

"At least 54 million people have never heard of or read about the Atlantic Charter, and more than 80 millions are unable to name even one of its provisions."

In the same address Gallup blamed the Federal Government for a large part of the public's ignorance regarding world affairs. Others have cited the newspapers, or the public schools or the distractions from serious matters provided by the radio, motion pictures, and other entertainment media. Regardless of where the responsibility lies, the fact remains: public opinion on major issues is not based on information, or, if so, it is, to a considerable extent, information which has been forgotten.

Man Is Credulous

In the light of what research in several fields—notably psychology, sociology and anthropology—has revealed, however, the widespread lack of correct information is seen not to be the primary factor anyway. The "don't know" responses to pollsters' questions may mount while newspapers are streamer headlining the answers daily. *Many wrong ideas, and conclusions based upon them, have persisted for centuries after the facts contradicting them have become easily available to all,* outstanding examples being many current superstitions, to be dealt with in Chapter 7.

In his chapter on "Our Credulous Heritage" in *Wish and Wisdom* (D. Appleton-Century Co., 1935), the late Joseph Jastrow wrote:

"Beliefs the mind must acquire to live at all; once started, they continue. Standards are derived from the test of experience; they mature with the slow growth of the ages. Until otherwise cultivated, the natural appetite of the mind is prone to accept the plausible, the congenial, the comforting, the thrilling, and is avid for the spice of wonder. . . ."

In *The Psychology of Conviction* (Houghton Mifflin, 1918) the same author wrote:

"We cannot lightly shake off the tenacity of our convictions, however obtained, nor the inertia that easily, and the incapacity that necessarily appeals to authority; we shall continue to yearn to believe what is agreeable and to resist unpleasant truths; we may still reserve some corner of our belief-chamber which shall be exempt from the intrusion of inquiry. . . .

"Retrospectively credulity attaches to the formation of beliefs under outgrown standards. A weak logical sense inheres in them; but more positively they result from prepossession which means a willingness to dispense with logical requirements in the interests of a cherished conviction."

Many another authority has attested to the fact that it is natural and easy to believe. A child accepts the world as he finds it and as he is told it is. He takes the word of those nearest him and can be made to accept any lie, from the customary ones about Santa Claus, fairies, and storks to more important ones concerning social, political, economic, and religious institutions and values. A baby seeks orderliness. Any mother knows that an infant can be more "sot in his ways" than a grandparent; he hates to have his routine habits disturbed once they have been established. Throughout his entire nonage his greatest desire and need is for a sense of security.

As it is with infants so is it with society as a whole. Customs, traditions, prejudices and the like are difficult to break. Primitive man had to seek explanations for the unseen, the fearful; had to arrive at a satisfactory view of an orderly universe; had to find the answers to the so-called "childish" questions of where he came from, and why, how he fit into the total scheme of things, where he was destined to go, and so forth. Once group explanations were devised and accepted, the social pressure upon and punishment of the disobedient and backsliders was great. It has been a long struggle to replace even some of the most outlandish and unprovable ideas which originated in cave man days and shortly thereafter with new ones based on scientific proof or likelihood. History is replete with the records of martyrdom in the interest of advancement of the truth. Every new iconoclastic thought has had to overcome the full weight of united social opposition.

The point seems so elementary as to require no elaboration. Every reader of this book certainly has heard of Socrates, Jesus, Galileo, Columbus, and hundreds or thousands of others who were made to suffer and even die because of their ideas. There is no viciousness to compare with that which men have shown toward other men who differed from them in ideas. "Widely different ideologies cannot exist in the same world" is the way persecution and murder often have been rationalized. Even in the name of religion based on the strongest teachings of tolerance and love, literally hundreds of thousands of lives have been taken in the effort to rid the world of all except the supposedly loving likeminded and consequently "fittest" to survive and breed.

Not only physical security but, equally or more important, mental security also is threatened by iconoclasts and heretics. As one locks his door or builds a higher and thicker wall for protection or seeks to destroy someone who might cause him bodily injury, so he does the equivalent with his infuriated bigoted defenses against any attacks on his mind. A characteristic summing up of the lamentable situation was that of James Harvey Robinson in *The Mind in the Making* (Harper, 1921):

"Few of us take the pains to study the origin of our cherished convictions; indeed, we have a natural repugnance to so doing. We like to continue to believe what we have been accustomed to accept as true, and the resentment aroused when doubt is cast upon any of our assumptions leads us to seek every manner of excuse for clinging to them. The result is that most of our so-called reasoning consists in finding arguments for going on believing as we already do."

With what psychiatric diagnosis would reveal concerning most of the news sources with whom he comes into diurnal contact, the newspaperman need not be concerned. It is, however, valuable for him to be able to understand some of the most commonplace symptoms, and, of them all, bigotry is hardly surpassed in importance. It is an unmistakable sign of insecurity and the louder a bigot shouts and the more vehement and unreasonable his remarks, the more insecure his analyst undoubtedly would find him to be. Ignorance, of course, is a certain breeder of intolerance. One fears the unknown and hesitates to explore it, just as a timid person stops fearfully at the door of an unlighted room. Ignorance, furthermore, is not an exclusive possession of the uneducated. Very often a highly specialized person is grossly uninformed regarding many if not most or all fields outside his own and consequently extremely boorish in his expression of opinions regarding them. Even the best brains that a society possesses may be considered pretty narrow by the succeeding generation. For instance, in 1846 one of England's greatest men of all times, Benjamin Disraeli, commented as follows on the then new theories of evolution: "What is the question now placed before society with the glib assurance which to me is most astonishing? That question is this: Is man an ape or an angel? I, my lords, am on the side of the angels. I repudiate with indignation and abhorrence those new-fangled theories."

But that, it may be objected, was more than a century ago, before the impact of Mendel, Lamarck, and Darwin had been felt; before Pavlov, Freud, Adler, and Jung; before Einstein and, particularly before the Manhattan Project. This is the age of the atom and radar, genes and chromosomes, vitamins and calories; in other words, truly the Age of Science. One could assume then that blind credulity, prejudice, and various forms of bigotry have given way to rationality.

Yet rather than decreasing the tendency toward gullibility, the scientific advancement of the past century has had exactly the opposite effect upon many. The "impossible" has happened so many times— bombs over Hiroshima, radar bouncing off the moon and girdling the earth, television and the like—that who would doubt that it could happen again? Whereas a short generation ago science was treated skeptically, humorously, or even belligerently in the press, and was considered an enemy of religion by many church groups, today the media of communication are almost reverent in their attitude. Nevertheless, people could still be taken in by an Orson Welles broadcast of a Martian invasion of New Jersey on Halloween in 1938, and several years later could be made apprehensive when radio and newspapers combined in spreading rumors of flying disks or saucers. In the early days of exploration, before many men had ventured onto the fearsome ocean, travelers were able to regale the gullible with fantastic tales of sea serpents, giants, and all kinds of freaks of nature. Today reputable editors and their readers must be vigilant to avoid being taken in by stories of prehistoric animals, missing links, haunted houses, curses, miracles, phony feral men and all sorts of tall tales and rumors.

Since the famous Scopes trial in 1925 at Dayton, Tenn., in which Darwinism won a moral but not a legal victory, newspapermen have not had to report many speeches similar to that of Disraeli on evolution. Some members of Congress, however, do still defend segregation of blood in Red Cross blood banks for fear a transfusion of Negro blood into a white man would cause him to have mulatto offspring. And in June, 1949 a member of the Illinois General Assembly opposed a bill to permit licensed colleges and laboratories to obtain unclaimed dogs in public pounds by declaring, "If the cure for blue babies is perfected, they (the experimenters) don't need any more dogs for this type of disease. Do they have to keep practicing in order to keep alive their abilities?"

The vast majority of newspaper readers have no way to distinguish fact from fiction. They do not possess the facilities with which to check the validity of most of the reports reaching them by press, radio or other media. Instead, they must rely on these "usually reliable sources" and most can say, with the late Will Rogers, that "all that I know is what I read in the newspapers."

In our modern complex industrial society the psychological necessity for order and certainty is vital. With the objects of interest and desire so many times multiplied, the dangers of disappointment and consequent frustration are correspondingly increased. Modern man does know more than his ancestors, but what he knows is smaller proportionately to the total amount of potential knowledge. The specialization which our economy demands breeds feelings of inadequacy in all fields other than one's own. It is natural that man should seek "short cuts" to understanding of their subject matter, which accounts for the popularity of outlines and stories of philosophy, history, chemistry, and all other subjects, news reviews and digest magazines, "inside dope" newsletters and "how-to" books on making friends and influencing people, living alone and liking it, and reading other books. To avoid feelings of gross inferiority modern man grasps at simple explanations—"definitions of situations," as the social psychologists say it. It is difficult for the "truth" to prevail against the preconceptions which result. Spreaders of knowledge, including newspapermen, often are up against mental stone walls.

It was Walter Lippmann, the one outstanding journalist who has made a sizeable contribution to the understanding of public opinion, who, perhaps better than anyone else before or since, described what happens in the thinking of the average man as a result of his inability to know and comprehend his complex environment. In *Public Opinion* Lippmann made use of a publishing term "stereotype" which since has been adopted generally by other scholars in this field. He used it to describe the "pictures in our heads" whereby we find shortcuts to understanding. Wrote Lippmann:

"Each of us lives and works on a small part of the earth's surface, moves in a small circle, and of these acquaintances knows only a few intimately. Of any public event that has wide effects we see at best only a phase and an aspect. This is as true of the eminent insiders who draft treaties, make laws and issue orders, as it is of those who have treaties framed for them, laws promulgated to them, orders given at them. Inevitably our opinions cover a bigger space, a longer reach of time, a greater number of things, than we can directly observe. They have, therefore, to be pieced together out of what others have reported and what we can imagine. . . .

"For the most part we do not first see, and then define; we define first and then see. In the great blooming buzzing confusion of the outer world we pick out what our culture has already defined for us, and we tend to perceive that which we have picked out in the form stereotyped for us by our culture. . . .

"They [stereotypes] are an ordered, more or less consistent picture of the world to which our habits, our tastes, our capacities, our comforts and our hopes have adjusted themselves. They may not be a complete picture of the world, but they are a picture of a possible world in which we are adapted. In that world people and things have their well-known places, and do certain expected things. We feel at home there. We fit in. We are members. We know the way around. There we find the charm of the familiar, the normal, the dependable; its grooves and shapes are where we are accustomed to find them. And though we have abandoned much that might have tempted us before we creased ourselves into that mould, once we are firmly in, it fits as snugly as an old shoe." [1]

In more orthodox social scientific language, stereotypes internalize symbols for or caricatures of objects of attention. They are centers

[1] From *Public Opinion*, by Walter Lippmann. Copyright, 1922, by The Macmillan Co.

around which basic attitudes and habits are built up. They are images and ideas of classes, situations and events in advance of personal contacts, by means of which individual members of groups and typical situations can be visualized and defined. This writer once obtained quite a shock when he met the late Sir Percival Phillips. Instead of a lean, tall, blond, monocled, humorless Britisher which one would expect anyone with that title and name to be, there was a short, pudgy, dark, balding, slangy Ohio-born American foreign correspondent who interviewed the writer in his underclothes.

Other popular stereotypes prove as unrealistic but nevertheless persist and have the effect of coloring one's expectations and not too often his observations. Not all old-maid school teachers are horse faced, old fashioned in dress, stern, and utterly lacking in sex appeal; but no cartoonist or casting director would think of violating the stereotype. In 1945 the Writers' War Board published a pamphlet, *How Writers Perpetuate Stereotypes*, the purpose of which was stated clearly in the introductory paragraphs as follows:

"During the year 1944 the Writers' War Board and its Committee to Combat Race Hatred came to the conclusion that the writers of the United States, because of their habitual employment of 'stock characters,' were unconsciously fostering and encouraging group prejudice. To investigate the truth of this conclusion, the Writers' War Board commissioned Columbia University's Bureau of Applied Social Research to make a study of the treatment accorded white, Protestant Anglo-Saxons in mass media as against the treatment accorded all other elements of the American population. When finally completed, this research material became the basis of a performance sponsored and staged by the Board at the Barbizon-Plaza theater, New York, on Jan. 11, 1945.

"An invited audience of 600 writers, editors, artists, publishers, broadcasters, and communications technicians was informed that the constant repetition of racial stereotypes was exaggerating and perpetuating the false and mischievous notion that ours is a white, Protestant Anglo-Saxon country in which all other racial stocks and religious faiths are of lesser dignity. It was promised that the Writers' War Board would prepare and issue a digest of the report of the Columbia University bureau. Here then is that promised report."

Of 889 identifiable characters in 185 short stories in eight nationally circulated magazines, 90.8 per cent were Anglo-Saxon whereas only 9.2 per cent were drawn from all other racial stocks in the United States, the study showed. The bureau concluded on this phase of its study: "The behavior of these fictional characters could easily be used to 'prove' that the Negroes are lazy, the Jews wily, the Irish superstitious and the Italians criminal." Also analyzed were stage plays, motion pictures, comic cartoon books, radio programs, newsreels and advertising copy with generally similar results.

Prohibitionists, with their stovepipe hats, blue noses, long dark clothes and frayed umbrellas; paunchy, bald, sometimes dollar-covered Babbitt-like businessmen; sly, unshaved, long-haired labor agitators with pockets bulging with either subversive literature or destructive weapons; mortar-board-covered, dreamy-eyed, brain-trusting college professors; Stepin Fetchit-type Negroes and Shylock-type Jews are among the most familiar stereotypes. The frequency with which an American tourist is informed by some native with whom he has made friends that, "You're not at all like other Americans," indicates that stereotypes of our own and foreign invention are international. The statement, intended as a compliment, really, of course, is insulting to one's group and consequently to one's self. So is the oft-repeated, "Some of my best friends are Jews," and, of course, any statement beginning, "You're just a typical—".

It is not only persons which are stereotyped. So also are ideas. Discussion of how it is done, by proverbs, slogans, labels and symbols will be found in Chapter 11.

Related to stereotypes are *social sentiments* and *prejudices*. A sentiment is a feeling of admiration or abhorrence, approval or disapproval, or resentment which one feels toward another, or with reference to some event or situation. They are emotional, as well as intellectual. They are influenced by previously formed opinions, but are not public opinion properly speaking since they are unfocalized. Familiar examples are the traditional hatred of Frenchmen for Germans, of capitalists for communists, of fanatical Protestants for Catholics. Sentiments are not only the causes of attitudes which are the bases of opinions but, in turn, influence other attitudes and opinions.

Prejudice means "to pre-judge." In its popular usage a prejudiced person, possessing attitudes and/or opinions based on preconceptions rather than personal experiences, is a bigoted person. He regards truth as absolute, static and unchangeable. Prejudices naturally are emotional and irrational and the prejudiced person is intolerant rather than open-minded.

The Importance of Absolutism

Between the wars a sizeable literature was produced on the subject of Western mankind's confusion over human values. Partly because of the effect of science and of the increased tempo of living in an industrial society, old standards seemed to be tumbling much faster than new ones were being created to take their place. Wrote Walter Lippmann in *A Preface to Morals* (Macmillan, 1935) which, with Joseph Wood Krutch's *The Modern Temper* (Harcourt, Brace, 1929), was about the best of the between-wars analyses:

"The creeds of modernity are so powerful that they do not tolerate a crystallization of ideas which will serve as a new orthodoxy into which men can retreat. And so the modern world is haunted by a realization, which it becomes constantly less eager to ignore, that it is impossible to reconstruct an enduring orthodoxy, and impossible to live well without the satisfaction which an orthodoxy would provide."

The extreme difficulty of getting the kind of cosmic view which science has demonstrated to be necessary has created a sterile period in philosophy during the past half century. With the exception of the humanists, few have even attempted to create "rhyme and reason" in such a fast-changing world, universe, and galaxy.

Regarding the effect of modern science and life on the intelligentsia Frederick E. Lumley wrote in *The Propaganda Menace* (Appleton-Century-Crofts, Inc., 1933) as follows:

"To the most cultured people truth is more partial and relative than it has ever been. To these people absolutisms are but relics of the days of ignorance and superstitions. Uncertainties are recognized everywhere. Consequently there is renewed enthusiasm for investigation; research is the guiding word today, research and change. More people than ever before in human history are less sure about what they know and how they know it, but more people are eager to know and to be sure. The evidence for these assertions is everywhere about us; the chief evidence is in the stupendous growth of modern science."

Not even scientists, however, have escaped the "curse" of *absolut-*

ism, another obstacle to the fact disseminator. Their search is for an orderly universe and once they think they have found it, they are not happy about having it overthrown. When, early in the century, the experiments of Michelson and Morley disproved the existence of an all-pervading ether and cleared the way for Einstein's special and general theories of relativity, there was great mental anguish in the scientific world. There ought to be an ether, just as there ought to be a Santa Claus. Life would be so much happier if there were one. Then there would be a plane of reference by which to "place" anything and everything. The thesis that "the only absolute is that there are no absolutes" isn't very conducive to peace of mind or productive of a sense of security.

The extreme absolutist in any field is a fanatic. His is the only true religion, politics, moral code, set of economic beliefs. Few fanatics are pleasant people in discussion or debate. A good antidote to exposure to fanatics of any one type is exposure to another group "on the other side" of the same issue. Fanatics are fanatics, whether of right or left, orthodox or heretical. A fanatic's world is one of blacks and whites, right and wrong, good and bad with no grays or extenuating circumstances. A fanatic is actually a person who is insecure but who "covers up" by becoming a bigot. Most people cannot properly be called fanatics, but there is hardly anyone who isn't "hipped" on something.

One vexatious and much discussed form that absolutism takes is bureaucratic-mindedness. Much of the abuse that has been heaped on government officials—bureaucrats—is undeserved. They are not all red-tape lovers, arbitrary, pretentious, and slaves to formal rules any more than are their counterparts in private industry. Bigness in either government or private industry means that rules and regulations multiply. These, however, *can* become so unwieldy as to slow up rather than hasten attainment of the ends which they were created to serve. Most persons revolt against such formalism, but some don't. Rather, they become enamoured with the order and consequent security which result from making what originally were means to an end become ends in themselves. Army officers and superfluous vice presidents in industry can be as bookkeeper-minded as any public administrator whose discretionary powers are strictly limited by hostile or critical Congressmen. The church, schools, labor unions, in fact, all institutions, are not immune and must guard against the disease. The chancery (equity) courts developed in medieval England when the courts of law became so tradition-ridden that appeals to the Crown multiplied in the attempt to obtain justice in matters not covered by existing statutes or precedents. The principle of *stare decisis* (let the decision stand) still is a stumbling block. Many a jurist has confessed, as did Federal Judge John Knox in *Order in the Court* (Scribner, 1943) that more than once he was compelled to render decisions contrary to his better judgment because of legal tradition. In his *Woe Unto You, Lawyers* (Reynal & Hitchcock, 1939) Fred Rodell takes some terrific cracks at legal-mindedness. He charges that society suffers because most lawyers believe there *is* such a thing as abstract justice which merely needs to be identified and applied to any particular case at hand. Another critic of absolutism in the law, and anywhere else it may be found, Thurman W. Arnold, wrote in *The Symbols of Government* (Yale, 1935):

"This struggle to formulate ideals and principles which are sound, systematic and consistent leads only to the building of utopias on the part of reformers and the defense of abuses on the part of conservatives. This is as true in small affairs as in large ones. The struggle for procedural reform in law offers us an example of the slowness of change in an institution whose critics and reformers refuse to think objectively."

It is through study of the extreme forms of human behavior that much of what is known about so-called normal behavior has been learned. The psychological differences between the fanatic or the bureaucratic-minded and the more tolerant person are qualitative, not quantitative. Even the most scientifically minded must look for the beam in his own eye before condemning the mote in another's. It is utterly impossible for anyone to avoid being suggestible in the direction determined by his previous conditioning. We all find it easier and more pleasant to believe what we want to believe and to reject whatever reaches our consciousness which does not square with our preconceptions. To become social beings we must learn to act and think in the ways considered proper within the group to which we are trying to adjust. Most of the simple elementary matters—table manners, correct forms of speech, and so forth—are learned early and are reduced as much as possible to the level of routine habits. At the same time, however, more important conditioning is taking place to instill in the child the religious, political, moral, and other ideas and ideals which influence his thought and action throughout the rest of his life. Despite the violent clashes of opinion recognizable within any culture, the similarities between those who are a part of that culture are greater than their differences. Not, as the preceding chapter explained, because of instincts, or group minds or rational thinking, but because of similarity of early social conditioning.

As society grows in size and complexity, however, clashes of interest multiply and the differences between persons become more fundamental and important. *With the highest conscious motives, persons with different backgrounds interpret the same objective facts in widely dissimilar ways.* Their thinking, we say, is "colored" by their religious, political or economic bringing up. Consequently, to restate a point made earlier in this chapter, one cannot place too much hope in reform of the press of any or all of its sins. Take the familiar example of lawlessness, filthiness, or illiteracy among slum dwellers. To the objective newspaper reporting of facts and pictures Reader A may respond: "See what happens to human beings when we allow such bad conditions to exist," whereas Reader B declares: "Riffraff will ruin any neighborhood and undermine American ideals if not squelched." Dislike of a person or of the group he represents makes one more likely to believe the worst about him. Anti-Catholics, for instance, are predisposed to accept as true a scandalous bit of gossip regarding a priest, whereas some Catholics find it easy to do the same when a Protestant clergyman is concerned. It's perfectly normal to be that way. Nobody can help it. One shouldn't need any course in abnormal psychology to recognize and understand such phenomena. Rightness or wrongness has nothing to do with it, if for no other reason than that ideas of what is right and what is wrong differ as between individuals and groups at the same time and within the same groups at different times. The "devil theory" of human motivation gets one nowhere in trying to understand his fellows. The fanatical left-winger who regards the dyed-in-the-wool conservative as a vicious, mean, greedy plutocrat whose chief pleasure is seeing others suffer so he may prosper, is just as much "off the beam" as the fanatical right-winger who thinks every workingman should be frisked to see how many bombs he's carrying in anticipation of blowing up everything just for the fun of it.

The Experimental Laboratory

The findings of both the experimental and clinical psychological laboratories support the central thesis of this chapter: not much reliance can be placed on the axiom: "Give the people the facts and they will find the way."

The work of Ivan Pavlov on conditioned responses is familiar to everyone who has had a high-school course in biology. The Russian scientist rang a bell while showing food to a dog. After a while the animal salivated at the sound of the bell only, without the sight of the food, the original stimulus. Some authorities have gone so far as to say that all learning, even prenatal, is the result of chain-action, conditioned responses. Such is substantially the thesis of the behaviorists as set forth in *Behavior*, by John B. Watson (Holt, 1914) and of Edwin Holt in *Animal Drive and the Learning Process* (Holt, 1931), to cite two leading references. Even though this point of view may be considered extreme, it is undeniable that once learning has occurred, by whatever process, future behavior is conditioned by the habits and attitudes that have been formed.

Watson's famous experiments with infants were among the first. Using Pavlov's techniques he induced different emotional reactions in babies by associating loud noises with harmless animals and by similar situations. All sorts of attitude tests reveal differences between subjects with variegated racial, religious, economic and other backgrounds. Popular among some psychiatrists are the Rorschach ink blot tests whereby clues to personality are obtained by the interpretations those taking them give to the meaningless figures. Word association tests serve a similar purpose: unusual or delayed responses provide the clues. In such tests subjects are read lists of words and asked to respond with other words which those asked suggest. For instance, if the experimenter says "white," the subject may answer "black," or he may say "surrender" or "house" or any of a number of things. Years of analysis of thousands of cases has made it possible to form some judgments of those who give certain answers.

Many experiments to determine suggestibility are also (or primarily) ones in conditioning. For instance, before taking any kind of opinion test subjects may be told what the viewpoint of experts or of the majority is supposed to be. Invariably the results show a tendency to agree with what apparently is the "correct" point of view, whereas other, similar groups with which no attempt was made to precondition the subjects respond differently. Many and many a class in psychology has been victimized by professors who attempt to demonstrate to the students their own gullibility. An orthodox experiment is to tell the young people to raise their hands when they hear a sound or smell an odor or see a light. Even though there may be no sound, odor, or light, an astonishing number of the "victims" always accept the suggestion that the opposite is so. A modification of the experiment is actually to flash a light or make a noise several times at regular intervals; when the time interval is changed, subjects continue to respond in accordance with the pattern which has been established.

"We may define suggestion as a form of symbol-communication by words, pictures, or some similar medium inducing acceptance of the symbol without any self-evident or logical ground for its acceptance," writes Kimball Young in *Social Psychology* (Appleton-Century-Crofts, Inc., 1947).

A pioneer in the experimental study of suggestion, Boris Sidis, wrote in *The Psychology of Suggestion* (Appleton, 1898):

"Suggestibility is a fundamental attribute of man's nature. We must therefore expect that man, in his social capacity, will display this general property; and so do we actually find the case to be. What is required is only the condition to bring about a disaggregation in the social consciousness. This disaggregation may either be fleeting, unstable—then the type of suggestibility is that of the normal one; or it may become stable—then the suggestibility is of the abnormal type. The one is the suggestibility of the crowd, the other that of the mob. In the mob direct suggestion is effective, in the crowd indirect suggestion."

Nobody ever stripped man to his psychological nakedness more thoroughly than did Everett Dean Martin in *The Behavior of Crowds* (Harper, 1920) from which come the following often-quoted extracts:

"My thesis is that the crowd-mind is a phenomenon which should best be classed with dreams, delusions, and the various forms of automatic behavior. The controlling ideas of the crowd are the result neither of reflection nor of 'suggestion,' but are akin to what, as we shall see later, the psychoanalysts term 'complexes.' The crowd-self— if I may speak of it in this way—is analogous in many respects to 'compulsion neurosis,' 'somnambulism,' or 'paranoiac episode.' Crowd ideas are 'fixations'; they are always symbolic; they are always related to something repressed in the unconscious. . . .

"The unconscious egoism of the individual in the crowd appears in all forms of crowd-behavior. . . . The 'censor' is less active in the crowd than in most phases of mental life . . . the 'compulsive' character of the mechanisms frequently . . . well nigh reduces the individual to an automaton, the crowd is one of the most naive devices that can be employed for enhancing one's ego consciousness. The individual has only to transfer his repressed self feeling to the idea of the crowd or group of which he is a member; he can then exalt and exhibit himself to almost any extent without shame, oblivious of the fact that the supremacy, power, praise, and glory which he claims for his crowd are really claimed for himself. . . .

"The crowd does not think in order to solve problems. To the crowd-mind, as such, there are no problems. It has closed its case beforehand. This accounts for what LeBon termed the 'credulity' of the crowd. But the crowd believes only what it wants to believe and nothing else. . . .

"The crowd-mind is everywhere idealistic, and absolutist. Its truths are 'given,' made-in-advance. . . . To the crowd-mind a principle appears as an end in itself. It must be vindicated at all costs. To offend against it in one point is to be guilty of breaking the whole law. Crowds are always uncompromising about their principles. They must apply to all alike. Crowds are no respecters of persons."

Mob-mindedness can exist without the physical existence of a crowd. "Everybody's doing it" is the point of view of the wastrel who breaks a moral law, the motorist who exceeds the speed limit, the domestic who "totes," or the businessman who "chisels" his customers or evades the income tax, anti-trust, or other laws. More seriously one may taunt, cheat or commit physical violence on a member of an unpopular group; or he may be "carried away" by a craze, movement, or other manifestation of mass hysteria.

A strong factor in any experiment to test suggestibility is the prestige of the experimenter or of authority to whom appeal is made or of the medium used. Professors as a rule get better results than instructors or assistants unless, of course, they are extremely unpopular with their classes. If the experiment is one to test alleged agreement or disagreement with an authority, the extent to which the person cited is a controversial figure will influence the results. Use of the ordinary media of communication—newspapers, magazines, books, radio, motion pictures—increases the likelihood of a subject's being uncritical when the suggestion is put. Innumerable experiments have been conducted to demonstrate almost unbelievable carelessness on the part of highly intelligent people in putting their names to incredible petitions. In November, 1947, for instance, 26 of 40 prominent Northwestern University student leaders solicited signed a petition recommending that a pile of lumber on the campus be removed to the reserve room in the library. In *Making of a Reporter* (Putnam, 1942) Will Irwin related a successful stunt involving much more important victims at the Versailles conference in 1921. The perpetrators were a group of San Francisco newspapermen. Wrote Irwin:

"In language burlesquing these manifestoes and proclamations we drew up a declaration of an autonomous California. We demanded Nevada on racial and economic grounds. 'This territory was settled by people who started for California and never got there,' and 'San Francisco is the main support of Reno's leading industry.' We wanted the Columbia River neutralized—'It is the breeding ground for the California salmon; and we hold it intolerable that this purely Californian fish should during its vital years of infancy and early maturity live under the domination of an ethnically alien people.' On the other hand, we left Los Angeles and vicinity to the United States as an enclave 'on account of the ethnic influence of Iowa.' We peppered the document with a few jokers such as calling M. H. deYoung, owner of the ultraconservative *Chronicle*, 'leader of the militant labor unions.' Then I put on my uniform and solemnly delivered a mimeographed copy to every propaganda bureau in Paris; and one of our men took a copy to Berlin. All the recipients, including the Germans, on first sight took it seriously. The experiment was a success." [2]

The author's *Hoaxes* (Macmillan, 1940) is replete with similar examples of the ease with which human beings can be taken in by the most outlandish of pranks, serious and otherwise. The following is from that book's introduction:

"Throughout history mobs have formed and become hysterical;

[2] From *The Making of a Reporter*, by Will Irwin. Copyright, 1942, by Will Irwin. Used by permission.

governments have fallen; reputations have been made and destroyed; international relations have been strained, and wars have been fought, all as a result of hoaxes which were exposed too late. Scholars have met in serious conclave, or have traveled to all parts of the earth; navigators have sailed the seas; audiences have filled halls; the stock market has risen and fallen; newspaper offices have been raided and closed and court trials have dragged on for months merely because some person or persons had to have his or their joke."

When a person is suggestible in the direction of his interests or desires, he is said popularly to engage in "wishful thinking." That means an inclination to see what one wants to see, to believe what it serves one's purpose or flatters his ego to believe. This human trait affects one's ability to observe and recall correctly and is a handicap to accurate reporting and to court testimony. A typical experiment in simple eye witness reliability was reported by the United Press on June 30, 1936, as follows:

Minneapolis.—(UP)—Eye-witness testimony, often vital in law courts, has been tested in an experiment at the University of Minnesota department of psychology.

The experiment consisted of an unusual incident in a classroom where 216 psychology students were listening to a lecture by Prof. Kenneth Baker. Despite simplicity of questions asked following the incident, the students gave widely varied answers.

The experiment was conducted in this manner:

Prof. Baker's lecture was interrupted suddenly by Prof. Howard P. Longstaff, who walked to the platform carrying a slip of blue paper. He wore a brown overcoat and a red baseball player's cap.

CLASS IS SURPRISED

"Mr. Professor," he said, "here is a telegram for you."

Prof. Baker tried not to accept the paper, but it was forced into his hand and the messenger left the platform. The action was staged with no fore knowledge of the class.

The procedure lasted 15 seconds. Immediately after the students were asked a series of questions. The results follow:

Virtually all of the class said Prof. Longstaff wore a brown coat. Forty-five said he had on a baseball cap, 10 just said "cap," and 30 said a red cap. Several, however, said he wore a hat, two said he had nothing on his head, and others described the headpiece as a skull cap, stocking cap or tam.

AT VARIANCE ON TIME

Estimates on time varied widely. Only 18 said 15 seconds, while the majority of the class estimated 30 seconds or more, 27 said a full minute and a few said as high as two minutes.

Out of the entire class, 53 admitted they had no idea of what time the demonstration took place. The majority of estimates were fairly accurate.

Most of the class said the message was on blue paper, but 28 said it was yellow, and nine said white.

GREATEST ERROR ON CONFLICT

The greatest error occurred on the question as to which person struck the other. Although neither man struck a blow, 62 students said the messenger struck the lecturer, and 119 said the lecturer struck the messenger. Only 18 said no blow was struck.

Professor Longstaff, the messenger, had previously lectured before the class for six hours and conducted two quizzes. Yet 58 were unable to identify him, and six gave wrong identifications.

Only 70 of the 216 said the messenger addressed Professor Baker as "Mr. Professor." Eighty-four asserted he said "Professor." Others said the messenger called him "Professor Baker," "Mr. Baker," "Mr. Teacher," "Hey, mister," "Teacher" and other variations.

The late Webb Miller, long-time United Press correspondent in Europe, confessed in *I Found No Peace* (Simon, Schuster, 1936) to the psychological obstacles in the path of the reporter dedicated to the cause of obtaining the truth that will set men free, as follows:

"The most important thing I learned professionally was that the truth about anything is difficult to obtain; that the more I studied the various aspects of any particular subject, the more qualified, the less definite and clear-cut my opinions became. Twenty centuries ago Greek philosophers discovered there is no exact truth except in mathematics.

"Even when I witnessed an event myself I saw it differently from others. When I questioned eye witnesses, persons who had no reason to distort the truth, each told a somewhat different story. I had to strike an average of their stories and temper this with my judgment of the circumstances and interests involved to come somewhere near the truth. I found that even when people with the best will in the world tried to tell the truth and nothing but the truth they could not do it. Each one saw something different. Every man's imagination unwittingly distorted what his eyes saw." [3]

In *The Psychology of Rumor* (Holt, 1947), Gordon W. Allport and Leo Postman reported on a number of experiments reminiscent of the parlor game of transmitting information from one player to another down a line or around a circle for the purpose of a laugh at the end over the extent to which distortion had taken place. In the Allport and Postman experiments Player No. 1 studied a picture which he then described to Player 2 and so on, usually through six or seven steps. It takes several chapters to relate the multitudinous and multifarious ways in which the descriptions became modified. Typical finding was that whereas 92 per cent of the proper names included in the test pictures were given correctly in the original description, on the first retelling only 51 per cent were correct, 18 per cent incorrect and 31 per cent "leveled out"—that is, ignored. By the fifth retelling only 18 per cent of the proper names were given correctly, 5 per cent were given incorrectly and 77 per cent were leveled out.

The findings of the experimental laboratory, to summarize, are one-sided. Regardless of the technique used, and many have been tried, the results invariably show that man is highly suggestible, especially in the direction of his interests and preconceptions. He also is a poor observer and transmission of his eye-witness reports is unreliable, increasingly so as the process continues. The freest press conceivable, trafficking only in strictly objective facts, is at best only a small part of the answer to the problem of how to obtain the utopian society.

The Clinical Laboratory

In addition to the experimental laboratory, during the past century and a half—importantly the latter half of that period—there has been the clinical laboratory where attempts to relieve mental suffering have led to important new concepts regarding the basic motivations of human behavior.

Modern clinical psychology is not, strictly speaking, a denial or refutation of all, or of any appreciable part, of what preceded it. Rather, it is a divorce from, a virtual ignoring of, most of the animism, philosophy, theology, metaphysics, epistemology, and even outworn

[3] From *I Found No Peace*, by Webb Miller. Copyright, 1936, by Simon & Schuster, Inc.

biology with which the psychology of the past was associated. Present-day psychiatrists accept man as he is here today, in his mundane existence, without too much concern over where he came from or where he may be going.

One basic tenet of the modern clinical psychology is that *the difference between so-called normal and so-called abnormal behavior is one of degree rather than kind.* As some wag put it: the abnormal are just like we are, only more so. Richard Muller-Freienfels in *The Evolution of Modern Psychology* (Yale, 1935) declared: "At any rate we can safely say that even the most bizarre pathological phenomena are not wholly different from manifestations of normal mental life but are either quantitative or qualitative variants of what are considered to be 'normal' states. This enables us to understand mental abnormalities to a certain extent. In turn, hyper-intensities, subnormalities, and other abnormal variants shed interesting light upon normal cases. Pathological states are often distortions of normal experience in which certain normal features appear in an exaggerated form, or in sharper focus. Thus, pathological melancholia is the profound intensification of the 'blues,' which are still considered normal, while the 'fixed ideas' of mental patients correspond to the 'single-track' associations of otherwise normal people."

Of equal importance is the prevalent modern belief that *one's psychological present is the consequence of his psychological past.* Orthodox psychiatric procedure is to attempt to discover the childhood experiences and other causes of a patient's present unhappiness or personality difficulties. With well over 50 per cent of all hospital beds in the United States occupied by mental patients, and as a result of the popularization of psychiatry through its use during World War II by the armed forces and by the motion pictures, magazine articles, and book authors, this branch of medicine is growing rapidly. More important, the stigma formerly attached to having been a mental patient is being overcome and it seems safe to predict that the time is not far off when psychiatrists will be consulted as freely and with no more shame than are physicians and surgeons today.

The greatest influence in the development of psychiatry and of the preventive mental hygiene movement was, of course, Dr. Sigmund Freud of Vienna who developed the therapy known as psychoanalysis as a substitute for hypnosis and theorized elaborately on the basis of more than a half century of clinical practice. It is not germane to the purpose of this book to go into elaborate description of Freudian psychology with its seemingly exotic terms, such as ego, superego, libido, and id. Familiar is the fact that Freud emphasized sex as the most important life force. According to him each human passes through four stages in his sexual development: autoerotic (during which the primary interest, to the infant, is his own body); Oedipus (approximately from two to five years of age during which the child is deeply attached to his mother and regards the father as a rival); homosexual; and heterosexual. Neurotic behavior results if the passage from one stage to the next is retarded or incomplete.

Although the extreme importance of early sexual experience is recognized by present-day neo-Freudians, there has been a considerable revolt against accepting the sexual urge as the complete key to the riddle of human behavior. Even more widely known than Freud's concept of the Oedipus complex is that of the inferiority complex postulated by one of the father of psychoanalysis' early disciples, Alfred Adler. To the latter, who called his theories "individual psychology," generally considered a misnomer, the basic drive is not sexual but successful adjustment to social living. The challenge of life, Adler taught, is to win prestige by conquering life's difficulties. Failures cause frustrations which lead to inferiority complexes and attempts to overcome (or compensate for) those feelings. Neuroses develop as unsuccessful attempts at such adjustments. Neurotics, in other words, are discouraged slaves of ambition.

Another early Freudian disciple, Carl Jung, desexualized the libido and talked about psychic energy. Everyone, he said, has so much energy and it may be degraded and dissipated in sex or utilized in religion, art, and other socially approved ways. Jung saw life as a process imbued with the elements of the remote past, and his psychology is the portrayal of a conflict against this archaic past.

It would be possible to go on and on to name numerous others who have modified or supplemented Freud's theories or advanced ones of their own. The master's greatest contribution of all, however, has remained virtually unchallenged, although unfortunately ignored to a considerable extent by Adler. That concept is the existence of *an unconscious mind which exists as a reservoir of memories which influence subsequent behavior even though one is consciously unaware of them.* Without this concept there would be virtually no modern psychiatry. To simplify Freud's original concept: there is a mental censor which suppresses unpleasant but important desires or thoughts. During sleep and other dissociated states the censor is weakened. Just as daydreams are always wish fulfillments, so are night dreams, Freud declared. Psychoanalysts still consider their patients' night dreams as containing important clues to the causes of their anxieties; they attempt to interpret the symbolism characteristic of many dreams and to correct the distortions, at least in recall, which are common.

Others have emphasized more than Freud the cultural factors which determine what is to be censored and thus shoved into the unconscious. The more complicated the environment, it is contended, the greater the number of things which are forbidden and consequently the greater danger of frustration and neurotic behavior. The differences between Freud and Adler and others regarding the importance of the sexual urge or as regards "life and death instincts" (Freud), "collective unconscious" (Adler), and "masculine protest" (Jung) become decidedly secondary. Certainly, at least, that is true when the purpose is to study and understand public opinion. Many of the phenomena with which the newspaperman comes into contact are mass demonstrations of the operation of unconscious "defense mechanisms" by means of which the supposedly normal, as well as the abnormal, seek to avoid frustration. The following discussion concerns a number of the most important defense mechanisms.

Rationalization. Unless we could "salve" our consciences life often would be unendurable. Nobody can live permanently with a strong sense of guilt for having sinned against the laws of either God or man. To accept the fact that one is mean, cruel, or otherwise reprehensible is virtually impossible without considerable assistance which —from whatever source—amounts to psychiatric treatment.

To avoid the maladjustment which might otherwise result from admission of one's real motives for a questionable action, we unconsciously advance better—meaning more socially acceptable—reasons. For instance, we say that the cruel slap or kick we give an animal or child is "for its own good" and we may repeat the old saw about its hurting us more than it does the victim. If we are timid about speaking up in a meeting we rationalize that we are being tactful, biding our time for a more opportune moment, refraining from showing our hand, or avoiding suspicion of agreeing with radicals which would impair our future usefulness. By such mental gymnastics we actually can make ourselves feel virtuous for having done the wrong rather than the right thing. The motorist who refuses aid to an accident victim rationalizes that he was in a hurry, had to keep an appointment in the next town, or that he was unaware of the seriousness of the injured person's injuries, didn't believe there was anything he could do, believed that more and better assistance would be forthcoming soon, and so forth.

Illness is a common excuse for avoiding doing the disagreeable. Long before the term "psychosomatic medicine" was coined, keen-minded laymen as well as psychiatrists and their predecessors were able to recognize the real motivation for the sick headache which conveniently comes just in time to make it impossible to perform an unpleasant task. All of us commit what the experts call Freudian errors, some of which assist us in obtaining legitimate excuses to avoid doing what we don't want to do. Typical example is the man who cuts himself badly while shaving, thus making it impossible to keep an appointment which he unconsciously wanted to break anyway. Many forms of abnormal behavior serve the same purpose. Amnesia, for example, not only provides good newspaper copy, especially when the victim is prominent, but, more important, gives the victim the escape from reality that he unconsciously desires. Thus, the businessman who leaves his home for the bank where he is to sign a paper which is very distasteful to him suddenly, before reaching his destination, swerves in his path and goes, instead, to the nearest railroad station. There he purchases a ticket to some far-off place. Arriving there, under a different name, he leads a life entirely different from that to which he is accustomed. Days, weeks, months, sometimes years later, as suddenly as he changed his resolution the day he was on the way to the bank, something happens to his consciousness. He seems to awaken as from a dream. He recalls his real name, remembers his departure from home and his walk to the bank, wonders where on earth he is and how he got there. It's good newspaper copy and usually enough time has elapsed so that it no longer is necessary or perhaps even possible for the amnesia victim to do what he really ran away to avoid doing.

What makes rationalization a normal way to avoid facing reality whereas amnesia is considered an abnormal way of doing the same thing is merely the fact that the former method is much more frequent. According to Kimball Young in *Social Psychology* (Appleton-Century-Crofts, 1947): "It has often been implied and even openly stated that rationalization is a pathological and somewhat evil type of behavior. Rather, however, this device serves man admirably in soothing his conscience, or his socially conditioned sense of right or wrong. It provides a defense against the exposure of violent, anti-social, or unethical motives. The genuine motives can often be brought to light only by careful analysis of past behavior and usually only by persons who are sufficiently outside one's social picture to reexamine one's conduct objectively. Rationalizations, at least those acceptable to one's group, make for smooth and uninhibited behavior. It is hard to live in the world of our fellows, to participate in social life, if we are constantly aware of the true foundations of our conduct. In fact, the usual interpretation of one's own conduct or of one's own culture is likely to be an elaborate rationalization."

Just as there are both individual and public opinions so, as Young intimated, are there public as well as individual rationalizations. It is common practice, for instance, for newspapermen to excuse the shortcomings of their profession by asserting they "give the public what it wants." Lynchers "defend Southern womanhood" and "keep the Negro in his place." Manufacturers who employ labor spies or goons to break strikes rationalize their immoral and sometimes illegal behavior by asserting they are defending the industry they represent, possibly the American free enterprise system as a whole, against communist-inspired rebellion.

Much of what has been considered the world's best philosophical, historical, religious, economic, political and other types of theorizing has been essentially rationalization. Some of the earliest important examples were provided by the Greek philosopher Aristotle who justified both human slavery and capital punishment through application of his celebrated principle of "the golden mean." The divine right of kings thesis certainly was a rationalization to justify the existence of absolute monarchy. With the age of exploration the feudal system became archaic, unable to produce sufficiently to meet the new commercial needs. A number of philosophic theories about the innate equality of man arose to justify the democratic revolts against political and economic tyranny of the seventeenth, eighteenth, and early nineteenth centuries. Few Americans would argue that the results were not good or even question the value of the "all men are created free and equal" thesis. Nevertheless, Rousseau, Locke, Voltaire, and Jefferson *were* rationalizers in the interest of justifying the revolt of the underdog in many countries.

Familiar to readers of Rudyard Kipling are the phrases, "white man's burden" and "manifest destiny" by means of which the European imperialist attempted to rationalize expansion in order to establish worldwide empires. Many a colonial administrator has justified repressive measures because the alleged inferiority of the natives rendered them unfit to rule or make decisions for themselves.

Economic man, "laws" of supply and demand, and misapplications of the findings of the evolutionists regarding struggles for existence and survivals of the fittest are among the rationalizations of ruthless exploitation in the field of economics.

One common form of rationalization, important to recognize in the study of public opinion, is "everybody's doing it." This is a cynical point of view which enables one to flout the codes of correct conduct even when not buoyed up by the physical presence of a lawless crowd. It is a form of mob-mindedness without the mob. "It's all right if I sneak this book out of the library," the student rationalizes, "because all of my classmates do the same thing." The extent to which this, or any other rationalization, achieves its purpose of easing the conscience and maintaining mental poise, depends upon the reality and strength of the social code which one rationalizes he is observing regardless of how much his behavior violates other codes. In other words, attempts at rationalization are not always successful and many of the beds for mental patients are occupied by persons who failed in theirs. If there were a bed for everyone who ever tried rationalization, of course, the total would be the same as that of the population as a whole.

Compensation. Even without going "the whole hog" with Alfred Adler regarding the primary importance of the urge for prestige, it is difficult to deny that one's failures will "get one down" unless there is a psychological means of escape. The familiar term to describe this method of avoiding frustration is compensation, "the substitution of one goal for another or of one method of reaching a goal for another," to quote Young again.

The child who is neglected at home may compensate for his low status there by becoming a hard-working and brilliant student at school. The rejected lover may throw himself into business or politics or some other effort. The homely wallflower who never can become a social butterfly may become a scholar. And so on through many similar simple situations which the reader easily can think up for himself. Note, however, the "may" in each case cited. There is no inevitability. Instead of becoming a brilliant student, the neglected child may become just the opposite in the unconscious effort to win attention at home by badness instead of by goodness. Instead of "pitching into" some hard work to overcome his sorrows, the rejected lover may jump into the lake or remain a broken-hearted failure. The social misfit may become a snob, sometimes described as "a social coward," or a cynic, generally someone who "can't take it," as the slang expression goes.

Compensation may take several socially important forms. One, as pointed out by Adler, is *overcompensation*. The boisterous, back-slapping and somewhat obnoxious extravert may in reality be an overcompensated introvert overacting in his attempt to acquire the kind of personality necessary for popularity in his cultural environment. Whatever other attributes he may have, if a person in our society cannot overcome a "cold fish" personality, he runs the constant risk of social ostracism, the most severe form of social punishment. In our culture it would be difficult to find a social group in which one would attempt to simulate introversion or asceticism in order to get along better. Such, however, might well be the case in another part of the world or in our own geographical area at some other period. The forms compensation takes, in other words, are culturally determined. If one wishes to probe further into the subject he should examine the factors which cause a cultural group to place a high premium on one form of behavior rather than on an alternative form. In the next chapter attention is directed to this basic problem.

Another socially important form of overcompensation, certainly originating with an inferiority complex, is the *superiority* complex. This is the form of escapism which may be used by members of minority groups which are objects of unjust discrimination. Among Chicago Negroes, for instance, are to be found cults whose "bibles" have been written to explain that Adam and several generations which followed him were black. By some act of medical magic some humans changed their skin color to white and, by gross chicanery, gained control of the earth. It is, however, written in the sacred books accepted by these cults that the wrong ultimately shall be righted. Similar "messianic hopes" have been held by other downtrodden groups unable to find solace in the promises of orthodox religion that in the afterlife the last shall be first, and so forth. Whipped up by the proper amount of evangelical fervor, such hopes can become paranoiac, with groups as with individuals. The paranoid is one who has delusions of grandeur or of persecution, really the same thing, as he believes his persecution results from his importance. The incidence of such psychotic behavior among American minority groups, need it be pointed out, is slight. In this phase of life, as in all others, the possible psychological reactions are many. One alternative reaction is aggression; another is meek compliance—Uncle Tom behavior—the child-like attitude which seems to say, "If I'm good and act like you want me to, you won't hurt me." There are also always some masochists who accept their plight as their just deserts because of some transgression, real or imaginary, personal or inherited from one's ancestors. And there are those who try to escape physically by accepting Jim Crow and ignoring the other world from which they are excluded anyway. This by no means exhausts the possible avenues of escape but should be enough to serve as a warning against too glib generalizing. Whenever one form of compensation is widespread to the exclusion of others, there is a reason which only careful and thorough investigation can disclose.

Two other recognizable forms of compensation are *substitution* and *sublimation*. The former, also sometimes called *transference* or *displacement,* means the giving up of one form of behavior for another which is more socially approved. A frequently cited example is that of a young man whose mother disapproved his engagement. Unwilling or unable to abandon his intention to marry for that reason, the poor fellow developed an illness which gave him a reason which he could justify to himself and to others. To sublimate is to substitute for a lower form of behavior one which has high moral approval. The jilted girl who enters a nunnery, for instance, is sublimating. So is the person who overcomes his inferiority by going in for art or poetry or classical music. Childless couples adopt orphans, old maids become nurses or kindergarten teachers—beautiful ways to overcome their disappointment at not being parents in their own right.

A final outstanding form of compensation is *vicarious escapism*. Bewildered and belittled by the size and complexity of one's environment, one may seek an outlet in adventure stories, exciting romances, hero worship of athletes or popular entertainers, or in riotous entertainment. In every important culture known to Western civilization there have been avenues of mass vicarious escapism. Arenas, bull fights, parades, ceremonies, Coney Islands, world fairs, professional sports, and many others easily come to mind. In our times the motion pictures perform an important function in this respect by creating a world of fantasy which serves as a conventional outlet for unfulfilled desires. Radio soap operas do the same, and there has been "trashy" literature for the frustrated at every period of history. These media may or may not fall short of providing the satisfaction equivalent to that which comes from participant activities, such as folk dancing, player rather than spectator sports, travel, fishing, hunting and the like. In the secret society one obtains both the opportunity to participate, his ego exalted by high sounding titles and gorgeous costumes, and to dwell in a fictitious dream world of mysterious signs, omens, slogans, and hand grips. It's an unreal environment but dwelling in it temporarily makes the colder reality of everyday life more endurable.

Regression. Otherwise perfectly healthy, physically and mentally, a dishwasher nevertheless delighted reporters and photographers by succumbing to an irresistible urge to walk backwards on the crowded streets of Denver. Psychiatric diagnosis was easy: symbolic regression. Because he was dissatisfied with his employment, the man wanted to return to an earlier job in which he was happy.

Regardless of whether the stages through which he passes are those enumerated by Freud or some different ones, there is no doubt that a person grows up and that behavior considered normal at one age level becomes queer at least at another. As St. Paul put it (I Cor. 13:11) "When I was a child, I spake as a child, I understood as a child, I thought as a child; but when I became a man, I put away childish things."

Failure to mature socially is called *fixation*. It is not so common as regression which is the resumption of the behavior of an earlier age.

It is a way of escaping from frustration through failure to succeed at a more advanced age. In its Feb. 1, 1938 issue *Look* gave a page of pictures and comment to Mrs. "Chebby" Cohen, British housewife, who, although 23 at the time, dressed like a 10-year-old and played house and dolls with children. In the February, 1937 *Virginia Medical Monthly,* Dr. Beverley R. Tucker reported on an extreme case of regression. It was that of a middle-aged woman who could not adjust to widowhood after a lifetime of pampering, first by her mother and later by her husband. First she adopted the dress and mannerisms of a younger "merry widow," then by regressive stages became an adolescent, a child and an infant. Finally, she "assumed the foetal posture," to quote Dr. Tucker, "breathing gently being her only movement." In comment the doctor wrote: "Regression as a personality reaction is not uncommon. The vicissitudes and complexities of life bring out many and varied reactions. Certain individuals meeting particular situations with which they feel an inability to cope compensate by regressing in their personalities to a period which to them is more simple and more satisfying to their feeling-tones. However, those who regress usually stop and stick, either permanently or for a while, at some specific period. Many of these, as the causative circumstances clear, return to normal."

Among older children thumb sucking (imitative of infant nursing), bed wetting, and temper tantrums may be forms of regression. Some authorities contend that much homosexuality is the result of regression after the subjects have made unsuccessful attempts at heterosexual adjustments. Weepy, baby-talking, clinging-vine women are using childish tricks to obtain advantages, usually from men whose egos are flattered by the apparent evidence of dependence on them.

At the collective behavior level, crowds revert to the savage or precivilized level when they disregard contemporary law or moral codes in carrying out their sadistic impulses. Most of the time, everyone, not only Chambers of Commerce, talks about and believes in progress. In times of crisis, however, when danger seems to threaten, there always are "back to" movements. Their appeals are greatest in periods of economic insecurity when the need for "something to cling to" becomes keen. When things seem to be going bad there is talk of the "good old days," "the old-fashioned religion," "the little red school house" and so forth. Orators appear to castigate audiences for having strayed from the straight and narrow so as to bring down their own punishment upon themselves. The three *R*'s were good enough for grandpa when he went to school; our kids would be better off if the curriculum hadn't been cluttered up with a lot of new-fangled courses and theories. When the economy wave hits boards of education in times of economic depression, it is the so-called frills—vocational education, aesthetics, personality development classes and so forth— which are doomed to go first in the inevitable retrenchment. No matter how much they may have complained about the old disciplinary subjects during their youths or in retrospect, the good burghers who hold the pursestrings feel safer and sounder by regressing to them in times of stress.

Unhappily for those who try regression—groups as well as individuals—the past cannot be relived, only inadequately imitated. Time *does* march on. Maybe life was more pleasant in frontier, horse-and-buggy days, but huge urban centers are here, and so are Big Business and Big Government. The isolationism of pre-telephone, telegram, radio, radar, airplane, and atomic bomb days is gone and gone forever. Nations, like individuals, must adjust to changing conditions. When growth occurs rapidly it is not to be wondered at that many find it difficult to keep up. Regression, however, is one of the most hopeless, albeit one of the most common, defense mechanisms. It usually fails and one remains or becomes more frustrated as the rest of the world moves ahead while he tries futilely to turn the clock back.

Identification. For a child to imitate the gestures, facial expressions, tones of voice, and mannerisms of his parents and others with whom he comes in close contact is normal. He is both loyal and submissive to those upon whom he is dependent until adolescence when revolt against authority also is a normal stage in one's maturation.

As a defense mechanism identification enables a person to obtain a feeling of security through attachment to some other person or group or cause. As Young puts it, "Identification may be defined as the taking over of the acts, tones of voice, gestures or other qualities of another person and making them, temporarily or permanently, one's own." Identification may result when one compensates by vicarious escapism. It may assume the character of hero worship or extreme devotion to a leader or to a cause. One may "throw himself into" church work or lodge activities or into promotion of some ideology. And his spirits rise and fall with the fortunes of the person, object, or idea with which he has identified himself.

Although one seemingly belittles himself by making his own interests subordinate to those of another, he gains strength and a feeling of security because the other, to him at least, is stronger and firmer. Identification, furthermore, may result in aggressive campaigning as well as in abject fellowship; in either case, however, it is the cause which counts.

As in the case of regression, extreme forms of identification on the collective behavior level are more likely to occur in times of stress and strain. When large numbers of persons are out of work, for instance, they seek causes and leaders in which they can believe in order to better their lot. At all times it is possible to keep one's mind off one's troubles by active participation in some organized social activity with an apparently unselfish motive.

A common form of identification is to ape one's supposed betters. Much of the make-believe of childhood is play acting in which the child imitates some favorite of story book, cinema, or real life. So imaginative are the little ones that they come close to convincing themselves they actually *are* the characters that they assume. Lovers psychologically may be virtually one rather than two entities. It is nonsense to dismiss love as merely "a state of mind." Of course, it's a state of mind; so is every other emotion. It is the state of mind in which one's happiness becomes identified with that of the other person.

The rabid fan identifies himself with a team or a particular player; he is jubilant over victory, despondent over defeat. Similar strong attachments may be made to a political party, a church, labor union, secret society—in fact, to any association. Love of alma mater, the old home town, one's native state or nation are ordinary forms of identification. One takes pride in the achievements of any member of a group with which he is associated, shares any disgrace suffered by any member. Pride of country—patriotism, that is—is highest in times of crisis, particularly warfare, when, without such identification, the individual would feel very small and insecure indeed.

Projection. Mr. A. stumbled over his son's tricycle in the dark, picked himself up and administered a healthy kick to the velocipede.

Mrs. A, adept at prevarication herself, accused her husband of lying to her with his story of having to work late at the office. Her spinster sister, observing through darkened window that the girl next door lingered in the car with her boy friend for quite some time after they parked in front of the house, started a scandalous rumor concerning the two. Her brother, reprimanded by his foreman for a poor job at the factory, thundered about the poor quality of his tools. His son became equally vocal in condemning his teacher who, he insisted, "had it in" for him, accounting for his bad grades.

All of the A family were projecting their own faults or shortcomings into others, either blaming them for mishaps or accusing them of having the same habits and attitudes that the A's refused to admit they possessed themselves. *Projection is essentially scapegoating* and its everyday practice is pretty widespread. Almost any emotion, idea or thought can be projected to escape a sense of guilt or inadequacy. The results, furthermore, are not always sinister. One may, for example, project a latent sadism into a crusade to fight cruelty against animals or children. Likewise, the results are not always bad when a parent projects upon a child his own suppressed desires. It may, in fact, be a good thing for the youngster to slave at the piano even though he is making up for the fact that his mother was thwarted in her ambitions to become a musician; or it may be beneficial for him to study engineering or law or even journalism because that is what his father once wanted to do himself.

In wartime, furthermore, the opportunity afforded to project and focus one's hate on the enemy has therapeutic effects. It is a fact, attested to by numerous authorities in most countries, that civilian morale was not broken by terrific bombings. Rather the victims of the destruction were compelled to stop brooding about their personal troubles, which came to seem trivial, as they united with others to meet the common threat. At the beginning of World War II the British hastily constructed several new hospitals which they thought would be necessary for mental patients caused by the frightfulness the government correctly anticipated. After the buildings had remained idle for many months, they were converted to other uses. There were no patients. Dr. Robert D. Gillespie, chief psychologist of the Royal Air Force, declared that his wartime service was the quietest in his lifelong career.

Projection, on the other hand, is evil when the projector seeks to punish, or even to reform, the scapegoat upon whom he heaps unreasonable blame. The injustice inflicted increases in proportion to the needs of the frustrated projector. The more disappointed the old maid, in other words, the faster her tongue wags. And the more widespread the sense of shame, guilt, or insecurity, the more avidly do others help spread her poison. It does anyone who is consciously or unconsciously worried about his own conduct good to hear and relate a juicy bit of gossip about someone else; he then realizes he's not the only or perhaps the worst undiscovered sinner at large.

There may be honor among thieves, but among most classes of persons suspicion is rife that those with whom one has dealings would like to swindle him in the same way he'd not be averse to swindling the other fellow if possible. Individuals and groups, including nations, do not come by feelings of mutual trust easily. Especially is this true if one has been once caught off his guard. As the brave is supposed to have said: "White man fool Indian once; shame on white man. White man fool Indian twice; shame on Indian."

Scapegoating ebbs and flows with the need for it. When times are good, with jobs and high wages for everyone, there is comparative harmony and widespread brotherly love. At such times there is enough to go around so the need does not exist to project blame upon someone else for depriving one of his just deserts. In times of scarcity, however, exactly the opposite condition prevails. Out of a job the little fellow seeks explanations, and there is no dearth of those offering to supply them. "The Jews! You are unemployed because they have all the good jobs." Or "the niggers," or "the reds," or some other minority group unable to deny the charges or to fight back effectively. In recent times the outstanding example of successful mass scapegoating was that provided by Messrs. Hitler and Goebbels who projected all of Germany's post-World War I ills on the negligible number of Jews—less than 1 per cent of the country's total population. Postwar reconstruction periods are productive of scapegoating; for example, there were Ku Klux Klans after both the Civil War and World War I. In each case, when "normalcy" was restored, the Klan decayed.

This chapter has been intended as a cursory review of what psychology—empirical, experimental, and clinical—reveals regarding the

reasons why man acts and thinks as he does. The intention has been
to throw whatever light could be found through such a study on the
validity of the principle that if man can only obtain the facts—the
pure, unadulterated, objective, uncensored facts—he can, as the saying goes, "find the way." It should be clear by now that such is not
the case. In addition to the purveyor of news there is the recipient of
it, and he is, figuratively, quite a hard nut to crack. This chapter has
dealt primarily with what the newspaper reader is; in the next chapter
the emphasis will be upon the sociological factors which contribute to
causing him to be that way.

CHAPTER THREE

THE NATURE OF SOCIETY

The customs, institutions, ideologies, and other aspects of his culture largely determine how man acts and thinks.

Customs

When in Rome (or London or anywhere else) you do as the Romans (Londoners or whatever natives are involved) do. And if you don't and are prominent enough, you become newsworthy, as witness the following which appeared in the Chicago *Daily News* for June 30, 1949:

London—(AP)—Marlene Dietrich smoked at the wrong moment and came within inches of getting her knuckles rapped.

She smoked at a luncheon given for her at the Savoy Hotel before the toast to the King was drunk. In Britain, that is the height of something you don't do, and Marlene forgot.

The toastmaster didn't like Marlene's improperly timed cigarette and he banged his gavel with a sharp rap close to Marlene's fingers and in booming tones proposed the traditional toast to the King. Then with a rasp in his voice he said:

"Ladies and gentlemen, you may now smoke."

Marlene was knocked from her poise for a moment but recovered swiftly and said to the toastmaster: "It's some time since I've been in Britain, and I'm terribly sorry."

The toastmaster, John Mills, a stickler for etiquette, said afterwards:

"Angry? How could anyone be angry with such a lovely woman? Besides, she wasn't the only one smoking, and some of the others should have known better."

What happens when you deliberately, rather than innocently as in the case of Miss Dietrich, break a custom and, more importantly, try to persuade or compel others to do likewise, was suggested by an earlier article in the same newspaper. The following is from the issue of Sept. 9, 1946:

Are they rationing LOVE now?

This was the startled query of marriage-license seekers in the County Building today when told of the edict of the Rev. Walter Schlie, pastor of the Immanuel Evangelical Lutheran Church in Batavia.

The pastor has banned kissing at the altar after a marriage ceremony, maintaining that a handshake is "a sufficient sign of affection."

* * *

"I didn't sweat out four years overseas for a handshake," demurred Milton E. Cochran, 22, of 5200 E. Emerald av.

"What's this—another prohibition deal for the serviceman?"

Milton will wed Harriet Petroff, 21, the girl who lives upstairs, on Saturday.

* * *

"I waited a year for my first kiss," said Florian Falk, 24, of 11300 Vincennes av. "You mean you can't even kiss—after it's legal?"

Falk and his pretty blond fiancee, Anne Majewski, 20, of 720 W. 116th st., will wed Sunday at St. Catherine of Genoa Church.

* * *

Not only the traditional wedding kiss, but also secular music and the throwing of rice ("a heathenish custom") were banned in the Rev. Mr. Schlie's church.

"I can see why the throwing of rice might be prohibited to conserve food," offered Lt. (j.g.) Lee Harrington, 27, of Trenton, N. J. "But as for kissing—!

"My fiancee is coming here from the West Coast to be married. We chose Chicago as midway between our homes.

"Do you think we'll settle for a handshake?"

* * *

Elaine Owsiak, 19, of 3448 W. Rutherford av., admitted she was having trouble getting enough rice for rice giblets for the wedding breakfast.

"But I haven't noticed any shortage of kisses," she asserted, glancing at her beaming escort, Klemence Adamski, 24, of 4901 W. Roscoe av.

Adeline Rozek, 22, of 8835 Manistee av., and Edward Biernacki, 23, of 8241 Saginaw av., agreed that handshaking was fine—for business associates.

* * *

Batavia's first handshake wedding took place yesterday, when the Rev. Mr. Schlie officiated at the marriage of his sister-in-law, Esther Hohenberger, to Henry Meyer, Jr., both of Batavia.

"I agree that too great a display of affection would be inappropriate in a place of worship," commented Judge Arthur W. Elliott, of Fairfield, Ill., sitting in Cook County Marriage Court.

"But here I even suggest the marital kiss to seal the bonds of matrimony. I get varied responses, but usually a lot of cooperation."

The Rev. Mr. Schlie was, of course, absolutely correct as to the non-Christian origin of rice throwing. Most wedding customs, in fact, have descended from pagan times. They began as attempts to shield the happy couple from evil spirits. Thus, the veil was originally a disguise; the best man, bridesmaids and other attendants were for the purpose of confusing the lurking demons as to the identity of the principals. Throwing things at the newlyweds and teasing them originated partly in the attempt to fool the spirits into believing the occasion was one of sorrow rather than of joy. Also, relinquishing an old shoe once was a symbol of exchange of a property right. So too may have been rice throwing although most authorities think the main purpose was to appease the spirits by feeding them. At any rate, in medieval times either rice or wheat was a sign of fertility and if the grain, or some product of it, touched the bride, it became lucky. Wedding cakes and bridal bouquets (flowers symbolized sex energy) still are sought as souvenirs by wedding guests. Kissing the bride, the practice to which the Illinois clergyman particularly objected, is one of the few current wedding customs of comparatively recent origin—not earlier than the so-called Middle Ages—and it is estimated that about half the people alive today have yet to receive their first kiss, nuptial or any other kind.

Tracing modern customs to their ancient origins is a fruitful form of research for the feature writer. Anthropologists and other social scientists are inclined to consider it antiquarianism and largely a waste of a scholar's time. It is, however, an effective way to take some beneficial swats at ethnocentrism, a common definition of which is that of Herskovits in *Man and His Works* (Knopf, 1948): "the point of view that one's own way of life is to be preferred to all others." It might, for instance, be good for some of the dignitaries who gather solemnly for a cornerstone laying to know that the traditional ceremony originated in primitive times when living humans were sealed into new buildings as sacrifices to the gods to pacify them for man's usurpation of the land on which the new building was to be erected. Later, animals, plants and other forms of sacrifice were substituted, but the original purpose lingered, for centuries, well into the present era.

A great many more of our contemporary customs and institutions —perhaps a majority of them—are of ancient origin. The toastmaster who threatened Marlene Dietrich's knuckles, for instance, performed a function which began as an attempt to keep heavy drinking parties from getting "out of hand" through appointment of someone to preserve order. He first was known as a tablemaster. Today it is impolite not to conceal a yawn with one's hand; originally the gesture was to prevent an evil spirit from flying into the open mouth. Blessing a sneeze, by saying "Gesundheit," "God bless you," or some similar phrase, had the same preventive purpose through use of a magically potent word or phrase. The handshake originally was a means whereby fighters made certain their opponents would not violate a truce. Tipping the hat began as a gesture of obedience by a slave or servant to a master. The military salute developed from the gesture that knights made to indicate they were shielding their eyes from the dazzling beauty of the Queen of Beauty at a tournament. Mourning grew out of fear of the departed souls. And so, in all phases of modern life, much that is considered proper and even necessary is merely a residual corruption of a bygone practice, the original meaning of which may have been considerably different from the contemporary.

Of whatever origin or nature, customs are of extreme importance in determining what is normal behavior and in providing a sense of social security through their observance. No social group is without them. Every family develops its own, and guests in the home, unless they do not care about being considered boorish, do their best to obey them. A person may repress a snicker and feel very superior about his own ways of doing things but to avoid ostracism or worse he conforms as best he can. If he dwells for any length of time among people with different customs, when he returns home he must be careful to avoid creating the impression of "putting on airs" by continuing to act as he learned to do while away. If the period he has been gone was protracted, this is not easy to do as his personality, as well as his attitudes, opinions, and beliefs, are moulded largely by his associates. Miles Vaughn, long-time United Press Far Eastern correspondent, told in *Covering the Far East* (Covici, Friede, 1936) of the shock he experienced upon returning to the United States when he realized that his Orient-born children were strangers in their own country, experiencing difficulty in getting along with other children their own age. Scientific investigations have revealed the difficulties aliens have with their American born children. No matter how many physical clues to their racial or nationality origin may remain, their cultural conditioning has been American; hence, their attitudes and opinions have little if any resemblance to those of people in the Old Country from which their parents or grandparents emigrated. The conflicts to be noted in the children of aliens result when the old folks accommodate themselves to the new environment more slowly than do their schoolgoing offspring and try to impose standards of another world upon youngsters trying to adjust in a new one. Similar clashes, of course, occur between older and younger generations of families with American roots in colonial times.

Social psychologists distinguish between a *custom* and an *institution* and relate both to the *folkways* and the *mores*. Some acquaintance with their lingo is essential if the newspaperman is to attempt to follow the recommendation of this book, that he be a student of his culture as well as a mere chronicler of its superficial foibles. "An institution," writes Herskovits, "is defined as 'any fixed mode of thought or behavior held by a group of individuals' which can be communicated, is genuinely accepted, and the violation of which causes disturbance." Robert I. MacIver and Charles H. Page in *Society* (Rinehart, 1949) call them "established forms or conditions of procedure characteristic of group activity." The difference between an institution and a custom obviously is one of degree rather than kind, the former really being customs which have obtained definite and widespread recognition. Whereas we use customs to describe accepted ways in which people act in personal relations, institution pertains to group activities. A further distinction must be borne in mind between an institution and an *association*. As MacIver and Page put it: "If we are considering something as an organized group it is an association; if as a form of procedure, it is an institution." Every association has its characteristic institutions, and every institution has external insignia or means of recognition, which is not true of customs.

The difference perhaps can best be clarified by examples. Whereas a church is an association, its sacraments are institutions. The family is an association, but monogomy is an institution. So is the wedding feast, but most of the means by which the courtship was furthered (gifts, rides, dances, shows, and so forth) are customs. Obviously, customs are more likely to change than institutions. At one time it was customary to court a girl by an evening's conversation with her on the family sofa, or by walking her home from prayer meeting. Times obviously have changed. The example suggests what some authorities mean when they distinguish between the *material* and the *immaterial* culture and contend that changes in the former usually precede changes in the latter. Many and many another phase of living underwent changes when the automobile replaced the horse.

Customs which become common to a group are its folkways, a term originated by the late William G. Sumner in *Folkways* (Ginn, 1907). As instruments of control of social behavior the folkways become the mores when they are given a higher degree of social sanction as being necessary to group welfare. They are "folkways with a sanction." Since it is a matter of degree, it is difficult to think of any folkways which do not compel some obedience upon threat of social ostracism or loss of prestige at least. Traditions, conventions, proper etiquette, rituals and ceremonies must be observed in customary fashion. *Social codes* compel obedience; *taboos* forbid disobedience. As society becomes more complex legal codes supplement religious, moral, and social codes in prescribing and proscribing conduct. Unless, however, a law is consistent with the mores, it is difficult of enforcement as those who lived through the era of prohibition in the United States well know. In some groups, as a matter of fact, it is not merely customary but virtually mandatory to break the legal codes in order to "stand in" with one's coevals. Much of the confusion over defining delinquent or criminal behavior results from attempts to apply the standards of one group in judging members of another group. For instance, if a youngster reared in a family in which the older siblings and their neighborhood associates engaged in purse snatching, jackrolling, shoplifting, and similar illegal activities would be abnormal if he didn't act likewise. The tattletale, stool pigeon, or informer is shunned and despised by his fellows. To be one means that one just about has to change the social group in which he wishes to have status. One reason why the results of settlement house and social service work in general have not been better has been because of the missionary approach which has been used. Denizens of one cultural group have invaded the territory of another in the attempt to convert them to the moral standards of the area from which they came. Several years ago a number of feminine believers in clean elections from Chicago's north side suburbs were run out of the river wards where they tried to be poll watchers. Their presence was resented as much as would have been the case had the situation been reversed and the "hoods" had appeared in the wealthy precincts as kibitzers. Much of the lament which goes up about the extent to which undesirable political elements have "captured" a given constituency might be omitted if intended as sorrow for the plight of the supposedly enslaved. Quite frequently the elected representation is not merely what the voters deserve but actually what they want.

In his reportorial work the newspaperman encounters widespread failure, often amounting to stubborn refusal, to recognize the cultural aspects of social behavior: among lawmakers, public officeholders, judges and other court officials, even old-line social workers. Just make, administer, and enforce laws and instill in persons a desire to obey them is the traditional philosophy. Today the growing popularity of psychiatry indicates an increased realization that there are at least mitigating circumstances often to be found in the personal histories of wrongdoers and a desire to understand misbehavior even while continuing to use old methods of coping with it. Among the leading organizations with a cultural point of view is the Chicago Area Project, affiliated with the Institute for Juvenile Research which is part of the Illinois Department of Public Welfare. In its own words, in 1939 after five years: "The Chicago Area Project is an experiment to determine the extent to which constructive changes in social environment may result in a reduction in the volume of delinquency. It has as its objective the discovering of facts regarding the social and cultural origins of delinquency and crime, and the utilization of this knowledge in a demonstration program which may lead to an improvement of present methods used in the prevention and treatment of delinquency." In 1941, in another report, appeared the following: "Evidence that most forms of delinquency in which children engage in low income areas are learned and transmitted through association can be derived from many sources. The large number of autobiographies and other personal documents secured from delinquents by the writers and their colleagues during the last twenty years, give ample evidence that boys acquire their knowledge of the various forms of stealing and the essential techniques through contacts with other persons in the play group, gang, street corner crowd, and in other groups in the community, and with delinquents in detention homes, industrial schools and other such institutions. Further evidence has been revealed in a study of the records of delinquents in the Cook County Juvenile Court. This study showed that many of the boys who appeared in the court in 1938 had been in the court with others in 1936, while many of these had been in court with still others in 1935. By this method of investigation, it was possible to show that there has been an unbroken continuity of relationships between delinquents who have appeared in the court year after year, from the early years of the court's existence to the present time.

"This tradition of delinquency which exists in the low-income areas of the city, while only a part of the total community, becomes embodied in the life and practices of play groups, gangs, crowds, and other groups of such influence and prestige as to instill in their members a powerful incentive to engage in delinquency, and to sustain them in delinquency in defiance of the law. These groups come into being spontaneously, and derive their power both from the fact that they are a natural product of the dynamic forces in the life of the community, and because they provide protection, security, recognition and other human satisfactions in the lives of their members. They are so much an integral part of the community that they can probably be dealt with only by altering those aspects of the life and organization of the community that produce them, and give them sanction and prestige."

This point of view is quite different from that traditionally held by social agencies which continue to send workers into delinquent and other "problem" areas to preach and teach for the purpose of winning converts from bad to better behavior, or, at any rate, to provide sufficient recreational opportunities so that the kids will lack time and/or energy for mischief or worse. Not only do these agencies fail to attract those most in need of character education but they are also unable to put a stop to the continued breeding of new problem children to replace those who have passed on. The Area Project conception is that only when a community takes an interest in its own problems and through its own leaders and indigenous associations attempts to change its codes of behavior will there be lasting or important results.

Ideologies

The differences in viewpoint between the old-line social workers and the Area Project are mostly over methods of procedure rather than ideology. A clearcut ideological difference in this field would exist between one person who believed delinquents are born and not made and another who held the opposite: that they are made and not born.

It is in such ideological bases that the opinions which make up public opinion are rooted. Properly labeled, "delinquents are born and not made" is an attitude in the current social psychological usage of the term. Attitudes, as the preceding chapter made clear, may arise from many sources, personal experiences prominently included. They also grow out of ideologies which are widespread systems of thought by which explanations are given of the interrelationships between various aspects of life and by which even the meaning of life itself may be provided. To distinguish between an ideology, a philosophy, and a religious tenet often is difficult. Furthermore, what one authority calls a primary attitude as distinguished from a secondary attitude may be what another means by an ideology. Whatever the end of the lexicographical evolution of the theorizing, the important fact remains unchanged that different levels of conditioning of the mental state with which one begins (or ends) will be recognized to exist, call them whatever you will.

For instance, a person who holds that "all delinquents are born, not made" may have a fatalistic attitude or philosophy as regards life as a whole. The same person would be likely to believe that saints also are born, not made; and the same for sinners, geniuses, and others. He therefore forms his judgment on specific matters, such as the social workers versus Area Project approaches, on the basis of his deeper convictions, consciously or unconsciously. There is, however, no simple uniform 1-2-3-4 development in the thought processes of different persons who think alike on any matter at any ideological or attitudinal level. For example, several persons who believe that "delinquents are born and not made" may disagree as to what should be done about it. Mr. A may argue for lifetime incarceration, Mr. B for capital punishment, and Mr. C for humanitarian treatment. In each case, obviously, other factors come into play to complicate the conditioning process. Mr. B's hardboiled point of view may be characteristic of him as a scorner of religious and philosophic glorifications of the importance of the individual, or he may accept the Aristotelian concept of restoring social balance by expiation. Mr. C may be kindly from having suffered personally or from strong belief in certain religious precepts such as virtue or charity.

Any ideology or philosophy or religious or other concept can influence any other at any level, making the possible combinations of cause and effect almost illimitable. The apparently basic attitude of fatalism even may result from diametrically opposed points of view; either an all-powerful deity who has predestined everything, or a purely mechanistic explanation by which, theoretically, every phenomenon can be traced back to the first Adam or atom. It is for the psychoanalyst to probe for the train of sequences whereby individual attitudes and opinions are formed. The moulder of public opinion takes advantage of the opportunity afforded at each stage of their development to alter their direction. He recognizes the importance of ideologies (or whatever they are called) to be as great as that of customs and all of their repercussions in influencing social thought and action.

As is true of all other aspects of a culture, in small, simple communities there is a minimum of alternative or conflicting ideologies in any field. As society becomes more complex and interdependent, and as populations move about, the number increases and the separate ideologies come into contact, which often means conflict, with each other. For the individual this may mean mental storm and stress. Karen Horney, eminent American psychiatrist, in *The Neurotic Personality of Our Times* (Norton, 1937) says neuroses are the price man pays for civilized progress.

When a new major ideology arises the almost automatic response is to brand it as heresy, condemning and persecuting its adherents. That failing, in time there may come tolerance (a "live and let live" attitude) or attempts at accommodation ("it's really not inconsistent or dangerous anyway"). Finally, the opponents of the new may become so reconciled to defeat that they "save face" by actually taking credit for the heresy, which now becomes orthodoxy. Pertinent case in point is the contemporary Catholic school text which praises Galileo, the seventeenth-century scientist who was tried and convicted and forced to recant his belief in Copernican astronomy by the Inquisition. Instead of disproving the existence of a deity and of an orderly planned universe, science now is said by many, including some of the leading scientists, to do exactly the opposite. Although radicalism may be tomorrow's orthodoxy, the lag between appearance and acceptance of even a successful new idea is as strong in one generation as in the next.

As was intimated in the preceding chapter, the most basic ideologies originated in efforts to obtain understanding of the universe and of the nature of things, including man himself. As such they provided a mental sense of orderliness and security for the believer. Ideologies also originate as rationalizatons of what has become widespread thought or behavior or to justify new forms not easily defended in terms of old ideologies. Examples are racial theories to "prove" the innate inferiority of colonial or persecuted people; messianic hopes by the downtrodden themselves; divine right of kings; *laissez-faire* economics and all of the great "isms," including democracy. The strongest of such ideologies are those which carry conviction that they are based on "natural law," or embody "the will of God." May it be repeated here that declaring that an ideology is based on unscientific premises or is a mere rationalization is not tantamount to denying its worth-whileness as a working principle. When the supernatural is successfully invoked, however, there is greater likelihood that it will endure. The sanctions, including hope of Heaven and fear of Hell, are greater than any man-made equivalents. Condemning something as atheistic is stronger than to call it un-American, un-democratic, or merely impolite.

Once in existence, from whatever source, ideologies influence thought on widespread fronts. They are frames of reference by which the immediate and specific can be understood. They can take a great deal of buffeting and still endure through constant reinterpretations— mostly rationalizations, of course. Take, for instance, absolutism—belief that there are eternal and unchangeable rules of nature or of God. Men can and do differ in what they consider the absolutes to be but have in common the faith that there are some. More specifically, the Bible may be interpreted differently both to justify and to condemn card playing on the Sabbath or any of a large number of other practices. One's dogmatism may become mitigated to the point that he accepts the assumption that there are "many roads to salvation," but remain absolutistic in his conviction that it is essential to obey the rules of whatever pathway one selects to follow. There is abundant secular as well as ecclesiastical literature dedicated to the purpose of seeking elusive Truth.

Without any interest whatever in attempting ourselves to find an answer to Pilate's question, let us examine how some strongly held and widespread ideologies have affected society. A few examples should suffice to demonstrate to the student of public opinion the extraordinary power and importance of ideologies.

Until comparatively recently medical students had to be ghouls to obtain cadavers on which to experiment because of the deeply rooted belief that God had set fixed spheres of animal and plant life; hence scientific classification was un-Godly. More important, man had been created in God's image, so autopsies and dissections were heathenish. Even today some antivivisectionists—though by no means a majority —oppose animal experimentation because it upsets the divine plan. And although there are widespread differences as to what the revelations are or mean, there still is belief in the idea that most of the increases which occur in man's knowledge and understanding result from such revelations in accordance with an inscrutable law, not vouchsafed man to comprehend.

Of the importance of the ideology of ancestor worship, Lewis Browne wrote in *This Believing World* (Macmillan, 1926): "Man, once so terrified by the ghosts that he fled at the least suspicion of their presence, now dared to go right up to them and implore their aid. Ancestor worship arose. Tribes often depended for their solidarity upon the sole bond of supposed descent from a common ancestor. Failing that, the tie that served to hold them together was a common ritual. Ceremonies at birth, puberty, marriage, and death were the things that bound those clansmen into a compact group. The same was true of the annual festivals. And thus, by and with religion, the living together of men was made possible."

Continuing, Rabbi Browne elaborated upon the ramifications of an essential point of view, on how it permeates and affects all phases of life: "More than that: by and with religion the living together of men was made not only possible, but also desirable. Religion clothed and adorned the cold nakedness of primitive existence with shreds and patches of beauty. All that grace and color which transmits mere existence in Life—in a word, all Art—may truly be said to have arisen out of religion. Sculpture had its origin in idol-making, architecture in temple-building, poetry in prayer-writing, music in psalm-singing, drama in legend-telling, and dancing in the season worship of the gods.

"It may seem to us incredibly rude, this conglomeration of terrors and hopes, of clutchings and gropings, of stupidities and yearnings, which for want of a better name we call Primitive Religion. But for all that, it was holy—for it saved mankind."

Of the evil force of similar ideas, Norman Angell wrote in *The Public Mind* (N. Douglass, 1926): "It would not be true to call the burner of witches, the torturer of heretics, the fomenters of patriotic wars, murderers or assassins. Usually they have been passionately convinced that they were doing right, obeying the will of God. It is the ideas that were assassins. The men who held those ideas had merely failed to examine credentials, to see whether, as an old illustration has it, the Deity who had spoken to them and aroused their feelings so intensely, was in fact God—or Satan. They 'meant well' in their cruelty and devastation, their motives were pure, as are often, for instance, those of judges who send innocent men to their doom."

The power of ideas has been eulogized time and time again. Not so frequently or so well done have been efforts to point out the ramifications of an idea to show how it influences thought and action in many, sometimes seemingly unrelated spheres. Anthropologists can do it for cultures not their own. It is not so easy to do it for one's own culture. Hence, many of the best books about the United States have been written by foreigners. In *The Chrysanthemum and the Sword* (Houghton Mifflin, 1946), a leading American anthropologist, Ruth Benedict, attempted to explain the Japanese, somewhat in terms of parallels and differences in American culture. In part she explained and summarized her purpose and findings: "When we stated to Japan, therefore, just before Pearl Harbor the high moral bases on which the United States based her policy in the Pacific, we were voicing our most trusted principles. Every step in the direction in which we pointed would according to our convictions improve a still imperfect world. The Japanese too when they put their trust in 'proper station' were turning to the rule of life which had been ingrained in them by their own social experience. Inequality had been for centuries the rule of their organized life at just those points where it is most predictable and most accepted. Behavior that recognizes hierarchy is as natural to them as breathing. It is not, however, a simple Occidental authoritarianism. Both those who exercise control and those who are under others' control act in conformity to a tradition which is unlike our own, and now that the Japanese have accepted the high hierarchal place of American authority in their country, it is even more necessary for us to get the clearest possible idea of their conventions. Only so can we picture to ourselves the way in which they are likely to act in their present situation."

Easy to understand, of course, is the fact that people reared to believe in the divinity of their emperor and their own blood relationship with him will think differently from people who believe that "all men are created equal and are endowed by their Creator with certain unalienable rights." Not clear, without elaborate study, putting oneself mentally in the place of another to the fullest extent possible, is what forms the differences take. Even to do so in our own culture is difficult. There are innumerable pitfalls, among which one of the most serious is not detecting misapplication of an idea or principle legitimate in one field to establish a point of view in another. An example is the justification by Burke, Peel, Spencer and others of poverty as natural. In fact, so are almost all of the widespread attempts to adapt the principles of biology to economics, notably the "survival of the fittest" ideas of Darwin to justification of ruthlessness in business com petition. It is too soon for the full effect of Einstein's relativity to be known. Already, however, it has affected social scientists to the extent that they are pragmatic about the chances of a culture, or any part of it, lasting longer than its usefulness. In other words, ideas like objects, are good as long as they work. If they persist after they really are outworn—as certainly does happen—it is because alternatives either have not been presented or have not yet been demonstrated to be as workable. Even so, hypocritical lip service may continue to be paid obsolete concepts long after they are obeyed more in the breach than in the observance, because of the tremendous resistance to change that is characteristic of all societies, including our own. A major transition in thinking is a slow and painful process. In addition to the original negative resistance, there usually develops a positive counterrevolutionary movement which may masquerade as progress but actually is for the purpose of turning the clock back.

Ideals

History no longer is taught as a succession of names and dates. Rather, the emphasis is upon the causal relationships between important events and upon long-time trends and their significance. Naturally, historians differ in their interpretations, and even the best of them must beware of the pitfall of unconsciously making the facts fit the theory. Nevertheless, it is a significant step toward understanding the past—by which the present becomes more comprehensible—to recognize that economic, social and political trends *do* exist and are as important as battles, war lords, and monarchs.

In the lexicon of most historians today "change" and "progress" are not necessarily synonyms. Laymen are inclined to be a bit schizophrenic on the subject. On the one hand there is the tendency to look down upon earlier cultures as inferior and to shun the old fashioned and obsolete. On the other hand, there is the frequent eulogizing of the "good old days" before men made the mistake of adopting dangerous new ways. At a higher level, college students may argue the equivalent of whether the South Sea islanders were better or worse off before the white man discovered them.

The answer as to what is better and what worse naturally depends upon the set of values which one uses as a standard. Since all such yardsticks are man-made, there is bound to be no unanimity. Nevertheless, certain goals or ideals do exercise greater influence at any given time or place than others, and, as in the case of all the other social phenomena so far considered, there are social as well as individual ideals.

According to an orthodox dictionary definition, an ideal is "a perfect type; a model to be imitated; what one would wish to be." Idealism similarly is defined as "an acting according to one's ideals of what ought to be, regardless of circumstances, or of the approval or disapproval of others." Throughout history philosophers, religious prophets, and exponents of utopias have postulated their ideas as to what is the best society and, in some cases, even the second best in the belief it might be more attainable. A comparatively recent treatment is that of Bertrand Russell in *Prospects of Industrial Civilization* (Century, 1923): "For my part I should judge a community to be in a good state if I found a great deal of instinctive affection rather than hatred and envy, a capacity for creating and enjoying beauty, and the intellectual curiosity which leads to the advancement and diffusion of knowledge." In *Civilization* (Harcourt, Brace, 1923) Clive Bell lists (a) a sense of values, and (b) reason enthroned as the prime qualities of what he considers a civilized state. Bell is among the writers who use "civilization" as virtually synonymous with "culture" as the latter term has been employed in this book, which is the way orthodox among social scientists today. To some writers the two words *are* synonymous. To others civilization means the entire product of man's works, whereas culture is any part of the total product studied at a particular time and place. Usually, however, civilization has a qualitative connotation. He who calls one person or group civilized whereas another is not means that the former is, in his eyes, superior to the latter; which brings us back to the original declaration that "it's all in the point of view."

The foregoing is not tantamount to saying that, despite the lack of an olympian perspective by which to evaluate cultures and/or ideals regarding them, such attempts have not been made and are not important. The ideals that groups have held, regardless of the amount of hypocrisy which may be involved in paying homage to them or how far short of the goal actual attainment has fallen, have been of tremendous importance. Bell eulogized ancient Athens for having sacrificed comfort to beauty as a communal ideal, even to the extent of exonerating a sculptor who tortured a model when the work of art he produced as a result was displayed. Bell, of course, recognized the particular instance as evil but cited it as an extreme illustration. Renaissance Italy honored its artists above its politicians but, according to Bell, fell short of attaining civilized greatness because it was appreciative and imitative, mostly of the Greeks, rather than productive. Although the data are inadequate, ancient China is supposed to have apotheosized the scholar. Aldous Huxley wrote in *Ends and Means* (Harper, 1937): "Every age has had its ideal. The ruling classes in Greece idealized the magnanimous man, a sort of scholar and gentleman. Kshatriyas in early India and feudal nobles in medieval Europe held up the ideal of the chivalrous man. The *honnête homme* makes his appearance as the ideal of the seventeenth-century gentleman; the *philosophe* as the ideal of their descendants in the eighteenth century. The nineteenth century idealized the respectable man. The twentieth has already witnessed the rise and fall of the liberal man and the emergence of the sheep-like social man and the God-like Leader. Meanwhile the poor and downtrodden have always dreamed nostalgically of a man ideally well-fed, free, happy and unoppressed."

Worship of an ideal, as Huxley implied, can become fanatical as in the case of Nazi Germany or sun- and emperor-worshipping Japan. These were contemporary examples also of extreme ethnocentricism as narrow as that of the Greeks who considered all non-Greeks to be barbarians. A certain amount of such group conceit is inevitable even when ideals are taken less seriously. A campus fraternity, for instance, which puts a premium on athletic prowess considers itself made of much sterner stuff than another which emphasizes scholarship as its ideal. The better students, of course, look down upon the he-men as all muscle and no brain. All groups, including families, have ideals by which they judge their own members and others. Maybe it is musical ability or skill at carpentry or fishing or even acrobatics. It is a great temptation to say that a group which sets its sights on aesthetic achievement is aiming higher than one which idolizes mere brawn, but, in the interest of scientific objectivity the author refrains from doing so. The point which he hopes he has made is that group ideals are important in influencing thought and action and, consequently, public opinion.

Trends

If a yardstick set of values or a social philosophy is necessary to understand the past—to determine whether change should or should not be considered progress—it is many times more important in attempting to prognosticate the future.

Of books telling where we are going, usually because of where we have been, there are an abundant number, authored by Oswald Spengler, Count Herman Keyserling, Karl Marx, James Burnham, Friedrich Hayek, Arnold Toynbee, and others. It would be impossible as well as superfluous to attempt to analyze, or even to summarize, their contents here. When one is a rider on "the wave of the future" it is difficult to know toward which shore one is being swept. For all practical purposes, as far as one's everyday living is concerned, it doesn't make too much difference either, as one continues to "go along" most of the time. Of course, if one is convinced that the millennium is imminent, he may spend his supposed last hours either in riotous entertainment or prayerfully, depending upon his disposition. With most of us most of the time, however, either doom or salvation does not seem quite that immediate, and we don't spend much time and effort preparing ourselves for the next great era of mankind.

In understanding the events which he reports as individual phenomena the reporter will be aided by a social philosophy, provided it is acquired by experience, not prejudice, and provided he struggles to remain open-minded. Despite the great logic which has characterized many of the historical projections of the past, there never has been an infallible large-scale long-time prophecy. There exist statisticians who can draw curves to show the ups and downs of this or that from Babylonian days to the present. To these cyclists all civilization is rhythmical and consequently predictable. The author, however, has observed two equally good curve drawers use substantially the same data and come out with almost exactly the opposite conclusions. After the crash of 1929 a small compilation of the roseate predictions of many of the world's supposedly best economic authorities, all of which were proved wrong, was entitled *Oh Yeah,* which was about the way most Americans felt about "prosperity is just around the corner" and similar remarks by the alleged seers. During the closing months of World War II all of the "best" economists, from the extreme left to the extreme right, predicted an immediate postwar depression—or at least recession—while industry was reconverting from war to a peacetime basis. Talking about 60 million jobs was brushed aside as the idle pipedream of idealists.

Just as the Roman citizen must have been unaware that he was rising or falling, so the modern finds it difficult to determine whether capitalism and democracy are still suffering from growing pains in early stages of development or are decaying after having reached their pinnacles of success and usefulness. At any time what men think is true is as important as or even more important than what subsequent events prove to have been the case. At the same time, of course, regardless of what he thinks is happening, one is affected by the actual turn of affairs. To illustrate, the German who believed Hitler was destined to rule the world and acted accordingly was caught as short as the fellow who bet two dollars on the wrong horse or subscribed to the wrong issue of utility stock. On the other hand, from the broader point of view, the entire Hitler movement and Word War II might be considered as mere episodes in a more significant world trend. There are many authorities willing to shed light on the problem. Unfortunately, few people read their books or listen to them. The trends, if any, that the average man is aware of are short-time and comparatively unimportant. If, however, there is a drift toward immorality, or, vice versa, toward greater virtue, for instance, he will be affected by it regardless of his perspicacity. It will influence his day-by-day attitudes toward his family, friends and business associates. If he philosophizes at all he'll do so on the basis of all of the types of conditioning which have been considered in preceding pages.

Social Relationships

A few more fundamental social psychological concepts, most of which have been touched upon in one way or another by what has preceded, are significant in connection with this chapter's purpose of "laying a groundwork" for understanding contemporary American society.

In-Groups and Out-Groups. A sense of belonging, or "we" feeling, as it often is called, is an important feature of the relationship between an individual and any group, organized or unorganized, to which he belongs. The person identifies himself with the group, projects, and makes its well-being his also. He suffers disgrace brought on by any other member and takes pride in any accomplishment of any other member, living or dead. Fraternity and club house walls are covered with pictures of former members who achieved fame, and mantels are cluttered with the loving cups and other trophies of yesteryear.

Pride in group—which increases with the personal psychological need for it—leads to the concomitant feeling that those who do not belong are outsiders. Whether this generates an attitude of hostility depends upon the intensity of the interest holding the group together. If a group is in real or imagined competition with another, the feeling is strong. And the strength increases with the feeling of insecurity which leads to projection (scapegoating). At its comparative best the hostility attitude is merely irritating smugness.

Social Distance. This is the feeling one has of the difference between himself and members of any other group. It may be "horizontal" or "vertical." If the former it is held that the different groups are on a par in value but are so separated either by distance or interest that they do not consider themselves as being competitors. Most Americans, for instance, have such an attitude toward Australians. We don't look down upon Australians, nor do we look up to them. We think of them, when we do so at all, as just too far away for there to be much in common between us. Doctors and lawyers, to illustrate social distance based on interests rather than geography, generally have a mutual respect for each other, regarding each other as social equals, but not in competition economicaly or, as groups, in any other way. Any rivalry which exists between a particular doctor and a particular lawyer is in relation to an interest which they have in common and unrelated to their occupational interests.

Entirely different is vertical social distance. It is predicated on the assumption that the groups involved *are* in competition and that the relationship between them is that of superior and inferior. Power and prestige are the possession of the upper class or classes and those beneath them on the social scale are expected to know and to keep their place—on the proper side of the social tracks. If any hunk of superior clay marries "beneath" him or consorts unduly with "lower level" folks, he suffers ostracism by his peers; if he consistently supports the points of view of the masses, he is accused of being a traitor to his class. In democratic societies, without hereditary titles and privileges, it is social pressure which defines and preserves class. The older a society becomes, no matter how democratic in political and legal setup, the more class-ridden it is likely to be. Family counts more and more with each generation; class consciousness and superiority attitudes develop among the older residents or those higher on the social scale. Passage from one class to another, either up or down, becomes more and more difficult. One's social status is determined by the accident of birth, regardless of personal ability or achievement. Without governmental fiat the class system develops its own form and its own sanctions which, in primitive societies, often included elaborate taboos for violations of thinly drawn lines of proper behavior.

The ultimate end which a class system may reach is caste. In a caste system there is a complete barrier to mobility between classes; there is a thorough stratification of classes. Membership is entirely hereditary so that there are no *nouveau riche* crashing the gate, or at least opening it so that their children can enter and be accepted. Despite the religious rationalizations and seemingly complicated social codes to define and enforce it, a caste system simplifies societal existence. Everyone's place or status is known and the rules which he is expected to observe are clearcut. The conditioning process to make him accept his status in life does not begin before birth, as in Aldous Huxley's satirical utopia, *Brave New World* (Harper, 1932), but it does start shortly thereafter so that by the time the child becomes old enough to comprehend, he has pretty well accepted his unchangeable role.

The socially evil aspects of class and/or caste obviously are its discouragement or stifling of individual initiative and ability. Every country which has had a hereditary line of kings has gone through periods of being ruled by incompetents, even morons, elevated to thrones because of the mere fact of royal birth. Precedence and power are the keystones of class and caste, rather than ability as brought to the top through equal opportunities of competition.

Although class and caste are terms usually applied only to large societal or national groups, the principles can be observed in operation in associations of any type. Nepotism exists in business as well as in government. Churches, civic organizations, labor unions, school systems, even groups interested in aesthetic matters, may be plagued by class or clique control. Consciously or unconsciously, in filling a vacancy in business or on the executive committee of a private club, class consciousness may be the determining factor. Obviously the class principle is clearest to detect when status is associated with a single controlling factor around which others cohere. In modern society as a whole this factor is generally the kind and amount of wealth, but it may be religion or race or skill or birthplace or family history or any of a number of other factors. In some colleges sons and daughters of former students occupy social positions higher than others. On some faculties, graduates of certain colleges enjoy advantages. Old settlers, like elder statesmen, rate higher in public prestige often than comparative newcomers to a community. Any influx of persons with different backgrounds into almost any kind of social group is resented and even suspected as motivated by a desire to "take over." In times of economic or other insecurity these "foreigners" become natural and easy scapegoats upon which to place the blame for any disaster or threatened disaster. To summarize, support of clique, class, or caste is a way to protect oneself against competition on the basis of the principle of "let the best man win." Such support may become paranoiac, with the members of the privileged upper crust actually coming to believe in their superior worth through the sheer accident of birth or inheritance. As Thorstein Veblen so ably pointed out in *Theory of the Leisure Class* (Macmillan, 1899), they then develop superficial external habits and customs by which to distinguish themselves from their supposed inferiors and are resentful when the inferiors, reacting naturally, tend to emulate such superficialities. Always good for a laugh in plush circles is a caricature of the lady of the house glaring at her cook wearing a hat similar to her own. Imitation of the appearance and mannerisms of one's supposed betters is resented both by them and by other members of one's own class. The former regard such behavior as "upstart" or "crashing the gate," whereas to the latter it is "putting on airs," or "buttering up the boss."

Rare, probably nonexistent, is the community in which the investigative reporter does not find examples of the class system at work. To "get anywhere" in some unit of government, or branch of business enterprise or private association, he will find, it is necessary to be from the right sides of the tracks, or be of a certain national, racial, or religious origin, or belong to a certain social set or have acquired the right classmates at school or in some other way made himself potentially eligible. Early in the war the welcoming committee for a returning war hero was greatly embarrassed when it was discovered the soldier lived in an unphotogenic slum area. The press generally obliged by not taking pictures of it. Similar situations have arisen when members of minority groups have won civic prizes of which, on more than one occasion, they subsequently have been deprived. In recent years, to its everlasting credit, there has been an increasing tendency on the part of the press to "go after" such instances of undemocratic behavior. Typical situation was that described in the following editorial, "Harvey Jones Gets an Auto," from the July 18, 1947 Chicago *Times*:

It must have come as a surprise to members of the Kiwanis club in Ahoskie, N.C. that anybody would give a hoot about the way they tried to gyp Harvey Jones out of the $3,200 Cadillac he won in their raffle.

When Harvey's name was drawn, the club committee decided he wasn't eligible to win because he was a Negro. They ordered a second name drawn and gave Harvey back the dollar he had paid for the winning ticket.

It was their own affair, wasn't it? That's what they thought. How wrong they were!

The small-minded Ahoskie Kiwanians failed to realize how seriously Americans take pride in sportsmanship and fair play. They failed to realize that even in North Carolina there are white men who would disagree with their decision.

In spite of their efforts to keep the story mum, the "Independent" at nearby Elizabeth City printed the facts. Editor G. W. Haskett called the gyp a "rotten, ungentlemanly, unsportsmanlike transaction." There was an American upholding the best traditions of the American press.

The story went out over news wires and soon most of the American reading public was boiling with indignation. Kiwanians in other cities were embarrassed. After all, the Kiwanis is an organization of business and professional men interested in "promoting the adoption and application of higher social, business and professional standards," and in "intelligent, aggressive and serviceable citizenship."

In Salisbury, N. C. Dr. Charles W. Armstrong, international president of the Kiwanis clubs, ordered the Ahoskie club to give Harvey Jones another Cadillac. The club agreed. It looks as though Jones will take cash instead.

The incident should help impress on those people who see no harm in pushing around Negroes or other minorities that most Americans are against such practices. And the weight of American public opinion can make itself felt even in isolated centers of prejudice such as Ahoskie.

When the popular will of all our people got behind Harvey Jones and forced justice in his case, it was a good day for America.

CHAPTER FOUR

THE NATURE OF PROPAGANDA

The propagandist cannot easily bring new attitudes and opinions into existence, but he has developed techniques which he uses skillfully to utilize existent attitudes and opinions for his own purposes.

In two minutes over Pearl Harbor the Japanese did more to end American isolationism than the Committee to Defend America by Aiding the Allies (the William Allen White committee) had been able to accomplish in two years.

Drastic events affecting one's personal well being always are more potent than any amount of the most skillful propaganda. In politics it is the "pocketbook appeal" that is most important. Dust storms, William Allen White used to say, have defeated more Kansas governors than exposures of official corruption. In 1932 probably any candidate nominated by the Democratic party would have been elected president because 12 years of Republican rule had ended in disastrous depression from which almost everyone suffered. In succeeding presidential elections the expenditure of millions of dollars for propaganda and the opposition of the overwhelming majority of the daily newspapers failed to convince a majority of voters that they were not better off under Democratic administrations than they had been under the Republicans.

On matters less cataclysmic than wars and depressions a significant experience also is the leading cause of a rapid change in personal opinions. "I considered her one of my best friends and one of the most honest and forthright persons I ever knew until I caught her going through my purse" suggests how it can happen. Change the last clause of the quotation to "until I was told that she was picked up for shoplifting" and the pitfalls that the propagandist can create are suggested. It is not necessarily what actually is true but what is believed to be true that counts. Inadequate or incorrect information or no information at all, misrepresentation of the facts or wrong judgments as to wherein one's best interests lie, can cause public opinion to support what perspective later reveals to have been harmful rather than beneficial measures.

The Power of Propaganda

Man, however, is not putty in the hands of a clever propagandist. The most skillfully devised and ably presented appeal will fail if it collides head-on with deeply rooted attitudes and convictions. For extreme example, you could select the most eloquent and competent committee of Baptists to be found the world over, provide it with unlimited funds and propagandistic know how and turn it loose on the Roman Catholic College of Cardinals. One would have to give tremendous odds to find anyone willing to take a bet that the most elaborate and protracted efforts on the part of the Protestant committeemen would convert a single one. Similarly laymen with strong convictions—religious, economic, political, or otherwise—are impervious to propagandistic appeals which do damage to these convictions. "It is not very difficult to persuade people to do what they are all longing to do," wrote Aldous Huxley in "Notes on Propaganda," in the December, 1936 *Harper's.* "But," he explained later in the article, "in general, if people behave as well as they do it is not because they have read about good behavior and the social or metaphysical reasons for being virtuous; it is because they have been subjected during childhood, to a more or less intensive, more or less systematic training in good behavior. The propagandists of morality do not rely exclusively or even mainly on the written word." Examination of the effects of numerous attempts to influence human thought and action at different stages of history led Huxley to conclude: "Political and religious propaganda is effective, it would seem, only upon those who are already partly or entirely convinced of its truth."

The widespread fear of red propaganda in the United States was expressed in an editorial in the July 13, 1949 New York *World-Telegram* which stated:

RED AND NOT RED—HOW?

When the American Assn. of University Professors upheld this week the right of teachers to be Communists it bent over backward, in our opinion, in its effort to guarantee the right of academic freedom.

The association said it believes there should be no ban on any teacher because he is a Communist as long as he keeps his politics out of school and doesn't preach the party line.

That line of reasoning might be all right if it would work. But we doubt that a teacher-Communist, his life dedicated to spreading the Red doctrine, will refrain from trying to do all he can to inject the Red philosophy into his students.

There are ways he can do this without inviting trouble from his college. The clever Red educator can inject, bits at a time, his philosophy into classwork that apparently is a model of objectivity. An idea here, a phrase there, a page of this book, a quote from that one, and at the end of the course the student's thinking has been influenced.

The Communist professor can spread his line not only in the classroom, but even more effectively outside school hours. He can be the companionable, sociable and popular campus favorite. Quite an opportunity for a Red propagandist to get students to absorb his thoughts.

Schools and colleges have a tough problem to decide where the basic educational principle of academic freedom should end to guard against Communist infiltration. The best answer seems to be for the institutions to exercise the greatest vigilance over the activities of their faculties and be extremely cautious that academic freedom never is used as a license to destroy itself and the kind of government that makes it possible.

The above quoted editorial is an example of how the potency of a Communist professor's influence on a student, hence of the Marxian "line," is exaggerated. The editorial writer forgets that over against the effectiveness of "an idea here, a phrase there, a page of this book, a quote from that one," there were the ideas of all of the rest of his teachers throughout his entire educational career; there were the ideas, phrases, pages and quotations from all the other books read; there was the influence of all of his relatives, friends and associates which served as a powerful counter propaganda. Furthermore, the editorial writer takes for granted a degree of gullibility on the part of the American student which is far from reality.

Neither communistic nor any other kind of propaganda is anywhere near that effective. To quote from the Huxley article once more: "Social and political propaganda is effective, as a rule, only upon those whom circumstances have partly or completely convinced of its truth. In other words, it is influential only when it is a rationalization of the desires, sentiments, prejudices or interests of those to whom it is addressed. . . . Men accept the propagandist's theology or political theory because it apparently justifies and explains the sentiments and desires evoked in them by circumstance." As for communism it never has taken hold in the United States because this nation's entire cultural heritage has been inimical to it. For the Marxist thesis to have validity there must develop a class consciousness among the proletariat. The open class system growing out of American frontier conditions has been an insuperable barrier.

The most successful propaganda in this country during the past quarter century or more has been the propaganda against propaganda, and for the reason Huxley suggests: events made people susceptible. A brief resume of those events will serve to illustrate how the attitudinal groundwork making possible the success of a propaganda campaign is laid; how, in other words, the soil in which the propaganda seed will grow is created.

The closest this country ever has come to achieving national unity through belief in the sacredness of a common purpose and a consequent manifest destiny, was during World War I. For an overwhelming majority of Americans our participation in that war was a holy crusade to save the world for democracy and to end all wars. Because the conviction was so intense, the subsequent disillusionment was severely bitter.

Long before World War II broke out, millions of Americans painfully had concluded that our entrance into World War I had been a mistake—rightly or wrongly being unimportant now. As it is with individuals, so it is with nations. When one errs, or thinks he has erred, he seeks an explanation which will be self exonerating—the psychological device known as projection discussed in the preceding chapter, or scapegoating if you use the propaganda analyst's term. So we ran through the gamut of excuses: (1) the pro-Britishness of Woodrow Wilson and his close associates, Colonel House and Ambassador Page in particular and/or their diplomatic blundering; (2) the machinations of the House of Morgan and other Wall Street financiers who allegedly stood to lose heavily in the event of a German victory because of their loans to the Allies; (3) the munition makers —merchants of death they came to be called—who were said actually to operate as motion picture thrillers frequently showed them doing: stirring up wars and revolutions all over the world for the sake of profits.

Unfortunately none of these facile explanations could endure scholarly, or even congressional scrutiny. The fourth and final alibi, however, defied analysis. It was that we had been victimized by a secret British weapon, invisible as the wind and just as capable of blowing us hither and yon against our will. That effective terroristic device was propaganda. Maybe, if World War II had held off a little longer, that explanation would have gone the way of its predecessors. Probably not, however, as rebuttal was virtually impossible. It's difficult to fight something you can't see. At any rate that was the situation before 1939.

Postwar disillusionment had caused the debunking period of the twenties not just, or even primarily, of the atrocity stories of World War I but of history, especially historical biography. Strongly against our will we nevertheless had to recognize that the game of power politics again was being played the world over. Reluctantly we recovered from a mental orgy of idealistic thinking. Especially after the Kellogg Peace Pact was proved to be only a pious hope, pacifism became popular, patriotism unpopular. Skepticism and cynicism increased. Since almost fanatical faith in high ideals once had failed to achieve practical results, it seemed to follow that belief in any ideals was unintellectual. Youth, thousands of whom had taken the Oxford oath, almost had to be dragged to training camps when selective service began a year before Pearl Harbor; and once there they talked of Ohio—over the hill in October.

Before World War I a "literature" on the subject of propaganda was almost nonexistent as a cursory examination of *Reader's Guide* or a library's card index file will verify. As a matter of fact, there was virtually nothing on the entire subject of public opinion as such. Then in 1927 appeared Harold D. Lasswell's *Propaganda Technique in the World War* (Knopf) which was the first of a number of books and articles seeming to confirm the growing conviction that we had been duped into accepting the 1914–18 conflict as being something which it wasn't. In October, 1937, the Institute for Propaganda Analysis made its debut and, despite the splendid work that it did in making a decade of school children less gullible, it nevertheless had the negative effect of helping to make "propaganda" into a smear word. Propaganda against propaganda increased and was tremendously effective. The word became accepted as a virtual synonym for "lie." Typical definition was that by Frederick E. Lumley in *The Propaganda Menace* (Appleton-Century-Crofts, Inc., 1933), "Propaganda is promotion which is veiled in one way or another as to (1) its origin or sources; (2) the interests involved; (3) the methods employed; (4) the content spread; and (5) the results accruing to the victims—any one, any two, any three, any four or all five." To clinch it Lumley also wrote: "Propagandists are not truth seekers. They are social fixers; their commodity is not the naked truth; when it is not wholly lies it is what we may. call reconditioned truth; it is truth arrayed to serve as means to a desired condition."

The Institute was not so extreme. It defined propaganda as "expression of opinion or action by individuals or groups deliberately designed to influence opinions or actions of other individuals or groups with reference to predetermined ends." Nevertheless, the Institute helped make the populace propaganda-conscious. As interpolated, the exposés of the Institute and other authorities came to mean that all our national ills were traceable to our having once been taken in by propaganda. Millions who, during World War I, with open-minded gullibility had believed almost anything, now were in a state of emotional disbelief of virtually everything. Anyone who correctly identified the war clouds as they began to gather, and who declared that American interests were affected, was called a propagandistic warmonger, notably Franklin Delano Roosevelt from the time of his Chicago quarantine speech in October, 1937 on. In the spring of 1939 the late Senator Borah announced he had better information than the administration and knew positively that there would be no European war that year.

When Adolf Hitler crossed the Polish frontier to begin his infamous "counteroffensive with pursuit," C. Hartley Grattan rushed into print with *The Deadly Parallel* (Stackpole, 1939) to prove World War I was just being resumed after a long armistice; to point out it was none of our affair; and to warn against our succumbing to British propaganda to the contrary a second time. Some Americans— just a handful—did awaken as early as 1931 with the first Manchurian invasion; others when Ethiopia was invaded; or when Spain became a proving ground for the Italians and Germans; or when the Rhineland, or Austria or Albania was overrun; or when Czechoslovakia was sold out at Munich; or when Poland, or the Lowlands, or Norway or France or Russia was invaded or Britain threatened. Millions, however, slept blithely on, muttering "America First" in their nightmares until the bombs fell on Hawaii. Irrational fear of propaganda had helped to blind altogether too many Americans to reality.

Examination of our social behavior since "propaganda" entered the lexicon of the majority of Americans reveals several things: (1) the most effective propaganda is that which seems to warn against or create fear of other propaganda. Thereby many acquire the idea it is necessary constantly to be on the alert because the propagandist, like the goblins, will "git" you if you don't watch out, and they close their minds to the invasion of all new ideas, for fear some will be dangerous; (2) otherwise, the propagandist's effectiveness is in his manipulation of existent attitudes and opinions rather than in his ability to create such attitudes and opinions; (3) the social conditioning which determines what those attitudes and opinions are results from the impact of events and situations rather than from skillful use of the propaganda devices.

Much has been written about the elaborateness and effectiveness of the German propaganda machine as operated by Dr. Paul Joseph Goebbels. The pertinent fact to be borne in mind is that neither Hitler nor anyone else could have come to dictatorial power in Germany had he not capitalized upon the economic distress and insecurity of the German people. In his early stages *der Fuehrer* had plenty of rivals whom he had to eliminate by outshouting, absorbing, or liquidating. Granted that another leader might have steered a different course, if the Weimar Republic had been satisfactory to a larger proportion of Germans, if their economic status had been less insecure, neither the Nazi nor any other alternative movement would have made headway. Revolutionary change never is sudden. The Declaration of Independence is largely a long recitation of grievances and of the efforts the colonists had made to obtain redress through peaceful means. Intolerable disregard of the plight of the masses brought on the French Revolution. Czarist Russia was a black spot on the world's map. After World War II the Chinese masses turned to the communists not because they had been indoctrinated with propaganda or because they had any understanding of Marxist doctrines, but because the Chiang Kai-shek regime had become hopelessly inept and corrupt. In all of these cases the revolutionists had capitalized upon discontent but were not the main factor in creating it.

Another comparatively recent example of the extent to which preconditioning affects the chances of success by the propagandist was provided by the first Russian-Finnish war which began Nov. 30, 1939. The emotional upsurge in the United States was way and beyond the feeling which had been exhibited during any of a series of previous violations of national sovereignty by the Italians and Germans: in Ethiopia, Spain, Austria, Albania, Czechoslovokia, and Poland. When the Soviets pushed forward their frontier at the expense of the Finns, the reaction of a large proportion of Americans was expressed by one leading Chicago businessman who called it "the greatest crime since the crucifixion." Because of the comparatively lackadaisical attitude that most Americans had toward the events of Italian and German aggression in preceding years, the explanation is not to be found in the heinousness of the Kremlin's action. Rather, it is to be found in the existent attitudes of the American public. On the one hand there were positive sentiments of liking for little Finland, long admired because of her record, unique among nations, of continuing payments on her World War I debts, one even coming after the Soviet invasion began. Finland also was the native land of one of the world's leading musical composers, Sibelius, whose works were very popular in this country, and she could boast of a couple of fellows able to run faster than anybody else. Even more important, however, were the negative attitudes of dislike and hatred for the Soviet Union. Here at last, after more than twenty years, was an opportunity to do something about it. So Herbert Hoover, famed for his World War I relief work, came out of virtual retirement and figuratively began passing the hat for the benefit of Helsinki. Before much could be collected and transmitted, however, the fighting was over, much to the surprise of those who had followed American newspaper accounts of it. According to those press dispatches little Finland was giving big Russia a surprising beating. Pictures showed Soviet equipment abandoned on snowy roads and Russian soldiers frozen into the most outlandish positions because of poor stamina resulting from inadequate food, clothing, and supplies. Adding up uncontradicted stories of Finnish mileage gained would have put the Finnish army in Stalingrad by the time hostilities ceased rather than in its own capital accepting surrender terms. The fault in this case was the refusal of both sides to permit correspondents at the front.

One of the most important effects of the many books on World War I propaganda, beginning with Lasswell's and including *Propaganda for War,* by H. C. Peterson (University of Oklahoma, 1939), *Spreading Germs of Hate,* by George Sylvester Viereck (H. Liveright, 1930), *Falsehood in Wartime,* by Arthur Ponsonby (G. Allen and Unwin, 1925), *The Growth of a Legend,* by Fernand Van Langenhove (Putnam, 1916), *War Propaganda and the United States,* by Harold Lavine and James Wechsler (Yale, 1940) and *Atrocity Propaganda, 1914–1919,* by James Morgan Read (Yale, 1941), was on the attitudes of Americans as regards wartime atrocity stories.

During World War I without question the most effective type of anti-German propaganda in the United States was the atrocity story. Virtually every rumor, no matter how grotesque, was believed, especially after the German Outrages Inquiry Committee, an official British body created by the distinguished Lord James Bryce, gave its report in 1915. A subsequent protest by five American foreign correspondents covering the warfronts had little effect. Wrote Read: "The real secret of the power of propaganda from 1914 to 1918 lay in the unpreparedness of its victims. They hardly knew what the word 'propaganda' meant; they certainly had no institutes devoted to running analysis of propagandist output."

Nor did most Americans have any idea of the real causes of the war. Before 1914 American newspapers and press associations followed a policy of strict objectivity in the reporting of foreign news. The small staffs abroad were restrained from venturing upon interpretation. The result was that when a comparatively minor incident such as the assassination of a member of the Austro-Hungarian royalty threw most of Europe into armed conflict, American editors were as dumfounded as their readers. During the month of negotiations between the murders at Sarajevo and the first shot of the war, many American papers played the running story on inside pages, so little did they realize its significance. By contrast, when war broke out in 1939 it came as a virtual anticlimax after the Munich crisis of the preceding year. In the interval between the wars the newspapers and press associations did not revert to their former policy; instead, they peopled the world with first-rate scholars who provided both play-by-play accounts of what was happening and explanations of events as well, so that American newspaper readers came to recognize the inevitability of conflict.

Just as a blank slate is better for writing purposes than one covered with chalk marks, so is an empty mind the best potential material for the propagandist at work. In 1914, so unprepared were Americans and so uninformed, that public opinion was divided as between the Germans and the Allies. There was, however, no radio in those days and the British effectively cut the Atlantic cables and stopped the mails so that, until the final months of the period of American neutrality, the Germans were virtually cut off from all communication with this country. And when contact was established it was only by means of a powerful dots-and-dashes wireless station.

"The picture of the Germans painted by British propagandists was fantastic," wrote Peterson, "but it was accepted as long as the people being propagandized were kept away from Germans in the flesh. . . . Out of an untrue interpretation of what was happening, American leaders arrived at an utterly fallacious conclusion as to what could be achieved. In other words, the propaganda was not only responsible in a large degree for American entry into the war, but it was also responsible for the temper and irrationality of the peace treaty and the vindictiveness of the post-war years." [1]

Unproved as the charge that propaganda was largely responsible for this nation's entry into the war may be, it certainly is true that propaganda—especially the atrocity story—greatly affected American public opinion, especially after we became a participant. Belgian babies without hands; French women without breasts; Canadian soldiers crucified to barn doors; holy places, especially Rheims Cathedral, bombed without provocation; sacred treaties guaranteeing the neutrality of Belgium and other small nations torn into scraps of paper at the Kaiser's feet were accepted as actualities without question. Despite contemporary proof that the boat was armed and con-

[1] Reprinted from H. C. Peterson, *Propaganda for War.* Copyright, 1939, by the University of Oklahoma Press. Reprinted by kind permission of the publisher.

Carl A. Rudisill Library
LENOIR RHYNE COLLEGE

sequently subject to attack under international law, sinking of the British *Lusitania,* with the loss of 128 of 197 Americans aboard, was taken as proof that the modern Germans in sooth were descendants of the Hun and Boche, which is what they came to be called. In fact, the entire German program of submarine warfare—something new in World War I—was atrocious, causing some authorities to define atrocity as some new means of waging war of which the enemy thinks first, so that this war's atrocities became the next war's orthodox methods of fighting. The shooting by the Germans of Edith Cavell, a nurse who assisted about 250 Allied soldiers to escape, was legally legitimate and consistent with what the Allies themselves had done in more than one similar situation. Nevertheless, Edith Cavell became a World War I heroine and her killing was related with telling effect in neutral countries. It was especially effective in Italy, some authorities even saying it was mainly responsible for the Italian entry into the war on the Allied side in violation of a solemn treaty obligation to aid the Austrians and Germans. In China, the most effective propaganda item was the picture of German war dead allegedly being hauled away to a soap factory, a stunt accomplished by shifting the captions on two pictures, one showing dead horses being taken to the factory, the other showing dead soldiers on the way to decent burial.

In addition to these and some other widely circulated stories, there were literally thousands of anecdotes supplementing and confirming the major ones. No wartime speech—of which there were hundreds of thousands or millions—was complete without some. School teachers related them to classes; friends and business associates exchanged "the latest" whenever they met. One felt chagrined if he did not have "a new one" to relate on any occasion. Few if any doubted the authenticity of any of them, even the most hoary which were revived from Spanish-American, Boer, Franco-Prussian or even Civil War days.

Made sheepish by the interbellum scholarly exposés, which the general disillusionment conditioned people to accept, millions resolved never to be "taken in" again. So, when the stories of German and Japanese brutality began to arrive in World War II, the prevailing attitude was entirely different. Instead of uncritical credulity, there was stubborn refusal to accept as true even the most authenticated accounts or, if believing them true, a disposition to shrug them off with an almost unbelievable indifference. The writer recalls showing newspaper photographs of Generals Eisenhower, Bradley, and Patton, other military leaders, members of Congress and representatives of the American press, at Buchenwald in the spring of 1945. A good-sized majority of approximately 60 university juniors and seniors believed the pictures either were faked ("there is no proof the bodies are not those of Americans killed in battle," one student typically remarked) or to be taken only as evidence that "modern warfare is frightful." There was little shock, almost no indignation. The same reaction occurred when pictures of emaciated former American prisoners of the Japanese were shown and accounts of the Death March from Bataan were published. "Our soldiers kill unarmed prisoners and strafe lifeboats" was a frequent explanation for failure to get excited over Dachau, Belsen, or Auschwitz. Explanations that atrocities committed by individual soldiers or even ordered by underlings are different from wholesale slaughters in accordance with deliberate national policies of extermination, failed to have much effect. The point we are concerned with here, however, is not the rightness or wrongness of the reaction but its great difference from that of a generation earlier to unverified accounts of much less frightful occurrences. Whereas once Americans believed almost anything without proof, on a later occasion they refused to believe almost everything, even when supported by seemingly irrefragable evidence.

What Is Propaganda?

The most effective propaganda, the preceding discussion should have made clear, is that which supports what those to whom it is directed already believe, which gives them what they want to hear. In such cases the propaganda really is superfluous if the purpose is to create basic attitudes, but it has a morale-building effect and fortifies believers in their convictions. Thus, the demagogue who shouts about white supremacy at a Ku Klux Klan conclave is greeted with enthusiastic cheers; so is the orator who damns the Vatican in a gathering of Jehovah's Witnesses, the agitator who screams at Wall Street to a cell of reds, the National Association of Manufacturers speaker who warns against communists, and so forth.

In all such and similar cases the propaganda either is not recognized as such or is labeled as "good" propaganda, the exception to the rule that all propaganda is bad. From the standpoint of those who are condemned, however, the propaganda—and there is no doubt in their mind that it *is* propaganda and not education or something else —is decidedly bad. Limiting any definition of propaganda to the dissemination only of evil consequently is seen to be difficult, almost meaningless, as it leaves so much that goes on in the effort to influence thought and action outside its scope. The attempts of Lumley and others to restrict the meaning of the word to encompass only what is concealed or deceptive leads to the same difficulty. According to such definitions the harangues suggested in the preceding paragraph would not be classifiable as propaganda because they were open and above board.

Theoretically it probably makes no difference how you define propaganda as long as you and others understand its limitations and suitable words are invented to cover phenomena thereby excluded from the definition. It certainly, however, is much simpler to accept an objective scientific definition such as that of the Institute for Propaganda Analysis (see page 97) with its emphasis upon the motivation of the propagandist rather than upon the social effects of his work. Acceptance of this point of view eliminates the necessity of making exceptions to the "badness" principle, to exclude propaganda for churches, colleges, charitable organizations, and the like toward which most people have favorable attitudes. If one feels that all efforts to influence the thoughts and actions of others are wrong, regardless of the cause, he faces the necessity of declaring that most of life from the beginning of time has been evil. When one condemns the propaganda of a cause in which he does not believe he often is really condemning the cause itself, not the arguments. There is, of course, a legitimate field for condemnation of unethical practices in this as in all other fields; that is, to deplore most of the evils which Lumley and the others consider are inherent in all propagandizing. But in so doing one runs the risk of magnifying the maliciousness of the opposition and of exonerating his own teammates. Either propaganda for his side doesn't seem at all reprehensible or he easily rationalizes that the end served justifies the means taken to achieve it.

To repeat, propaganda—or whatever you want to call it—which coincides with the existent attitudes of its intended "victims," is the most effective. That, however, is not the propaganda that is feared.

Rather, it is propaganda from "the other side" which causes one to form opinions which, if translated into action, would lead to results detrimental to one's best interests. People, in other words, are afraid of being fooled or tricked into something. The answer of the ethical propagandist is that such is not his purpose; rather, he is attempting to persuade and convert. Again, ethical considerations become foremost and each case must be decided on its own merits.

There is no doubt, under whatever definition is accepted, that the propagandist operates with a purpose: to influence others to his way of thinking or acting. Consequently, the theoretical difference between propaganda and education is clear. The educator is supposed to be engaged in imparting knowledge without intent to promote any particular cause. That there is a great deal of propaganda passing as education there can be no doubt; the distinction is, to repeat, theoretical, to be found in the intents of the propagandist and educator rather than in their methods or effects. Even so it is not easy to draw the line. Is, for instance, the sociologist who points out that there is a correlation between bad housing and juvenile delinquency educating or propagandizing? What about the biologist who explains the theories of evolution? The political scientist who explains that such-and-such a law was passed because of the pressure exerted by certain special interests?

Presumably the educator can defend himself by giving "both sides" of any subject, by merely telling his classes what certain philosophers, historians, eugenicists and others have said and then referring them to adverse criticism of each in turn. Still the line often is a thin one unless a fact is so widely accepted that there is no popular "other side" believed to exist. The teacher can declare that he conscientiously tries only to "make his students think," but the extent to which his unconscious motives may be different cannot easily be determined. The only possible criterion is whether the educator does the most honest job of which he is capable, seeks for the truth to the best of his ability and imparts it to others as he discovers it. Deliberate suppression or distortion without question makes him a propagandist. Expressing heretical ideas doesn't. The importance in a democracy of allowing the scholar the widest range possible is apparent.

Whereas educators are searchers after truth, propagandists are advocates of causes. This is not tantamount to declaring that propagandists disregard truth. As a matter of fact truth often is the very best propaganda. The propagandist, however, goes out to seek those to whom he would impart it; the educator waits for those also interested in truth-seeking to come to him. Hence, the cloistered tradition which keeps many teachers from active participation in public affairs, a characteristic of American life deplored by many as depriving us of the public benefit of what are supposed to be our best-trained minds.

It would be possible to go on and on casuistically. This author, who has been both, recognizes a decided difference in purpose between the educator and the propagandist. Even easier to detect is the distinction between propaganda and advertising. The latter is just one kind of the former in which the purpose is polarized and clear: to induce customers to make purchases. It is because he knows what the advertiser wants him to do that the average citizen does not fear advertising so much as he does other forms of propaganda: those in which the propagandist tends to conceal his ultimate aims. There exists in the United States a healthy skepticism regarding the lavish claims of some advertisers, partly as a result of having been induced to purchase inferior products as a consequence; and a considerable amusement over some advertising efforts to attract attention. These attitudes, however, in no way approach the widespread suspicion of propaganda used for purposes other than to promote commercial sales.

In considering those forms distinction must be made between them and events which have a propagandistic effect. The Japanese attack on Pearl Harbor is a case in point. It was not a propaganda stunt promulgated by the Roosevelt administration or Fight for Freedom people. Nevertheless, it had the effect of convincing millions of hitherto unconvinced people that the United States was menaced by the Axis powers. A public report may be seized upon by a propaganda group as tending to support its point of view. The Copeland bill to strengthen the food and drug acts was given little chance of passage over the efforts of pressure groups which had spent millions of dollars to fight it. Then there occurred several deaths because of the marketing of improperly tested sulphanilamide in liquid form and opposition to the measure crumbled. A federal law permitting the Federal Bureau of Investigation to enter kidnapping cases passed easily after the kidnapping-murder of the son of Charles A. Lindbergh; it is, in fact, popularly called the Lindbergh law.

Most propaganda efforts are directed, not to establishing new attitudes but to manipulating those which already exist. An argument is most certainly won if the judge of it—that is, the subject to whom the propaganda appeal is directed—becomes convinced that *the matter at issue is not really one of opinion at all but rather one of belief*; that is, something which is not properly controversial but easily resolved by application of a settled conviction as a yardstick. In static primitive societies that is the way most matters could be decided. There truth was static, the rules were known and were absolute and consequently easily discovered, applied, and enforced in any particular situation. Situations, to use the social psychologist's jargon, were defined in terms of customs, traditions, prejudices, stereotypes, sentiments.

In modern times it is not so easy to settle an argument by appeal to authority or axiom because, as pointed out in the preceding chapter, old standards and ideals have broken down with the result that much that formerly was sacred no longer is. The range of the discussable has widened greatly, and the process continues with the spread of scientific inquisitiveness. Nevertheless, even today change is not so rapid that regressive appeals to the past are not effective. Rationally men may accept new iconoclastic ideas but emotionally they still cling uneasily, often unhappily, to the past. And so, as already pointed out, in times of distress "back to" movements flourish and frustrated persons seek to recover "the good old days" when the order and sense of certainty which all men crave reputedly was more nearly attained. In the Feb. 14, 1937, New York *Times Magazine*, Goebbels, a master propagandist was quoted as believing:

> The ordinary man hates nothing more than two-sidedness, to be called upon to consider this as well as that. The masses think simply and primitively. They love to generalize complicated situations, and from their generalizations to draw clear and uncompromising conclusions.

Appeals to the past are most valuable for the propagandist who seeks to defeat some departure from it, for the counter-propagandist, that is. Thus, public housing is un-American; prison reform proposals are the result of maudlin sentimentality, and so forth. The device is that which the Institute for Propaganda Analysis called *name-calling* and almost always involves label-pinning on what is being opposed. Anyone can make up a list of effective "smear" words: red, communist, nigger-lover, bureaucrat, fascist, reactionary, warmonger, etc. Several of the foregoing are useful in discrediting proponents of the new and in indicating that the propagandist's side is that of the tried and tested, the eternally true and just which it is his intention to defend and preserve.

Appeals to the old and sacroscant also can be made by advocates of new ideas as well as by their opponents. Politicians try to show that they are on the side of the angels, that they merely are proposing what is orthodox in support and protection of the well established: nothing new, nothing radical, nothing inconsistent with experience and deeply rooted belief. In *Words That Won the War* (Princeton, 1939) James R. Mock and Cedric Larson wrote of the Committee on Public Information, 1917–1919, the so-called Creel Committee of World War I: "The committee performed an almost incredible task in the marshaling of opinion, in building strong walls of national solidarity. But it is important to realize that the committee was no inner clique imposing unwanted views on the general public. Scarcely an idea may be found in all the work of the CPI that was not held by many Americans before war was declared. The committee was representative of the particular majority of American opinion. What the committee did was to codify and standardize ideas already current, and to bring the powerful force of the emotions behind them. It is true that the whipping-in of stragglers through application of social pressure held a vitally important place in the work, but the greatest effort was directed toward vitalizing convictions already held and toward developing the will to fight for ideas already familiar."

The propagandist tries to convince others that their best interests will be served by adoption of his thoughts or actions. This may mean either adhering to the old or championing the new, as the case may be. "It is just what you've been waiting for" combines elements of both psychological appeals. St. Paul, masterful propagandist, used this technique when, according to Acts 17:22–23, he told the Athenians: ". . . Ye men of Athens, I perceive that in all things ye are too superstitious. For as I passed by, and beheld your devotions, I found an altar with this inscription, TO THE UN-

KNOWN GOD. Whom therefore ye ignorantly worship, him declare
I unto you."

The extent to which the proselyting appeal works is dependent upon
the extent and intensity of recognition of need. At war's end the salesman of commodities whose production has been curbed during the
hostilities has an easier time than when there is greater abundance.
Then part of his job must be creation of desire which he does by
appealing to every possible yearning prevalent in the culture: to save
labor, to be in style, to "keep up with the Joneses," to appear a little
superior to the Joneses, and so forth. The late William I. Thomas,
eminent sociologist, postulated four wishes which, he declared, men
always have regardless of their culture. Not instincts but necessary
ambitions in order to be well-adjusted, no matter how differently
attainment of them may be sought in different cultures, they are: (1)
a sense of security; (2) recognition by others; (3) affectional response; (4) new experiences. Insurance company advertisers specialize
in appealing to the first; correspondence schools and clothing manufacturers to the second; cosmetic and patent medicine advertisers to
the third; and travel bureaus to the fourth. All propagandists, of
course, try to combine all of the appeals, the broad basic ones cited
by Thomas and all of the others postulated by almost everyone else.
Their talents really are put to a test when a distinct conflict of interests
exists. Such occurs when a new need comes in conflict with an old
principle. As already intimated, if the need is vital and the old is
really obsolete, time will take care of the situation. It is the propagandist's job, however, to speed up the process, or, if he is on the
other side, to slow it down. Always it is the propagandist's own
interests that are most important, but his forte is to make others
believe he is operating unselfishly in their interests or that the interests
of the propagandist and of the propagandized are mutual.

Propaganda Techniques

Although it contributed to the exaggerated fear of propaganda that
affected most Americans, the Institute for Propaganda Analysis performed a valuable function in analyzing and classifying many of the
important propaganda appeals. In an article, "The Analysis of
Propaganda: A Clinical Summary," in the *American Journal of
Sociology* for September, 1945, Alfred McClung Lee, executive

director of the institute, now a Brooklyn college sociologist, refined and extended the list of devices as follows:

A. Techniques of basic procedure
   1. Selecting the issue
   2. Case-making or card-stacking
   3. Simplification
B. Use of omnibus words (basic propaganda shorthand)
   4. Name-calling
   5. Glittering generality
C. Techniques of identification
   6. Transfer
   7. Testimonial
   8. Plain folks
   9. Band wagon
D. Strategic techniques
   10. Hot potato
   11. Stalling

Lee is the first to admit that this is an incomplete and more or less arbitrary list, but, he insists, "The techniques are workable. Anyone, with practice, can use them." He meant workable and usable by the propaganda analyst and also by the unskilled. Naturally, there were organized propagandists long before the word was invented. The term dates at least from the designation of a Cardinalitial Commission de propaganda fide by Pope Gregory XIII (1572–1585) and from its successor, the Congregatio de propaganda fide, established in 1622 by Pope Urban VIII to spread Roman Catholic doctrine. In his everyday efforts to win friends and influence people, almost everyone is an unconscious propagandist. It is utterly fallacious to separate the study of propaganda from that of human behavior as a whole, to consider propaganda as a secret or unusual skill which is the possession of the elite only. The matter of ethics also is not involved in this or in any other classification. The "big lie," in the efficacy of which the Nazis believed, can be told while using any or all of the devices. Likewise, the absolute truth (if such there is) can be used similarly.

The Institute for Propaganda Analysis devoted virtually all of its attention to the written or spoken word. In the discussion to follow that also will be the emphasis, but the additional attempt will be made to point out how the same effects can be obtained through actions.

Selecting the issue. According to Lee this "refers to the effort of the propagandist to select and state the issue upon which he would like to make his stand in a social competition or conflict. From a current tactical standpoint, the issue that is accepted by a public as the crucial one in a contest has a considerable bearing upon where the struggle begins, its support, and the relative advantages of such a starting-point to the partisans."

For example, a measure for federal aid to education is before Congress and is the object of only moderate debate. Its passage seems likely because its need easily can be demonstrated to be great. Then, however, an amendment is introduced requiring that distribution of funds shall be in accordance with population rather than need; or that aid shall be denied states in which racially segregated school systems exist, or states in which parochial schools benefit in any way from tax revenues. Immediately the issue is changed and the entire bill goes down in defeat. Sometimes the mover of the amendment is a sincere advocate of it who would prefer to see the measure lose if his addition is excluded; on other occasions he may be an opponent of the original proposal who cleverly seeks to defeat it by introducing the new element which he knows will "stir up a hornet's nest."

Without amendment opponents of a measure may divert debate into consideration of only one aspect of it. Does it or does it not violate states' rights? Is it or is it not too expensive? Is or is not the fact that communists favor (or oppose) it important? And so on. When Hugo Black was nominated by President Roosevelt to be a member of the United States Supreme Court, the main issue on which Senate confirmation hinged was the importance of his one-time membership in the Ku Klux Klan. Since the point was raised by some whose own views didn't seem to be greatly different from those of the Klan, there was ample cause for suspecting hypocrisy. The Klan issue was, in fact, termed "a red herring" by Senator Black's supporters who argued that his views and actions in the intervening years were contradictory to those which could be considered pleasing to the hooded heroes.

The red-herring issue is, of course, a superfluous issue; as the dictionary puts it, "something used to draw attention away from the real issue." Although everything said in debate of it may be absolutely unquestionable, the mere act of raising it is propagandistic in purpose. So is the "wait until we see the white of their eyes" technique: that of delaying attack on a measure until the strategic moment, when the attention of opponents is diverted to some other pressing matter or when proponents of the measure need the support on some other matter of the attackers who then are in a position to make "trades" of support. The newspaperman, especially he who covers any legislative body, should realize that correct timing is a great attribute of anyone in public life. Franklin Delano Roosevelt possessed the ability to know when to speak up and when to keep silent. Often he drove his advisors to the verge of nervous prostration by his apparent indifference to attacks by his enemies. Then, at what usually would prove to be the strategically best moment, FDR would let loose. His Teamsters' Union speech during his last campaign was, from this standpoint, his greatest. Pleading the pressure of presidential duties imposed by the war, the president allowed the Republicans to pile up argument after argument against him, disregarded rumor and malicious attack of which in an earlier campaign he might have been expected to take cognizance more promptly. What FDR apparently realized more than other party leaders was that his silence did not work entirely against him; rather, it helped to create the impression of a national leader too devoted to the public interest to take time out to defend himself. When he did speak he capitalized upon that attitude by sweeping the board clean of virtually everything. To spike the canard that had been making the rounds that the Navy was put to great expense and danger by sending a battleship back to an Aleutian island to rescue Fala, the White House scottie, candidate Roosevelt referred to his patience when he, his wife, and children had been the victims of lies; when they started to pick on his dog, FDR declared, he could remain quiet no longer.

Case-making. "This," Lee explains, "is the ordering of facts or falsehoods, illustrations or distractions or distortions, logical or illogical statements, in such a sequence that the best or worst possible impression will be made. . . . When deliberately unfair, it may be called card-stacking."

Often, the case is on the way toward being made by the mere selection of the issue, as the examples given suggest. Wading through the "bunk" or worse that is the stuff of which most public discussions are made demands the best that any newspaperman possesses. Even when the cause is one in which he believes, he may sicken at the manner in which its proponents pull out the stops to allow emotion to flood the place and come near to causing a lachrymose drowning of the real issues. Take, for example, the following passage from the address, "The Tragedy of the Lusitania," which Wesley Frost, former American consul at Queenstown, Ireland, delivered in World War I days according to Mock and Larson:

"It was black out there on the Atlantic, and in the blackness the lifeboats alternately rose on the crests of the waves and sank into the black valley between. The boats carried women and children whose hair hung in icicles over their shoulders and their half frozen bodies yielded to the rolling and pitching of the frail boats. Now and then a half-dead passenger uttered a shriek of pain or of anguish as she realized that a friend or relative had died in her arms. Meanwhile, in the dark hull of the German submarine, the captain watching through the periscope finally turned his head away. Even this man, agent of Prussian cruelty, had witnessed a scene upon which he did not care to gaze."

Card-stacking is the technique of the half-truth. One of the best jobs of analyzing a journalistic example of the technique was written by an anonymous Washington newspaperman under the title, "The Smear Technique," for the January, 1948, *Nieman Reports*. Reproduced with the permission of that publication, it was as follows:

"The smear story," the Professor of Journalism told his class, "is at once one of the most rewarding and the simplest to write. The damaging results to the victim of the smear are usually lasting, and if only the simplest regard is observed for the rules of libel, the victim has no recourse. The barest minimum of rules are required for a craftsmanlike smear:

"1. Use a half-truth, if possible, rather than an outright lie. It is more difficult to disprove.

"2. Choose the half-truth in such a way that it may be stated in a sentence whereas its refutation or explanation will require at least a paragraph.

"3. Effect the smear by innuendo rather than direct statement.

"4. Do not be discouraged or forestalled from your effort by the fact that there is no damaging evidence against your victim. Create it yourself. This is accomplished simply, usually through the connective 'and.' Just mention the man you are smearing in the same sentence with whatever invidious organizations, persons, philosophies and activities that come to your mind.

"In view of the simplicity of the smear technique, it is discouraging to find so many smear stories which fall short of optimum efficiency.

"An example at hand is from the Washington, D.C. *Times-Herald* of July 17, 1947. It is by no means the worst smear story in the world; it includes some imaginative and distinguished passages. But technically it leaves much to be desired.

"Let us proceed with its analysis. The story, by James Walter, is in the left-hand column of notes which will now be distributed to the class. In the right-hand column are comments on the facts and implications, for most of which I am indebted to a speech of Representative Chet Holifield, in the House, on July 22."

Times-Herald	*The Facts*
Dr. Albert U. Condon, who played an important role in the development of the atom bomb before taking his present job as head of the United States Bureau of Standards, where vital information concerning American industrial research is accumulated, will be called before the House Un-American Activities Committee, for questioning about Russian A-bomb know-how, this newspaper learned last night.	Dr. Condon's first name is Edward.
	The lead is scarcely newsworthy. In a magazine article several weeks earlier, Chairman J. Parnell Thomas of the Un-American Activities Committee, declared he was going to call Condon to the stand. Thomas' smear technique, incidentally, was more gifted than the reporter's: Thomas said he was going to "subpoena" Condon, thus creating the impression that Condon was a recalcitrant and unwilling witness, when, in fact, he had never even been requested to testify. On reading the magazine article, Condon promptly wrote Thomas that he would be glad to testify and help the Committee in any way, a fact which the *Times-Herald* reporter probably knew but did not mention.

Times-Herald	*The Facts*
Dr. Condon will be quizzed because the committee feels his contacts with Russian scientists and pro-Communist sympathizers in this country qualify him to discuss Soviet atom research, according to Representative Thomas, Republican of New Jersey, chairman of the Un-American Activities Committee.	Rather nice. Fairly deft usage of a technique known as damning with faint praise. The reporter is not specific about the "contacts" referred to. This was a wise and also necessary omission, since there were no such contacts.
This newspaper learned that after Condon left as head of the research department of the Westinghouse Electric Co. in Pittsburgh to join the Manhattan project, his leftish associations were under continuous scrutiny by military intelligence personnel.	He did not leave Westinghouse to join the Manhattan project; he was assigned to it by the company in connection with its work on the project. He was not head of Westinghouse research, but rather associate director. No doubt he was under scrutiny. He, and everyone else of importance on the project was, or should have been. The important thing is that this scrutiny failed to uncover any derogatory information, for Condon continued with the project off and on, until almost its end.
Before coming to Washington he directed atom-smashing experiments with the Westinghouse cyclotron, only instrument of its kind owned by an industrial laboratory in this country.	It was not a cyclotron, but a Van de Graaf electrostatic generator.
He worked on the A-bomb project three times and later the Soviet Government violated diplomatic courtesy by secretly inviting him to the two hundred twentieth anniversary of the Russian Academy of Science in Moscow, but permission for him to leave this country was refused upon request of the Army.	He was not invited by the Russians, secretly or otherwise. They invited organizations to send delegates; Condon was chosen as delegate of the American Institute of Physics.
At that time a group of scientists in this country was vigorously at-	No doubt of the fact that Groves refused permission for Condon to

Times-Herald

tempting to wrest control of scientific secrets from the Army. The request to keep Dr. Condon "at home" presumably came from Maj. Gen. Leslie R. Groves, who masterminded the Manhattan or A-bomb project in New Mexico.

Of this contemplated trip Dr. Condon told the *Times-Herald*:

"Other scientists were permitted to take the trip to Russia, but the military thought it best that I remain here."

While Groves would not admit direct intervention in the Condon case, he did tell the *Times-Herald*:

"I would have been remiss in my duty if I had consented at that time to let anyone who knew about the possibilities of the Manhattan project go to such a meeting so soon before the bomb was to be used."

The visit, it developed, was to have been made just 30 days before A-bombs were dropped on Nagasaki and Hiroshima, to force the end of the Japanese-American war in the summer of 1945.

The Un-American Activities Committee also is interested in hearing Dr. Condon for the following reasons:

1. Condon, while working for Westinghouse, also served on the science committeee of the American-Soviet Friendship Society.

The Facts

leave. He also tried to stop Dr. Irving Langmuir, but the latter proved to the War Department that his connection with the bomb project was extremely remote, and he was allowed to proceed. Groves' decision in regard to Condon was not particularly bright; the last-minute withdrawal of the only nuclear physicist in the Moscow-bound party caused much comment and provided the Russians an unmistakable tip-off some 30 days before the bomb was dropped.

Condon had no part at that time with the efforts of the scientists to "wrest control" from the military. Incidentally, the scientists were not trying to wrest control of the "secrets" from the Army. They had the secrets already. They wanted—and got—civilian control of the atomic project. This made Groves and the *Times-Herald* unhappy.

The trip had had White House sponsorship. President Truman had ordered the Army to fly the group to Tehran.

As it happened, Condon had gone back to Westinghouse in February, 1945, severing all connection with the A-bomb project. He was unaware that the bomb had been successfully tested or was about to be used.

Presumably this refers to the National Council of American-Soviet Friendship. In 1944 and 45 when Russia was our ally, the Council's sponsors included Senators Thomas (Utah), Capper and Saltonstall, Bishops Wells and Peabody, Mrs. J. Borden Harriman,

Times-Herald	The Facts

| Dr. Frank Aydelotte, Karl Compton, Albert Einstein and Dean Christian Gauss. Dr. Condon severed connections with the Council after the end of the war.

2. During this same time his wife, Emilie, a native of Czechoslavakia, was corresponding secretary for the Pittsburgh Council, American-Soviet Friendship Society. | Mrs. Condon is a native of Chicago. She worked for the Russian War Relief, an agency headed by Winthrop W. Aldrich of the Chase National Bank.

3. After moving to Washington, Dr. and Mrs. Condon attended a meeting of scientists at the home of Mr. and Mrs. J. Terry Duce, 3014 Woodland Drive NW, where Mrs. Condon's expressions of admiration for Russia were so strong that she was taken to task by one member of the Senate and two members of the House. | Mrs. Condon was not taken to task by anybody for expressions of admiration for Russia on this or any other occasion.

4. Condon was a close friend of Dr. Harlow Shapley, named in 11 Communist-front organizations, among them the Joint Anti-Fascist Refugee Committee, 16 of whose members have been convicted of contempt of Congress. | Good technique here, but it should have been developed further. Shapley, in turn, is at Harvard, which John Reed attended. It should also have been pointed out that Condon reads German, in which language Das Kapital was written.

5. Condon was also a close friend and occupied the New York apartment of Edwin S. Smith, named in 21 pro-foreign groups by the House Un-American Activities Committee, which had him under fire in 1940 for reputed Communist sympathies while he served on the National Labor Relations Board. | Smith was in the group, above-mentioned, which went to Russia. Condon met him first at that time. Smith put him up in his apartment for two nights because Condon was caught without a hotel room during that crowded time in New York.

6. Condon was constantly checked by military authorities for security reasons at the same time, | Presumably everyone on the project was checked, unless Groves fell down on his job. As mentioned

Times-Herald   *The Facts*

but not as frequently as Dr. Frank Oppenheimer, card-carrying member of the Communist Party, whose brother, Dr. J. Robert Oppenheimer, led the team of physicists who exploded the first atom bomb in the western desert.

above, the checking apparently never disclosed anything unfavorable about Condon.

But the reporter is to be congratulated on this paragraph; it has the right touch and method.

Oddly, Condon was born on March 2, 1902, at Alamogordo, N. Mex., not far from the scene of the atom-bomb experiments. He quit his $15,000-a-year job with Westinghouse to work for the Government at a little more than $9,000.

Nothing odd about it; it was a perfectly normal delivery.

A true burst of genius by the reporter. This is a new technique and worthy of emulation by every smear writer. The innuendo that a man will accept a lower-paying Federal job only for sinister purposes has limitless possibilities for future exploitation.

He was eased into his job as head of the Bureau of Standards under the aegis of Henry Wallace.

He was appointed by President Truman and "eased in" by a unanimous Senate vote of confirmation. He was also appointed by the Senate Committee on Atomic Energy as its scientific advisor.

Thomas said last night that because of Condon's record of reported Communist sympathies his activities had been under surveillance for a long time by committee investigators, who would continue their inquiries.

The "record" never established, is now properly taken for granted.

Condon's offer to testify and otherwise aid the committee is ignored. The impression that we are dealing with a furtive and recalcitrant fellow is felicitously reinforced.

The American-Soviet Friendship Society with which Condon served is listed by the Un-American Activities Committee as a Red-front group. At one time it solicited $500 each—a total of $22,500—from 45 American corporations to pay for publication and distribution in Russia of certain books.

Efforts of the Un-American Activities Committee to get at books

Notably good craftsmanship here. God only knows what the reporter is talking about, an excellent thing in smear stories. The reference is probably not to the above mentioned National Council of American-Soviet Friendship, but it may be another, unconnected organization, the American-Soviet Science Society. This group, which the Un-American Activities Committee has

Times-Herald	*The Facts*
and records of the American-Soviet Friendship Society proved as difficult to get as those of the Joint Anti-Fascist Refugee Committee. As a result the Reverend Richard Morford, executive secretary of the A.S.F.S., has been indicted and is waiting trial for contempt of Congress.	never asked for any information or records, exists for the purpose of translating Russian scientific papers into English, not the other way around. It is backed by a $25,000 grant from the Rockfeller Foundation. It has never solicited funds from American corporations. Its trustees include Winthrop W. Aldrich, K. T. Compton, and John Foster Dulles; its acting chairman is a member of the Rockefeller Institute for Medical Research; its members include, besides Condon, Drs. E. C. Lawrence, R. E. Millikan, W. D. Coolidge, Irving Langmuir. However the word "Soviet" is in its title, and no smear writer worthy of the name would neglect that opportunity.
A little more than a year ago the Communist-owned New York *Daily Worker* carried stories about Condon and others headed "U.S.-Soviet scientists swap information." Condon was quoted as welcoming the cooperation for peaceful and constructive purposes.	Condon does not read the *Daily Worker* or give quotations to it, but references to the *Daily Worker* in a story of this sort is traditional; its omission would have been inexcusable.
Condon was also closely associated with the Southern Conference for Human Welfare, listed by the Un-American Activities Committee as a Communist group in which Wallace also was active.	The reporter knew in detail Condon's "close" association, for Condon had told him the circumstances. He had never heard of the group until he was requested to let his name be used as a sponsor at one of its local dinners. He consented after being assured that among the other sponsors were Senator Morse, Mrs. Gifford Pinchot, Mrs. J. Borden Harriman and Mrs. Wiley Rutledge, wife of the Supreme Court Justice. This was Condon's one and only association with the group.

Another analysis of the handling of the newspaper accounts of the attack on Dr. Condon was given in "Trial by Newspapers" by Joseph T. Klapper and Charles Y. Glock in the February, 1949 *Scientific American*. A paragraph-by-paragraph analysis of a different news story, similar to the *Nieman Reports* piece, was entitled "How to Read the Chicago *Tribune*," by Milton Mayer in the April, 1949 *Harper's*.

Six years later the Associated Press paid the National Maritime Union $7,500 to settle a libel suit out of court and publicly retracted in its entirety a story which received sizeable newspaper treatment from coast to coast in January, 1943. Appearing originally under an eight-column streamer, "Ship 'Strike' Irks Guadalcanal Fighters," in the Akron *Beacon-Journal*, the story charged that members of the union had refused to unload a merchant ship containing war supplies on Sunday because of a union regulation. The original story, which the AP picked up and broadcast, was attributed to six Guadalcanal veterans supposedly on visits to Akron. Its appearance added important ammunition to the supply of those who were engaged in anti-labor propaganda during the war years. That the retraction appeared more than six years later indicates the difficulty that victims of lying attacks, journalistic or otherwise, have in setting the record straight. The incident also is a caution to newspapermen and readers about accepting at face value the testimony of "three marines, two sailors, and a Navy pilot."

How effective is this sort of thing? Who knows? Editors and others with an antilabor bias accepted the 1943 story as gospel truth, taking it as additional confirmation of what they had known all the time. Pro-laborites, on the other hand, either disbelieved or minimized the importance of the story. If it happened, they held, it was an isolated incident and only those directly involved should be considered culpable, not the entire labor movement as some of its detractors seemed to believe. Of concern to both sides were the reactions of the great number of "in-betweens," citizens without pro- or antilabor axes to grind, the "neutrals" who hold the balance of power in deciding any controversial matter. As only one of many antilabor stories, the Guadalcanal account had a cumulative effect; it probably helped condition some people, to cause some of the "on-the-fencers" to fall off on the antilabor side. When they returned home and discovered that most of the accounts of absenteeism and strikes and other forms of

alleged unpatriotic behavior on the part of labor were gross exaggerations or entirely false, however, many members of the armed forces
reacted against their misinformants. It would be pleasant to believe
that a lie always will be found out and the liar punished, but unfortunately such is not the case.

The "straw man" technique is a form of card-stacking. This involves creation of a false issue for the sake of being able to refute it.
It amounts to a misrepresentation of the argument of the other side
so that it will appear weak. "Would you want your sister to marry
one?" interjected into a discussion of any proposal to improve the
status of the Negro is an example. The horrendous pictures of bureaucratic inefficiency that are drawn often are in the same category.
Cartoonists opposed to President Roosevelt's seeking the counsel of
some university professors created the stereotype of the brain truster,
and editors asked if readers wanted to turn over the running of the
country to such long-haired and wild-eyed dreamers. "Clear it with
Sidney," referring to advice FDR was supposed to have given his
political lieutenants at the 1944 Democratic convention (denied by
both FDR and the other principals) conjured up images of the chief
executive with an open telephone wire to the desk of Sidney Hillman,
long-time president of the Amalgamated Clothing Workers of America.
The straw man issue is obviously a false one serving the same purpose
as the red herring: to divert attention from the real issues and to
becloud the situation.

Simplification. This, Lee wrote, "refers to the reduction of propaganda materials to formulas which approach in brevity and dogmatism
as nearly as possible the form of a slogan." It represents the type of
thinking against which the semanticists have declared war (see Chapter 11), that of considering any issue as dichotomous: all black or all
white, no grays. "The issue is simply this: are we going to keep
church and state separate or aren't we?" elucidates the opponent of
released time for school children to receive religious instruction. "It's
simply a question of whether we still have freedom of religion in
this country so that parents can bring up their children with the kind
of education they see fit," is the simple rejoinder of someone on the
other side of the argument. Each, of course, speaks on the basis of a
different set of values, a different philosophy of life, a different point
of view as to what freedom of religion and separation of state from

church mean. Getting such opponents together with a meeting of minds is an insuperable task; the best that can be achieved is a compromise with which neither is likely to be pleased.

Slogans, as Lee suggests, simplify discussions as many of the most popular indicate: "54–40 or fight," "back to normalcy," "remember the Alamo" (or the Maine or Pearl Harbor), "rum, Romanism, and rebellion," "have you had enough?" are among the best known. Any propagandist appealing to someone with a strong prejudice would like to make him believe the point at issue involves a simple choice between acceptance or rejection of that prejudice. So he says, "You've just got to decide whether you want your taxes doubled or not," completely disregarding the benefits supposed to accrue from whatever proposal it is that might cause a rise in taxes and probably grossly exaggerating the extent to which the burden would be increased. "It's just an attempt of the unions to take over the city," or "Unless you take this action nobody's home will be safe," suggests attempts at simplification.

Name-calling. Using a bad name to describe an opponent and impugning his motives are old and familiar ways of waging a fight. The effectiveness of stereotyped labels on a person or idea has been mentioned (see page 41). So has scapegoating (see page 67). All forms of name-calling are intended to simplify the issue by belittling the opposition. Scapegoating performs the additional function of diverting attention from the real issues. It is projection of the causes of misfortune onto another, often involving the personification of some evil.

During World War I the Allied propagandists had to create the "devil" upon whom to project blame for the holocaust and focalize hate. They were successful in scapegoating Kaiser Wilhelm II, whose position as head of the German state made him an easy if not the natural subject. The emperor, furthermore, lent himself well to the attack because of his personal appearance and the ease with which some of his words could be interpolated. His upturned mustachios suggested arrogance to his detractors and his withered arm was made to have the same effect that a hunched back or other deformity often has; it made him different and hence, with proper rhetoric, gruesome and awesome. His "Got mit uns" easily became "Me and God," and the national song, "Deutschland über Alles" was interpolated to signify that the Germans had ambitions of world-wide imperialistic control.

By contrast World War II propagandists had an easy time. Their scapegoat already was in existence and hardly anyone can deny that Adolf Hitler "asked for what he got." His ribald oratory was impressive at the lavish Nuremberg rallies but Americans who heard his shrieks over short-wave radio never could understand why. Hitler's palpable lies and his unmistakable ambitions made him an easy target. Once he was dead, or at least out of the picture, the attitude of many of his enemies softened considerably toward his followers. It was almost a personal war against *der Fuehrer* and postwar Germans undoubtedly benefitted because of that fact.

Of scapegoating, Ellis Arnall wrote: "The fundamental factor, of course, is the feeling of the average man that he is powerless to assert his individual will, to express his individual personality, or to influence his personal fate. His dignity as a man is assailed, and in anger he turns to seek any enemy. Then the hatemonger presents him with a ready-made victim, whispering in his ear, appealing to his eye with his nasty little pamphlets, telling him: 'All your troubles are due to the polacks and the kikes and the niggers. They are plotting against you. They are burying guns back of the church or the synagogue or the lodge house. They are going to rise. They are going to kill you. They are going to get you unless you get them first. Kill them! Kill them!'

"It is an old trick. It was not new when the anger of hungry Rome was diverted from the monopolists who were stealing the Egyptian corn crop to the timorous followers of Peter and Clement, hiding in the catacombs and scrawling their professions of faith on the rocks that underlaid the Seven Hills. It was old when Philip of France directed the hate of his people toward the Templars. It was no novelty to the Tsars, who always found it convenient to substitute another pogrom for needed agrarian reforms. It was handy at Nuremberg and Berlin and Munich. It is always handy; it is always more economical to substitute the blood of men for the bread that men are seeking." [1]

Glittering generality. The concomitant technique to calling the other side bad names is to use "virtue" words to describe yourself or your ideas. "Plumed Knight," "Silver-Tongued Orator," "Happy War-

[1] From *The Shore Dimly Seen.* Copyright, 1946, by J. B. Lippincott.

rior," "Vinegar Joe," and "Old Blood and Guts" are among the nicknames that had strong appeals in recent times. When one newspaper opposed to a bill before the state legislature to permit animal experimentation labeled it a "dog-torture" bill, its rival, in favor of the measure, countered with "child-saving" bill.

Usually the prestige-building or favor-finding words and phrases are more vague, intended to mean all things to all people. A good job of exposure was done by Sam Tucker in his column, "As I View the Thing," in the Oct. 29, 1937 Decatur (Ill.) *Herald* as follows:

ORATORY IS THE ART of making pleasant sounds, which cause the hearers to say, "Yes, Yes" in sympathy with the performer, without inquiring too closely exactly what he means. Nearly all so-called political debate is oratory, by this unflattering definition. So also, I am compelled to admit, are nearly all newspaper editorials, most of the lectures on economics, and most sermons.

Let us, just as a laboratory experiment, and not for any practical purpose—far less, for any purpose of discrediting the speakers—examine two typical paragraphs, from two recent political speeches. . . .

Specimen No. 1

Liberty and freedom should mean a fair distribution of the rewards of production and should prevent an unhealthy concentration of wealth and economic power in individual hands or government.

Specimen No. 2

True liberalism does not start as an economic system. An economic system flows from it. The only economic system which will not destroy intellectual and spiritual freedom is private enterprise, regulated to prevent special privilege or coercion.

The first word is "liberty." Tell me, please, exactly what liberty is. Where does it begin, and where does it leave off? And while you are working at this problem, notice please the second noun in the sentence: "freedom." Presumably it means something different from "liberty," because our great political leader would not have considered it necessary to couple the two if they meant the same thing. . . .

After you have worked out these definitions, I invite you to look back again at the two quotations from the Great Minds. There are a lot of further questions I have for you. What is a "fair distribution"? Does it mean the same thing to you as to your housemaid, your hired man, or the machine operator in your factory? What are the "rewards of production"? Again, I want you to be definite, not furry. How much concentration of wealth is an "unhealthy" concentration? What is "government"? If you think that last is easy, I will undertake to give you a bad half-hour in conversation.

In the Specimen No. 2, following the same stern effort to get at some real kernel of meaning, under rank flowering jungle of verbiage, I want to know your definition of "liberalism," and of "economic system." I invite you to set down in specific terms on paper, in firm, solid terms a plain man can understand, what distinction you make between "intellectual and spiritual freedom," as the words are used by the speaker. Tell me what, exactly, is "private enterprise"? Does a man who runs a tavern, selling liquor to minors, operate a "private enterprise"?

Perhaps you will be able to do better with all these problems than I can. Sincerely I hope so. For the fact is, that, after earnest study of these sonorous examples of oratory, substituting the word "blah" for every well-sounding word I cannot turn into a firm meaning, I get this translation of two famous speeches:

No. 1

Blah and Blah should mean a Blah-blah of the blah of blah, and should prevent an blahy blah of blah and blah power in individual hands or blah.

No. 2

True blah does not start as a blah blah. A blah blah flows from it. The only blah blah which will not destroy blah and blah blah is blah-blah, regulated to prevent blah-blah or blah.

If either speech contains any more precise meaning than that, you'll have to prove it, and then you'll have to prove that the meaning you read into it carried into the intelligence of anybody else, beside yourself.

Transfer. Lee says: "Transfer carries the authority, sanction, and prestige of a respected institution over to something else, in order to make the latter more readily acceptable, or it does the opposite."

No public meeting devoted to consideration of an important matter would be complete without an American flag on the platform. Even the Bundists used to display it as well as pictures of George Washington, Abraham Lincoln, and other national heroes. "In the name of home, mother, the little red school house, and the spirit of liberty" is a glittering generality but it also is an attempt to transfer some of the emotional response the omnibus words inspire to support of the measure at hand. There is no real connection between a pretty girl and a can of soup, yet advertisers (not only of soup but of most commodities) know the value of sex appeal. Animals also strike a sympathetic chord, so we have kittens directing attention to railroads, dogs helping the sale of talking machines, and cows speaking up for dairy products.

The flag, the cross, the Statue of Liberty, Niagara Falls, Mount Rushmore, and other symbols are more than mere attention-getters. The favorable responses they evoke are intended to be transferred to the persons or objects or causes with which the propagandist associates them. Much of the political cartoonist's skill is directed to creating such associations. A picture of a well-groomed Uncle Sam approving or disapproving something packs a wallop.

Basking in the light of another's fame is far from an unusual practice. "George Washington slept here" may be a joke because of its overuse, but he who lives near an historic site or possesses a precious relic associated with greatness has an exalted ego. Chambers of commerce advertise the town's landmarks, business concerns and organizations take the names of famous persons or places. According to Roger Butterfield in "The Legend of Will Rogers" in the July 18, 1949 *Life,* "In Oklahoma, still the Indian Territory when he was born there, Will Rogers is regarded as the greatest man the state ever produced, and, more than likely, the greatest American who ever lived. In its cities and towns and along its roadsides his name is encountered as often as 'Dr. Pepper' or chili and beans. There are Will Rogers high schools and Will Rogers airports, Will Rogers libraries and Will Rogers rodeo grounds, Will Rogers hotels and Will Rogers motels, even a Will Rogers 5¢ and 10¢ store and a Will Rogers Methodist church. The Frisco Railroad's best train through Oklahoma is called The Will Rogers Special." Not all of this memorializing is due to the sheer belief in the former cowboy's greatness; a considerable portion of it resulted from the desire to gain prestige by capitalizing upon his name. And the same is true of similar use of the names of other great ones. The kid who goes to an Abraham Lincoln school "has something" on the youngster who attends the Harold E. Smith school even though the Mr. Smith so honored at some bygone time was a local celebrity.

Testimonial. Motion picture stars endorse cigarets, tooth paste, and many other products, and grin joyously from billboards as encouragement to other consumers to go and do likewise. So do famous athletes, aviators, and, less frequently, politicians and others with status as public heroes. In such cases the opinion of the Great Name isn't any better than that of anyone else, but advertisers know that the appeal gets results. Of the same opinion are political leaders who seek their endorsements. When Irene Dunne comes out for the Republicans, the Democrats counter her with Katharine Hepburn and as many more as will "come out" publicly. Organizations for the support of this or in opposition to that parade their entertainers on the stage at mass meetings, both as an added attraction to draw crowds and to win converts.

In any field the opinion of a leading figure carries considerable weight in any argument. Educators are influenced by what an outstanding university president says on a controversial matter; lawyers cite other lawyers and jurists; doctors wait to learn what specialists have to say about some new announcement in medicine, and so on. When the matter relates to something factual, as the authenticity of a scientifically testable claim, such reliance on expert testimony is, of course, rational. When it concerns something which is a matter of opinion only, even outside the field of special interest, it is emotional.

High school debaters are prone to quote authorities for both facts and opinions. Usual rebuttal procedure is to advance some other quotation from the same source to indicate the authority didn't mean exactly what the original words seemed to imply, or that he changed his mind. Or some equally important authority is cited in the attempt to counteract the first. On one occasion, however, a youthful arguer answered in somewhat this fashion: "Yes, we know the eminent authority cited by our opponents favors their side. That is what we are debating here tonight: whether this person's opinion is right or wrong. They say he is right and we say he is wrong. Let me give you our reasons." The audience gasped but the judges, either impressed by the audacity of the approach or amused by it, or both, gave the polemical heretic their votes. It is not so easy to handle a propagandistic testimonial when one does not have a visible audience all attending to him.

Plain folks. If, as an after-dinner speaker, you feel you must be "reminded" of a funny story, for maximum effectiveness, make it one "on" yourself. In that way you not only will get whatever laughs the anecdote deserves but you also will create the impression that you are a "regular" fellow who hasn't lost "the common touch," one who still is able to take a joke on himself—just "plain folks" like all of your hearers.

Kissing babies has been a little overdone and so is in disrepute as a candidate's method of ingratiating himself, but shaking hands and calling on people in their homes or talking to them in the streets are still in vogue. It's called "getting next to the people" and is more effective than a formal platform speech, with or without questions and heckling and personal introductions at the end. More so than in any other country in the world, austerity is disliked in the United States. Harry Truman's business failure subsequently became a political asset to him, as good as having been born in a log cabin was for candidates in the preceding generation.

At the same time as wanting their leaders to be sprung from the same origins as themselves, people expect them to demonstrate some superior qualities. Thus, the "plain folks" technique can be overworked. It is doubtful if anyone who reeled onto a platform roaring drunk would make many votes, no matter how eloquent his speech might turn out to be. Dignity as well as evidence of superior intelligence is required of a popular leader. Douglas MacArthur's greatest handicap has been the impression he created of being egotistical and snobbish. Lindbergh, on the other hand, ingratiated himself with millions by his use of "we" in telling of his historic solo flight across the Atlantic, indicating that he believed his airplane, the Spirit of St. Louis, should share in whatever glory he had earned. Upon his return from the war General Dwight D. Eisenhower displayed a becoming modesty, giving credit to the troops under his command and to the folks who stayed at home and produced the material. He cautiously refrained from adverse criticism of anyone and ignored questions seeking to get him to commit himself on political matters.

Band wagon. This is the appeal which urges people to join the happy throng and not be queer outsiders. "Everybody's doing it" is the thought, tending to create what the sociologist Floyd H. Allport calls "the illusion of universality." The propagandized is given to understand that the proposal, whatever it is, must be right or so many others wouldn't favor it. Nobody wants to be isolated or ostracized; rather, the urge to conform is necessarily strong in any social being. So when Men of Distinction change to a certain brand of whiskey, one is impressed, not only by the testimonial but by the fact that if he doesn't hasten to do likewise, he'll find himself all alone drinking an inferior brand. At least that's what the advertisers hope will happen and it apparently does in enough cases to keep the distilleries open.

"Don't throw your vote away," the ward heeler informs all who possess the suffrage in his precinct, meaning, "Better be on the winning side which is ours." The band wagon appeal capitalizes upon the American's admiration of bigness (see pages 167 ff.) as well as upon the universal desire to be a part of the crowd and popular. The longer the list of names on a petition becomes the easier it is to obtain new signatures. Attempts to start new rival veterans' organizations after World War II met with less than moderate success; the well-established American Legion enrolled the majority of the newly eligible. It was "the thing to do," as it also is safest to patronize the largest and best-known stores and purchase the most familiar brands of goods. While he is getting started a businessman has to rely on references and testimonials; after he has attained sufficient growth he can use sales and other figures in his recruiting of new customers.

The negative aspect of the band wagon appeal is the threat, expressed or implied, that if one doesn't get aboard he'll be left "out in the cold," friendless, helpless, and alone.

Hot potato. In everyone's closet there is at least one skeleton. Lucky is the propagandist who possesses the keys to those closets, even though he may never use them. To "get something" on one's opponent is to possess potential power over him. If one uses his damaging information it may well be a red herring or straw man. Lacking any such information the propagandist faces the necessity of creating situations which will cast the same kind of discredit on his enemies.

Called "hot potato" by Lee, the technique was labeled "propaganda of provocation" by the Institute for Propaganda Analysis in its bulletin, "Speaking of Rudolf Hess," Vol. IV, No. 7, which appeared in 1941. The Institute cited the Nazis' burning of the Reichstag in 1933 and Rudolf Hess' flight to Scotland in 1941 as outstanding examples.

Violence on occasion has been provoked by employers during strikes in the almost certain belief that the workers would be blamed for it. "Planting" evidence is a crude and reprehensible way of convicting a criminal, but frequently an effective one.

Stalling. This "involves a play for time, the use of plausible delaying tactics that may permit the opposition to lose vigor, interest, or support before the real struggle occurs. It may take the form of the appointment of an investigating committee, the insistence upon adhering to 'the proper sequence' (red tape), as well as the more familiar 'memo-passing,' " according to Lee.

It might be called the "yes, but" technique whereby a hypocritical supporter of a measure keeps his record clear but achieves his real purpose nevertheless. Henry Cabot Lodge and his cohorts succeeded in killing ratification by the United States of the League of Nations by stalling tactics and by weighting the protocol down with amendments, all the time insisting that they were in favor of it.

"I'm in favor of your objectives but I want to investigate to make certain your methods are the best by which to achieve them" is the answer that the staller often gives. Further weasling out of a situation may involve a quantity of mealy-mouthed hypocrisy. "I am," says Senator Bloke, for instance, "one of the greatest friends the Negro has. Why, some of my best friends are Negroes. And it is because I am such a friend of the colored man that I would not want to handicap his rise to his proper station in life by voting for this measure which would inspire more discrimination against him, more hatred of him, than it ever would prevent. For we must realize that all other men do not possess the sympathetic understanding of the Negro's problem that we possess," and so on and so on, blah blah blah, in the attempt to explain a vote against a fair employment practices or other civil rights act.

"The time is not opportune" is a slightly more honest evasion. To altogether too many who use it, however, the opportune moment never does arrive. They keep putting it off to avoid disagreeableness in the hope that agitation will die down or wear itself out. Beware of the excessive procrastinator in promulgation of any cause; in most cases he really is not a friend but an enemy.

Propaganda By Action

Mostly the propaganda devices with which the foregoing discussion has been concerned are utilized to manipulate and capitalize upon existing opinions and attitudes. As explained in the early part of the chapter, to create new attitudes is a long, tedious process. Developing out of complex social relationships they change slowly. Secondary or specific attitudes derived from basic attitudes—or sentiments—may be capable of alteration by propaganda, but to affect a primary attitude one would have to set in motion an elaborate chain of causes and effects, a prodigious undertaking for even the most efficient public relations counsel.

To illustrate the point of the preceding paragraph, it would be possible by skillful propagandizing to change the reputation of a person through convincing others he was either more or less virtuous than hitherto believed. To alter the basic moral code by which the person is judged to be good or bad, however, is a different matter. The attitude toward the specific individual is a secondary attitude derivative from more general and much more deeply held sentiments.

The Big Business which public relations has become, its purposes and methods, will be considered in Chapter 15. In essence, public relations counsel who really are that and not mere publicity directors or press agents who have adopted a fancy name, try to emulate nature as much as possible. That is, they seek to create situations out of which the results they desire will come as though naturally. They generally recognize that "actions speak louder than words" and create good will for their clients by guiding their behavior so as to deserve it. Much of modern philanthropy is traceable to the advice of public relations counsel; so also is a considerable amount of the society-page activities of public figures and their families. The psychology motivating the planned behavior of those seeking public favor is sound, but one shudders to conjecture what life will be like if the time comes when one's every action is directed by experts. Human relations certainly would be so artificial as to mean our dearly prized individuality would be lost. Today royalty and their American equivalents, including especially our entertainers, live in goldfish bowls and are deprived of the freedom, even of the streets, which their fans enjoy. Although they may yearn for more privacy and naturalness in their lives, they know full well that when the autograph seekers stop coming they had better start worrying.

Censorship

It is not so that what one doesn't know doesn't hurt him. Ignorance, though blissful, can be extremely injurious. Certainly when the

Founding Fathers wrote guarantees of freedom of the press, speech, religion and assembly into the Constitution—that part of it known as the Bill of Rights—they considered adequate information a prerequisite for a workable democracy.

Censorship, consequently, can be more important than propaganda in determining public opinion. Censorship, in fact, properly considered is the negative aspect of propaganda, and the effectiveness of any propaganda proper increases with the extent to which competing propaganda is eliminated.

When most people think of censorship they conjure up visions of governmental dictators burning books or at least of officious bureaucrats with scissors and black ink. Censorship by private individuals and agencies, however, is just as important—perhaps more so. Anyone with anything to hide keeps his mouth shut and does his best to prevent what it is becoming known in any other way. Such censorship "at the source" is the most frequent and most important kind. Newspapers and other media of communication altogether too often are scapegoated for not printing information which it has been impossible to obtain because of the lack of cooperation on the part of the only potential news sources.

Byron Price, Associated Press official, who became director of the Bureau of Censorship, recognized that Americans reared in a proud heritage of freedom of speech and of the press considered any censorship as distasteful. Almost from the start of the Republic, the Bill of Rights had promised a cherished freedom of expression. Even in wartime, the people believed that their rights should be jealously guarded—that they should be able to criticize acts of the government and that the public should be given all information which could be consistently disclosed. Nevertheless, it is a fact that not only are most people "hush hush" as regards embarrassing matters concerning themselves, but also, and more important, virtually all of the governmental censorship that we do have has resulted from the efforts of pressure groups to influence law-making bodies. Twentieth-century man has his taboos, legal and otherwise, just as much as did any of his predecessors (see Chapter 7). To ignore someone is more detrimental to him than to smear him as many a politician given the silent treatment knows.

The most effective censorship naturally is that which exists without those affected by it being aware of its existence. When, as in wartime, censorship is admitted, its effects are bound to boomerang to some extent—a price that it is known must be paid. Whenever it is known that concealment is taking place, whether by an individual in peacetime or a government in wartime, there is bound to be guesswork as to what really is going on. And that leads to the manufacture and dissemination of rumors, some of which are more injurious to morale than the truth would have been.

Traditionally it is considered wise policy to hold up or minimize bad news from the battlefront until able to announce some counteracting good news simultaneously. Paradoxically, two studies, both reported in *Public Opinion Quarterly* for Summer, 1943, tended to disprove the wisdom of this policy. The articles, announcing the results of studies of the effect upon morale of newspaper treatment of war news, were: "Do Rosy Headlines Sell Newspapers?" by Elizabeth Winship and Gordon W. Allport and "Building War Morale with News Headlines," by Floyd H. Allport and Milton Lepkin. A few quotations from the latter epitomize the findings: "Headlines which stress how well we are doing or how badly off the enemy is bring out significantly weaker reactions, less desire to participate in the war effort. . . . Bad news makes people want to do more than good news. . . . The important thing to remember is that it is the bad news headline which will stimulate war activity over the long haul."

As for the other, supposedly more important function of wartime censorship—to keep valuable information from the enemy—doubt of its efficacy also has been spread by postwar revelations of the content of official enemy documents. Nevertheless, the effort to conceal the truth and thus save the lives of one's fighting men is still considered justifiable, just as, on the positive side of opinion formation, psychological warfare is undoubtedly here to stay. In wartime as in peace, however, the propagandist can do little more than utilize to his advantage the opinions and attitudes which are already in existence. Hitler and Goebbels terrorized many of their intended victims by propaganda before they turned loose their armed might. They successfully disseminated propaganda to divide and conquer, but they did not create the innate weaknesses or the schisms in Poland, Norway, France or any other nation. They just turned what existed to their own advantage.

PART II

CULTURE AND
PUBLIC OPINION

CHAPTER FIVE

GENERAL CHARACTERISTICS
OF AMERICAN CULTURE

What Americans are today they have become because of their comparatively brief but unusual heritage. Their opinions today are influenced by the conditioning of past generations.

A modern Cinderella who spent her girlhood in a modest home in Chicago's stockyards area will be married in Palm Beach, Fla., after midnight tonight to Winthrop Rockefeller, the nation's most eligible bachelor.

Rockefeller, at 36, is the only unmarried grandson of the late John D. Rockefeller, the almost legendary founder of the Standard Oil Co. and possessor of a fortune once estimated at 1½ billion dollars.

The bride was identified in the official announcement, made by Rockefeller's Socony-Vacuum office in New York, as Mrs. Barbara Sears, divorced wife of Richard Sears, Jr., Boston socialite.

LICENSE ISSUED TUESDAY

The announcement followed a Palm Beach newspaper's discovery that the couple's marriage license was issued Tuesday in Okeechobee, a Florida town 75 miles northwest of Palm Beach,

The 1942 social register lists Mrs. Sears as Jievute Paulekiute.

Records showed that a pretty Englewood High School junior so named, who lived in a fourth floor flat at 3121 S. Morgan st., was crowned 'Miss Lithuania' in July, 1933 at the Century of Progress exposition here.

Then, like a jig saw puzzle, the fairy tale story of Eva's rise to fame was fitted together—her short-lived career on the stage, her marriage to Sears, her divorce and return to the tenements (this time on New York's Third av.)—and now her engagement to Rockefeller.

MINING TOWN NATIVE

Eva was born in the little mining town of Noblestown, Pa. near Pittsburgh, in 1916. Her parents soon thereafter were divorced. Her mother brought her to Chicago and married Peter Nevechas. The family lived in

[137]

a Lithuanian colony. Her mother and step father, now moved to a farm near Lowell, Ind., still speak English with the accents of their Lith homeland. . . .

————Chicago *Daily Tribune,* Feb. 13, 1948

To declare, as some might be tempted to do, that no such story as the foregoing could originate anywhere except in the United States would be inaccurate. After all, commoners married Edward VIII of England and former King Michael of Rumania, and both rites were performed far across the sea. It is no exaggeration, however, to assert that only in this country would the romantic tale receive headline attention comparable to that usually reserved for the obituaries of presidents, declarations of wars, and international spy scares.

From the standpoint of the American newspaperman, the Rockefeller wedding story had about everything: romance; rags to riches; love conquering all in the good old democratic tradition; success for the underdog; youth and beauty, and a resultant vicarious thrill for an army of otherwise frustrated readers. Jievute proved it still "can be done" in this great land of freedom and free enterprise. Regardless of how ill chosen some of the headline-fitting labels applied to other stories may be, "Cinderella" was exactly apt in this instance. And the Cinderella theme is the most popular and sure-fire in American journalism and in American literature, playwriting, radio, and motion pictures as well. To understand why this is so requires a consideration of the nation's cultural heritage and historical development.

Democratic Idealism

Although the Daughters of the American Revolution and a few others complained, most Americans felt so secure economically during the prosperous twenties, that their reaction to the rather sizeable amount of iconoclastic historical and biographical writing of the period was amusement rather than anger or fear that American institutions were being undermined. As a result the emboldened debunkers were able to wreak havoc with George Washington's cherry tree, Paul Revere's horse, Betsy Ross' flag and many another object of traditional patriotic adulation. Not only were legends ferreted out, identified, and often deplored as such. More important, fresh anecdotes were presented to checkmate the apotheosis of some national heroes. Most important of all, the humanizing process went so far as to include a reevaluation of the motives of many of the Founding Fathers to reveal that either certainly or in all likelihood they were activated by selfish economic as well as by philosophic and altruistic considerations.

What all the scholarly skeptics of the twenties or of any other period could not do; what all of the critics, native and foreign, have failed to do, is to shake the faith of the ordinary American in the democratic ideal. Although he may question the intentions of some of the Pilgrim Fathers, Minute Men and members of the Constitutional Convention, and although he may be highly critical of some contemporary governmental activities, he nevertheless is steadfast in his conviction that the American dream expresses the best form of life toward which men should strive. Despite any contradictions in his own conduct, he pays lip service to the principle that what is needed is more, not less democracy. Even American Negroes who have been denied full participation in the blessings of that democracy have firm faith in it according to the Swedish observer, Gunnar Myrdal, in his colossal *The American Dilemma* (Harper, 1944). It would be difficult to find any appreciable number of Americans of any kind who would deny that their country has become great largely because of the extent to which it has practiced the democracy it preaches and that its most important shortcomings derive from failures to enlarge on the practice.

The essence of traditional American idealism is stated succinctly in the philosophical second paragraph of the Declaration of Independence: "We hold these truths to be self-evident, that all men are created equal, that they are endowed by their Creator with certain inalienable rights, that among these are life, liberty and the pursuit of happiness. That to secure these rights governments are instituted among men, deriving their just powers from the consent of the governed." This was deliberately taken by Thomas Jefferson from John Locke, the British philosopher who also inspired the Puritan revolution of 1688 in England, the first of the modern revolts against absolutism in government, sometimes called the "bloodless" and sometimes the "glorious" revolution which eventually brought William and Mary of Orange to the British throne. The significant change which Jefferson made was to substitute "pursuit of happiness" for the Lockian "property."

In common with Jean Jacques Rousseau, the great French philosopher whose "natural rights" theories influenced the leaders of the

French Revolution of 1789, Locke and his American disciples—Jefferson, Madison, Paine and others—believed in the basic equality of men, regardless of racial, religious, or national origin or economic status and disbelieved in any class distinctions based on any of those or other factors. Accepting this basic equality, for which there is overpowering contemporary anthropological evidence, the early American idealists believed in the ability of the great masses to govern themselves rather than to be ruled by a superior race, nation, or class. Abandoned was belief in the divine right of kings; and in human slavery, either actual as we knew it in this country until the Civil War, or virtual as existed throughout medieval Europe under the feudal economic system. Human values came first: the dignity and civil liberties of the individual with which neither an overbearing church nor an overbearing state should be allowed to interfere.

Properly to understand the American experiment in attempting to put those ideals into practice it is necessary to have some historical perspective as to how they originated and developed. Locke, Rousseau, Jeremy Bentham, and others who theorized regarding political democracy did not philosophize in a vacuum. They were affected by the same forces that gave rise to Martin Luther and the Protestant Reformation in religion; the Renaissance in the field of aesthetic interest; John Stuart Mill, Adam Smith and other believers in *laissez faire* in economics. After the approximately five hundred years of domination of the church lasting from the fall of Rome through the Middle Ages had been broken, nationalism—as expressed in an equally tyrannical state—had become just as much an interference with the "life, liberty, and pursuit of happiness" of the individual.

Freeing that individual from the shackles of feudalism became, not a mere matter of humanitarianism but one of absolute economic necessity as the age of exploration and colonization advanced. Much of the theorizing and philosophizing, to glorify the natural or other rights of the individual, was, as always is true, rationalization to justify the freeing of the serfs to the end that the production of surplus commodities needed in an expanding world trade could become possible. The Cromwells consequently reduced feudal privilege in England and gave impetus to the British mercantile system which depended on self-sufficiency and native industry. The new capitalism offered an opportunity to accumulate wealth. It led to the creation of a legally "free" wage-earner class. It offered to millions a chance to own and operate the means of production.

Mill and Smith saw monarchial government as a restraint on the development of exploration, colonization and world trade, hence, *laissez faire*. Hence also Jeremy Bentham's idea that that government is best which governs least. The first economic liberals were those who fought the restraints of government on economic activities. Because the English kings, representing British business interests, placed more restraints on the Americans than the latter were willing to bear, the colonists revolted. Even the English later admitted—many of their intellectuals did, that is—that it was beneficial to break the control of George III, and our revolution accomplished that feat in the Old as well as the New World.

Those then were the American ideals and that was how they originated. The Declaration of Independence set forth the principle and the Constitution of the United States established the machinery by which it seemed best at the time to make possible the achieving of those ideals. Its Preamble reads: "We, the People of the United States, in order to form a more perfect union, establish justice, insure domestic tranquillity, provide for the common defense, promote the general welfare and secure the blessings of liberty to ourselves and our posterity, do ordain and establish this Constitution for the United States of America."

Because of the then recent Old World examples, there was understandable fear of a strong central government, with the result that there are numerous constitutional provisions for what are called checks and balances. The division of the work of the Federal Government into legislative, executive, and judicial departments, each with some veto power over the other two, is one example. States' rights, implied or expressed, is another. Both the Federalists of Alexander Hamilton and Thomas Jefferson's Democrat-Republicans, furthermore, feared the possible despotism of an unbridled majority. Hence, the Supreme Court to protect minorities from repressive legislation.

Quite obviously, if the masses were to govern themselves, it was in the public interest that they be as informed and educated as possible. Also, it was important that they be permitted to criticize and change their government as need arose. Hence, the Bill of Rights, establishing primarily freedom of speech, freedom of the press, freedom of religion, and freedom of assembly—all intended as means to an end, not ends in themselves, which is an important point for modern journalists never to forget.

Independent of the Constitution—though, of course, consistent with its provisions—through legislation, other means to achieve the same ends have been established. Among the first great moves to strengthen American democracy was establishment of the free public school system. Public ownership of the post office has made cheap communication possible. More and more the general welfare clause of the Preamble is entering into congressional debate and judicial decisions as a yardstick by which to determine the wisdom or legality of matters of moment.

If the foregoing resume—superficial as it admittedly is—seems an unnecessarily tedious or a superfluous buildup to explain the "naturalness" of the journalistic appeal of the Rockefeller nuptials story, it still is justified, as would be any subterfuge for reminding newspapermen and newspaper readers of the nature of American democratic idealism in its pristine state. However, a much more practical purpose is served by laying the groundwork in this way, because the contemporary American character is the outgrowth of the inevitable conflict between idealism and reality as it has occurred during the past three centuries.

Early America obviously was the ideal place for the working out, deliberately or otherwise, of the democratic philosophy. The New World was a continent of seemingly unlimited opportunity, where, for several centuries, there were abundant natural resources. Thus, it became, as it was called, the Land of Promise, the melting pot of the world, the haven of the oppressed of the Old World. Said Andrew Jackson: "Behold it as the asylum where the wretched and the oppressed find a refuge and support."

The ever-present frontier, whose importance in shaping the American heritage was first emphatically pointed out by Frederick Jackson Turner in the 1893 annual report of the American Historical Association, encouraged individualism. In fact, it demanded strength, hard work, stamina, and courage. There *was* a struggle for existence, and the fittest *did* survive. Self-reliance, later eulogized by Ralph Waldo Emerson to the dismay of a couple of generations of schoolchildren, *did* flourish. Pioneers had to look to their own resources and efforts rather than to government. Frontier justice necessarily was crude and swift, and there was firm belief, based on pragmatic experience, in the adage about that government being best which governed least.

A log-cabin-to-White-House tradition developed. It is reflected today in our myths and legends (see Chapter 6) and is buttressed by innumerable true examples of rags-to-riches careers—Lincoln's rise from rail-splitting and Henry Ford's penniless start being among the outstanding. The tradition is strongly perpetuated in our literature. Until comparatively recently school children reared on the McGuffey readers were taught almost nothing else. The Horatio Alger novels, the Rover Boys, and similar books for juveniles stressed the opportunity which America offers to anyone to rise from a lowly beginning, overcoming obstacles by obeying the rules of honesty and diligence. Home, school, church, the press, and, more recently, the motion pictures and radio have helped in the indoctrination. Politicians always have capitalized upon the public attitudes thereby engendered. We now have developed to the stage where presidential candidates no longer can claim to have been born in log cabins. Today they show pictures of humble frame dwellings instead. An era will have ended when the rival nominees are ones who entered the world in germicidal maternity hospitals.

The self-reliance of the frontier, contemporaneously called "rugged individualism," helped develop the American national character. About the turn of the century, an English visitor, Dr. James F. Muirhead, wrote in *Land of Contrasts* (J. Lane, 1902) of ". . . a very distinctly American note, different in pitch and scale from any note in the British concert." This note, he explained, "includes a sense of illimitable expansion and possibility; an almost childlike confidence in human ability and fearlessness of both the present and the future; a wider realization of human brotherhood than has yet existed; a greater theoretical willingness to judge by the individual than by the class; a breezy indifference to authority and a posiitve predilection for innovation; a marked alertness of mind and a manifold interest; above all, an inextinguishable hope and courage."

Not all foreigners have been so kind. To some the go-getter, cocky attitude of some vacationing Americans has been more than a little obnoxious at times. To denizens of older, stabler cultures Americans often seem in too much of a hurry, too impatient of delay and inefficiency, too restless and eager to accept change for its own sake without adequate testing of whether the new really is better than the old. There is, of course, much latent admiration and considerable envy for the high standard of living which Americans have achieved regardless of the reasons. Although admitting that abundant natural resources and a west to which until recently Horace Greeley could advise young men to go, had something to do with it, most Americans would insist that devotion to the democratic ideal was of prime importance.

Certainly the frontier encouraged belief in the idea of equality. Man's capacity, not his forebears, was what counted. Class barriers probably were broken down more completely than they have been anywhere else at any time. Neighborliness and easy friendships grew out of the necessity for cooperation for self-protection against mutual enemies: Indians, wild animals, and nature. As a concomitant there also developed belief in the virtues of charity and brotherly love. Generosity and a helping hand were essential. There was a positive communal obligation on the part of those who succeeded to share with others, to assist in restoring loss resulting from natural enemies. The current belief in charity and philanthropy has deep roots in this country.

To protect this fairyland from foreign encroachments, it is not strange there developed a strong belief in isolationism in foreign affairs. Washington and Jefferson sternly warned the agrarian politicians, who neither imagined ever could become a minority, against alliances with Old World governments. So, throughout most of our history we have cared to have as little as possible to do with the rest of the world, except, of course, as might be necessary to make money from it. The Monroe Doctrine was an early form of self-protection; so were our purchase of Alaska and our Open Door policy in China.

The so-called "American System" developed by Henry Clay involved a combination of protective tariffs and internal improvements. Always we have been idealistic about waging war, dreading that any action on our part should be interpreted as imperialistic in intent. In 1898 we "came of age" with our easy defeat of Spain and taking from her the outposts of empire, but our entry into that war was preceded by a tremendous journalistic propaganda drive to convince us we really were in it for the sole purpose of protecting the Cubans from Spanish butchers. In 1917 we undertook to save the world for democracy and to fight a war to end all wars. In 1941 we were drawn into World War II in probably the only way we ever would have gotten into that conflict—by the unprovoked attack at Pearl Harbor.

Only during World War I have the American people ever approached anything like a fanatical crusading zeal. But when the high purposes for which we honestly thought we were fighting didn't automatically come with the military victory—when, that is, the world we saved for democracy decidedly didn't stay saved—we quickly reverted to an even stronger and, as subsequent events proved, blinder nationalism. In the thirties, an unreasonable disillusionment and defeatism became widespread, especially among students. Because one set of values had proved false—or rather unworkable—or at least they hadn't been achieved, the idea spread that no sets of values were any good. Because we didn't easily achieve an ideal, some young people came to believe that all ideals are sissy, impractical, almost un-American. It was a cynical point of view which led to the taking of a lot of pacifistic Oxford oaths by young men who fortunately forgot all about them after Dec. 7, 1941. There was a reaffirmation of the belief in the disinterested righteousness of American foreign policy, in the absolute absence in our diplomats of any but the most altruistic and humanitarian motives.

A final characteristic worth mentioning here as derived in part from our idealistic democratic tradition of individualism, though having stronger roots in our capitalistic tradition from which our democracy cannot be divorced, is the American idea of what constitutes success. Unquestionably it is largely victory over someone else as the result of competition. Today progressive educators are attempting to combat this attitude, but parents find it extremely difficult to become used to report cards which comment only on the extent to which a son or daughter has lived up to his own possibilities. Those who grew up when a grade of 87 meant you were just that much better than a classmate who got an 86 ask the modern teachers, "But how does he (or she) compare with the others in the class?" and are bewildered if not resentful when modern teachers are reluctant or unable to supply the answer.

Our Business Civilization

Unable, because of the war, to continue roaming the South Seas, Margaret Mead turned her expert anthropological attention to her fellow countrymen, producing a brilliant book, *And Keep Your Powder Dry* (Morrow, 1942), and numerous magazine articles. In her discussion of "Has the 'Middle Class' A Future?" in the February, 1942 *Survey Graphic,* she wrote: "The most typical element in the success system, best exemplified by middle class fringes in Europe, and by the bulk of Americans, may be described as a moral attitude toward life, a belief that success is the result of effort, the reward for saving, self denial and hard work, and a dependence upon the self for one's fate in the world. Coupled with this attitude which developed concurrently with the emergence of the middle class in Europe, there is another element, the element of fear and guilt. As success is the reward of virtue it is also the proof of virtue; to fail is to be branded as having sinned." A little later in the same article, she summarized: "America is essentially a success system country in the attitudes which we foster and by which we live."

Partly, as already elucidated, this characteristic is the outgrowth of our democratic tradition and the influence of the swashbuckling frontier upon our development. It is impossible, however, to separate study of the history of American democratic ideals from that of our business and industrial machinery. Cognizant of their record of prodigious and unparalleled development in a comparatively short time, Americans believe in progress. Each generation is bound to be an improvement on the preceding one, and, because opportunities are almost illimitable, anyone who fails in the economic struggle is either innately inferior or a blunderer who gets what he deserves.

It is not surprising that ours is what it is called the world over—a business civilization—or that the prevailing attitude regarding success should be what it is. It is virtually inevitable that such should be the case in view of our history. Until two generations ago, there was free or cheap land for almost anyone who wanted it. There was a new place to which to go if discontented or unable to achieve one's goals in one's original locale. Nobody had to be a stick-in-the-mud. There was work to be done clearing a continent, building cities, and erecting mammoth industries. Everyone was needed and the fellow who invented a better mousetrap did find mankind trooping to his door. There was originally so much to go around that nobody gave a hang about posterity. It seemed unbelievable that the time ever could come when the lack of forests, well water, good soil, or any other natural resources would be a problem for anyone.

Conditions have, of course, changed drastically. Jefferson envisioned a nation of small landowners and considered industry "the maidservant of agriculture." In his day more than three-fourths of the population still lived on farms; today fewer than one-fourth do. When all of the arable land was taken up near the end of the nineteenth century, there were about six million farms. There never can be many more without decreasing the chance, already very tough, for the individual farmer to make a living, unless new scientific methods of farming exceed many times the highest expectations now held for them. Whereas, at the beginning of the nineteenth century, more than 90 per cent of the farmers owned their own farms, by the middle of the twentieth century barely half of them, if that many, did so. In the thirties large-sized farms—those over 1000 acres—increased in number by 25 per cent whereas those under 50 acres decreased 15 per cent. About one million of the six million farms were on marginal land, and no matter what the administration in power in Washington since World War I, it has had a "farm problem" on its hands. With about 465 million acres the maximum capable of cultivation, and nutrition experts agreeing that two and a half acres is the minimum needed to support an American in good health, population experts today are re-reading *Essay on the Principle of Population as It Affects the Future Improvement of Society,* published in 1789 by the English economist, Thomas Robert Malthus. Two recent books, repeating the Malthusian warning that population always tends to outstrip ability to provide sustenance, are *Our Plundered Planet* by Fairfield Osborn (Little, Brown, 1948) and *Road to Survival* by William Vogt (Sloane, 1948).

As regards industry, the situation is similar. The end result of competition is, of course, monopoly; when someone wins a competition, others naturally must lose. The growing problem first was recognized shortly after the frontier disappeared and we made a gesture or two of protest during the final decades of the nineteenth century, with passage of the antitrust laws, creation of the Interstate Commerce

Commission and the Federal Trade Commission. Those brakes, as is commonly known, were woefully inadequate. With the Supreme Court deciding that only "unreasonable" restraints of trade were culpable and with lax enforcement in general, mostly due to inadequate congressional appropriations, in almost sixty years not a single person ever went to jail for violation of the Sherman Antitrust Act.

Just before World War II broke out in Europe, the Temporary National Economic Commission, headed by Senator Joseph C. O'Mahoney of Wyoming, conducted an exhaustive survey of the trend toward monopoly in this country. Among other findings the TNEC discovered that three automobile companies controlled 86 per cent of automobile production; three can companies controlled 90 per cent of production in that field; three cigaret companies controlled 80 per cent of the output; four corn binder companies, 100 per cent; two plate glass companies, 95 per cent; three steel companies, 60 per cent, and so on. Corporations with less than $50,000 in total assets comprised over 50 per cent of all companies but had only 1.4 per cent of the assets. Six per cent of all corporations owned 85 per cent of all the assets.

That was before Pearl Harbor. Understandably, to speed war production the government favored industrial giants. The war-end report of the Smaller War Plants Corporation indicated what happened. In 1904 big corporations controlled only 30 basic products; by the end of World War II the 250 biggest corporations controlled two-thirds of the nation's usable manufacturing facilities. Small corporations—those with an annual net income of $250,000 or under—dropped from a 23.4 per cent share of corporate income in 1918 to an 11.6 per cent share in 1942. In 1939, small firms—those employing under 500—accounted for 52 per cent of the total manufacturing output; in 1944 they accounted for only 38 per cent. In 1944, 2 per cent of all American firms employed 62 per cent of all American workers.

In April, 1947, the Federal Trade Commission made a special report to Congress which showed that since 1940 big firms had swallowed up over 1,800 smaller ones. They had taken over plants which had assets totalling 4.1 billion dollars, or nearly 5 per cent of the total assets of all manufacturing corporations in 1943. The country's 62 biggest corporations came out of the war with 8.4 billion dollars of net working capital, much of it in liquid form and readily available for buying up competitors. Nearly one-third of those merged were absorbed by the largest corporations, those with assets of over 50 million dollars. Seventy-five per cent of the buying-out was by corporations with more than 5 million dollars, meaning that the shakedown in the number of American businessmen has not come about by mergers of little fellows attempting to become a little larger.

In July, 1948, in another report, the FTC declared: "The current merger movement, under way since 1940, has resulted in the disappearance of more than 2,450 formerly independent manufacturing and mining companies. These firms held assets aggregating some 5.2 billion dollars, or more than 5 per cent of the total assets of all manufacturing corporations in the country." The FTC concluded with this warning: "A definite choice must be made. Either this country is going down the road to collectivism or it must stand and fight for competition as the protector of all that is embodied in free enterprise."

In the matter of family income the 1947 survey of the Federal Reserve Board shows the following situation:

Above $7500 ..... 8% of the families..got 30% of the income
$5000 to $7500....13% of the families..got 20% of the income
$4000 to $5000....11% of the families..got 13% of the income
$3000 to $4000....17% of the families..got 15% of the income
$2000 to $3000....20% of the families..got 13% of the income
$1000 to $2000....18% of the families..got 7% of the income
Under $1000......13% of the families..got 2% of the income

It was the report of the National Resources Board covering the fiscal year 1935–36 that caused Franklin Delano Roosevelt to direct attention to "one-third of the nation, poorly housed, poorly clothed, and poorly fed." When the National Emergency Council reported in late 1938 on economic conditions in thirteen Southern states, FDR declared: "It is my conviction that the South presents right now the nation's No. 1 economic problem—the nation's problem, not merely the South's." Among other things, the report showed that the richest Southern state had a smaller per capita income than the poorest state elsewhere. In 1937 the average annual southern income was $314; for the rest of the country it was $604. The South was educating one-third of the nation's children on one-sixth of the nation's school income. In

Arkansas in 1933–34 the average teacher's salary was $465 as compared with $2,361 in New York State. Other findings were similar.

By 1948 the situation had improved somewhat according to the Department of Commerce. In that year the per capita income for the nation as a whole was $1,325, more than double the average of $608 for 1929. Proportionately the South had improved more than other sections of the country but still lagged far behind. In the eleven southeasternmost states, for instance, the increase was from $344 in 1929 to $883 in 1947, a 157 per cent gain. By contrast, the Middle Eastern states increased from $926 to $1,559, a 68 per cent gain.

The foregoing figures and many, many more that could be cited indicate beyond possibility of doubt that the economic situation in the United States has changed considerably. Over-all averages are misleading in view of the inequalities which exist as between individuals and sections of the country. Pertinent to the study of public opinion, what has *not* changed much is the average American's attitudes toward the capitalistic system. And it is clear that radicalism in this country had made very little headway up to the mid-point of the century. This was so largely because the fomenters of discontent had to buck attitudes which had been more than three centuries in the making.

The most important of these already has been mentioned: that, no matter how maldistributed the wealth and income may be, there still is plenty of room at the top for the ambitious and talented. This attitude has been fostered by the American system of open rather than closed classes which it in turn helps perpetuate. In the United States marriages *do* take place across the tracks. The majority sympathizes with the young couple, sincerely in love, which defies or circumvents parental opposition because of some kind of prejudice. Admittedly, when it happens in one's own family one is not so broadminded, but at the theater he applauds so loudly that *Abie's Irish Rose* becomes one of the all-time dramatic successes. In the motion picture houses audiences root for the poor waif whom the scion of the blue-blooded family brings home and announces to his horrified mother and father he intends to marry. She, of course, always turns out to be a "diamond in the rough" or if a he, to have a "heart of gold," which is the way many underprivileged Americans regard themselves.

In the United States sons do not have to follow in their fathers' footsteps. As a matter of fact, if they do so, they lose rather than gain the respect of their fellows, even of the fathers themselves who expect their offspring to begin where they left off, not where they themselves began. American parents place a great deal of faith in education and want their children to go further in school than they were able to do. Children who leave home for college rarely return to their home towns following graduation; instead, they seek greener pastures somewhere else. Instead of taking pride in the Old Homestead where many generations have resided, American consider themselves failures if they are born, live, and die in the same locality. "Where are you from?" or "Where did you come from originally?" whichever is pertinent, is a frequently put question by anyone attempting to "size up" another. Most Americans, however, jealously guard as secret the amount of their income and pretend to be better off financially than they really are. In this effort they receive encouragement from advertisers who constantly appeal to them to "keep up with the Joneses."

Money unquestionably is the leading standard by which success is judged in this country. By thrift and wise investment one can stretch his inheritance or income to create an impression of greater opulence than he really possesses. The possibilities of such pretense are strictly limited, so, as will be elaborated upon in Chapter 9, there is a considerable amount of imitation of the more expensive necessities and luxuries of the wealthy. It is in the American open-class tradition not to admit that those wealthier are one's betters. They are just the luckier or more fortunate; given an even start, any he-man from the lower income brackets could show up any one who was born with a silver spoon in his mouth.

In other words, the masses of low income-receiving Americans never have developed an inferiority complex nor feelings of despair. This is due, in large part, of course, to the happy fact that, by comparison with their counterparts almost anywhere else in the world, their standard of living has been high, not low. Shortly before World War II the Chicago Motor Club, after a study of Department of Commerce figures, revealed that 75 per cent of automobile-owning families in the United States received incomes under $1,000 a year. Three times as many cars were owned by families with incomes below $1,000 a year as by families with incomes over $3,000. It was the sight of the American workingman going to and from the factory in his jalopy, for fewer hours of work, listening to his radio in his home by electric light, reading inexpensive newspapers and magazines and books, going to the movies and taking weekend trips, that very correctly created the impression that the standard of living of the average American is way and above that of the citizen of any other nation in the world. Our highways, skyscrapers, neon signs, jazz bands, chewing gum, cheap soft drinks, bathing suits, drug stores, bowling alleys, barber shops, and other evidences of comfort are the envy of all of the rest of the world.

In a provocative article, "World Revolution, American Plan," in the December, 1948 *Harper's*, Isabel Cary Lundberg wrote that it has been the American example, not Soviet propaganda, which is chiefly responsible for the post-World War II yearnings of subject peoples the world over for independence. "To millions of the world's colonial populations," she wrote, "America has for generations symbolized liberty and freedom from oppression." In another part of the same article, she explained: "For us, in America, suddenly to see ourselves as 'the terrible instigators of social change and revolution' demands so painful a mental readjustment as to be well-nigh impossible at first. For we have not the slightest conception of the revolutionary potential hidden in our national products, in the articles we use every day of our lives; and we have as a rule no conception whatever of the nature and needs of the billions who populate the other continents in both the eastern hemisphere and our own: human beings who have never seen the inside of a school, much less a bathroom; who never see a shop window and have never touched money."

Because the American way has been such a very good thing for so many and comparatively a better thing for almost everyone, those who otherwise might consider themselves a disenfranchised and exploited class never have developed that kind of psychology. Rather, they have wanted to maintain the system, keeping the opportunities open in the hope, at least, that their children will be able to climb higher on the ladder of success than they. The ideology of the American Federation of Labor traditionally has been one of support for American capitalism. Neither it nor the rival Congress of Industrial Organizations is revolutionary in purpose or program. Job, not industry control, has been the goal, to be achieved through the closed shop and maintained by means of the checkoff, maintenance of members, and similar devices. The trade and industrial union movements in this country have been far from proletarian rallying points. They have, in fact, always had hard sledding, as industry has drained off a great deal of the potentially best leadership to make them part of management; as so-called welfare capitalism has competed with them in meeting workers' needs; as white-collar workers have considered themselves professionals rather than laborers, and as a public, hostile to any threats that its creature comforts might be jeopardized, has made its mistakes costly. At no time has much more than 25 per cent of the total laboring force been unionized. When times are good the need for organized protection does not seem to be acute; when they are bad it is too late to join or too expensive to pay dues.

To shake the faith of the American worker in the fundamental soundness of the American capitalistic system would require widespread and protracted disaster, and even then there would be no certainty about it. Certainly during the depression of the thirties attempts to organize the unemployed failed dismally. Clients in relief stations were the most rugged of rugged individuals, lacking in camaraderie and realization of any common interests. Each was there to get as much as he could for himself and many were not hesitant about spying upon and reporting fellow sufferers who chiseled. Among WPA employees there was much more anti-WPA feeling than taxpayers who liked to believe they were all shovel-leaning, lazy good-for-nothings believed existed.

The Protestant Tradition

A third original influence which has helped determine the American heritage is Protestantism. Volumes have been written to prove and disprove that capitalism was an outgrowth of the Reformation, and a sizeable library exists on the subject of that early form of Protestantism known as Puritanism and its importance in the New World, past and present.

In *The Protestant Ethic and the Spirit of Capitalism* (Allen & Unwin, 1930) Max Weber contended that Protestantism created the moral and political conditions favorable to the growth of capitalism. Vigorously dissenting, R. H. Tawney, in *Religion and the Rise of Capitalism* (J. Murray, 1936) insisted that both Protestantism and capitalism were products of the same conditions. He admitted, however, that once started they gained strength from each other, especially in America. In *The American Public Mind* (Columbia University, 1936) Peter H. Odegard traced the American ideals of industry, sobriety, frugality, and thrift to the frontier and to Calvinism. Many another historian and sociologist has done likewise, although wide differences of opinion exist as to the importance of the Protestant influence and as regards the contemporary manifestations of its Puritan form. H. L. Mencken in his essay, "Puritanism as a Literary Force," in *A Book of Prefaces* (Knopf, 1922) declared: "Puritanism . . . has been a dominating force in American life since the very beginning. There has never been any question before the nation, whether political or economic, religious or military, diplomatic or sociological, which did not resolve itself, sooner or later, into a purely moral question." On the other hand several orthodox historians believe that Jefferson successfully liquidated the remnants of political Puritanism, and declare that the gloominess and austerity of the settlers of Massachusetts have been exaggerated. *The General History of Connecticut,* published in 1829 by the Rev. Richard Peters, and drawn upon heavily by historians ever since for information regarding colonial blue laws, has been debunked as grossly inaccurate and largely faked. And, although nineteen men and women were hanged during the witchcraft hysteria at Salem, none was burned to death as was long believed to be true.

Regardless of the causal relationship which did or did not exist between them, there is no doubt that individualism was of the essence of both capitalism and Protestantism. Puritanism throughout the seventeenth century was only the religious aspect of the general dissatisfaction which existed in England. The Pilgrims, who came in the *Mayflower* and landed at Plymouth Rock in 1620, were separatists who revolted against the Anglican church. The Puritans, who reached Massachusetts Bay in 1630, were reformers who wanted to remain in the Anglican church but to rid it of all vestiges of Catholicism. "Puritanism," wrote Harry Grant Plum in *Restoration Puritanism* (University of North Carolina, 1943), "was really the attempt to seize and apply the spiritual elements of the Reformation movement, to eradicate Roman forms, and to organize the English church so as to make possible the fullest use by the individual, laity and clergy of his historic liberty as established under the law. . . . Its real significance arises not in the establishment of any sect, but in the repudiation of the great Roman tradition that papal authority may override individual thought and become the *sine qua non* of man's relationship to his Maker."

Thus the type of Protestantism which first reached these shores was revolutionary as well as individualistic. "The fundamental reason for the Puritan migration to Massachusetts," wrote Allan Nevins and Henry Steele Commager in *The Pocket History of the United States* (Pocket Books, 1943), "was to establish a church-state and not to find religious freedom." The subsequent history of the Puritans bears out this judgment because, although democratic to the extent of having resented the dominance of the Anglican church, the Puritans were far from being such in administering their own government. Only church members could vote or participate in civic affairs. There was strict discipline and little tolerance for backsliders or heretics. Roger Williams, believer in the strict separation of church and state, was forced to flee the commonwealth through the snow to Rhode Island.

Protestantism, in particular Puritanism, emphasized the responsibility of each person to discover directly, on his own, and obey the will of God. The Bible, not the church, was law and guide. Virtue and industry, it was taught, are rewarded on earth as well as in Heaven; unworthiness is punished. Because of the intense fear of damnation which was instilled in him, the Puritan became habitually to consider first the moral aspects of any matter. Success, Lewis Mumford points out in *The Golden Day* (Boni, Liveright, 1926) was the Protestant miracle that justified man's ways to God. Addressing the National Council for Parental Education on Nov. 11, 1936, Prof. Joseph K. Folsom, professor of sociology at Vassar College, cited five values of Puritanism which have survived:

"1. Accumulativeness and thrift, with a fondness for showing others the results, as by a well-spread table.

"2. A 'trade and profit pattern' not merely for acquisition but for its own sake as well.

"3. Exaltation of manual work, as illustrated when the employer works with his employee.

"4. Exaltation of housekeeping as an end in itself, as shown by performances of tasks not really necessary.

"5. Demand for freedom from personal dictation, mingled with obedience to cultural values."

The Puritan influence which Mencken and others deplore is allegedly that which expresses itself in vice crusades, censorship of literature and art because of alleged sexuality, strict Sabbath laws, prohibition movements, and excessive circumlocutions in everyday speech to avoid offending the most squeamish.

Although Protestantism—all branches taken together—still is dominant in the United States, Roman Catholicism rapidly is catching up with it. The original stock has mingled with that of latecomers from all other parts of Europe, even the world. As each new wave has arrived the immigrants have been compelled to start at the bottom economically, doing the dirty work of ditch digging, hog killing, and the like; living in slums and being unaccepted socially. Second-generation newcomers, no matter where from, however, have revolted, and assimilation, except in the case of those of pigmented skin, has been pretty well completed by the third generation. According to Margaret Mead, we are a third generation nation with status dependent on length of residence in the country rather than upon original antecedents or special personality characteristics.

One factor which old- and late-comers had in common, regardless of origin, was a rebelliousness of spirit. In general those who have emigrated to this country have been the misfits, often considered the riffraff and undesirables in their places of origin. They have been the adventurous among the oppressed of other lands, even though some arrived in prison ships or with a price on their heads. Tracing genealogies is only a recently cultivated hobby among old-line Americans. There must be as many ancestors hanging from their necks as from their tails on many and many a family tree now considered among the most stalwart in our clime.

No matter what their national origin, race, or religion, late-comers to these shores have been affected by the entire American tradition, including Protestantism, for whatever importance it has. This includes Puritanism, even though one is Anglican, Roman Catholic or non-Christian. No nation, of course, ever before has been built out of so many different types of material. The extent to which standardization of customs and ideologies has occurred in this country is astounding. Already folklorists are organized in the attempt to preserve at least a record of regional cultural forms before they succumb to the leveling process which speedy transportation and communication, including the newspapers with their syndicated material and all kinds of advertising, are quickening.

Aestheticism

Although the evidence linking whatever prudishness still remains in this country to its fundamentalist ancestry may be circumstantial, there is little doubt that many other aspects of contemporary American life are traceable to one or more of the factors discussed so far in this chapter. Certainly there is no denying that ours is a European-based culture. The original pioneers brought with them the customs, habits, language, religions, traditions, and other bases for mannerisms and determiners of thought and action which were characteristic of the Old World. There still lingers more evidence of that influence along the Atlantic seaboard, especially in New England, than farther west.

Puritanism may have been a factor but doubtless more important was the frontier in retarding the development of the arts and aesthetic interests in the New World. The pioneers just didn't have time or facilities to write novels or poems, to draw or paint or mold or compose music. The rugged existence which conquering a continent entailed didn't attract the aesthete anyway, and it was not until gadget-making had progressed almost to its present stage that even the women had the leisure time to produce or appreciate the so-called finer things of life. It wasn't much more than a generation ago that some Englishman quipped, "Whoever reads an American novel?"

That the criticism was justified Americans had to admit. When they thought about it at all, they felt inferior; or else they overcompensated by branding all art as "sissy stuff." When the author was a boy he stuck his roll of music under his coat and went down alleys so that the fellows wouldn't know he was taking piano lessons. That he was taking them very much against his will would not have been considered an adequate alibi.

Even the excuse employed in the preceding paragraph—that the exigencies of frontier life were too time-consuming—has been called a rationalization to cover up the disproportionate standard of values, emphasizing materialism rather than the spiritual, which is admittedly an American characteristic. Foreign critics accredit the American lack of creativeness to our inordinate love of the Almighty Dollar. In their eyes we are too busy making money to know how to enjoy it once it is earned. We judge an object by its price tag, not its beauty; ask "What's it good for?" and scoff at the idea of "art for art's sake," despite Ralph Waldo Emerson.

In *The Story of Utopias* (Boni, Liveright, 1922) Lewis Mumford described Coketown, the factory center, in which all standards are quantitative, not qualitative. The supreme aesthetic achievement is the self-made man. Everything that contributes to the physical necessities of life is called comfort and everything else is luxury. Things are made to wear out, consumption is a social duty, and family status is determined by the size of the rubbish heap in the alley. Obviously, a satirical exaggeration but poignant criticism nevertheless. Escapees from Coketown inhabit the country house where the emphasis is on collection, not creation. There art and literature are appreciated but not created.

To reach our present state, in which we need no longer feel inferior to others in this matter of artistic creativeness, Americans passed through several stages. The first attempt to remedy the situation which foreign critics finally convinced us we were in—that of aesthetic infantilism—was to imitate and to borrow European models. Then, when we developed the wherewithal, American millionaires literally overran Europe and the rest of the world in quest of art treasures which then were boxed up and shipped back home. As we vigorously sought beauty to cover up the bleakness of our existence, our conception of culture became that of the museum. So, until we became old enough to value our own antiques, we scoured the Old World for artifacts to add to our collections. Ultimately the governments of most foreign countries had to clamp down to halt the alarming exportation of their precious relics. Still, however, we could continue to entice their living artists by promises of greater financial reward. And that we did, so for a long time there was very little English spoken in the orchestra pits or backstage at grand opera or concerts in America.

It was all pretty superficial, up to and even beyond World War I. Instead of causing Europeans to conclude we had acquired good taste, it made them scoff at us for using our almighty dollars to buy what we were incapable of producing ourselves. That hurt too, because it also was true; and once the war was over the rush of young Americans eager to study abroad and even to become expatriates if necessary to escape philistinism was resumed. But things had changed, and within a decade the sober bohemians came drifting home. Some of their first efforts after their rediscovery of their homeland shocked and infuriated many, as for example Grant Wood's famous portrait of the Daughters of the American Revolution and many of his other pieces. Regional painting, however, was followed by regional fiction and almost a mad antiquarian rush to discover or manufacture the American folktale, tall story, architecture, and other art forms. Reservation Indians became the objects of artistic attention, and the cultural projects of the depression's Work Projects Administration did a marvelous job of collecting, cataloguing, and preserving Americana.

Radio and the motion pictures helped change the attitude of schoolboys regarding music. Public schools in cities of even small size established bands and orchestras. Little theater groups sprang up and writers' conferences became the thing. Admittedly a great deal of what passes as aesthetic interest still is so shallow as almost to constitute fraud. It probably is true that those who really understand and appreciate opera still are to be found in the galleries, not the photographed boxes. And no other city ever has been able for any length of time to rival Broadway as a producer of original plays. Writers still converge on Greenwich Village and some of the typical New Yorker's condescending attitude toward everything west of Poughkeepsie is justified by the facts. Nationwide hookups, however, now carry the Metropolitan Opera and the New York Philharmonic Symphony from coast to coast and several slightly jazzed-up versions of classical music, first introduced in some motion picture or other, have been hummed throughout the land. American authors and poets now are winning their share of international Nobel prizes, and since the early thirties the United States has had no reason to feel inferior regarding either the quality or quantity of its artistic production.

Nor do we have to be as ashamed as formerly of the sight of the rear ends of our buildings. Or of their fronts either. Recently built factories are not eyesores but, in many cases, masterpieces of utilitarianism and beauty. Throughout the ages the producers of beauty have been wont to starve and suffer unless subsidized. In the United States the role of the princely sponsor of Cellini's days has been assumed by Big Business. The serious drawback suggests itself: he who pays the piper calls the tune. As a result there have been more than one public battle between artist and sponsor over a mural or piece of sculpture. One notable clash of this kind was that which occurred in 1933 when the Mexican artist, Diego Rivera, included Lenin in a mural on the elevator bank of the RCA tower in Radio City. Thomas Hart Benton's murals depicting Missouri history in the state's capitol at Jefferson City also aroused a storm of adverse criticism, typical comment being that of Representative Max Asotsky: "They'd go swell in a lot of Kansas City barrooms." Newspapers are quick to give full coverage to such incidents as, in fact, they are whenever any matter involving attempted censorship of any of the arts is at issue.

Although no polling evidence exists to establish the fact, the voluntary response to incidents of this sort, as a newspaperman sees it, would indicate that the public generally favors freedom of artistic expression and opposes censorship. Certainly it is virtually impossible any more, even in Massachusetts, for a Society for the Suppression of Vice or a Watch and Ward Society to win a law suit against a sincere novel on the grounds of salaciousness. At the same time, to balance this democratic attitude, there is high popular disdain for the long-haired and highbrowed. "Brain truster" was an opprobrious term in early New Deal days, and a cartoonist's favorite subject is the wild-eyed, horn-rimmed spectacled, mortarboard-covered, gowned professor. There is, in other words, strong suspicion of the intellectual in America. Parents may put great faith in education, including higher education; but they still react to any unpopular idea expressed by an academician with, "Has he ever met a payroll?" and they adhere to the bromidic axiom, accredited to George Bernard Shaw, "Those who can, do; those who can't, teach."

Thus, despite the great improvement in both production and appreciation of the past quarter century, the United States still is a long way from heroizing its creative artists and academicians, or granting them social status commensurate with their ability and achievement. According to Clive Bell in *Civilization*, there never has been a civilized democracy. Rather, all great civilizations have either been imposed by the will of a tyrant or maintained by an oligarchy. Others have contended that the price society must pay for an artistic class is slavery or its equivalent for all but the privileged few. It is, of course, all a matter of relative attainment; and America seems well on its way toward overcoming its slow start on the road toward aestheticism.

The Moralistic Viewpoint

As Mencken pointed out, Americans take a moralistic attitude toward most public questions. In private the citizen may admit, even boast, of his own foibles and deviations from "the straight and narrow," but publicly he is firmly on the side of the angels. In this respect he is probably just human, as a certain amount of hypocrisy may be noted in every culture. In the United States, however, the trait assumes some unique and extreme forms.

One is the tendency to believe that a moral matter can be settled by a public going on record in favor of righteousness and against sinfulness. Our tendency to "pass a law" and smugly celebrate victory for our side has been noted by many foreign observers. Probably no other people in the world took the Kellogg Peace Pact of 1928 so seriously as did Americans; a majority of us actually accepted the international treaty at its face value. So, for us, war was eliminated because it had been outlawed legally. Not only did the pact carry the name of the American secretary of state, but the origin of the idea was traced to a Chicago lawyer, Salmon O. Levinson. Much of our pre-Pearl Harbor isolationism resulted from our disgust with the British and French for not living up to the obligations that they had assumed.

Our experiment, noble or otherwise, with prohibition is perhaps the most frequently cited example of the American tendency to go on record piously in behalf of virtue and then vigorously to ignore the action. Our antitrust laws are another example. Thurman W. Arnold, onetime head of the antitrust division of the Department of Justice, in *Folklore of Capitalism* (Oxford, 1937) takes heavy raps at our hypocrisy in respect to their enforcement. Instead of preventing monopoly they actually encouraged it, he contends, by deflecting the attack into purely moral and ceremonial channels. Law, as many a newspaperman with experience in covering the courts knows, is what critics of our legal system charge it is—really a game in the United States. A court action is something to be won, from the standpoint of contending counsel, regardless of the sacred quotations about justice which may be chiseled into the marble over the courthouse entrance. The big American crime is getting caught. If you can "get away with it," you still are innocent even in the eyes of those who know or strongly suspect the facts. Rats never deserted a sinking ship as fast as your friends cold-shoulder you, however, if you get "caught with the goods," even though the same friends may have trespassed with impunity in the same way more frequently themselves. This is a trait which most Americans privately will admit, sheepishly too, but one which they are unwilling or unable to break. "The guy took a chance and wasn't clever enough to avoid being caught," is the viewpoint. "I'm no worse than anyone else," fails to obtain public sympathy or to win acquittals except in matters about which the statutes are palpably inconsistent with morals. Prosecutors, for instance, hardly ever ask the extreme penalty any more for husbands who kill adulterers; in such cases the unwritten is stronger than the written law, and juries just cannot be depended upon to take a life for a life.

Capital punishment, as a matter of fact, is inflicted today with an increasing rarity upon any kind of murderer, and the reason is not because killers buy their way out with high powered "mouthpieces." Rather, it is because of a combination of other factors, most important of which probably is the fact that American society no longer feels so endangered by the waywardness, even to the point of homicide, of any one of its members. On the frontier the opposite was true. Thieving, cattle rustling and similar forms of misbehavior just could not be tolerated; there were too many external dangers toward which the community had to present a united front to permit internal enemies as well. So, frontier justice was swift and sure; as a result it quite often wasn't justice. The equivalent of the frontiersman's frantic attitude toward crime in his midst is observed in a neighborhood where a purse snatcher, rapist, or molester of children is known to be at large and undetected. In understandable fear the citizenry demands action by the police; if necessary it forms vigilante groups.

In comparatively recent years, however, a great change has occurred in public attitudes once the criminal has been apprehended. There are fewer and fewer lynchings or threats of violence, more and more reliance upon authorities to handle the matter from there on in the belief that safety has been restored when the offender is removed from circulation. This change has come to a large extent from a more enlightened attitude as regards the nature and causes of crime. Psychiatry is winning the battle against classical theories of criminology that criminals are either born or are persons who deliberately choose to use their God-given free will to be misfits rather than conformists. Today the growing attitude is that there must be something radically wrong with someone who commits a particularly atrocious crime. Those who cry out, in a fit of regression, for an end to maudlin sentimentality, easy sentences, coddling of prisoners and the like, are fast becoming a minority. Legislatures have been slow to pass laws in conformity with the findings and theories of twentieth-century criminologists and penologists, but the day of the hue and cry decidedly is gone as far as the general American public is concerned.

That the United States should have a lawless tradition is only natural in view of its history. From 1607 many of the early settlers were considered the most undesirable element in the countries from which they came. Once here they had to become more, not less, tough, and there were still wide open spaces to which to flee in case of trouble. The habit of carrying weapons existed of necessity from the start, and the spirit of competitiveness encouraged the cutting of corners in the race for success. Rugged individualism on the frontier often meant getting the Indians drunk so as to cheat them. There seemed to be so much to go around for so long a time that an easy, swaggering attitude toward things in general easily developed. Many of the stories of the wild and woolly west undoubtedly are gross exaggerations, but travelers on the first transcontinental railroads for a long time *did* take pot shots at buffaloes from car windows. Entertainment on any frontier always is raucous, due partly to the absence of women and partly to the necessity to "blow off steam" after a hard day's work. The defiantly independent attitude which typifies American youth by comparison with the youth of any other land is descended from the carefree, rough and tumble days of their great grandfathers.

This lusty, gusty existence led to excesses which were intolerable when the settling-down period was reached and vigilante groups were organized for the purpose of cleaning out the ruffians. It was not so much, however, conversion to righteousness as self-protection that was the motivating force. Brigandage had to become more refined as it did during the period of the so-called "robber barons." In general Americans were as proud of their first millionaires as is any family or home town if one of its boys goes to the city and makes good. Before they got over being proud the "boys" had cornered almost all of the good land and natural resources in which they had only a pirate's interest and were well on their way toward "hogging" the whole economic show. Statistics regarding the drift toward monopoly control in this country and the depletion of natural resources were given earlier in this chapter.

Americans are adept at romanticizing their existence and they certainly have done so in regard to those aspects which relate to love and marriage. Despite the fact that about one out of every five marriages now ends in divorce, movie makers and novelists still grow rich by repetition of the old theme that all problems involving the sexes end at the altar. Americans are extremely sentimental about anything concerning womanhood. Whistler's painting is the stereotype whenever mother is mentioned, and at every age the female is expected to be better—that is, more virtuous, kind, honest, and so forth—than the male. The so-called emancipation of woman and her entry into business have caused a great deal of the superficial chivalry of the immediate past to disappear, but even practical males can react violently at any insult to one of their own womanfolk.

What we call "popular" music is devoted mostly to sorrowful laments about how lonesome someone is about "you-ooo." There is no newspaper photography with greater pulling power than that with pretty girl appeal, which also monopolizes the covers of most popular magazines month after month. On the one hand some of this descends to frank and cheap sex appeal; on the other it is surrounded with an aura of romance, and the girls worth knowing are the clean wholesome type like the kids next door with whom one played and grew up.

The same romantic attitude typifies the average American's undergraduate knowledge of the business world. The inevitable consequence of the Horatio Alger myth is a tremendous letdown on the part of the young idealistic graduate when as the commencement orators tell him, he "departs from the school of life to enter life's school." In a paying job he quickly learns that some of the lampooning of his professors for being impractical theorists and rosy picture painters is justified. The disillusionment stimulates a dangerous type of cynicism which contributes to the "I'm going to get mine" attitude which often makes a mockery of law, both statutory and moral. No matter how un-scrupulous he may become in his money-making activities, however, he is likely to remain sentimental in his personal relations and to be kind to his mother, wife, children, and pets. He can be ruthless in fighting organized labor in his plant and yet donate heavily to the Community Chest which distributes charity to the same persons and their families. The average merchant is so responsive to a hard-luck story that Chambers of Commerce try to enforce strict rules regarding solicitors as an act of self-protection. Even the harshest bailiffs, police, and gentlemen of the press will pass the hat for the spinner of a tear-jerking tale.

Class Consciousness

Some of this charity is in the spirit of *noblesse oblige* (persons of noble rank should behave nobly) and is salve for the conscience of those uneasy about how they attained their positions of comparatively superior ease and comfort. America's classes are open and there is little class consciousness among those in the lower income brackets. At the other end of the scale, however, the opposite is becoming more and more true.

It is a compliment to be told one has not been spoiled by fame or fortune, and it is derisive to declare that the opposite is true: that one's success has "gone to one's head." On the whole the American well-to-do are much more informal than is true in other cultures. They have to be, or pretend at least to cultivate a democratic façade. At the same time, however, they cannot help but be conscious of their com-paratively superior status. Nor is it easy to avoid the belief that it is deserved. Snobbishness is to be found more frequently among second-generation wealthy than among the *nouveau riche*, because of the realization, unconscious at least, that one has acquired his position through inheritance rather than his own efforts. Such, naturally, is a fact which nobody can admit to himself so he rationalizes that it is heredity which counts. Thus, the poor are recognized to be such because they are lacking in ability; the rich have risen to the top be-cause of their superior capacities which they then pass on to their progeny. A generation ago the eugenicists who spun long tales about Jukes and Kallikaks found ready believers among the upper crust. More recent proofs that intelligence is not a Mendelian unit characteristic and that there is nothing to doctrines about racial superiority haven't been so well received.

All of this is just another way of saying that whatever class consciousness exists in the United States is to be found at the top, not the bottom, of the economic scale. And that among the well-to-do it grows whenever the spread between the extremes widens, which always is a harbinger of trouble ahead. It was during the long regime of Franklin Delano Roosevelt that much of this class consciousness solidified because in FDR there was a personification of the threats to entrenched interests and an object upon which resentment and hate could be focalized. The squire of Hyde Park was, in the opinion of his peers, a traitor to his class, and all the rebuttal arguments that FDR really was trying to save them from themselves were to little avail. The crash of 1929 and the resultant lean years of depression inspired so much fear in so many blue-blooded as well as red-blooded hearts that a scapegoat was essential.

The monumental work on how a self-conscious upper crust develops and its characteristics is Thorstein Veblen's *The Theory of the Leisure Class* (Macmillan, 1899) which ranks with Lincoln Steffens' *Autobiography* (Harcourt, Brace, 1931) on any newspaperman's *must* reading list. In its practice of conspicuous consumption and conspicuous waste, the leisure class develops mannerisms and standards which, superficial though they may seem, come to be accepted as absolutes and are emulated by the less privileged. Not intrinsic merit but successful imitation of these outward manifestations of wealth and social position becomes the yardstick by which others are judged. Such superciliousness in time leads to a gulf of misunderstanding between social groups, with the upper class attitude verging on that implicit in Marie Antoinette's supposed saying, "If they don't have bread, let them eat cake." Whenever one "crosses the tracks" he must guard against applying his own standards of correctness in matters of dress, table manners, speech, morals and other aspects of social behavior so as not to see only evidence of inferiority and return grateful to be different.

Despite the growing evidence to the contrary, most everyone still likes to think of himself as middle class, as numerous experiments have revealed. Since class is largely a matter of consciousness this situation has caused the United States to earn and deserve the sobriquet of a middle-class society. The population, however, is growing; the neighborhood and community are disappearing; businesses are so big that employer-employee contacts are infrequent and *ésprit de corps* among workers something which must be artificially created if possible; specialization required throughout the business and professional world is drawing people in all fields further apart rather than closer together; conflicts—rural versus urban, aged versus youth, male versus female, rich versus poor—are developing; government is a huge undertaking carried on more and more indirectly through representatives with the individual voter further and further removed from it. Class distinctions, prejudices, and scapegoating are increasing dangers. The homogeneity which rapid transportation, easy communication and standardized consumption as the result of large-scale production and advertising foster is offset by the heterogeneity which contemporary living compels.

"Bigger and Better"

This bigness is not recognized by the average American as the breeder of evil. Quite the contrary, it is almost an object of worship, because it has been accepted as the symbol of progress. Outdoing the other fellow, city, state, or nation becomes an obsession as we apply the quantitative yardstick to every aspect of our life.

This is, of course, the age of the giants in industry and in government. Competition among industrialists has resulted in bigger and better consolidations so that the day when the billion dollar corporation was a novelty is long since past. We now have corporations with assets totaling more than 5 billion dollars. Many of them have assets totaling more than those of some of our states.

"What size is it?" is the inevitable question which one American asks another upon learning that the party of the second part is from an unfamiliar place. Nothing wounds civic pride more than a drop in population. The superiority complex from which most New Yorkers suffer hardly has been exaggerated by envious critics fom the hinterland. Big city thinks it is better than small city; small city thinks it is better than town or village; village and town look down upon "hickish" farmers.

Aside from the matter of total population every inhabited place boasts of some unique distinction. Chicago has the world's largest hotel, the world's biggest office building, the world's longest streetcar line, the world's greatest newspaper, the world's largest Polish settlement outside of Poland itself. A Hoosier proudly relates that Indianapolis is the largest city in the world not on a navigable river. Folks in Nevada call Reno "the biggest little city in the world." Milwaukee leads in breweries, although Cincinnati and St. Louis dispute that fact. Atlantic City is the leading convention city. Los Angeles has Hollywood and both California and Florida have the best weather. The efforts of Chambers of Commerce to discover and exploit the distinctive are reminiscent of the judges at a pet show in which three children entered turtles. To save face for everyone there were three prizes; for the best large-sized turtle, for the best small-sized turtle and for the best medium-sized turtle. All three youngsters went home happy.

The American idea of progress as identified with bigness is a stereotype according to Walter Lippmann in *Public Opinion* (Macmillan, 1922) in which he wrote: "The stereotype represented by such words as progress was composed fundamentally of mechanical inventions. And mechanical it has remained, on the whole, to this day. In America more than anywhere else, the spectacle of mechanical progress has made so deep an impression that it has suffused the whole moral code. An American will endure almost any insult except the charge that he is not progressive. Be he of long native ancestry or a recent immigrant, the aspect that has always struck his eye is the immense physical growth of American civilization. This constitutes a fundamental stereotype through which he views the world: the country village will become the great metropolis; the modest building a skyscraper; what is small shall be big; what is slow shall be fast; what is poor shall be rich; what is few shall be many; whatever *is*, shall be more so. . . . To be sure, the ideal confuses excellence with size, happiness with speed, and human nature with contraption. . . . The desire for the biggest, the fastest, the highest, or if you are a maker of wristwatches or microscopes, the smallest; the love, in short, of the superlative and the 'peerless' is in essence and possibility a noble passion."

This pride in size is, of course, rooted in reality. As Chester Bowles pointed out in *Tomorrow Without Fear,* "Although in number we Americans made up only 7 per cent of the world's population, we possessed 40 per cent of the world's petroleum reserves, 18 per cent of the world's iron, 50 per cent of the coal, 20 per cent of the copper, 17 per cent of the tillable land, and 27 per cent of the effective water power. . . . In 1940 we owned and used 70 per cent of the world's automobiles and trucks, 50 per cent of the world's telephones, we listened to 45 per cent of the world's radios, we owned and used 35 per cent of the world's railroads. We consumed 59 per cent of the world's petroleum, 56 per cent of the world's silk, 53 per cent of all coffee, 50 per cent of all rubber and 25 per cent of the world's sugar." [1]

It is not strange that the world over the United States has become the personification of the "bigger and better" idea. Commissioned by the promoters of Chicago's Century of Progress—one of a series of prewar world's greatest fairs—the historian Charles Beard edited a symposium, *Century of Progress* (Harper, 1933). In his own contribution to it, Beard pointed out that the concept of progress, as we know it, was unknown to classical writers or thinkers of the Middle Ages. Democracy, science, and technology all have contributed to its development since, according to Beard, it emerged in 1737 with *Observations on the Continuous Progress of Universal Reason* by the French Abbe de Saint Pierre. In America, Beard wrote, "the natural resources, intellectual climate and social order were highly favorable to the growth of the new concept. Here nature had provided an enormous and diversified material endowment which could be used to establish a high level of life and sustain the continuous advancement of standards if intelligently and efficiently used. Here the population was ready for secular enterprise. While many had migrated to America in search of religious freedom, the great majority who came voluntarily had come for mundane reasons. . . . And the factors which contributed to the generation of the idea of progress in America were respect for industry and labor, a preoccupation with secular enterprise and a spirit of experimentation and invention."

The principal purpose of the promoters of the Century of Progress was to make it the biggest and best of the succession of extravagant world's fairs from 1853 up to that time. Four years later the New

[1] From *Tomorrow Without Fear,* by Chester Bowles. Copyright, 1946, by Simon and Schuster, Inc.

York World's Fair sought to outdo the Middlewestern effort in depicting The World of the Future. Symbolic of the American point of view
were the Dali-like trylon and perisphere (the spike and ball, as they
were called by the irreverent), as symbolic of the skyscraper, a distinctly American architectural invention without at least one of which
no city can call itself grown up.

Charles Merz, now editor of the New York *Times*, in *The Great
American Bandwagon* (John Day, 1928), Stanley Walker, former
city editor of the New York *Herald Tribune,* in *Mrs. Astor's Horse*
(Stokes, 1936), John Tunis, widely known sports writer, in *$port$,
Heroic$ and Hy$teric$* (John Day, 1928), and Silas Bent, also a long-
time newspaperman, in *Ballyhoo* (Boni, Liveright, 1927), are among
those who have exposed and satirized the extent to which the "bigger
and better" ideal has permeated all aspects of American life. Although
the books are all at least two decades old now they still are valuable
antidotes to excessive chauvinism. Typical quotation from the Merz
book is the following: "This is a good life we lead. It has plenty of
bath tubs, open forums, good roads, laundries, high schools and
department stores. . . . This is the day of the non-stop flight, the
million-dollar gate, the moving picture queen, the new Ford, the
White House Spokesman, and the English channel . . . six tube sets
and tinted stucco . . . goose-neck putters and semi-balloons . . .
patriots discussing Lloyd and Chaplin, Ruth and Gehrig, Jones and
Hagen, the widow's defense and the state's prosecution. . . . We
turn casually to the day's news at breakfast with no thought of acquiring a new hero on this particular morning, and in bold type spread
the full width of a front page find that a new hero has sprung full-
panoplied from the news like Minerva from the head of Jupiter. Some
bold deed performed lone-handed, some spectacular and unexampled
feat, some service to a cause worth while but hitherto quiescent, leaps
out at us in giant headlines. . . . The whole nation reads the news.
The whole nation rings with it. . . . When the bandwagon lumbers
down the street we hop aboard it."

Today some of the names naturally would be different, but the
spirit of the quotation would be about the same, granted that the
speculative twenties were comparatively somewhat excessive. Illustrations of the extent to which the bigger-and-better idea has permeated
all phases of our life are plentiful. Many rich Americans specialize in

outdoing each other in building bigger and better houses, some of which almost exceed Veblen's wildest dreams as examples of conspicuous consumption. Thousands of dollars have been spent on such extravagances as perforated toilet paper which plays tunes when unrolled in the manner of a player piano, gadgets which set off chimes, and others which release a shower of confetti. Since Hollywood movies specialize in such settings, with movie stars talking over the telephone while taking milk baths, they become the highest standards toward which moderns the world over can strive and, in their ignorance, millions of people in foreign lands conclude that most Americans enjoy such luxuries.

Competition exists as to the number of houses one can acquire. J. P. Morgan spent millions acquiring palatial residences in all parts of the world, many of which stood empty most of the year. Morgan had a town house on Madison Avenue, New York; an estate at Glen Cove, Long Island; Wall Hall, a place in Hertfordshire, England; a town house in Grosvenor Square, London; Cannochy Lodge, where he went for the shooting, in Forfarshire, Scotland; and a hideout in Bermuda.

In the late twenties "Daddy" Browning, a New York real estate man and *bon vivant*, released to the press a list of the gifts he had given his fiancée and future wife, Peaches. It included one ermine coat, one fox trimmed coat, one Russian sable coat, one other fur coat, 60 dresses, one fox neckpiece, three ensembles, 175 overcoats, 20 hats, 30 pairs of shoes, one ostrich fan and other gifts of jewelry.

Crimes of the century; pugilistic contests of the decade; beauty queens; a succession of fairs and public ceremonies each exceeding its predecessor in length, grandeur, or expense; any or all of these features characterize glamorous twentieth-century champion-minded American life. Many murder trials resemble a three-ring circus. In 1935, for instance, when Bruno Richard Hauptmann was on trial for the kidnapping-murder of Charles A. Lindbergh, Jr., three hundred newsmen covered the occasion and filed more than ten million words. The sheriff made a neat profit by charging ten dollars for main-floor seats and five dollars for balcony seats, and also collected a quantity of good bonded liquor and expensive cigars. The local hotel owner obtained options on all available rooms in town for one dollar a night and charged newspapermen five dollars for room and board. After the trial he paid off the mortgage on the hotel and bought a new sedan. Souvenir salesmen overran the place, many of them selling miniature ladders advertised as "exact duplicates" of the famous ladder used in the commission of the crime. The warden of the jail sold the paper spoons, forks, and plates the prisoner was compelled to use for fear he might commit suicide. While the jury was deliberating the attorney general sat in the jury box and amused the spectators with his wit. The prosecuting attorney sat in the witness chair and burlesqued the testimony of witnesses. A local restaurant advertised a "trial lunch" which included "writers cramp soup, Lindbergh steak, Hauptmann beans, Jury pie and Press custard."

When the career of Dion O'Bannion, a Chicago gangster, was cut short by the guns of a rival mob, his funeral cortege contained 26 cars full of flowers. Frankie Yale, an important personage in New York's underworld, read the account of O'Bannion's obsequies and expressed the wish that his funeral would be just as good and, if possible, better. He got his wish, being put to rest in a coffin reputed to have cost $15,000. There was a five-mile funeral parade through the streets of Brooklyn. Thirty-eight automobiles were filled with flowers, said to have cost $37,000. "Joe the Baker," a Bronx racketeer, was buried in a coffin costing $15,000. His funeral procession had forty cars full of flowers.

Education today is a big business in the United States. Veterans taking advantage of the educational provisions of the GI Bill of Rights preferred the large universities to the small colleges. To attract students, especially in lean times, the modern brain factories scour the country for the best brawn available for martyrdom on the field of football glory, and rules regulating the solicitation and subsidizing of athletes are observed about as strictly as are the antitrust laws. Some serious studying still is done on college campuses, but the rah-rahism which the movies and pulp writers like to extol also exists. A college degree is more and more becoming an economic necessity, and a fraternity or sorority pin of equal or greater importance socially. Students go to college or university to obtain a degree as distinguished from an education, and the modern liberal arts college grinds them out wholesale as unable as are the diploma-happy graduates themselves to say what it is they are educated for. Anyway, it's not "what have you learned?" but rather "how much education have you had?" that counts nowadays.

Neuroticism

It all sounds a little crazy, and it is. Nevertheless, most Americans can take it "in their stride" or at least learn to tolerate their "bigger and better" fellow countrymen. Wrote Robert Lynd in *Knowledge for What?* (Princeton, 1939), "Most of us Americans are not super-aggressors, most of us are not successes-in-a-big-way, and life consists for most people in just living along. This just living along quality is a large part of American culture. But its numerical predominance does not render it either emotionally predominant or emotionally self-contained. It represents, rather, in American life an enforced second best, a coming to terms with the situation in which one finds oneself caught. At every point our young, optimistic culture thrusts forward its gains rather than its costs and losses. It plays up in print and symbol the pace-setting ways of life of its more successful members. . . . Those who cannot get what they want do not generally commit suicide; they go on living, but their living takes place in a welter of coercive values . . . one may not crave a Packard, but there are always new Chevrolets. . . . The drama is simply reenacted in a humbler arena."

And so we find the timid bookkeeper or clerk on lodge night donning a splendiferous costume and hearing himself called by an awe-inspiring title, going through a prescribed ritual of hocus pocus which is bigger and better than that of which any other secret society can boast. "Our ritual," says the Fraternal Order of Beavers, "stacks up with any other in existence—brief snappy opening ceremonies, including beautiful Patriotic Flag exercises . . . special dramatic degree exemplifying the Beavers in the valley of the Turquemenau and their conflict with the Iroquois." Similarly says the Ancient and Illustrious Order of the Knights of Malta: "Our ritual is the sole repository of the rites and ceremonies practiced during the Middle Ages, preserved in their entirety but presented in more exquisite style by the aid of modern invention."

America is, as Merz and others have called it, a nation of joiners. According to Mumford in *The Golden Day*, the meagerness of the Protestant ritual begat a starvation which found surcease in the jamborees of the Odd Fellows, Elks, Woodmen, and countless other fraternities. James Truslow Adams' explanation in *Our Business Civilization* (A. and C. Boni, 1929) is the lack of hereditary titles in the United States.

Life conditions in every culture give rise to some fears, Dr. Karen Horney declares in her book, *The Neurotic Personality of Our Times* (Norton, 1937). In our culture competition is a problem for everyone. Quite differently from many other societies, past and present, we put a premium on success and prestige. Neurosis, she says, is the "stepchild" of our culture. Everyone cannot be "bigger and better" and nobody ever can be certain that he is big or good enough. As the objects of desire multiply, the chances of failure in obtaining them increase correspondingly. Excessive mothering of children in the attempt to give them a better start onward and upward creates an excessive need for affection and disappointment when the romantic love for which we are taught to yearn and to expect is not obtained.

Every people have had their equivalents of our Coney Islands, vicarious or escapist outlets such as chariot races, bull fights, and the like. No others, however, have ever exceeded us in the zeal with which we've gone at our tearing up of telephone books to shower over parading heroes, our swoonings over crooners, and the outlandish stunting to which we have resorted to feel important. In his famous motion picture, *Modern Times*, Charlie Chaplin depicted the contemporary need for leisure-time highjinks to relieve the strain. Working on the assembly line of a modern factory, Charlie, typifying, as always, the underdog, went berserk because of the robotlike behavior it entailed. No galley slave or coal digger ever had his working life more routinized than the present-day laborer who screws on bolt number such-and-such for dismal hour after dismal hour until someone is able to invent a machine to do it faster and more efficiently. Large-scale production means not only that the worker no longer has any ownership or control over the product of his labor. More important, he has opportunity for little or no craftsmanship and often doesn't even understand the nature of the finished product on only one small part of which he works. He is just a living cog in a big machine. And such he is likely to remain no matter how much industry may be socialized. It would be just as boring to push and pull a switch for the government as it is for a private owner. In fact, according to one of the foremost critics of the factory system, Ralph Borsodi, in *This Ugly Civilization* (Simon and Schuster, 1929): "Complete socialization would be the final step in the process of making man the servant of his own machines, the first step of which was taken when factories were first erected."

In another part of the same book, this great exponent of "back to the homestead" charges: "The real genius of our age is engaged in thinking about how to abolish labor instead of how to ennoble it." Another typical Borsodi quote is the following: "Our factory-dominated civilization is making us into an overfed, constipated, nervewracked, physically inferior race." Unless management, which is becoming increasingly aware of the problem, finds the solution, the sensational and flamboyant in leisure-time activities are going to become increasingly, not less, attractive to the human robot. And our hospital beds are probably going to continue to fill up with mental patients who have been unable to "stand the gaff."

Nevertheless, it still is significant that the American flag never dips in honor of any supposedly superior person, including the head of a state—a king or a president. It is the individual, in theory at least, who still counts in the United States. It is the individual who, though he often acts as though he doesn't realize it, still is the government. The state, if he uses it rightly, is his agent, his tool in attaining the kind of life which twentieth-century inventive genius makes potentially possible. And here, of course, is where public opinion comes in.

CHAPTER SIX

LEGENDS; FOLKLORE; MYTHS

What one believes about the past seriously conditions his opinions regarding events of the present.

Legends

According to the best evidence available, mostly gathered by an Oxford University historian appointed by the British government to investigate (*The Last Days of Hitler*, by H. R. Trevor-Roper, Macmillan, 1947), Adolf Hitler is dead. The evidence, however, might not be worth much in an American court. It is entirely circumstantial: some charred bones which might be anybody's, and the contradictory recollections and conjectures of a number of servants and others who supposedly were with *der Fuehrer* a few hours or days before his alleged suicide.

There is no corpus delicti, and nobody has testified that he actually saw Adolf breathe his last. As a result, there has hardly been a month since the supposedly fatal April 30, 1945, that there has not been a rumor that Hitler and Eva Braun, his wife or mistress, are alive and in hiding in the Bavarian mountains, Spain, Japan, Patagonia, Queen Marie island in Antartica, or someplace else. One of Eva Braun's former maids has been reported to say she saw her ex-mistress in Munich as late as July, 1945; a Polish newspaper in October, 1947 quoted a former German air force pilot as insisting he flew the couple to Denmark shortly before Germany's capitulation. Martin Bormann, missing one-time deputy to Hitler, has been reported seen in Sydney, Australia, among other places. It is not surprising that in May, 1947, Gallup pollsters found 45 per cent of those included in a nation-wide poll believing Hitler still is alive.

Press associations and newspapers may be expected to continue to give space to the rumors as they arise. Even if incontrovertible proof of Hitler's death were forthcoming, the legend-making already has had too much of a headstart to be stopped. Witness the following account by Fred Sparks which appeared in the June 1, 1949, Chicago *Daily News*:

Rittersbach, Germany—Hitler still is alive, living in a gigantic Bavarian cave with a goodly number of his roughs waiting for der tag.

That is one bedtime story being told in the hamlets of Deutschland these nights as the rationed electric lamp blinks.

There always has been something of the mystic about the German, that blond "superman" who came within an ant's sneeze of conquering the whole wailing world.

So I am not at all surprised to come to this typical tiny town—homesite of 700 Germans—and find the citizens hereabouts delighting in ghosts and witches and fantastic tales.

* * *

After all, Germany is the land of Grimm's fairy tales, and Siegfried the Gorgeous, who was almost impossible to bump off, and Wotan, prancing prince of war.

Now that the herrenvolk are getting back on their feet, legends of past power and future victories again are circulating.

The current silly, which I extracted from crusty citizens after a fistful of schnapps, follows:

Der Fuehrer, dear kinder, did not go up like a toasted marshmallow in his Berlin bunker, as the saps have been led to believe.

* * *

Nein. He took 100,000 of his most magnificent muscle-men and retired to a great cave in the heart of the Bavarian Alps—a cave the address of which is unknown to the nasty occupying powers.

There he lives quietly today, nursing his nerves and lecturing his hearties. When he is particularly peeved about some Allied trick, he will make one of his speeches, causing the clouds to clap thunder in approval, the winds to howl and bolts of lightning to slash through the sky.

Someday when the time is ripe—or maybe sooner—he will emerge with his hordes, pitch out the foreign swine, and unite the torn Reich.

* * *

Following this act of liberation, Hitler & Hosts—after becoming accustomed to the sunlight—will goose-step across the flabby face of a decadent democratic world and create a truly German universe, in which every Teuton is indeed a triumphant tyrant.

Sieg Heil!

Judging from numerous historical instances of heads of state and heirs apparent whose deaths were mysterious or unexplained, it may be well into the twenty-second century before the repercussions of Adolf's uncertain fate cease to be serious. In other words, Hitler dead under the existent circumstances may become a greater threat to the peace and tranquility of the world than had he escaped to some impregnable redoubt with a large proportion of his army.

It will be some time—five or ten years would seem to be the absolute minimum—before Adolf Hitler, if alive, will want to disclose his identity. Likewise, impostors will be dissuaded from making claims for at least that long. It is difficult to believe, however, that fifteen or twenty years from now there will not be as many "living" Hitlers all over the world as there now are supposed hideouts for the hunted couple. If political events should take such a turn that a revival of Naziism in either Germany or any other country seems possible, their appearance will be hastened. Otherwise, they will be septuagenarians about whom there no longer is any reason for international worry.

Some of the future Hitlers will be obviously deranged persons whose life histories will be easily ascertainable. Others will appear as from nowhere. Each will have a different plausible story of how he escaped death in May, 1945, and of his whereabouts during the intervening years. These accounts either will be difficult or impossible to check or will be heavily supported by documentary evidence.

Many of the "confessions" will be on deathbeds to credulous persons who will spend lifetimes in attempts to prove them and to persuade others to believe. By 1970, there will be at least a half dozen cemetery headstones in different parts of the world purporting to be erected over the remains of the man who set the world on fire in the thirties and early forties. A mummy or two will be making the rounds of the world's fairs. Magazine-article writers and book authors will become effete living off checks and royalties for pros and cons regarding each pretender.

The living Hitlers will provide even more dramatic "copy." They will be the trusted servants of important employers, successful business or professional men, perhaps college professors, who suddenly "reveal" themselves to close associates. They will have amazing knowledge of Hitler's private life and of secrets of state, by which they will persuade their dumfounded confessors to become their patrons. Not a few of these Hitlers will be exposed to the scrutiny of relatives, associates and diplomats of all nations who knew the real *Fuehrer*. The whole world will be stupefied to learn that such visitors were recognized immediately and had their memories refreshed regarding anecdotes which could be known only to them and the real Adolf.

The absence of proof, in the form of documentary evidence or personal belongings, will be explained easily in view of the hasty departure Hitler must have made from Berlin. And Adolf's known propensity for flying into a rage or becoming sullen will serve any pretender in good stead when questions become embarrassing.

More than one public or private commission will be appointed to investigate. It is not inconceivable that hundreds of thousands, perhaps millions, of dollars will be spent by them. The effect of adverse reports upon the discoverers of the supposed Hitlers will be only to cause them to redouble their efforts to establish their cases. If, by any chance, Eva Braun shows up living, it is quite conceivable that she will accept one or more of the impostors as her returned lover or husband.

The one circumstance which could prevent any or all of this from happening would be the continuation of danger to a reincarnated Hitler, no matter how venerable and politically impotent. In such case—in fact, in any case—the versions of Hitler's fate to which we shall be subjected for decades will in themselves be serious. Some ex-Nazis may find it to their advantage to come out with new versions of Hitler's death or escape. Because the Russians were in sole possession of Hitler's last known whereabouts for weeks before the Americans and British arrived, they are especially susceptible to versions with political implications, as that they captured *der Fuehrer* alive and kept him incommunicado until the opportune moment, possibly at a conference of heads of states or foreign ministers at which a threat to turn Adolf loose had a strong effect in putting across some Soviet point.

Finally, about a half century from now, it will have to be admitted that Hitler no longer possibly could be alive. Since he and Eva already are rumored to have had offspring, by then the principal concern of those who make pretenders and impostors a hobby will be alleged sons and daughters, grandsons and great grandnieces. Their sponsors will support their claims for compensation for personal property belonging to Hitler, possibly the royalties from sales of translations of *Mein Kampf*. As early as January, 1946, British authorities were reported from Herford, Germany, to be holding an eighteen-year-old girl who claimed that *der Fuehrer* was her father. Her mother, she said, had been his mistress in the late twenties. Almost two years later, in December, 1947, Helmuth Riegge, a mothball salesman from Hanover, was reported to have swindled credulous Germans out of $50,000 to defray expenses of a secret mission to rescue an alleged Hitler son living incognito in a castle inside the Russian zone.

Hitler's alleged progeny into the third and fourth generations will be potential threats as figurehead leaders of revived Nazi movements the world over. Most of them, however, probably will eschew political for economic gain, and they will plead that they should not be persecuted for the crimes of their ancestor. They will be vaudeville, lecture platform, drawingroom, and Hollywood favorites. Even if their claims are disproved and their deceptions exposed, they may continue to make good livings as does Harry Gerguson, the onetime Imperial Highness Prince Michael Alexandrovitch Dimitry Obelensky Romanoff, who gets by as a famous West Coast restaurateur because of amused admiration of his colossal gall.

In case any of the foregoing seems far fetched or impossible, there isn't a supposition contained in it that does not have an historical precedent. What it has been imagined *could* happen as an aftermath of Hitler *has* happened in the past, in many instances more than once. A few accounts of "living legends" should be helpful to the newspaperman who hardly can expect to complete a lifetime's career without encountering some such stories.

Among the most pathetic chapters in English history is that of the two little princes whose skeletons were not discovered in the Tower of London until more than twenty years after their deaths. They were the sons of Edward IV who died in 1483. The older, thirteen, was on his way to be crowned Edward V when he and his younger brother, Richard, Duke of York, were taken prisoner by their uncle, Richard, Duke of Gloucester, who promptly became Richard III. Rumors of the deaths of the princes spread, but it was two decades before Brackenbury, the Tower constable, revealed that he had refused to obey orders to kill the boys and that their murderers were Sir James Tyrrel and two servants who smothered them with pillows and hid their bodies.

In 1492, the year Columbus first sighted the New World, Yorkist sympathizers became impressed with the regal bearing of a living model of a Breton merchant. They took him to Ireland, where, five years earlier, they had crowned a ten-year-old boy, Lambert Simnel, as Edward VI, claiming that he was the Earl of Warwick, although the real Earl of Warwick was in London. That attempt at regaining power failed when a force of Irish and Germans under Sir Thomas Fitzgerald was defeated by Henry VII in Lancashire. Richard Simon, the instigator, was imprisoned, but the phoney Edward VI, now plain Lambert Simnel again, was pardoned and later became the royal falconer.

Perkin Warbeck, the new discovery, wasn't so easy to convince of his own royal blood. He swore before the mayor of Cork that he was not the Earl of Warwick and also denied that he was the bastard son of Richard III. His protests that he was not Richard, younger of the two princes killed in the Tower, however, were to no avail. His sponsors wore Perkin down and he finally consented to play the role of pretender to the English throne. He was taken to France where Margaret of Burgundy acknowledged him as her nephew. He attended the funeral of Frederick III in Vienna, corresponded with Queen Isabella of Spain and traveled with Maximilian to Flanders where he was acknowledged as the new emperor and rightful king of England. He married Catherine Gordon, cousin of James IV of Scotland.

On July 3, 1495, from shipboard, Perkin watched the troops of Henry VII trap and annihilate the Yorkists who, intent on making him king, tried to land at Kent. Two years later Perkin himself went ashore at Exeter during a second invasion attempt and was taken prisoner. On Nov. 23, 1499, he was killed for allegedly attempting to escape from the Tower. The same year one Ralph Wilford, who claimed to be the real Earl of Warwick, met a similar fate.

A century later, Czar Ivan the Terrible died, leaving two sons. The older, Feodor, in 1584, succeeded his father to the throne of Russia but came under the spell of Regent Boris Godunoff, his brother-in-law. The younger son, Demetrius, was virtually exiled with his mother to an estate at Uglich, about a hundred miles from Moscow. There, one day when the boy was ten or twelve, he was found dead with his throat slashed. The official explanation was that the child accidentally fell on a knife while playing. The villagers, however, blamed Bitiagofski, the guard whom Boris had assigned to the child. They lynched Bitiagofski and two hundred of them were executed in revenge.

About five years later, after Feodor also had died and Boris had become czar, a Polish Prince, Adam Wisniewicky, was scolding a servant. Suddenly the menial turned on him, saying in essence, "If you knew who I really am, you wouldn't dare talk to me like that." Then he confessed that he was Demetrius, explaining that a plot against his life had been suspected and another boy employed as a double. After the double's death the real Demetrius escaped to a monastery. Prince Adam, convinced, presented the young man to King Sigismund of Poland who either also believed in him or at least decided to use him against his Russian enemies. In 1604 a Polish army invaded Russia. Boris died in April, 1605 and, two months later, Demetrius was crowned czar in Moscow amid wild acclaim. Almost a year later, however, his popularity dissolved when he imported a Polish wife, Marina Mniszek, daughter of the Palatine of Sandomir. In May, 1608, Demetrius was killed during a successful insurrection.

The False Demetrius, as history knows him, is believed to have been a monk named Gregory Ostrepieff. Within a year after his death a new Demetrius appeared, declaring that another had been mistaken for him during the revolution. Marina accepted him immediately as her husband, and the Poles backed his contentions. He was killed at Kaluga in 1609, but it wasn't long before there appeared two more Demetriuses, each claiming to be the son of the original. Both were captured and executed before 1613.

That the New World should become a haven of harassed European royalty was natural. Throughout the eastern half of the United States today there are markers to indicate where a number of them are alleged to have sought refuge. Sanford, Maine, for instance, has a tavern where Louis Philippe supposedly stopped in 1797, only Stephen Roberts has pretty well proved that he didn't. Bardstown, Ky., is convinced that the rich paintings in its St. Joseph's Roman Catholic Proto-Cathedral were presented by Louis Philippe in appreciation for medical services rendered him by a local priest. On Muller Hill, near Hogansburg, Madison County, N.Y., there is a shack which, local legend has it, was the secret hangout of Charles X of France about 1800.

Commemorating the most dramatic incident of all, however, is the stone which the Jean Nicolet chapter of the Daughters of the American Revolution erected Oct. 27, 1937, at Green Bay, Wis. It reads in part: "This tablet marks the landed estate of Eleazar Williams, who served in the U.S.A. during the War of 1812 and who was reputed to be Louis XVII, dauphin of France."

Sober historians are agreed that Williams was a part-Indian missionary. Neither his parents nor any other relatives ever could be persuaded to say he was anything else. Nevertheless, in February, 1853, Williams was author of an article in *Putnam's Weekly* claiming that he was the Lost Dauphin of France. He was made aware of that fact, he confessed, in 1842 by Prince de Joinville, son of Louis Philippe. De Joinville denied ever having heard of Williams, and others pointed out the unlikelihood of the French king's inviting more trouble than he already had.

The accepted story of the Lost Dauphin, son of Louis XVI and Marie Antoinette, is that he died in prison in Paris in 1795 from scrofula and inhuman treatment by his Republican jailers. Because he was buried in an unmarked grave and because the doctor who performed a post mortem on his body died mysteriously a few days later and, perhaps largely, because many wanted terribly for the potential Louis XVII not to be dead, before 1850 there were at least fifty Lost Dauphins all over the world. Williams, because of his magazine article, received more attention than most, and Mary Hartwell Catherwood wrote a best selling novel, *Lazarre,* about him. Another Dauphin, Pierre Brosseau, who died about 1875, is buried in the Evanston, Ill. Calvary cemetery. He always insisted that he remembered being smuggled to Canada.

Evidence that "living legends" continue to be news long after they cease to be "living" is the following press association story which appeared in the June 1, 1947, Chicago *Sun:*

Oneida, Wis., May 31.—(UP). A quiet plot in the Oneida Indian Mission churchyard today became the final resting place of Eleazar Williams, a missionary who died in 1885, claiming to be the lost Dauphin of France.

Williams long maintained that he was the son of Louis XVI and Marie Antoinette—and therefore entitled to the French throne. He claimed that conspirators stole him from the French Bastille when the king and queen were beheaded.

Then, he maintained, he lost his memory and did not recover it until after he came to America in 1795.

Williams was said to have led a secret corps of rangers on espionage missions in northern New York during the War of 1812 and then helped Indians migrate to Wisconsin. Later he married a 14-year-old half-breed and became an Episcopal missionary and teacher.

He returned to New York, where he died in 1885 and was buried in St. James Cemetery. Recently his body was taken from its eastern grave and moved to the scene of his missionary work.

As the remains of the "Lost Dauphin" were lowered into the Wisconsin soil, Episcopal Bishop Harwood Sturtevant and the Rev. William Christian recited simple prayers.

Their prayers were for Eleazar Williams, missionary and teacher.

There was no mention of the "Lost Dauphin."

Of the "dauphins" who remained on the other side of the water, Charles William Naundorff proved the most irritating to the French government. He not only recalled how he had been drugged by friends, declared dead in his coffin, and rescued, but he also related subsequent escapades, including his imprisonment and his escape to Germany. After several years there working as a watchmaker, he returned to France. He died at Delft, Holland, where his tombstone reads: "Here lies Louis XVII, Duke of Normandy, King of French courts." After his death his son took up the royal claims, suing in French courts in 1851 and 1874 for recovery of the property of his alleged grandparents, Louis XVI and Marie Antoinette. A grandson for years held court as John IV in a Parisian wineshop.

Another American landmark is the grave, in the Third Creek Presbyterian Church cemetery near Cleveland, N.C., of Peter Stuart Ney, schoolteacher, who thousands still are convinced was really Marshal Michael Ney who led the last charge of the Old Guard at Waterloo and was called "the bravest of the brave" by Napoleon Bonaparte. Officially Ney was tried and executed Dec. 7, 1815, in Luxembourg Gardens for having deserted to Napoleon after the escape from Elba. According to the legend, the firing squad was composed of soldiers

who formerly served under Ney and helped him to escape to the
United States. Ney supposedly arrived at Charleston, S.C. in January,
1816, was recognized by French refugees at Georgetown and moved,
first to Brownsville and, in 1830, to Iredell County, N.C. He read
French history in the library of nearby Davidson College and fainted
when told of Napoleon's death on St. Helena. The record is not clear
as to whether the Tarheel Ney ever claimed to be the famous French
general. In Paris Père-Lachaise cemetery there is a monument to the
marshal.

The following is from the Sept. 30, 1946, New York *Times*:

Cleveland, N.C., Sept. 29—Peter Stuart Ney, a school teacher, who
was buried near their community a hundred years ago in the cemetery of
the Third Creek Presbyterian church, was unquestionably Marshal Ney
of France, one of the most brilliant generals of Napoleon's armies. This
assertion was made today by Dr. Howard E. Rondthaier of Winston-
Salem, president of Salem college, and vice president of the newly organized Ney Memorial Association.

In commemoration of the centennial of Ney's death in this vicinity, a
large assemblage paid tribute to his memory. Dr. Rondthaier and Senator
Clyde R. Hoey, of Shelby, were the principal speakers. Latta B. Ratledge
of Mocksville, president of the Memorial Association, was in the chair.

Dr. Rondthaier offered evidence in support of his theory that the French
Marshal escaped death before a firing squad and came to America to live
in disguise in an isolated spot.

At times, this school teacher, while under the influence of intoxicants,
and on his deathbed maintained he was the Marshal of the French Armies,
Dr. Rondthaier said.

In his address, Senator Hoey said that he was not unmindful of the
"isms," national debt and other current trends which might make Americans pessimistic on the future. He said he expected, however, that the
United States would emerge soon as a much finer land. He called attention
to the standards of law, morality, education, freedom and faith cherished
by the Founders of the country, and urged that modern citizens revive
those fundamental principles that Christianity can solve.

International problems may threaten the peace and security of the
world, too, he emphasized, but he warned that peace and cooperation
could not come over night.

Representative R. L. Doughton, chairman of the House Ways and
Means Committee, also spoke briefly. . . .

Neither Williams nor Ney ever attempted to interfere with European politics, but another refugee who sought safety in America pre-

sumably would have done so had the opportunity arisen. She was the supposed Anastasia, youngest daughter of Nicholas II who miraculously escaped death while her parents, brother, and three sisters were destroyed by the Bolsheviks July 16, 1918, at Ekaterinburg.

The girl first attracted public notice in 1920 when Berlin police prevented her from committing suicide by drowning. For years she was confined to a hospital for the mentally ill where she was thought to be a Polish peasant, Franziska Schanzkowski. To fellow patients about to be released, however, she told a different story which in short time reached czarist sympathizers. One of them, the Duke of Leuchtenburg, relative of the Romanoffs, befriended her in his castle until 1927. There, to many girlhood acquaintances of the dead czar's youngest daughter, she told how she was left at the scene of the mass murder supposedly dead from bayonet wounds. A young Red soldier, however, rescued her. They fled together to Rumania where she married him, becoming Mme. Tschaikowsky. A son was born but died in a foundling home, and the husband was killed in an automobile accident.

A commission representing several European monarchs called her an impostor. Members of the czar's household and relatives, however, were amazed at the girl's ability to identify them without prompting, and at her knowledge of intimate family affairs. She also resembled photographs of the real Anastasia and she had a protruding bone in her left foot. Sascha, the real Anastasia's nurse, believed in her, and Gleb Botkin, son of the czar's physician who had played with Anastasia as a child, began an energetic campaign to establish her claim.

Mrs. William B. Leeds, of Philadelphia, the former Princess Xenia of Russia, was convinced and brought the girl to the United States. In 1935 a New York court dismissed her suit to obtain about 7 million dollars which the czar's government had kept in American banks. The girl later fell out with Mrs. Leeds and today is believed to be back in Europe.

Accompanied by a quarter page of pictures of Czar Nicholas and members of his family, under the six-column headline, "Czarist Princess Slips Through Soviet Net," the following article by George Weller appeared in the July 8, 1949, Chicago *Daily News*. It puts the Anastasia story in a different light.

Rome—The Princess Tatiana reportedly the last of the Romanoffs, has slipped away from her nursing post in a German displaced persons camp. The presence of Soviet agents on her trail made her flight necessary.

Under British protection, she has moved to England and is living there under an assumed name, it is learned here from sources close to the supposed princess.

The princess, now 53, escaped the wholesale Russian execution of the Czar's family. Aided by Gen. Ludendorff, she made her way to Berlin.

She lived in Berlin from 1923 under an alias, using the Lithuanian passport with which the German field marshal provided her.

ALIAS PENETRATED

At the end of the war her alias was broken when an American reporter disclosed enough clues to where she was to put the Soviets again on her trail.

Through a British envoy in Central Europe it was arranged by friends that Tatiana go to England.

Tatiana's whereabouts are being closely protected, not only against Soviet agents but because she would become an important figure politically in the event of an upheaval in Eastern Europe.

Her circle of friends do not believe that a restoration of monarchy would follow closely any anti-Communist split in Russia. But they assert that the alleged Tatiana, a quiet and earnest woman now devoted to the cause of refugees from Communist Europe, might play a later political role of importance.

EVIDENCE LACKING

Whether the woman whom the British authorities have sheltered is actually a cousin of the House of Windsor, or an impostor, is a matter which Tatiana's supporters admit will be difficult to prove. Documentary evidence is lacking.

They are eager, however, to avoid such a fiasco as occurred in the years following World War I when a so-called Princess Anastasia appeared in New York with the support of the Vanderbilt family.

The theory among the supporters of "Princess" Tatiana is that the so-called Anastasia was put forward not so much as a careerist but as a Soviet ruse, to draw Tatiana from behind her alias in Berlin.

LOST HEART TO PRINCE

Tatiana never married. In her early years it was expected that she might be betrothed to Edward, Prince of Wales, who met her in Moscow when she was 16 and he 19.

Later she fell in love with Prince Joachim, son of the Kaiser of Germany. Joachim, apparently believing that she was killed by the Soviets and unaware that Ludendorff was helping her to escape, committed suicide only a few days before Tatiana reached Germany.

A plea for legal recognition of her title has been placed by Tatiana before the British courts. If it were recognized, she would become heir to that portion of the Romanoff jewels, including the Orlov gem, which were sent by Nicholas II to England to be held in safe keeping by his cousins of the House of Windsor.

A typical "discovery" story, also involving the czarist court, came out of Alaska in early 1946. As reported by the United Press it was as follows:

Anchorage, Alaska, Jan. 16 (UP).—The far north today yielded a strange, new story—the possibility that Rasputin, mad, dissolute Russian monk, is still alive on a lonely Alaskan island.

The tale, gathered from superstitious Russian-Aleutian Island natives, and many not-so-superstitious Alaskans of Yankee extraction, is that Rasputin is watching the grave of a Russian priest on a desolate spruce island off Kodiak.

Gregory Rasputin, the "Mad Monk," was reported assassinated in Leningrad in December, 1917. He allegedly had exercised mesmeric influence over Czar Nicholas II and the Czarina.

For years a number of Alaskans have believed that in the activity and physical appearance of an aged Russian monk, named Gerasim Schmalz, is a clue that may combine two of the eeriest stories of Czarist Russia and Alaska.

One hundred and forty-seven years ago, a Russian priest named "Father Herman," told his followers in Moscow, before departing for Alaska, that he would return in 150 years.

Father Herman died in Kodiak that same year and was buried on the island. Since then his tomb has been guarded religiously by members of the Greek Orthodox church.

In 1919, Gerasim Schmalz arrived at Kodiak and took over the task of guarding the wind-swept tomb.

Natives and the few whites who saw him said he closely resembled Rasputin. Angered by repeated questioning, Schmalz went into hiding.

Eustace Ziegler, famed Alaska artist, surprised Schmalz at his hideout one day and photographed him, returned to his studio and super-imposed the gaudy ceremonial robes worn by Rasputin on the picture of Schmalz. Ziegler says the resultant photograph was identical with pictures of Rasputin.

The final, and to many Alaskans, main point in the speculation that Schmalz is Rasputin is that the Russian monk very well could be alive, as he would be 73 years old.

According to history, Rasputin was slain by Prince Yussopoff, of the Royal Russian household, after the monk's increasing power over the Czarist court caused the grand duke and others to decide his death was imperative.

Yussopoff was said to have fed Rasputin poisoned cakes, shot him, beat him over the head with a heavy iron poker and to have thrown his body through a hole in the ice in the Neva river.

Largely because of at least three motion-picture versions that have been hits in this country, Americans are familiar with the 60-year-old mystery of Mayerling involving the deaths of Archduke Rudolph, son of the Austro-Hungarian Emperor Francis Joseph, and the beautiful Baroness Marie Vetsera, granddaughter of a Greek banker.

The *New International Encyclopedia* says laconically, "Under cir-circumstances never explained he was found dead in his shooting lodge at Mayerling near Baden." That was Jan. 29, 1889, and there are at least fifty versions of what happened. Taking your pick among them, you believe either that Rudolph and Marie were or were not lovers; that the emperor did or did not command his son to break off a clandestine affair and return to his wife, the Archduchess Stephanie, daughter of Leopold II of Belgium; that the pair fulfilled a suicide pact or that one killed the other and then did away with him or herself, or was murdered by a third party. In March, 1949, appeared *Rudolph; The Tragedy of Mayerling* (Scribners) in which Carl Lonyay debunked the entire romance between the prince and Mary Vetsera. The dead girl, this Hungarian count related, was just fascinated by the prospect of being found dead in Rudolph's bed as a result of a joint suicide.

In February, 1937, Henry W. Lanier, son of the famous poet, Sidney Lanier, made the headlines by insisting the Mayerling Mystery was a gigantic hoax to permit Rudolph to escape from an embarrassing personal situation. According to Lanier the archduke escaped to South America where he lived until 1914. A son, about sixty in 1937, supposedly became an American citizen. Although Lanier's version was more detailed than most, it was not the only or the first to suggest that if any man was found dead at Mayerling, it was not Rudolph. Anyway, if Rudolph did get away he was one Hapsburg who lost interest in thrones. Much truer to form were the dozens of impostors who said they were Archduke John Salvator of Tuscany, another Hapsburg, who disappeared in 1890 while sailing around Cape Horn. Because he ran off with one Milly Stubel, a commoner, the archduke had been disinherited. He took the name of plain John Orth and became a soldier of fortune. All 28 who accompanied him on the ocean trip presumably were drowned, but John Orth kept appearing all over the world for two decades.

It is, of course, not only royalty who "die hard." The two Tichbourne trials are among the most famous in English history. They also resulted from a death at sea: that of Roger Charles Tichbourne, believed drowned in 1854 off the coast of Brazil. Although his estate was settled the next year, his bereaved mother refused to believe that her son was dead. She employed detectives to find him and advertised in publications all over the world. About ten years later, from Wagga Wagga, New South Wales, there arrived a man of suitable age and appearance whom the mother accepted as her son. Two long court trials followed and the impostor, Arthur Orton, was convicted of perjury. The testimony revealed the tremendous efforts to which he had gone to acquaint himself with family lore. The mother, however, still refused to have her illusions destroyed, and when Orton died in 1898, his coffin was inscribed, "Sir Roger Charles Doughty Tichbourne."

In July, 1932, Captain Alfred Loewenstein, Belgian financier, was reported by the pilot to have fallen into the English channel during a flight from Croyden, England, to Brussels. Because his death was bound to affect many adversely, they were easy believers of seemingly endless rumors that the captain had been seen in different parts of the world. Exactly the same occurred after the suicide of Otto Krueger, Swedish match king, in Paris. The most widely circulated tale was that the coffin sent to Stockholm carried a wax mummy. Krueger was supposed to have feigned suicide to escape the wrath of those affected adversely by the crash of his financial empire.

Col. T. E. Lawrence, the celebrated Lawrence of Arabia, was killed in an automobile accident in England but shortly afterwards was "seen" in Italy on his way to Africa and Asia to resume his troublemaking. On Aug. 20, 1946, the Louisville *Courier-Journal* used the following Associated Press story with a two-column AP wirephoto captioned, "He or history is wrong," showing the appeal this sort of thing has, to news editors at least:

New York, Aug. 19.—White-bearded Edward James Monroe of Jacksonville, Fla., was introduced at a press conference today by the publisher and physical culturist, Bernarr Macfadden, as 131 years old and a son of the fifth President of the United States.

Monroe said at the conference at Macfadden's office that he was born July 4, 1815, on the outskirts of Richmond, Va., a son of President James Monroe by a third wife.

"How can this be?" a reporter asked Macfadden after he had learned from an encyclopedia that Monroe had one wife and was survived by two daughters.

BERNARR TAKES HIS WORD FOR IT

"Well," said Macfadden, "we have only his word for it. He certainly is an old man."

Monroe, clutching a cane in one hand and a Confederate flag in the other, surveyed the quizzical reporters and answered questions.

Any life-prolonging hobbies?

"The Golden Rule. I want done to me what I do unto others."

Girls?

"I love them. You can't do without them."

Food?

"I eat anything."

Tobacco and liquor?

Monroe, removing a cigar from his mouth, said he seldom smokes. He said he drinks whiskey only "to make it sociable."

The reason for his self-acclaimed great age, Monroe said, is his habit of sleeping 15 hours at a stretch on sandy beaches.

"There is a magnetic current in the earth," interjected Macfadden, "and the body absorbs it."

The reason for the press conference?

Neither Monroe nor Macfadden offered any.

In the "letter" column of *Life* for June 20, 1938, appeared the picture of a nonogenarian who, a Chattanooga correspondent wrote, had convinced a large audience in that city that he was Jesse James, notorious Missouri outlaw who presumably was killed in 1882 by Bob Ford. The old man's story, supported by 54 depositions and other proof, was that the body mistaken for his was that of Charles Bigelow with whom he had switched clothes and weapons. He, James, had lived for 51 years in Colorado as Jim Walker, he claimed. The furore created by this claimant was nothing compared with that which followed the streamer-headline story, "Jesse James Is Alive," in the May 10, 1948 Lawton (Okla.) *Constitution,* the writing of which gave Frank O. Hall, city editor, the greatest thrill of his career, according to his account of the story in the May 28, 1948 *Editor and Publisher.*

J. Frank Dalton, the Lawton Jesse James, also said it was Bigelow who was killed in 1882. The novelist, Homer Croy, "took care" of the situation rather well in the Nov. 14, 1948 *American Weekly* and in his book, *Jesse James Was My Neighbor* (Duell, Sloan, and Pearce, 1949). Upon interviewing Dalton, Croy noticed that the impostor's third finger on the left hand was intact whereas James had shot off the digit's last joint when fifteen years old. Nor did Dalton correctly identify Red Fox, a race horse belonging to James, nor did he recall correctly the number of children born to James or other historical details.

The American badman who posthumously has kept more showmen and authors alive than all the others combined, was John Wilkes Booth, the crazed actor who assassinated Abraham Lincoln on April 14, 1865 in Washington's Ford Theater. Still on exhibition is a well-preserved mummy, identified as that of John St. Helen who died in 1903 at Enid, Okla. where he had been known as David E. George. Years earlier, believing himself to be dying, he had confessed to Finis Bates, a Memphis lawyer, that he was, in sooth, the tragedian. His corpse is fractured and wounded to correspond with Booth's bodily characteristics, and an X-ray reveals in the stomach a signet ring marked with either a B or S.

Although the story which Bates put together in book form has been investigated and declared fantastic many times, the Booth controversy goes on, hardly a year passing without a fresh contribution to the literature. St. Helen or George, of course, was not the only claimant; there were scores of others, each with his coterie of believers. According to Prof. Frank J. Foster of the University of Alabama, at least 200 collectors claim to have the pistol with which Lincoln was killed.

It all could have been avoided had there been less secrecy regarding the post mortem examination and burial of John Wilkes Booth following his suicide or fatal shooting by a soldier, Boston Corbett, as he emerged from the burning barn on the Richard Garrett farm near Bowling Green, Va., April 26, 1865. The testimony of the hotel clerk and surgeon who identified the body has been given an historical going-over such as no cross examiner ever attempted of a living witness. Articles and books have been built around minor discrepancies in it. The legend is kept alive and may never die.

Neither, to return to Adolf Hitler, will his. To date it is not even nicely started. Before many years it will not be merely the incorrigible German Nazis who will yearn, "If Hitler had only lived." It really should be, "If only we had irrefragable proof that he didn't." Those who objected to publication of the upside-down picture of Benito Mussolini and his girl friend will wish that there had been another like it, with a Berlin dateline.

Living legends, all that has preceded in this chapter should have made clear, are both fruitful of journalistic copy and important in influencing public opinion on political matters. Of greater and more lasting importance are what, by contrast, may be called "dead" legends, or legends concerning historical persons or events. Throughout history they have been a leading factor in the establishment and promotion of group solidarity, especially nationalism.

By definition legends are greatly exaggerated or untrue accounts of some persons or incidents that may have had some basis in fact but which have been distorted in the telling. They may arise in many ways; imposture, of which several examples have been given, is only one. Incorrect interpretations of experiences, false inferences from actual occurrences or from incidents that might have happened or from incidents that actually happened but not to the person to whom accredited are among the sources of origin. Mostly those that are important on a large scale concern national heroes who, however, may become heroic partly or largely as a result of legendary accounts concerning them. Regarding the origin of local traditions, Lord Raglan wrote: "There are various ways in which a local tradition, so called, comes into existence. In the first place there is to be found, in most rural areas, some clergyman or schoolmaster with a smattering of history or archeology who enjoys speculating about the past and invariably ends, if he does not begin, by regarding himself as a more than sufficient authority for his own statements. He is regarded as the expert, and nobody dreams of questioning what he says, or of checking it with even the most readily accessible works of reference.

"Then there is the person who seeks to add interest and romance to a house or a neighborhood by transferring to it some story which he, or more often she, has heard or read in some other connection. The lady's story or the vicar's statement may gain a temporary vogue, and being taken down from the lips of some rustic by a collector of folklore or local historian, be accepted as a piece of genuine 'folk memory.'

"Then there is the snowball type of story, which grows as it goes. The process is somewhat like this:

"Stage 1—This house dates from Elizabethan times, and, since it lies close to the road which the Virgin Queen must have taken when traveling from X to Y, it may well have been visited by her.

"Stage 2—This house is said to have been visited by Queen Elizabeth on her way from X to Y.

"Stage 3—The state bedroom is over the entrance. It is this room which Queen Elizabeth probably occupied when she broke her journey here on her way from X to Y.

"Stage 4—According to a local tradition, the truth of which there is no reason to doubt, the bed in the room over the entrance is that in which Queen Elizabeth slept, when she broke her journey here from X to Y." [1]

Other legends originate as deliberate lies, to enhance a reputation or to increase the sale of a book or out of high motives of patriotism. Captain John Smith started one of our most romantic legends—that of his heroic rescue from death by Pocahontas—after the Indian princess had married John Rolfe and was being lionized by London society. Smith, very much "down on his luck" at the time, came out with *General Historie* in 1624. It contained the rescue story which had not been included in his *True Relation,* published in 1608, in which he told of his excursion to Chickahominy where he fell in with hostile Indians, became the intended target for about 25 of their arrows and finally was captured by them. According to his earlier report he talked his way out of the predicament by convincing the chief that the English king would seek tremendous revenge in case anything happened to him. His only mention of Pocahontas was that she was adept at turning cart wheels. At the time she must have been about twelve years old. Although none of the historic markers at old Jamestown today relate the dramatic rescue tale, there are to be purchased there post cards which make Pocahontas appear to be at least in late adolescence, beautiful of course, and very appealing as she

[1] Reprinted from *The Hero,* by Lord Raglan, by permission of Methuen & Co., Ltd. Copyright, 1936, by Methuen & Co., Ltd., London.

flings herself between her kinsfolk and the unfortunate John whose head is resting on the chopping block.

"So what?" asks the product of the public schools in which the Pocahontas story has been related solemnly to a dozen or more generations of boys and girls. "It's a good story and it doesn't change history very much. Certainly it doesn't hurt anybody. In fact, it helps because it's a good example of courage and because justice triumphs." Such an attitude, of course, epitomizes the importance of legends. They glamorize the past; in fact, in a young country, they help create a past of which to be proud. Thus they help prove that a nation (or any group to which they pertain) has a noble heritage, and make for unity and *esprit de corps*.

Legends make natural heroes seem more heroic, better models for youngsters to emulate. They help establish ideals to live up to. They teach lessons and help establish rules of conduct and maxims for future generations to follow and obey. Who can measure the effect on American thought and conduct of one of the most familiar and famous legends of them all: the George Washington cherry tree yarn? That story, which has the youthful George escaping punishment for destroying the tree by confessing, "Father, I cannot tell a lie; I did it with my little hatchet," was a plagiarism by Parson Mason Locke Weems in the fifth edition of his *Life of George Washington,* published in 1806, of a story included in *The Minstrel* by Dr. James Beattie, published in 1799 in London. The spurious anecdote is undoubtedly the best-known of all concerning the Revolutionary hero, despite its being dropped from their story-telling repertoire by many modern pedagogues.

When Weems wrote, the United States of America was still a mere infant, badly in need of patriotic feeling. Albert Bushnell Hart wrote in the January, 1910, *American Historical Review* that it was "a period when it was thought a moral duty to look upon the patriots of the Revolution and the fathers of the Constitution as demigods." After William Holmes McGuffey included the tale in the second of his famous Eclectic Readers, it was well on its way toward immortality along with the boy who stood on the burning deck, the young shepherd who cried "Wolf, wolf" too often, Mary and her woolly lamb, and hundreds of other old favorites.

Although immeasurable, as is almost every other factor connected with public opinion, the influence of historical legends can be imagined from a listing of a few of the best-known which, taken as true by school children, have been remembered more vividly than most so-called "straight" history, for example: Paul Revere whose ride was eulogized by Henry Wadsworth Longfellow although actually Revere was arrested by redcoats before he was able to awaken "every Middlesex village and farm"; Betsy Ross, who supposedly made the first American flag although proof that she did so is sadly lacking; Barbara Frietchie, glamorized by John Greenleaf Whittier although the window from which she defied the Confederates to "shoot if you must this old grey head" wasn't on a street over which "Stonewall" Jackson's men marched; John Brown, whose famous body mouldered, containing as murderous a soul as any fanatic ever had; Marcus Whitman, whose famous trip from Walla Walla to Washington has been proved to have been entirely unrelated to any effort to save Oregon Territory for the United States; the Bixby letter, supposedly written by Abraham Lincoln to a mother who lost five sons in the Civil War, which, if actually written, was a beautiful blunder as not all of the lady's sons became soldiers and not all who did so were killed, and so on.

There are legends about every important person in American history. Since they are mostly anecdotal they do not alter greatly one's understanding of the broader aspects of history. It is significant, however, that often it is the fiction that outlives the fact and may be all that the so-called average person knows about a particular historical figure. For example, to a majority of those who have heard of him at all, Captain Miles Standish probably would be identified as the fellow who sent John Alden to propose to Priscilla for him. The best-known anecdote concerning John Quincy Adams is the apocryphal one that Anne Royall, editor of *Paul Pry,* stole his clothes while he was in swimming so as to obtain an interview with him, given currency by another president, Harry S. Truman, in a press conference as recently as March, 1948.

By means of legends some persons, whose contributions to national security or progress or civilization or what have you were comparatively meager, are made posthumously into heroes. The role of the famous McGuffey readers, of which a total of 120 million were sold over a period of 75 years, in magnifying and perpetuating some of them has been mentioned. There also have been thousands if not millions of orators on the Fourth of July and other occasions and writers galore who perpetuated legends. There also was Elbert Hubbard whose periodical, *The Philistine,* books, and pamphlets, and especially his *Scrapbooks,* had an effect on adults up to his death May 7, 1915, on the *Lusitania,* similar to that which the McGuffey readers had on school children. Typical sample of Hubbard effulgence was the conclusion of the piece, "The Message to Garcia," wherein he magnified the importance of a minor Spanish-American War incident: "My heart goes out to the man who does his work when the boss is away as well as when he is at home. And the man who, when given a letter [actually it was an oral message] to Garcia, quietly takes the missive, without asking idiotic questions, and with no lurking intention of chucking it into the nearest sewer, or of doing aught else but deliver it, never gets 'laid off' nor has to go on strike for higher wages. Civilization is just one long, anxious search for such individuals. Anything such a man asks shall be granted; his kind is so rare that no employer can afford to let him go. He is wanted in every city, town and village—in every office, shop, store and factory. The world cries out for such; he is needed and needed badly—the man who can 'Carry a message to Garcia.' " The man, incidentally, was the late Maj. Andrew S. Rowan.

The real importance of legends is the glamorous aura with which they surround many of the best-known historical personages and events, which means the general attitudes towards a nation's past that they help create or fortify. It makes a difference whether people believe their presidents, generals, and other leaders were supermen or rakes. Any group has a tendency to forget or ignore its less reputable predecessors and to apotheosize its worthy ancestors. Once built up as demigods they become accepted as having had infallible wisdom and prophetic vision so that their words continue cogent in political and other debate for centuries after their decease. The quickest way for any would-be moulder of public opinion to kill his influence with some patriotic groups is to question publicly whether the halo with which a dead hero has been endowed was entirely deserved. Rather, it is almost sure-fire to be able to ring in a couple of great names as those of men who unquestionably would favor what one is proposing were they still around to participate in the discussion. Motion pictures with historical themes contribute to the collective picture of America's past greats as impeccable. How successful, for instance, would the cinematic version of "Custer's Last Stand" have been had it shown the Indian fighter to have been a colossal blunderer who virtually sacrificed his two hundred men because of an "insatiable glory-lust," to use the descriptive phrase employed by E. V. Westrate in *Those Fatal Generals* (Knight, 1936). It simply could not be done.

Folktales

When it is recognized as such a legend loses much, if not most or all of its effectiveness. Not so the folktale which, though known to be make-believe, is influential because of the moral involved, the lesson it teaches, or the extent to which it "catches" the spirit of an era. As regards a number of figures of antiquity it is not known whether they are legendary or folklore characters. In this category are Helen of Troy, King Arthur, Roland, William Tell, and Robin Hood. The United States is too young to have any comparable list, the closest candidate probably being Johnny Appleseed, supposed to have been an itinerant preacher, Jonathan Chapman, who traveled through what is now the Middle West planting apple trees. Such heroes of American folklore as Paul Bunyan, John Henry, Pecos Bill, and Kemp Morgan never have been taught as anything but purely imaginative characters and many of the tales told of them are of contemporary rather than pioneer origin. They can, however, have as important an effect upon story lovers, as witness the influence of the Grimm brothers' fairy tales, Aesop's fables, Arabian Nights, Mother Goose, Tyll Eulenspiegel, Baron Munchausen, and even Robinson Crusoe.

Paul Bunyan certainly exemplifies the American spirit. For him and his blue ox, Babe, no job was too difficult. For the lumbermen who invented him he doubtless provided a boost to morale and surcease from the privations which their labors entailed. Likewise, John Henry personified the aspirations of railroad workers threatened with unemployment because of mechanical inventions. In folktales the narrative, not the historical, sense is uppermost. They are "good stories" which succeed mostly to the extent that they "catch" the spirit of the times and endure to the extent that they express the spirit of *all* times as far as the group which they glorify is concerned.

Just which of the American folktales will survive with the force of real legends (fortified by their association with real names) it is impossible to tell. Whole bookloads of American folktales now are appearing, among the best being *The American Imagination At Work,* by Ben C. Clough (Knopf, 1947) and *Tall Tale America,* by Walter Blair (Coward-McCann, 1942). Says Clough in his Introduction: "For the American story-audience, fortunately, is not hypercritical. The good reader or listener will gladly suspend disbelief if he can. The dialect may be wrong, the plot unlikely, the incidents impossible; no matter, if the narrative gift is there. As a matter of fact, a little improbability has never seemed amiss in American narratives. It is likely that from the days of the *Mayflower's* adventurous trip to those of the hardly credible atomic bomb our romantic history has predisposed us toward fantastic fictions."

If this appraisal is correct, a word of warning might be thrown in here for the newspaperman to watch out for some of the "old standbys" of the type which Alexander Woollcott used to be so fond of collecting, which crop up with fiendish regularity in speeches by famous persons, contributions from readers, and even over press association wires. One such is of the son who returns home wealthy after many years and is murdered by his aged parents before he has a chance to reveal his identity to them. Another is the wedding party sacrificed one at a time to a pack of wolves so that the bride and bridegroom might escape—a yarn pooh-poohed often by Viljhalmur Stefansson who says wolves don't travel in packs. Since World War II there have been a series of folktales, or rumors if you will, concerning undertakers (morticians, as they prefer it), the most prolific of which concerns a mixup in shipping two bodies east so that some unknown gets buried in Arlington Cemetery while an admiral or a general is discovered in the coffin at a simple rural or small-town burial.

Perhaps the strongest bid for immortality in recent times was made by those who invented and helped perpetuate the exploits of an American fighting man named Kilroy. How the practice of inscribing "Kilroy was here" all around the globe originated nobody knows. One popular version is that a sergeant in the Pacific whose name actually was Kilroy once went A.W.O.L. and when he returned to his base discovered that his outfit had moved on. In the hope that his comrades in arms might trace him, Kilroy wrote his famous message all along

the route he took in the attempt to find them. Regardless of how it
started, as Bill Davidson wrote in "Who's Kilroy?" in the Dec. 27,
1946, *Collier's*: " 'Kilroy was here' is lettered on the very tip of the
torch of the Statue of Liberty, on the bullet-scarred base of the Marco
Polo Bridge in China, and, reverentially, near the eternal flame of the
Unknown Soldier under the Arc de Triomphe in Paris. When a
famous steeplejack was hired recently to do some work on the top-
most structure of the George Washington Bridge in New York, he
found these words tauntingly inscribed in the most inaccessible section
of one of the towers."

In his column, "It Takes All Kinds," in the Chicago *Sun* for Jan. 12,
1947, the late Lloyd Lewis compared Kilroy with a fictitious Cogle
during the Mexican War.

Myths

If a folktale of the Paul Bunyan, Kilroy, or Cogle type is believed,
it becomes a myth. That means, to paraphrase Martha Warren Beck-
with in *Folklore in America* (Folklore Foundation, 1931), that it
becomes an imaginative account to explain something that is otherwise puzzling about nature, life, or social usage. Accepted as true,
any one of the stories would fit the definition given by Hamilton Basso
in *Mainstream* (Reynal, Hitchcock, 1943): "By myth is meant specifically a parable, allegory or folktale that ostensibly relates some historical event, usually of such character as to explain some practice,
belief or institution."

Thus, given credence, the Paul Bunyan tall tales would settle the
argument as to the origin of the Great Lakes, St. Lawrence River,
Thousand Islands, Rocky Mountains, and much of the rest of the
geography of the North American continent. The existence of an
invisible or at least extremely elusive Kilroy would explain signatures
and probably all other markings, to be found in out-of-the-way places;
and all military blunders could be blamed with impunity upon the
equally difficult-to-find Cogle.

That any such credulity could exist in our supposedly enlightened
and scientifically minded age seems impossible. The trend is away
from belief in venerable myths which, shattered, either disappear or
at best linger as folktales. Typical example of operation of this process
—the exact reverse of that whereby a folktale becomes a myth—was

described in the Aug. 5, 1946 *Life* as follows: "Like the Vikings ten centuries ago, the tradition-loving British of the Isle of Man met in the open on Tynwald Hill on July 5 to hear the laws passed by their local Parliament which, after Iceland's, is the oldest in the world. The procession to the hill was led by the swordbearer, followed by Air Vice Marshal Geoffrey Bromet, the new lieutenant governor. They followed the same path, 365 paces long and strewn with reeds to ward off evil, that 'Orry the Dane' walked a millennium ago. By custom any Manxman could protest at this time against any injustices of law.

"Beside tailless cats, the Manxmen also possess some of the world's best tales. They say their island was formed when Finn MacCool, an Irish giant, hurled a clod of earth across the Irish Sea at a Scottish giant—and missed. Later the Little People came and they are honored with a bridge. Whenever a Manxman passes, he tips his hat and says, 'God day, Little People, I wish you well.' "

Fantastic as the Bunyan and MacCool tales may seem to be, they are no more so than most of the explanations which peoples of all kinds have given for similar phenomena. Primitive myths unquestionably originated as part of man's early quest for understanding and certainty. Sun, moon, planets, and stars; day and night; the seasons; birth and death; winds and tides and similar natural phenomena were frightening unless rationalized by means of myths. Most popular mythology of the past, probably because it was so beautifully recorded, was that of the Greeks who postulated scores of gods and goddesses to account, not only for every geographical and astronomical phenomenon but for human emotions and aspirations as well. Not of factual origin, myths deal mostly with the supernatural; in fact, they might be considered to be legends regarding the supernatural. Many of them pertain to bygone days when deities presumably walked the earth and talked to men.

It is a gross error, however, to believe that myths are merely fantastic, imaginative, make-believe stories which appeal to only the primitive, ignorant, and illiterate. In the entire world today there are more people who believe in scientifically disprovable myths than there are those who do not. Virtually every great religion has its stories of how the universe and man originated. Because these accounts are inconsistent and contradictory, they cannot all be true. Nevertheless, each is sacred to its believers, unrecognizable by them as mythological, whereas those of all other groups are outlandish, superstitious, profane, and heathenish.

This, of course, is just another way of saying that no person is aware of his own myths as such. To him what another might call myth is true, as Santa Claus, the Easter Rabbit, and the stork are jokes to adults but actualities to children. Certainly the Japanese people did not recognize the fallacy (if that is what it was) of their belief that their emperor is a direct descendant of the sun god. Nor do Mohammedans believe that their prophet merely suffered from auditory hallucinations. Says Kimball Young: "The myth and legend are adult extensions of the infantile world of fantasy and make-believe. For the adult they furnish socially acceptable frameworks for understanding the past and the present and for defining future responses. They give continuity to social reality. They are part and parcel of the social world in which we live and move and have our being. The particular errors of perception and memory which play a part in the rise of myths and legends are merely the natural psychological processes by which the social reality grows up through group participation. They gratify the wish to appear superior to other groups. Our own egos expand as we participate in groups imagined sacred or motivated by the highest ideals. All myths and legends are self-justificatory. In this way they are like rationalizations; but they are more continuous, more integrated and furnish something of order and meaning to the world. While myths may have less basis in fact than legends, the psychological mechanisms in their development are much the same. There is more than a dash of imagination in the myth. There is perhaps less concrete fact at the outset, but it remains, nevertheless, as important as the legend in serving as the foundation of ideologies and as an interpretative tool in getting about in our world. We may say that legends are modified accounts of the past events and of historic personages, whereas myths are imaginative accounts of the meaning of life. In this sense they are the basis of philosophy. In other aspects they are a projection of our wishes into the future. Yet the differences between myth and legend are rather of degree than of kind." [2]

Of the relationship between myth and ritual, which obviously is close, there is a difference of opinion among scholars. Some say rituals originated to symbolize and perpetuate myths; others believe

[2] From *Social Psychology*. Copyright, 1947, by Appleton-Century-Crofts, Inc.

that myths arose to explain rituals. Centuries later it doesn't make too much difference, certainly not in the study of public opinion, except as exposés of the paganish origins of some rite which he considers sacred might cause someone to be less superstitious. A study of the history of religions leaves no doubt that they all borrowed from each other, often in the attempt to proselytize.

Myths explain and justify the *status quo*. A myth-ridden society is a stable one, but it also is a static one. In it truth is eternal, moral values are absolutistic, heresy is punished severely. *Excessive belief in myths handicaps and even neutralizes whatever powers of independent investigation a man may possess. Such a man changes his attitudes and opinions much less frequently and more slowly than he who has been emancipated from acceptance of unscientific explanations of origins and meanings.*

Not all myths are supernaturally sanctioned, and the social effect of many which are largely or entirely divorced from religion or superstition is as great as of those which supposedly do obtain support from the unseen. There are myths in every department of human thought. Some are of long standing or recurrent; others merely transitory but of great influence while they last. Mention of a few which have come to be recognized for what they are (or were) should suffice to illustrate that fact.

Military. Not only the French but the peoples of almost every other nation in the world, the Germans excepted, before 1940 considered the Maginot Line to be impregnable and France unconquerable because of it, the best-trained army in Europe and the greatest living military genius, General Gamelin. Hitler's armies shattered the myth in short order but a year later had the myth of their own invincibility destroyed by the Russians. Hitler never got to realize his ambition of sleeping in the Kremlin. Much of what was believed about the armed strength of the Russians and the Japanese was proved by events to be pure myth. The same was true in both world wars of what the Germans thought about the United States' inclination and ability to fight.

Nationalistic. All of our wars, American school children are taught, were righteous conflicts into which we were forced against our will. Other nations teach much the same regarding their own history, but not of that of each other. The Germans were not the only or the first to believe themselves the greatest people on earth. Myths of nationalistic superiority have gotten a good many would-be world conquerors into trouble. Millennial hopes have helped many downtrodden people to endure persecution. Excessive chauvinism also may be a characteristic of an area, as a state, within a nation, or of a city. Distorted maps to indicate a New Yorker's idea of America are not too grossly exaggerated; nor is there anything unreal about many of the jokes as to what a Texan thinks of his homeland.

Racial. Myths of the alleged superiority or inferiority of particular races or of nationality and other groups mislabeled as races, have resulted in horrible persecutions and slaughters. Hitler's exploitation of the racial superiority myth is familiar; so also is the use the Ku Klux Klan makes of it. The subject of prejudice, including the angle of mythology connected with it, will be considered in Chapter 8.

Historical. Although a great many of the first settlers in the New World arrived here a step or two ahead of the sheriff, the myth is developing that every pioneer was a high-minded, moralistic man or woman of courage who fled his native land solely to enjoy freedom of religion, speech, press, and assembly. To be descended from super-selfmade men is even better than to have the sun as an ancestor. The myth of a glorious past is a part of any mature nation's heritage. It fortifies belief that its foreign policy always has been correct and that its domestic affairs have been conducted with such wisdom that it could not escape becoming what it believes itself to be—the best of all possible places to live.

Political. The Constitution is the most perfect document devised by man, and any suggestion of change is considered unpatriotic despite the fact that it has been amended more than twenty times. The Supreme Court is sacrosanct and appointment to it denotes the possession of great judicial knowledge, although the wisdom and even the patriotism of individual justices have been questioned. Attempts to increase the number of justices ("packing") is tantamount to undermining American institutions. Despite the development of governmental activity, there is still a lingering idea that government is best that governs least. In the face of global orientation of American foreign policy George Washington's attitude regarding entangling alliances is an article of faith as is his attitude regarding a third presidential term.

Science. The late Joseph Jastrow edited *The Story of Human Error* (D. Appleton-Century Co., 1936) to which an impressive array of leading scientists contributed chapters regarding the obstacles which had to be overcome in the fields of their specialties. A few random extracts from Jastrow's introductory chapter, "The Procession of Ideas," will suggest the conclusions to which most of them came: "Mind in the making follows no straightforward progression; its many wanderings in the quest for truth compose a cyclopedia of error and vain solutions far more than orderly annals of successful advance. . . . With little insight into physical operations he (meaning primitive man) creates a world of psychic magic, peopled with gods. . . . Current popular mentality still bears the impress of the ancestral primitive mind. . . . Not only *motive* but the *level of method* shapes inquiry; the beliefs of astrology proceed on the folklore level, elaborated by learned doctrine; the conclusions of astronomy are framed —with whatever measure of error and imperfection—on the scientific level of investigation. . . . Logically, settling things by authority is just a false method of arriving at conclusions; its practical utility and psychological satisfyingness override this objection. . . . The deference to authority, as well as the absorption in dialectic, becomes a habit of mind, defeating inquiry. . . . It is unfortunate that scholastic deductive logic came to be regarded as the model of logical procedure. . . . All argument by analogy is weak at best and treacherous besides. . . ." Among the myths which had to be overcome, Jastrow's study revealed, were: pre-Copernican astronomy; all astrology; the Hippocratic humours; phrenology; instincts; free will and rational thought; born criminals; lunacy as derived from the influence of the moon; vitalism; the fixity of species; inheritance of acquired characteristics; and many, many more. Developing today is a myth of a different kind which may prove to be the most dangerous of all: that science is bound to find the answer for every human problem.

Sociological. The social contract and other natural-rights theories describe the way in which organized society should have begun: by free men of their own volition electing to band together for mutual protection through obedience to and enforcement of law. It's good to conduct political and governmental affairs as if such were the case, but obviously isolated men could hardly antedate society itself. Much social work has proceeded in accordance with the Spencerian adage that poverty is natural and inevitable. A great many precepts which formerly had the strength of myths in influencing thought in this field today are being challenged: that delinquency is primarily the result of broken homes; that broken homes result from alcoholism; that alcoholism results from irreligion; that capital punishment prevents crime; that reformatories for juveniles prevent adult lawlessness; and so on.

Legal. With its fictions, presumptions, and axioms, the law, as it has developed from Anglo-Saxon days, is loaded down with mythology: that a corporation is to be considered as an individual; that anyone absent for seven years is dead; that no child under seven years of age is a reliable witness; that anyone able to distinguish between right and wrong is sane and strictly responsible for his acts; that anyone is innocent who has not been proved guilty beyond a reasonable doubt; that there is such a thing as a reasonably prudent man; that there is no wrong without a remedy; and so forth.

Moralistic. Americans are highly moralistic, and there always has been a Poor Richard, William Holmes McGuffey, Horatio Alger, Elbert Hubbard, or Edgar Guest around to encourage them in cultivation of the trait. Hence, no matter what inconsistency or even hypocrisy he may display in his actual behavior, there is hardly a citizen who would want to argue the negative of such axioms as: honesty is the best policy; virtue is its own reward; love finds a way; most sexual problems can be settled by marriage; every boy has an equal chance to become president; and many more like them.

The importance of the 120 million McGuffey readers in shaping the national character already has been mentioned. Typical of the simple homilies by which American idealism was taught was the following from the *Third Eclectic Reader*: "A poor widow, in a great need, approaches a merchant and asks for five dollars. The merchant gives her a check for the amount, which the widow presents at the bank for payment. When the banker pays out fifty dollars, the widow protests. The banker carries the story back to the generous merchant who then gives the widow five hundred dollars, 'for such honesty is poorly rewarded by even that sum.'" Another example, from the *Fourth Eclectic Reader*: "A traveler once fed a hungry Indian whom he happened to meet on the road. Many years later the traveler is captured by Indians, but manages to escape with the aid of the same Indian whom he once befriended," obviously a variation on the "Androcles and the Lion" theme.

Summarizing the effect of the McGuffey readers, the St. Louis *Star-Times* in its May 7, 1936, issue said:

Into his readers, William Holmes McGuffey, a Miami university professor, had crammed nuggets of knowledge he had mined during years of hard study.

They presented classical gems, rewritten proverbs, adapted fables, folklore, and myths, psalms, the cream of oratory and drama, fiction and history, and utterances of sage, statesman and poet.

In them, too, were combined proper proportions of adventure, love, humor and pathos; with perhaps an overdose on the subject of death and how properly to prepare for it.

Hardly a text in any of the books failed to emphasize some lessons in patriotism, honesty, politeness, courage or industry.

Another excellent study of the subject was "Social Ideas in McGuffey Readers," by D. A. Saunders in *Public Opinion Quarterly,* Winter, 1941.

Many a prominent American writer, especially during the roaring twenties when cynicism was an understandable literary reaction, has taken a rap at inconsistencies and hypocrisies in the American character. One of them was the Nobel Prize-winning Theodore Dreiser who contributed the following to the June, 1936 *Partisan Review and Anvil*: "Americanism, as I see it, is an illusion of national individuality, held by the great mass of our people in more or less emotional form, through which ideas of reform of government, of social systems, of art, etc., can be focused; essentially, it is the emotional, intangible, and often unconscious frame of reference with which most Americans compare whatever ideas they have or come into contact with. Americanism involves the associated illusions of such words as: individualism, the land of the free and the home of the brave, liberty, self-made man, pioneers, this is the best country in the world and you ought to be proud you were born here, the stars and stripes, etc. As I think of it, it is these deeply rooted, powerful associations, close to the very essence of feeling, and as such a positive force. It grew out of the cultural conditions of Western Europe, and is opposed to it in the same way that an acorn is opposed to an oak."

In his address to the 1935 graduating class of the University of Chicago, Robert Maynard Hutchins described some of the social

myths which he believed motivate the average American in his everyday activities: " 'Getting on' is the great American aspiration. And
here the demoralizing part comes in: the way to get on is to be 'safe,'
to be 'sound,' to be agreeable, to be inoffensive, to have no views on
important matters not sanctioned by the majority, by your superiors,
or by your group. We are convinced that by knowing the right people,
wearing the right clothes, saying the right things, holding the right
opinions, and thinking the right thoughts we shall all get on; we shall
all get on to some motion picture paradise, surrounded by fine cars,
refreshing drinks and admiring ladies. So persuasive is this picture that
we find politicians during campaigns making every effort to avoid saying anything; we find important people condoning fraud and corruption in high places because it would be upsetting to attack it; and
we find, I fear, that university presidents limit their public utterances
to platitudes. Timidity thus engendered turns into habit, and the
'stuffed shirt' becomes one of the characteristic figures of our age."

In *Knowledge for What?* Robert Lynd listed some "outstanding
assumptions in American life" with comments as follows:

"1. The United States is the best and greatest nation on earth and
always will remain so.

"2. Individualism, 'the survival of the fittest,' is the law of nature
and the secret of America's greatness; and restrictions on individual
freedom are un-American and kill initiative.

"*But:* No man should live for himself alone; for people ought to
be loyal and stand together and work for common purposes.

"3. The thing that distinguishes man from the beasts is the fact
that he is rational; and therefore man can be trusted, if let alone, to
guide his conduct wisely.

"*But:* Some people are brighter than others; and, as every practical
politician and businessman knows, you can't afford simply to sit back
and wait for people to make up their minds.

"4. Democracy, as discovered and perfected by the American people, is the ultimate form of living together. All men are created free
and equal, and the United States has made this fact a living reality.

"*But:* You would never get anywhere, of course, if you constantly
left things to popular vote. No business could be run that way, and of
course no businessman would tolerate it.

"5. Everyone should try to be successful.

"*But:* The kind of person you are is more important than how successful you are.

"6. The family is our basic institution and the sacred core of our national life.

"*But:* Business is our most important institution, and, since national welfare depends upon it, other institutions must conform to its needs.

"7. Religion and 'the finer things of life' are our ultimate values and the things all of us are really working for.

"*But:* A man owes it to his family to make as much money as he can.

"8. Life would not be tolerable if we did not believe in progress and know that things are getting better. We should, therefore, welcome new things.

"*But:* The old, tried fundamentals are best; and it is a mistake for busybodies to try to change things too fast or to upset the fundamentals.

"9. Hard work and thrift are signs of character and the way to get ahead.

"*But:* No shrewd person tries to get ahead nowadays by just working hard, and nobody gets rich nowadays by pinching nickels. It is important to know the right people. If you want to make money, you have to look and act like money. Anyway, you only live once.

"10. Honesty is the best policy.

"*But:* Business is business, and a businessman would be a fool if he didn't cover his hand.

"11. America is a land of unlimited opportunity, and people get pretty much what's coming to them here in this country.

"*But:* Of course, not everybody can be boss, and factories can't give jobs if there aren't jobs to give.

"12. Capital and labor are partners.

"*But:* It is bad policy to pay higher wages than you have to. If people don't like to work for you for what you offer them, they can go elsewhere.

"13. Education is a fine thing.

"*But:* It is the practical man who gets things done.

"14. Science is a fine thing in its place, and our future depends upon it.

"But: Science has no right to interfere with such things as business and our other fundamental institutions. The thing to do is to *use* science, but not let it upset things.

"15. Children are a blessing.

"But: You should not have more children than you can afford.

"16. Women are the finest of God's creatures.

"But: Women aren't very practical and are usually inferior to men in reasoning power and general ability.

"17. Patriotism and public service are fine things.

"But: Of course, a man has to look out for himself.

"18. The American judicial system insures justice to every man, rich or poor.

"But: A man is a fool not to hire the best lawyer he can afford.

"19. Poverty is deplorable and should be abolished.

"But: There never has been enough to go around, and the Bible tells us that 'The poor you have always with you.'

"20. No man deserves to have what he hasn't worked for. It demoralizes him to do so.

"But: You can't let people starve." [3]

In *Man Against Myth* (Little-Brown, 1947), Barrows Dunham attacks ten social myths, most of which he says are antidemocratic, aimed at freezing the *status quo*. His list, with brief summaries of his chapter-long discussions of each, follow:

1. *You can't change human nature.* A society in which nobody did anything for others could have no division of labor. Man is not inherently selfish.

2. *The rich are fit and the poor unfit.* There is confusion between natural and moral and legal law. A biological theory is not a sociological one also. The fit may not be good. Few qualities making for survival have moral value.

3. *There are superior and inferior races.* All scientific knowledge indicates the contrary. "In the whole of history, no Negroes or Jews, no members indeed of any 'inferior' races, have inflicted upon mankind sufferings which remotely compare with those inflicted by the self-styled 'superior' races."

4. *There are two sides to every question.* If there are only two alternatives and they are contradictory, one must be false. "The prin-

[3] From *Knowledge for What?* Copyright, 1939. by Princeton University Press.

ciple becomes simply a counter which is moved about in an effort to forestall defeat."

5. *Thinking makes it so.* Muddiness often is mistaken for depth. The earth existed for 500,000 years before human beings inhabited it. We don't know for certain that there is no cosmic consciousness, but we do know that for all scientific purposes the hypothesis is unnecessary.

6. *You cannot mix art and politics.* It is unlikely that there can be many works of art which have no reference to life and to the problems of living. Utility doesn't necessarily corrupt beauty. "To decide the beauty of a work of art is one thing and to decide what effect it will have because it is beautiful is quite another."

7. *You have to look out for yourself.* A ruling elite has many blindnesses, but the most dangerous is its belief that people never learn. Ethics is an instrument of power because it is an instrument of justification and persuasion.

8. *All problems are merely verbal.* "Every devout semanticist regards himself as an island of sense in an ocean of absurdity." If the views of the semanticists are correct, there can be no science of anything.

9. *Words will never hurt me.* The real meanings of words are fixed by social conventions and they change. Pinning of bad labels on persons and movements is injurious to them.

10. *You cannot be free and safe.* Security is itself as much an incentive as profits. It "is not necessarily incompatible with incentive and cannot be a source of universal idleness."

Only a reading of this splendid book in its entirety can give an adequate impression of the author's clever refutation of these and other popular platitudes.

Economics. In our business civilization, the "folklore of capitalism" constitutes perhaps our most important mythology. In his book, *The Folklore of Capitalism* (Yale University, 1937) Thurman W. Arnold wrote: "It is a national mythology which gives the great industrial organization an established place in society. This business myth has affected psychological motives in our daily life." To summarize Arnold's book here is impossible. It is a cogent roundup of the many ways in which generation after generation is indoctrinated with the idea that *laissez faire,* or—to use its modern name—free enterprise is the best of all possible economic systems and that governmental activity, in the public interest, if unwanted by business, is evil. Whereas the private corporation can count as valuable assets any capital improvements, when government invests in a new building or other public works, it goes on the liability side of the balance sheet.

Despite the many failures of classical economists to predict correctly, using their cycles and curves and applying their supposedly immutable laws, belief that such absolute economic laws exist is persistent. Presumably there is such a thing as an Economic Man who heeds the laws of supply and demand, marginal utility, diminishing returns, and so forth as reverently as though they were God-made and not merely man-made. Attempts still are made to draw analogies between the biological and commercial worlds, with emphasis upon struggles for existence and survivals of the fittest. Such fallaciousness helps justify the *status quo*. And that is the original purpose and main function of myths of any kind which cease to be effective only when they are recognized as such. It is in the best interests of everyone who profits from the existing order to do his utmost to prevent that from happening.

CHAPTER SEVEN

TABOOS; SUPERSTITIONS

Major obstacles to clear thinking regarding contemporary problems are unscientific ideas and mental habits inherited from prescientific times.

Taboos

A sports announcer was broadcasting a football game over a nation-wide network. Late in the final quarter a halfback broke away from his tacklers and dashed down the field, apparently headed for a touchdown. The crowd "went mad," as the saying goes, and the announcer was so carried away by the excitement in the stands that he completely forgot himself and exclaimed into his microphone: "Look at that son of a bitch run!"

Immediately he was cut off the air, and the station played a few minutes of organ music instead of completing the broadcast of the game. The announcer subsequently was fined $1,000 and suspended from broadcasting. He had broken a taboo.

Although President Truman made the familiar expression somewhat less disreputable by using the initials, "s.o.b." in referring to a newspaper columnist and radio commentator in the spring of 1949, it probably will be some time before it can be used with impunity by most other public officials, or by schoolteachers, editorial writers, and broadcasters. Within the past decade, however, it *has* become possible to use the expression spelled out, rather than with initials and dashes, when it appears in direct quotation in a newspaper story. Magazine-article writers, book authors, and playwrights have enjoyed the freedom for an even longer period as is usual in cases involving matters of public taste.

The unhappy announcer's punishment was loss of his job. It is
doubtful whether in addition he suffered from social ostracism. Such,
however, might very well have been the case had he used any of a
number of four-letter words of Anglo-Saxon derivation which are
taboo in almost all mixed companies. Or if he had committed any of
an interminable list of other offenses, of either act or word, the exact
nature of which would depend upon the public involved. In every
social group there are things which just are not done, subjects which
simply are not proper topics of conversation. A sizeable part of a
child's lesson in what constitutes good manners is what one does not
do in public, what one does not mention outside the family circle or,
in some cases, even within it. Such proscriptions, in other words, are
social in origin and nature. They are a forceful means of social control, defenders of the *status quo,* and *obstacles to the development of
a public opinion which might tend to bring about change, because they
stifle frank and open discussion or conduct.*

As popularly used today a taboo, according to Archibald Lyall in
The Future of Taboo in These Islands (K. Paul, Trench, Trubner,
1936) is "an unwritten and largely arbitrary regulation which governs
the conduct of daily life, and for the breach of which the penalty is
also unwritten, ill-defined but always social in its character." Strictly
speaking, however, a modern social "thou shalt not" is not a taboo.
Properly used that word, one of the few of Polynesian origin in the
English language, describes the elaborate system of supernaturally
sanctioned prohibitions which Captain James Cook and other explorers observed in the South Seas in the last quarter of the eighteenth
century. As defined by Hutton Webster in *Taboo* (Stanford, 1942),
"Taboos are prohibitions which, when violated, produce automatically in the offender a state of ritual disability—'taboo sickness'—
only relieved, when relief is possible, by a ceremony of purification." [1]

As they existed not only among the Polynesians but the world
over among primitive peoples, including the ancestors of civilized
Western man, taboos were in effect the negative mores of a society.
A taboo signified both a sacred and an impure or forbidden thing. It
was something that a person believed he could not approach, touch,

[1] Reprinted from *Taboo,* by Hutton Webster, with the permission of the author and
of the publishers, Stanford University Press.

or name without grave danger. Sigmund Freud in *Totem and Taboo* (Moffatt, Yard, 1918) compared taboos to Emmanuel Kant's "categorical imperatives" which tended to act compulsively and rejected all conscious motivation. Freud distinguished between a taboo and a religious rule, the former not being derived from a commandment from a deity. He discovered their origin in the ambivalence of emotions, meaning the simultaneous attraction to and repulsion from an object or idea.

Other scholars, almost all of them taking an anthropological approach, trace the origin of taboos to animism which Freud himself considered to have been the "first world system," that is, the first conception of early man to explain the forces dominating his environment. The animistic world was one in which unseen or supernatural forces dominated the activities of humans. In fact, the principal if not the sole activity of the spirits, goblins, witches, fairies, pixies, elves, leprechauns, demons, or whatever they were, presumably was to make man's lot happier if pleased with his behavior, quite the opposite if displeased. Consequently, it was good sense to observe carefully the relationships between causes and effects so as to determine what the unseen favored and what they disfavored. Then to devise ways to court favor, avoid disfavor and, particularly, to undo the harm that might otherwise result through even innocent violation of a law formulated on the basis of such experience.

How many specific taboos originated is suggested by the reports of anthropologists. One reported that a member of the Central Australian Warramunga tribe ate some forbidden fruit which was considered sacred and only fit to be consumed by the chief. No one was surprised when he became seriously ill. Actually, the observer contended, he was suffering from an acute case of dysentery but the natives thought they knew better. Similarly another anthropologist told of a Maori woman who died shortly after eating food set aside for the chieftain's children. Her guilt, in her own mind, was not lessened by the fact that she did not know the food was taboo when she ate it. Her death probably was due solely to fright.

Primitive man believed that any illness or accident was punishment because he had broken a taboo. Thus he blamed any misfortune upon some unusual experience in case he was unable to trace it to any already existent taboo; and so new taboos came into being. By the time comparatively modern scholars got around to studying them, the systems were elaborate and often complicated; significantly, they were not the same for all groups. What they had in common was their all-inclusiveness and their retrospective expediency. In taboo fear is systematized. It is, in fact, the most ancient legislative code of humanity, meaning that man's relationship to other persons, especially as regards their most important activities, was regulated, as were his relationships with places and objects.

It would be impossible as well as superfluous to attempt to list even the most important taboos. In addition to those which originated as the result of observing the coincidences between events and misfortunes, there were some imposed by rulers in the attempt to protect their own persons and to preserve certain foods, places, and things for their own use. So there developed sacred persons as well as sacred things and places. Many rulers were not allowed to set foot on the ground, or they carried heavy umbrellas to shield themselves from the elements or from the eyes of their subjects. In pre-V-J Day Japan, even to gaze upon the emperor was taboo. Days of the week or year, numbers, strangers, corpses, objects destroyed by lightning or other so-called "acts of God" were tabooed. Taboos preserved and protected tribal customs regarding marriage, family life, property ownership, respect for authority, and almost everything else. Once established they were self-enforcing as the punishment was believed to be automatic. Consequently even innocent violators of a taboo might be killed or ostracized for the protection of the rest of the group, or, in some cases, they underwent purification ceremonies. These might include self-mutilation or sacrifice or symbolic rituals.

It is natural that there should develop experts in ridding afflicted persons of their taboo sicknesses, so passing of the taboo from one of a lower station to one of a higher order, such as a medicine man or priest, became common. One typical way was for a witch doctor to place his feet on the abdomen of the person who had eaten forbidden food so that the transfer could take place. Another was for a helper to touch a stick to the taboo victim, tie it to his own body and then submerge himself in water. There he untied the stick and threw it as far as possible. In that way the taboo was transferred from the man to the stick and thence to the sea where it could do no harm.

These acts are entirely irrational, of course, but hardly more so than the precautions some moderns take in particular situations; as, for example, throwing a pinch of spilled salt over the left shoulder, saying "God bless you" or "Gesundheit" after sneezing, or knocking on wood when making a statement regarding one's good fortune. These and similar practices are vestiges of animism as popularly understood. Most of those who engage in them laughingly explain they are just making fun, but often the laugh is more than a wee bit strained and nervous-sounding. Just to satisfy curiosity, the best research indicates the following: (1) salt once was used as money, explaining the expression "to earn (be worth) his salt." Possessing value, it was used frequently as a sacrifice to the gods, and its loss was important. Evil spirits were believed to hover on one's left side; hence the direction in which salt was thrown to appease them; (2) as explained in Chapter 5 the post-sneeze expressions had their origin in the belief that evil spirits could enter or leave the body unless controlled by magical expressions; (3) knocking on wood may have originated in the days when men lived in frail huts outside of which evil spirits supposedly lingered. The knocking in such cases would be for the purpose of noise-making when speaking of matters about which the spirits might become jealous.

As explained in Chapter 3 many wedding customs likewise originated in attempts to prevent jealousy on the part of evil spirits. Mourning probably began in attempts to convince the ghosts of the deceased that the mourners were in no way responsible for their deaths. Some primitives used to carry out corpses feet first so that they could not look back upon their abodes. When hardly any death was recognized to have resulted from natural causes, the dying often were isolated, abandoned, or buried alive to safeguard the living. Death houses usually were taboo; whole tribes might leave a death scene or abandon crops or other near-by objects. The deceased's possessions might be destroyed or buried with him in the belief the ghost would be angry if anyone were to use his things. Tracing genealogies among some primitive tribes was virtually impossible because of the belief that a person's name was part of him and died with him. To avoid summoning their owners from the shades, the names of the dead never were spoken except by sorcerers imploring their aid in some matter. It was an important development when man changed from fearing to worshiping his ancestors, but both systems tended to fortify the *status quo* and to discourage the development of public opinion as we understand it today.

Censorship

Wrote Sir James George Frazer in *Garnered Sheaves* (Macmillan, 1931) "On the taboo were grafted the golden fruits of law and morality, while the parent stem dwindled slowly into the sour crabs and empty husks of popular superstition on which the swine of modern society are still content to feed." Superstitions, with which a major portion of this chapter will be concerned, however, are only one manifestation of outworn concepts. There also are customs, manners, and written laws. Of all the "unwritten laws whose transgression brings admitted shame," to use a phrase from Lyall, none are more powerful than the sex taboos and their close relations, the lavatory taboos. The primitive and fundamentalist Christian traditions unite in our culture to give us the association of sex with dirt and sin. This association permeates our entire culture and gives rise to many secondary taboos on words, dress, recreation, expressions of feelings and so forth.

A "bad" language, mostly oral, developed. Since publication of James Joyce's *Ulysses* (Limited Editions Club, 1935) and a few other best-sellers dealing frankly with sex, however, some of the "Twelve Unprintable Monosyllables" are seen occasionally in print. The single use of only one of them, it is true, caused Lillian Smith's *Strange Fruit* (Reynal, Hitchcock, 1944) to be banned in Boston in 1944. On the whole, however, similar efforts by the New England Watch and Ward Society, the New York Society for the Suppression of Vice, and other literary vigilante groups have failed during the past two decades. About the only other major attempt to obtain legal censorship of a novel for alleged obscenity which has succeeded upon appeal to a higher court since World War I was that against Edmund Wilson's *Memoirs of Hecate County* (Doubleday, 1946). In March, 1949, Judge Curtis Bok, son of the one-time great editor of the *Ladies' Home Journal,* Edward W. Bok, in Philadelphia cleared James T. Farrell's *Studs Lonigan* trilogy and six other books of charges of obscenity and indecency.

Neither Judge Bok's decision nor any other, of course, affects all of the nation. Several states still have laws promulgated or inspired by the great vice crusader, Anthony Comstock, who founded the New York Society for the Suppression of Vice in 1873. The federal law banning use of the mails to any printed matter found to be obscene or indecent still exists. It is the judicial interpretations of these laws which have changed in recent years. Each library board, school board, and city council, however, is virtually a law unto itself and there is hardly a book, including many of the classics, in which sex is dealt with in any way, which is not still on a taboo list someplace. The Index Librorum Prohibitorum of the Roman Catholic Church has been kept up to date ever since 1559 and contains approximately 8,000 titles at present. Obscenity, of course, is only one of many reasons why a book may be listed.

Since 1934 likewise the Catholic-inspired Legion of Decency has performed a careful watchdog function as regards motion pictures. Self-censorship is exercised by the Motion Picture Producers and Distributors of America, Inc., formerly headed by ex-Postmaster General Will Hays and more recently by Eric Johnston, one-time president of the United States Chamber of Commerce. Of the many pressure groups of which the Johnston office must take cognizance, the Legion of Decency unquestionably is the most important with the result that the Legion's list of condemned films has become shorter with the years. Principal theme of the Production Code to which motion picture producers must conform is: "No picture shall be produced which will lower the moral standards of those who see it." Among the most important articles of the code, which indicate the extent to which sexual taboos are dominant, are the following:

Crimes Against the Law. These shall never be presented in such a way as to throw sympathy with the crime as against law and justice or to inspire others with a desire to imitate crime.

Sex. The sanctity of the institution of marriage and the home shall be upheld. Pictures shall not imply that low forms of sex relationship are the accepted or common thing.

Vulgarity. The treatment of low, disgusting, unpleasant, though not necessarily evil, subjects should conform always to the dictates of good taste and a regard for the sensibilities of the audience.

Obscenity. Obscenity in word, gesture, reference, song, joke, or by suggestion (even when likely to be understood only by part of the audience) is forbidden.

Profanity. Pointed profanity (this includes the words *God, Lord, Jesus, Christ*—unless used reverently—*hell, S.O.B., damn, Gawd*), or every other profane or vulgar expression, however used, is forbidden.

Costume. *Complete nudity is never permitted.* This includes nudity in fact or in silhouette or any lecherous or licentious notice thereof by other characters in the picture.

Dance. Dances suggesting or representing sexual actions or indecent passion are forbidden. Dances which emphasize indecent movements are to be regarded as obscene.

Religion. No film or episode may throw ridicule on any religious faith. Ministers of religion in their character as ministers of religion should not be used as comic characters or as villains. Ceremonies of any definite religion should be carefully and respectfully handled.

Locations. The treatment of bedrooms must be governed by good taste and delicacy.

National Feelings. The use of the Flag shall be consistently respectful. The history, institutions, prominent people and citizenry of other nations shall be represented fairly.

As in the case of the laws pertaining to literature, it is the interpretation of these rules that is important. In a pictorial display in its July 18, 1938, issue *Life* listed a few "specifics" as follows: (1) Up to 1934 in *Tarzan* pictures, Maureen O'Sullivan wore one provocative flap of leather in front, another behind and a tunic; since then she has been well covered by a tunic; (2) beds are strictly censored. Unmarried characters may not occupy the same bed nor kiss in a horizontal position; (3) drunkenness must not be made attractive. In *The Thin Man,* characters drank continuously but apparently never got drunk. Drunkenness must be followed by a hangover; (4) in a Russian film, *Peter the Great,* the emperor was shown jubilantly kissing the rear of his infant son. In American movies the human posterior may be freely kicked but never anything else; (5) marriage may no longer be used for laughs as in early slapstick comedies. If a marriage scene is to be funny the ceremony must be performed by a justice of the peace. England will not allow the Lord's Prayer in a film. Quebec forbids mention of divorce; (6) illicit love must not be made attractive as it was, for instance, in *Queen Christina,* a 1933 picture; (7) incest is strictly taboo; a scene hinting at it in *The Barretts of Wimpole Street* was deleted; (8) stockings, as a rule, may no longer be taken off by girls themselves, much less by men as happened in the 1926 picture, *What Price Glory*. Men may not take off their pants though they may be caught with them off; (9) thighs must not be visible between top of stocking and underclothing. If stockings are not worn, the outside of a woman's thigh is permitted but the inside is taboo; (10) prostitutes may be shown only when essential to the plot and must be made unattractive. *Of Human Bondage* with Bette Davis showed prostitution at great length but sordidly. In *Dead End* the prostitute's syphilis was changed to tuberculosis; (11) kisses must be restricted to lips, avoiding neck, arms, back. Kisses must not be too long nor too passionate. Japan cuts kissing scenes, substitutes twittering birds.

Some of the typical "don't's" issued by the Hays office in 1941 included the following, the parenthetical explanations being those of the office:

Words and phrases to be omitted from all pictures:

Alley cat (applied to a woman)
Broad (applied to a woman)
God, Lord, Jesus, Christ (unless used reverently)
"Fanny"
Fairy (in a vulgar sense)
"Fire"—cries of
Goose (in a vulgar sense)
Hot (applied to a woman)
"In your hat"
Lousy
Nuts (except when meaning "crazy")
Razzberry (the sound)
Tomcat (applied to a man)
Buzzard (too similar in sound to bastard)

Words and phrases invariably deleted by political censor boards:

Bum (England)
Punk (England)
Stick 'em up (U.S. and Canada)
Shag (British Empire)

Words and phrases particularly offensive to patrons in foreign countries:

Frog (French)

Kike (U.S. and England)

Spig (Mexico and Central America)

Wop (Italian)

Millions of words have been written, pro and con, about motion picture censorship. Every controversy over any type of censorship, of course, is first-rate newspaper copy. The following article by Albert Deutsch in his column in the March 29, 1944, *PM* casts light on the prevalence of one type of taboo without as well as within the motion picture industry:

The obstacles raised by the Legion of Decency against the general release of Walter Wanger's anti-syphilis film, *To the American People,* highlights once more the age-old struggle of public health to break through outworn moralistic strictures against the dissemination of vital truths.

The taboo against public discussion of venereal disease—broken in the press and the radio after a long, uphill struggle—still holds the movies enthralled.

The recent struggle given to the dramatic potency of the sulpha drugs and penicillin in venereal treatment has lulled a lot of people into the false feeling that the venereal problem is as good as licked. Far from it. Selective Service figures show that nearly five out of every 100 men of draft age are infected with syphilis. About three times as many are victims of gonorrhea. Venereal disease is still one of the greatest cripplers of military man power. Alarming wartime rises in the venereal disease rate among teen-age Americans have been reported.

We know how to prevent syphilis and gonorrhea. We know how to cure the twin scourges quickly and effectively. Medical science has given mankind powerful chemical weapons for dealing a death-blow to venereal disease. The chief remaining block along the path to final conquest is public ignorance.

The Wanger film, exhibited nationally through commercial movie houses (on a non-profit basis), could help tremendously to bridge the gap between scientific knowledge and public ignorance. It has been produced with taste, intelligence and tact. It can be seen by people of all ages. Experimental showings in seven or eight towns have received a very favorable response from movie-goers.

The film was made under the sponsorship of the California State Health Assn., and the U.S. Public Health Service. The War Activities Committee of the OWI has approved it as a genuine contribution to the war effort. The film includes introductory talks by Surgeon General Thomas Parran of the U.S. Public Health Service and Surgeon General Norman T. Kirk of the U.S. Army.

Parran, a Catholic, is the foremost American crusader against venereal disease. He has done more than any single contemporary to check its inroads.

The general distribution of the Wanger film, completed about six weeks ago, has been halted by objections emanating from the Legion of Decency, a Catholic organization which passes on the moral values of feature film productions. The Legion's objections appear to rest on three main grounds:

The picture violates the Motion Picture Production Code, which bans all films dealing with "sex hygiene and venereal disease."

The Legion objects to all such pictures, even good ones, because it feels they might open the way to unscrupulous exploitation by unethical producers.

This particular film, while not condoning immorality, does not stress continence as the chief means of preventing venereal disease.

Impartial experts offer these answers to the Legion's objections:

The movie industry code was set up only for commercial producers and distributors. It does not cover Government-sponsored productions.

Every human activity is subject to abuse. You don't suppress good pictures in order to prevent bad ones. Discrimination is needed.

The film was made on a straight public health basis. The morality angle was not stressed because it has failed to check venereal disease in the past. Since, however, sex promiscuity is one of the main causes of syphilis, it may be expedient to stress the point in the film. The Public Health Service's advisory council on venereal disease education has criticized the film for omitting the moral factor. It can be included in the film without too much trouble.

The Public Health Service is loath to enter into a full-dress controversy over this film. If the Legion of Decency can work up powerful pressure against it, the ensuing debate might imperil Congressional appropriations sorely needed for other Service activities.

I trust that a satisfactory agreement can be worked out by all parties. The picture is too valuable to be tossed on the scrap heap.

Radio today is more restricted than the motion pictures; stage plays are allowed more freedom. So are newspapermen usually when they write about attempts to censor the arts.

The comparative freedom enjoyed by the professional stage is not shared by amateurs. When a small college put on *Elizabeth the Queen,* a great deal of cutting was necessary, as the coach explained, "to save the ears of the chancellor and other bigwigs who will be out in front." So, when Essex called his mistress a "bitch of brass," according to Maxwell Anderson, it had to be a "witch of brass," according to the collegians. In the film version the expression was entirely missing, illustrating the rule that if a sinful entertainment reaches a smaller or more educated audience, it is not nearly so sinful as when it finds wide and popular circulation. For instance, *Tobacco Road* on the screen was a very much expurgated version of the foul-mouthed Broadway version. Burlesque is more or less permitted on the stage but not for nation-wide consumption on the screen. Boccaccio and Ovid may be sold in the United States if the shocking portions are left untranslated. Presumably they will not be injurious to such as can read Italian or Latin. This aspect of taboo is far from logical which is to be expected from the irrational nature of the whole taboo structure, past and present.

Again, books, even though kept somewhat in check by the various societies of Comstockery, enjoy a wider freedom than periodicals. James Branch Cabell's *Jurgen* was banned at first but later allowed to circulate. However, he never could have been printed in *Red Book, Cosmopolitan,* or any of the other popular home magazines. Indeed, fear of violating the strict sex taboo made Ray Long, editor of the latter magazine, reject Somerset Maugham's equally famous *The Book Bag,* a story concerned with incest and murder. Not even in the confession pulp magazines can the heroine fall openly into sin. All sin must be by suggestion, never by open portrayal. As a pulp editor once said, "Let the shadow of a bed be on every page but never let the bed appear." Publications intended for juvenile readers must hold understandably to even stricter purity requirements.

In the Spring, 1938, *American Speech,* Edwin R. Hunter and Bernice E. Gaines reported in an article, "Verbal Taboo in a College Community," on one experiment to determine the extent of squeamishness among freshmen, seniors, and faculty members in Maryville College in eastern Tennessee.

They chose 62 words that once were or still are widely considered offensive, asked the students and teachers to indicate whether they used the words: (1) as freely as "cat" or "dog," (2) with a feeling of being bold or modern, (3) only when talking to intimates, (4) never if they could avoid it, or (5) never under any circumstances.

The investigators found the college freshmen most finicky, the seniors most free-spoken, the faculty betwixt and between. The women had more taboo words than the men. Some of the words, and the proportion of each group that used them freely:

Coffin: freshmen, 89 per cent, seniors, 96 per cent, faculty, 90 per cent, men, 89 per cent, women, 90 per cent

Corset: freshmen, 47 per cent, seniors, 57 per cent, faculty, 51 per cent, men, 58 per cent, women, 42 per cent

Guts: freshmen, 16 per cent, seniors, 22 per cent, faculty, 18 per cent, men, 27 per cent, women, 10 per cent

Pregnant: freshmen, 21 per cent, seniors, 43 per cent, faculty, 50 per cent, men, 26 per cent, women, 20 per cent

Prostitute: freshmen, 24 per cent, seniors, 48 per cent, faculty, 48 per cent, men, 35 per cent, women, 29 per cent

Whore: freshmen, 9 per cent, seniors, 15 per cent, faculty 7 per cent, men, 11 per cent, women, 8 per cent

Bastard: freshmen, 8 per cent, seniors, 20 per cent, faculty, 39 per cent, men, 12 per cent, women, 16 per cent

Bitch (most taboo of the list): freshmen, 7 per cent, seniors, 9 per cent, faculty, 17 per cent, men, 10 per cent, women, 7 per cent

Of the admonition that "The Lord will not hold him guiltless who taketh his name in vain," Robert Graves wrote in *The Future of Swearing and Improper Language* (K. Paul, Trench, Trubner, 1936): "This commandment seems to have a double force, recording in the first place a taboo against the mention, except on solemn occasions, of the tribal god's holy name (for among certain savage tribes it is still considered unlucky to use a man's real name, often known only to himself and the priest), and in the second place, a taboo against even a decent pariphrasis of the god's name; for the act of calling him to witness any fear or condition, or the summons to curse or destroy an enemy, must involve elaborate purifications or penalties."

In some sections of society it is almost a social requirement to be a good swearer, and so the taboos against profanity and obscenity are rebuilt into anti-taboos. When anti-taboos are formed it seems just as necessary to those affected to keep them as it is for others to observe the original taboo. Between the devout churchgoer who says "gosh darn" and the street arab who uses the original expression there seems to be a wide gulf, but the difference is only that between a taboo and an anti-taboo.

There is also a way, by circumlocution, to avoid the word taboo while seeming to obey it. Thus "witch of brass" for the original "bitch," "bustard" for "bastard," "gol darn" for "God damn," "cripes" for "Christ," and so on, all reminiscent of the Polynesian who changed the names of things similarly named when a high sacred chief died. The Englishman likewise says "ruddy" and "blooming" for his illogically tabooed "bloody" and refers to his backside as "the back porch" or "the covered way," to feel free from taboo violation. Another English euphemism which has all the earmarks of an old taboo is the use of "Uncle's" for "pawnbroker's," which is calling something feared by a proprietary name.

In many of the instances cited, a modern taboo violator would experience a feeling of uneasiness, or a sense of guilt comparable to that of the primitive transgressor. The contemporary word for such an attitude is "conscience," but he who breaks the commandment against taking the Lord's name in vain, or any of the other commandments for that matter, may experience a feeling of dread that is more than remorse. So may he who desecrates a holy place or violates the injunction to observe the Sabbath in a certain way, or eats the wrong food on the wrong day or disobeys any other religious rule. In other instances, in which the religious sanction is lacking, he may dread social ostracism or financial loss as the result of having committed a *faux pas.*

Superstition

It is not to be wondered at that prehistoric man took so much stock in the supernatural. From the beginning man had to fight for his very existence. Huddling fearfully in a dark cave he listened with terror to the wild screeches of the wind, the crashing of thunder and lightning, and the growling of lurking beasts. All his universe seemed charged with danger. Earth and sea and sky seemed set against him, bent upon his destruction. There came the natural projection: all things are alive and meaningful; nothing happens by chance; all hurt is intentional on the part of unseen forces.

No wonder that in his quest for safety primitive man sought to understand the unseen and then to control it as best he could so as to ward off evil and obtain favors. With an almost total lack of instruments by which to measure and test, most of the conclusions to which he came regarding the nature of the earth, the universe, and himself were incorrect. From one standpoint the entire history of civilization —and perhaps it is the most important standpoint from which to view the history of civilization—can be written in terms of man's struggle away from his unscientific ideas. Every step has been taken with great struggle. Centuries and centuries were necessary to convince a majority that the earth is round. Every scientific advance has been fought vigorously because the new knowledge upset old and cherished beliefs.

Today many mysteries remain. Man has not learned to create life. He cannot always cure disease. He is powerless to prevent death. The tides and weather remain uncontrollable and earthquakes, hurricanes, and tornadoes are still unpreventable. Nevertheless, science has progressed to the point where it should be recognized that a scientific explanation of what remains unknowable is possible. Just because the answer has not yet been found, as, for instance, to the causes of cancer or the common cold, in the light of what science *has* revealed, it would be grotesque to conclude that those diseases result from the caprices of spooks. Nevertheless, that such kind of thinking not only persists but is widespread, by no means confined to the ignorant and lowly, cannot be denied. Superstition, which may be defined as a belief which persists in the face of scientific verification to the contrary, and which involves faith in some unscientific, supernatural forces at work, is the most important contemporary descendant of ancient taboos, myths, and legends and other notions regarding the unseen.

In a Northwestern University Reviewing Stand discussion of "Have We Outgrown Our Superstitions?" March 30, 1947, over WGN, the moderator asked, "But aren't a lot of these superstitions relatively harmless? What if you do knock on wood, what if you do throw salt over your left shoulder, what if you do believe in Santa Claus and in the Easter Bunny? Aren't they relatively harmless things?" and again, "For example, might not certain superstitions and illusions provide comfort to people in distress, escapes from reality which contribute to peace of mind?" Answering, the Rev. John Nicholls Booth of the Unitarian church of Evanston, Ill., said in part: "Well, you know Eugene O'Neill's play, *The Iceman Cometh*, expressed a view similar to that. The idea was that the moment man loses his illusions, his life isn't worth living. The disadvantage comes in that as long as you are living in this aura of illusion, you can be relatively happy, but when the day comes of disillusionment, when you discover that what you believed was important and true isn't important and isn't true, then the props are knocked out from underneath such people. The cold water of reality is hard to take. It results in disillusionment, cynicism and defeatism.

"I think the classic example is what happened in Great Britain during the war. They had a number of days of prayer there, hoping to get good bombing weather so they could bomb Germany. They also asked for good weather for landing on D-Day. You know what happened. Clouds obscured Germany and they had some of the worst bombing days at critical times. Two of the temporary piers were washed away in the Channel. They had quite a time there on D-Day. They had to postpone it one or two days, if I remember correctly. The result was that people began to leave the churches by the thousands. In our own papers they told of church leaders gathering together and saying this is a serious problem. These people have lost faith. Well, of course, you are going to lose faith when you put your eggs in the wrong kind of a basket, when you are trying to back up a falsehood. And that is exactly what you are doing when you are supporting these superstitions."

This author, also a participant in the program, then remarked: "What you are really saying, Booth, is that the superstitious person is inclined to be absolutistic in his thinking. He thinks in terms of all white and all black. He not only has false hopes and fears, but he is a sucker for demagogic appeal. He is inclined toward racial prejudice, disregarding all the anthropological evidence to the contrary, and in a time of insecurity he will fall for any kind of new Messiah that comes along to create a proper scapegoat for him to lay the blame on for any of his own shortcomings. You can say that may give him mental peace and comfort, yes, but the social consequences of it far outweigh the feeling of comfort that he may get." Earlier on the same program this writer declared, "The hangover of unscientific thinking is an obstacle to the proper solution of all social, economic, and political problems. A person who believes in black cats and umbrellas and all of these other everyday superstitions is less likely to think logically and clearly in any other field. He is continuing in an unscientific frame of mind at a time when the clearest type of scientific thinking is essential."

Athletes, sports writers know, are notoriously superstitious. According to Herb Graffis, noted columnist, "There used to be a fellow who made a pretty good living at it named Evil Eye Finkel. He would hire out to some fighter to sit and put the Evil Eye on the opponent. And there is Sid Luckman. One time the Bears told me that when he jumped out on Wrigley Field if he put his right foot on the sod first he was going to play a fine game. Horton Smith always used to put that wood tee in the ground with his left hand. Bobby Jones, if he was going good, would never change his sweater or knickers."

Mel Ott was reputed always to touch second base on his way from the dugout to the outfield. Answering "What is your special jinx?" in the July 15, 1949 Chicago *Sun-Times* Talkies, an inquiring reporter column, Bob Chipman, Cubs pitcher, said:

I have many jinxes, not just one special one. For instance, I always throw my glove face down. If it lands face up, it's a bad omen. Also, I wear a special sweatshirt till I lose a game and then I'll change to a different one. I think I have prolonged effects of the superstition I observed as a kid—if you step on the cracks of a sidewalk you'll break your grandmother's back. Well, when going to bat or walking to the pitcher's mound, I'll always step OVER the foul line. To avoid another jinx, I pick up the resin bag before pitching a game.

In the same symposium, "Rube" Walker, catcher, confessed that he never likes to change his uniform during a winning streak and is wary of having his photograph taken before a game; Dave Philley, White Sox fielder, said he always touches two bases, second and third, on his way in to the dugout and never changes bats during a hitting streak; Luke Appling, veteran shortstop, admitted he picks up ladies' hairpins because "they bring me base hits."

According to Helen Welsheimer in "She Debunked 8,000 Superstitions!" in the Nov. 24, 1935 Philadelphia *Record* Weekly Magazine, a professional debunker, Claudia de Lys, believes "practically every member of royalty has one or more superstitions." Of the dowager Queen Mary of England, Miss de Lys reputedly declared:

At a ceremony in Edinburgh in 1927, Queen Mary had to cut a ribbon and was given a pair of golden shears. She insisted upon paying sixpence before using them, declaring that otherwise it would be bad luck.

In 1947 when the queen's granddaughter, Princess Elizabeth, was married, her bridegroom, the Duke of Edinburgh, was reported in the newspapers to have touched a chimney sweep for luck on the way to Westminster Abbey.

According to Miss de Lys: ·

Superstitions seem to abound everywhere, among all people. Verree Teasdale and Adolphe Menjou refused to be photographed together before their marriage, because they believed it would bring them bad luck. Barbara Hutton believes jade is her lucky stone. Vincent Lopez dotes on astrology and numerology.

Cecil de Mille is afraid that bad luck will pursue him if he fails to wear a certain leather jacket while directing a picture. The jacket is one that he wore 22 years ago when he made his first production, "The Squaw Man."

Grace Moore is superstitious about a pair of red baby shoes which she wore when she was learning to walk. She won't appear on the stage, before a camera or sing over the radio without having them near her.

Richard Dix has two neckties which he believes bring him luck. He wears one if he wants things to go right, such as a new venture or the signing of a new contract. He will never turn off the radio or phonograph before the piece is finished, he will never change dressing rooms on a lot, and he believes that three on a match is an omen of death.

Jack Pearl wears his mother's wedding ring on his left hand and never removes it. He attributes his good luck to it.

Who can deny that many of these strictly personal superstitions are reminiscent of the taboos that the South Sea islanders obeyed? These are supposedly successful and intelligent people. Books have been written about the superstitions of the Ozark and Cumberland mountaineers and other less educated people. The origins of some of the most common superstitions can be traced or imagined; the sources of many more are yet to be discovered.

Most of the superstitions so far mentioned can be divided roughly into (1) unlucky objects or actions, to be avoided, and (2) lucky omens or actions or ways to avoid ill luck. In the recapitulation and listing to follow will be found many fantastic beliefs of the educated and illiterate alike. What the chemistry and/or physics of many of these superstitions possibly could be defies the imagination.

Bad Luck. Prof. George J. Dudycha found that 92 per cent of 853 freshmen and 95 per cent of 305 seniors in seven Middle Western colleges believe that "one who breaks a mirror has seven years of bad luck." He reported his findings in an article, "The Superstitious Beliefs of College Students," in the January-March, 1933 *Journal of Abnormal Psychology*. Origin of this superstition is believed to have been in the animistic concept that the reflection is the person's soul which momentarily has departed the body.

Some say fear of the number 13 originated in the belief that the devil rules covens of 12; others that the superstition began with realization that there were 13 at the Last Supper. Anyway, 95 per cent of Dudycha's seniors and 91 per cent of his freshmen believed that "Friday the 13th always brings bad luck." The Friday the 13th feature is, of course, almost a "must" in every newspaper office although in recent years there have been an increasing number of stories telling of persons or organizations dedicated to defiance of the superstition. Some such organizations sprang into being when businessmen realized they were losing business on the fearsome days. A typical debunking Friday the 13th feature was that sent out by the United Press associations March 13, 1936, as follows:

EDITOR'S NOTE: The following Friday the Thirteenth story was written for the United Press by the only surviving chief ruler of New York's "13 club," the original organization of its kind. The writer also contends he also is the oldest living hotel detective.

By J. Arthur Lehman
Former Chief Ruler of the 13 Club of New York
Written for the United Press

New York, Friday, March 13.—(UP)—My advice to anyone that wants real luck and happiness and health is to break every possible known superstition today.

I intend to open an umbrella in the house, light three on a match, and walk under any ladders I can find.

Our "13" club was founded and chartered in 1882. It started out as an organization devoted only to breaking down superstitions. All the members of the club that I can remember had good luck.

I joined the club in 1884. I'm the only living former chief ruler of the organization. I'm 78 now and I defy you to find anyone happier or healthier than I am.

I look only 50 and I feel a lot younger than that.

The club operated chiefly as a social organization but the members, nevertheless, didn't believe in superstitions.

We used to hold our dinners on the 13th, sitting 13 at a table. If it was Friday the 13th that was all to the good. Every member sat down under an open umbrella. Each spilled salt. There were 13 candles on each table.

Anyone who had a black cat cross his path on the way to the dinner was considered especially blessed.

The ice cream was served in coffin-shaped containers. The skull and crossbones decorated our menus and we tried to find dishes that had 13 letters in their name.

The only unlucky thing that ever happened to us was that the club folded up in 1914 because of the war. It has been out of existence since but I'm figuring on reviving it. Just think, we'd been 54 years old now if we'd kept going right through.

The late Presidents Theodore Roosevelt and Woodrow Wilson were honorary members of our club. They were lucky, weren't they?

And me, well, all the good looking blondes in my office building rush up to me and throw their arms around me.

All you men should go out and break a few mirrors right now. I'm going to do it just to be sure my luck holds.

Despite the efforts of such modern iconoclasts hotels rarely have thirteenth floors or rooms numbered 13. An *American Weekly* feature for June 9, 1939, told of the attempt of Chicago's Hotel Morrison to solve the problem of what to do when the hotel books a family dinner, a luncheon group, directors' meeting, or wedding party at which exactly 13 persons appear. In such cases an extra place is set and is occupied by a department store dummy, Louis XIV, who takes the hex off the occasion.

Reporters often strain themselves to get a "13" story as witness the following from the Sept. 14, 1946 Chicago *Sun*:

The number "13" started swarming all over Francis Crones yesterday (Friday the 13th) in the Municipal court of Judge Oscar S. Caplan.

Crones, who has 13 letters in his name, runs a cartage company at 1313 W. Randolph St.

Accompanied by his son, Francis, Jr., who was celebrating his 13th birthday, Crones found himself listed on line 13 of the court sheet for speeding 43 miles an hour in a 30 mile zone—that is, 13 miles an hour faster than the law allows.

Crones asked for a continuance.

Assistant City Prosecutor William M. Barth (13 letters in his name, too) suggested a continuance to Oct. 13, because, as he pointed out, that is his 13th wedding anniversary.

"My word," said Crones, "My brother's birthday is Oct. 13."

Judge Caplan granted the continuance, then hastily counted the letters in his own name, and heaved a sigh of relief.

"Only 12," he said, "I couldn't have stood it otherwise."

Among other common "dangers" which the superstitious avoid are the following: walking under a raised ladder, which probably originated in the recognition that to do so was to break a triangle, symbol of the trinity; allowing a black cat to cross one's path; looking at a new moon over the left shoulder, through a doorway, or from an ocean liner; opening an umbrella inside; returning for some forgotten object after beginning a trip; counting the cars in a funeral procession; allowing a tree, post, or other object to come between one's self and a walking companion; beginning a task on a Friday (94 per cent of Dudycha's seniors and 91 per cent of his freshmen wouldn't do it), and many, many more.

Good Luck. To ward off evil there are amulets, talismans, charms, St. Christopher and other medals, lucky stones, words, and sayings. Before the era of the automobile to find a horseshoe was good luck. Nailed over a doorway with the open end up, it "pointed up luck" and allowed the evil spirits to flow upward and outward. Four-leaf clovers and rabbits' feet also are lucky. So is getting the larger portion of a chicken's wishbone which two persons pull apart. Some people spit on the palm of the hand when they see a white horse or a crosseyed man or a hunchback. It is better luck to rub the hunchback. There is a familiar ditty to recite fast when seeing a falling star (really a meteor) in order to benefit by the experience. To avoid misfortune when you happen to make the same remark simultaneously with another person, you must say "bread and butter" in unison with him. Crossing the fingers is an old way of warding off evil, frequently used today when consciously telling an untruth. Because all doorways once were considered sacred, bridegrooms still frequently carry their brides across the threshold of their new homes to insure a happy wedded life. Likewise, so as not to break the charm, wives may never remove their wedding rings.

Significant was the following advice by Father Hugh Calkins, a leader of Chicago's perpetual novena of Our Sorrowful Mother, in his monthly *Novena Notes* in January, 1943: "Superstition comes from ignorance or fear. . . . During wartime, superstition leaps sky-high in popularity. During danger periods, medals receive attention all out of proportion to their value. So the service men are being weighed down with medals and good luck charms (too often put in the same class). Department stores are advertising 'St. Christopher Good Luck Pieces.' And non-Catholics are being 'converted' to the phony brand of faith that says: 'Wear this medal and nothing can happen to you.'

"Meantime millions of good Catholics wonder if the only road to Heaven is metallurgical. . . . To be sure of God's help and protection over body and soul always keep yourself in God's grace. Then you won't even need medals, though you may use them. And if you are not in God's grace, you are not pleasing to Him . . . though you be wearing more medals than Goering. . . . Wouldn't it be better for many drivers to drive well and carefully and not depend so much on overworked St. Christopher? God still runs His world; it's not run by luck or charms. . . . Wear medals? Sure, but understand them. Put first things first."

Signs and Portents. Some people believe that when their ears burn it is a sign that someone is talking about them. Physicists probably would be hard put even to imagine the kind of tests to conduct to discover how sound waves convert themselves into heat waves and seek out and find the one and only person for whom intended, sometimes at a considerable distance. Likewise the way in which unannounced guests can make their intended host's nose itch is difficult to explain in the light of modern knowledge.

Even more difficult to understand is it how animals and birds are supposed to be able to foretell the future and, especially, why, knowing it, they have an interest in conveying their knowledge to humans. Nevertheless, even some of the strongest believers in the doctrine of free will instead of predestination contend that a howling dog or hooting owl is a warning of death; likewise, a bird in the house or on the window sill. Probably these superstitions originated when objects of nature were thought to be merely the habitats of spirits and animals were supposed to be gods, often able—on unusual occasions at least —to talk the language of humans. A disagreeable cry, such as a crow's caw or a raven's croak, was associated with an evil spirit. On the other hand, pleasant appearing and sounding animals and birds were either good spirits in disguise or messengers from them. That such ideas persist was evidenced by the widespread agreement with Eddie Rickenbacker's explanation of how a sea gull happened to light on his head while he was floating around in a lifeboat in the South Pacific during World War II.

Even insects are credited with supernatural powers, especially katydids and crickets who are supposed to be able to predict the weather. Because of the perpetual struggle that primitive man had to wage with the elements, it is not surprising that so many superstitions regarding them persist today. As for katydids, their "singing" is supposed to mean frost in exactly six weeks. Crickets are said to make louder noises when hot weather impends than when it is to be cold. Squirrels are given credit for being better prophets than human weather bureaus; they grow heavier pelts when especially cold winters are in the offing.

Although occasional journalistic features are written about some of the other weather superstitions, St. Swithin's Day, and, more importantly, Groundhog Day are "musts" on the assignment sheets in many newspaper offices. The former comes on July 15 and the superstition consists in the belief that if rain falls on that date it will continue for 40 days. The belief originated in the 40 days' delay because of rain during funeral services for St. Swithin. Because that was such an unusual occurrence its failure to recur has caused a diminution of credence in the portent. Not so Groundhog Day which falls on Feb. 2 or 3.

The following represents one of the comparatively few attempts—by newspapermen or anyone else—to "follow up" the original story. It appeared in the March 16, 1949 Kansas City *Star*:

Well, it has been six weeks since the ground hog emerged into the sparkling sunlight, saw his shadow, and went back into his hole in expectation of six more weeks of wintry weather.

There are those who say Mr. Ground Hog, by his act, exhibited the superhuman acumen which long has been attributed to his species. However, J. R. Lloyd, chief weather forecaster for the Kansas City district, says the ground hog was somewhat off the beam this time—and Lloyd has records to prove it.

A LOOK AT RECORDS

"If you think we've had really bad weather in the last six weeks, you're thinking of January," Lloyd said. "Let's get down to brass tacks. Let's start with temperatures."

Rustling through some papers on his desk, Lloyd came up with some blue curves and green-checkered graphs.

"Here's February," he said, pointing to a row of figures. "We finished that month with the average temperature running one and one-third degrees above normal. So far this month—in March—we've been about 1.8 degrees above normal. I'd say that makes things about even Steven."

Precipitation last month was 1.36 inches, as compared to the normal, 1.49 inches. So far in March the total is .33 of an inch, about one-third of the normal .97 inch. These figures, Lloyd said, showed the 6-week period to be quite deficient in precipitation. The total to date for the year, 6.91 inches—far ahead of the normal 3.16—received its big boost with the snow and sleet of January.

Mr. G. Hog, Lloyd observed, still is not the answer to long range forecasting. Incidentally, Lloyd said, it is too wet for any St. Patrick's day potato planting. . . .

Animals. Because wild animals were as threatening to primitive man as the elements, a considerable mythology concerning them developed. Good and bad spirits were believed on occasion to assume animal form. It was the custom to eat certain animals in the hope of acquiring their characteristics: strength from the lion, courage from the tiger, cunning from the panther, and so on. Today, most potential man eaters are behind bars in zoos and circuses, so the abundant amount of misinformation concerning animals probably should be classified under the heading "ignorance" rather than "superstition." Nevertheless, stories of unusual intelligence or ferocity still are popular with editors and often include superstitious beliefs, as, for example, accounts of angleworms and frogs falling to earth during rainstorms, cats which suck the breath from sleeping children, dogs who talk, horses able to count, toads who survived for decades or centuries in cornerstones, pets able to sense impending danger so as to to warn their masters, and so forth.

Louis T. Stone of the Winsted (Conn.) *Evening Citizen* became known as the Winsted Liar because of the many tall tales, most of them concerning animals, which he originated and which the press associations helped to disseminate throughout the country. Typical of Stone's yarns were those which concerned the following: a deaf and dumb pig; a cat with a hare lip that could whistle "Yankee Doodle"; a cow that grazed on a patch of horse radish and gave scalding hot milk; a squirrel that shined his master's shoes with his tail; and a pair of frogs who became inebriated with applejack and painted the town a greenish red. In his *Hoaxes* (Macmillan, 1940) the author gave the details of many more of Stone's masterpieces and of similar generally harmless tall tales concerning man's feathered and furry friends.

Not so harmless are the stories about sea serpents and land monsters which recur with almost scheduled regularity every few weeks, especially just before the tourist seasons are about to begin at Loch Ness, Scotland, Lake Como, Italy, or along either American coastline. Many of these stories illustrate gullibility rather than superstitious belief, as will be explained in Chapter 9. A contributing factor to the hysteria which causes posses to form and people of all ages to become panicky, however, is lingering belief in the existence of horrendous creatures, perhaps prehistoric atavisms about which bold travelers in the early days of explorations used to relate wild tales to credulous listeners. No matter how skeptical he may be, an imaginative newspaperman can produce some exciting copy when assigned to a monster hunt.

Health. Despite the great progress that has been made in medical research and in public health education, an incredible amount of superstition about diseases, their cause, prevention, and cure, persists. Through regular health advice columns and special articles, newspapers contribute to dispelling the fog. It is, however, a discouraging uphill fight, and unconsciously the newspaperman on occasions may allow a hoary one to slip into his copy, as, for example, that drowning persons always go down three times or that hair stands on end or turns gray overnight or suddenly because of a great fright.

There are many current superstitions concerning food, diet, and cooking, among them being the following: that oysters should be eaten only during months in the English spelling of which occurs an "R"; that fish are brain food; that walnuts, the shape of whose meat resembles the human brain, are brain food; that fish and milk should not be consumed at the same meal; that cucumbers and milk do not mix; that canned food never should be allowed to remain in a can once it is opened; that cooking with aluminum is dangerous; that green apples cause colic, and so forth. Commonly held causes of ill health, all superstitious, include: handling toads causes warts; rusty nails cause lockjaw; baldness comes from wearing hats; swallowing seeds will cause appendicitis; enormous appetites are a sign of tapeworm.

To prevent sickness the superstitious may wear red flannel underwear as a protection against smallpox; carry horse chestnuts to ward off rheumatism; wear amber necklaces to prevent goiter; brush their teeth to prevent decay; swallow baking soda to aid digestion; eat raw onions to avoid colds. Among the fictitious and sometimes dangerous cures are the following: cobwebs for wounds; coral for nosebleed; whiskey for snakebite; lemon juice for freckles; sulphur and molasses for spring fever (whatever that is); a broth of lizards boiled in milk for asthma; a poultice of red clay and vinegar for a sprained ankle or wrist; a gold ring for a sty; and a key down the back for nosebleed.

Among the primitives some of the strictest taboos concerned menstruation, pregnancy, and childbirth, some of them originating before the connection between intercourse and pregnancy was recognized. Modern superstitions regarding birthmarks had their prehistoric counterparts when pregnant women avoided geese so that their children would not have long necks; did not tie knots so that their deliveries would not be difficult, and refrained from turning locks so that the baby's fingers would not be bent and powerless. A pregnant woman had to keep quiet in a rainstorm so that it would not develop into a thunderstorm or destructive lightning. When a child was born, it was believed that a part of the father's soul left him and entered his offspring; consequently, one twin would be killed so that the father's loss would not be too great. On the other hand some primitives were known to consider twins a sign of the deity's pleasure.

Among moderns there are those who warn against rocking an empty cradle lest it interfere with the baby's sleep once he is placed in it; those who believe that if a woman holds a newly born infant on her first visit she will become a mother soon herself; that if a married woman is the first to see a new infant, she will become pregnant; that to lay a coat and hat on a strange bed is to invite motherhood; that a mother who fails to nurse her baby soon will have another; that the number of future children can be determined by counting the knots in the umbilical cord; that no infant should look in a mirror or have his hair cut within a year so that he will not waste away; that a baby's fingernails should not be cut within six months to prevent his dying within six years; that a mother sacrifices a tooth for every child: that wearing necklaces means easy teething, and so on.

Character Analysis. The good work that newspapers do through cooperation with the medical profession in attempting to debunk health superstitions is offset by the extent to which many of them continue to espouse quackery in the related fields of psychology and psychiatry. When a particularly heinous crime is committed, they may take pictures of suspects to phrenologists, handprints to palmists, and samples of handwriting to handwriting analysts. An example of the kind of nonsense which results is the following from the March 30, 1936 Chicago *Herald and Examiner:*

By C. A. Bonniwell
Noted Character Analyst

Even a casual study of the features of the principals in this latest, solved murder mystery, emphasizes the astonishing similarities of all four of them in certain characteristics.

Three of them have eyebrows in color and growth that are very similar and which because of their quality indicate an almost utter lack of imagination, while the fourth one has little more. Under the circumstances, since they apparently never were bothered with any imagination, they never considered the results of their actions.

Their noses are similar in general characteristics and they all show a lack of character and a certain bestiality that now they have confessed, can easily be appreciated and understood.

The very small mouths and thick lips almost tell their own story. Here you have selfishness and utter lack of consideration of others, related or strangers. Satisfaction of their own selfish desires was the dominating motive of all of their actions.

It is seldom that you find all four parties to any action with almost identical ears, in that none of them have any lobes in the full sense of the word. Once set to a course of action they were no more amenable to reason than an army mule.

The relatively small space between the opening of the ears and the back of the head shows a ruthlessness in the consideration of others that is difficult for the ordinary person to understand. Astonishingly enough all four are alike in this respect. While human beings are generally gregarious animals none of these four seem to be, although they worked in a pack like so many wolves.

Possibly in this quintet of similarities and more particularly in those selfish, petty mouths, so typical of their actions, is a clue to their abnormalities.

Selfish, petty people never consider any but themselves and their own interests.

Their ego must be satiated and lacking the virile qualities to accomplish their ends on innate ability, they follow what to them seems to be the easier course.

Accompanying the article were separate pictures of the four young men with arrows leading to numbered portions of their facial features and brief written analyses of what the characteristics indicated.

In December, 1945, the unknown murderer of Miss Frances Brown, former WAVE, wrote in lipstick on the wall of her hotel room: "For heavens sake catch me before I kill more. I cannot control myself." On its front page Dec. 11, 1945, the Chicago *Daily News* ran a three column facsimile of the message and a two-column artist's sketch of what the murderer looked like based on analysis of the handwriting. The accompanying story follows:

By Jack Mabley

The killer of Frances Brown is a short, swarthy man whose instincts are guided by gluttony and self-love.

This is what "the handwriting on the wall" tells Leon York, noted Chicago graphologist who has spent 35 years judging persons from their handwriting.

"I visualize this man as about 36 years old, about 5 feet 4 inches tall, and weighing 174 pounds," York told the Daily News today.

* * *

"He is an introvert type given to sulking and self-pity," York said. "I can see a throw-back to being tied to a woman's apron strings."

York gave unhesitating opinion as he scanned a picture of the note written on the wall of Miss Brown's apartment: "For heavens sake catch me before I kill more. I cannot control myself."

The most dominating factor in the handwriting is the killer's gluttony, York said. He lives for his appetite, which undoubtedly affects his sexual instincts.

* * *

In rare instances cases are encountered when women write like men, and vice versa, York said, but it is extremely unlikely in this instance.

The killer probably was right-handed, York deduced.

"The roundness of the R, the beginning of the M's, and formation of the K in 'kill' and 'sake' show a man who above all is a sensualist through domination of appetite.

"A definite amount of perversion is shown. He is independent, a bachelor rather than a family man. Or if he had been married, he obviously is a widower."

* * *

The ease with which he wrote the B in "before" indicates that letter may be an initial of his name, York opined.

"The beginning of the stroke on the M shows definite primitive instincts," York continued.

"He is a simple individual, yet has a certain amount of native cunning. He has the shrewdness, astuteness, impulsiveness to dare to do things on the spur of the moment.

"A sex crime is not necessarily premeditated, but brought on by turbulence such as dominated his makeup."

The actual murderer, of course, was a frail seventeen-year-old University of Chicago student, William Heirens, who bore no resemblance whatever to either the artist's sketch or the description when he was picked up for burglary more than six months later. Nor did his interests coincide at all with those ascribed to him by the Chicago *Times* which, in its Dec. 11, 1945 issue, headlined "Hunt Musician as Maniac Killer" and "Murdered to Music?" In both articles it was suggested that the writing on the wall indicated that the author had received a musical education. A psychiatrist was quoted as authority for the belief.

One might think that the experience would have soured the paper's editors on handwriting analysts. Not so. Rather, in March, 1949, the paper, by then the Chicago *Sun-Times,* began giving away $1,500 each week to readers who sent in samples of their penmanship expressing wishes. Amy Grant, *Sun-Times* graphologist, daily decided the prize winners and composed such gibberish as: "Let's make an analysis of Whittingham's handwriting and see what it reveals to me. Notice the U-shaped 'm's' and 'n's' with small vowels. It showed he knows how to handle people and has a strong sense of responsibility."

No wonder psychiatrists and leaders of the mental hygiene movement have a tough time combatting such superstitions as that brunettes are more trustworthy than blondes; red hair indicates a quick temper; a recessive chin means a weak will; a square jaw is a sign of courage; smart people are physically weak; hair on the chest is a sign of virility; heavy hair is a sign of strength (remember Samson and Delilah?); brains and beauty do not go together; a "lean and hungry" look. is a sign of deceitfulness as are also shifty eyes. The following debunking column by Sydney J. Harris in the June 4, 1947 Chicago *Daily News* was a journalistic rarity:

By Sydney J. Harris

Superstitions die hard. Science has conclusively proved that you can't tell anything about a person's character from his looks—but most people keep right on judging others by childish standards.

We still cling to the outworn belief that red-heads are hot-tempered. that man with a recessive chin is weak-willed, that a square jaw indicates manly courage and aggressiveness. Even those who should know better often fall into such delusions.

In Gen. Mark Clark's story of his African adventure, he quotes King George VI as telling him that Adm. Darlan was not a man to be trusted. "I remember seeing Darlan at a luncheon," the king said. "He had shifty eyes." Darlan was a *rat,* but because his ethics were shifty, not his eyes.

A couple of months ago, Dr. David W. Cook told the American Management Association that most so-called "systems" used by personnel departments in hiring employees are "the bunk."

"Generalities can't be applied to individuals because of their physical makeup," he told his audience, and employers will sadly agree that many a lad with an All-American face turns out to be an embezzler just as often as the fellow with the ferret puss.

SHOWUP

A beautiful demonstration of this fallacy was given by Prof. Fred August in his criminology class at the University of Kansas City some years back. He passed out 75 photographs to his class, asking them to identify the criminal types and the noncriminal.

You may remember the payoff—50 per cent of the students chose J. Edgar Hoover's picture as that of a criminal. On the other hand, not one student selected "Baby Face" Nelson, the notorious desperado.

For every Einstein who looks the part, there are hundreds of philosophers and mathematicians who look like insurance agents, doormen, plumber's assistants and truck drivers. The first time I saw Bertrand Russell, he reminded me of a dishonest jockey. And everyone has remarked that New York's most distinguished dowager resembles a washerwoman on a gin jag.

It shouldn't be necessary to point out such obvious facts at this late date in human history; but, unfortunately, millions of people still think they can size up a person at a glance. That's why we have to have such large con-fidence-men squads on our police departments. The suckers persist in trusting the wrong face.

Despite Harris' excellent piece his own paper, as well as many others, gave serious space to a couple of members of the Illinois Gen-eral Assembly who, in March, 1949, persuaded the legislature to inves-tigate the University of Chicago and Roosevelt College for alleged com-munism because of the impression made by a number of students from those institutions who went to Springfield to lobby against bills which they believed violated freedom of speech, press and assembly. In the process of the debate Sen. William J. Connors, Democratic leader in the Senate, called the students "a dirty greasy bunch of kids with their hair not combed," and asked, "How can they be clean inside if they're so dirty outside?" and Sen. G. William Horsley declared: "These young people do not have the clean-cut American youth look."

As Harris indicated in his column, scientific experiments to test ability to judge character by facial expressions always have negative results. There have been many such tests, some of them appearing in newspapers and magazines. *Life,* for instance, in its March 10, 1947, issue printed the pictures of 14 criminals and as many reputable citi-zens and invited its readers to tell the difference. In such tests sub-jects answer on the basis of their stereotypes of "men of distinction," dope peddlers, Tarzans, and the like.

If any correlation ever is found between bodily characteristics and personality traits it will come from careful, patient scientific experi-mentation of which there already has been quite a bit. Ernest Kretsch-mer, a German psychologist, made the first important classification. In his *Physique and Character* (Harcourt, Brace, 1925) he cited three leading types and described their personality traits as follows: (1) asthenic—long and thin, given to melancholia; (2) athletic—well rounded physically and well adjusted psychologically; (3) pyknic—round and ruddy in appearance, jolly in disposition, overcompensated extraverts. Modern leader in this field is Dr. William Sheldon who describes the endomorphic (fat), mesomorphic (athletic), and ecto-morphic (lean) in *Varieties of Human Physique* (Harper, 1940). He also ascribes personality traits to the physical types. The endomorphics, for instance, are viscerotonic, love physical comfort, good food, good company, polite ceremony, and sleep; they are good family men. The mesomorphic are somatotonic emotionally, loving physical adventure, risk-taking and physical exercise and being in general most uninhibited. The ectomorphic are the cerebral type, alert and oversensitive, generally introverted, tense and restrained, adapting themselves to active routine, as military life, only with difficulty.

But if study of a sufficient number of cases establishes the validity of either this or some other attempt to correlate physical types with personality types, it will not necessarily prove that the explanation is anatomical. What shapes and sizes and behavior traits are considered best is socially determined. A person's personality may well be the outcome of his counterreaction to his fellows' reaction to his appearance. It would be difficult, for example, for a cripple used to being shunned and ridiculed to avoid developing a disagreeable or shy personality as a defense reaction.

Numbers. In addition to the unlucky 13, the numbers 3 and 7 are of particular significance. The former, of course, suggests the trinity and so generally is lucky. The latter is mentioned many times in the Bible. God made the world in six days, rested on the seventh; Pharaoh dreamed of seven in several different connections. For centuries there were only seven known planets; to be the seventh son of a seventh son supposedly endowed one with special powers.

Among the primitives all numbers had significance. In general odd numbers were masculine, even numbers feminine. Everything and everybody had his number, the compilations often being mixed with astrology. Today the superstitious have lucky and unlucky numbers, important to them particularly when they gamble but also kept in mind when requesting automobile license numbers or telephone numbers and on similar occasions.

Typical of the "number magic" of the present are the following examples which have appeared in numerous magazines and newspapers.

It may prove interesting to your readers to tie up Hitler's career with certain prophecies in the Book of Revelation. I quote the 18th verse of the 13th chapter: "Here is wisdom. Let him that hath understanding count the number of the beast; for it is the number of a man, and his number is six hundred threescore and six."

By using an old cipher in which A is 100, B is 101, C is 102, etc., we find only one man whose name is 666.

H	107
I	108
T	119
L	111
E	104
R	117
	666

	Mussolini	Stalin	Hitler	FDR
Born	1883	1879	1889	1882
Came to power	1922	1924	1933	1933
Years in power	18	16	7	7
Age	57	61	51	58
	3880	3880	3880	3880

3880 divided by 2 = 1940

The following sentence from a pre-game football account in the Oct. 10, 1947 Chicago *Sun* is typical of what may be found quite frequently on any sports page:

Although he admits having but little faith in superstition, the Rocket mentor was quick to point out that, perhaps the number "7" might hold something favorable in store for his boys.

Despite the miserable record that most ex-sports writers have made upon attempting to become writers in other fields, there probably are not many sports editors at least so stupid as not to realize they are helping to perpetuate nonsense in this way. Maybe not, however. If governors of states are not more intelligent, why expect it of lesser men? The following, indicating what is meant, is from the daily column of John Dreiske, political editor, in the May 15, 1947 Chicago *Times:*

HE HAS GOV. GREEN'S 'NUMBER'

Springfield, Ill.—Victor Georg, who ranks high among Gov. Dwight H. Green's advisers in his professional capacity as a numerologist, is not able to sustain himself on numerology exclusively and so has a job as a field investigator in the state department of agriculture.

It was Georg who accompanied Green to the Republican strategy conference attended by GOP senators, governors and others at Mackinac island in 1943. He has been a potent factor in helping to make up the governor's mind on more than just this one occasion.

Georg regularly holds numerologal clinics in the Flamingo room (a bar with a carpet) of the Leland hotel attended by the governor's intimates. What the governor doesn't hear in person concerning what he ought to do with the state's affairs and be right with the numbers is relayed to him by members of this clinic.

One Georg recipe for success is outstanding. It concerns Supreme Court Clerk Earle Benjamin Searcy. Along about the time it became definite that Searcy, a former state senator from Springfield, was to be the candidate for Supreme court clerk, he, as a member of the Georg clinic for better numbers, was advised to no longer be known signature-wise as "Earl B. Searcy."

He was induced to change his signature and ballot name to "Earle Benjamin Searcy," and the numbers would take care of the rest. Well, this proved to be a great boon to Georg's numerology business because after that Searcy, Earle Benjamin, that is, was elected.

There was one exception to Georg's string of successes. He told State Director of Agriculture Arnold P. Benson that, according to the numbers, he was a cinch to be elected secretary of state in 1944. However, even Babe Ruth struck out now and then.

Fortune Telling. On the authority of the Better Business Bureau, *Look,* Sept. 4, 1945, called fortunetelling a "$200,000,000 racket." That was in wartime when fear of death and uncertainty about the future always cause a boom in the trade of the card sharks, tea-leaf readers, palmists, numerologists, crystal-ball gazers, mind readers, astrologers, and similar fakes. To expose the local soothsayers and necromancers is not an infrequent assignment. The *Look* article includes the contradictory prognostications obtained by two investigators each of whom visited six different seers. The following is typical of the kind of story which results from such an assignment.

By Hyman Goldberg

I am very confused.

The other day I happened to be walking along Madison Ave. and the fresh air got sort of overpowering so I dropped into a saloon.

The name of the place is Cerutti's, and it is a very nice place and they have good medicinal whiskey and after a while I felt better.

Well, after a while a lady comes up to my table, a nice motherly looking sort of lady who looks like a teacher I used to have in PS 42 and she says she would like to tell my fortune.

So of course I asked her to sit down because it is only the polite thing to do when a lady comes up to you in a saloon and talks to you. It seems you can't go to a saloon nowadays without somebody grabbing your hand, or your head, to tell your fortune.

She said her name is Mary Talley, and she pulled out a deck of cards and said:

"Cut them three times."

I did.

TWO GOVERNMENT LETTERS

"You are going to get two Government letters soon," she said, "one of them asking for more information."

"From my draft board, or from the Internal Revenue?" I asked.

She said she didn't know, but anyway she saw uniforms all around me. The uniforms were going to surround me very shortly. Then she said there were many women in my life. I asked her if they were the ones wearing the uniforms. She disregarded that.

"There are also three babies in your life," she said, "but they're not yours."

She didn't know what they were doing hanging around me if they're not mine.

"One woman loves you intensely," she said intensely, "and another woman, whom you haven't seen for a long time, will come back. She will ask a favor."

A man at the next table, who had been listening intently to my life secrets, snorted.

"Hah," he said, "they always ask for favors."

Miss Talley and I disregarded him.

GOOD NEWS

In 1942, said Miss Talley, I am going to have more stability. She said I was going to make more money. You listening, boss?

When Miss Talley got through with my fortune, she told me that she feels things about people in her stomach.

"I don't eat until 2:30 a.m.," she said, "because I keep feeling things about people in my stomach and if I ate it would interfere."

I left Cerutti's and went for a long walk and thought about the things that are in store for me according to what Miss Talley said, and I got upset, so when I found myself at 123 E. 54th St., which is, oddly enough, a saloon called "One-Two-Three," I went in for a little refreshment.

I was sitting there and I guess I must have looked worried or something because the bartender said:

"What's the matter, bud?"

So I said I was worried about my future.

"You don't have to be," he said, "because we have the best astrologer in the world here, name of Myra Kingsley."

So I sat down at Miss Kingsley's table and she asked me when I was born. I am a Leo, for which I am sorry because I know a couple of guys named Leo and I don't envy them a bit.

Miss Kingsley took one look at me and at her book and she said:

"You have had a very sheltered life; you have never had to struggle."

She was perfectly right. I have never been out of work since I was 15 when I got my workies.

Miss Kingsley said she didn't see any uniforms around me at all. So there, Miss Talley. She said I was very fortunate and would make a lot of money. There must be *something* in all this, don't you think, boss?

About this time I thought maybe I should try one more fortune teller and let two out of three win, so I went over to Armando's on 55th St., where a young lady named Julienne, like in potato, came over and dropped a card on my table which said:

"Julienne, you certainly hit the nail right on the head—you should be a member of the Dies Committee."

It was signed: "J. Parnell Thomas, Dies Committee, Wash., D.C." And he should know because who knows better than the Dies Committee about crystal bowls?

Julienne looked at my hands with a flash light, and she said:

"You did a great deal of traveling between the ages of 14 and 17."

She was right. In those years I moved three times, from College Ave., to Seabury Pl., and then to Crotona Park East, practically all over the Bronx.

She said she saw in my life a lot of women, and a lot of money, which made me feel pretty good, so I went on to Willie Henderson's saloon and hung around there for a long time until Willie took my head in his hands and said:

"You better go home now, because if you don't, you are liable to get a hole in your head."

And that is closer than any of the fortune tellers came, because I *would* have got a hole in the head.

—*PM*, Nov. 16, 1942

In the same papers which like to do such things, however, are likely to be found daily horoscopes. Or they have an avidity for such side-bars as the following, from the Jan. 25, 1944 Chicago *Daily News:*

By Robert Faherty

Mrs. Frank Starr Williams was more interested in money than love, said a Chicago astrologer today, an hour before the safe deposit box of the slain Mrs. Williams yielded $250,000.

The woman astrologer, who has a North Side consultation room and has given readings to Mrs. Williams, found in the stars, she said, that Mrs. Williams was very ambitious and energetic, and that her talent and determination were applied to material things.

Adele Born Williams' sign is Sagittarius, ruled by the money planet, Jupiter, the astrologer found, but the influence of Gemini also was strong.

"By reading her charts I knew her past," said this woman, who is consulted by hundreds of women in all walks of life. "People in Sagittarius do not like to have their readings disclosed—for fear they will be called dominating. But she was a Sagittarius!"

There was also a reading of "accidents"—showing that Mrs. Williams was subject to mishaps, of which the shooting in the Drake Hotel might be called one.

This leader of the horoscope trade offered what appeared to be advice to the detectives trying to solve the mystery. With what seemed disappointment, she said: "In her chart there are no highlights—no history of romances and intrigues—there is money, mostly."

She added: "The charts of movie people and sailors show highlights."

Or they give space to such bunk as the following:

Paris, Dec. 26.—(UP)—French astrologers see the Allies winning the war by the end of 1940 and predict that at least one of Europe's leaders will die violently during the new year.

French newspapers give prominence to the predictions of well-known astrologers.

Typical was the comment of "Madame F," who said that Adolf Hitler would die like "Robespierre," who was guillotined. She said Hitler is more agitated and nervous than ever as a result of dissension among his chiefs. He also has "lost face," she said.

"Madame F" thought the war would not end in bloody battles but would be won through economic means.

"I see an end to the war relatively soon, followed by a period of contentment," she said. "After a period of obscurity in the first year, naval battles will be resumed suddenly, with decisive victories for the Allies. Germany will lack able leaders and will soon begin to harvest what it has sown. Hitler will be replaced by another as authoritative as he. That is why his removal will not immediately bring peace. Then will follow a period of great activity, particularly in the diplomatic field."

"Madame N" predicted two assassinations in "neighboring countries" but said they should not disturb the Allies. One assassination, she said, would be followed by a revolution that would be "advantageous to us." There also will be a death in "a royal family to the South."

Outstanding dates will be Feb. 11 and July 31, "Madame N" said.

Others said the war would last 420 days, would be extended to the Balkans, would find Belgium joining the Allies after an attack by Germany, would see the end of the Rome-Berlin axis and finally would result in war between Germany and Russia.

—Chicago *Daily News*, Dec. 26, 1939

Space does not permit detailed discussion of astrology and the other phoney sciences. The preceding story needed only time to refute it which is the case with most such predictions. One factor operating in the fortunetellers' favor is the disposition some who consult them have to follow their predictions as though they were advice and then illogically to give the soothsayer credit for great powers. Mostly, however, they remember only the good guesses and overlook the bad. Some important persons patronize quacks. In the April 9, 1938 *Liberty*, Madame Marcia confessed that she gave clairvoyant readings to a president of the United States and his wife and added: "Now I had senators and cabinet members and congressmen and judges, bankers, lobbyists, diplomats, and heads of great corporations coming to my home on R Street to beg for astrological readings and clairvoyant guidance." Is it any wonder that dream books and their like are so popular with frustrated clerks and stenographers?

Astrology, which teaches that human actions are influenced by the stars and other heavenly bodies, originated in early biblical days or earlier. Then, and until comparatively recent times, the earth was believed to be the center of the universe and the stars and planets to have fixed positions. Knowing the exact moment of a person's birth the astrologers say they can tell, by the positions of the stars, what the newly born's luck is likely to be for the duration of his life. When we say a person is moonstruck we are using astrological language. Our word "lunatic" also comes from the Latin "luna," meaning "moon." Making wishes when seeing "falling stars" and talking about lucky and unlucky stars is to reveal the influence of what should be recognized as utterly unscientific belief.

Premonitions. Especially in the early days of his syndicated "Case Records of a Psychologist," Dr. George W. Crane debunked many fallacies. The following, which appeared in the Feb 11, 1936 Milwaukee *Journal,* was typical:

Case B-174: Albert S., 48, is the head of an automobile agency and a very competent business man.

"Last Saturday night I felt a presentiment that all was not well," he told me at a banquet which we were attending, "and that night I had a dream that my mother was dying.

"Now I had not heard from her for more than a week but in her last letter she had said that she was not feeling very well. When we had visited her a month or two before she was able to be up and about the house, so there was no reason for my worrying about her.

"But before breakfast the morning after my dream I received a telegram stating that she had suffered a stroke during the night and had died within a few minutes.

"Dr. Crane, if this isn't mental telepathy, how in the world can you explain it?"

THE DIAGNOSIS

In the first place, we should keep in mind that it is redundant to speak of "mental telepathy." Telepathy refers to thought transference and therefore we should never put the word "mental" in front of "telepathy." Since I believe the great majority of people are guilty of this error, I point it out.

Telepathy has been a debatable topic for generations and it is the bed-rock of spiritualism. But psychologists never have been able to demonstrate direct influence of one mind by another when two persons are in different rooms or different cities.

IS TELEPATHY POSSIBLE?

In our modern shockproof age scientists do not say that telepathy is absolutely impossible but that it has never been proved. Chance occurrences of similarity in thought between two persons, however, do not prove the existence of thought transference.

To have validity in the scientific world a thing must be capable of being repeated under controlled conditions, and thus far telepathy has failed absolutely to stand this rigid test.

Psychologists will admit, of course, that if two persons have had the same experiences, then objects which confront them will often give rise to the same ideas or memories. If I were to ask you to give me the first thing that comes to mind when I say "white" I know that a large percentage would say "black." This is not telepathy, but an example of common experiences with the same situations.

FOREBODING AND PREMONITION

Albert's premonition during the evening is probably simple enough if we had all the facts. He admitted that he thought his mother looked a little pale when he last visited her. And her usual weekly letter to him had not arrived that morning.

One of his business friends had been hurt in an automobile accident that same day and taken to a hospital. Does it seem a great stretch of probability that Albert's thoughts about his friend's accident may have led to a thought of death?

Death in his own family might be the next thought. Who would be the most likely candidate? His mother's pallor and the failure of her usual letters could easily get him into a brooding mood and thus could have continued into his dreams. This is probably a case of "hunch" or intuition and doesn't need telepathy for its explanation.

(Copyright, 1936 by the Hopkins Syndicate.)

Of late years more than logical columns of that sort have been needed to offset the predilection of press associations for playing up premonitions or their lack in almost all cases of accidental death. For instance in the United Press' Jan. 31, 1948 report from New Delhi following the murder of Mohandas K. Gandhi appeared the following:

It was revealed today that he had a premonition of death. Retiring Thursday night, Gandhi said to his 18-year-old granddaughter Manu:

"This is a strange world. How long can one be at the game?"

Rising early yesterday, Gandhi said to his personal attendant:

"Bring me all my important papers. I must reply today. Tomorrow may never be."

A year earlier the rival Associated Press originated the following:

New York, Jan. 26.—(AP)—Interviewed in Copenhagen only a few days before the plane disaster that killed her and 21 others, Grace Moore, American operatic soprano, told a reporter:

"It is wonderful to live and sing."

Miss Moore had left the United States last July for a European concert tour and appearances before American occupation troops.

'GREAT . . . TO HELP OTHERS'

Last week, apparently without premonition of tragedy, she told a reporter for a Copenhagen newspaper, the Berlingske Tidende. . . .

Another from the United Press in 1947:

Seattle, Feb. 2—(UP)—Two young children were buried and crushed to death early today when a landslide of tons of earth and rock smashed through their bedroom at Kirkland while their parents were obeying a premonition to move them to a safer place. . . .

And once again from the Associated Press in 1947:

Detroit, Jan. 12.—(AP)—An unexplained premonition of danger prompted one passenger hastily to scribble out a will before boarding an airliner that crashed today near Galax, Va.

Mrs. Chloe Newman, 42, of Port Huron, Mich., who was killed in the crash, was driven here by three other women to catch the Miami-bound plane. They stopped in a restaurant before proceeding to the airport.

A nervous condition which caused Mrs. Newman to visit her physician a short time earlier struck her again at the dinner table. She pulled an old envelope from her purse and drew up the will.

Long before Freud became interested in them, dreams were the object of fascinating, awesome interest. Primitives believed that dreams were the experiences of the soul which departed the body during sleep. It is dangerous, psychiatrists agree today, to generalize regarding the meanings of dreams. Similar dreams may have different interpretations for different persons. As *Look* pointed out in a pictorial article, "Your Dreams," by Dr. Robert Clark in its June 8, 1937, issue: "If you dream of finding yourself at a dinner without clothes on, you may be cold and in need of covering. This dream also may indicate a feeling of inferiority or immoral tendencies which you wish to hide." Whereas Dr. Clark wrote, "Falling dreams may be due to worry, perhaps of a 'falling out' with a loved one, or to a fear of failure in love," in the April, 1940, *American* there appeared a "table for interpreting common dreams based on the findings of widely known psychiatrists" which interpreted a "falling" dream as meaning, "You have an urge to do something which you consider wrong." Dr. Clark said a flying dream may "indicate a longing for greater freedom in love or a desire to escape from an unpleasant situation," but the *American* interpretation of such a dream was, "You are ambitious to rise above some sort of limitations." What some creditable psychiatrist would say is unknown, because creditable psychiatrists wouldn't take part in such journalistic hokum. At that, such explanations are much to be preferred to the bilge that is to be found in dream books for sale on almost any newsstand unless all sold out as happens with considerable rapidity. Some day maybe a scientific dream book will be available. If such happens, however, it is pretty certain that it will not foster the unscientific notion that the future is revealed in one's sleep.

Telepathy. It is fairly certain also that if scientific experimentation ever establishes the fact of thought transference between persons there will be seen to be nothing supernatural (or supernormal, as some prefer) about the phenomenon. As of this writing expert opinion is divided over the experiments which Professor J. B. Rhine has been conducting for a couple of decades at Duke University into what he calls extrasensory perception. Probably a good-sized majority of other psychologists still are incredulous, although they have given their colleague a fair hearing.

The point for newspapermen to note is that the Duke experiments are conducted with the strictest of scientific controls and nothing except the simplest transferences between two people not far apart has been claimed. They are described in Professor Rhine's *New Frontiers of the Mind* (Farrar, Rinehart, 1937) and *The Reach of the Mind* (Sloane, 1947). Regardless of how they may feel about the evidence herein contained, psychologists are of one mind regarding the vast majority of the professional mind readers, clairvoyants, crystal gazers and other professional entertainers who without doubt perform amazingly skillful tricks but by means which it is not difficult for anyone, with a modicum of experience in magic, to figure out. That goes for the youthful Patrick Marquis, twelve-year-old Los Angeles schoolboy, who received fulsome newspaper and magazine attention in 1936 for doing the familiar X-ray eye trick, purchasable from any dealer in magical secrets and equipment for a reasonable sum. That goes also for Joseph Dunninger who, until the smell of the fleshpots clouded his reason in recent years, began and ended every performance by emphatically declaring his performance to be entertainment only. As for laymen who think they cause people to turn their heads by staring at their backs—well, nothing about them; they're too silly to mention.

Spiritualism. Suffice it to say about this much-discussed subject that no medium ever sought to obtain the $10,000 which first Harry Houdini and later Joseph Dunninger offered to pay for any psychic phenomenon incapable of being duplicated by trickery or explained by natural means. Table-tappings, ectoplasm, levitations, trumpeting, slate and other written messages, ouija and planchette boards, spirit photographs, and other tricks of the professional medium's trade have been exposed and explained over and over again. It takes a professional usually to do it so an investigative newspaperman, unskilled in magic, runs the risk of being taken in by the eerie sights in store for him if he starts nosing around.

That man should crave everlasting life and consequently communication with those who already have attained it is understandable. Wrote Joseph Jastrow in *Fact and Fable in Psychology*: "Spiritualism represents a systematization of popular beliefs and superstitions, modified by echoes of religious and philosophical doctrines; it thus contains factors which owe their origin to other interests than those which lead directly to the occult. Its main purpose was to establish the reality of communication with departed spirits; the means, which at first spontaneously presented themselves and later were devised for this purpose, were in large measure not original. The rappings are in accord with the traditional folklore of ghosts; their transformation into a signal code (although a device discovered before) may have been due to the originality of the Fox children; the planchette has its analogies in Chinese and European modes of divination; clairvoyance was incorporated from the phenomena of artificial somnambulism, as practiced by the successors of Mesmer; the 'sensitive' or 'medium' suggests the same origin as well as the popular belief in the gift of supernatural powers in favored individuals; others of the phenomena such as 'levitation' and 'cabinet performances' have their counterparts in Oriental magic; 'slate writing,' 'form materialisations,' 'spirit messages' and 'spirit photographs' are, in the main, modern contributions. . . . Spiritualism thus appeals to a deep-seated craving in human nature, that of assurance of personal immortality and of communion with the departed. Just so long as a portion of mankind will accept material evidence of such a belief, and will even countenance the irreverence, the triviality and the vulgarity surrounding the manifestations; just so long as those persons will misjudge their own powers of detecting how the alleged supernatural appearances are really produced, and remain unimpressed by the principles upon which alone a consistent explanation is possible, just so long will spiritualism and kindred delusions flourish." [2]

The experiment described in the following article which appeared in the Oct. 31, 1936 Philadelphia *Record* ended in failure.

By the Associated Press

Hollywood, Calif., Oct. 30.—The last conscious effort by Mrs. Harry Houdini to communicate with the ghost of her husband, Houdini, the great necromancer, will be made Saturday night—the 10th anniversary of his death.

"If there is no contact then," she said tonight, "I will be forced to one of two conclusions—either that personal survival after death is a falsehood or that there is no hope for any of us to reach those who have gone on."

The Hallowe'en seance will be held on the roof of a Hollywood hotel, from 8:30 to 9 p.m. (P.S.T.)

[2] From *Fact and Fable in Psychology*. Copyright, 1900, by Houghton Mifflin.

16 CITIES JOIN IT

At corresponding hours in 16 cities of the United States, and in London, England, Melbourne, Australia, and Victoria, B.C., other groups will gather to assist her, she said. They will be composed of spiritualists, scientists and close friends of the great magician.

Houdini died in Detroit, October 31, 1926.

"It's just a coincidence that this attempt to reach him falls on Hallowe'en, the night when spooks are supposed to be out," Mrs. Houdini laughed. "But our agreement was to last exactly 10 years following his death.

"The seances will be held on the last hour of that period."

FORTUNE FOR INQUIRIES

Following the death of his mother, Mrs. Houdini said, he was told by spiritualist mediums that she transmitted messages to him through them.

"He spent a fortune investigating such supposed phenomena," she said. "Inasmuch as he was himself a past-master of all the tricks and illusions magicians use, he frequently exposed supposed 'contacts' with the spirit world as impostors."

So far as she knew, she said, Houdini never found a scintilla of evidence to support the belief of spirit-visitations.

Nevertheless, they made a compact that Houdini would attempt to communicate with her after his death. It involved a code message—which has never been delivered—and other mechanical manifestations of his spirit presence.

10-YEAR COMPACT

"Beatrice, I'll come to you somehow, even if I have to go through hell," she said he told her on his death-bed.

The compact was to last 10 years and no longer. At 9 o'clock Saturday night, the last moment of it will have run out. The last set time for Houdini's ghost to speak will have gone.

The seance will merely be a gathering of a few people, one a Superior Court Justice of Los Angeles county. Seated at a round table, beneath a ruby light, they will remain silent, in a "receptive" frame of mind.

Mrs. Houdini said certain pre-arranged signals and evidences known to her alone, will indicate if Houdini's spirit is at hand.

Similar experiences were conducted by Howard Thurston, great magician, and other friends of the agnostic lawyer, Clarence Darrow, for years after his death in 1938 also with negative results. The good that stories of such attempts to raise the dead do, however, is more than offset by yarns such as the following:

Baltimore, Aug. 9—(AP)—Police combing the cluttered apartment of a murdered medium came up with a "voodoo" curse today. They reported discovery of a prescription bottle with the paper-doll figure of a man suspended, head down, inside.

The name "Mike Pappas" was scribbled on the doll three times. Police explained voodoo practitioners use such devices to bring death or illness to enemies.

A Baltimore restaurateur, Mike Pappas, was one of the persons questioned in connection with the slaying of the spiritualist, 60-year-old Mrs. Emma A. Kefalos. He was described as an acquaintance both of her and her second husband who has been dead four years.

Fellow mediums of Mrs. Kefalos tried to put a supernatural finger on her slayer at a seance, but no important clue came through from the spirit world. Police, meantime, rounded up Baltimore mediums and spiritualists, crystal ball gazers and fortune tellers. They also asked Mrs. Kefalos' clients to come in.

Her body, bound hand and foot, was found yesterday in the raspberry-tinted, second-floor apartment where she presided at seances and gave spiritual readings. She had been strangled with an ironing cord.

Mrs. Ora Dunn, 45, told detectives that Mrs. Kefalos—her best friend—had premonitions.

"She was scared to death," reported Mrs. Dunn. "She was even afraid to go to sleep. She knew she was going to die the way she did."

Mrs. Kefalos lived alone with a plump tabby cat. A fellow medium said she was a "wonderful lady but a mediocre spiritualist who had a lot of trouble with men friends."

—New York *Daily Compass*, Aug. 10, 1949

Ghosts. The English are way ahead of Americans in the matter of ghosts. Their countrysides abound with haunted houses and legends of eerie adventures. In recent years, however, this country has been doing pretty well in this, as in many other respects, in catching up with the Mother Country. There already is a sizeable literature of "true" ghost stories, such as William O. Stevens' *Unbidden Guests* (Dodd, Mead, 1946) and also a few good iconoclastic pieces, including *Ghosts I Have Talked With,* by Henry C. McComas (Williams, Wilkins, 1935). Neither believers nor skeptics venture publication until after what they consider thoroughgoing and scientific investigation. Nevertheless, a newspaper will rush into print with any kind of unfounded ghost story such as the following which was accompanied by front and inside page pictures:

Belleville—While St. Libory residents whispered in awe about the eerie "visitor" at the Greten farm, Catholic officials began an investigation of the mysterious "spiritual manifestations."

Mr. and Mrs. Tony Greten report they have been visited almost nightly since May 1 by a "spirit" which writes messages, shakes beds and hurls pencils in anger.

The Greten farm is in Washington County, about 280 miles southwest of Chicago.

NOTES EXCHANGED

The Catholic investigation began after the Rev. Edward Dahmus, pastor of St. Liborius Church where the Gretens are parish members, visited the farm and said he exchanged notes with the "spirit."

The "spirit" according to Mrs. Greten, apparently is attached to her 11-year-old son, Jerome. There are nine other children.

It makes its bed-rattling appearance, Mrs. Greten said, only after Jerome goes to bed. It rattles only his bed, she said, and will not touch it if anyone other than Jerome is lying there.

It wasn't until they told Father Dahmus of the mysterious visits that they realized it might be a "spirit," Mrs. Greten said.

PENCIL TAKES WINGS

They then put down a piece of paper and a pencil and asked in writing: "What do you want? Why are you here?"

"The pencil just flew across the room," Mrs. Greten said.

Next they tried pen and ink. But, according to Mrs. Greten, the bottle of ink moved across the table and spilled on the floor.

At Father Dahmus' suggestion they laid out an indelible pencil. This time, Mrs. Greten declared, the pencil wrote "mass."

Mrs. Greten said they then laid out a box of crayons and the "spirit" wrote "1,000." None of the family could attach any significance to the number.

PRIEST ASKS QUESTION

When Father Dahmus wrote, "Are you a good or an evil spirit?" Mrs. Greten said the pencil was hurled at the priest. He then said it must be an evil spirit.

Hundreds of persons pass nightly by the Greten farm to peek at the home but few work up the courage to go to the door.

Ten "spirit" experts went to the home and came away shaking their heads.

"There are more knockings and bed shakings when we come to visit," one woman said. "It seems the spirit is objecting to our presence."

Most of the 300 residents of St. Libory frankly admit they are afraid to look into the mysterious happenings.

NO CHURCH COMMENT

Bishop Albert R. Zuroweste of the Catholic diocese at Belleville said it will be some time before an official church opinion is formed. Until then, he said, there will be no church comment.

Father Dahmus described the Gretens as "normal, happy and devout people." Their farm is modern, well kept and prosperous.

Mrs. Greten, who becomes angry if anyone refers to the "spirit" as a ghost, said she had hoped it would be a "good spirit." The Gretens said they are not afraid and will not move.

—Chicago *Sun-Times*, June 27, 1949

Witchcraft. "Thou shalt not suffer a witch to live," its supposed author, Moses, wrote in Exodus 22:18. Thus, belief in witchcraft is seen to be of ancient origin. By Charlemagne's time it was so widespread the emperor had to put a ban on it. From the thirteenth through the seventeenth centuries it was a generally accepted belief despite four or five papal bulls against it. Since Luther, Erasmus and Calvin all believed in witches, the Protestant Reformation had no effect. Throughout history hundreds of thousands of persons actually have been put to death because others convinced courts of law that they were in league with the devil and using their fiendish powers to the detriment of the accusers.

If anyone thinks "those days are gone forever" he hasn't read William Seabrook's *Witchcraft* (Harcourt, Brace, 1940), nor has he kept up with his periodical, including newspaper, reading. Witness the following typical stories:

Detroit, Jan. 20.—(UP)—A Negro woman's fears of being "sacrificed to Allah" in a pot of boiling water led today to evidence that activities of a voodoo cult extended to New York, Chicago and Canada.

Investigation indicated, police said, that a Japanese deported after a cult murder in 1932, was directing the organization's weird ceremonies from a Canadian hideout.

Verlen McQueen, Negro, who calls himself Verlen Ali, was arrested on complaint of his wife that he was preparing to boil her and their 11-year-old daughter alive at a gathering of "worshippers of Allah. . . ."

—Philadelphia *Record*, Jan. 21, 1937

New York, Oct. 2—(UP)—Father Divine took credit for the punching power behind Heavyweight Champion Joe Louis' fists today, and warned the champ not to be critical of this claim "because if he does, he will lose out."

Divine, in a sermon in his paper "The New Day," said:

"When he (Joe Louis) was born, the transmission of the spirit of my prophecy and declaration was reincarnated in him for the world for which he was predestined to reign as king in . . . he did not know anything about it; his parents did not know anything about it."

Divine said he got the idea of creating another Negro heavyweight champion when Jack Johnson lost the title "and it was declared that another so-and-so would never ascend to the ring, would never become to be the world's heavyweight champion."

Divine said color had nothing to do with Louis' success. . . .

—Chicago *Sun*, Oct. 2, 1946

Brooklyn—(UP)—The Rev. Bennay J. F. Benson, pastor of the Brooklyn Dutch Reformed church, knelt on the steps of Borough Hall today and prayed for the Brooklyn Dodgers.

He asked that they receive an even break in the pennant race with the St. Louis Cardinals, and added:

"If the Lord gives Brooklyn an even break, they're good enough to win."

* * *

About 200 persons gathered around the steps of Borough Hall at noon. Just as a large clock started booming 12 times, Benson took off his hat, kneeled and prayed:

"O Lord, we're praying for those Dodgers. Their chances don't look so good right now. Everybody is praying for the Bums to win.

"O Lord, give we pray, give to the Dodgers an even chance to win the pennant; like the man in the woods who is crossing the stream on a fallen tree trunk, who met a bear in the middle, coming his way—

" 'O Lord,' he prayed, 'I only ask if You don't help me, don't help the bear either.' "

After the prayer Benson was asked whether other Brooklyn clergymen approved of his actions.

"They gave me the double E," he said.

"What's the double E?"

"Envious Eyebrow."

He will pray on the Borough Hall steps daily until the National League pennant race is decided.

—Chicago *Daily News*, Sept. 25, 1946

Gil Dodds, track star and holder of the world's indoor record for the one-mile run, told 700 fundamental Protestant youth yesterday that he won races because people like them prayed for him every time he ran. . . .

Chicago *Sun*, March 31, 1947

William Seabrook began an article, "Witchcraft—Does It Exist Today?" in the April, 1939, *Cosmopolitan* as follows:

"In 1929 a lady in Allentown was murdered, her body literally covered with anti-witchcraft amulets,* and in 1931 a young matron of

---

* Miss Verna Octavia Delp was murdered.

Wilkes-Barre, graduate of a New England college, killed an alleged witch with a knife.† 'She had cast a spell over my husband,' said this college girl, 'and it was her life or mine.'

"Belief in witchcraft, far from being dead today, still holds more than half of humanity all in a grip of basic but unreasoned fear that often leads to horror, homicide and murder. Rational efforts to wipe it out by destroying superstition have failed because they have been based on false logic. It is always assumed that, since rationally there can be no *supernatural* power in witchcraft, it possesses no power of *any sort*. False logic can sometimes lead to true conclusions, but in this case the conclusion is also false. . . ."

† Matron who killed Millie Dilley was Mrs. Carl Thomsen.

Still available also are copies of a pamphlet, *Begone Satan!* subtitled, "A Soul-Stirring Account of Diabolical Possession. Woman Cursed By Her Own Father, Possessed from 14th Year Till Her 40th Year. Devils Appearing: Beelzebub, Lucifer, Judas, Jacob and Mina," published by the Rev. Celestine Kapsner, O.S.B., St. John's Abbey, Collegeville, Minn. It is the story of an exorcism in 1928 at Earling, Ia., by Fr. Theophilus of St. Anthony's monastery of Capuchin Friars at Marathon, Wis. Write-ups appeared, among other places, in *Time* for Feb. 17, 1936 and the Milwaukee *Journal* for March 1, 1936.

And in the Ozarks today they still drive spikes in effigies to get rid of enemies and go in heavily for charms and potions to bring lovers to time. Read about it in *Ozark Superstitions* by Vance Randolph (Columbia University, 1947). It'll keep you on the lookout for the Evil Eye for the rest of your days.

Curses. But why read it, after all, when the newspapers provide such entertaining stuff as the following from the Springfield (Ill.) *State Journal* of Jan. 28, 1940?

Hollywood, Jan. 27.—(INS)—Grimly stalks the "curse of Cahuenga pass" today in the ghoulish annals of its legend, with another life listed among its victims.

Of course, modern skeptics who don't believe such things, smile and say "it's all coincidence."

But, nevertheless, Henry (Hank) Jones, the adventuresome mining man who scoffed at the oft and long whispered legend, was dead today . . . dead just as are eight others who sought the Benito Juarez fortune in the vicinity of Hollywood Bowl. . . .

Outstanding "curse" stories of recent years have pertained to the tomb of King Tut-Ankh-Amen, opened in 1922, and the gigantic Hope diamond whose last owner was Mrs. Evalyn Walsh McLean, widely known Washington, D.C. socialite. Despite disproof of the rumor that there was a written curse in the Egyptian mummy's sarcophagus, directed at anyone who disturbed the dead monarch's bones, whenever anyone who had anything to do with the opening of the grave died the legend of the curse was revised journalistically. Efforts to prove that the deaths were from natural causes and that most of those present at the excavation fulfilled their normal life expectancies were futile. Execution of the terms of Mrs. McLean's will may put an end to the superstition regarding the famous jewel. On the other hand, chopping up the stone may tend to make it all the more dangerous. Who knows?

Visions; Revelations. As explained earlier in this chapter coincidence was a major factor in the origin of primitive superstitions. That the type of thinking which led the caveman to believe that his magic worked still exists is evidenced by the following article, the climax of which is in the last paragraph, which appeared in the Feb. 4, 1948 Chicago *Sun-Times:*

By Edward Uzemack

A handful of relatives and friends came yesterday to pay a last tribute to Cader Timberlake, 42.

They gave him the best funeral they could. Yet Cader was a stranger to them. Among the group, there was none who could say he knew this man during the last 15 years.

Cader had come back to them as mysteriously as he had drifted away from the family fold when he was a young man of 27. Vance Timberlake, his brother, could only marvel at the meeting with Cader before death.

DERELICT NOTICED

Vance, a salesman who lives at 4301 N. Richmond St., on Jan. 23, saw a pathetic man in ragged clothing trying to warm himself in the lobby of the Wrigley Building.

Vance tried to talk to him. The stranger appeared dazed. Vance followed him outside and watched with horror as the human derelict walked into the side of a passing auto. Vance then noticed a deformity of the hands—the same as his brother had. Anxiously he went through the stranger's pockets and found an old Social Security card to confirm his suspicions.

DEATH FOLLOWS

Timberlake rushed his long lost brother to his home, where he bathed and shaved him and called a doctor. The doctor ordered Cader taken to a hospital, where he died a few days later.

The doctor explained that Cader Timberlake apparently had been wandering around for several days with a skull fracture.

But no one could explain the mysterious force that, in a city of 3,500,000 persons, had led Cader to a spot where his brother could find him.

Hardly a fortnight passes without some new "wonder" being reported from some part of the world. Among the most newsworthy of them are visions of the Virgin Mary, Christ, or God, publicity which attracts thousands, even hundreds of thousands of persons to view the site and the individual claiming to have had the experience. One of the most notable of such occurrences was the succession of visions to which a nine-year-old boy in the Bronx attested in November, 1945. With scientific detachment Albert Deutsch reported the story as follows in the Nov. 16, 1945, *PM*:

No well sprang out of the rocks in the dreary Bronx lot Wednesday night where Joseph Vitolo, the "miracle boy," kept his last vigil while a crowd of 30,000 waited vainly for the expected wonder to be worked. One woman in the crowd claimed her child's palsy had been cured, several spectators went into hysterical fits, one woman had a heart attack, and a lot of people may have caught cold, standing for hours in the wind-swept rain.

It may be presumed that the large Vitolo family will now settle back into the degree of normalcy that their spectacular 16 days of local fame will permit. The morbid, the miserable and the intensely religious will probably continue to visit the spot where nightly visions of the Virgin Mary were claimed, dwindling in numbers as time dissipates the present excitement. Later, perhaps, learned psychiatric and theological studies will be published on the meaning of the alleged miracle of The Bronx.

QUESTIONS

Several questions come to mind in speculating on the Bronx incident. A newspaper article is obviously not the place for a deep medico-theological discourse. I can merely make passing comment on some of the questions people are asking.

Did Joseph Vitolo really see a vision of the Virgin Mary?

We have the word of the nine-year-old boy, together with statements by several of his playmates that they saw a "bright light" on the rocky ledge of the lot where they had been playing around a fire at night.

These factors must be considered in speculating on the vision: Joseph, and probably his playmates, had seen *The Song of Bernadette*, based on the famous "Lourdes miracle," wherein Bernadette Soubirous sees repeated visions of the Blessed Virgin, a well springs out of the rock, and miracle healings occur on the spot. The impact of movies on the highly suggestible minds and emotions of children has been revealed in numerous incidents.

PRE-HALLOWEEN

Further, this was the night before Halloween, when witch-riding and other wondrous things are anticipated by imaginative children. Might it not be possible that the "holy light" was really a phosphorescent substance glowing through the murky night from a castoff article on the ledge? Again: oculists tell us that apparitions are not uncommon among people who have gazed long and intently on bright lights or fire.

History reveals innumerable cases of apparitions of saints and demons arising in the overwrought minds of children and adults alike. Our mental hospitals are filled with unfortunate people who regularly see visions of divine and demonological figures, and even commune with them. In times past, it was considered quite normal to see saints and devils in one's everyday routine.

Epidemics of mass hysteria, where many people, in moments of high tension, claimed to have seen identical apparitions, have occurred frequently among simple and credulous people. Often, innocent people were burned or hanged as witches as a result of these hysteria-produced visions. Apparitions occur more frequently in periods of great stress and anxiety, such as the present.

Perfectly normal people often are struck by apparitions suggested by peculiar cloud-like shapes that suggest some legendary or real-life figure. A classic instance of the power of suggestion is the famous dialogue between Hamlet and Polonius in Shakespeare's play:

Hamlet: Did you see that cloud? That's almost in shape like a camel.
Polonius: By the Mass, and it's like a camel indeed.
Hamlet: Methinks it's like a weasel.
Polonius: It is back'd like a weasel.
Hamlet: Or like a whale?
Polonius: Very much like a whale.

On the night of Joseph's last vigil, a spectator pointed toward a white figure apparently swaying in mid-air behind Joseph and cried: "The Vision!" The "vision," UP reporter Robert Richards says, "proved to be a woman spectator, dressed in a glistening white raincoat standing precariously on a fence."

Such is the stuff of apparitions.

Do "miracle cures" really work?

This is the subject of ceaseless debate. Both theologians and scientists are agreed that definitely authentic cures have been wrought at the world's most famous healing shrine—that at Lourdes, in France. Orthodox believers naturally ascribe these cures to miraculous healing.

Skeptical scientists point out:

A large number and variety of human ailments are not caused by physiological defects, but are "functional" in character, produced by psychological causes. Many cases of apparent physical paralysis, for instance, have been diagnosed as arising from mental or emotional maladjustment. Many seeming cripples—some of them unable to walk for years—have been treated and cured by psychiatrists through psychological means. They are known as "hysteria" cases.

The so-called shell shock of World War I offers a good example of hysteria. One American soldier, at the moment when his regiment went over the top at zero hour, fell back into his trench, crying: "My hands are paralyzed!" His arms were truly frozen at an upreaching angle, and he was hospitalized as a paralysis case. A psychiatrist who recognized the case as one of hysteria cured him some months later through routine psychiatric procedure.

A number of invalids flocking to healing shrines are really hysterical cases. In their case, the confidence in help, the pervading belief in a miracle, the will to be cured, the intense excitement at the shrine, all provide favorable factors for the clearing-up of symptoms.

Some medical writers have observed that many "miracle cures" have been only temporary in nature, with the old symptoms returning after the initial excitement wears off. They also raise this question:

It is said that about one-tenth of the ailing people who make their pilgrimage to Lourdes "feel better" after their visit. But what of the devastating despair that seizes many of the others who receive no benefit from their visits. . . .

Emile Zola, in his great novel, *Lourdes*, offers one major reason why so many people seek out healing shrines. He observes that they hold out to suffering masses the "delicious bread of hope for which humanity ever hungers with a hunger that nothing will ever appease."

My old friend, the late psychiatrist, Dr. William Alanson White, a wise and sympathetic observer of the human scene, once wrote on the meaning of "faith cures."

"Faith healers have come into existence because of a need which many people have. The restless multitude, seeking for peace of mind—for happiness, for fulfillment—express that need, and so along comes a whole host of medical, religious and even political and sociological sects which minister to this cry for help.

"The chronic invalid will almost surely and quite naturally take the advice of a man who says confidently: 'I can cure you.' Who would not? Wouldn't you and I, if we had been pronounced hopelessly ill, if we had spent years in fruitlessly seeking health, only to see it gradually failing us? Why not at least try—it can do no harm. People have been cured by everything under the sun—by little pieces of metal, by bottles of medicine, by slaves, by electricity, by hypnotism, by suggestion, and finally, by religion."

Healing shrines and "miracle workers" have been known to every age and every people—pagan, Christian, Buddhist, Jewish, Moslem, etc. They probably will flourish as long as the miseries, fears and anxieties of men find no solution or satisfaction in our overrated civilization.

In wartime, as might be expected, visions and revelations are particularly plentiful. In the New York *Times* for Jan. 28, 1940, Krishnalal Shridharani discussed "Miracles in War" as follows:

From the time of the heroes of Homer down to the present day the annals of war contain passages of pure mysticism. Soldiers in every struggle have had visions, and besieged cities have witnessed miracles. The present armed conflict in Europe recently added one more legend.

According to a report from Helsinki, this latest of war miracles took place around Hameenlinna. A Finnish Army captain heard the story from a wounded brother-officer. This officer and nine of his soldiers, fighting on the Eastern Front north of Lake Ladoga, had seen an angel in the sky, "facing Soviet Russia with arms outspread as if protecting the Finns."

A similar story of miraculous intervention was widely circulated in the undeclared war between China and Japan: The Chinese population of the Nantao quarter of Shanghai was said to have received the whispered tidings that the Nantao city god, a huge wooden Buddha, had left the temple and appeared in the streets to comfort Chinese troops in the Chapei area—a supposed sign from heaven that a Chinese victory was ahead. No one bothered to explain how the image got back to its niche in the temple in time to receive the homage of Shanghai's millions of devout Chinese.

Four years ago the Ethiopian warriors were similarly buoyed up by what they took to be divine assurance of the ultimate defeat of the invading Italians. A dispatch from Harrar pictured the women of the town, together with a group of native troops, watching with rapt-upturned faces as the tricolor Ethiopian flag was painted in the sky. The Ethiopian soldiers had halted in the square before the Coptic Church on their way toward a battle in the south. While they knelt to receive a blessing a green cloud emerged out of the east. A little later a rose-colored cloud appeared to the south. The yellow tinge of the sunset completed the green, rose and yellow flag of Ethiopia.

Witnesses reported that the women cried out in awe and that the ebony faces of the men shone with the sureness of victory. Then, the story continues, the natives, with a little aid from the Coptic priests, were able to distinguish the symbol of the cross in the remaining clouds. The dispatch quoted the priests as saying that the sign of the cross over Harrar signified that God had taken the side of the Ethiopians.

In India in 1930, although the Civil Disobedience Movement was ordinarily nonviolent, there were many instances of alleged miracles. One old woman in a small town in Bardoli announced that she saw Gandhi every evening addressing meetings. As it happened, the Mahatma at that time was serving a term in a jail 290 miles away. But the woman made her story sound so credible to so many people that the legend of Gandhi's nocturnal vaporizings through prison walls can still be heard in her district.

The comfort which men and women derive from mystical experiences in wartime is illustrated by the story of a vision which appeared before British troops in Belgium in the early period of the World War.

At Mons, in 1914, the Tommies were worn and heartsick—according to the legend—and were on the verge of utter annihilation. They were hopelessly outnumbered in men and machines. Ten thousand Germans were hemming in 1,000 British soldiers. Suddenly a British lieutenant fell to his knee and prayed to St. George, England's protector. The sky opened in a blinding flash, the story goes, and hundreds of old English bowmen appeared on the horizon. They smashed the German line.

The French Army in the World War founded another legend, "Le Comrade Blanc." The White Comrade was apparently a sublime combination of nurse, doctor and priest. He bent over those who lay in the field and eased their pain.

Over and above these widely circulated tales there is a treasure trove of supernaturalism in stories told by individual soldiers. It was not uncommon for soldiers on the edge of No Man's Land to hear the "call" which they believed predicted death.

Men who heard the "call" but still live say it was a terrifying experience. Usually, however, the visions of the battlefield provided an emotional release for hair-trigger nerves, solace to those in despair, and, above all, fresh courage.

When someone claims to have had a vision what can a reputable reporter do? In July, 1949 Irving Pflaum, foreign editor of the Chicago *Sun-Times,* was in the vicinity of Lublin, Poland when word spread that a portrait of the Virgin Mary was shedding tears. More than a half million Poles were said to have made pilgrimages to the cathedral before the government, which suspected a clerical political plot, stopped all means of transportation there. At least one woman was trampled to death and nineteen others injured before the hysteria ended. The following is Pflaum's "confession" as to what he observed:

Lublin, Poland—In the midst of hysterically weeping and praying men and women, the miraculous weeping Virgin of Lublin seemingly shed a tear Sunday in the Lublin Cathedral while a demonstration took place in the town square.

Sun-Times Correspondent Dennis Weaver, Mrs. Weaver, Mrs. Pflaum and the writer stood within four feet of the painting of the Madonna when a tear apparently appeared and moved down her face.

There is divided opinion among the four *Sun-Times* witnesses as to whether the tear moved, but they all agreed that the dark faced Virgin seems to have a large, darker tear-shaped mark below the right eye.

Mrs. Pflaum and Mrs. Weaver believe they saw the mark grow longer and deeper. Weaver flatly says he didn't see it move and I'm not sure what I saw.

POLES SHOUT

But there's no doubt that the Polish faithful watching the picture thought they saw the tear move.

"Tears," they shouted in Polish, and real tears ran down their faces.

The emotional tension was terrific in the crowded cathedral as the priests tried to quiet the crowd.

The attitude of the priests and apparently the official attitude of the Catholic authorities is one of great reserve.

Lublin Cathedral Vicar General Steniak has tried to get official approval for temporary closure of the cathedral to discourage pilgrims.

While the Lublin government refused to close the cathedral, the Warsaw government has suspended rail and bus traffic to Lublin.

SONG CLASH

Outside the cathedral Sunday disturbances mounted rapidly until the police had to use fire hoses to dispel the madly singing crowds. It was a combat of songs, the church folks singing, "My Chemy Boga" which means "We want God," and the government demonstrators singing, "Czerwony Sztandar," the Red Banner Socialist song used by the Communists in place of the unpopular "Internationale."

It was apparently a political clash in which the police showed restraint and prevented bloodshed by using cold water. When we left Lublin for Warsaw in the late afternoon an atmosphere of tension remained.

Incidentally, no obstacles were placed in our way on the long drive through Southeastern Poland over the week end.

—*Chicago Sun-Times*, July 18, 1949

There is one type of revelation story which no longer receives much journalistic play. That is the "end of the world" prophecy, and the reason for editorial skepticism obviously is because too many faithful have been left stranded on mountains at dawn or dusk in the past to cause a newspaperman to "go out on a limb" again. Should the journalistic timidity end there would be no dearth of material because every few years some prophet appears to announce he has been divinely appointed to prepare the world for Judgment Day which he usually is able to set within reasonable limits. Unless he attracts an exceptional following or creates a public disturbance, he usually obtains a more or less polite "brush off" from the press.

So, also, do most publicity seeking professional soothsayers. There are, however, exceptions as witness the following account of what is easily recognizable as a simple sleight-of-hand performance, which appeared in the June 20, 1947 Columbus (Ohio) *Citizen*:

Pittsburgh, June 20.—(UP)—Robert Nelson, the Columbus, O., mentalist, is a poor bet as a possible newspaper subscriber.

The reason—he knows what the headlines will be even before the paper rolls off the presses.

Wednesday morning before witnesses which included police officers and reporters, Nelson wrote his predictions of three headlines which would appear in Thursday's editions of Pittsburgh papers.

He placed the predictions in an aspirin box, which in turn was put in a Bisodol tin. Then he tucked the tin in a mass of dough which was baked in a loaf of bread.

The bread was taken, under police escort, to the Syria Mosque last night and opened by Safety Director George E. Fairley.

Fairley took the paper from the aspirin box, unfolded it and read the predictions to the audience.

The results—nearly three right out of three.

From the Pittsburgh *Sun-Telegraph:* "Nathaniel Spear Dies, Dean of Merchants Here."

Again, the *Sun-Telegraph:* "Pirates Break Slump, Beat Giants 12–2."

And from the Pittsburgh *Press:* "16 Killed in Clipper Crash."

That was his only slip. Actually the headline read that 15 were killed.

He also predicted correctly the runs, hits and errors for both the Giants and the Pirates.

Nelson's act was one of the standout performances of the four-day International Brotherhood of Magicians convention here.

While Spear had been ill for some time prior to his death, it was a surprise to the general public. There had been no publicity of his illness.

As to the Pirates, they had just lost five straight games—absorbing a 12–5 walloping from the Giants the day before. Yesterday they suddenly turned on the Giants, marking up their biggest total of hits—16—in any game this season.

The plane which crashed had not been reported missing when Nelson made his prediction.

Col. Fairley admittedly was completely mystified. Nelson just stroked his goatee and smiled knowingly.

Miraculous escapes. An Associated Press Wirephoto used in the Chicago *Sun* for Jan. 30, 1948, was captioned, "Crucifix Unscathed as Quake Levels Church," and the cutlines were: "Untouched by havoc, Crucifix is only object left standing in church of Immaculate Conception at Oton, in Philippines. Like string of giant firecrackers, a series of more than 50 earthquakes rocked wide area . . . leveled many towns. Heavy death toll is feared."

Such occurrences can be interpreted as mere freaks of disaster. They have journalistic pulling power, however, far beyond any picture, for instance, which would show a chair or a table or any other ordinary object left undamaged in the midst of chaos. Likewise, a crucifix which had been wrecked, as many have been in storms and fires, lacks dramatic appeal.

Similarly, narrow escapes by humans are awe-inspiring whereas the deaths of others, even in the same disaster, are considered normal though sad. The wearer of a St. Christopher medal, for instance, who survives a battle or wreck may give credit to the medal, but what of the dead victims also with medals on their persons? In the mine disaster to which the following short side-bar refers, 110 persons lost their lives.

(By Times Staff Correspondent)

Centralia, Ill., March 26—"I had a bad cold, but that was the Lord's way of taking care of me," said Albert K. Gates today, 65-year-old veteran of 30 years of coal mining.

"I begged off work yesterday," he explained. "That's why I missed the explosion. That's why I'm here."

"The Lord just took care of me," he repeated fervently.

—*Chicago Times*, March 26, 1947

A picture which accompanied the following story from the May 9, 1949 Chicago *Daily News* was paired with another showing the wreckage of an airplane which crashed near Buffalo, Mo., killing three.

Vancouver, B.C.—(UP)—Two plane crash survivors, rescued after 6 days on rugged Mt. Hozomeen's icy slopes, arrived here Monday certain that "Someone upstairs" had looked after them.

"Someone upstairs was looking after us. That's for sure," said Miss Sheila Cure, 28, student nurse and Bill Grant, 28, pilot.

They survived a plane crash 50 feet from the top of the 8,080-foot mountain, a snow slide and six days of hunger. They lived on chocolate bars.

A crowd of 200 was at Sea Island Airport when they stepped from a Royal Canadian Air Force bomber. They had been led to safety Sunday by their parachute rescuers.

Grant said their greatest fear during the week-long ordeal was a snow slide after their light plane crashed.

If "someone upstairs" looks after survivors why does he not also care for the victims? If the sea gull which lighted on Eddie Rickenbacker's head was on a divine mission, why did not other sea gulls save others adrift on the ocean? Is it to be concluded that God spares the virtuous, which is what the statements of survivors indicate that they often think they are, and destroys the wicked? Or is it the other way around, the good dying young and the evil being allowed to live? Either way, the thinking doesn't square with what the churches teach about the ways of the Almighty.

Faith healing. As Albert Deutsch pointed out in the feature article appearing on page 263, modern psychiatry does not deny the existence of faith healing. In fact, it explains it in thoroughly scientific terms. The current name given to research into the relationship between bodily disease and mental health is psychosomatic medicine, and many of the clinical case histories which a fairly good-sized library on the subject now contains are more remarkable than most of the sensational journalistic accounts which appear with such frequent regularity.

Several magazines have had excellent stories on the subject in recent years. Notable among them have been "Psychosomatic Medicine," by Francis Sill Wickware in the Feb. 19, 1945 *Life*; "Psychosomatic Medicine," by J. F. Brown and Carl-Gustaf Tillman in the July 7, 1941 *New Republic* and "What Makes You Sick?" by Gretta Palmer in the May, 1945 *Ladies' Home Journal*.

What can be said to summarize and conclude this lengthy chapter? That twentieth-century man, despite his genius for mechanical invention, manufacture, and manipulation, still has a long way to go to escape the unscientific habits of thought of his primitive ancestors. Superstition is everywhere; it distorts the mental processes of even some of the world's most prominent leaders. It inspires and perpetuates fears and suspicions. *The superstitious-minded is not a clear thinker. His contribution to the public opinion of his times is of questionable value.*

By incessantly capitalizing upon manifestations of superstition the newspapers help perpetuate them. With few exceptions the entire press, including the press associations and syndicates, is guilty. Many of mankind's leading problems never will be solved until superstitions, which are an obstacle to their even being viewed in proper perspective, are removed. But, to take a more businesslike view, a story with a superstitious slant is a certain circulation builder.

CHAPTER EIGHT

PREJUDICES

The solution of many problems is delayed or prevented be-
cause prejudice prevents insecure persons from recognizing or
admitting the facts of a situation.

The Nature of Prejudice

Of all the disagreeable persons with whom a reporter
comes in contact, none is more exasperating than the uncooperative
news source who "has no use for newspapermen." Often he is someone who has become "soured" as the result of a single unhappy experience with an inaccurate or unethical newsgatherer on the basis of
which he has concluded that "they're all alike." Even a more pleasant
subsequent experience with the press may cause such a person to
relent only to the extent implied by the statement, "You aren't like
the rest; one never would take you for what you are," which any loyal
newspaperman will regard as an insult rather than as a compliment.

Rare, indeed, probably nonexistent, is the person who does not
have some prejudices. Of considerable importance in the formation
of opinion, both private and public, a prejudice differs from a dislike
which, according to the *Thorndike Senior Century Dictionary* (Scott,
Foresman, 1941), is "a feeling of not liking." A dislike occurs after
one has had some contact with another person, thing, or idea. Meaning "to pre-judge," a prejudice, on the other hand, according to the
same dictionary, is "opinion formed without taking time and care to
judge fairly." Prejudice implies a negative attitude in the absence of
first-hand or adequate contact with the object of the prejudice, or the
irrational extension of a dislike for a single representative of a group
(as reporters) to include all other members of the group without discrimination.

As defined in a wartime Army talk on "Prejudice: Roadblock to Progress," to be found in the Appendix to the *Congressional Record* for Aug. 1, 1945, "A prejudice is an opinion or emotional feeling which isn't based on fact or on reason. It is an attitude in a closed mind." The dictionary gives as a synonym, "bigoted," which it defines as "sticking to an opinion, belief, party, etc., without reason and not tolerating other views; intolerant; prejudiced."

Prejudices are not inborn or inherited. They are learned. As stated in the Army talk: "All of us inherit certain characteristics such as color of our skin and the shape of our head. But we do not inherit our prejudices. When we are born we have only the capacity to develop love and hate and the other human emotions. Whom we learn to like or dislike, love or hate, depends on our experiences—in our home, in our school, in our neighborhood—and the effect these experiences have upon us. The language we learn, our religion, ideas, feelings and attitudes, our manners and prejudices—all these come from our environment.

"As children, we imitate not only activities of those around us, especially our parents, but also feelings, attitudes and opinions. Prejudices, too, are absorbed unconsciously from our parents and other people in our environment.

"By the time we have grown up we already have 'pictures in our mind' of many people with whom we've had little or no contact. We may have a stereotyped picture of Negroes as lazy, stupid, happy-go-lucky; of Jews or Scots as stingy and money-mad; of Irishmen as hot-tempered, brawling, whisky-loving. These stereotypes are being constantly reinforced through newspapers, movies, conversations and jokes, books and radio. A single story, comic strip or movie may not make too deep an impression. However, when time after time the Negro is presented as a crap-shooting, shiftless character; the Latin as a gangster or racketeer; the oriental as a slinking, mysterious and crafty person—then deep and lasting impressions are made which go to form attitudes and prejudices."

Some prejudices originate as generalizations based on personal experience. If one is injured or repelled in any way by another his dislike or hatred may be extended to include all of the members of that person's family, fraternity, church, school, race, city, state, or nation. His reaction is like that of the child knocked off his feet by a large dog who remains frightened by dogs all the rest of his life, or until cured of the phobia by a psychiatrist. As the semanticists put it, Dog 1 is not Dog 2; neither is Redhead 1, Redhead 2; or Jew 1, Jew 2. Even after a person has had considerable contact with Catholics or bankers or labor leaders or any other group, if his thought processes were absolutely rational he would recognize the possibility of exceptions to whatever conclusions he has formed regarding them as a class. Likewise, if he were thoroughly rational, he would recognize that his dislike of members of a particular group as a whole is based on only one or a few phases of the life activities of those people. To "have no use for any part of them" often is to close one's mind at times when one's own interests would be served better by being less sweeping in one's condemnation.

Once in existence prejudices fortify and perpetuate themselves. The prejudiced person interprets each new experience in any way related to the object of his prejudice irrationally. In "How to Poison Your Mind," in the Dec. 16, 1939 *This Week Magazine*, widely circulated newspaper supplement, Andre Maurois related the anecdote of a student who tested his conviction that his English professor had an intense personal dislike for him. Instead of an original short story, which had been assigned, he turned in a translation of one of the best by the master short-story writer, Guy de Maupassant. The teacher's comment was: "Commonplace writing. Subject dull, details badly selected. You simply don't understand how to tell a story." In the same article Maurois quoted from an epilogue which George Bernard Shaw wrote to one of his plays:

"Is it a good play?" the heroine asks the critics.

"Whose is it?" they ask in reply.

"I'll tell you that later," she says.

"O, no!" they protest. "You'll have to tell us that now. If it's by a good author, it's a good play. If it's by a bad author, it's a bad play."

In "Motes, Beams and Foreigners," in the March, 1931 *Harper's,* Dorothy Canfield analyzed the ways in which tourists in foreign lands obtain the impressions of the natives that they are predisposed to receive. Most travelers, her summary amounts to, see what they want to see, think what they are prepared to think; in other words, have their stereotypes of the persons and places they visit confirmed. Among other anecdotes she related was that of an eminent Frenchman who wrote vitriolically about the United States as a whole following an experience in a New York hotel. Because she knew the visiting lecturer was worried about the health of a member of his family, a woman associated with a group sponsoring one of the Frenchman's lectures went to his hotel room to deliver a letter she had received in his name. Hardly had he read the letter which contained sorrowful news, and as he was standing stunned in his sorrow, an official of the hotel phoned to inform him that entertaining women guests was forbidden to men. Miss Canfield contrasted this anecdote which, she wrote, caused the Frenchman subsequently to emit "one eloquent wail of sorrow over Christopher Columbus' betrayal of humanity" with another concerning an American schoolteacher who was refused service when she visited a French cafe unescorted and cried out about the foul-mindedness of all citizens of the republic. What is wrong, Miss Canfield concluded, is that visiting Americans do not compare French night-life women with American night-life women, but with mothers, wives, and sweethearts; and the same, in reverse, is true of Frenchmen visiting America, or of anyone of any nationality visiting any other country.

The prejudiced person generalizes without adequate facts. He is motivated by a strong "consciousness of kind" or "in-group" feeling. If it is traditional for members of the group to which he belongs to be prejudiced against those of another group, he would be a rebel, perhaps a pariah, if he failed to conform. Particular prejudices, in other words, become part of the mores of a particular group to be obeyed as much as are any customs or taboos. As stated in the introduction to the Army talk to which two references already have been made: "Practically every one of us has prejudices. Some of us may shudder at the idea of eating frogs and other foods we've never tasted but which other people enjoy. Or we may be prejudiced against bow ties or purple shirts. But these are meaningless prejudices which don't hurt us. There are other prejudices, however, which affect our lives very much. A prejudice against a necktie because of its color is harmless—but a prejudice against a person because of his color, race, nationality or religion can do plenty of damage."

In other words, it is the group or social prejudices that are most important, certainly in public opinion formation. And they originate very much in the same way as do personal prejudices. Among children, primitives, and others of little experience, there is a tendency to be cautious as regards strangers. Anything different is suspect. It is a common defense mechanism to scoff at whatever one does not understand, to consider everything different to be inferior to one's way of doing things and to fear that the better may be defiled by the poorer unless the latter is eliminated. So fearful were some primitive peoples of strangers that they killed them upon sight.

With both individuals and groups prejudices serve the psychological purpose of helping to maintain self-confidence or to "cover up" feelings of insecurity. Prejudices help to simplify life and to exalt the ego. *The prejudiced person, in other words, needs his prejudices* to be at peace mentally with himself and with the rest of the world. As in the case of the defense mechanisms (see pages 56 to 68), they enable him to avoid the disastrous effects of frustrations as a result of fear or failure. Wrote Dr. Julius Schrieber in "Doing Something About Prejudice," in the February, 1948 *Survey Graphic*: "Prejudicial attitudes and actions usually reveal a personality disturbance within the prejudiced individual. So long as the prejudice is not acted upon or does not lead others to follow in similar irrational behavior patterns (an optimistic and unreal hope), the tragedy and its consequences are a problem of the individual. But when prejudice is implemented—translated into some form of unfair discriminatory practice—it is no longer an individual problem; it becomes a social problem calling for social concern and social action. . . . Make no mistake about it. Prejudice undermines the mental health of all men—aggressor and victim."

Of primary importance in evaluating the role of prejudice in public opinion formation is the fact that few prejudices are held with equal intensity at all times, except by fanatics. With most people prejudices remain more or less latent until the psychological need to blame someone for one's misfortunes arises. During good times, it is true, an employer with a prejudice against Jews will refuse to hire them. He is very likely, however, to rationalize his action by explaining that his employees or his customers would object. Let his business slump, or an economic crisis become widespread, national or world wide, and he is a potential recruit for the demagogic appeal that it is the Jews who are responsible. *The extent to which prejudice is rampant, therefore, is an index to the extent to which people feel secure,* and the bigot who sounds the most positive when he recites his convictions usually is actually comparatively among the least secure; in fact, he probably is frightened and to avoid acceptance of the fact of failure on the part of himself or of others in whom he has had confidence or in the workability of ideas which he cherishes, he seeks a scapegoat on whom to place blame. Thus, a prejudice-ridden community is a sick community just as a prejudice-haunted person is a sick person.

How prejudice *per se* ebbs and flows with the times has been illustrated by its ups and downs in the United States during the past decade. Despite a plethora of predictions that the contrary would be the case, during World War II the civil liberties of Americans were not severely impaired. In fact, it would be closer to the truth to declare that between Pearl Harbor and V-J Day, prejudice and persecution were at unusually low ebb in the United States.

The explanation is to be found in the fact that the attitudes of fear and insecurity which cause prejudice to become intense were absent. Families naturally were anxious regarding their relatives in the armed services, but the nation-wide confidence as to the outcome was so strong that the government several times warned against over-confidence. Even at times of worst military reverses, it hardly occurred to anyone to doubt that the ultimate result would be victory. It was just a matter of time, and there was some impatience over what seemed to be needless delay in completing a comparatively simple job: that of defeating the pint-sized Japanese and the boisterous Germans over whom we had proved our superiority once, just a quarter of a century earlier.

For millions of Americans the war meant better jobs and higher wages than they had enjoyed in years. As long as the war lasted everyone's immediate purpose in life was clear. There existed national unity and a feeling of "we-ness" which included everyone regardless of race, religion, national origin, or economic class. No scapegoats were needed because there was no consciousness of weakness or failure.

Once hostilities were ended there was an almost immediate change in public attitudes. First it was fear of a recession during the reconversion period with the potential labor force augmented by 14 million returning soldiers. When the danger of recession passed, there developed fear of inflation, mostly realized, followed by worse fears of deflation and depression. As regards international affairs most Americans within a year became as disillusioned over the permanence of the fruits of military victory as it had taken the preceding generation 15 years to become after World War I. By the end of 1946 hope that the United Nations would preserve peace better than the League of Nations had done had almost vanished, and, as has happened often in history, two major former allies had fallen out and there was talk of the possibility of World War III. After enunciation of the Truman Doctrine in March, 1947, discussion in many quarters of whether there would be another war changed to conjecture over when it would start.

By contrast with the war period the conditions which give rise to widespread prejudice were existent in the postwar era: namely, feelings of insecurity and fear of the future.

The Incidence of Prejudice

There is no group without prejudice. Neither is there any group of importance which has not at some time been the object of prejudice.

Nero fed Christians to the lions and used them as scapegoats on whom to blame the burning of Rome. Catholics have persecuted and murdered Protestants, and Protestants have persecuted and murdered Catholics. Both have done the same to Jews and Freethinkers.

Although they came to the New World partly to escape discrimination against themselves, the Puritans were as intolerant of backsliders and heretics as their tormentors had been of them. Roger Williams had to flee to Rhode Island. At Salem the need for scapegoats led to the torture and killing of innocent people as witches. In most of the colonies Catholics were outlaws; only Maryland, Delaware, and Pennsylvania allowed them to vote. The Jesuits were blamed for French and Indian wars and many other Indian uprisings were believed to have resulted from "popish plots."

Even after adoption of the Bill of Rights with its guarantee of religious freedom, attempts were made to obtain federal aid for Protestant institutions. In 1811, for instance, President Madison vetoed two bills: one would have incorporated the Protestant Episcopal church at Alexandria, Va., and the other would have made a land grant to the

Baptist church at Salem Meeting House. Some of the vilest writing ever done on this continent was directed against Catholics. Much of it allegedly exposed convent life, notably Rebecca Reed's *Six Months' Residence in the Convent,* Mrs. Arthur Butt Sherwood's *The Nun,* and several tracts by Maria Monk. The mid-nineteenth-century leader of the anti-Catholic movement was Samuel F. B. Morse, inventor of the telegraph. The complete story, including the burnings of convents and churches, was told by Gustavus Myers in *History of Bigotry in the United States* (Random House, 1943) in which also are related stories of persecution of Mormons, Masons, Jews, Jehovah's Witnesses, and others. In fact, as intimated, there is hardly a racial, religious, or nationality group which does not receive mention and any omissions probably were the result of oversight.

Primitives hardly reacted in more hostile fashion to strangers than some groups have to every wave of immigrants to the home of the brave and land of the free. As the Germans, Irish, Swedes, Poles, Italians and others arrived to escape intolerable conditions at home, they were forced into American ghettos, compelled to do the most menial labor, and exploited by politicians and any others who could figure out a way to do so. The newcomers lived on the "wrong" side of the tracks and were called wops, polacks, dagos, bohunks, sheenies, and other opprobrious names to indicate that their users considered themselves to be of superior clay. About the middle of the nineteenth century there arose the Know Nothing movement "in which the anti-immigrant sentiment crystallized, was a national phenomenon," according to Stow Persons in "Americanization of the Immigrant," in *Foreign Influences in American Life,* edited by David F. Bowers (Princeton, 1944). After the American frontier passed, Persons related, the "new" immigrants "had to overcome handicaps never imposed upon their predecessors. Although chiefly of peasant stocks, bred to the land, they found most ready opportunities as cheap labor in urban industrial and construction projects. With frontier settlement no longer possible, a few found their way to abandoned farming lands in the East. The majority, however, settled of necessity in the slum areas of the large cities, where 'Little Italys' or 'Little Polands' arose to disturb the exponents of Americanization. Social isolation more complete than had ever surrounded the frontiersman was now the lot of the newcomer."

Nevertheless, as James G. Leyburn pointed out in the same symposium: "The millions of immigrants who came to our shores before the 1880's have been so completely absorbed into the body of American life and culture that we no longer think of them as constituting problems. . . . We still have thousands of first-generation immigrants, and millions of second-generation ones. . . . Given time, and a continuation of our present restrictive immigration laws, there is every reason to expect the absorption of the newer stocks."

Such, however, will not come about without more Niagaras of congressional oratory ascribing to the "alien menace" almost all of the social and economic ills with which we may be afflicted at the time. All Americans, probably including the Indians, are by ancestry aliens, but it always has been only the newer arrivals who have been the objects of fear, suspicion, and hate to combat which they have been virtually helpless. The quota system under which we have admitted immigrants since 1924 uses as its base 1890 so as deliberately to prevent continuation of a heavy influx of southern Europeans and to encourage the older types of immigrants. During the depression, when even the small quotas were not being filled and emigration was exceeding immigration year after year, Rep. Martin Dies of Texas and other "100 per centers" advocated deportation of all first-generation Americans as a solution for the unemployment problem. Another perennial is for some "statesman" to advocate deportation of aliens to rid the country of crime. This despite the fact that the Federal Bureau of Investigation revealed in 1941 (the last year for which such statistics were included in the bureau's semi-annual *Uniform Crime Reports*) that the law-breaking rate per 100,000 for the foreign born was 104 compared with 317 for native whites. After World War II the attorney general instituted a drive to "send back where they came from" almost any alien whom he could find an excuse to so treat, claiming that in that way he was protecting the nation from communism and other forms of radicalism.

When, as a wartime measure to improve relations with an important ally, it was proposed to repeal the Chinese Exclusion Act of 1882 and admit about 100 Chinese immigrants a year under the quota system, one of the leaders in opposition was William Green, president of the American Federation of Labor which throughout its history has favored all types of immigration restriction. Explained Green: "A

Chinaman's always a Chinaman." Thus is suggested the importance of the economic factor in racial and nationality prejudice. It is when a group is in real or supposed competition with one's own that fear and dislike of it are greatest. If there is enough to go around—jobs and good incomes for all—this feeling remains latent; when times become bad, however, it intensifies. One of the best statements on the subject is to be found in *The Police and Minority Groups,* a manual prepared by Dr. Joseph D. Lohman of the University of Chicago for the Chicago Park District Police Training School. Wrote Dr. Lohman in part: "The idea of racial superiority has been formulated in struggles between the upper and the lower economic class, between the rich and the poor, between the natives and the foreigners, between despotic rulers and the masses of people, and between aristocratic 'blue bloods' and the 'common man.' The ideas of racial and national superiority have likewise been introduced into the claims and aspirations of whole communities of men, even nations, in their bid for power over other communities and nations. We have just witnessed the catastrophic effects of such a nationwide phobia in the peoples' fascism of Germany and Japan.

"In similar manner, religious and cultural groups have seized upon racial dogma as a means of justifying their actions toward the infidel and the heretic. In nearly every sphere of human activity can be heard the cry of racial superiority as men find themselves sorely pressed in justifying persecution and conflict."

For the most part, second or third generation Americans have been able to overcome the prejudices directed against their parents and grandparents. They have become assimilated at least in the economic life of the nation and, to an increasing extent, socially as well. Anglicizing their names, so as to make them easier to spell and pronounce, has hastened the process for some. The late Sen. Theodore Bilbo (Dem., Miss.) actually caused laughs in the United States Senate when he read the names of Slavic origin signed to letters he had received.

The assimilation of members of most nationality groups has been facilitated because they have not had to overcome too much discrimination in obtaining employment and gaining promotions on the job, in joining labor unions, gaining admittance to colleges and universities, exercising the right to vote and renting or purchasing housing wherever they desire. The two groups which have suffered in the past and which continue to suffer most from these and other forms of discrimination are the Jews and the Negroes. Because the newspaperman is bound to encounter anti-Semitism and anti-Negro feeling in many of their aspects, he should be acquainted with the facts regarding the most important arguments advanced by those who dislike Jews and Negroes to rationalize their unjust behavior toward those minorities.

Anti-Semitism

There are approximately 4,500,000 Jews in the United States, constituting slightly more than 3 per cent of the total population. They are not a race any more than are Americans of Swedish, Scotch, Syrian, or any other descent. Rather, they are a people, their cohesiveness the result of a common culture, the most important element of which is their religion. As anyone can discover for himself by comparing Jews of his acquaintance, they do not all resemble each other in appearance. Some are tall, others short; some blonde, others brunette; some dark-complexioned, others light, and so on. The stereotypes made familiar by anti-Semitic caricaturists are a distortion of what anthropologists recognize as the Mediterranean type, one of the three major types of Caucasoids, the other two being Nordics and Alpines. The hooked nose and dark complexion which the cartoonists exaggerate are characteristics of many Arabs, Italians, Syrians, and others originating in the Mediterranean area. Many other Jews are fair-skinned, blue-eyed and tall as are other Nordics, originating in northern Europe and including Norwegians, Swedes, Danes, some Germans, and others. Still other Jews are Alpines, with in-between skin color, and stocky, as are many French, Germans, and Slavs.

Other nationalities, as the Poles and Czechs, have kept alive their nationalism for decades or centuries, but they have done so while continuing to inhabit the same geographical area that they have yearned to have restored to them for the purpose of reestablishing a political state thereon. The Jew, on the other hand, has been a wanderer although keeping alive, wherever he is, the hope that some day the land of the founders of his religion, Palestine, would be restored to him. Within the past half century, during which the Zionist movement grew strong, however, Jews, especially American Jews, have by no means been united in their support of it. Some Jews have abandoned adherence to old Jewish customs, including the religion, and have become Christians, agnostics, or atheists; they naturally resent still being classified as Jews. Others, while retaining devotion to the Jewish tradition, believe that they should be able to retain it while becoming assimilated in all other respects wherever they happen to live. Often the familial residence of such Jews is centuries old and the foster-home ties consequently are much stronger than those to the mythical land of the Old Testament. There is a third class of Jews which adheres strictly to all of the old beliefs and customs; they inhabit a cultural island wherever they are, mixing as little as possible with others. They are the orthodox, or, as the Christian term would be, the fundamentalist Jews.

Religion. American Jews are more inclined than Gentiles to explain anti-Semitism by the fact of religious differences. For centuries in Europe the heresy of the Jews, from the Christian point of view, undoubtedly was a major factor in causing them to be persecuted as they have been in every century in virtually every country. The demagogues of early days of intense religiosity were able to capitalize on the Jews' strangeness in the field of most people's major interest. Especially fiendish periods of persecutions and massacre followed Constantine's edict establishing Christianity as the official religion of the Roman Empire in 378 and from the eleventh through the fourteenth centuries, the period of the Crusades. Jews who became usurers when the Christian scriptures still were interpreted as forbidding the practice, were taxed heavily to support both church and state. Louis IX of France at one time cancelled one-third of all debts owed to any Jew "for the benefit of his soul." Jews were banished from almost every European country, several times from France, England, and Spain. They were blamed for the Black Death of 1348 and the London Plague of 1666. They suffered terrible martyrdom during the Spanish Inquisition and were slaughtered in Czarist Russian pogroms during the nineteenth century and by the German Nazis in the twentieth.

In the United States Jews are sometimes referred to as "Christ-killers" and their synagogues and cemeteries often have been desecrated by brotherly-loving Christians. As the practice of religious education in the public schools increases, the differences between Jews and Gentiles are accentuated in the minds of children. Nevertheless, most of the complaints commonly heard about Jews in America do not relate to their religious beliefs, and the discrimination against them hardly is traceable to the attempts of Christians to win grace by converting or annihilating nonbelievers or to vent their spleen because Jews do not attend mass or Epworth League. American Christians just don't feel as strongly about their faith as did medieval Europeans. The Jew continues to be a convenient scapegoat, if for no other reason than because it has been his historic role throughout Christendom. The rationalizations, however, have changed considerably.

Personality traits. The excuse generally given for the "gentlemen's agreements" that exclude a Jew from clubs, fraternities, schools, and other places is because he possesses personality traits distasteful to Gentiles. Specifically, he is charged with being loud, flashy, pushy, clannish, and vulgar. Fighters of anti-Semitism reply that if any Jew possesses these or other disagreeable traits they are *the result, not the cause* of anti-Semitism. Sigmund Livingston wrote in *Must Men Hate?* (Harper, 1944): "The Jew was persecuted for many centuries. He was herded into ghettos; by law he was compelled to wear a yellow badge on his outer garments to identify him as a Jew; for the same purpose he had to wear certain headgear; he was denied the privilege of owning or cultivating land; he was denied the right to engage in handicraft; he could not join the guilds. Ordinary vocations and avocations were denied to him, and he was regarded as no more than the chattel of the ruler. These and many other impositions and deprivations left their indelible impressions upon him."

It is inconsistent to accuse the Jew of being both pushy and clannish. Often he has little choice of where he lives as restrictive real estate covenants have barred him from many residential areas. If he must live in a ghetto, even a white-collar ghetto, he hardly can help being clannish. Such stratification creates a strong "in-group" feeling and a "stick-togetherishness" for mutual protection. Since the early thirties thousands of American Jews, including many with no allegiance to or even knowledge of Jewish culture, have been forced by events in Hitler Germany to become aware of their Jewishness. The rapidity with which not a few of those reverted to their assimilationism following the war with the rationalization that "Hitler is dead; the danger is past," indicates that much of the clannishness is forced upon Jews and is not of their own choosing.

It would be phenomenal if some Jews who have studied their own history or who have followed events during their own lifetimes did not develop persecution complexes. Such attitudes hardly are delusionary because Jews *have* been persecuted; they still *are* persecuted. To expect people with such a background not to be affected would be to expect the impossible. It would be difficult to prove, however, that Jews as a group are more "this" or "that" than any others. There are aggressive and obnoxious members of every race, nationality, and religion. The difference lies in the fact that a supercilious Englishman is disliked as an individual and a vulgar Dutchman is less likely to bring down condemnation upon all of his countrymen. Let one Jew misbehave, however, and all Jews suffer as a consequence.

Economic monopolists. Jews are not accused of being mentally inferior. Quite the contrary, they are called so clever that any Gentile dealing with them has to be constantly on the alert to avoid being taken in or cheated. Supposedly unscrupulous in their business practices (the Shylock stereotype), the Jews constantly are rumored to have taken over large segments of American business. The facts, however, just don't substantiate the accusation.

In "Anti-Semitism Is a Danger to the Nation," in the Jan. 27, 1942 *Look,* Vincent Sheean revealed the utter baselessnes of the oft-heard charge that Jews controlled the important media of communication, pointing out the following: of the 60 top officials in the three large radio chains, only five were Jewish; of the country's 1,974 daily newspapers, 15 were Jewish-owned (incidentally, the most important of these, the New York *Times,* usually is considered America's fairest and best); of 19 banks in the New York clearing house one was Jewish-owned; of a total of 80,000 corporation directors, 4 per cent were Jewish.

Jews *do* predominate in the scrap iron and steel business, probably owning about 90 per cent of it. Jews also are heavily represented in the tobacco-buying business and in the rayon underwear and dress-cutting trades. In the communications field they are heavily represented in the motion picture industry. They are, however, insignificant in number and importance in banking and investments. There are very few international Jewish bankers. In insurance, automobile, coal.

rubber, shipping, and transportation Jews are virtually unrepresented. Certainly there are few Jewish names in any who's who of industrial giants of past or present in America—Morgan, Harriman, Carnegie, Schwab, Sloane, Ford, du Pont, and so forth.

To explain why Jews are concentrated in a relatively few commercial and industrial fields, Carey McWilliams wrote in *A Mask for Privilege* (Little, Brown, 1947): "Generally speaking, the businesses in which Jews are concentrated are those in which a large risk-factor is involved; businesses peripheral to the economy; businesses originally regarded as unimportant; new industries and businesses; and businesses which have traditionally carried a certain element of social stigma, such, for example, as the amusement industry and the liquor industry. Not being able to penetrate the key control industries, Jews have been compelled to occupy the interstitial, the marginal, positions in the American economy. . . . The types of business in which Jews are concentrated, by their very nature, fail to invest ownership with social power and prestige. . . . Much of the job discrimination that Jews encounter in the United States today reflects a determination on the part of the majority to keep certain sectors of the economy in non-Jewish hands."

In law and medicine—professions to which many Jews turned after being barred from business but from which they are increasingly being excluded by school quotas—their representation in New York was about equal to their proportion in the population. However, Jewish lawyers do not get the same quality of business that non-Jewish lawyers do. They are more frequently to be found in court rooms which most lawyers try to avoid. The most satisfactory and most lucrative law work is for large corporations. Jewish lawyers do not obtain such employment to anywhere near the extent which would seem reasonable and fair. Jewish lawyers, in other words, get the work which other lawyers consider least attractive. A similar situation exists as regards medicine. *PM* pointed out in its Nov. 26, 1943 issue that in 420 American cities of more than 10,000 there is not a single Jewish physician.

An even more cogent argument in answer to the charge of business or professional monopoly by any group in a democracy would be "so what?" Who cares whether Greeks own all the restaurants or Chinese all the laundries. which, of course, is entirely untrue in either case? If the United States is the melting pot of the world, what difference does it make who does what so long as it is well done?

Radicalism. Completely disregardful of his inconsistency, the anti-Semite who rants against the Jews because they are international bankers and monopolists (which the foregoing section shows they are not), also condemns them for alleged radicalism. Apparently the Jewish capitalists just want to own everything so that they can turn it over to the Jewish proletariat. In some quarters the New Deal was called the Jew Deal and President Roosevelt, Secretary of Labor Frances Perkins, and many other members of the administration were incorrectly called Jews. The labeling, of course, was done with the purpose of capitalizing upon anti-Semitic feeling; the whispered accusation was supposed to be as damaging as to say its subject was a wife-beater, adulterer, embezzler, or alcoholic. On March 7, 1935 Franklin Roosevelt made answer in a letter to Philip Slomovitz, editor of the Detroit *Jewish Chronicle* who had sent him "evidence" made public by former Gov. Chase S. Osborn of Michigan that FDR was of Jewish descent. In transmitting the information to the president, Slomovitz had written that "it is with a considerable sense of regret that I must comment that we have grave doubts as to whether we may hope to feel so deeply honored. . . . However, there is always a chance that there is an honor in store for us somewhere, even though unexpected." President Roosevelt's answer was as follows:

The White House
Washington, March 7, 1935

Philip Slomovitz, Esq.
Editor, The Detroit Jewish Chronicle
525 Woodward Avenue, Detroit, Mich.

My Dear Mr. Slomovitz: I am grateful to you for your interesting letter of March 4. I have no idea as to the source of the story which you say came from my old friend, Chase Osborn. All I know about the origin of the Roosevelt family in this country is that all branches bearing the name are apparently descended from Claes Martenssen Van Roosevelt, who came from Holland sometime before 1648—even the year is uncertain. Where he came from in Holland I do not know, nor do I know who his parents were. There was a family of the same name on one of the Dutch islands and some of the same name living in Holland as lately as 30 or 40 years ago, but frankly, I have never had either the time nor the inclination to try to establish the line on the other side of the ocean before they came over here, nearly 300 years ago.

In the dim distant past they may have been Jews or Catholics or Protestants—what I am more interested in is whether they were good citizens and believers in God—I hope they were both.

Very sincerely yours,

Franklin D. Roosevelt.

In 1935, *Fortune* estimated, between 3,000 and 4,000 of the supposedly 27,000 American Communists were Jews, a surprisingly small number when the true causes of conversion to Communism—persecution, frustration, and the like—are considered. Only 2.6 per cent of the Bolshevik party at the time of the Russian revolution in 1918 were Jews; only one of 17 members of the Politburo shortly before World War II was a Jew. In prewar Germany there were 550,000 Jews, less than 1 per cent of the total population. If every one of them —men, women and children—had voted Communist, there still would have been 5,760,240 non-Jewish Communist votes in the last free election before Adolf Hitler assumed power.

Karl Marx, spiritual godfather of present-day Socialists and Communists, it is true, was born of Jewish parents; but he was baptized at six and his education and environment were Christian. Nicolai Lenin was not Jewish nor is Josef Stalin. Earl Browder and William Z. Foster, recent Communist leaders in the United States, both came from very old native American stock.

World-wide plotters. To attack the absolutism of Napoleon III, in 1864 a French lawyer, Maurice Joly, published in Brussels a satirical *Dialogues in Hell*, between the shades of Machiavelli, symbolizing dictatorship, and Montesquieu, exponent of democracy. Thereby was laid the basis for one of the most colossal hoaxes of all history, *The Protocols of the Learned Elders of Zion*, which first appeared under that title in 1905 in Russia under the editorship of a minor church official, Sergei Nilus. The purpose at that time was to frighten the vacillating Czar Nicholas II into taking more vigorous action against revolutionary elements. It was easily recognizable as a plagiarism of Joly's tract with some borrowing also from a novel, *To Sedan* by Herman Goedsche, published in 1868. In the intervening years numerous interpolations had been made, but the essential change was to accredit most of the words advocating a devilish plot to control the world to Theodore Herzl at the first meeting of the Zionists, in 1897, in Basle, Switzerland.

First important expose of the *Protocols* was by the London *Times* in its Aug. 16, 17, and 18, 1921 editions. They also were declared forgeries, after scholarly analysis, by Prof. Hugo Valentin of the Swedish University of Upsala. In 1934 the South African Supreme court declared the *Protocols* to be "an impudent forgery, obviously for the purpose of anti-Jewish propaganda," and in May, 1935 a Berne, Switzerland court called them "a forgery, a plagiarism and silly nonsense." Nevertheless, from 1920 to 1927 the Dearborn (Mich.) *Independent*, owned by Henry Ford (only American to be mentioned favorably in Hitler's *Mein Kampf*) waged a vigorous campaign against Jews during which the *Protocols* were reprinted as true. Faced with a lawsuit in 1927 Ford publicly retracted and apologized, saying he had been duped. Publication of his vicious book, *The International Jew*, however, continued with translations to be found all over the world, especially in Latin America. Likewise, William J. Cameron, editor of the *Independent* series, continued as editor and as commentator on the celebrated prewar Ford Sunday Evening Hour, an hour of music over the radio which was interrupted for a talk by Mr. Cameron on "The American Way," which contained some of the most convincing Old Deal propaganda ever disseminated in this country. Furthermore, many of the leading anti-Semites of recent times, including the Rev. Charles J. Coughlin and Gerald L. K. Smith, operated for long periods almost within the shadow of the Ford factories in the Detroit area, and Charles A. Lindbergh, who in 1941, at Des Moines, under the auspices of America First, accused American Jews of trying to get the United States into the war, became a Ford employee.

In addition to the *Protocols*, to smear the Jews as international warmongers and revolutionists, there have been repeated attacks on the *Talmud* which contains the writings of more than 2,000 rabbinical scholars expressing their individual opinions which are in no way binding upon other Jews. It is possible to lift some of these writings out of their context to construct a bad case against Jewry, as many of its enemies have discovered. Another comparatively new favorite, dating from 1934, is an alleged letter or speech by Benjamin Franklin advocating restriction of Jewish immigration. It was given currency by William Dudley Pelley, head of the Silver Shirts, who went to prison for subversive activities during World War II, but this letter was denounced as a hoax by the Franklin Institute in Philadelphia, chief

depository of documents on Franklin, and by Charles A. Beard, Carl
Van Doren, and other scholars. Commented Livingston: "It has been
frequently noted by authorities on the subject that in relating a falsehood the perverted mind will go into detail so as to give credence to
misstatements. This very detail often convicts the author of the falsehood. In this instance, the fictitious speech was said to have been taken
from the Pinckney journal or diary. There is no such journal or diary.
It is also claimed that the original of the journal or diary is in the
possession of the Franklin Institute, when, as a matter of fact, neither
the original nor any copy thereof has ever been in the possession of the
Franklin Institute. It is therefore evidence that the perverted mind
which invented this fiction, instead of giving it a semblance of credence, defeated its own purpose."

On the broader subject of Jewish internationalism, McWilliams
commented: "Those who charge the Jews with a conspiracy to dominate the world are themselves the real conspirators and their conspiracy is the reality hidden in the fable."

War record. Jews have played their part in every war in which the
United States has been engaged. Jewish colonists on the whole supported the Revolutionary War, one of the leaders in helping to finance
it being Haym Solomon of Philadelphia. During the Civil War there
were about 6,000 Jews in the Union army; of them nine were generals, 18 colonels, and 600 officers of lower rank. A leading member
of the cabinet of the Confederacy was Judah P. Benjamin. The first
volunteer during the Spanish-American War was a Jew; also the first
American soldier killed during that war. There were 15 Jews on the
Maine when it sank.

In 1917 of the approximate 103,000,000 Americans, 3,300,000 or
3.2 per cent were Jews. The total American fighting force during that
war was 4,355,000 or 4.3 per cent of the entire population; among
them were 250,000 Jews, or 7.5 per cent of the Jewish population.
There were 13,000 to 14,000 Jewish casualties, 3,400 of them fatali-
ties. Distinguished Service Crosses were awarded 150 Jews, and 175
American Jews got the French *croix de guerre.*

Despite this record, which could be augmented considerably, a
record better than that of which most other racial or nationality
groups can boast, the Jew has been accused of being unpatriotic, a
malingerer, and a bad soldier. During World War II a particularly

filthy attack, unquestionably Nazi-inspired, circulated in the form of a compilation of *World War II Facts* as follows:

"The first American to be wounded in battle was Private Michael Murphy.

The first American to be killed in an aeroplane engagement was Captain Colin Kelly.

The first American to be wounded in action was Private Patrick O'Flaherty.

The first American to be decorated for bravery was Corporal Terrence O'Rourke.

The first American to be captured as a prisoner of war was Sgt. Joseph O'Brien.

The first American to obtain four rubber tires was Abie Cohen."

One of the most dramatic scenes in the history of the Illinois General Assembly occurred March 17, 1943 when a Jewish member, Sen. George D. Mills of Chicago, arose to comment upon the reading of the "facts" by another member of the Senate. The following were Senator Mills' remarks:

"Mr. President:

"I find myself in a very embarrassing position, for it becomes necessary for me to criticize a fellow member of the Senate—a task which is never pleasant, but one which has been made necessary by what has just occurred here on this floor.

"The senator who has just read this card does not know, and perhaps you gentlemen do not know, that since 1936 the Axis powers have spent and are spending millions of dollars every year for propaganda which seeks to divide you from me and all of us from each other, so that we shall fail against them in the end.

"The senator read that card most innocently, but it did not come into his hands either innocently or by accident; it was placed in his hands deliberately, and by the design of sinister forces who would destroy us. Perhaps you gentlemen do not know, but hundreds of thousands of these cards are being distributed at this moment throughout our country. Someone has gone to the trouble and expense of printing and illicitly distributing them, and it isn't being done for the purpose of advancing the cause of humor in America—for if you examine the implications of the card carefully, you will see that it contains no humor whatsoever.

"If the senator had read this card in a hotel lobby or some other public place, I could have talked to him privately and shown him the error of his ways, but the senator has seen fit to read this card on the floor of the Senate, and through his lips the State of Illinois speaks. As senators we are presumed to be leaders of public thought, and we are supposed to know what we are talking about; and if one of our members speaks heedlessly, it becomes our duty to correct our erring member.

"The senator read the name of Captain Colin Kelly, which appears on the card. All of us honor that great American hero and cherish his memory, but it is to be remembered that on that same airplane in which Colin Kelly went to his death rode Sergeant Meyer Levin, the bombardier who dropped the bomb that destroyed the Japanese battleship. Meyer Levin's life was spared, and up until three weeks ago, he continued his fight against Japan—and then he, too, was killed; and he too, now, is a dead American hero.

"Senator, without intention, no doubt innocently and ignorantly, but notwithstanding, you insulted the memory of a great American hero.

"The spirit of O'Connor and Goldberg [a shoe store] has made my city of Chicago a great city, and this spirit has made our country a great country. For united, you and I and all of us together will win the war and will write a peace that we can live under; but once you divide us, either by suspicion, by hatred, or by ridicule, we shall all fall together."

In the Dec. 23, 1942 *PM* John C. Cullen, included in other versions of the tract as "the first American Coast Guardsman to detect a German spy," was quoted as follows:

I understand my name is being used, without my consent, in a leaflet called the "First American." Persons putting out that leaflet have no right to use my name. We are in this fight together, Jews, Catholics and Protestants. We are all trying to do our part. Anybody who tries to stir up hatred against a race or religion is playing the Nazi game. I hope every good American who sees this leaflet, or any leaflet attempting to divide us, will tear it up.

Sigmund Livingston wrote "I would like to take the author and all those who have helped him to circulate these venomous lines on a little journey to some of the Cohens, his fellow citizens, whom he so lightly maligned. I would first stop at the house of Sergeant Schiller Cohen of New York City. He is 23 years of age and holds the Distinguished Flying Cross, the Air Medal, ten oak-leaf clusters and a squadron citation. He was with the first American aircraft to bomb Nazi-held Europe. He flew with the first Fortresses to attack enemy territory in North Africa and participated in the opening aerial assault on Italy. Altogether, he flew on 52 bombing missions and has to his credit 252 hours of air combat." Livingston's account continued with "visits" to the homes of a number of other Cohens.

Real reasons. When an abnormal number of cases of vandalism directed at Jews occurred in New York in war days, William B. Herlands was appointed to investigate. He concluded that "such acts are not accidental, or fortuitous, and they are more than juvenile delinquency in the ordinary sense." In his 200-page report, examining 31 case histories involving 54 suspects, he wrote: "Vandalism and violence are not the roots of the problem, they are only the symptoms. They are a sign of undemocratic, un-American thinking. The vandals and offenders have been inspired by the same kind of anti-American and anti-Semitic propaganda used by the Nazis as part of their technique to 'divide and conquer.' Such propaganda originated in Germany and was adopted by such domestic organizations as the Christian Front and the Christian Mobilizers, among others. One of the objectives of such propaganda was to plant the seeds of racial and religious hate. The commission of certain acts of vandalism and violence cited in this report is attributable to propaganda sponsored by the Christian Front and the Christian Mobilizers. Whether this constitutes 'instigation' or 'inspiration' is at best a matter of definition."

But why the Jews? How does it happen that it is so frequently they who are selected as scapegoats if, as has been demonstrated, none of the most commonly advanced criticisms of them hold up under analysis? Partly, of course, the explanation in modern times is to be found in the mere fact that they have been persecuted before. As McWilliams put it, "Anti-Semitism has long been a socially sanctioned and culturally conditioned mode of expressing aggressive impulses." After pointing out that "there is not a single accusation against the Jew which was not directed against the Christians during the first four centuries of the Christian era," Livingston adds, "A delusion, whenever it has saturated the mass mind, becomes a common faith. The denial of that faith is heresy. This is the reason that the delusions of men have been so obstinate and enduring. . . . Once they have possessed the mass mind, the destruction of delusions is a slow process."

As the Herlands report indicated, demagogues, hate mongers, and, during wartime, the enemy help keep alive the delusions. *The answer as to why anti-Semitism persists is to be found not by studying the Jew but by studying the anti-Semite.* Why does he need to continue his hate? For all of the reasons given earlier in this chapter for the existence of prejudice of any kind. In addition, it is natural to resent those whom one knows he has injured. A persecuted victim is on his persecutor's conscience. He resents it because the object of his hate has made him act badly. If it weren't for the hated object, his twisted reasoning leads him to conclude, he would have remained an admirable person.

Throughout history the Jew has been an ideal scapegoat for the frustrated because he has been homeless and comparatively helpless. In the United States anti-Semitism is of comparatively recent origin, partly because the tighter immigration laws have helped to eliminate other potential minority groups which could take some of "the heat" off him. McWilliams dates the beginning of overt anti-Semitism in the United States to the refusal of the Grand Union Hotel of Saratoga Springs in 1877 to rent a room to Joseph Seligman, prominent New York banker. "As prosperous and successful merchants, bankers and traders, the German Jews could not be altogether excluded from the civic and social life of the communities in which they had settled; but they could be made to feel a subtle sense of rejection, and limitations could be imposed against their further encroachment on the citadels of power," McWilliams wrote. "The erection of these invisible barriers at the top levels of society was largely prompted by the feeling that, at this level, they were to be regarded as serious competitors for place and power."

Thus the economic basis for the urge to be prejudiced is suggested. Successful activation of prejudice removes a potential competitor and the urge to do just that increases with the necessity, as in times of economic insecurity. To quote McWilliams once more: "Perhaps the answer is that anti-Semitism is a strange mixture of cause and effect. A symptom of unrest and disorganization, it is consciously used to spread unrest and disorganization. . . . Obviously, anti-Semitism is a social disease . . . the great waves of anti-Semitism have always occurred during periods of sharp social conflict, or pronounced social change, of immense social upheaval."

To repeat, the real answer as to why prejudices of any kind exist is to be found, not through a study of prejudice's victims but of the prejudiced. A final McWilliams quotation: "The groups that spawn anti-Semitism are socially sick groups. The appearance of overt forms of anti-Semitism is always a warning sign. The society that produces the seat or fever of anti-Semitism is a sick society—how sick, in fact, can be largely determined by the number of anti-Semites. When the fever chart shows a rise in anti-Semitism one can rest assured that society, in some of its parts, in some of its relationships, has begun to show the symptoms of deep-seated maladjustment and disorganization. The pathology of anti-Semitism leaves no room for doubt on this score. The social function of anti-Semitism seems to be to provide people with an escape from a reality that has become intolerable."

More vehemently, in perhaps the most vitriolic attack ever delivered against anti-Semites, Ben Hecht wrote in *A Guide for the Bedevilled* (Scribner, 1944): "It is murder, foul murder, that stirs the anti-Semite. It is the foul need of warming the dead places in the human skin with the sight or thought of blood spilling that stirs him against the Jew. It stirs him sometimes only to oratory, sometimes only to the bird-brained chatter of the 'exclusive' dinner tables, sometimes only to the cousinly deeds of calumny, robbery and political action. Sometimes the anti-Semite is too civilized to kill, and murder degenerates into a tic—a spasm of distaste, a twitch of arrogance. Or he is too pious, too purring, too masked, with love and learning to shed blood. Then murder becomes books of theology, anthropology and unpretty fiction. But it is always murder. It is always murder that bubbles under the mask of anti-Semitism."

White Supremacy

For more than three hundred years the overwhelming majority of those who have come from overseas to make their homes in the New World have been in search of greater freedom and/or opportunity. On the whole either they or their progeny have been successful in the quest. Not so, however, either the ancestors of America's 14,000,000 Negro citizens or their descendants. The first colored people to arrive here did not come of their own volition. Nor, since the first twenty slaves were unloaded in 1619 at Jamestown, to the present, have freedom or opportunity comparable to what white men enjoy, been their lot. Quite the contrary, in fact, has been the case, so that today the world's leading democracy has the world's largest and most important minority problem.

To cite the innumerable adverse criticisms ordinarily made of the Negro seems superfluous because they all are ramifications of a single idea—that, because of his race, he is inferior and consequently must be kept "in his place" which means something less than first-class citizenship such as that allowed the white population. Because this fundamental assumption, this major premise, is so colossally untrue, the rationalizations to justify the inhuman treatment that the colored 10 per cent have had to endure are correspondingly grotesque. To engage most white Americans in a calm, rational discussion of the situation is virtually impossible. Backed into a corner with anthropological, sociological, and other scientific refutations of all of his arguments, the prejudiced person shouts "nigger-lover" and invariably winds up with what he considers his *tour de force*: "Would you want your sister to marry one?"

If he is to do a competent job, the newspaperman must shy clear of such polemics. He cannot report accurately about something of which he has inadequate or incorrect knowledge. Here then are the facts, as they are best known today, regarding the White problem as it relates to Black America.

Race. There is a Negroid race as distinguished from the Caucasoid and Mongoloid races. The most important difference between members of the three races is skin color. In general, people who—since at least the beginning of recorded history—have lived closest to the hot equator, have had dark skins, while those farther away have had light skins. How it came about—by separate acts of creation, by natural selection, by acquired characteristics or in some other way—is not known and, in the light of more important information regarding racial differences, is of comparatively insignificant importance.

It is not true, a cursory examination of history is sufficient to establish, that members of different races have an "instinctive" or "natural" aversion for each other, whereas members of the same race get along well. Most of the world's most bitter wars have been fought between people racially similar: Chinese versus Japanese; Sioux versus Pawnees; French versus Germans. With the exception of South Africa virtually nowhere else in the world is there anything comparable to the anti-Negro sentiment prevalent in the United States. Englishmen, Frenchmen, Italians, and other Europeans have only as much anti-Negro prejudice as has been taught them by American tourists and servicemen. On the Pacific Coast it is the yellow rather than the black man who is the major object of hatred, and in the Southwest it is the brown man of Mexican, which means mostly Indian, descent. What we are wont to call a racial problem consequently really is a minority problem difficult of solution only because the members of the minority are easily distinguishable. To put it in another, more accurate way, anyone who is set apart because of his physical appearance is a convenient scapegoat.

There is a considerable misinformation concerning physical differences, other than skin color, between races. Height, for instance, is not a distinguishing characteristic, as there are tall and short species in every race. As Ruth Benedict and Gene Weltfish pointed out in *The Races of Mankind* (Public Affairs Pamphlet No. 85, 1943), for instance, the Shulluk Negroes in the Nile valley average about 6 feet 2 inches tall whereas their neighbors, the brown pygmies, are only 4 feet 8 inches. Hopi Pueblo Indians in Arizona are 5 feet 4 inches whereas their Mohave neighbors are nearly 6 feet.

Neither is head shape a distinguishing characteristic: there are long and round heads of all races. Nor, despite some Southern members of Congress, are the blood types different. Members of all three races are likely to have any of the four types of blood known to medical science.

Even color is losing its importance, or value, as a distinguishing feature. Neither Hitler nor many of the rest of his Nordics were fair-skinned, blue-eyed and blond-haired. Most Caucasoids today are "in-between" types, especially in the United States where people of all nationalities have been intermarrying for generations. As for the Negro, Professor Meville Herskovits, anthropologist of Northwestern University and one of the world's leading authorities on that race, has declared that probably not more than 20 per cent of those today classified as American Negroes are of pure African origin. Most of the mixture was with Indians during colonial days, although a sizeable amount of "lightening" resulted from the libidinous activities of plantation masters not thought to be too reprehensible when Negroes hardly were considered human and laws were passed with heavy penalties for anyone attempting to educate them. The fact of such miscegnation, however, tends to contradict the contention that members of other races are repugnant to whites.

Dr. Edwin R. Embree, who was president of the Julius Rosenwald Fund for many years up to the time it completed its function in 1948, declared in *American Negroes* (John Day, 1942) that a new race, Brown Americans, is developing in America. It is variously estimated that annually from 20,000 to 60,000 members of what are considered Negro families "pass over" and become part of the white population. The "natural selection" practiced by Negroes themselves is hastening the lightening process, as the light-skinned avoid marriages with the dark-skinned. Wrote Embree: "Even if there is no more infusion of white blood, a few more generations of mingling among Negroes themselves will bring about so general a distribution of strains that it is likely that every Negro in America will have some white ancestry and most of them some Indian blood." Nevertheless, legally in most Southern states, anyone who is as much as $\frac{1}{64}$ Negro is a Negro. Even in the North there are social if not legal penalties attached to such a heritage, as Sinclair Lewis emphasized in *Kingsblood Royal* (Random, 1947). In the Aug. 30, 1949 *Look*, Walter White, long-time secretary of the National Association for the Advancement of Colored People, in an article, "Has Science Conquered the Color Line?" reported on a recently discovered chemical which, he wrote, "could hit the structure of society with the impact of an atomic bomb." It is monobenzyl ether of hydroquinone which, White said, already has caused some Negroes to lose the pigmentation in their skins. In the Aug. 27, 1949 *Science News Letter*, Dr. Louis Schwartz, a retired skin specialist of the U.S. Public Health service, denied the efficacy of the treatment.

Negro-haters like to point to other physical characteristics which, they allege, indicate that the Negro is closer in the evolutionary scale to the anthropoid apes than is the white man. It is true that a broad nose, long arms, short trunk, lower hairline, and wider space between the eyes are more apelike than their opposites. However, the white man more nearly resembles the monkeys in hair texture, short legs, heavier brow, thinner lips, and lighter skin. Scientists scoff at any attempts to prove anything about human races in any such way.

Mentality. In fact, scientists know that any claims that one race is superior to any other race mentally or intellectually are fallacious. It is true that American Negroes usually rate lower than whites in standard intelligence tests, but the phenomenon is to be explained sociologically rather than psychologically inasmuch as the best I.Q. tests depend upon the amount of information subjects have, and information can be equal only when opportunities to obtain it are the same. Proof of the greater importance of environmental factors was provided by a breakdown of the results of the Army Alpha tests given all draftees in World War I as follows:

Median Scores on A.E.F. Intelligence Tests

Southern Whites:
Mississippi 41.25
Kentucky 41.50
Arkansas 41.55

Northern Negroes:
New York 45.02
Illinois 47.35
Ohio 49.50

It was because the Benedict and Weltfish pamphlet included these facts that Southern Democrats, led by Rep. Andrew Jackson May of Kentucky, obtained congressional action to ban its circulation among servicemen during World War II.

Commented Professor Otto Klineberg, Columbia University anthropologist: "The real test of Negro-White equality as far as intelligence tests are concerned can be met only by a study in a region in which Negroes suffer no discrimination whatever, and enjoy exactly the same educational and economic opportunities . . . It is safe to say that as the environment of the Negro approximates more and more closely that of the white, his inferiority tends to disappear."

In 1949, Dr. Benjamin Pasamanick of Yale University's Child Development Clinic, received the annual Hofheimer award of the American Psychiatric Association for a study under conditions approximating those set forth by Professor Klineberg. Subjects were 53 Negro infants and 57 white infants of New Haven families, the Negroes generally being on a lower economic level than the whites and inhabiting poorer housing. However, Dr. Pasamanick reported, "The Negro mothers probably received the best diets in caloric and vitamin value that they had ever enjoyed during their lifetime because of the rise in living standards obtained by all people in spite of wartime scarcities. Almost all of these mothers received prenatal care in New Haven clinics, with supervision of and instruction on prenatal diets. And finally all the infants received adequate dietary supervision during infancy." The conclusions included the following:

"1. The average New Haven Negro infant of this study is fully equal in behavorial development to the average New Haven white baby.

"2. No outstanding characteristic was found which could be called a 'racial' difference, with the possible exception of the definite acceleration in gross motor behavior displayed by the Negroes. In the spheres of fine motor, adaptive language, and personal-social behavior the Negro babies did at least as well as the white children. There were no very pronounced differences in personality structure. The Negro infants, despite less favorable examination circumstances, adjusted well to examination, displaying more equanimity and restraint than white infants."

Despite the denials of some American white Christians, the church's teaching that all human beings are alike in the eyes of God seems to have a scientific validity. Despite the evidence and despite about 200 Negro doctors of philosophy, innumerable members of Phi Beta Kappa, George Washington Carver, Marian Anderson, Hazel Scott, Langston Hughes, Paul Dunbar, Paul Robeson, Willard Motley, Richard Wright, Jackie Robinson, Joe Louis, Larry Doby, W. E. B. DuBois, James Weldon Johnson, Duke Ellington, Canada Lee, Katherine Dunham, Hattie McDaniel, Lena Horne, Jesse Owens, Ralph Metcalfe, A. Philip Randolph, Ralph Bunche, Bill Robinson, Ethel Waters, Arna Bontemps, Josephine Baker, and a host of other "arguments" to the contrary, these frustrated white supremacists probably will persist in pointing to Stepin Fetchit, Rochester, Amos and Andy, and minstrel-show end men as the correct stereotypes of the American Negro. It would be too big a blow to their pride to admit they had been wrong for so long. More important, it would be to contradict much of their childhood teaching and their adulthood experiences.

Characteristics. Those experiences have taught them that many Negroes are illiterate or at least ignorant, disease-ridden, happy-go-lucky, delinquent and criminal, bad housekeepers, shiftless, and lazy. The last charge—the charge of indolence—can be dismissed as ridiculous in view of the fact that proportionately more Negro than white backs have been strained building the nation's highways, railroads, and buildings. To the extent that it originated with julep-drinking aristocrats who thought it up while engaged almost full time in nothing more strenuous than the practice of chivalry, it is doubly ridiculous.

Many of the other charges cannot be dismissed so lightly. It is extremely important, however, that they be explained. To epitomize what scores of authorities on the subject have pointed out: if you impose the conditions which create second-class citizens, you get second-class citizens. That is, you reap what you sow. Slum housing, inadequate medical attention, poor schooling, insufficient parental attention because both parents must work to keep the family together, improper diets, and the realization that one is trapped as far as escaping such an environment is concerned, breed frustration, bitterness, and hate which lead to delinquent and criminal behavior, neuroses, and exaggerated behavior in attempts to overcompensate for the inevitable sense of insecurity.

It is traditional that the Negro is last hired and first fired. Employers and employees alike make his employment and advancement difficult. He is barred from joining many labor unions, Jim Crowed in others. He seldom gets the opportunity to acquire much seniority where he works. From many skilled trades, and white collar and professional jobs, he is barred completely. Dr. Lohman pointed out in his Chicago Park District survey that "Although the Negroes make up 10 per cent of the population of Chicago, they occupy only 2 per cent of the 'clean-work' jobs and perform 34 per cent of the servant work. Sixty per cent of all white male workers are classified as skilled, business and professional, or clerical. However, only 25 per cent of all Negro male workers have such jobs." He cited the National Resources Board survey which revealed that for 1935–36 only 3.1 per cent of Negro families had incomes of more than $2,000 whereas 41.6 per cent of all white families were in that category. In North Central cities, white families averaged $1,720 per year whereas Negro families averaged $1,095.

Without enough money nobody can afford the necessities to produce good citizens. Even when the Negro can pay, furthermore, he is not permitted to buy in accordance with his means. His educational, recreational, and cultural opportunities are decidedly limited. Embree pointed out that in ten southern states in 1936 the per capita educational expenditure for white children was $49.30; for Negro children it was $17.04. The national average at that time was $80.62. In 1945, according to the October, 1947 *Southern Patriot,* the corresponding per capita expenditures in 17 states and the District of Columbia where separate schools are maintained by law were $73.67 for whites and $32.46 for colored. Because they insist on operating two separate school systems, the comparatively impoverished Southern states are unable to provide adequate schooling for children of either race. A few but not many good colleges and universities for Negroes exist, but it is difficult to obtain adequately trained teaching personnel because of the refusal of white institutions to admit colored students. In recent years several long-fought court battles, culminating in the United States Supreme Court, have compelled or induced several Southern colleges and universities to admit Negro students to their professional schools when they are unable to maintain equal opportunities on a Jim Crow basis. In the 17 states and the District of Columbia which maintain separate school systems, there is one white doctor for every 843 of the white population but only one Negro doctor for every 4,409 of the Negro population. Similarly there is one white lawyer for every 702 whites and one Negro lawyer for every 24,997 Negroes; one white engineer for every 644 whites and one Negro engineer for every 130,700 Negroes. The same situation exists in all of the other professions.

Negro health is decidedly inferior to that of whites. According to the Bureau of the Census, in 1940 the life expectancy of white males was 62.6 years; that of Negro males, 52 years; white women might expect to live 67 years; Negro women, 55.2 years. In 1945, according to the Metropolitan Life Insurance Company, the expectancies were as follows: white males, 64.4 years; Negro males, 56 years; white females,

69.2 years; Negro females, 59.62 years. In almost every category Negro morbidity and mortality are greater than that of whites. Ignorance of proper hygienic methods, inadequate medical and hospital facilities and disease-breeding living conditions are responsible.

Bad housing is the cause, not the result of social evils. Lohman pointed out that in the Chicago ghetto "there are square-mile areas where the density is over 50,000 per square mile. Indeed, in certain smaller sections the staggering density of 90,000 per square mile has been reached," and explained: "The incredible congestion on the Negro South Side is a direct result of segregation, buttressed by restrictive covenants and intimidations which deny Negroes access to other sections of the city." Other extracts from the same report follow: "Great numbers of Chicagoans are crowded into ancient structures. Many have long outlived their usefulness and suitability as human habitation. . . . Attempts on the part of individual Negro families to move into what, traditionally, have been white areas are not, as some would have us believe, the result of a mere desire to live among whites. Rather, it represents the compelling need for, and drive after, a decent home in which to live and raise one's family. . . . Questionable conduct is often mistakenly regarded as an evidence of racial inferiority. It is more likely to come from limited education and social opportunities. . . . Insufficient family income is the major reason why many in our population must withdraw their children from school at the earliest permissible age. . . . It is not, as some have too hastily concluded, a reflection of a lower native intelligence on the part of individuals residing in these areas."

In comment on the incidence of delinquency and crime in Negro areas Lohman pointed out: "Wherever there are found places or hangouts for street corner gangs, one finds the natural setting for many racial incidents. Juvenile delinquents as a hardened and venturesome lot are more readily disposed toward violence and possess the daring that is requisite to the initiation of conflict." He also referred to the findings on which the program of the Chicago Area Project is based (see pages 75 to 77), that delinquency and crime rates remained substantially the same in many areas where the racial and nationality complexions changed completely several times over a period of years. This indicates that social behavior is determined by social conditions, that criminals are made and not born. A few specifics regarding Negro crime rates, which are admittedly high: (1) there is a greater avidity on the part of police to arrest a Negro. They are more frequently victims of police "dragnets" and "roundups" than are whites, and they receive rougher treatment while in custody; (2) they have been the victims of wrongdoing oftener than they have been the perpetrators of it. Ever since they were forcibly brought to the New World they have been exploited, cheated, deprived of their legal rights, beaten up and murdered, often "to protect Southern womanhood" and, in general, to preserve the illusion of white supremacy.

Bergen Evans in *The Natural History of Nonsense* (Knopf, 1946) says of the charge that Negroes are sexually more potent and aggressive than whites that "it seems more a product of that itching interest, usually disguised as horror or moral indignation, which all people take in the sexual behavior of other groups." He points out that the Chinese have similar myths regarding whites. Embree pointed out that "Contrary to popular belief, sex offenses are not the chief causes of lynchings." Of 2,522 cases carefully studied, only 477, or less than 20 per cent, were even accused of rape. That Negroes have an obnoxious odor because of their race is pure myth. If they are overly superstitious, it is because of their poor education. As the preceding chapter illustrated, they have plenty of white company in all of their unscientific beliefs.

Under the subtitle, "Customs Not Racial," Benedict and Weltfish wrote:

"Differences in customs among peoples of the world are not a matter of race either. One race is not 'born' to marry in church after a boy-and-girl courtship, and another race to marry 'blind' with a bride the groom has never seen carried veiled to his father's house. One race is not 'born' equipped to build skyscrapers and put plumbing in their houses, and another to run up flimsy shelters and carry their water from the river. All these things are 'learned behavior,' and even in the white race there are many millions who don't have our forms of courtship and marriage and who live in shacks. When a man boasts of his racial superiority and says that he was 'born that way,' perhaps what he's really saying is that he had a lot of luck after he was born.

A man of another race might have been his equal if he'd had the same luck in his life. Science insists that race does not account for all human achievements."

The Price of Prejudice

Prejudice is expensive, not only in a monetary but also in other ways, several of which were cited in the Army talk referred to earlier (see page 274).

Prejudice is contagious. Declared the Army talk: "History has taught us that when we discriminate against one segment of the people, we set a pattern that may be used against other groups. Hitler's persecution of the Jews, trade unionists, Communists and Socialists was later directed against Catholics, Protestants, liberals and eventually the people of the world.

"In 1855 Abraham Lincoln understood this when he said: 'As a nation we began by declaring all men are created equal. We now read it "All men are created equal except Negroes." When the Know Nothings get control it will read, "All men are created equal except Negroes and foreigners and Catholics." '

"Consideration for the Negro, the Jew, the Catholic, the foreign born, or for any other minority group rests not merely on the grounds of humanity and justice; it rests on the solid base of self-interest."

Prejudice makes us all poorer. To quote from the Army talk again: "We can't have an enlightened democracy with minority groups living in ignorance. We can't have a prosperous democracy with minority groups so poor that they can't afford to buy the goods America produces."

The costliness to the South of maintaining separate school systems has been mentioned. In 1946 the Wisconsin Welfare Department found that it cost $150,000 to keep residents of Milwaukee's blighted 6th Ward who had been convicted of crimes in the state prison and reformatories; those "sent up" from the city's best ward, the 18th, cost only $3,523. The San Francisco Planning and Housing Association compared a slum area and the Marina district, an average well-kept neighborhood, both with about 12,000 inhabitants, and discovered that there were 36 times as many cases of tuberculosis in the slum area; twice as many fires occurred there; there were three times as many infant deaths; while 39 Marina adults were arrested there were 4,771 adult arrests in the slum area. The cost to taxpayers was twice as great for fire protection, four times as great for the maintenance of juvenile courts, 89 times as great for police protection, and 100 times as great for public health protection. Atlanta slums a few years ago paid 5½ per cent of the tax revenue but received 53 per cent of city services.

Prejudice robs us of minority talents. Although fewer than 1 per cent of pre-Nazi Germans were Jews, one-third of the 43 Nobel prizes awarded to Germans went to German Jews. When Hitler came to power all living prize winners were forced into exile, and the nation was deprived of their talent and of that of many other intellectuals, not all Jewish, who were murdered, allowed to deteriorate in concentration camps, or compelled to flee.

Similarly, in this country, we fail to utilize the talents of minority groups when we establish quota systems, acknowledged or furtive, in colleges and universities; when medical, legal, and other professional associations ban or make admittance difficult for doctors and lawyers; when we hang out "Gentiles Only" or "Whites Only" or "Christians Only" signs and refuse to employ the best potential talent available, or, having employed without discrimination, do not make promotions on merit, in private industry, government service, or the armed forces.

It is impossible to say whether Alfred E. Smith would have made a better president than Herbert Hoover, but in 1928 he was defeated in large part because of his Catholicism. In 1949 Ralph J. Bunche, who won the Nobel peace prize after he brilliantly mediated the Arab-Jewish dispute for the United Nations, declined an offer to be an assistant secretary of state partly because he refused to subject his family to the strict Jim Crow enforced in the nation's capital. In the same city and elsewhere whites "cut off their noses to spite their faces" by refusing to rent halls to Negro entertainers or lecturers. Constitution Hall in Washington, D.C., several times has been refused to the colored contralto Marian Anderson, to the pianist Hazel Scott, and to others by, of all groups, the Daughters of the American Revolution. The Knoxville, Tenn. censors cut out a scene featuring Lena Horne in the motion picture, "Ziegfeld Follies of 1946."

Prejudice blinds us to real situations. By making scapegoats of minority groups we do not face the realities of a situation. You can no more lick a depression by blaming it on the Jews or the Negroes or the labor unions or the liberals or anyone else than a primitive man can cause the death of an enemy by sticking knives in an effigy. In fact, by dissipating our energies through scapegoating, through fostering internal dissension, we retard rather than accelerate solution of any difficulty. In time of crisis teamwork, a united front of all affected, is needed but seldom obtained as different groups have as their major concern the attempt to pin responsibility on each other.

Prejudice weakens the United States' position throughout the world. In Berlin, after the defeat of Germany in 1945, the victorious allies agreed that "All Nazi laws which . . . established discrimination on grounds of race, creed or political opinion shall be abolished. No such discriminations, whether legal, administrative or otherwise, shall be tolerated." It is very difficult for American statesmen to pose as exponents of democracy throughout the rest of the world when Negroes are lynched in Georgia, their homes burned in Chicago, their lives taken in street fighting in Detroit and their human dignity disregarded almost everywhere. After all, about 75 per cent of the peoples of the entire world are what we call colored. The press of nations unfriendly to the United States jumps at every opportunity to headline a true story of discrimination or violence against some minority member or group in this country. Unfortunately, they are able to run such stories with considerable frequency. They also do not have to resort to any journalistic exaggerations when they tell their readers that a large proportion of American Negroes are not even allowed to vote, in absolute violation of the United States Constitution, in the "one nation, indivisible, with liberty and justice for all." When the Freedom Train, carrying the original copies of the Declaration of Independence, Emancipation Proclamation, and other documents failed to stop at Memphis and a number of other places because the natives refused to relax their Jim Crow customs even long enough to permit American citizens equal before the law to view the exhibit, millions of foreigners were shocked.

In November, 1948, appeared the report of the National Committee on Segregation in the Nation's Capital, which has headquarters at 4901 Ellis Avenue, Chicago 15. A condensed and illustrated summary, *Segregation in Washington*, was written by the late Kenesaw M. Landis and was indeed a shocker. It included accounts of an African foreign minister refused admittance to a white hotel; a Bolivian educator refused service in a chain restaurant; a Hindu woman refused service at a drugstore soda fountain; West Indian students forced to stand at a counter to eat; a Panama visitor asked by a priest to leave a white Catholic church; a Puerto Rican senator forced to sleep on a couch in a government office, and many others. In Washington there even are separate cemeteries for the dogs of colored and whites.

Prejudice degrades everyone. Wrote Landis in the final section of his brilliant summary: "When people are divided by a master-race theory, liberty and justice are impossible. Nowhere is this plainer than in the capital, where one-quarter of the population is segregated according to color. Here we have been building ghettos of the mind, body and spirit.

"The physical ghettos are the most obvious of all. They breed disease and crime, and give racism a base by the Lincoln Memorial. The ghettos of the mind have darker passages. They are built behind the walls of the segregated school system where children are taught not to know each other. They extend into the universities, into the minds of educators, doctors and divines.

"The ghettos of the spirit are hardest to define, but their darkness is the worst. These are blank spaces in a common humanity where men step on each other and take pride and profit in doing so. These are the ghettos that cramp the soul of the nation in the place of its pride, and lessen the meaning of life."

It is not only, or perhaps primarily, the victim of prejudice who suffers; his tormentors are depraved and debauched also. Theirs is a bad conscience, a violated morality, an heretical religious conduct. All that is best in man is reflected in democratic behavior in the spirit of the American Declaration of Independence and Bill of Rights. Lip service to the noble ideals of those documents while violating them in practice makes a mockery of our pretensions as a nation. Prejudice is the most shameful feature of American social, economic and political life. Also, pertinent to the subject matter of this book, *it is one of the most important, though corrupting forces in determining what American public opinion is on many matters.*

"We need no further justification for a broad and immediate program than the need to reaffirm our faith in the traditional American reality," declared the President's Committee on Civil Rights in its report, *To Secure These Rights*, in February, 1947. That sentiment was included in the 1948 platform of the Democratic party. In November of that year, not enough liberal Democrats—or liberal Republicans either—were elected to Congress to put it into effect, so strong is the force of prejudice in the United States.

Prejudice as News

"In the whole of history," wrote Barrows Dunham in *Man Against Myth* (Little, Brown, 1947), "no Negroes or Jews, no members indeed of any 'inferior' races, have inflicted upon mankind sufferings which remotely compare with those inflicted by the self styled 'superior' races."

It is when violence occurs that prejudice becomes newsworthy. Articles telling of discrimination in employment, education, housing or other aspects of life necessarily must be "dug up" in most part, through diligent detective work on the part of some energetic reporter. Or else they pertain to court actions intended to force granting of one's civil rights. When fists fly, however, the American press can be depended upon to take full advantage of the situation unless it is dissuaded from doing so, as the Chicago newspapers have been convinced by the Mayor's Commission on Human Relations that it is wise to soft-pedal news of violence at interracial housing projects or when Negroes move into formerly restricted areas and are greeted with bombs and torch throwers.

Although some groups interested in promoting better race relations deplore such suppression, believing that the public should be given the facts so that it can protest acts of terrorism, the hush-hush treatment is much preferred by them to the handling frequently given such incidents. In the fall of 1945, for instance, Evanston, Ill., was thrown into an uproar by a completely phony crime wave created by one Chicago newspaper and picked up by all of its rivals. Knowing that the sensational journalism had been inspired in vengeance after his refusal to give a reporter a certain item of news, the chief of police froze up and refused to comment, expecting the frenzy to die down. The mayor and other public officials also adopted the silent treatment, understandably but, as it turned out, unfortunately. For more than a week the perpetrator of every unsolved crime within a wide area was reported by the Chicago press as being sought in that suburb. Sheriff's cars began patrolling the city, especially the west side section largely inhabited by Negroes. Later, when local excitement became intense, local police joined the fun, arresting scores of colored people found on the streets after dark, flashing automobile searchlights into the windows of Negro residents and in general terrorizing the neighborhood. Some American Legionnaires in South Evanston called a meeting attended by nearly 200 incensed citizens and virtually threatened to form a vigilante group to protect the city if the city fathers refused to act. They stormed a meeting of the City Council, but the following week another group of alarmed citizens also filled the Council's chambers to indicate their alarm was not over the fictitious crime wave but because of the extent to which hysteria was endangering the civil liberties of many. At that meeting the mayor finally released statistics to show that rather than increasing, crime, by comparison with the same period the previous year or the preceding month, was on the downgrade. Even after that statement, the Hearst paper continued to publish its series (probably already written) about the Evanston wave of lawlessness. The other papers, however, called it off and the citizens believed their mayor that they were not in imminent danger of having their throats cut.

Perhaps the most significant aspect of the Evanston crime scare was the fact that there was absolutely no proof that, if the denizens of the suburb were responsible for all the unsolved rapes, robberies and burglaries committed on Chicago's north side, it was the colored element that was to blame. The closest anyone ever came to identifying any fugitive as a Negro was a woman who screamed and ran when she saw approaching her, about a half block away on the other side of a dark street, a figure which she thought was a Negro man. Nevertheless, public opinion accepted the suggestion of the newspapers, accentuated by the behavior of the law enforcement officers, that it must be the Negroes who were responsible. In such ways do prejudices warp the judgment of otherwise sound-thinking people.

The Evanston incident ended without casualties. The same unfortunately has not been true on innumerable occasions when similar situations have arisen in other parts of the country. One of the worst examples of irrational prejudice gone rampant was the so-called "zoot suit" rioting in June, 1943, in Los Angeles. After three nights of sporadic street fighting, on the evening of June 7 about 1,000 uniformed men stormed through the city's downtown area stopping street cars to drag out youths of Mexican descent, breaking into theaters, restaurants, and other places for the same reason, beating up any dark-skinned adolescent encountered anywhere.

As so often happens, it was the victims rather than their tormentors who were arrested. Although photographs of those taken into custody by police showed that no more than half wore zoot suits, the press dubbed them all "zoot suiters" and explained that the violence occured when soldiers and sailors acted in self-defense against zoot-suit gangs which had been annoying them and their girl friends. Doubtless the newspapers' use of zoot suit instead of Mexican resulted from the complaint of the Office of War Information against the former use a year earlier during what was known as the Sleepy Lagoon case, when one Mexican was killed and 22 arrested following a fight between two gangs of juveniles of Mexican extraction.

The zoot suits which gave their name to the west coast hoodlumism consisted, in the jargon of those who adopted the costume, of "reat pleats, stuff cuffs, a zest vest, svelte belt and a 'won my wings' tie." Translated, that means elaborately pleated trousers, extremely tight cuffs, a belt line just a little below the armpits and a huge bow tie. The equipment might also include a "dog chain," or an extra-heavy watch chain reaching below the knee, a knee-length coat with large lapels and a broad flat hat, usually with a feather. This outlandish outfit had been worn by adolescents, white and colored, for a long time before the June incidents. In fact, for many months the Los Angeles *Times* had run a comic strip in which a zoot suiter was a sort of superman.

Once the rioting occurred, the opinions of psychiatrists all over the nation were sought to explain why adolescents would masquerade in such fashion and how the incidence of juvenile delinquency could be affected by the wearing of such clothes. While the Los Angeles City Council solemnly banned the wearing of zoot suits under penalty of 30 days in jail, the mental hygienists answered with virtual unanimity that there is no way to judge or predict a person's criminal tendencies by his raiment and ventured similar explanations as to what makes youngsters want to be conspicuous in appearance. "The wearing of exaggerated clothing as a means of achieving distinction and recognition denied in other fields is a well recognized phenomenon," wrote Ruth D. Tuck in "Behind the Zoot Suit Riots" in the August, 1943

Survey Graphic. "The desire for flashy, bizarre clothes is natural in practically all adolescents," commented Albert Deutsch in the June 14, 1943 *PM*. Referring to Dr. Lawrence B. Reddick, the latter writer cited "the craving for attention" as another adolescent urge and then stated, "In underprivileged areas, and especially among minority groups, the 'sharp' sartorial get-up has become a badge of defiance by the rejected against the outside world and at the same time a symbol of belonging to the inner group. It is at once a sign of rebellion and a mark of conforming. It carries prestige."

"They are 'children' obsessed with a sense of dissatisfaction with things as they are," explained Dr. Paul L. Schroeder, former director of the Institute of Juvenile Research in Chicago who examined Hermann Goering before the Nuremberg trials. "They are drawn together and become aggressive because of their strength of numbers. That undoubtedly brought about their trouble with the servicemen. The servicemen, on the other hand, dislike the zoot suits because they feel they are giving American youth a bad name. They expressed their resentment by stripping the zoot suiters."

None of the experts spoke or wrote in any different vein. Almost a year later, in an article, "A Psychiatrist Looks at the Zoot Suit" in the February, 1944 *Probation*, organ of the National Probation Association, Dr. Ralph S. Benay called the zoot suit craze an outward manifestation of "adolescent neurosis" which, he wrote, was symptomatic of the sexual chaos in present-day adolescents, revealing itself in a bizarre reversal of normal male and female dress, marked aggression, a sense of gross inadequacy, and of tormenting insecurity. He wrote: "A striking symbolism for the masking of masculinity is the long coat and upper bagginess of the trousers, completely hiding the genital characteristics. The wearer is in glaring contrast with the sailor in his short blouse and tight fitting trousers, emphasizing his masculine development. . . . The hat is extremely feminine with its wide brim and its feather twice the height of the crown. The vivid colors of the band add to its effectiveness. There is the long hair which is often neck length with curls. The shoes show feminine shape of ornate type, with much tooling, pointed Dutch toes and high heels."

The situation, Dr. Benay pointed out, is reversed with zoot suit girls. Their attire is oversexed, not undersexed like that of the male zoot suiters. These girls, "instead of disguising their sexuality in the simplest of clothes, emphasize their secondary sexual characteristics in the very tight sweaters and Basque shirts with broad vertical stripes of many colors."

Most of the theorizing by authorities took place in publications published at long distances from Los Angeles. There the official and public attitude was typified by the testimony given by a representative of the sheriff's office at the time of the Sleepy Lagoon case that Mexicans are "biologically" predisposed toward criminal behavior. For more than a year before the June, 1943 riots, observers on the scene report, the police had acted in the same manner as did the Evanston law enforcers during the hectic week of alarm in that city. They constantly prowled about in the sections inhabited by Mexican-Americans, 98 per cent of whose youth, incidentally, are of American birth. Mexican youths were picked up on slight provocation, frisked, held incommunicado, denied civil rights. Whereas during 1942 the juvenile delinquency rate for the city of 2,500,000 as a whole was 1.6 per cent, the rate for the Mexican population of 219,000 was 3 per cent. Actually, however, juvenile delinquency had increased less during war years among the Mexicans than it had among other elements in the population, and, as noted earlier in this chapter, the greater avidity of police to arrest and prefer charges against members of unpopular minority groups make official statistics of questionable value.

Wrote Carey McWilliams in the June 21, 1943 *New Republic*: "Immediate responsibility for the outbreak of riots must be placed upon the Los Angeles press and the Los Angeles police. For more than a year now the press (and particularly the Hearst press) has been building up anti-Mexican sentiment in Los Angeles. Using the familiar Harlem 'crime-wave' technique, the press has headlined every case in which a Mexican has been arrested, featured photographs of Mexicans dressed in 'zoot suits,' checked back over the criminal records to 'prove' that there has been an increase in Mexican 'crime' and constantly needled the police to make more arrests." In similar vein Ruth Tuck wrote: "Most of the press stood for harsh repression, with little consideration of underlying causes or interest in long time treatment." There were the blatant headlines that might be expected, to explain, "Zoot Suit Gangsters Plan War on Navy" (Los Angeles *Daily News*, June 8, 1943) and "Mayor Pledges Two-Fisted Action, No Wrist Slap" (Los Angeles *Examiner*, June 10, 1943). To counteract such treatment there was hardly a word of sane comment in any newspaper. The situation finally quieted down when the armed forces belatedly declared Los Angeles out of bounds and Governor Warren appointed a commission to investigate.

During World War II, much to the delight of German and Japanese propagandists, there were race riots in several large American cities where Southern hillbillies and colored workers were thrown together in war industries. The worst was that which occurred during the week of June 20, 1943 in Detroit. It ended, after 34 had been killed, more than 1,000 injured and more than one million man hours of work had been lost, when army troops moved in to restore order. What happened in the interval was best told by Alfred McClung Lee and Norman D. Humphrey in *Race Riot* (Dryden, 1943). Near the beginning of their account (page 5) the authors, both Wayne University sociologists at the time, wrote: "Riots are the products of thousands upon thousands of little events that have affected the habits and emotions of thousands upon thousands of people both future rioters and future innocent bystanders," and near the end (page 96) they explained: "The sources of anti-Negro, anti-White, and similar prejudice are not in the schools, the churches, and like organizations. Sentiments of prejudice begin in the intimate social relationships of home and play-group, and they develop and solidify into deepest habit patterns chiefly through ignorance—ignorant mothers and fathers who try to give their children a feeling of status through 'running down' other groups and races—ignorant associates in play and work activities. All this ignorance that we have failed to dispel through positive preparations for democratic living. These prejudices provide emotional satisfactions, which are then fanned by irritations of all kinds, by demagogic orators, by organizations that feed upon hate, and by such subversive groups as the Christian Front, the Black Legion, the Ku Klux Klan and the many others that proselytize the psychologically conditioned with wonderfully satisfying 'panaceas.' "

Dr. Lee also prepared a pamphlet, *Race Riots Aren't Necessary*, No. 107 in the Public Affairs series. Earl Brown wrote "The Truth About the Detroit Riot" for the November, 1943 *Harper's* and Public Affairs pamphlet No. 87 *Why Race Riots? Lessons From Detroit*. Ernest A. Gray, Jr. wrote "Race Riots Can Be Prevented" for the December, 1945 *Harper's*. All were in substantial agreement with

Justin McCarthy who began his story from Detroit for the June 22, 1943, Chicago *Sun*: "Hitler won a battle in Detroit today."

Nineteen centuries earlier the Hitlers of that time also won a victory. As related in Acts 7:54–60:

"When they heard these things they were cut to the heart, and they gnashed on him with their teeth.

"But he, being full of the Holy Ghost, looked up steadfastly into heaven, and saw the glory of God, and Jesus standing on the right hand of God.

"And said, Behold I see the heavens opened, and the Son of man standing on the right hand of God.

"Then they cried out with a loud voice, and stopped their ears, and ran upon him with one accord,

"And cast him out of the city, and stoned him; and the witnesses laid down their clothes at a young man's feet, whose name was Saul.

"And they stoned Stephen, calling upon God and saying, Lord Jesus, receive my spirit.

"And he kneeled down, and cried with a loud voice, Lord, lay not this sin to their charge. And when he had said this, he fell asleep."

Prejudice and hate always have been major factors in determining what public opinion is and in shaping the affairs of the world. No student of public opinion can avoid paying an extra amount of attention to the vicious side of the subject.

CHAPTER NINE

MENTAL EPIDEMICS

Much stupid thought and action results because "everybody's doing it," and nobody wants to be different except in socially approved ways.

Fashions

"Ladies of Utah, in my amazement and in my dismay, I beseech you:

"Surely you will strike—a wildcat strike would be just the very thing—before you meekly (or weakly) accept this unkind thing. . . . this cruel wrong that the deep dyed plotters behind the pages of your fashion books are about to inflict on you for their private—and generally ill-gotten—gain. . . ."

So wrote Vivian Meik in the Aug. 30, 1947 Salt Lake City *Deseret News* regarding the attempt of dress manufacturers to persuade women to purchase longer dresses and skirts than they had been wearing for years in order to attain what they called the New Look.

From the pulpit of Washington's fashionable All Souls Unitarian church, the Associated Press reported Sept. 15, 1947, the Rev. A. Powell Davies denounced long skirts as "immoral," "moronic," and "a crime against human decency" because they "waste the material that is desperately needed by the world's suffering people . . . because they represent the foolish and grotesque in a world that is crying out for wisdom and sanity."

And from several other cities came reports similar to the following:

Dallas, Tex., Aug. 23.—(AP)—With a band playing old-time songs and half its members dressed in grandmother's clothes, and Little Below the Knee Club women stopped downtown Dallas traffic today with a parade proclaiming long skirts old-fashioned and impractical.

"Shall it be this?" and "Grandma wore this" were the banners on early model cars filled with women dressed in the long skirt styles of the '90s and the '20s.

"Be sensible" and "be practical" were the placards on the snappy new convertibles filled with girls sitting on the back of the seats, legs crossed, dresses a little below the knee.

"Don't know what they're trying to do but guess it's a good idea" was a comment on the street.

* * *

Josiah D. Malcolmson, almost 75 and a veteran of the Spanish-American war with "a medal to prove it," knew. "The shorter the better," he declared.

Malcolmson put on his old campaign hat and rode in a truck in the parade under a sign "old soldiers still have young ideas." Directly in front of him rode a pretty young girl, legs crossed, skirt a little below the knee.

Spectators leaned out of downtown office buildings, lined the sidewalks and pushed out into the street along the five-block route of the 20-minute parade. They whistled at the girls in the convertibles and laughed at the old-fashioned styles.

* * *

Mrs. Warren J. Woodward, the Dallas housewife who started the L.B.K. Club two weeks ago, said that almost 2,000 women have written her that they were in sympathy with her rebellion against fashion's decree of longer skirts for women. She has received inquiries about the L.B.K. Club from a group in Juneau, Alaska, as well as from dozens of cities in the United States.

Men, too, have written, explaining buying new dresses with longer skirts for their wives was expensive and, anyway, they liked the shorter skirts.

The marines who composed today's color guard to lead the parade weren't exactly sure how they'd gotten in.

"Well, the marines always get there first," Master Sgt. Charles L. Pryor of Littlefield, Tex., explained.

Organized and unorganized, the opposition served only to provide millions of dollars of free publicity for the new style so that the advertising departments were suspected of having inspired it. Feature writers, columnists, photographers, and cartoonists kept the "controversy" alive for several weeks. Then the girls calmed down and began hoarding their pennies so that they could be among the first to appear on the streets in the new finery.

Although fashion undeniably is highly commercialized in the

United States, it decidedly is not so that consumers are at the complete mercy of producers. Fashion designers and manufacturers must "guess right" with each new product with which they hope to effect a widespread change in buying habits. To do so successfully they must be "in tune" with the times, meaning that they must appeal to a potential if not an actual buyers' demand. In *Economics of Fashion* [1] Paul H. Nystrom cited several expensive campaigns to bring about important style changes which failed. Likewise, he recalled occasions on which manufacturers were put to heavy expense to meet new demands which arose quite independently of their efforts and sometimes contrary to their wishes. An example was the sudden popularity in the early twenties of men's shirts with collars attached. A typical passage from Nystrom's book follows: "Ever since 1918 there have been a number of outstanding efforts to change or control the trend of fashion, all apparently fruitless. A great amount of time, thought and money have been applied during the last ten years to bring back or to reintroduce fashion movements for women's suits, shirtwaists and separate skirts. Apparently every season this effort is repeated in spite of the fact that every available figure and index of sales in these items of goods showed a steady decline up to the end of 1927."

Throughout history church and state, medical men, oldsters, and others have made innumerable attempts to regulate or influence how men and women, especially young ones, shall dress and otherwise adorn their bodies. Mostly it has been a futile effort as the function of clothing is more than merely to provide warmth and protection. As J. C. Flugel pointed out in *The Psychology of Clothes* (Hogarth, 1939), the primary motive—more fundamental than modesty—is decoration, and, as is true of all forms of art, standards of beauty change with the times; they are, in fact, a reflection of those times. "Fashion," wrote James Laver in an article, "War and Fashion," in the December, 1940 *Living Age,* "far from being a frivolity, is always the epitome of an epoch and in it can be seen reflected, as it were, in miniature, the whole of an age." Similarly, Pierre Clerget pointed out in "The Economic and Social Role of Fashion," which appears in the 1913 annual report of the Smithsonian Institution, "The appearance of a new style or garment is the visible sign that a transformation is

[1] Paul H. Nystrom, *Economics of Fashion.* Copyright. 1928. by The Ronald Press Company.

taking place in the intellect, custom and business of a people." Clerget illustrated his argument by reference to the abandonment by the successful Chinese revolutionists of the queue and their adoption of Western clothing.

Other authorities cite the extent to which changes in habiliment symbolized the social upheaval brought about by the French Revolution. Marie Antoinette, whose chief if not only talent seems to have been to appear decorative, favored towering headdresses and billowy hoop skirts. Both sexes among the upper classes wore highly decorative clothing made from rich materials, mostly brocaded silk with many trimmings. Among the underprivileged the shabby pantaloon was standard attire. Their victory secure, that costume and variations of the long trousers became a symbol of the Era of the Common Man and were worn by everyone who did not want to run the risk of being taken for an aristocrat. Once the Terror was passed it became the mode to admire all things Greek and Roman because the new regime was acclaimed as the spiritual inheritor of the democracy of those earlier periods. So, women became pseudo-classical in appearance, with diaphanous loose clothing sometimes over pink skin tights.

Approved, if not, as some claim, introduced into England by the famous style dictator, George Bryan (Beau) Brummell, long trousers caught on there despite exhortations against them as vigorous as any ever resolved by a Chamber of Commerce or Women's club against bobbed hair, shorts or scanty bathing suits in modern times. Cambridge University in 1812 decreed that students appearing in hall or chapel in long trousers should be considered absent. The Duke of Wellington, despite his heroic fame, was refused admittance to London's most famous restaurant because he was an early addict to the new style. In 1820 one section of the Church of England ordered that no preacher who wore long trousers should be allowed to occupy a pulpit. Even today knee breeches still are proper attire in the English court although even the king appears almost everywhere else in what for more than a century has been orthodox garb.

Laver reviews history to conclude that in times of peace clothing reflects the comparative social stability of the era. Waistlines of women's garments remain at normal location, and there is a tendency toward more elaborate hairdressing. Come war or revolution or some other social upheaval, however, and the women abandon their corsets, cut their hair and wear less but more masculine clothes. Unrestrained, the waistline is free to go where it will. In 1800 generally it went up; in 1920 it came down.

Men, too, participate in the trend toward sartorial simplicity in times of stress. For example, during World War I they shed their long underwear. World War II resulted in at least partial abandonment of both the superfluous necktie and suit jacket in hot weather, and a general loosening of the entire getup. The following article from the July 5, 1949 Chicago *Daily News* indicates the newsworthiness of such revolutionary behavior and suggests the social pressures which slow down change.

By Jack Mabley

A revolutionary change in men's hot weather clothing appears to be at hand.

The staunchest strongholds that dictated that men wear coats and ties in the hottest temperatures are surrendering to a trend toward comfort in dress.

Men without coats and ties now can get in restaurants and hotels in Chicago where a year ago they would have been given the bum's rush.

Headwaiters on diners of crack streamlined trains will show tieless men to tables without a word of protest.

Ralph Freeman, manager of the Sheraton Hotel, announced, "Until this year coats were required in our dining rooms. Now the trend all over the country is to comfort. If men don't wear coats at home, they don't need to wear them here."

A publicity representative of the Hotel Ambassador's Pump Room said: "Men must wear coats and ties. I've seen good people turned away hungry."

However, Ernest Byfield, president of the Ambassador and Sherman hotel corporations, stated, "We like to see coats and ties in all our dining rooms, but we don't throw anyone out.

"We used to be rigid about dress in the Pump Room, but now if a man is neat and tidy the waiter will seat him. Maybe I should keep the rooms so cold you'd have to wear a coat. You need earmuffs now."

George W. Kerner, superintendent of the Fred Harvey dining car system, said: "We have no restrictions. The days of requiring coats and ties are gone. Today comfort is the word."

A North Western Railroad spokesman said, "We'll go along with the national trend. We never call attention to a diner's dress. The public sets its own standards."

A diehard is the Empire Room at the Palmer House. A waiter captain said, "We don't allow anybody without a coat or tie. However, we keep several ties in the check room in emergencies. We prefer proper dress. If someone comes in with one of those two-toned sports outfits, we put him in an inconspicuous place, you know."

The champion of comfort for men is Chicagoan Bill Veeck, president of the Cleveland Indians baseball club.

"I believe every person should dress for comfort, not style," Veeck asserts. "I'm comfortable without a tie, hat, coat or collar. If you're happy with a tie, go ahead and wear one. They strangle me."

Ernie Byfield said Veeck will be welcome in the Pump Room.

There are, of course, some universal and possibly eternal factors which operate to the advantage of would-be fashion dictators. Principally there are the desires, on the one hand, for change—something new and novel—and, on the other hand, once a fashion has been established, to conform to it so as not to be considered old-fashioned and queer. In the United States—a young and rapidly changing but highly industrialized country—both of these factors are particularly strong.

Always productive of laughs is an inspection of the family photograph album showing grandmother's hoop skirts and bustles, mother's high-necked and long-sleeved wedding gown and her high-piled hairdo, grandfather's whiskers, and father's youthful moustache, sideburns, and high stiff collars. To the youngsters it seems incredible that their ancestors could stand to look at each other, much less share feelings of love or even of admiration. And, regardless of how defensive they may be in response to juvenile jibes, the oldsters find it difficult not to believe that they have acquired better taste with increasing maturity. They even glance at faded pictures of the Gibson girl, Lillian Russell, Little Egypt, Mary Pickford, Clara Bow, Theda Bara, and other glamorous pinup girls of yesterday and wonder how they ever considered them alluring.

What it all proves is that standards of beauty, including fashions, are socially determined and differ by time and place. In Egypt feminine corpulence is admired; Padaung women stretch their necks and wear metal collars; some Australian tribal women make severe scars on their faces; Ubangi stretch and distort their lips until they resemble ducks' bills. Within modern times in this country it has been considered attractive at intervals to be hippy, with or without an hourglass figure, and to possess a boyish shape. Waistlines have gone up and down; curves have been accentuated and disguised. Nobody has ever produced convincing evidence that there is any correlation between obedience to any moral code and the presence or absence of clothing so those who worry about current styles should relax.

To repeat a point—in fact, *the* point of this part of the chapter—while an individual or group of individuals can determine the particular mode or fashion, *more fundamental changes occur only as aspects of broader and more important social trends*. Some changes are utilitarian in origin. Men's clothing, for instance, became drab and colorless following the Industrial Revolution when the soot, smoke, and dust of the early factories ruined more gaily colored garments. When mass production replaced tailoring, masculine garb became standardized in design as well. The bicycle was a factor in causing skirts to shorten late in the nineteenth century. The post-World War I revival of individual participation in games had a further effect of loosening and lightening sports clothes for both sexes. During World War II several communities modified ordinances which forbade women to wear masculine garb, as dresses and skirts just could not be worn on many war industry jobs. Wrist watches became popular during World War I as part of a foot soldier's equipment; identification bracelets, introduced during World War II, continued to be worn for years thereafter. One of the earliest specific campaigns of American suffragettes was for adoption of freer and more masculine clothing for women. Mrs. Amelia Jenks Bloomer's name still is used to describe one such piece of wearing apparel. Not much progress, however, occurred until other factors combined to advance the so-called emancipation of women.

Within the limits indicated style leaders can be influential in determining what shall be popular during a particular season. Once the tastes of queens and kings' mistresses were emulated. England in the seventeenth, eighteenth, and early nineteenth centuries had a series of masculine fashion leaders, each given the popular *beau* title. Col. Robert Fielding, Richard Nash, George Bryan Brummell, and Count Alfred D'Orsay were among the most famous. In our business civilization most new fashions used to originate with or for the upper economic classes, the "400." What Mrs. So-and-So wore at the opening of the opera, horse show, or presidential inauguration gets fulsome treatment on the society page provided the grand dame has a bank account well into six figures. Before 1930, it is estimated, about 85 per cent of American-made dresses were modeled after Paris creations, only the rich being able to purchase the originals, which is what they did to the fullest extent possible. World War II just about finished whatever was left of Paris' world leadership in this field. One of Hitler's first edicts after his capture of the French capital was that French fashions henceforth should "reflect the ideals of material and domestic love, the kitchen and purification." The effort failed as designers sabotaged the order and French women refused to buy. Since World War II the Parisian influence on American fashions has been almost nonexistent. Of far greater importance are motion pictures which over a long period of years have been responsible for as many style innovations as Prince Albert and his famous coat, all other visiting royalty, and the native rich together. Examples: as long as cigar smoking was associated only with villians, sales suffered; when Clark Gable undressed in *It Happened One Night* and revealed he wore no undershirt, their sales dropped; in other films Gable made amends with another part of the clothing industry by glamorizing turtleneck sweaters. Tail coats nearly reaching the heels resembling that worn by Robert Montgomery in *The Duke of Chicago* came into brief demand after showing of that picture; Marlene Dietrich popularized slacks on and off the screen; Shirley Temple hairbands once were the vogue; when Charles Boyer ordered pink champagne for Irene Dunne in *Love Affair*, the wine industry underwent a miniature revolution. Greta Garbo's dark glasses were emulated by many, as were Jean Harlow's platinum blonde hair and Sonja Henie's white skating shoes. Popeye, both in comic strip and on the screen, is credited with having increased the consumption (or at least the sale) of spinach by about 40 per cent. How important (and consequently newsworthy) one aspect of motion picture influence on fashions became during wartime is indicated by the following article:

Hollywood, Feb. 16.—(UP)—The federal government cracked down on Veronica Lake today as a menace to the war effort; it claimed too many lady airplane workers imitating her peek-a-boo bob had scalped themselves in the machinery.

Miss Lake said okay. Said she was tired of looking at the world through one eye, anyway, and that henceforth she'd wear her hair on the top of her head.

"Any woman who wears her hair over one eye is silly. I never have worn it that way, myself, except in pictures. It made a good trade mark on the screen, but it was hard to see where I was going."

The situation concerning 20,000 Veronica Lakes trying to operate turret lathes in war plants all over the nation first reached the desk of Mary Brewster White of the womanpower division of the War Manpower commission.

To Monroe Greenthal of the War Production Board she sent an inter-office memo: "Subject, Veronica Lake's hair."

"The working gal's indifference to the dangers of long flowing hair-does has driven personnel directors to the last stages of profanity," wrote Miss White. "Veronica Lake has had a tremendous influence because of her unfettered mane upon too large a percentage of ladies engaged in turning out the ammunition."

Miss White added that she was delighted to note that Miss Lake's hair had gone up in her last movie ("So Proudly We Hail") and said she believed the War Manpower Commission and the War Production Board should do everything possible to keep La Lake's topknot on top.

—Chicago *Daily News,* Feb. 16, 1943

Fads

Even if the government had not found it necessary to interfere, the peek-a-boo hairdo undoubtedly would have disappeared shortly anyway, for it was a fad rather than a fashion. The difference is this: a fashion is the prevailing style at any given time, style being defined as a characteristic or distinctive mode or method of expression, presentation, or conception in some field. When a style is widely accepted and followed, it is a fashion, and the psychological appeal is the urge to conform. To be fashionable means to be up to the minute, to be like others. By contrast, a fad is a miniature fashion which affects only a comparatively small group which desires not to be alike but to be different. The appeal of a fad is novelty. Consequently, fads are short-lived because when too many adopt the same fad its distinctiveness vanishes, and the faddist has to seek a new means of satisfaction.

Whereas, as explained, fashions generally are set by the so-called upper classes, after which they are copied by those below them on the economic ladder, fads generally originate nearer the bottom and may or may not be adopted by their originators' supposed betters. When such does happen, the fad is likely to develop into a fashion as was the case with bobbed hair after World War I, cigarette smoking, and much of the lightening of the feminine wardrobe. The faddist must not be confused with the chronic rebel who wears long hair when almost everyone else has his cut short and who goes in for exotic forms of dress—berets, poets' ties, zoot suits, and so forth—to symbolize his defiance. There likewise is the chronic faddist who takes up almost every new one that comes along in many or all different fields. Such a person doubtless is a neurotic who uses faddism as a means of off-setting his frustration. *The extent to which an entire social group or nation suffers from a sense of insecurity can be deduced from the extent to which fads develop mass followings and succeed each other in rapid succession.* There were fads during the prosperous twenties—crossword puzzles, mah jongg, miniature golf, the Charleston, "Yes, We Have No Bananas," raccoon coats, loafers, sneakers—but they were tame by comparison with their successors after the depression set in and war fears grew. The thirties were the period of chain letters, Bank Nights, "The Music Goes Round and Round," Confucius say, "knock knock," handies, monopoly, jigsaw puzzles, the Big Apple, Black Bottom, marathon dances, and goldfish swallowing. In March, 1939, a Harvard freshman won a $10 bet by chewing and swallowing a live goldfish. Three days later at Franklin and Marshall College a student salted, peppered, and swallowed three goldfish. A little later another Harvard man polished off 24. He also offered to eat a bug for a nickel, an angleworm for a dime and a beetle for a quarter. A University of Pennsylvania student gulped 25 goldfish; a University of Michigan undergraduate swallowed 28; a Boston College gulper disposed of 29; a Northwestern University student ate 36; and the grand champion, at Clark University, downed 89.

Russian boots, sloppy galoshes, Princess Eugenie hats, peg top trousers, barrel skirts, sloppy joe sweaters, garterless socks, bobby socks, babushkas, and saddle shoes come and go; so do conga lines and jitterbugs, Kewpies, fox tails, and shmoos, jive and be bop, "The Maine Stein Song," "The Big Bad Wolf" and "Open the Door, Richard," and an incessant succession of slang expressions and "apt" phrases: 23-skidoo, oh you kid, oh yeah, how come? says who? Who's Yehudi? Does your mother know you're out? natch, but definitely, and drop dead. When King Tut's tomb was opened the ancient Egyptian motif became strong for awhile; whenever Walt Disney invents a new cartoon character it becomes familiar as a doll and as decoration on scarfs, chinaware, children's furniture, wall paper and almost every other imaginable place. In 1949, after a year, gross sales of schmoo novelty items exceeded 25 million dollars. Several newspaper publishers protested to United Features Syndicate against such commercialization of a leading comic strip character. Typically T. R. Waring, managing editor of the Charleston (S.C.) *News and Courier*, was quoted in the Sept. 3, 1949 *Editor and Publisher* as saying, "The schmoo's value as a news feature to us has deteriorated since he became a soap salesman."

Most of the fads of dress, speech, music, and entertainment are popular primarily with youth. Each succeeding generation of parents is driven wild by the so-called "popular" music of the hour and scandalized by the dressing, dancing, and other forms of recreation of their offspring. It should be some consolation to realize that the worrying mothers of today were the "flappers" of the post-World War I period whose parents were as concerned over their morals and safety as they are now over those of their sons and daughters. Taking up the bizarre is a normal form of adolescent behavior, and if a youngster gets into trouble it is unlikely that his having had his friends write their names on his gaudy raincoat or his addiction for quiz shows had anything to do with it. Nor is a polychromous face, fingers, or toenails the harbinger of a career of prostitution for the teen-aged girl. It must be admitted, however, that the Selective Service Board found that tattooed draftees were one and a half times more likely than others to be psychoneurotics.

Almost all of the fads and fashions so far mentioned in this chapter were in their heyday the recipients of journalistic attention. Not much of the writing, at least to this author's knowledge, indicated much depth of perception of the actual social psychological nature of the phenomena. Rather, each in turn is more likely to be written up "on its merits" as an isolated phenomenon. One zany World War II fad which was good for a number of attention-getting feature articles in both newspapers and magazines actually involved only a comparatively few persons. It was the short snorter fad which is believed to have begun well before wartime, in 1925. In that year Joe Crosson is supposed to have started it in Fairbanks, Alaska with rules which made anyone making a trans-oceanic airplane flight eligible and subject to one dollar penalties to be paid to all Short Snorters present if ever unable to produce his short snorter dollar, containing signatures of flight companions, upon demand.

More familiar and interesting to a much larger number were the wartime peregrinating Kilroy and the ubiquitous gremlins. The former was discussed in Chapter 6 (see pages 199 to 200). The latter apparently were postulated by Royal Air Force pilots during the Battle for Britain in 1942 to explain otherwise unexplainable errors and breakdowns of equipment. Maybe some aviators actually believed that there were aerial pixies who bored holes in their planes' wings, jammed landing gear, knocked machine gun sights out of line, punched holes in flying boat wing floats, and otherwise made a nuisance or a serious menace of themselves. If so the gremlins were a case of orthodox myth making. On the whole, however, the gremlins were accepted as fanciful and a comparatively harmless wartime diversion. Cartoonists and advertisers introduced them plentifully in their copy. At least one comic strip, "The Gremlins," was begun, Walt Disney immortalized gremlins on the screen, and there were newspaper and magazine feature articles galore and even several books. It became common practice to blame every lapse of memory or error, Freudian or otherwise, on the gremlins, and the excuse usually met with charitable response. Anyone "passing the buck" to gremlins really was saying, "I didn't mean it; to err is human." Thus the screwball fad may have had a good effect by increasing tolerance of the shortcomings of others.

There follows a typical short newspaper feature of the period:

Like their cousins, the pixies and the leprechauns, the gremlins—those little gnomelike creatures who ride with aviators on their bombing expeditions—are more mischievous than harmful.

And, according to Dr. Wilfrid Dyson Hambly, curator of anthropology at Field Museum, who is the authority for that statement, they are quite in keeping with the times, although they are likely to disappear after the war.

"Belief in 'little people,' " said Dr. Hambly yesterday, "may have had its origin in observations of African pigmies, but it has existed down the ages.

"War and sudden danger, the uncertainties of life, always bring beliefs of this kind to the surface. It is as natural for aviators to believe in gremlins as it is for children to believe in Santa Claus.

"Even in the modern world, belief in pixies and fairies has by no means died out. Like gremlins, these little people are always up to pranks, but are never vicious. Pixies, for example, turn your pockets inside out or make you lose yourself in the fields. And if you ever find a leprechaun, he may direct you to the source of hidden treasure.

"In the last war, we had the angels of Mons, and Joan of Arc appeared before the defenders of Verdun. So it is not remarkable that in this war we should have gremlins. One placates a gremlin or paints him on the cockpit of a bomber as a mascot, just as one would wear a rabbit's foot or any other charm or amulet."

Dr. Clark Kuebler of the classic language department, Northwestern University, compared the gremlin to the daemon of the ancient Greeks. The daemon, he explained, was not to be confused with the demon. He was rather a good spirit, a guardian angel; the opposite of the furies who personified the conscience.

"Thus," he said, "if you keep on the good side of a gremlin, you can expect a safe journey and a happy landing."

According to the gremlinologists, only aviators can actually see gremlins or aerial pixies. The female gremlin, or the fifinella, flies only for the fun of it, and is never up to mischief, and it is the baby gremlins or widgets who get behind the aviator's ears and tickle him.

Chicago *Sun,* Dec. 13, 1942

"The country is back to normal," wrote commentators, in essence, all over the United States as a new pastime, originating in California, swept eastward to the Atlantic seaboard. The inspiration for much sardonic reporting and multitudinous headaches for law enforcement and other public officials was the Pyramid Club, a get-rich-quick venture reminiscent of the chain letters of 1935. Although the mathematical odds against their ever making much were prodigious, over a several weeks' period early in 1949 thousands of persons joined clubs at $1 or $2 for membership and gathered nightly, usually with coffee and doughnuts for refreshments, to check up on the efforts of other members to recruit newcomers so as to keep the play going. Theoretically, if each new member obtained two more, in 12 days a person would become top man and stand to gain $2,048 on a dollar investment. Actually, few if any such winners were reported from anywhere, and the fad died out shortly. Chief beneficiaries probably were the telephone companies as the clubs avoided the mails so as not to run afoul postal regulations as the chain letterites had done. Participants also testified to the opportunity the Pyramid Clubs provided to make new acquaintances and to the democratic composition of many of the club meetings. Jim Moran, press agent who allegedly introduced the fad into the nation's largest city was quoted in the March 12, 1949 *New Yorker* as saying: "Pyramiding is good for the nerves. It's far better than talking to yourself, and I'm sorry to say that the number of people who are talking to themselves on the streets of this country is increasing by leaps and bounds."

Crazes

Some writers called the Pyramid Clubs a craze, and in some localities the designation probably was apt. For the nation as a whole, however, the fad did not become as epidemic as had several of its predecessors, certainly including the chain letters of more than a decade earlier, miniature golf, bank nights, "Open the Door, Richard," and some other songs. Sociologically defined, a craze is a fad or fashion that is accompanied by considerable crowd excitement or emotion: one that has "gone wild," that is. Social annals record mental epidemics which seem fantastic in retrospect.

Whatever the craze involves becomes "the thing to do" or "to think," and the bandwagon effect operates to break down the resistance of many of the supposedly most sober and rational. All of the factors which operate at any time to compel conformity of thought and action of any kind are fortified by a greatly heightened intensity of feeling which makes life unpleasant or dangerous for the noncomformist. It takes considerable courage to avoid being swept along by the majority point of view when not to do so imperils one's very safety. The entire atmosphere during the height of a mental epidemic is conducive to conscious or unconscious acquiescence. That is, the individual has strong motivation to give in and to rationalize his orthodoxy. If there are martial music, parades, ceremony, oratory, and other public manifestations of enthusiasm, "holding out" becomes increasingly more difficult.

The first great period of mental epidemics during the Christian era was that of the pilgrimages and Crusades which lasted almost three hundred years, from the beginning of the eleventh until near the end of the thirteenth centuries. It is estimated that approximately seven million lives were lost in the futile attempts to recapture Jerusalem and the rest of the Holy Land after its conquest in 1076 by the Seljukian Turks.

"Listen to nothing but the groans of Jerusalem," Pope Urban II explained to a multitude at the second Council of Clermont. First intense silence and then sobs which became more and more hysterical greeted him as he continued, "And remember that the Lord has said,

'He that will not take up his cross and follow Me is unworthy of Me.'
You are the soldiers of the cross; wear, then, on your shoulders the
blood-red sign of Him who died for the salvation of your soul!"

Similar emotional appeals by Peter the Hermit and others helped
whip Western Europe into a state of religious frenzy. Leaving fields
and towns, serfs and petty traders joined up as members of the holy
forces intent upon doing God's will by murdering their fellow men.
The proper reply to any skeptic was: "He who will not follow Me is
unworthy of Me." Men of all races and nationalities, with their wives
and daughters, with infants taken from the cradle, grandfathers on
the verge of the grave, and many sick and dying, came from every
direction, all ready to help in the conquest of the Holy Land. Miracles,
revelations and visions were almost a daily occurrence and the mental
climate was such that to doubt was heretical. In 1212 occurred the
most pathetic and tragic of all the incidents connected with the craze:
the Children's Crusade. Like the legendary youngsters who trooped
after the Pied Piper of Hamelin, about 50,000 boys and girls, many
from eight to ten years of age, left their homes, some running away,
to follow a teen-ager, Stephen of Cloyes. Contrary to their prophet's
expectations, presumably based on revelations, the seas did not open
before them as they supposedly had for the Children of Israel. Instead, almost all of the little ones were either lost in shipwrecks or
captured and sold into captivity as slaves or prostitutes.

The colossal failure of the Crusades, whose real motivation several
authorities consider to have been more economic than religious,
caused some disillusionment regarding the efficacy of revelation. By
others, however, it was interpreted as evidence of God's displeasure
with man because of his sinfulness. From the thirteenth through the
sixteenth centuries there were organized attempts to take advantage of
virtually every sizeable catastrophe to proclaim the wrath of God
against corruption and to invite sinners to atone for their transgres-
sions. Most important were the Flagellantes who probably originated
in Italy after the plague of 1259. They traveled from town to town in
somber raiment, preaching and exhorting and publicly inflicting severe
physical punishment upon each other. They invited others to join them
in endurement of physical torture, declaring that their blood had a
share with that of the Lord to atone for sin. The most severe outbreak
of flagellantism came during and after the Black Plague which from

1347 to 1349 caused 13 million deaths in China, 24 million in the rest of Asia, and 25 million in Europe. Flagellantes and other religious fanatics were able to whip up a maddening sense of sin among members of all economic classes. It was a great period of religious revivals of all sorts and of brutal treatment of Jews and nonbelievers. In 1252 Innocent II ordered rulers to compel seized heretics to confess "by torture which will not imperil life or injure limb." As late as 1751 the king of Portugal forbade the Inquisition to burn anyone to death without governmental license.

One important chapter in the history of mass hysteria is that of the dancing mania which began during the last quarter of the fourteenth century and lasted for almost two hundred years. Clerks and artisans, nobles and slaves, and people of all other sorts danced in the streets until exhausted. Some even became so ecstatic that they killed themselves by banging their heads against walls in tune to music. The mania was called the St. Vitus dance because a visit to the saint's chapel sometimes ·worked a cure. Today it generally is referred to as Tarantism after a wild Neapolitan folk dance, the Tarantella. The Italians believed that wild dancing was the only cure for the bite of the tarantula. Actually, the spider's bite is not poisonous. Nevertheless, a victim usually displayed hypochondriac symptoms including weak-sightedness, loss of the power of speech, and insensibility to ordinary causes of excitement. At the sound of music such patients, obviously the victims of hysteria, awoke from their lethargy and started a passionate dance. The behavior of those who participated in the religious frenzy of the period was similar.

At the end of the fifteenth century Pope Innocent VIII appealed to Catholics to rescue the church from the power of Satan. Europe already was a vast asylum of paranoiacs and monomaniacs possessed with fear of persecution by infernal agents. The papal appeal had the effect of starting them on an incessant search for witches and sorcerers. The sixteenth and seventeenth centuries have been called the period of demonophobia, and the tortures and horrible deaths inflicted upon thousands of innocent persons form a dismal chapter in the annals of mankind. A German inquisitor, Sprenger, worked out a whole system of rules by which the guilty might be discovered. The suspect, for instance, was to be asked whether he had held any midnight meetings with the devil; whether he had attended a witches' sabbath; whether he could raise a whirlwind; and whether he (or she) had had sexual intercourse with Satan.

Getting rid of supposed witches reached maniacal proportions in all parts of Europe. In Italy, Cemanus burned 41 women in one province alone; in Germany Sprenger's victims totaled 900 in a single year. The German commission appointed by the pope condemned to the stake upward of 3,000 victims. In the American colonies, mostly in 1692, 32 alleged witches were executed, 20 of them at Salem. In *The Devil in Massachusetts* (Knopf, 1949) Marion L. Starkey relates how the epidemic there was started by two mischievous girls. Reviewing the book in the Aug. 23, 1949 New York *Compass*, Prof. S. E. Lind of Rutgers University wrote:

> Charge followed charge until the jails of the neighborhood overflowed. Justice, administered by magistrates unlearned in law but heavily reliant for guidance upon the Puritan clergy, who in effect governed the community, consisted of the accused futilely attempting to deny that they had assumed the shape of monsters and had tormented the girls. When the accused protested too strongly, their young accusers went into hysterics in the courtroom, forcing the defendants then to prove that their "familiars" were not at that very moment engaged in their evil work! Against such charges neither sanity nor truth could prevail.
>
> The hysteria spread until even some of the accused admitted—a few with perverse pride—their witchery and wizardry. Long standing neighborly malice or enmity came to a head in accusations of devilish alliance, husband against wife, families disintegrated. It was not until the whole population threatened to become engulfed—and, not without significance, several irreproachably high-placed citizens had been accused—that the waves of madness subsided.

Since the United States became a nation, violence against others has not been a characteristic of religious fanaticism. The Ku Klux Klan, Christian Fronters and other hoodlums who have attacked Catholics, Jews and others hardly have been motivated by religious zeal. In other respects, however, participants in a series of religious revivals during the nineteenth and twentieth centuries have behaved not much differently than their predecessors. That is, they have shouted, jumped, sung, prayed, cried, and fallen into convulsions at the mourners' bench and have preached damnation almost as loudly.

Waves of religious mania spread over the United States in 1800, 1815, 1832, 1840, 1867, 1893, and during the 1920's. What is called "The Great American Revival" began simultaneously in New Haven and New York in 1832. According to Boris Sidis in *The Psychology of Suggestion* (D. Appleton, 1898), "In many places the religious epidemics took the form of laughing, dancing and barking or dog manias. Whole congregations were convulsed with hysterical laughter during holy services. In the wild delirium of religious frenzy people took to dancing, and at last to barking like dogs. They assumed the posture of dogs, moving about on all fours, growling, snapping the teeth, and barking with such an exactness of imitation as to deceive any one whose eyes were not directed to the spot!" Sidis quotes a description of the revival given by Albert S. Rhodes in the Dec. 11, 1875 *Appleton Journal* which contained the following:

The apple of Sodom grew out of this religious mania; the followers soon became incapable of sin. . . .

"And when a man becomes conscious that his soul is saved," proclaimed one of their spiritual leaders, "the first thing that he sets about is to find his paradise and his Eve." The leaders could not find paradises in their own homes, nor Eves in their own wives, and sought their "affinities" elsewhere. . . .

Before long the spiritual union was found to be incomplete, and it assumed the ordinary character of that which exists between man and woman who live together in close intimacy.

Such goings-on during the present century have been confined mostly to small cults and have been far from epidemic. The career of more than one Messiah has ended in police court, and others have been the object of more scorn and ridicule or, at best, amusement than of reverence. Usual journalistic practice, unless a cult engages in illegal practices, is to treat it with decent restraint. To the nonbeliever, however, even the most objective attempt probably is more damning than proselyting. An example of such writing is the following from the Sept. 17, 1936 St. Louis *Star-Times*:

New York, Sept. 17—"Thank you Father!"

"So glad you came!"

These greetings rang loud in the headquarters office of Father Divine when the writer squeezed inside recently to get a look at the little Negro preacher whom thousands hail as God.

At least 500 of his flock were packed into the narrow quarters at 20 West 115th street in the heart of Harlem—present kingdom of 150 "kingdom extension offices" all over the United States, Canada, the British West Indies and Switzerland.

It was a touching sight. Grey-haired white women sat alongside Negro women and street urchins at "banquet tables," eating food provided free for the poor by the Rev. Divine.

The flock took up every bit of standing room in the place.

OTHERS STAND ON BENCHES

Others stood on benches lining the walls and stared rapturously. Occasionally the magnetism of the good father would prove too powerful and they would swoon away or sink dizzily to the floor.

Suddenly the crowded congregation began a solemn hymn, half-singing, half-chanting.

The rhythm was contagious; the writer found his foot sneaking a few taps. Abruptly the hymn ceased. Some women screamed hysterically. Then began an avalanche of testimonials:

"Oh, Lord, you gave me a brand new body.

"A brand new mind.

"A brand new home.

"Thank you, Father!"

One white man, young and well-tailored, arose and reviewed recent court cases in which Father Divine's enterprise—such as his peace garage and peace restaurant—were ruled to be nonprofit making, and therefore did not come under the workmen's compensation law.

The speaker concluded:

"The magistrate freed you, Father—for you are God. And I thank you for filling me with the sweetness of holy truth and making me clean and good once more."

TESTIMONIALS CHEERED

Lusty cheering greeted each new testimonial.

Seated at the end of the center table, directly beneath a microphone suspended from the ceiling, was Father Divine, sacred cynosure of all eyes—reading a newspaper!

The writer learned this was quite appropriate, however, for he was digesting his own publication—the "New York News," devoted to his work and preachings. A semi-weekly magazine, "The Spoken Word," is also published in New York for Father Divine's peace mission movement.

Suddenly a squat white woman pressed close to the writer and urged:

"My good man, why don't you talk to Father Divine and be converted to the most wonderful movement for goodness on earth?"

The well-wishing woman bobbed up and down as she spoke.

"I first heard about the Peace Mission movement in California," she related.

"I found the true faith—Father Divine. I came to New York to be close to him."

"How much money have you donated to the movement?"

"Not one penny! He won't take money."

This was indeed puzzling. "Then how does he buy the food for the poor?"

"Father Divine says to find out where he gets his power and then we will know where he gets his funds."

FOLLOWERS BELIEVE IN HIM

There is no doubt that Father Divine's proselytes firmly believe him to be God. His followers are reminded of this constantly, for the "church" hall is littered with signs to that effect.

A frenzied roar interrupted the sign reading, followed by an oppressive silence. Father Divine had arisen.

After two hours of waiting the writer was anxious to hear him speak. He stood quietly a few moments, a benign, bald-pated little fellow, gazing through half-closed lids at this small fraction of his idolizing populace.

Many hundreds more were eagerly waiting for him to preach—in rooms above, in his restaurant, next door, and outside in the street. They watched the loud speakers, connected with the microphone in the main hall.

But the good father did not speak. He simply smiled adieu and sauntered to a private office upstairs.

"Why didn't Father Divine give a sermon tonight?"

"Oh, he never preaches unless he feels like it," she said. "We never know when he'll speak. We are blessed just to be able to see him."

Abundant similar copy was written during the revivalist twenties about Aimee Semple McPherson who built the one and a half million dollar Angelus Temple in Los Angeles to house her Four Square Gospelites who contributed the money to make it possible. Also, in former years, about John Alexander Dowie and Wilbur Glenn Voliva and their Christian Catholic Apostolic church at Zion, Ill., Billy Sunday, "King" Benjamin Purnell and his House of David at Benton Harbor, Mich., the Mighty I Am cult and numerous practitioners of voodoo, snake worshippers, faith healers and even flagellantes. Because it attracted several important statesmen, businessmen, athletes, actors, and others the world over, the movement led by Dr. Frank Nathan Daniel Buchman, variously called the Oxford Group and Moral Re-Armament, perhaps should be considered the most important of the modern movements. In explanation of how its "soul surgers," "God control" and other appeals caught on, Franklin Fearing wrote in "MRA and the World of Reality" in the November, 1939 *American Teacher*:

"In times of stress when social change is accelerated and the hard-

won and long-established securities and, particularly, the privileges
of entire classes are undermined, some of these familiar verbal
formulae lose their potency. Those which have become rigid and
stereotyped no longer 'fit' the world of social reality. Many persons
because of inadequate education and class-limited social experience
are unable to renovate and reorder their systems of belief to meet the
demands of a changing reality. The result is the appearance of anxiety
and near panic in large segments of the population. These individuals
seek to escape the situation by minimizing or simplifying their problems. This avoidance reaction may even take the extreme form of a
denial of the existence of the factors which precipitated the catastrophe. It is then that individuals and groups search desperately for those
affirmations, however superficial, which will appear to re-establish
order in a world which seems to have gone mad. It is then that individuals and groups crave yea-saying rather than nay-saying, and require soothsayers who will declare that God is in His Heaven and
that prosperity is just around the corner."

Chain letters, Pyramid Clubs and other contemporary get-rich-
quick schemes which attained epidemic proportions, had their medieval counterparts. About 1634 suddenly tulip-growing became a craze
in Holland. People of all economic classes participated in the tulipo-
mania which ended as suddenly as it began, ruining thousands. While
it lasted the tulip market underwent a tremendous inflation. As much
as 100,000 florins were spent for just 40 bulbs. People even sold their
homes to invest in the tulip market, and foreign money began pouring
into the country. Neither the French nor the British, however, learned
anything from the experience because less than a century later they
both had financial crazes of their own which wiped out a sizeable
number of fortunes.

In 1717 a canny Scotsman, John Law, obtained authorization from
French authorities to establish a trading company on the west bank
of the Mississippi River. Because the riches of the New World were
known to be enormous, 300,000 applied for the first 50,000 shares of
stock in Law's company. Buying and speculating went on furiously
for a short time. Then suddenly everyone wanted to sell, and the
bottom fell out of the market. In 1720 the story of the South Sea
Company across the channel was similar.

In the United States there have been constantly recurring periods of financial boom and bust. Usually boom days are characterized by widespread stupid ventures into the stock market by rank financial amateurs, all trying to turn over an easy dollar. There also were the frenzied gold rushes to California in 1849 and the Klondike a half century later, the land rush into Indian Territory, now Oklahoma, in 1912, and the Florida land boom in 1925.

Partly as a result of the last-mentioned, Miami, a city of 10,000 at the turn of the century, became a metropolis of 150,000 in the midst of the "new paradise," and began planning for 1,000,000 in another decade. The whole city became a frenzied real estate exchange as "pioneers" rolled in from all other parts of the country to buy land "worth its weight in gold" for a comparatively few dollars. Approximately 2,000 real estate offices and 25,000 agents helped them satisfy their longings. Shirt-sleeved crowds, hurrying to and fro under the widely advertised Florida sun, talked of binders and options and water-frontages and $100,000 profits. The city fathers had to pass an ordinance forbidding the sale of property in the street, or even the showing of a map, to prevent inordinate traffic congestion.

And what was taking place in Miami was taking place on an equal scale in other parts of the state. Thousands of orange groves in the ridge country were destroyed to make way for town sites. The road from Jacksonville to Miami, more than 300 miles long, was practically a city street, with mushroom settlements along practically its entire length.

The public bought anything, anywhere, as long as it was in Florida. One had only to announce a new development, be it honest or fraudulent, be it on the Atlantic Ocean or deep in the wasteland of the interior, to set people scrambling for house lots. "Manhattan Estates" were advertised as being "not more than three-fourths of a mile from the prosperous and fast-growing city of Nettie," although there was no Nettie. Speculation was easy—and quick. No long delays while titles were being investigated and deeds recorded; such tiresome formalities were postponed.

The Miami *Daily News* and the Miami *Herald* said the city was not only "The Wonder City," it was also "The Fair White Goddess of Cities," "The World's Playground," and "The City Invincible." Fort Lauderdale became "The Tropical Wonderland," Orlando "The City Beautiful," and Sanford "The City Substantial."

Daily the stream of rhetoric poured forth to the glory of Florida. It reached its climax in the joint proclamation issued by the mayors of Miami, Miami Beach, and Coral Gables (who modestly referred to their county as "the most richly blessed community of the most bountifully endowed state of the most highly enterprising people of the universe"), setting forth the last day of 1925 and the first two days of 1926 as "The Fiesta of the American Tropics—our season of fiesta when love, good fellowship, merrymaking and wholesome sport shall prevail throughout our domains."

Presumably the fiesta was successful. But by New Year's Day of 1926 the suspicion was beginning to insinuate itself into the minds of the merrymakers that new buyers of land were no longer so plentiful as they had been in September and October; that a good many of those who held binders were exceedingly anxious to dispose of their stake, and that a lot of people were not going to be able to complete payment on their land.

The boom began obviously to collapse in the spring and summer of 1926. It was aided by two hurricanes which showed what a "soothing tropic wind" could do when it got a running start from the West Indies. The people fell back on their heels, awakened. The craze died as rapidly as it had begun.

Mass Hysteria

Genesis of most if not all mass hysterical behavior is fear. That it should turn to panic in cases of disaster—fires, earthquakes, shipwrecks and the like—is understandable. He who remains calm at such times is considered brave or heroic. Merely to list a fair sample of instances in which people have "lost their heads" over nonexistent serpents, monsters, fiends, and other supposed threats to their safety, however, would add many pages to the length of this book. In his *Hoaxes* (Macmillan, 1940) this author cited several score examples of extreme suggestibility, many merely illustrative of the extent to which human gullibility can go but some saddening because of their tragic consequences.

Immortal in the annals of this subject is the 1938 Hallowe'en broadcast by Orson Welles' Mercury Theater of the Air of H. G. Wells' *War of the Worlds.* The most nearly complete account is to be found in *The Invasion from Mars* (Princeton University, 1940) by Hadley

Cantril, Hazel Gaudet, and Herta Hertzog. Coming just a month after the Munich crisis, during which time millions of listeners kept on their radios for hours at a time, the dramatic account of horrendous living things emerging from space ships grounded in New Jersey caused thousands of persons to leave home in quest of safety. All over the nation otherwise responsible citizens reported to police, newspapers and radio stations that they had seen signs that the Martian invaders were landing in other areas.

Since the American broadcast, radio dramatization of the same book has caused similar hysteria on at least two other occasions. In November, 1944, people were reported to have panicked in the streets of Santiago, Chile, with several resultant accidents and a few deaths from heart attacks caused by fright and excitement. In February, 1949, an indignant mob caused $350,000 damage when it set fire to the El Comercio building in Quito, Ecuador, where HCQRK, which put on the show, is housed. Deaths totalled 15 and injuries numbered hundreds. Police were slow to arrive at the scene of the disturbance because they were out hunting the Martians. It took tanks and tear gas to end the episode.

There have been other realistic broadcasts which have had similar consequences. In February, 1946, Paris, France, was thrown into turmoil by a fictitious account of atomic waves crossing the Atlantic from North America, the probable result being atomic disintegration of the earth. The technique used on that broadcast was that which Welles had made popular, or—should it be—terrifying. The program began with what purported to be a speech by an American professor which was interrupted for the soul-shaking "news."

A May, 1947, phony news broadcast over WVTR in Tokyo resulted in the release of three enlistees and a civilian officer from the Armed Forces Radio Service. Their frightful brain child was a 20-foot sea monster which supposedly rose out of the bay, upset small vessels, chased people from the street and finally identified itself as the "reluctant dragon" come to wish the AFRS a happy fifth birthday anniversary.

"I just ran out of jokes. I got to thinking that maybe nobody listened," was the explanation given by an announcer for KWLM at Willmar, Minn., in February, 1949, for having faked a news account of a circus carload of wild animals loose in the community. As in all of the other cases mothers frantically gathered up their children and stayed behind locked doors. Men with rifles reported for volunteer duty at the police station. Communities for miles around were affected by the hoax.

Such incidents, of course, are journalistic bonanzas. Investigators of many instances in which fear has been rampant because of some nonexistent terror have been adversely critical of the press for its role in spreading the hysteria. In all fairness, however, such incidents have been occurring almost since the beginning of time, long before Gutenberg ever was heard of. One of the best studies of a recent case was that on which Prof. Donald M. Johnson of the University of Illinois reported in the April, 1945 *Journal of Abnormal and Social Psychology*, entitled "The 'Phantom Anesthetist' of Mattoon: A Field Study of Mass Hysteria." Whereas Professor Johnson chastised the newspapers of the southern Illinois community of 15,000 for streamer headlining accounts of complaints which the police investigated with entirely negative results, he concluded that the approximately 30 "victims" were mostly hysterical women below the average educational and economic level of the community as a whole.

The Mattoon story, which the press of the entire nation took up, began Sept. 1, 1944, when a woman reported to police that someone had paralyzed her by spraying sickish sweet-smelling gas through her bedroom window. After the newspaper reported the incident under a sensational headline, "Anesthetic Prowler on Loose," other "victims" began to report similar experiences and hundreds testified to having seen prowlers or to having observed other clues. Professor Johnson demolished the theory that there was at any time a "mad gasser" not only by pointing to obvious lack of motive, since none of the attacks was accompanied by any burglary, but also by pointing out the impossibility of any gas's causing the symptoms it did without affecting other members of the household, including pets, and without leaving a trace. Nevertheless, the leading paragraphs of the Chicago *Herald-American* article Sept. 10, 1944 on the Mattoon hysteria were as follows:

Groggy as Londoners under protracted aerial blitzing, this town's bewildered citizens reeled today under the repeated attacks of a mad anesthetist who has sprayed a deadly nerve gas into 13 homes and has knocked out 27 victims.

Seventy others dashing to the area in response to the alarm, fell under the influence of the gas last night.

All skepticism has vanished and Mattoon grimly concedes it must fight haphazardly against a demented phantom adversary who has been seen only fleetingly and so far has evaded traps laid by city and state police and posses of townsmen.

Professor Johnson began his conclusions: "Analysis of records available at Mattoon together with the results of interviews with most of the victims leads to the conclusion that the case of the 'phantom anesthetist' was entirely psychogenic."

One of the author's earliest memories is of his father retiring at his usual hour May 18, 1910, with the explanation, "If I'm going to meet my Maker before morning, I want to be rested." It was a bold, brave thing to do because all over the world that night other people were gathered in groups for "end of the world" parties. Others sought out caves, mines, and other hiding places; still others attended all-night religious services, and some even committed suicide. Cause of the hysteria was the approach of Halley's comet which becomes visible every 76 years. For weeks the newspapers had been full of the comments and predictions of astronomers and others. Although on the whole the scientists were not worried, fearful people were affected by the prediction of Gen. Ballington Booth, head of the Volunteers of America, that there would be deluges of water and fires and by the advice of W. E. Corey, president of the United States Steel Corporation, to his friends, to call in their money.

Many other "end of the world" scares have occurred, but most of them have resulted from revelations reported by prophets or by fanatic interpretations of Revelation or other parts of the Bible, and have not been so widespread as that which the heavenly wanderer caused.

In defense of those who suffered paroxysms because of Halley's comet: there *was* a comet and it was visible to the naked eye for several nights in the southwestern sky where this writer recalls having seen it. Hardly as much can be said in apology for thousands, perhaps millions, who kept their eyes glued heavenward during the summer months of 1947 looking for what came to be called "flying disks" or "saucers." Possibly some planes, meteors, birds and other objects were observed by aviators and others. The report issued in mid-1949 by the Air Material Command at Wright Field, Dayton, Ohio, definitely admits the possibility of there having "been something" to some of the reports which began with that of a Boise businessman, Kenneth Arnold, that he observed nine saucerlike objects in formation at 1,200 miles per hour during a flight June 24, 1947, from Mt. Rainier to Mt. Adams in the State of Washington. It is quite certain, however, that the overwhelming majority of those all over the United States and in some foreign countries who made the headlines suffered from hallucinations or spots before the eyes.

Inspired in part by two magazine articles ("The Flying Saucers Are Real," by Donald E. Keyhoe, and "How Scientists Tracked a Flying Saucer," by Commander Robert B. McLaughlin, in the January and March, 1950, issues of *True*), flying saucers reappeared in the headlines early in 1950. Newspaper and radio offices were deluged with inquiries after a Los Angeles salesman, Ray L. Dimmick, declared he had seen the wreckage of an ultra-streamlined flying saucer that crashed into a mountain in Mexico containing a 23-inch pilot. It turned out that all Dimmick had seen was a piece of scrap which someone told him was from the wreckage of whose existence the Mexican government pleaded ignorance. The recrudescence of flying disk stories was significant because of the different treatment accorded by the press. Whereas two years earlier the journalistic attitude had been one of fulsome respect which stimulated credulity on the part of readers, the revival of hallucinations was treated humorously or cynically, albeit with fulsome headlines, artists' drawings, and full-length articles.

The Red Scare

Almost immediately after the end of World War II what came to be called the "cold war" between the United States and the Soviet Union began. Although both nations, now the world's most powerful, ratified the charter of the United Nations as evolved at the San Francisco conference during the summer of 1945, the Security Council of that body soon became deadlocked because of irreconcilable differences between them.

To block the decisions of the majority of the Council, the Soviets made frequent use of the veto. Despite strong objections from the United States, furthermore, they proceeded to strengthen their hegemony over their small neighbors, with only Yugoslavia able to resist successfully. As a result of an almost incessant series of "incidents" in the diplomatic struggle between the Russians and Americans, featured by much vituperative oratory at Lake Success and other places, there developed a tremendous disillusionment in the United States over the fruits of victory in World War II and an increasing fear that the world was plunging rapidly toward World War III. Existence of the atomic bomb and reports that the hydrogen bomb, many times more destructive, was being manufactured, increased the fear for the future and helped produce a nationwide state of "jitters."

Probably as an inevitable consequence of the precarious international situation, there developed at home a drive to discover, expose and render helpless any and all persons and groups which might be considered subversive and a threat to national security in the event of war with the Soviet Union. Historical perspective will be needed properly to evaluate this period of American history during which the effort to discover "reds" became an obsession with many and left almost none unaffected. As early as February, 1947 the President's Committee on Civil Rights, in the report, *To Secure These Rights* which became a major 1948 campaign issue, warned: ". . . public excitement about 'Communists' has gone far beyond the dictates of the 'good judgment' and 'calmness' of which Holmes and Brandeis wrote. A state of near-hysteria now threatens to inhibit the freedom of genuine democrats . . . If we fall back upon hysteria and repression as our weapons against totalitarians, we will defeat ourselves. Communists want nothing more than to be lumped with freedom-loving non-Communists. This simply makes it easier for them to conceal their true nature and to allege that the term 'Communist' is 'meaningless.' "

Four and a half years later, August 14, 1951, in a speech helping to dedicate a new building housing the Washington headquarters of the American Legion, President Truman called upon that veterans' organization to help stop "scare mongers and hate mongers" who he asserted were curbing the free speech and other constitutional freedoms of the American people. Said the President:

"These people claim to be against communism. But they are chipping away at our basic freedoms just as insidiously and far more effectively than the Communists have ever been able to do. These people have attacked the basic principle of fair play that underlies our Constitution. They are trying to create fear and suspicion among us by the use of slander, unproved accusations and just plain lies. They are filling the air with the most irresponsible kinds of accusations against other people. They are trying to get us to believe that our government is riddled with communism and corruption when the fact is that we have the finest and most loyal body of civil servants in the world. These slander mongers are trying to get us so hysterical that no one will stand up to them for fear of being called a Communist."

Less than a fortnight earlier President Truman, in a Detroit address, also referred to a July 4 stunt by a reporter of the Madison (Wis.) *Capital-Times* who drew up petitions headed "Preamble to the Declaration of Independence and the Bills of Rights" and circulated them among picnickers in a public park. Only one of 112 persons solicited was willing to sign.

Although President Truman did not mention him by name in his speech to the American Legion, he undoubtedly had most in mind Senator Joseph McCarthy of Wisconsin who, for more than two years, had been making attacks on the floor of the Senate against employes and associates of the Department of State. Most dramatic of the many ramifications of Senator McCarthy's campaign were the hearings by a Senate subcommittee regarding the activities of Professor Owen Lattimore, Far Eastern expert of Johns Hopkins University. The result was exoneration for Professor Lattimore who related his experiences in *Ordeal by Slander* (Little, Brown, 1950).

Despite the President's outspoken criticism of the "witch hunting" of the 1945 to 1951 period, there were many who contended that the chief executive was himself far from blameless. That was because of his Executive Order 9835 in March, 1947 which called for the establishment of loyalty boards to investigate the Americanism of all federal employees.

In 1948 Bert Andrews of the New York *Herald Tribune* won the Pulitzer, Sigma Delta Chi and American Newspaper Guild prizes for his newspaper exposé of how the loyalty investigators operated in apparent disregard of the democratic principles for which Anglo-Saxons struggled for centuries: that a person is considered innocent until proved guilty beyond a reasonable doubt; that an accused shall know the nature of the charges against him and that he shall have the right to face his accusers in open court and cross-examine them. Instead, Andrews revealed in his newspaper articles which he later expanded into a book, *Washington Witch Hunt* (Random House, 1948), governmental employees were dismissed without a hearing or even a statement of the charges against them. In its issue of August 11, 1947, the *New Republic* revealed that its investigation indicated more than 50 per cent of those dismissed were Jews or married to Jews.

The American Civil Liberties Union and similar groups expressed frequent and grave alarm over the authority given the attorney general to list organizations (approximately 150 by mid-1951) as subversive without giving them the opportunity to defend themselves. Similar lists were prepared by Un-American Activities committees in several states and cities (see *Guide to Subversive Organizations and Publications,* House Document No. 137, May 14, 1951) and widespread use of such lists was made by private employers as well as public officials.

The adoption of the principle by the Department of State that anyone having "habitual or close association" with a person "believed to be" a Communist should be considered suspect was condemned as unfair "guilt by association" by civil liberties groups, but the United States Supreme Court, on several occasions, upheld or refused to review lower court decisions defending it. One of the most vigorous attacks on the loyalty and security programs of the federal government was that by Alan Barth, Washington *Post* editorial writer, in *The Loyalty of Free Men* (Viking, 1951), in which he charged that criticism of administrative policies was improperly being taken for disloyalty. Strong warnings against the nationwide concern over "spies" and "subversives" also were sounded by Jerome Davis in *Character Assassination* (Philosophical Library, 1950), Carey McWilliams in *Witch Hunt* (Little, Brown, 1950) and O. John Rogge in *Our Vanishing Civil Liberties* (Gaer, 1949).

In *Security, Loyalty and Science* (Cornell University Press, 1950), Professor Walter Gellhorn of the Columbia University School of Law, contended that the loyalty programs were seriously interfering with the progress of scientific research in the United States.

Many American atomic scientists, indignant at the treatment accorded Dr. Edward U. Condon (see Chapter 4) expressed their feelings in the results of a poll published in their association *Bulletin* for June, 1948. In answer to the question "How did the manner in which charges were made against Condon affect your willingness to accept responsible positions?" 63 per cent said "made me reluctant to accept," and 12 per cent replied "I would decline such an offer." Some American scientists were resentful over the manner in which the loyalty investigations were conducted at Oak Ridge. One scientist was suspended on the following charges:

1. After he moved out of a house, his landlord found some magazines left behind, among which may have been a copy of the *New Masses*.

2. A neighbor believes one of his relatives by marriage is a Communist.

3. Another relative by marriage is reported to have been a member of the Joint Anti-Fascist Refugee committee.

4. Another relative by marriage was reported to have been a member of a camp which is reported to have had Communist connections.

During the many hearings by the House Un-American Activities Committee organizations and individuals frequently were accused of subversive activity without an opportunity to clear themselves.

By far the most dramatic "show" put on by the House committee during the Rankin-Thomas period of control was the public hearings into the affairs of the motion picture industry. Robert Taylor objected to having been required to take a part in "Song of Russia"; Adolphe Menjou identified a fellow traveler as anyone who applauds the singing of Paul Robeson; and Walt Disney, until corrected, designated the League of Women Voters as a Communist-front organization. No evidence was introduced that any Hollywood production had contained communist propaganda, but ten prominent film writers were cited for contempt for refusal to answer questions regarding their political beliefs. In May, 1949, the ten brought suit for 52 million dollars under the Sherman Anti-Trust Act against the film producers who discharged them following their contempt convictions. Six months earlier one of the ten, Lester Cole, was awarded $75,000 back salary and was restored to his job by a federal jury in Los Angeles. In April, 1950, however, the United States Supreme Court refused to review the lower court's upholding of the contempt orders, and the Hollywood ten began prison terms.

Even a desultory reading of the *Congressional Record* for the period should suffice to establish the fact that it was a time of frenzied vituperative oratory. Every critic of any phase of American foreign policy was suspected of subversive activity; every gesture by any organization in the interest of peace was called Moscow-inspired; liberal foreigners, even legislators and government officials, were denied visas to enter the country; many liberal Americans could not obtain passports to travel abroad. The proposed Mundt-Nixon (80th Congress) and the Mundt-Ferguson (81st Congress) bills virtually provided for the disbanding of any organization arbitrarily listed by the attorney general as subversive. In September, 1950, the McCarran-Wood bill, passed over President Truman's veto, contained all of the important features of its predecessor bills and, in addition, a provision for concentration camps.

Most of the states considered and about half of them passed subversive activities laws. The chief targets of the epidemic of name calling in 1949 and 1950 were the teachers. Most of the state laws and city ordinances were directed primarily at them. A number of schools were investigated officially in the attempt to root out Communists on the faculty. There were numerous firings of professors and public school teachers of liberal or radical political leanings. The National Education Association adopted a recommendation by a committee which included Gen. Dwight D. Eisenhower, president of Columbia University, and Dr. James B. Conant, president of Harvard University, that Communists should not be allowed to teach. The American Association of University Professors, however, resolved just the opposite, and Harvard, Yale, and Chicago were prominent among the universities which refused a request of the House Un-American Activities Committee that they submit lists of textbooks.

What really caused this extreme fear? Some, including President Truman, said "post-war jitters—nothing to worry about." Others recalled the warning of Charles Evans Hughes in an address June 21, 1920, at the Harvard Law School: "We have seen the war powers which are essential to the preservation of the nation in time of war exercised broadly after the military exigency has passed and in conditions for which they never were intended and we may well ponder in view of the precedents now established, whether constitutional government as heretofore maintained in this republic could survive another great war, even victoriously waged." Still others recalled Huey Long's prediction that if fascism came to the United States it would be in the name of anti-fascism. Other postulates included the following: that the administration deliberately encouraged fear to stifle opposition to its policies; that the existence of the atomic bomb made fear of another war so great that men acted unreasonably; that recollection of the depression of the thirties created anxiety and frayed nerves; that some American interests which had been sympathetic with and even helpful to Adolf Hitler were conditioning the United States to finish the job which the Nazis started; that the United States, with 80 per cent of its federal governmental expenditures going for war purposes, was on an artificial war economy the only end to which could be either depression (if the spending were terminated) or war.

Just which explanation or group of explanations was correct this author admits he is not wise enough to say with finality. The point he wishes to make here is that *the hysteria was not an isolated phenomenon* and that most of the current reasons given for it were utterly naive. In the preceding chapter (see pages 277 to 279) the change from wartime feelings of security, which kept violations of civil liberties at a minimum, to postwar attitudes of fear and insecurity was mentioned. If our democracy survives, so that there are those left to write freely, the indiscriminate accusations of the post-World War II period, with the resultant threat to traditional civil liberties, probably will take their place in history as another outstanding example of mass hysteria.

That Americans did not surrender their right to differ is exemplified in the dissenting opinions of Justices Black and Douglas, who, in the case of the eleven communist leaders, vigorously disagreed with the majority decision of the Supreme Court handed down June 4, 1951. Chief Justice Vinson in announcing the judgment of the Court stated: "Petitioners intended to overthrow the government as speedily as circumstances would permit. Their conspiracy to organize the Communist party and to teach and advocate the overthrow of the government of the United States by force and violence created a 'clear and present danger' of an attempt to overthrow the government by force and violence." Justice Douglas on the other hand proclaimed ". . . free speech is the rule, not the exception. The restraint to be constitutional must be based on more than fear, on more than passionate opposition against the speech, on more than a revolted dislike for its content. . . . Some nations, less resilient than the United States, where illiteracy is high and where democratic traditions are only budding, might have to take drastic steps . . . To believe that petitioners and their followers are placed in such critical positions as to endanger the nation is to believe the incredible."

Rumors

In the spread of hysteria no factor is more important than that of rumor, defined by Gordon W. Allport and Leo Postman in *The Psychology of Rumor* (Holt, 1947) as "a specific (or topical) proposition for belief, passed along from person to person, usually by word of mouth, without secure standards of evidence being present."

To the importance of rumor in influencing human thought and action many leading thinkers testified long before any attempts were made to study the subject scientifically. Typically, early in the eighteenth century, Jonathan Swift wrote: "What some invent, the rest enlarge." It is doubtful if there ever has been a war, outbreak of violence or mass hysterical phenomenon of any kind which has not been preceded, accompanied or followed by rumors.

So important is rumor upon morale that one of President Franklin Delano Roosevelt's first warnings to the nation after the Pearl Harbor disaster was "to reject all rumors, those ugly little hints of disaster that fly thick and fast in wartime." Readers of this book need not be reminded how rapidly and completely that advice was forgotten. As regards the Pearl Harbor losses, to which it specifically referred, for instance, a survey in Boston revealed that 60 per cent had heard they far exceeded official acknowledgments, and of that group, one-third accepted the rumors as closer to the truth than the government's report. Wrote Allport and Postman: "In wartime, rumors sap morale and menace national safety by spreading needless alarm and by raising extravagent hopes. They menace the security of military information and, most damaging of all, spread the virus of hostility and hate against loyal subgroups within the nation. In the years of postwar strain rumors are only slightly less destructive in their effect."

Not only opinion but overt action as well frequently can be traced to a flurry of rumors. Riots, as an instance, virtually never start without rumors to incite and intensify the violence. A serious riot in Harlem in August, 1943, followed rumored versions of an incident in a Harlem hotel lobby between a Negro soldier, who was injured in the shoulder, and a white policeman, also wounded. Rumor had it that the Negro was shot in the back and killed by the officer. Likewise, at least two rumors about a fist fight between a Negro and a white man preceded and accompanied the Detroit riot (see pages 315 to 316). In that instance the "white" rumor told that a white baby had been tossed from a bridge by Negroes, while the "black" rumor said it was a Negro baby tossed by whites. Of the role of rumors in the Detroit riot, David J. Jacobson wrote in *The Affairs of Dame Rumor* (Rinehart, 1948):

"The tides of intergroup strife soon turned as the twisted chatter captivated all Detroit. Within minutes after the fighting broke out the rumors were spreading like a gasoline fire through the white districts: first it was that a white woman had been raped on the park bridge; then it was that she had also been killed. . . . Later it was said that she had also had a baby in her arms at the time, which her assailant had tossed from the bridge into a river to drown. And before long, in the swollen rumors, it was said that two white women had been attacked by Negroes."

About 200 B.C. Plautus commented: "I believe there is nothing among mankind swifter than rumor." In this respect, as in all others, the improvement (?) made possible by rapid communication is to be noted. Typical of several wartime attempts by newspapermen to test the speed with which rumors traveled in the national capital was that related by Bert Andrews in the Aug. 30, 1941 New York *Herald Tribune*. While one of two experimenters remained in downtown Washington had passed his rumor that a high administration official had decided to resign, the other took an eight-minute taxi ride to the capitol. Three minutes after he entered the House of Representatives side of the building, he heard the story in the form of "Don't tell anybody but—."

Although rumors flourish in times of stress, as a war, they are a part of the fabric of everyday word-of-mouth communication at all times. Whenever a person passes along a tidbit of gossip with the tag-phrase, "I hear" or "they say," the chances are he is rumor-mongering. As Allport and Postman emphasize in their definition, rumor deals with specific persons and events, always topical, as, for example: the

Russians use lend-lease butter to grease their boots; WACs and WAVEs are used as prostitutes; bodies of soldiers from sunken troop ships are washed up on eastern beaches; a draft bill soon will force women into war work; and so forth.

Two other important characteristics of rumor are that (1) they express and gratify various emotional needs of the individual or community, and (2) they give current information. A legend, by contrast, may be a rumor which has "solidified" over the years to express a more or less constant theme (frequently national pride) of cultural importance (see pages 176 to 198). Also, rumors represent value-judgments of those who are mongering them. Thus, he who reports the spurious information that "The Jews are getting all the best jobs in the Army" is at the same time telling his listeners that he dislikes Jews. Wrote Robert K. Knapp in "A Psychology of Rumor," in the Spring, 1944 *Public Opinion Quarterly*: "Rumors express the underlying hopes, fears and hostility of the group."

Classification of rumors. Rumors have been classified in at least three ways: by speed or frequency; by subject matter, and by motivation. The temporal classification, used by D. A. Bysow and cited by Allport and Postman, includes: (1) *creeping* rumors, usually dealing with misfortune and sinister *sub rosa* doings by prominent persons; (2) *impetuous* rumors, dealing with immediate threats of violence or catastrophe; and (3) *diving* rumors, which are of short duration but recur when conditions giving rise to them are duplicated. Many atrocity stories which circulate in war after war, only slightly changed to fit immediate circumstances, are of this type.

Using the second method of classification, that of subject matter, Knapp analyzed rumors current in 1942. He found approximately two-thirds of them hostile in their intent and divisive in their effect. About 9.3 per cent were anti-Semitic, 3.1 per cent anti-Negro, 21.4 per cent anti-administration, and 19.6 anti-armed forces. Jacobson, concerned mostly with wartime rumors, used six categories: pipe dream, bogey, atrocity-type, hate, wonder, and fantastic. He thereby suggested the third classification scheme which is explanatory and not merely descriptive. As utilized by Allport and Postman it is four-fold: (1) fear or bogey; (2) pipe dream or wishful thinking; (3) wedge driving, and (4) unclassified, mostly curiosity.

The rumors exaggerating American losses at Pearl Harbor were bogey rumors, derived from fears and anxieties. So were most atrocity stories and rumors of fifth-column activities and secret enemy weapons. Pipe-dream rumors express the wishes and hopes of those among whom they circulate as, for example, that Lloyd's of London was quoting 10 to 1 odds that the war would be over by such and such a date; that Hitler, Mussolini, or Tojo was dead or mad; and, in the last weeks of the war, that surrender had taken place. Wedge-driving or aggression rumors, reflecting hate and hostility, were for the purpose of "dividing and conquering." The Nazis were especially adept at this sort of rumor. In addition to their "strategy of terror" to spread conviction of their invincibility and the terrible fate certain to befall anyone opposing them, they took advantage of the period of the so-called "phony" war in late 1941 and early 1942 to persuade French soldiers, idle and jittery in the Maginot Line, that stay-at-home civilians were making love to their wives and sweethearts and to breed suspicion of their British allies through asking, "Where are the British? Fighting until the last Frenchman."

In the United States wedge-driving rumors were intended to set class against class. Every minority—Jews, Negroes, Catholics and so forth—was accused of evading the draft, hoarding and getting rich unpatriotically. All over the country there were rumors of Eleanor clubs, named for Mrs. Eleanor Roosevelt, the colored feminine members of which pledged themselves not to do housework for whites, and of "push" days on which Negroes supposedly banded together to make nuisances of themselves in stores, on streetcars and buses, and in other public places. So prevalent and harmful did such rumors become that the Federal Bureau of Investigation investigated, but with negative results. There were also a great number of anti-labor rumors, exaggerating the importance of strikes and absenteeism; and, of course, an increase in those which appealed to political opponents of Franklin Roosevelt. All sorts of official blundering in the conduct of the war was charged, especially in the handling of rationing which, of course, caused some inconvenience to civilians.

Psychology of rumors. "Rumor," wrote Allport and Postman, "travels when events have importance in the lives of individuals and when the news received about them is either lacking or subjectively ambiguous." Formulawise, the two psychologists summed up the essence of rumor-mongering as follows: $R \sim i$ times a. Translated, it means the *amount of rumor* in circulation varies in direct proportion with the *importance of the event* multiplied by the *ambiguity* of the news about the event.

Obviously, residents of Vermont will not be terribly excited about rumors of a swarm of grasshoppers headed in the direction of Kansas; the threat would not have sufficient importance for them. When, as during a period of wartime censorship, confidence in the adequacy of information obtained through the ordinary communications channels is diminished, anxious people are "suckers" for those bulging with supposed "inside dope." Lack of adequate news alone is not sufficient to breed rumors. As a matter of fact, rumors about the losses at Pearl Harbor increased rather than diminished after full accounts of the government's official declaration appeared in the press. On the other hand, there were few rumors in London during the period of the blitz, because the English people knew from personal experience just how serious the situation was. When people know the worst they do not need to invent rumors to make things darker. Few, however, know the worst, or the best, about many things in the modern complex world.

All of the factors elucidated in Chapter 2 to explain human credulity are operative in intensified form when rumors circulate. Rumors form an important part of the process by which the ordinary person seeks order and routine in his environment. It is easier to accept than to reject them, and once a rumor is underway there is social pressure to believe it. Basically, however, as Allport and Postman wrote, "most rumors circulate because people have an ax to grind or a nest to feather or a ghost to lay. In short, they circulate because of some form of self interest." Thus, rumors have considerable therapeutic value. To quote the same source once more: "By permitting one to slap at the thing one hates it *relieves* a primary emotional urge. But at the same time—in the same breath—it serves to *justify* one in feeling as he does about the situation, and to *explain* to himself and to others why he feels that way. Thus rumor rationalizes, while it relieves." Thus, the person who explains his failure to obtain employment or to advance in a certain organization because he is not a Mason, or a Knight of Columbus, or of Danish descent, or whatever the group may happen to be, is slapping at what he hates, giving "good" reasons for his hate and elaborating upon the reasons.

Simple expectancy also causes rumors to fly. They are, in fact, likely to be most frenzied when a momentous event is expected to occur. If one is eager to hear a piece of news and is expecting it momentarily, he is conditioned to believe it has happened before it actually has. A person, for instance, may think he hears someone knocking at the door when he is awaiting a visitor. Similarly the American people gave birth to thousands of rumors shortly before V-E Day simply because the press was speculating on the German surrender and everyone was awaiting the news momentarily. A conditioning factor also was the desire of most people for the war to end. Quite obviously wishful thinking is at the basis of many a rumor; get-rich-quick schemes find readier victims in times of depression when many want desperately to obtain economic security.

People also believe rumors because they contribute to national or group pride and appeal to vanity. Some rumors, furthermore, appeal to the listener's thirst for thrills, and in some instances to his sadistic tendencies. If one likes a story he frequently "makes believe" the story is true, just as a child breathes real life into a favorite comic strip or literary hero. Not to be omitted, finally, is a secondary motivation factor: rumor mongers may be seeking attention and prestige, or they may simply be trying to fill an otherwise awkward gap in conversation.

Another way of putting much of what has been said is by use of the psychiatrist's term *projection* (see pages 65 to 68). A person is said to project when his emotional state is reflected, unconsciously, in his interpretation of his environment. He tends to believe rumors which conform to his own secret interpretation of reality. How this element of projection, or simply wish, can channel a gossipy yarn into a full-blown rumor was illustrated by Karl Menninger in *The Human Mind* (Knopf, 1930) as follows:

"Mrs. Adams to Mrs. Beck: 'Where is Mrs. King today? Is she ill?'

"Mrs. Beck to Mrs. Clark: 'Mrs. Adams wonders if Mrs. King may not be ill.'

"Mrs. Clark (who does not like Mrs. King) to Mrs. Davis (who does): 'I hear Mrs. King is ill. Not seriously, I hope?'

"Mrs. Davis to Mrs. Ellis: 'Mrs. Clark is saying that Mrs. King is seriously sick. I must go right over and see her.'

"Mrs. Ellis to Mrs. French: 'I guess Mrs. King is pretty sick. Mrs. Davis has just been called over.'

"Mrs. French to Mrs. Gregg: 'They say Mrs. King isn't expected to live. The relatives have been called to her bedside.'

"Mrs. Gregg to Mrs. Hudson: 'What's the latest news about Mrs. King? Is she dead?'

"Mrs. Hudson to Mrs. Ingham: 'What time did Mrs. King die?'

"Mrs. Ingham to Mrs. Jones: 'Are you going to Mrs. King's funeral? I hear she died yesterday.'

"Mrs. Jones to Mrs. King: 'I just learned of your death and funeral. Now who started that?'

"Mrs. King: 'There are several who would be glad if it were true!' "

An example of wish-and-fear projection was related by Elmo Roper in his syndicated column for April 8, 1949. The pollster told how two responsible newsmen called him by telephone from Washington to ask about an election survey that Roper was reported to have completed. They said they had heard that Henry Wallace had polled 11 to 11.5 per cent of the popular vote in a "secret poll" which Roper conducted for *Time.* Roper told his questioners that it was mere rumor. Nevertheless, a few weeks later the inquiry of the two newspapermen had become an "inside" story in *The People's World,* the west coast version of the Communist *Daily Worker.* By now the 11 per cent had jumped to 11 million votes. Then Walter Winchell reported that a Henry Luce poll showed Wallace to have 15 million votes. The New York *Daily Worker* said that Roper had given the results to Luce who, displeased, told Roper to repeat the poll. The second poll, according to the Communist paper, showed the Progressive party candidate to have more than 11 million votes. "By this time," said Roper, "the story had reached the Washington gossip-go-round and various letters-to-the-editor columns of New York and Chicago papers." The final rumored figure came out at 18 million votes.

How rumors travel. In addition to subconscious needs, rumor mongering is aided by the fact that most persons perceive, remember, and report imperfectly. Even trained observers, including newspaper reporters, are afflicted. An amusing account of faulty reporting was given by Vernon McKenzie in "We Saw It With Our Own Eyes" in the December, 1938 *Quill.* McKenzie compared three accounts of the entrance of Clara Zetkin, aged Communist, into the German Reichstag on the occasion of her presiding over it. One writer said Clara was carried in on a stretcher, another had her supported by a party member, and, according to a third, she walked down the aisle with the help of two girls. Actually Clara had entered the building on a stretcher, was helped a short distance by someone, and completed the walk with the aid of two young women. What happened was that each writer saw and reported only one part of the total action.

Wrote Jacobson: "A successful rumor must always be a good short story. It must have an exaggerated, familiar, simple, direct, striking or humorous plot. It must employ names, numbers or places which are known. It must always be attributed to an authoritative source." If it does not possess these qualities, Knapp's studies revealed, it is inclined to assume them to become successful. Rumors become distorted because of the human tendency to (1) level, (2) sharpen, and (3) assimilate. By leveling is meant the dropping of details so that the rumor, as passed on, grows shorter and more concise, thus more easily grasped and told. Unfortunately it usually is the qualifying details which fall by the wayside most quickly. To sharpen is to build up and focalize those details which are retained. Names, numbers and places, for instance, become exact and familiar and, if no authority is mentioned in the early versions, one is added that is recognized as reputable and important. Assimilation not only determines what details shall be leveled and sharpened but also "adjusts" the retained details in terms of an individual's past experience, cultural conditioning, linguistic habits, and personal motives and attitudes. This process is fortified by the fact that rumors tend to come in clusters; that is, many related to the same topic or intended to create the same effect, are contemporaneous. The tendency toward credulity thereby is increased. The principle is that of the big lie repeated over and over in complete disregard of any and all attempts at refutation. Hearers become disposed to believe that "where there's so much smoke there must be fire."

Two wartime examples, paraphrased from the Allport and Postman book, will illustrate how the characteristics of rumor mongering operate.

CASE I. In the summer of 1945 a Chinese teacher on a solitary vacation drove his car into a Maine community and asked his way to a hilltop from which he could obtain a pleasant view. The view was pictured in a Chamber of Commerce tourist guide which he carried. Someone showed him the way, but in a half-hour there was buzzing in the community this rumor: a Jap spy had ascended the hill to take pictures of the region.

Although, like most rumors, this one contained a kernel of truth, it had been distorted and twisted as follows: (1) *leveling*—the rumor, as passed, omitted details as to the courteous, honest, and timid approach of the stranger and the facts that his nationality was unknown, that he carried no camera but only a picture, and that he didn't use stealth; (2) *sharpening*—Oriental became Japanese, a tourist became a spy, and a picture carried in the teacher's hand became a camera. It was (3) *assimilation* which determined what details were to be retained and how they were to be sharpened. Considered in the light of the war against Japan and the stereotype of the Japanese-spy-taking pictures, assimilation in this case took an inevitable course.

CASE II. It was common enough during World War II for housewives to say over the back fence: "I hear that out at Camp X they have so much meat that they throw whole sides of fresh beef into the garbage."

A quick analysis for motivational factors reveals: (1) the meat shortage was a matter of importance to the housewife; (2) evidence was at least ambiguous, for she could not know what the army was doing with its meat; and (3) she was frustrated by the meat shortage, and consequently sought an explanation for it. She might have picked Hitler, but possibly because he was too remote a figure, she fixed the blame upon the army. It might be, moreover, that she had known a greedy army officer or that the army didn't treat her Johnny right. Finally, by passing the rumor she might have been easing pangs of conscience for having bought meat on the black market. This would be direct projection—projecting her own sin onto others and then castigating them for having it.

The rumors which sprang up in the wake of the 1947 flying disk scare also illustrate how rumors can operate, deleteriously, in a postwar period.

Most common rumor was that the Russians had launched a secret weapon, and, in the obvious light of previous postwar fears, such a rumor showed perfect assimilation. Another popular rumor told of undercover atomic energy experiments by the United States. Some months after the first flurry of disks was sighted, a story datelined Geneva, Switzerland, and syndicated by the North American Newspaper Alliance, "linked" the flying saucers to Generalissimo Franco of Spain. Or they might have come from Mars.

Considering the saucers themselves, they might well be called *visual rumors*. One reason they kept on being sighted is that of simple expectancy which was discussed earlier. Suggestible people, having read about the things in the press, expected, if not hoped, to see them, and so—they saw them.

Moreover, in many cases, sight of a disk can be ascribed to faulty perception or hallucination. This is evident in the many differing descriptions offered by those who had "seen" the somethings. In Rockford, Ill., they looked like a "large electric clock," a Montana flier described them as a "flying yo-yo," a California woman had them traveling in a pack led by a "mama disk," and a Chicago woman saw a disk with legs on it which she thought was going to come down and slap her in the face.

In many other cases, someone was just lying. Pilot Vernon Baird admitted that his earlier report of being chased by a disk which disintegrated in his plane's backwash was just a wild tale. He said he wouldn't do it again. How many others similarly lied cannot be known, but in tall-tale America, which loves to pass along a whopper, the numbers can be put down as quite large.

How rumors start. Rumors frequently are started as part of a deliberate campaign. Arthur Robb, in "Shop Talk at Thirty," in the Sept. 6, 1941 *Editor and Publisher*, commented: "Some members of Congress and some senators are no more backward in starting rumors that might help their causes than are the high-salaried lobbyists and press agents who seek the society of the newspaper clan."

The Nazis made use of rumors as a means of "softening up" the countries they were about to invade. Their brand of rumor-mongering was designed both to instill fear and to divide, and thus conquer.

Most World War II rumors, nevertheless, were bred by innocent folk with no ax to grind. A casual comment by a man that chimneys could hide anti-aircraft guns led to the rumor that Boston roofs were bristling with armaments, ostensibly in preparation for an imminent enemy attack. "Its [accuracy's] most dangerous enemies," as the

Oct. 12, 1942 *Life* commented, "are innocent folk who love to tell a tall tale."

These folk can be put down, for the most part, as highly suggestible people whose life is poorly structured, possibly furnished over-rigidly with stereotypes and prejudices. Frequently, also, they lack basic knowledge about the universe. Thus one-fourth of all people polled thought an atom-bomb explosion could set off a chain-reaction which could blow up the world. Likewise, a good part of the United States jumped out of its skin during the famous Martian broadcast by Orson Welles because people actually thought Mars had launched an invasion against the earth. This mass hysteria came at a time when there was world-wide depression and unrest, and people who believed the Martian invasion said they felt "anything could happen."

Those persons who do not rumorize, who may be called immune, usually are the skeptics, perhaps trained in semantics or social psychology or merely having the Missourian's supposed attitude of waiting for evidence. Secure people, moreover, usually do not fall for the fear and hate rumors, and so also those who are comparatively free of prejudice.

It should be realized that rumors have their own publics. Consequently, what might be passed on as rumor-fact among one collection of individuals might be scoffed at as a wild tale by members of another group, although the same amount of prejudice and ignorance might be found in each group.

In any event, because rumors are so psychologically necessary, they probably never will be eliminated from the mass of people. As long as men have fears and hopes, and as long as they have stereotypes with which to explain or fortify them, man will continue to exploit the rumor device.

Controlling rumors. Nevertheless, there exists a need for some kind of rumor control, especially in wartime. Purpose of such control would be not to eliminate rumor-mongering, which is impossible, but to shorten the life span of any particular rumor. Consequently, rumor control always will lag a step behind the rumor.

How one rumor was controlled is told by Allport and Postman in connection with a Feb. 23, 1942, fireside chat in which President Roosevelt spoke about Pearl Harbor losses. It so happened that three days earlier a group of 200 undergraduate students were polled on the question: "Do you think our Pearl Harbor losses were greater or less than officially reported?" with these results: 69 per cent said much greater and 31 per cent said the same or less. But two days after the President's speech another group of 200 students was polled on the same question. This time—significantly—the percentages were, respectively, 46 and 54.

The philosophy of the Office of War Information was that to repeat a rumor, even to deny it, helped to spread it. Partly they worked on the idea which the nineteenth century German Chancellor, Bismarck, once summed up as: "nothing is proved finally true until it is officially denied." Consequently the OWI devoted itself only to giving out lots of news.

On the other hand, rumor clinics set up by various newspapers sought to combat rumors in the opposite fashion. They nailed rumors with fact.

Both the OWI and the several rumor clinics erred, however, as Allport and Postman point out, by placing too much faith in facts and logic. As many an editorial writer knows, you cannot fight rumors —or anything else which feeds upon fears, hates and stereotypes—by marshaling facts. Nevertheless, a democracy is obliged to make a maximum appeal to whatever is rational in its citizens.

Originator of the newspaper rumor clinic was W. G. Gavin of the Boston *Herald-Traveler*. Starting in March, 1942, and ending in December, 1943, he edited a weekly rumor feature with the aid of Boston psychologists and others concerned with the problem. The idea quickly caught on elsewhere. More than 40 newspapers and a number of magazines in the United States and Canada experimented with the rumor clinic.

Typical of the many experiments along this line is the following column, partly reproduced, from the Boston *Sunday Herald* for July 18, 1943:

The Rumor Clinic

Today we consider a composite rumor. Some part of it you've surely heard.

RUMOR: Some minority group (Negro), (Jew), (Catholic), (or other) is not loyal to America, but is (planning a riot), (plotting to get control of the government), (evading military service).

Fact: Not one shred of tenable evidence has ever been produced to justify any one of these slanders against special groups of our fellow countrymen. Such rumors are bigoted and treacherous lies.

Analysis: . . . (Then follows a series of questions and answers.)

Obviously such newspaper experiments helped to spread rumors. At the same time, however, they clearly labeled them as phony, and few readers could help but notice such labeling. In any event there has been no evidence that rumor clinics, excellent as they may seem to the intelligent, served to cut rumors down.

Some radio stations adapted the rumor-clinic idea for the air, but studies based on the radio experiments definitely were unfavorable. Because many persons are dial-twisters, and because auditory stimuli differ from visual stimuli, most listeners were found to have remembered the rumors but not the refutations.

Quite successful in rumor control was the "silence" program of several war agencies. Loose talk diminished when such slogans as "Zip Your Lip and Save a Ship" were pushed in the press, on the air, and in posters.

Still another way, probably effective, was the teaching of the psychology of the rumor to the lay public. When people were taught, usually through magazine and news articles, how dangerous rumors could be, they were put on guard at least temporarily against the tales in circulation. It was found, however, that it did little good to label anything a rumor when telling people about it. They still tended to believe it, if the psychological setting was right.

Whispering campaigns. Politics frequently has thrived on rumor spreading, and presidential campaigns invariably are marked by a special form of rumor-mongering: whispering campaigns. Rumors travel on the "whisper" level when they become purplish, obscene, and slanderous.

The same "whisper" topics have persisted since the days of Washington. These are, as James Truslow Adams noted in an article, "Our Whispering Campaigns," in the September, 1932 *Harper's*: sexual relations, treatment of wives, drunkenness, and the alleged possession of Negro (sometimes Jewish) "blood." Reflected in these topics, it will be noted, are prejudices and attitudes which have bridged American history.

It was whispered that Jefferson kept a mulatto woman who had borne him a child; that "Gen. Jackson's mother was a common prostitute, brought to this country by British soldiers. She afterwards married a mulatto man with whom she had many children, of whom Gen. Jackson is one," and that Herbert Hoover had imported and oppressed Chinese coolie labor, besides being a pro-German who had procured the execution of Edith Cavell because she was about to "expose" him.

During the 1944 campaign there was circulated this bit of doggerel which FDR was supposed to have addressed to his wife:

> You kiss the niggers,
> I'll kiss the Jews;
> And we'll stay in the White House
> As long as we choose.

Such tales circulate during presidential campaigns because, Adams comments, American politics are primarily concerned with men rather than with measures and ideas.

Whispering campaigns also have been used to boost a commercial product, to knock a competitor's goods, and to break up labor strikes. An amusing discussion of one commercial whispering campaign was given in an article, "Whispers for Sale," in the February, 1936 *Harper's,* by Robert Littell and John J. McCarthy.

"Not long ago," they wrote, "a large and country-wide chain of restaurants discovered, (a) that in New York it was losing Jewish patronage because of a wave of whispering that it discriminated against Jewish employees, (b) that in Boston it was being boycotted by Catholics who heard that it hired only Protestants, and (c) that in upper New York State, Protestants were criticizing it for hiring only Catholics."

The owner of the chain had a sense of humor. He had these three contradictory rumors made public—in other words, helped to spread the rumors—and, because they cancelled one another out, the whispering campaigns shortly dissolved into laughter. It would be a much happier and safer world if it could be related that all rumors so treated ended similarly.

PART III

PUBLIC OPINION MEDIA

CHAPTER TEN

LEADERS, HEROES, AND FOLLOWERS

Clues to the temper and needs of a time are found in the types of leaders and heroes who rise and in the intensity with which others follow and/or worship them.

Leadership

Any newspaperman who has not read Lincoln Steffens' *Autobiography* (Harcourt, Brace, 1931) lacks adequate educational preparation for his job. Typical of many passages in the famous muckracker's lengthy memoirs, indicating how much there is to be learned therein about American society, is the following to be found on page 627 of the Literary Guild edition:

"We understand that there are bosses and heelers in politics, and we despise heelers, but we do not sufficiently recognize that there are leaders and heelers in business, in reform, in society. I have shown all through this book that instinctively always and sometimes consciously, I sought out the bosses, the men who were 'it' on newspapers, in politics and business, everywhere. And yet I had not quite drawn the conclusion that sprang out of this last of an accumulation of experience in muckracking, that:

"In every city, as in every walk of life, there are principals and there are heelers; the principals are few; the heelers are many. You can always tell them. Go to a man, put a proposition to him, and watch; if he decides for or against it on the spot for himself, he is apt to be a principal and worth talking to. But if he can't come to a decision, asks time and a chance to consult with his associates, he is a heeler, a 'yes' man; he is not worth talking to. To get anything done, one must find and win over the free principals, and it is an utter waste of time to talk or work with the heelers. They will take your argument or your book to their principal, and he can blast it with a phrase. So get the principals, and let them get their sheep." [1]

Thirty-five years after the events which inspired Steffens to write the foregoing, another great journalistic seeker of social cause and effect, John Gunther, wrote in the Foreword to his monumental *Inside U.S.A.* (Harper, 1947): "Everywhere I went I asked two or three main questions: . . . Above all, who runs it?" Time after time, seeking the principals whose importance Steffens stressed, Gunther asked in essence: "Yes, but who *really* runs it?" He did such a good job ferreting out the answers that a terrific congressional howl went up when it was revealed passages from his book were being used by the Voice of America.

There have been similar ululations in the recent past. One of the loudest occurred in 1929 when James W. Gerard, former ambassador to Germany, issued a list of 59 persons as "the men who rule the United States." It consisted almost entirely of corporation presidents, bank presidents, utilities men, motion picture producers, Andrew W. Mellon, secretary of the treasury, and six journalists: Adolph S. Ochs, publisher of the New York *Times*; William Randolph Hearst; Col. Robert R. McCormick, publisher of the Chicago *Tribune*; Joseph Medill Patterson, publisher of the New York *Daily News*; Cyrus H. K. Curtis, magazine publisher, and Roy W. Howard, president of the United Press. "These men," Gerard explained, "rule by virtue of their ability. They themselves are too busy to hold political office, but they determine who shall hold such office." ·

There have been other lists, including those in Ferdinand Lundberg's *America's Sixty Families* (Vanguard, 1937), John McConaughy's *Who Rules America?* (Longmans, Green, 1934) and George Seldes' *1,000 Americans* (Boni, Gaer, 1947). They make a lot of people mad, set some to yelling "Communist." Possibly it is naive to try to personalize the economic power which is a powerful factor in our political and social life because if Gerard, for instance, were to revive his list today, he undoubtedly would include the names of some of the successors in positions to those on his original compilation who have died, indicating that it is the position of power rather than the

---

[1] From Lincoln Steffens' *Autobiography*. Copyright, 1931, by Harcourt, Brace and Co.

personality which is important. The Steffens' discovery that at any time and place there are principals and heelers, even in a democracy, however, is not affected as any experienced newspaperman will admit if he is honest with himself.

In their studies of the role of leadership the sociologists have paid almost no attention to these "rulers behind the throne." Rather, they have concentrated upon the "front" men whom their followers have a part in selecting. Such research is all right as long as it is kept in proper perspective. That means, as long as it is recognized that, important as such leaders appear to be, they are comparatively unimportant if the Gerard thesis is correct: that public policy is determined largely by others whom the masses have little or no part in choosing.

As defined by E. S. Bogardus in *Leaders and Leadership* (D. Appleton-Century, 1934) a leader is a person who exercises influence over a number of other persons. Edouard C. Lindeman in *Social Discovery* (Republic, 1924) said a leader is "an individual whose rationalizations, judgments, and feelings are accepted [responded to] by the group as bases of belief and action." According to Ordway Tead in *The Art of Leadership* (Whittlesey, 1935), "Leadership is the activity of influencing people to cooperate toward some goal which they come to find desirable." Those definitions are orthodox among social psychologists. They obviously refer to leaders who are in direct face-to-face contact with those whom they lead. Distinction is made carefully between leaders and bosses, dominators, demagogues, and reformers so as to restrict the definition of leader proper to the democratic group phenomenon whereby someone steps forward and does the job which the majority believe they want done or which he is able to convince them they should want done.

The true leader in a democracy, as the connotation of the term is limited in sociological literature, then, is a symbol of group aspirations and derives his power from the group itself. By contrast the *boss* actually is indifferent to what are the best interests of his followers. He serves his own selfish ends. When he seems to be serving the people he is doing so in order to exact a payment or reward later. When he seems to be in the vanguard of those working for improvement, he is merely an opportunist boarding the band wagon because he has no alternative. Fundamentally the difference between the boss and the true leader is one of purpose or intent. Methodologically, the boss drives whereas the leader leads.

The distinction between the boss and the *dominator* is largely one of degree. Because he must seek support from the "powers behind the throne," the boss may be only a figurehead. He is, however, more inclined to try to make followers like what they get and what they have to do to get it. Possessed of power to punish disobedience, the dominator (or *dictator* or *autocrat*) need be less subtle. He can, in fact, be utterly lacking in sympathy, ruthless, shortsighted, selfish, cruel. He depends upon discipline rather than morale, as in the case of a democratic leader, and derives his authority from outside, rather than from inside the group. He uses his followers as a means to an end, his end. The difficulty of categorizing particular persons is seen in the fact that bosses and dictators often obtain not merely blind obedience but adulation from followers as well. Classic textbook in how it can be done is *The Prince* by Niccolo Machiavelli in whose spirit the master Nazi propagandist, Dr. Paul Joseph Goebbels, once wrote to the fascist Belgian leader: "Work exclusively by parliamentary methods. Fascinate and terrify the crowds by painting the Communist peril in darkest colors. Keep the ball rolling by resounding polemics. Send back every reproach like a boomerang at the head of your opponent. . . . Above all, know how to amuse and delight the crowd. Be more lively than the others; everything depends on that."

To achieve such ends it often is necessary to act as a *demagogue* who, by contrast with the true democratic leader, sways rather than leads in order to impose his own selfish will on the masses. Out of his political experience Ellis Gibbs Arnall, former governor of Georgia, wrote in *The Shore Dimly Seen*: "The South has had its share of demagogues. They can be divided into three species. The first, and in the South it is most common, is a charlatan, dedicated to the interest of absentee overlords; he is a Quisling; he is like those sheep trained to lead the lines of his fellows to the slaughter pen. The second is merely avid for power; usually a former member of the current political hierarchy, he seeks to build himself an individual and personal following by painting upon his face the symbols of a painful and righteous indignation and stomping like the dickens. The third deserves sympathy; he begins as the honest, sincere, well-intentioned politician who wishes to right obvious wrongs, and who fails to awaken the interests of the people by a simple assertion until, finally goaded to despair, he utilizes the tricks of the trade of the mountebank and attains to power; sometimes he dies of a broken heart, sometimes of an assassin's bullet, and sometimes of drunkenness upon the power he has bought at a price his conscience regards as somewhat excessive.

"To whichever group he belongs the demagogue is recognizable by three obvious traits. He promises a vague utopia in which milk and honey shall flow more opulently than in the New Jerusalem. He is flanked by a company of jackals who pluck the corpse of the state treasury to dry bones. He selects as an object of attack some religious or racial group that is weak and relatively defenseless and loads upon its back the sins of the people, preparatory to driving it into the wilderness as a sacrificial goat.

"To a demagogue on the Pacific coast the scapegoat very likely will be the Nisei. When he lived in Germany, before he put a bullet through his brain, his scapegoat was labeled 'Jew'; his soul goes marching on in Boston where he suppresses books, and overturns the monuments in graveyards, and writes filth on the walls of synagogues, and waylays little Jewish paper carriers on their way home at evening. If he lives in the South he hates 'niggers.'

"But wherever he lives he fears schools and colleges and teachers and students. He feels that they are engaged in a single gigantic conspiracy against his rule, his person and his way of thought. His instinct is both sure and accurate; they are. . . . But he is a good showman, whether at Nuremberg before a youth congress, or in Georgia at a political barbecue. He knows the tricks of the ham actor, the gestures, the tones of voice that can arouse passions. Always he dresses himself up as the little man, the common man come to life, grown to Brobdignagian stature and becomes the 'duce' or the 'leader' or, maybe, 'Ploughboy Pete.' " [2]

More altruistic but no more a true leader in the democratic sense is the *reformer*. Obsessed by a single idea or ideals, he substitutes fervor and excitability for firmness and discipline in his followers. He is likely to be a perfectionist, a utopian, a panacea chaser with a fanatical faith in his cause which he seeks, often by demagogic methods, to transmit to his followers, from whom he requests but can-

[2] From *The Shore Dimly Seen*, by Ellis Gibbs Arnall. Copyright, 1946, by J. B. Lippincott.

not compel sacrifices. He is the spirit of protest, and he is inclined to be impatient and intolerant of his opposition. Lacking practicality, he is likely to be a "flash in the pan" on the political or economic scene.

Of the difference between demagoguery and statesmanship, William Jennings Bryan once said: "The difference between a demagogue and a statesman is that the former advocates what he thinks will be popular, regardless of the effect that it may ultimately have upon the people to whom he appeals; the statesman advocates what he believes to be the best for the country regardless of the immediate effect which it may have upon himself. One is willing to sacrifice the permanent interests of others to advance his own temporary interests, while the other is willing to sacrifice his own temporary interests to advance the public welfare."

And so the question becomes pertinent: how much real democratic leadership is there, and how important is it anyway? Bryan, it can be argued, may have thought he was a statesman, but the sad fact remains that the Great Commoner was defeated three times for the presidency, didn't last long as secretary of state and died immediately after making a complete fool out of himself at the famous Scopes anti-evolution trial in Dayton, Tenn. Was it because, in addition to being statesmanlike, to be effective as a leader one also must be somewhat of the boss, dictator, demagogue, or reformer? Or was it because, as some of his detractors have claimed, Bryan's statesmanship was diluted by too much of the qualities of those types? Opinion is bound to differ, both during a prominent person's life and when his biographers start to work posthumously on him. It is impossible to name a single outstanding historical personage of which that was not true, and only God could settle the arguments. Did Huey Long, for instance, use demagoguery for statesmanlike or dictatorial purposes? Harnett T. Kane in *Louisiana Hayride* (W. Morrow, 1941) and numerous other biographers have made out strong cases for the latter contention, but their writings are not popular with a large segment of the state's voters who in 1946 chose the Kingfish's brother, Earl, to be governor again, and in 1948 sent Huey's son, Russell, to the United States Senate. The lives of many others are capable of similar varieties of interpretation: Thomas E. Watson, who seems to fit Arnall's description of a disillusioned crusader become demagogue; Theodore Roosevelt, Woodrow Wilson, Adolf Hitler, Benito Mussolini and, of course, Franklin D. Roosevelt, saint to many, devil to others.

Kinds of leadership. There remains unanswered also the vexatious question with which we began this chapter: who are the real leaders anyway? All of the Americans to whom reference has been made were elected democratically to public office. In all studies of leadership the tendency is to concentrate upon political leaders. But what, not only of the Gerard, Lundberg, Seldes and other lists of supposed "real" leaders in that field, but also of the so-called leaders of thought: the scientists, philosophers, authors, artists, composers, and others who have had tremendous effects upon the thought and action of others, often for many centuries after their deaths? When it is said they are "leaders in their fields" what often is meant is "they were (or are) the best of their kind." The democratic process presumably operates when sycophants choose to accept their ideas and ideals without coercion.

The social psychological vocabulary isn't very satisfying in applying the term "leader" to everyone who has followers of any kind. Clarification is attempted by lists classifying leaders of different types. Many of them, however, are merely descriptive, as, for instance, ones in which these types of leaders are listed: volunteer, drafted, general, specialized, temporary, permanent, conscious, reluctant, professional, and paid. Better are W. M. Conway's culturally conditioned social types —crowd representatives, crowd compellers, and crowd exponents— described in *The Crowd in Peace and War* (Longmans, Green, 1915). In *Human Nature and the Social Order* (Scribners, 1902), C. H. Cooley distinguished between four types of leadership: (1) *direct,* which deals with people rather than things, an example being Theodore Roosevelt with his Rough Riders at San Juan; (2) *indirect,* which sets in motion forces that sooner or later change human behavior, examples being the Chinese who invented paper and Thomas Edison; (3) *partisan,* in behalf of a particular interest group or individual; and (4) *scientific,* shaping the course of the future through an altruistic devotion to discovery of truth.

In *Leaders and Leadership*, Bogardus distinguished between (1) group manipulators, (2) group representatives, (3) group builders, and (4) group originators. The manipulators, sensitive to group emotions, are able to express in agreeable ways what their followers desire. Thus, they often enjoy wide popularity which makes it possible for them to cause people to seek false as well as real gods. While it lasts their influence may be close to hypnotic. Group representatives are spokesmen of the popular will, personifications of unexpressed feelings as well as of the formulated opinions of their followers. It is a frequent topic of debate in political science classes as to whether congressmen and state legislators should consider themselves experts, to vote as their best judgment dictates, or merely delegates to act in accordance with the majority opinion among their constituents, no matter how wrong they consider it to be. The public official who takes the latter point of view is hardly more than a symbol, serving without any effort to change the direction or purposes of his followers, making it difficult to consider him a real leader in any sense.

By contrast, Bogardus described the group builder as one who subordinates himself and tries to lead according to what serves the best interest of his followers. He doesn't try to conquer the group for his own purposes but to discover what is constructive for it and to weave these ideals into a form of life for his followers. Such a leader was the late Mohandas K. Gandhi. In some respects the great Indian also was a group originator, one who first is possessed by a great idea. The group originator preaches and wins disciples who then engage in either organized or unorganized efforts to spread what they consider the truth to be. Jesus and other founders of religions obviously belong in this category.

Other attempts at classification—amateur and professional, direct and indirect, reluctant and eager, and so forth—cast not much more light on the problem of the influence of leadership upon public opinion. Regardless of what list one uses he is bound to encounter difficulty in finding pure examples to illustrate each type included in it.

Qualifications for leadership. Even greater confusion and failure is encountered when the attempt is made to enumerate the qualifications necessary for attainment of positions of leadership. Examination of the literature reveals that just about every trait ever considered valuable by anyone has been cited by someone as indispensable. Even when the author of such a list confines himself to a single field, however, the skeptic encounters little difficulty in amassing examples from real life which are indisputably exceptions to the stereotypes which acceptance of the trait lists would create. To cite

one of the most obvious examples: the White House has been inhabited by many individuals of widely different temperaments. To
discover the common denominator to explain how they all happened
to realize the dream of every son's mother in terms of their personality
traits or political techniques is well nigh impossible.

What makes leaders? Forgetting what may be mere hocus pocus
anyway, what concerns students of leadership is: *why this fellow at
this time and not someone else?* Admittedly the successful bidder for
leadership must "have something" which others lacked. True, but it
still does not follow that there are any universals or absolutes. The
traits making for success at one time and/or place might be just the
ones to spell failure at a different time or place. Indisputable is it that
leadership is an inevitable concomitant of group existence. Even
socially minded birds and animals have leaders. Even they also change
them when circumstances make it seem wiser to have a different type.
It depends on the job to be done, and an emergency or crisis can
catapult a comparative unknown into high position of responsibility
to do the group's bidding. The crisis past, the temporary leader may
resume his previous wallflower role.

Such phenomena occur, of course, when a particular skill is required to meet an emergency. Maybe a group of tourists finds itself
unable to make its desires known in a foreign land. Suddenly the
pimpled introvert to whom nobody has paid much attention steps forward and displays a fluency in the strange language which saves the
day. When an automobile or other piece of machinery breaks down,
it is the comparatively most skilled mechanic who takes over; when
someone faints it is the one who has had a course in first aid. And so
on. In times of disaster, such as fire or flood or riot, many of the
traits commonly listed in the social psychology books seem to be
proved to be most important: courage, self-reliance, versatility,
originality, individuality, inventiveness, cheerfulness, mental flexibility,
sympathy and understanding, sense of humor, physical strength,
intelligence, and so on.

In his drama, *The Admirable Crichton,* Sir James M. Barrie
satirically demonstrated how different situations require different types
of leadership. On the desert isle the able butler became the undisputed,
despotic leader. Rescued and back home in England he resumed his
position as menial and had to endure overhearing his employer relate

his castaway exploits as though they were his own. As many a writer has pointed out, in simple static societies leadership is not so necessary as in heavily populated, complex societies calling for considerable specialized skills. Many frustrations are avoided by persons who learn to become proficient (that is, looked up to as leaders) in limited, probably unimportant or even useless, fields of activity. In such cases psychological necessity leads to the attainment of traits making for excellence in the chosen spheres. Vocational guidance and personnel work are developing to help young people discover the areas in which they have the greatest chances for success.

Because leadership is observed to develop on the playground, even among very small children, it sometimes is erroneously held that there are "born" leaders. Actually the answer is to be found in the psychiatric records of the tots. Even then, however, there is no universal pattern. Aggressiveness does not always result from the same or similar factors. In some cases skillful parental encouragement may be the cause, or the examples provided by other members of the family. On the other hand it may be overcompensation for deficiencies in the home in providing an adequate sense of security. The neglected child may become bossy with playmates as an outlet for his pent-up emotions. Biographers in these days of Freudian influence search for clues to the adult behavior of their subjects in their early experiences, and it is familiar to most everyone that a number of men of short stature—Napoleon, Mussolini, Hitler, and Stalin, for instance—had unhappy home lives and endured taunts because of their physical inferiority. All of them overcompensated with such intensity that they became dictators. It does not follow, however, that it is a safe prognostication that every adolescent runt who shows signs of wanting to bully will become a dogmatic leader of men after he has passed his nonage. As a matter of fact he has about as much chance of winding up in a reform school or mental hospital. Likewise, not every poor student in the lower grades who tinkers with hobbies at home to the neglect of his school work is going to become another Watt or Edison. In addition to ability, or traits making for potential leadership, *there also must be opportunity* and taking advantage of that opportunity. In other words, the time and circumstances must be correct. Although some may seem to be swept into positions of leadership contrary to their desires or expectations, it also seems generally true that there usually has to be a will to leadership, or at least a ready willingness to assume responsibility, even though thrust upon one.

Granted that each case is an object of individual study, it is held that statistical averages have validity. Much of the work that has been done, however, has at best been empirical. Plato was one of the first to try it. In *The Republic*, he listed the qualities desirable in his philosopher-kings as wisdom, courage, temperance, justice, strength, high-spiritedness and farsightedness. Plato, of course, had in mind a particular situation, but without explanation his traits are just nouns, and they are qualitatively, not quantitatively expressed. How much courage? What kind of justice? And so forth.

Much more recently Gustav LeBon in *The Crowd* (Unwin, 1925) listed as essential leadership traits: keen foresight, conviction, perseverance, tyranny, will (intermittent or permanent), energy, prestige, and dominance. Bogardus' list includes: superiority complex, marginal uniqueness, fine physique, mental energy and focalization, confidence, painstaking forethought, inhibition, emanatory achievement, organizing ability, mental flexibility, versatility, enthusiasm, physical energy and endurance, sociality and prestige. In *Political Parties* (Hearst International Library, 1915) Roberto Michels emphasized force of will, wider extent of knowledge than ordinary, Catonian strength of conviction, self-sufficiency, a reputation for goodness of heart and disinterestedness, and some form of celebrity.

Many, many more similar lists, compiled by some of the leading authorities, exist. L. H. Moore studied "Leadership Traits of College Women" (*Sociology and Social Research*, September-October, 1932) by asking students to judge and evaluate those traits most conducive to leadership. In order of importance the traits considered most desirable were: democratic attitudes, vitality, positiveness, friendliness, enthusiasm, sympathy, trustworthiness, perseverance, and intelligence. In *The Executive and His Control of Men* (Macmillan, 1917) E. B. Gowin presented the results of a study of the relationship of height and weight to leadership. He concluded that executive leaders tend to be taller and heavier than others. He obtained the following averages:

	Height	Weight
University presidents	5:10.8	181.6
Authors	5:10.2	158.0
Bishops	5:10.6	176.4
Sales managers	5:10.1	182.8

In an article, "Experiments in Testing for Leadership," in the May, 1947 *American Journal of Sociology,* Joseph W. Eaton summarized: "In a democratic society, it is useful to look upon the phenomenon of leadership as a social value and not merely as psychological traits." That means that, whatever else he may be, the democratically selected leader must be a symbol of the desires, ideals, or institutions of his followers, and that, in a democracy, the important object of study should be not only, or perhaps not even primarily, the leader, but rather his followers.

Why men follow. Even the most primitive people, when they select their own leaders, operate in accordance with the principle that the best qualified is the one who seems most likely to advance the group interest. The strong man, warrior, or hunter who becomes a leader is accepted, not simply because of admiration for his display of ability, but because he is best fitted to protect and provide for the needs of the group. Freudians call this the operation of the father image. Whatever it is, it is a common-sense observation that those who have the opportunity to choose are not going to decide on someone whom they believe to be inimical to their own best interests. Sometimes a group may go in search of such a person to lead it out of a particular difficulty. Usually, however, the initiative is on the part of the would-be leader to win conviction and confidence. In several other chapters the extent to which large publics can be and have been fooled into placing false faith in causes and leaders has been enunciated. Demagogue or sincere aspirant, the potential leader must crystallize public opinion around a program and give it direction. He must arouse and appeal to popular fears and hopes, forcing the attention of the group on a common object of interest or attaching this interest to something which previously was popular. He must seem to possess a sense of direction and to point the way toward achievement of group desires.

Public opinion is not created by oratory but is the outcome of the stimulation of deep-seated attitudes to the exclusion of others. Nevertheless, by clever manipulation of facts and interpretations, the would-be leader may enhance and emphasize some particular sets of public attitudes and inhibit others. In times of crisis, when the demand for strong leadership is intense, he may find it to his advantage to concentrate attention on himself as the potential deliverer. That was the technique which proved successful for Adolf Hitler, but *der Fuehrer* operated in a nation where strong leadership had worked in the past and its absence at the time he was making his bid for power seemed to be, partly at least, the explanation for most of Germany's woes. So Hitler capitalized upon the leadership principle, and put it into effect throughout his party and, later, governmental machinery. In the United States the cultural conditioning has been different. Americans do not have inveterate reverence for messiahs. Quite to the contrary, our rugged individualistic background makes us more inclined to believe that no man is indispensable. Nevertheless, throughout our history when disaster has threatened or struck, we have sought the Strong Man and we have supported presidents at such times in their fights to obtain more power from jealously reluctant congresses. As long as a chief executive has retained the confidence of the majority that he is using the power in its interest, there has been no standing on principle; it is a pragmatic point of view. Once the crisis is past, however, always to date there has been reaction away from too much power for the executive branch and a recrudescence of the prestige and influence of the legislative branch.

The same psychological principles are known to operate in any group at any time. We run home to mama, or to big brother or to our minister or psychiatrist or to someone else when we need, or think we need, help; and at other times we neglect or resent attempts to give us advice or discipline. Depending on the urgency of need, also, we insist upon the good, better, best, or very best. Consequently, the type of leader a democratic group selects at any time is an index to the feelings of that group. If it picks a strong-willed person and gives him leeway, it is pretty certain that the feeling of insecurity is great. Picking such a person may be almost an act of desperation. At such times, the strong personality, the egotist or at least the person with a strong sense of self-confidence, especially if he remains a little aloof so as to enhance the myth of superiority, is more likely to find potential followers wistfully and wishfully eager to be convinced that he has the answer to their problems. In other words, no problems, no need for leaders; big problems, big leaders. From the standpoint of the gifted potential leader, then, this means that there is a strong element of luck involved in whether it is to be he or someone else. A person has to be born at the right time and place or must suffer the pangs of realization that he was either behind or ahead of his times. Alfred E. Smith never got over lamenting that he "stuck his neck out" just four years too soon and thought some responsible for his not being renominated in 1932 were ungrateful.

At all times followers—which means all of us—want to feel comfortably at home in their environment, in every phase of it. As explained in earlier chapters, modern living makes such severe demands upon us that we must look to others for simple understanding of many of its phases. In times of comparative peace and security we want leaders who will preserve customs and social institutions and not "rock the boat." In times of fear and insecurity we want to believe our leaders know the way out. Thus we are inclined to create our leaders in our images. We want to trust them when we need them most; we identify ourselves with them and take vicarious joy in their achievements. They enhance our egoes, increase our confidence, allay our anxieties. And if they don't do that, we change them for others who seem to offer what they fail to provide. Nothing, of course, succeeds like success, and success to the average person means a full enough dinner pail.

Ever cynical, the late George Bernard Shaw defined democracy as a collection of idolators as contrasted with aristocracy which is a collection of idols. Others have said that only merit can choose merit, that the quality of leaders in a democracy is of less importance than the quality of the people whom they lead. Hitler scoffed at democracy because he said it fosters incompetence rather than its necessary opposite. Even the British are wont to criticize the American political system as less likely than theirs to produce trained leadership. And there are plenty of Americans who have sought to debunk the Horatio Alger myth that talent is bound to rise to the top in the United States. None of these comments on the actual working out of the democratic system of selecting leaders—or perhaps it is the capitalistic method which really is the target in many cases—destroys the basic psychological fact that followers try to select those best fitted to advance their own interests. This may seem selfish, but what else could be expected?

The power of leaders. Much of what has been written suggests the controversy, which has engaged the attention of a number of scholars, regarding the relative importance of the *great man* as opposed to *social forces*. During the nineteenth century a number of writers, notably Thomas Carlyle, eulogized the forceful personality. There are many tracts interpreting history in terms of its outstanding personalities. The German philosopher Nietzsche taught a philosophy of power which influenced Hitler, at least indirectly. Dictators always belittle the importance of the masses, consider themselves to be men of destiny, superior to the rabble, perhaps divinely appointed to rule. Any biological evidence of the basic inequality of individuals is pounced upon by the fascist-minded as justification for repressive measures by the minority in order to keep the majority in line—for their own good, of course. All that aside, what about the question, "Do great men make history or does history make great men?"

In *Fate and Freedom* (Simon, Schuster, 1945), Jerome Frank pointed out there was no unanimous demand for a Reformation during the centuries, decades or years preceding it; nor for discovery and exploration, *laissez faire* or any of the other great occurrences and important thoughts of all times. The concept of "inevitable trends," he concluded, is a myth, and "scientific" history writing is impossible. Nobody, for instance, can answer a great many historical "ifs" such as what would have happened if Giuseppe Zangara had succeeded in assassinating President-elect Franklin D. Roosevelt in Miami early in 1933.

On the other hand, it probably is correctly pointed out, neither Roosevelt nor anyone else elected in 1932 could have instituted such a program as the New Deal had the country not been in a receptive mood as the result of the deepening depression. True, if John Nance Garner had become president he might not have proposed anything resembling the NRA, CCC, or WPA, but he would have had to do something in the face of great need or have gone into political limbo along with Herbert Hoover. Similarly, Hitler capitalized upon the economic plight of the German people following failure of the Weimar Republic to bring about postwar economic recovery. Roosevelt and Hitler both delivered to the extent of putting the unemployed to work or at least of putting food on their tables. Certainly the leader at times of such crisis has it within his power to do this or that, but his choice is limited by the social, economic, and political necessities of the time. He has to seem at least to satisfy the needs of the majority at the moment, and whether he was wise or foolish often cannot be determined until long after his death.

The limiting factor with which any leader has to contend is the force of tradition. The deep-seated beliefs and attitudes which characterize any culture slow down what could be called progress. How far, for instance, would a bidder for political power in India get were he to base his program on the contention that his country is backward because it adheres to superstitious religious convictions? About as far as an American presidential candidate who thumped for communism and atheism. Fundamental change occurs slowly and as the result of the impact of events and a gradual awakening of, first, the intellectuals and then, through their influence, of the masses. According to the Marxists, capitalism has about run its course and will collapse because of its internal weaknesses. In *The Managerial Revolution* (John Day, 1941), James Burnham also declared that capitalism is doomed but predicted that, not the proletariat but the managers—those who control the manufacture and distribution of goods—will take over. Who, if either, is right will depend upon the outcome of a struggle between advocates of both points of view. Most Americans regard Italian fascism, German national socialism, and Russian communism as counterrevolutionary, turning back the clock and destroying centuries of progress toward greater freedom for the individual. Nevertheless, many of the most outspoken acclaimed Anne Morrow Lindbergh's *Wave of the Future* (Harcourt, Brace, 1940) with its warning: "There is no sin punished more implacably by nature than the sin of resistance to change. For change is the very essence of living matter. To resist change is to sin against life itself."

Change, yes, but change to what? That is where the leader comes in, with limited power to decide the direction that change is to take. Reading history it may seem that certain great movements were inevitable, but there remain, as Jerome Frank emphasized, the multitudinous "ifs" of history. At almost any time of crisis, a different leader might have capitalized upon the same situation to bring about drastically different results. And then, on the other hand, he might not have been able to do so at all. It is pretty fatalistic, however, to take such an attitude, and even the most avid patrons of the astrologers and other soothsayers would lead miserable lives if they actually believed it was all predetermined.

A new idea may catch on because it seems to satisfy the longings at the moment of a large number of followers. The conditions making possible the putting over of an apparently new program, however, are preexistent; and there must be spokesmen, trailblazers, and often martyrs before even what may be considered in retrospect to have been inevitable occurs. No leader, no matter how great, can completely upset things. Despite his great prestige, amounting to adoration in thousands of cases, John L. Lewis, in 1940, could not persuade even a sizeable minority of his United Mine Workers to vote against Franklin D. Roosevelt; so, to preserve his prestige, he had to carry out his threat to resign as president of the Congress of Industrial Organizations if Wendell Willkie were not elected. The example of Robert M. LaFollette, Sr., who carried his home state of Wisconsin in 1924 on the newly created Progressive party ticket for president, after a lifetime of running as a Republican, is the exception and, of course, a great tribute to "Old Bob's" prowess. Wisconsin was, however, the only state that the LaFollette and Wheeler ticket did carry, and his movement collapsed almost immediately after defeat.

In his fireside chat on economic conditions, April 14, 1938, Franklin D. Roosevelt described how important change occurs and, by inference, what power any individual has to affect it, when he declared:

"Democracy has disappeared in several other great nations—not because the people of those nations disliked democracy, but because they had grown tired of unemployment and insecurity, of seeing their children hungry, while they sat helpless in the face of government confusion and government weakness through lack of leadership in government. Finally, in desperation, they chose to sacrifice liberty in the hope of getting something to eat. We in America know that our democratic institutions can be preserved and made to work. But in order to preserve them we need to act together, to meet the problems of the nation boldly, and to prove that the practical operation of democratic government is equal to the task of protecting the security of the people. . . .

"History proves that dictatorships do not grow out of strong and successful governments, but out of weak and helpless ones. If by democratic methods people get a government strong enough to protect them from fear and starvation, their democracy succeeds; but if they do not, they grow impatient. Therefore, the only sure bulwark of continuing liberty is a government strong enough to protect the interests of the people, and a people strong enough and well enough informed to maintain its sovereign control over its government."

Heroes and Hero Worship

Franklin Delano Roosevelt was more than a leader. To millions all over the world he also was a hero, as evidenced by the genuine outpouring of grief when he died. He unquestionably was what Sidney Hook in *The Hero in History* (John Day, 1943) called an "event-making" man as distinguished from an "eventful" man. As explained by Hook: "The hero in history is the individual to whom we can justifiably attribute preponderant influence in determining an issue or event whose consequences would have been profoundly different if he had not acted as he did. . . . The eventful man in history is any man whose actions influenced subsequent developments along a quite different course than would have been followed if these actions had not been taken. The event-making man is an eventful man whose actions are the consequences of outstanding capacities of intelligence, will and character rather than of accidents of position. This distinction tries to do justice to the general belief that a hero is great not merely in virtue of what he does, but in virtue of what he is."

Hook elucidated further with other examples. The exploits of Columbus, Vespucci, Da Gama, Magellan, and other explorers, he pointed out, were not historically necessary but what they did was. They were colorful incidents in a course of development whose configuration can't be explained by the activity of particular individuals no matter how gifted. They are not historical heroes in the sense of eventful or event-making figures because they cannot be considered as having been indispensable to the discoveries with which their names are linked. Hook thus attempted to take a balanced middle position between the "heroic vitalism" of Carlyle and Nietzsche on the one hand and the social determinism of Hegel and Spencer and the economic determinism of Marx on the other.

What makes Carlyle, Nietzsche, and their disciples frightening to a believer in democracy is that they not only saw history as the sum total of the biographies of great men, but they advocated rule by supermen. Historian of an age of individual enterprise and violently contending states, Carlyle in *Heroes and Hero Worship* (Lovell, 1885) repudiated the Christian democratic concept. The fundamental life force, he believed, is the will to dominate, and he considered Napoleon, Oliver Cromwell, and Frederick the Great as among those who had come closest to its realization. In *Thus Spake Zarathustra* and other works, Nietzsche went further in extolling force as the law of life. Supermen, he philosophized, emerge out of the bitter struggle for survival and are the chief determinants of history, which is as it should be.

There is a sizeable literature, pro and con, regarding the theories of the heroic vitalists. The social determinists, preaching a virtual inevitability, contradict their basic assumption. They say the great man is primarily an expression of "the spirit" of his times or the "soul" of his culture, each age therefore getting the heroes that it deserves. The great man of thought, according to the Marxists, prepares the minds of men for revolutionary social change; the great man of action organizes participants in the actual class struggle. With its emphasis upon equality, struggle and the survival of the fittest, heroic vitalism is decidedly undemocratic so that no matter how accurate it may be as an explanation of past history, the better society will come only when it is destroyed, democratic philosophers contend. For an able discussion see *A Century of Hero-Worship* by Eric Russell Bentley (J. B. Lippincott, 1944). Similarly, all theories of social or economic determinism, with their varying emphasis upon inevitability, are belittling to the individual and hence inconsistent with democratic aspirations.

Although the strength of the democratic tradition (or myth, if you insist) is largely responsible for the fact that there have been few living American heroes, in the shaping of the American character hero worship has been and continues to be an important fact. In fact, as Dixon Wector brilliantly illustrates in *The Hero in America* (Scribner, 1941), it answers a national need and is a vital part of our patriotism. Since we are a migratory people, we never have developed a patriotic loyalty to a place as "patria," Shakespeare's England, *la belle* France, and so forth. Consequently, our collective symbols, as the flag, the Declaration of Independence, Constitution, and Supreme

Court, are precious. They nourish a feeling of national continuity and the words of the Founding Fathers become almost holy writ.

As Gerald W. Johnson pointed out in *American Heroes and Hero Worship* (Harper, 1941), the past that influences our lives is not what actually happened but what men believe happened, a thesis already discussed in Chapter 6, "Legends, Folklore, and Myths." As we grow older as a nation and develop a past, through our schools we increasingly teach a sort of ancestor worship with fulsome eulogies of the pioneers, Founding Fathers, and outstanding figures of our early history. It is not, however, their superman qualities which are stressed but their democratic characteristics: Washington's honesty, Jefferson's faith in the common man, Jackson's simplicity, Lincoln's humble origin and modesty. There are no Machiavellis among them, no snobs or dandies. Rather, they are self-respecting, upright, decent, honorable, possessed of a strong sense of fair play, men who attained their power through display of character rather than by force. One consequence is that it is possible for groups of widely different types to claim many of our national heroes as "their own," with a corresponding impetus for them to facilitate the development of legends to prove their points.

Tracing one's familial or organizational ancestry to a sainted principal is a potent way to strengthen a sense of group solidarity. Minority movements especially thrive on martyrdom, as witness the importance of the John Brown legend to the Abolitionists and of Horst Wessel to the Nazis. During New Deal days the Democrats undertook the apotheosizing of Jefferson to offset the prestige value that Lincoln long had had for the Republicans. To enhance the national ego as a whole, the myth- and legend-makers have glamorized almost everyone capable of being considered a saviour of any part of our heritage. Although the Hall of Fame at New York University contains the effigies of leaders of thought in many fields, the dead heroes who have been important as inspirations to American school boys and girls have been mostly political and military leaders. Scientists, inventors, artists, writers, clergymen, and women have not fit easily the pattern of heroic victories over adversity in the unselfish service of their countrymen.

Anyone, from no matter what station in life, however, can be a living hero to someone, if only his children. Hero worship is an

important part of any youngster's character development. In addition
to the historical and literary models that he is encouraged to admire
and, if possible, emulate, there are parents, older brothers and sisters,
other relatives, neighborhood and community acquaintances, teachers
and others to whom he looks up. During adolescence it generally is
considered normal, or at least not too unusual, to have "crushes" on
teachers, scout masters and other young adults. In adulthood the
attitude of the well-adjusted person, however, is admiration rather
than starry-eyed adulation. During a political rally, religious revival or
similar occasion, even the most sober and unemotional adult may be
"carried away" by the oratorical or ritualistic appeals; it's like having
a good cry at a play. Anyone, however, who is in almost perpetual
turmoil because of some object of hero worship or who goes into frequent ecstasies over different heroes displays neurotic symptoms. His
intense hero worshipping is a form of regression suggestive of feelings
of inferiority.

Whereas religious prophets, warriors, and politicians, in and out
of office, have succeeded in working thousands into frenzied states
throughout the history, not only of the United States but of the whole
world, it has been the entertainers—athletic, dramatic, and otherwise
—who have been responsible for the greatest number of laurel
wreaths, ticker tape, and other symbols of affection displayed (hurled)
by sycophants. Such actively expressed hero worshipping serves the
same psychological purpose as reading escapist literature, only it
serves it better since it permits active physical as well as passive mental activity. Slavishly following the career of a baseball player or other
athlete by means of newspaper accounts and broadcasts provides
vicarious release, but much better is a ringside seat or a position
along a line of march.

Best organized effort to take commercial advantage of the tendency
to overcome frustrations through hero worshipping of entertainers is
provided by the motion picture industry with its well developed star
system. Once he has attained popularity no Hollywood actor can
enjoy much privacy. It is not vouchsafed him to take a quiet walk
in any public place or to appear where crowds may gather without
actual risk of physical injury from well-meaning but selfish souvenir
and autograph hunters. Even foreign fans of American movie stars
have learned to treat visiting cinematic royalty in the manner to which

they have become accustomed at home. On Jan. 28, 1948, according to the Rome bureau of the Associated Press,

Tyrone Power and Linda Christian said their marriage vows Thursday while thousands of screaming Italian bobby-soxers surged riotously across police lines outside the church of Santa Francesca Romana. It was Hollywood-on-the-Tiber's show of the year. . . . In the crush outside the church, several women fainted and a man's finger was broken. A number of persons were bruised. . . . There were more than 10,000 in the throng.

And, according to the June 13, 1949 *Life*: "For the first time in living memory the staid British Isles were indulging in a type of worshipful hysteria only too common in the U.S. The object of this nationwide adulation, which affected young and old of both sexes, was . . . Danny Kaye of Brooklyn."

In this country in recent years no hero worshipping craze has equaled that of which the crooner, Frank Sinatra, was the object. In 1944, at the height of his popularity, 150 policemen were necessary to control 10,000 fans trying to get into New York's Paramount Theater where he was singing. Ambulances were kept busy carrying away those who were crushed and trampled. Once inside, often after waits of almost a half day, some of the devotees—mostly teen-aged girls—frequently stayed through several shows. In "The Voice and the Kids," in the Nov. 6, 1944, *New Republic,* Bruce Bliven reported that one bobby soxer attended 56 consecutive Sinatra performances. Another wore a bandage for three weeks on her arm where "Frankie touched me." Weeping and swooning were considered normal behavior in a Sinatra audience. An anonymous article in the Dec. 12, 1944 *Look* quoted "a prominent psychiatrist" as believing, "War rather than Frank Sinatra accounts for the thousands of teen age youngsters who make his programs hideous with their clamor." The unnamed authority explained that because their boy friends were away at war, the lonely, frustrated adolescents were forced to find a symbol upon which to lavish affection and enthusiasm. Frankie filled the bill better than any of scores of other singers partly because of his appearance: he looked as though he could use a little mothering. The unknown source of the magazine's analysis said that the girls obtained erotic pleasure from shrieking and fainting, but that the lasting effects would not be deleterious.

Wartime, being a period of anxiety, creates the need for a father image—that is, for strong heroes—among adults as well. During World War II the most intense hero worshipping among Americans was of Gen. Douglas MacArthur. It is not detracting one iota from the general's ability as a military leader to declare that the movement developed from necessity rather than from any exploits of his. Some way had to be found to assuage the badly wounded national pride after the humiliating defeats suffered at Pearl Harbor and in the Philippines. Right up to Dec. 7, 1941, it had been the preponderant belief in America that a war with Japan would be of short duration ending in an easy victory for our side. The Japanese, most Americans were convinced, are inferior people, half monkeys in fact, whom we had decided to exclude as immigrants almost a half century earlier. To be pushed around by them was almost too much to take. Hero worshipping of MacArthur, at a time when he had done nothing except retreat, filled the psychological need of the moment. It also, of course, enabled Roosevelt haters to pin their hopes to someone other than the logical wartime leader, the president. Thus, the MacArthur button wearers were able to make visible display of their loyalty without having to push "national unity" so far as to deify the hated occupant of the White House. As a matter of fact, part of the MacArthur myth involved rumored and spoken charges that the commander in chief was jealous of the arrogant Pacific leader and deliberately withheld supplies and authority from him and refused to bring him back to the mainland.

MacArthur's known greatness makes it impossible to categorize him as a synthetic hero although a certain amount of skillful press agentry did go into his buildup, especially as election time drew near and in some Republican circles he was considered as a possible candidate. For weeks in early 1948 the Heart newspapers filled columns and even pages to acclaim the absent general's virtues and to explain his availability for the presidency. It didn't work if for no other reason than that in 1944, in some imprudent letters to a member of Congress, MacArthur had indicated that he, like Barkis, was willing. American voters prefer to have their presidential candidates act as though they have no interest in the most important job in the country.

Synthetic is the only way to describe many sports heroes. In their manufacture, newspapermen often have taken a prominent part, especially in building college football stars. Sports writers of an area even have been known to agree at the beginning of a season to boost the reputation of a certain player or players with the end in mind of having him or them selected on some mythical all-American teams. That every important conference in the country usually is represented on such teams is more than a slight hint as to how some college football heroes are made. Keeping sports reporters happy and comfortable and refreshed at games is one of the most important tasks of the publicity department of any college or university which is on its toes today. Neither the writers, their hosts, nor the glamorized young men themselves, however, are the originators of the inhibitions which several hundred thousands or millions of fans attempt to overcome in the stadia every Saturday and, in interminable second guessing of coaches during the other days of the week each autumn.

Neither can the sports writer indefinitely keep alive the illusion that an athlete is better than average unless the object of their praise does a reasonable amount of "coming through." Because of the nature of the game, with 22 men participating at any one time, football lends itself easiest to journalistic deceit. In other sports, where individual play is easier to follow, to remain a hero the contender must continue to win or show merit. That is so because the adoring public is fickle. It may cheer a promising athlete while he is "coming up," but it is quick to turn on him and back a new "underdog" if he fails to live up to expectations. Of the cruelty of such fickleness, Walter White, long-time secretary of the National Association for the Advancement of Colored People, wrote in his syndicated column for Dec. 13, 1947 as follows:

As I listened to the crowd at Madison Square Garden boo Joe Louis for his unsatisfactory 24th defense of the heavyweight title, two ideas pressed on my mind.

I wondered if the eagerness to tear down the cleanest and best-loved idol of boxing of this or any other time was not a yardstick of the sickness which infects mankind today. Jennie Lee, the brilliant British writer and member of Parliament, stated in London the other day on her return from the United States that American newspapers and radio had fed their readers during the war tales of disaster and gloom which in turn had created a cynicism and pessimism which continue to pervade American thought.

Have we as a nation become so permeated with the desire to destroy that in sixty minutes we transform a public idol into a bum?

An expensively dressed and obviously prosperous stranger turned to me with frenzied manner to demand if, in my opinion, Walcott had not won the fight by a tremendous margin and if Joe Louis was a has-been. When I replied that I had never seen a championship won by the challenger running away, however shrewdly and successfully, the expression on the stranger's face was almost that of one who had been accused of a heinous crime.

FORGOTTEN

The second idea which depressed me was one of wondering what an individual had to do to merit steadfast recognition from a fickle public. Walcott's cleverness in keeping out of Joe Louis' reach and his effective counter-punching which kept Joe off balance wiped out, at least for the time being, all memory of what Joe Louis had done for organized sport. Forgotten was the fact that when he emerged on the prizefighting horizon the business of commercialized mayhem was in about as foul odor as the wrestling racket is today.

Joe Louis bluntly refused to have anything whatever to do with fixed fights. Joe's integrity surpassed that of any other contemporary boxer and was above reproach. Unlike his predecessors, he had given every aspirant a chance at the championship.

I don't want to be cynical, but a public which can so instantaneously forget a record like his and demand that the title be taken away from Joe Louis because a cagey opponent stayed out of harm's way makes one wonder about the mental processes of such a public.

—Chicago *Daily News*

In his almost ribald *Phantom Fame* (Simon & Schuster, 1931) Harry Reichenbach, one of the first of the modern press agents, told of how he "stuffed the shirts" of many newcomers to motion pictures. Not infrequently, the man responsible for their rises to fame and fortune related, the principals came to believe in their own greatness as it was created for them by Reichenbach. There have been many tragic tales of terrible comedowns for former college athletic stars when, after four years of seeing their names in the headlines along with those of presidents, kings, and dictators, they have been graduated into the cold business world as inexperienced job seekers.

As in the case of the followers of leaders, for an understanding of hero worship it is necessary to study the worshipper rather than the hero. It takes little knowledge of psychiatry to recognize that there is something wrong with the Cleveland Indians fan who climbed a flagpole in midseason, 1949, resolved not to descend until the team attained first place in the American League or the season ended. Obviously a sad mental case also was Ruth Ann Steinhagen who put a bullet into Eddie Waitkus, first baseman for the Philadelphia National League team, after having endured two years of a violent silent crush on him. One of the best pieces of writing regarding the latter case was that of Albert Deutsch in the June 19, 1949 New York *Daily Compass* as follows:

There are some extraordinary parallels between the senseless act of violence against baseball star Eddie Waitkus and the triple murder a dozen years ago by Robert Irwin in the famous "Gedeon case." A reading of the Gedeon-Irwin tragedy in Dr. Frederic Wertham's absorbing book, *The Show of Violence* (Doubleday, $3), provides some illuminating clues to the twisted personality of the hapless girl who tried to kill her hero.

On the basis of Ruth Steinhagen's statements to the police and on the known record of Robert Irwin, it may be assumed that both were driven by what psychiatrists call the "Herostratus complex." Herostratus was an unknown citizen in ancient Greece who deliberately set fire to the renowned temple of Diana at Ephesus in order, as he explained, to become famous. He did; his name has come down as part of a useful psychiatric term.

The Herostratus complex—the urge to gain acclaim and punishment at the same time, arising from a deep sense of frustration and inferiority—crops up often in psychiatric case histories. It was partly responsible for Irwin's murder of three innocents; it apparently played a part in Miss Steinhagen's act.

Irwin set out to kill a well-known model, Ethel Gedeon. He went to her home, where he had once been a boarder, and waited for his intended victim's arrival. She didn't come, but before the next day dawned Irwin had murdered her mother, her sister Ronnie, also a model, and a boarder.

Irwin, like Miss Steinhagen, had exhibited symptoms of emotional disorder for a long time. Like the Chicago typist, he had an inordinate love of collecting pictures. He had thousands of clippings and reproductions—mostly of Greek heroes, of Napoleon and of famous prizefighters. He was sent to a juvenile reform school once for cutting pictures out of library books. He had a theory of what he called "visualization"—to lead an ideal life by concentrating on pictures of great persons and dreaming up incidents in their company. After the murders, "he frantically went through every drawer for pictures of her (Ethel). He could not find any. He took two photos of Ronnie (the murdered sister)."

On several occasions he had expressed a desire to commit suicide—as Miss Steinhagen also apparently did. He once thought of killing an old lady who looked like his mother. "I wanted to kill her, so I would get hung," he said. Ethel Gedeon, his intended victim, reminded him of his mother, too. Miss Steinhagen told police that Eddie Waitkus was like her father.

After his homicidal acts, Irwin thought of giving himself up to Walter Winchell, then actually surrendered himself to the Hearst chain so that he could get a big splash in the papers. "I wanted the limelight, and I got it," Miss Steinhagen is quoted as saying.

Both Robert Irwin and Ruth Steinhagen had sought release from tremendous emotional tension through an act of violence, and expressed relief from tension after "finding a way" of dramatic emotional release. Irwin, some years before his tragic act, had clumsily and unsuccessfully tried to emasculate himself. They both went through what psychiatrists call a "catathymic crisis," a building up of great tension that finds release in a dramatic act. In a significant sense, the final act in both instances was a search for suicide through murder. Miss Steinhagen apparently planned to kill herself after shooting Waitkus, but couldn't go through with it. These people seek punishment, but invariably at the hands of others.

Irwin—who, incidentally, is now serving a life term in a New York state institution for the criminally insane—slipped through the hands of a number of psychiatrists before he committed his homicidal deed. Miss Steinhagen had contact, briefly, with two psychiatrists.

One was Dr. Abraham A. Low of Chicago. Reached by phone, Dr. Low explained that Miss Steinhagen visited him but once, on referral from another physician. On that occasion he gave her a physical and neurological examination and made an appointment for a second visit. She didn't show up a second time.

Dr. Low tentatively diagnosed his patient as a case of hebephrenic dementia praecox, a type of psychosis most frequent among young people. She complained, at the time, that "other people are talking about me." Dr. Low suggested that Miss Steinhagen become a member of the well-known organization of psychiatric patients and recovered patients that he founded many years ago. It is known as Recovery, Inc., and occupies a suite of rooms in a midtown Chicago building. Patients and ex-patients gather there for social affairs, relaxation and discussion. They gain comfort and strength from one another.

Miss Steinhagen apparently visited Recovery, Inc., once, but failed to follow up.

The close relationship between the idea of murder and the wish for self-destruction, so evident in the Steinhagen case, is one of the key points of psychiatric research, especially on the part of the Freudians.

Fortunately flagpole sitting and shooting of heroes never have become epidemic. Mobbing motion picture actors, however, unfortunately is. And during the roaring twenties any American who returned from abroad with any claim to fame was greeted by millions in New York and, on triumphant tour, in other cities all over the country. The quantity and quality of such behavior, of course, in-

creases with the psychological need for it, and its prevalence is a clue
to the temper of the people.

Also a clue is the type of hero most likely to arouse the worshippers.
Always in times of fear and insecurity, the presumed deliverer will
be wildly, almost pathetically acclaimed. FDR reached hero proportions with millions as soon as he spoke the words, "All that we have
to fear is fear itself," in his first inaugural. That was what the people,
tired of being told "prosperity is just around the corner" wanted to
hear. Huey Long, Father Coughlin, Dr. Townsend, Gerald L. K.
Smith, and other panacea advocates who offer to make every man a
king, share the wealth, or deliver a fat check or ham and eggs every
Thursday, draw audiences when times are rugged, but obtain at best
tolerant response otherwise. In wartime, as noted, dark days are more
conducive to the generation of heroes than when victory comes easily.
In modern American times, however, it is the common or unknown
soldier who is more likely to be heroized than the top brass. This is
so partly because of our democratic tradition, partly because the general or admiral who orders, "Don't shoot until you see the white of
their eyes," "We have just begun to fight," or "Don't give up the
ship," today is likely to do so by long distance message rather than
from a position within sight of the enemy. In both world wars Americans have respected and honored their generals, but it has been the
Sergeant Yorks and Colin Kellys who have stirred their deepest emotions.

In the late nineteenth century Americans took national pride in
their first millionaires who enabled them to hold their heads higher in
the presence of supercilious foreigners. Few crowds, however, ever
attempted to tear the clothing from a Carnegie, Rockefeller, Schwab,
Morgan, or Ford. The public attitude toward the industrial and financial giants has been more of awe and envy than hero worship. The log-
cabin-to-White-House or Wall Street characters who have inspired
youth have been mostly fictional—the brain children of Horatio Alger
and others—rather than real.

Outstanding courage or sacrifice always is admired, but the fame
from such heroism is not enduring. In 1904, Andrew Carnegie endowed the Carnegie Hero Commission with 4 million dollars to provide medals for outstanding bravery, but the names of the recipients
disappear soon from the headlines and are not remembered. Even he

who achieves distinction through some spectacular achievement, to
continue in the limelight, has to persist in soliciting it. Many a one-
time great has been found in a tenement attic surrounded by his scrap
books and other souvenirs and not much else. Like so-called "popular" music, popular heroes pass in parade; when one starts slipping
there is another there to take his place. Once in awhile a supposed
"has been" stages a comeback, as did the "mammy" singer, the late
Al Jolson, in 1948, with the aid of the first of two movies based on
his life story. His, however, was the exceptional case. Usually revelation that a former hero has been picked up out of a gutter or recognized in a bread line leads to a subscription campaign, often led by
a newspaper, to grub stake him back to a minimum standard of living,
pay his doctor and hospital bills or give him a decent burial.

CHAPTER ELEVEN

LANGUAGE

Skillfully used, the written and spoken word can be mightier than the sword in winning approval for one's thoughts and actions and in influencing the behavior of others.

What's In a Name?

What's in a name? that which we call a rose
By any other name would smell as sweet.
—*Romeo and Juliet,* Act II, Scene 2

In eight hours 26 customers examined and 11 bought "Soft-Textured Genuine Irish Linen Handkerchiefs; Special, 3 for 50 cents." Simultaneously six customers examined and two bought "Nose Rags, 3 for 25 cents." Displayed on adjacent counters, the two piles of merchandise were from the same consignment. Commented a salesman in the Chicago department store which conducted the experiment: "People don't examine the quality of what they buy."

Shown under its original title, the motion picture version of *The Admirable Crichton* was a box office failure; rechristened *Male and Female* it was a huge success. That was in the silent cinema days and the experience helped teach Hollywood a lesson which it has observed ever since, with the result that *Moby Dick* became *The Sea Beast; Anna Karenina* was renamed *Love; The Jewels of the Madonna* was shown as *Sin;* and *La Tosca* as *The Song of Hate.*

In the June, 1946 *Coronet,* Walter Winchell was quoted as follows: "A perfume called 'Lady' for some reason couldn't catch on; then suddenly it became a best seller. Its makers had changed its name to 'Hussy.' " In the August, 1943 issue of the same magazine, Dr. W. E. Farbstein wrote under the heading, "More Dignity," as follows:

"The 'numbah plee-eeze' girls of an Illinois telephone company have received a titular raise from operators to the awesome 'secretaries of communication.'

"Proverbial ice-man stories are likely to chill under the title several Midwest companies have given their frozen water carriers—they're 'ice attendants.'

"Farewell to the soda jerks of an Ohio town now rated, if you please, as fountaineers.

"Tulsans hope to disguise their municipal dog catcher under the less ominous 'city humane officer.'

"Will the candy-striped pole of the barber shop quartet be able to live up to the elevated 'chirotonsor' which Los Angeles barbers are asking to be called?

"Milwaukee hod carriers move up the ladder of dignity with their recent designation as 'mason laborers.'

"And ironically apropos is the Vichy ragman's new name—'city salvager.' " [1]

The tendency to invest the supposed lowly vocations with dignity has been traced to the early days of the republic when the smallest shopkeepers began calling their places "stores," a word reserved in Mother England for large establishments. With the comparatively recent success of real estate agents in establishing the loftier designation of "realtor" for themselves, some insurance agents tried, with not too much luck, to become "insurors" and some furniture dealers insisted they are "furnitors." Mixed has been the fortune of the undertakers who have pretty generally succeeded in getting themselves called "morticians" and to persuade the bereaved to purchase caskets, cases, or slumber-cots instead of coffins (a word which dates from at least as early as 1525). In September, 1917 about 200 eminent members of the embalming profession banded together to promote such creations as limousine for mourners' coach, funeral home or funeral parlor for undertaking establishment, and negligee for shroud. A few have advertised themselves as "sanitarians," and an occasional "mortuary consultant" or "funeral counselor" has appeared. To date, however, no "obsequial engineer" has offered his services, but the *Engineering News-Record,* publication of the original type of engineers, used to devote a weekly column to uninvited invaders of their craft.

[1] Reprinted from August, 1943, *Coronet.* Copyright, 1943, by Esquire, Inc.

A "favorite" was the bedding manufacturer who became first a mattress-engineer and then a sleep-engineer.

"Beauticians" in their "shoppes" and white-uniformed "cosmetologists" now are familiar successors to the hairdressers of mother's girlhood days. In 1928 the president of the National Fertilizers Association wanted to change the group's name to the National Association of Plant Food Manufacturers. In 1940, to add dignity to their work, members of the International Brotherhood of Red Caps changed their name to United Transport Service Employes of America. Garbage men and ash men have become sanitary engineers and in Pasadena they work for the Table Waste Disposal Department. Some bartenders today are mixologists; there are candy making "studios" and "collection correspondents" instead of "bill collectors." How careful a newspaperman must be in keeping up with the occupational terminology was indicated by the late Howard Vincent O'Brien in his Dec. 20, 1943 "All Things Considered" column in the Chicago *Daily News* as follows:

I have a singular talent for putting my foot in it. The other day I wrote an innocuous piece about a speech made by a financier before a convention of bookkeepers. It was a nice piece, I thought—quite flattering to the speaker.

But today comes a sizzling letter from the managing director of the Controllers' Institute of America. It ends with this stinging rebuke:

"The address was delivered before the annual meeting of this Institute at the Waldorf-Astoria Hotel in New York City, which was attended by 1,500 controllers and financial officers of the larger corporations of the United States. *They are distinctly not bookkeepers.*"

QUANDARY

I should like to apologize to Mr. Arthur R. Tucker, managing director of the Controllers' Institute of America. Obviously, his 1,500 controllers and what-nots must be pretty important people or they wouldn't be eating at the Waldorf. But if I apologize for calling them "bookkeepers," I'll make the bookkeepers sore. And there are a lot more than 1,500 of them.

This is a quandary, indeed.

The plain fact is: I'm behind the times. I haven't caught up with progress. To me, a plumber is a plumber—not a sanitary engineer. It's hard for me to think of an undertaker as a mortician; and I'm as averse to calling a person who makes permanents a beautician as I am to calling newspapermen, journalists.

VERBAL IDIOCY

In fact, if I could get newspapermen to consent to it, I should like to have columnists called newspapermen.

I'm sorry that the controllers and the money-men of our large corporations should be hurt at my calling them "bookkeepers." No offense was meant, since I have the highest regard for anybody who can keep books. And I really have no clear idea of what a controller or a finance officer is. I don't even know the difference between an auditor and an accountant.

I am one of those to whom an adding machine by any other name would smell as sweet. And language doesn't make much sense any more. It was bad enough when we had streamlined flatirons. Now I learn from the radio we have the verbal idiocy of a "high fidelity" cigarette. . . .

Let anyone inclined to believe that it is only laborers and lowly entrepreneurs who seek greater dignity through a change of title pause to reflect on how many employees of large corporations and businesses, who formerly were called something else, now are known as vice presidents.

As any parent knows, if full veto power is allowed both parties, selecting a name for a baby is no easy task despite the thousands of potential choices. "I think Ralph would be nice," ventures the mama-to-be. "The kid next door was named Ralph but we all called him Stinky, and he deserved it," snorts her spouse, "I wouldn't give a dog that name." And that is exactly the way each reacts to a considerable number of the others' suggestions: because of childhood associations they are inacceptable. As a result one in 20 boys is named William or John with James, George, Charles, Harold, Robert, Edward, Joseph, and Arthur close behind. For every obnoxious Bill one knows, there was an admirable Willie to counteract his memory, so the name is acceptable. Comparable in popularity for girls, and for the same reasons, are Mary, Elizabeth, Margaret, and Helen.

In "Choosing Names for Babies," in the December, 1940 *Rotarian*, James F. Scheer quoted Prof. William E. Walton, University of Nebraska psychologist, as follows: "The name which a child is given at his birth may be a determining factor in his development of personality, acquisition of friends, and, in all probability, his success or failure in life. Odd-sounding names and those with ambiguous meanings may handicap him throughout his entire life. A harmless name like Ima Virginia Bird provides at least the partial answer to why a person with such a name quite easily develops an inferiority complex."

Scheer warned against such "atrocities" as Pete and Repeat, Kate and Duplicate, Max and Climax for twins. Both he and Hal Borland in "From Algernon to Zebulon," in the Aug. 20, 1939 New York *Times Magazine,* pointed out that, reasonably or not, some names which have been borne by famous men, through some association—perhaps in literature or on the stage—have fallen into disrepute. Among them are Percival, Reginald, Clarence, Chauncey, Aloysius, Arbuthnot, Fauntleroy, and Marmaduke.

In Buenos Aires in 1943 a court ruled that parents have no right to give their children absurd names and inflicted fines on parents who named theirs Zoroaster and Jupiter, at the same time, however, letting off two who named theirs Floreal and Oreste. In Astoria, N.Y., in early 1943, Mr. and Mrs. Joseph Mittel were forced, because of the public clamor that resulted, to rename their seventh child Theodore Roosevelt instead of Adolf Hitler, their original choice. Pleading as much innocence as if he had picked Napoleon Bonaparte or Julius Caesar, Mittel commented: "The papers have fixed things now, all right. My wife can't get a job. Some outfit is trying to take my kids away from me. They're telling us we have to move into a place with another bedroom, and with windows in all the rooms. They don't tell us how to do this on $14 a week."

Every playwright and novelist knows the importance of selecting the right kind of names for his characters. Several, including John Bunyan, in *Pilgrim's Progress,* Charles Dickens, and the comic opera team, Gilbert and Sullivan, made it virtually impossible for anyone to misunderstand the type of person they intended each brainchild to be. "Alexander Throttlebottom" seemed to fit exactly the burlesqued vice president in the George S. Kaufman, Morris Ryskind, and Ira Gershwin musical, *Of Thee I Sing.* A more dignified name would have spoiled the caricature. George Jean Nathan, veteran dramatic critic, wrote in *The World in False Face* (Knopf, 1923): "The theory that a rose by any other name would smell as sweet is open to challenge. On this we have ample proof from the experiments in laboratory psychology. Play 'The Prisoner of Zenda' exactly as Anthony Hope wrote it, but give the characters Yiddish names, and observe the effect. Or play 'Uncle Tom's Cabin' precisely as it was written, merely changing the various names to O'Brien, Fitzpatrick, and Murphy, and sit back and listen. Write the finest romantic play you can and christen your hero Sigmund Dinkelblatz and see what happens. What would have befallen the beauty of Lillian Russell had her name been Lulu Lachenschnitzl? And how much of a matinee idol would John Barrymore remain if he were to change his name to Mischa Woodel?"

Hollywood stars and their mentors certainly agree with this criticism. So, Etienne Jacques Pelliser de Bujac becomes Bruce Cabot, and not just so the name will fit in the marquee lights. William C. Goebel would fit lights and headlines, but Clark Gable is more attractive. Likewise, Ben Kulbelsky is not so good as Jack Benny and John F. Sullivan is inferior to Fred Allen. The list of popular stars of screen and radio who have adopted professional names is lengthy. A few more examples: Claude M. Duckenfield became W. C. Field; Frederick Ernest McIntyre Bickel became Fredric March; Phyllis Isley became Jennifer Jones; Constance Ockelman became Veronica Lake; Charles S. Thornstein became Charlie Chaplin; Leonard Slye became Roy Rogers; Maria Margharita Guadalalupe Catillo Boada became simply Margo.

In only one branch of the entertainment world has it been profitable to have a foreign-sounding name. That, of course, is the field of music. As Joe Benton, a southern Illinois tenor failed to catch on; as Giuseppe Bentonelli he became a Civic and Metropolitan opera star. It has been comparatively recently that the United States has stopped importing European musical talent and feeling inferior in cultural attainment. Motion pictures are an American invention and so from the start Northern European and especially British names have been preferred.

The same also is true in most other branches of American economic life. Some Jews change their names to help them escape the bad effects of anti-Semitism. Others anglicize them to make them easier to spell and pronounce by English-speaking Americans. Thus, the Greek Papademetracopoulos becomes Poulos; the Hungarian Gyaliu goes to court for permission to call himself Lee; the Finnish Glkhhyson chooses Carlson; the Bohemian Srb adds a couple of vowels to become Sarbo, and the German Von Lansschaffschausen drops a syllable or two so as to be Lanschafen. From the American Council on Education's *Intergroup Relations in Teaching Materials,* published in 1949, comes the following:

"A subtle but effective way to instill in students an inadequate conception of Americanism, and to make many children of foreign extraction squirm with discomfort and self distrust, is to assign exclusively such names as Jones, Smith, Brown and Evans to characters in the stories they read.

"Take a typical third grade reader. In the story it tells, 'Miss Lee is the teacher (teachers and those in authority almost always have this type of name); other characters are David Hill, Mary Field, Bill Field, Ruth Hill, Mr. Boyd (the principal), Miss Cook (the new teacher), Tom White, Patty and Mr. Brown.'" Occasionally, the study explains, a reader will "go so far afield as to use Mr. McLeod, Sandy and Angie, and Mr. Kelso, but they are soon back with Todds, Hoopers and Wheelers."

Even more serious, to parents who want their children to get a more democratic education, is "the tendency to use only 'soundly American' names . . . particularly evident in the early grade readers, the very place where the impression may be lastingly made, that Smith is more American than Bolinski or Gerardo." The Writers' War board deplored the same tendency in almost all media of communication (see page 41.)

It is not difficult to imagine what one's business or political enemies can make of it if one's initials are N.U.T. or R.A.T. Some whose parents have been thoughtless, however, may attempt to "make the best of it" by taking full advantage of the carelessness. Thus, Mary Hoar changed the spelling of her first name to Merry; some Shysters and Skinners have become lawyers; and there have been dentists named Yankum and doctors named Aiken. Bunyan and Swallum are druggists in Goldfield, Iowa.

Such proper names, and many others, may be considered amusing; they may suggest stereotyped impressions of their possessors, but they are not taboo in so-called polite society as are many common nouns and adjectives (see pages 224 to 226). Why some of these, such as the English "bloody," became hush-hush it is difficult to determine. In the United States, however, it is clear that the most interdicted words are those which relate to the genito-urinary and gastro-intestinal tracts, and, to a much lesser extent, to the deity. Both centuries' old Anglo-Saxon words and modern scientific terms must be avoided.

It is not, naturally, the words themselves that are important; rather, it is what they stand for, and in our culture bodily functions, especially evacuation and sex, are not proper topics of conversation, presumably to control their misuse. It is really sex which is the object of the taboo, the old idea being that the longer you can keep children ignorant or everyone from talking, the greater the chance that virginity and monogamy will be protected. The excretory functions are forbidden topics because of their close association physically with the sexual organs.

Circumlocutions

The way to get around these "shalt nots" linguistically is by circumlocution—roundaboutness in speech. Thus, what is concealed socially can be mentioned by a different word or series of words. Everyone knows what is meant but a sense of security is maintained for having not broken the taboo directly. So legs become limbs; breasts become bosoms; pregnant becomes delicate or interesting condition; a whore becomes a prostitute and a whore house becomes a house of ill repute; rape becomes attack or statutory offense; syphilis and gonorrhea become social diseases; feminine underwear becomes unmentionables. As times change so do the circumlocutions to indicate either greater frankness in recognizing the "facts of life" or the contrary. What originally was a circumlocution may continue in the slanguage as an innocent expression, as "for crying out loud," recent synonym for "for Christ's sake." At all times the codes of different groups differ and any person concerned with his own reputation observes the taboos of whomever he is with. One of the surest ways to fail as a moulder of public opinion is to use language considered improper by the audience which one is attempting to influence.

Of considerable value to the propagandist of any cause is the capacity to use those forms of circumlocution known as *euphemism* (calling bad things good) and *cacophemism* (calling good things bad). In *The Wonder of Words* (D. Appleton-Century, 1938), Isaac Goldberg stressed the importance of euphemism partly as follows:

"Euphemisms abound on every side, so thickly we forget they are there. When a shop calls itself a *shoppe* it is employing what might be called orthographic euphemism; the archaic spelling seems to lend dignity or quaintness, as the case may be. When a firm names its wares 'Good Luck' products, it is either trading upon the suggestiveness of the words, or is indulging in a private superstition as to their commercial efficacy. When the manufacturer of Pig's Pancreas was advised to change that name to pepsin gum, he yielded to a very sensible suggestion. Even to ourselves we seem more humane when we *liquidate* our enemies instead of killing them; when we place persons in *protective custody* instead of imprisoning them; when we tell an *untruth,* or a *falsehood,* or a *fabrication,* instead of a downright *lie.*"

When the German army swarmed across the Polish frontier Sept. 1, 1939, Adolf Hitler called the invasion a "counteroffensive with pursuit." Rarely in any war does anyone ever retreat; rather he "withdraws to a better position." Rebels *assassinate* regular troops but are themselves *summarily executed.* The Japanese referred to their overrunning of China in 1937 as an *incident.* Domestically we say: *boom* instead of *inflation*; *recession* instead of *depression*; in the South *War Between the States* instead of *Civil War.* During the civil war in Spain, as a result of great pressure, the press associations stopped use of the descriptions Loyalists and fascists, substituting Republicans and Nationalists. Huey Long declared that if fascism comes to the United States it will come in the name of anti-fascism.

In an address, "Language and Human Welfare," July 26, 1947 at a Conference on Language in Human Relations sponsored by Northwestern University and the National Congress of Parents and Teachers at Evanston, Ill., the writer commented on the world situation—which hasn't changed much since—partly as follows:

"First, there is the undeniable effect of words spoken by our leaders. During the war, starting with the secret meeting off the coast of Newfoundland in August, 1941, of Winston Churchill and Franklin Delano Roosevelt, the periodic meetings of the leaders of the most important United Nations—the Big 2, 3 or 4—were of tremendous importance in their effect upon the morale of the entire world. Even the president's bitterest enemies approved of them, got a lift from them. This effect was achieved in considerable part because of the way in which the results of those conferences were publicized. No military secrets, of course, were divulged; but a breathlessly waiting world always was told that great decisions had been made: that FDR, Winnie, Uncle Joe and the Generalissimo had called a spade a spade, had met head on, had thrashed out their differences and had made progress. Franklin Delano Roosevelt exuded confidence. There were differences in viewpoint, he would report; serious ones, yes; but there was nothing insuperable. Franklin Delano Roosevelt accented, as we said—or rather as we sang—the positive, rather than the negative.

"How different have been the public announcements following every conference since Yalta, the last which FDR attended. It has been a singing of the blues; an invitation to, if not an insistence upon, pessimism.

"Note the stroke of semantic genius that went into calling the aid to Greece proposal the Truman Doctrine. The only previous doctrine known to American school boys and girls was the Monroe Doctrine which we all were brought up to believe was a good thing. Doctrine, from the public relations point of view, is a capital word; it is as good as Liberty League, or America First, or Americans for Democratic Action. Throughout the debate on the proposal, furthermore, the Doctrine was 'sold' as a relief plan for Greece. I heard Paul Porter, who headed a special commission to Greece, talk for one hour on it to the Chicago Council on Foreign Relations without once mentioning the fact that any of the money was to go for military supplies or assistance, and without once mentioning the fact that Turkey was to receive anything."

In retrospect it is clearer than it was then that an essentially military program was sold to the American Congress and people as a relief program. A year later an essentially relief program—the Marshall Plan—was put across as primarily a military program. The reason, of course, was that in the 12-months period public opinion had been conditioned. In 1947 it would not have supported a military program; in 1948 it had been sufficiently frightened by the Russians to back any proposal advertised as a way to stop the Kremlin.

Immediately calling the few words that Secretary of State George Marshall spoke June 5, 1947, to the Harvard University Alumni Association at Cambridge, Mass., a "plan" also was masterful semantically. Until Congress got to work many months later on the European Recovery Program, there was nothing but a mere statement of principle. To a nervous people, however, the word "plan" was a godsend. The majority of Americans wanted to believe that there was a plan, any plan, anything tangible.

Two other phrases which figured importantly in international political debate in the post-World War II period were "cold war" and "iron curtain," the former an example of euphemism, the latter of cacophemism. Despite the high wartime hopes of the American and other peoples of the world, almost immediately after the end of hostilities, as has happened so often throughout history, the victorious allies began to fall out, and there was a return to what always before had been called, by historians and political scientists at least, "power politics." That phrase, of course, suggests some degree of common guilt since power is the mutual objective. In war, cold or hot, it is traditional to consider the cause of one's own side entirely just and the other side's equally unjust.

"Iron curtain" has been traced to Paul Joseph Goebbels, but it was given world-wide currency March 5, 1946, at Fulton, Mo., by former British Prime Minister Winston Churchill who then proposed what within two years became an actuality—military alliance between the United States and the British Empire directed against the Soviet Union. The immediate reaction of a large segment of the American press and its readership was decidedly unfavorable, but as the mutual fear and suspicion between the U.S. and USSR became greater in succeeding months, the circumlocution "iron curtain" came to symbolize the abandonment by the Soviets of freedom of speech, religion, and assembly. Continuous use of the phrase perpetuated belief that Americans just didn't know what was going on in the Soviet Union and its closest neighbors, the satellite states. Actually, examination of American periodical literature in the postwar period probably would reveal that there was more written about the Soviet Union by experienced journalists who had been there than about almost any other nation in the world. The ignorance of Americans regarding other countries is notorious. Iron curtain hardly is the complete answer to why the average citizen is unable to discuss with any degree of knowledge conditions in Italy, India, Mexico, Brazil, Australia, or any place else including Russia.

Labels

The propaganda devices of "glittering generalities" and "name calling" were described in Chapter 4 (see pages 122 to 125). To discredit a person or idea the propagandist attaches a label to a disagreeable stereotype. In time the stereotype becomes dim but the term continues to be accepted as derogatory and invokes an unfavorable reaction, often vague and general rather than specific. In *The Virginian* (Macmillan, 1902) Owen Wister has his hero demand, "When you say that, smile," when another character calls him a dirty name. In similar fashion the effect of a great many terms depends upon the intention of their user or his manner. Such terms include wop, nigger, dago, hick, gringo, sheenie, kike, chink, bohunk, chinaman, frog, hun, boche, and red. When you hear one person call another "a dumb Swede" without the other's becoming angry, you may be certain the two are close friends. Sometimes, however, even a friend secretly resents a label, even though innocently used by another. In "Name Calling," in the June, 1944 *Survey Graphic,* Walter Kong told of the distaste with which Chinese-Americans hear themselves called Chinamen and, especially, Charlie. There once was, and maybe still is, an organization with a name something like Society for the Prevention of Calling Pullman Porters George. It had "screwball" emulators, too, including ones which recruited the Johns and the Fannys.

Phrase making often is aided and abetted by headline writers who, of necessity, must use short synonyms to fit the space available. "Cold War," "Iron Curtain," and "Fair Deal" were godsends for them. In other cases, the original was not much longer than the opprobrious substitute, as in the case of "child labor" bill which became "youth control" bill in unfriendly newspapers; "unemployment compensation" which became "idleness bill"; and "reorganization bill" which became "dictator bill." In the case of the last named, the proposal to consolidate federal agencies in the interest of efficiency and economy was bitterly condemned when it was proposed by Franklin Delano Roosevelt; virtually the same bill passed quietly without much opposition under Harry S. Truman, and when Herbert Hoover a few years later recommended even further streamlining, he was hailed as an outstanding elder statesman by the same persons who had screamed "red" or "fellow traveler" a decade earlier when his successor in the White House made the same proposal. Successful promulgation of the label "court packing bill" was largely responsible for defeating the Rooseveltian proposal to permit members of the United States Supreme Court to retire at the age of seventy and, in the event they did not do so, to appoint additional younger members to the court.

A rather optimistic, albeit sarcastic, comment on the practice of inventing deleterious political labels was the following column piece by Milburn P. Akers in the Sept. 10, 1949 Chicago *Sun-Times*:

CRYING "BOO" TOO OFTEN

Republicans continue in their penchant for word mongering. Statism is their latest coinage. John Foster Dulles, Republican, who will contest a New York senatorial seat with former Gov. Herbert Lehman, Democrat, contends that this is the issue: statism, a word he interprets as connoting all that is evil in American public affairs.

The word, an apparent successor to communism, socialism, the welfare state, and the host of others with which the GOP has tried unsuccessfully over the years to frighten the public, will now get its preliminary workout. If Sen. Dulles—senator by appointment of Gov. Dewey—is able to make effective use of the word, if he is able to make a majority of New York voters shudder and run for cover every time he utters the word, statism, whatever it may mean, will probably constitute the GOP's platform in 1952.

However, the GOP hasn't previously had much luck in such efforts. They over-worked the word regimentation until it was innocuous. They've done the same by communism, socialism, dictatorship and others. They've pitched each succeeding campaign on some such word; a word intended to frighten American voters.

That they have done so—that they've fought wholly negatively rather than affirmatively—probably explains their long series of defeats.

What the Grand Old Party needs is an idea, not a word.

Back in the days of Mark Hanna they had an idea. But it took more than a word to express it. They championed the full dinner pail. Of course, they'd shy away from that one now. It's almost synonymous, in meaning, with the welfare state. It sounds too much as though its advocates were concerned over the welfare of the working man.

* * *

Ideas, not words intended to be derogatory of ideas, have won elections: ideas such as 54–40, or fight; don't change horses in the middle of the stream; he kept us out of war, and a host of others. But all of those ideas stated or implied action; action that would meet problems of the day.

Statism, as used by Sen. Dulles, implies no action. It implies only opposition; it is merely an epithet. And it isn't even a good epithet.

If such words as regimentation, communism, the welfare state, socialism and dictatorship failed to make the public run for cover, it is doubtful if any one will shudder when the Hon. John Foster Dulles and other GOP orators thunder "statism" from the hustings. Some day the GOP may cease acting the part of the small boy who, jumping from behind the bush, yells boo at passersby.

When it does, when it substitutes ideas for epithets, it may win an election, for a change.

By contrast with the examples so far given there are other words which have become less opprobious with the passage of time and, of course, changing of conditions. One such is "socialism." Less than a generation ago it was considered as damaging a label as "communism." Among the factors accounting for the change was the personality of the long-time leader of the American Socialist party, Norman Thomas, a retired minister who used perfect English with outstanding oratorical flourishes and had excellent table manners. As he got around he destroyed the stereotype of the long-haired soapbox crackpot. More important, however, was the fact that as the early war clouds began to gather, pacifism became the most important plank in the native Socialist platform. People couldn't be very frightened at others dedicated to the Gandhi principle of nonviolence and passive resistance. During World War I there was an orgy of persecution of pacifists and conscientious objectors who were called slackers and sent to federal penitentiaries. During World War II no one feared or paid much attention to their counterparts who obtained comparatively fair and easy treatment. "Communism" has replaced "socialism" as the label to discredit anything which it is hoped to prove is the antithesis of "democracy," "rugged individualism" and/or "free enterprise," popular synonyms for American capitalism.

In its extreme and distorted usage communism has become synonymous with any kind of government activity of which its user disapproves. From one standpoint anything government does is socialism or communism—the public schools, streets, parks, army and navy, police, fire department, and so forth—and many times voters at the polls have approved nationalization (another "smear" word when applied to something one opposes) of a public utility such as the water works or transportation system. Language is the tool with which stereotypes are perpetuated and scapegoats created. Once the word has acquired an unfavorable connotation it can be used promiscuously with evil effect, and the victims of such propagandizing, eager to find "easy package" answers to complicated problems, are happy for the mental shortcuts.

The same service is provided by the *proverb* and the *slogan*. In primitive societies, where the range of opinion is narrow, the former is the language form which most clearly reflects social values. Proverbs help preserve the group's "practical wisdom" and are quoted to prevent expression of heretical ideas. They flourish in more or less static societies in which social judgments are similar, but disappear or become ineffective in complex, rapidly changing cultures. In democracies they have the same effect as aphorisms by dead heroes in times of national crisis as they are reminiscent of the supposed reasons why "the good old days" were so good. Like the stereotypes they are unreliable clues to reality. It often, for instance, is not true that "where there's smoke there's fire," or that "the truth is somewhere between the two extremes," or that "where there's a will there's a way." Use of proverbs in modern United States is generally limited to "wisecracking" after an event, when one may remark, "haste makes waste," or "too many cooks spoil the broth," or, its opposite, "two heads are better than one."

More important in the formation of public opinion today is the slogan, which originally meant a Scotch Highland war cry but now is defined as the rallying cry for any group—business, political, reform civic, fraternal, or otherwise—to advertise its purposes and create a favorable impression. A slogan to be effective must be simple to understand, easy to remember, and pleasant to repeat. It must define a situation or problem unmistakably in the interest of its promoters. Among the best in recent political history have been "full dinner pail," "kept us out of war," "back to normalcy," "New Deal," "have you had enough?" and "Fair Deal." Immortal are "Liberté, egalité, fraternité," "54–40 or fight," "remember the Alamo," "remember the Maine," "remember Pearl Harbor."

Similar in effect is the aphorism which becomes used for sloganistic purposes: "don't give up the ship," "I only regret that I have but one life to lose for my country," "we have just begun to fight," "damn the torpedoes, go ahead," "you may fire when ready, Gridley," "Lafayette, we are here," and (negatively) "the public be damned," and "rum, romanism and rebellion."

Although slogans are most frequent and effective on a nation-wide scale during political campaigns and wars, their daily use by advertisers is familiar: "eventually, why not now?" "ask the man who owns one," "watch the Fords go by," "when better cars are built, Buick will build them," "it floats," "Atlas Prager; got it? Atlas Prager, get it," "it's toasted," "something new has been added," "they're milder," "the skin you love to touch," "the beer that made Milwaukee famous," and so forth.

There have been numerous experiments, by pollsters and social scientists, to test the effectiveness of proverbs, slogans and catch phrases. Typical was the questionnaire answered by 218 University of Washington students as reported by Selden C. Menefee in the January, 1938 *American Journal of Sociology*. Whereas 42 per cent agreed with the famous epitome of Voltaire's thinking, "I may not agree with what you say, but I will defend with my life your right to say it," only 16 per cent agreed with the rewritten version, "One should face death rather than allow any person to be denied freedom of expression." A heavy majority, 72 per cent, agreed with the super-patriotic, "We must demand allegiance to the American flag, and the traditions of the founding fathers for which it stands," but the favorable responses dropped to 47 per cent when the flag-waving was emasculated to read, "We should require people to respect the flag and abide by the political philosophy of the pioneer colonists in this country." Similar results were obtained for numerous other paired statements, one including stereotypes and the other excluding them as much as possible.

Word Magic

Modern mothers are not so inclined as their grandmothers to wash a child's mouth out with soapsuds after he has spoken a naughty word. To adults administering such punishment, the act in most cases was just that: punishment. In others, however, and probably most always as far as the child was concerned, it was more than symbolic. Rather, the cleansing act was necessary ritualistically to cleanse the youngster of sin, to prevent reprisals from a wrathful deity.

Primitive people, the anthropologists and philologists assert, put great stock in chants and incantations, curses and blessings. Some of them believed that their real names must be kept secret lest enemies, learning them, cause injury similar to those they could inflict if in possession of strands of hair, nail pairings, or possessions of their victims. In such cases words were not merely symbols. They had the power to kill as effectively as an Evil Eye, or they could save as efficiently as the exorcist's commands to demons in possession.

Ernest Cassirer's theme in *Language and Myth* (Harper, 1946) is that a fundamental assumption of myth making is that name and essence have internal relations to each other; that, in fact, the name *is* the essence of the subject. "In the beginning was the Word and the Word was with God, and the Word was God," summarized the belief of many early men in attempting to solve the riddle of the origin of things. The folklore of centuries ago is full of tales in which magic is performed through knowledge of the proper words to be spoken on occasion. Ali Baba, for instance, caused the door in the mountain to open by saying "open sesame" as he had overheard the forty thieves say it. The princess bested Rumpelstiltskin by learning his name. "Speak of the devil and he appears" is of ancient origin, and helpful genii were summoned to one's aid as often by spoken word as by rubbing a lamp or performing some other magical act. Among the South Sea islanders in comparatively recent times there were many magical words.

Wrote Stuart Chase in *The Tyranny of Words* (Harcourt, Brace, 1938): "Word magic is common to all primitive peoples. In a certain West African tribe, before setting up housekeeping it is highly desirable to obtain a Sampa. A Sampa is a prayer written in old magic letters which evil spirits are most likely to understand. It can be purchased at any wizard's for a few cowrie shells. He makes it while you wait. Into a calabash he puts a bit of clay, a feather, some twigs of straw, or whatever strikes his fancy and over it chants a spell. Hindu parents who lose a first child by sickness may name the second some such term as 'dunghill' on the theory that the gods who recognize people only by their names will not bother to waste a curse on such a lowly creature. What is a curse itself but a word winged for carrying physical harm? Frazer gives many examples of word taboos to show the universality of the practice. When a New Zealand chief who was called 'Wai,' the word for 'water,' died, a new name for water had to be found. To cast a spell on a man's name was frequently considered as effective as casting it on his person. Names were therefore closely guarded. According to Dr. J. P. Harrington of the Smithsonian Institution, a terror of the dead was so intense among American Indians that their names were not spoken aloud. Since the dead commonly bore names like 'Blue Reindeer' or 'Strong Bow' relatives and friends after the funeral were forced to invent new words for common objects like reindeer and bow, or at least to change the word a little. This brand of magic inevitably resulted in a welter of different names for the same object, and helped to create a babel of more than 100 languages spoken by American Indians. How many trivial wars resulted from the babel Dr. Harrington does not attempt to compute. The more wars, the more dead, the more new names, the more dialects, the more 'foreigners,' the more wars, the more dead . . ."

It would be pleasant to be able to write that all such unscientific nonsense has disappeared from the modern world, that this section properly belongs in the chapter on superstitions. Unfortunately, however, sometimes consciously but more often unconsciously, twentieth-century man often is circumspect in his word usage for fear of supernatural reprisals. More frequently he acts as though words in themselves had power to determine human affairs. During the San Francisco conference in 1945 to prepare the United Nations charter, for instance, there was endless haggling over terms. True it is that different combinations of words mean different things, but there was almost childlike faith that if the proper combination could be found peace would be assured; if not there would be another war. Experiment should have taught the participating nations that not the words of a treaty but the spirit behind it is what is important. There was nothing structurally wrong with the League of Nations; what was lacking was the will to utilize it so as to make it work. No law of any kind—local, state, national, or international—is any stronger than the public opinion behind it. Americans certainly should have learned that as a result of the fiasco of their Noble Experiment with prohibition. If the will to make it work exists, even the worst constitution is good enough. If the will to make it work does not exist, even the most perfect machinery will fail.

Akin to word magic is belief in numerology and in prophecy as indicated by magic numbers (see pages 244 to 246).

"Like everything that is French, our language is always logical. But this English! Ah I know it; but I do not understand it. . . . What a language!"

So exclaimed a French visitor, Jules Ravel, to the United States as related in the Contributor's club in the April, 1930 *Atlantic Monthly*. And what was the Frenchman's trouble? Well, for example, there was the word "fast." As summarized by *Reader's Digest* in its February, 1938, issue: "A horse was fast when he was tied to a hitching post. The animal was also fast under exactly diametric circumstances— when he was running away. A woman was fast if she smoked cigarettes. A color was fast if it didn't fade. To fast was to go without food. Et cetera."

And again, in M. Ravel's words: "One must hear first and then remember word for word. I remember reading a description of a view from a mountain top. It said that from where the man stood he could overlook the whole valley. I knew but one meaning for 'overlook.' You overlook something you forget to pack up—your opera hat, perhaps. Or you ignore something. But here was a man overlooking a whole valley! There it was, spread out at his feet; and yet he overlooked it. In other words, as I thought, he said he could ignore it. But why should he want to ignore it?"

Such criticisms by foreigners today are greeted by most Americans with good humored sympathetic snickers or outright laughter—at themselves rather than at the perplexed visitor. Such an attitude, however, is of comparatively recent origin. Any middle-aged American can remember well one effect of a couple of centuries of "ragging" by English critics of American speech: continuous but generally futile attempts by their school teachers to get them to avoid words or usages not approved by the best dictionaries. Now that the United States has taken over world leadership from the British, the inferiority feeling has disappeared and, in our opinion, it is the stuffy Old Worlders who are "off the beam" for insisting that an elevator is a lift, that a shoe is a boot or that a corset is a stay. Nevertheless, although the old "purists" have been put "under the table" by the more liberal philologists and other language authorities, the problem remains of how peoples all over the world ever are to communicate with each other if a halt is not called to new word coinage at which Americans perhaps have become more adept than any other people throughout history. On more than one occasion the translators at the United Nations—whose ability is a cause of amazement on the part of anyone observing them—have been stumped because certain words in one language have no exact counterpart in another. Adlai Stevenson, later governor of Illinois, once caused great consternation by using the expression "a pork barrel floating on a cloud," which the translators into Chinese, Russian, French, and Spanish said they just could not make meaningful in other languages. When statesmen are talking face to face the difficulties are easier to overcome than when communication is by means of written diplomatic mumbo jumbo, but they are by no means eliminated. And in addition to the national leaders there are the two billion citizens of the world who speak a total of 1,700 different languages.

Consciousness of the problem is by no means new. About 300 different proposals have been made for a synthetic universal language, among the most important (together with their dates of origin) being the following: Volapuk (1880); Esperanto (1887); Idiom Neural (1898); Latin without inflexions (1903); Ido (1907); Interlingua (1908); Occidental (1922); and Novial (1928). Despite the efforts of the International Auxiliary Language Association, which came into existence in 1924, not much progress was made until World War II and none of the universal languages recruited a sizable number of recruits. In 1943, however, in a much-quoted international telephone conversation, the Soviet ambassador to the United States, Maxim Litvinoff, and his wife used Basic English, one of the best descriptions of which is contained in *Basic English and Its Uses* (Norton, 1943) by Prof. Ivor Richards of Harvard University, co-founder with Prof. C. K. Ogden of Cambridge University, England, of the Association and co-author with him of one of the pioneer books on semantics, *The Meaning of Meaning* (Harcourt, Brace, 1923).

Further impetus was given Basic English in 1943 by Winston Churchill in a lecture at Harvard. There followed a rash of articles on the chances that the system, involving 850 simple English words, including only 18 verbs, has of becoming "the answer" to the problem of how to reduce international babel to mutual understanding. The following press association article was a fair summary of the main features of Basic English:

Basic English has leaped into prominence in this country since Commissar Litvinoff used it in a trans-Atlantic telephone conversation with his wife. It's designed as a sort of easy medium of conversation for all nationalities. The following explains it.

Washington, Dec. 19.—(U.P.)—The writing of this story is in Basic English, the new language of 850 words, which has the approval of many leaders in education.

If it sounds clumsy in the writing, that is because of the scarcity of words in the language. Basic English uses many words to tell the same idea that old languages tell in one word.

Prof. C. K. Ogden of London is the inventor of the language. He is of the belief that it will be in use soon in all countries of the earth.

Mme. Maxim Litvinoff, the woman the Soviet commissar is married to, is in approval of the language. H. G. Wells, the British story teller, is in approval. Many other leading men are in approval.

They are in the belief that Basic English will help unite the earth and keep its nations out of war.

The language is simple. It is put together of six kinds of words:

Operators—Words like come, get, give, keep, let, make, put and be.

Natural substances—Words like air, blood, butter, chalk, coal, copper, cork and cotton.

Necessary names—Words like act, additon, adjustment, agreement, amount and animal.

Common things—Words like angle, arch, arm, baby, bag, ball and basket.

Collectives—Words like approval, behavior, brass, bread, care, clothe and comfort.

Qualifiers—Words like able, angry, awake, black, boiling, bright and broken.

The language is to tell general ideas. It is not to tell specific things and so has to be used to describe foods (for instance) in this way:

A white root that makes the eyes water (onion).

A green plant food with a round heart (cabbage).

A sweet red root, used as food (beet).

A green-yellow berry with hair on the skin (gooseberry).

A cake rolled thin and cooked two times (cracker).

The language is lacking in grace. It is easy to learn. Prof. Ogden, Mme. Litvinoff and they who think the same way are of the belief that its lack of grace is not so important as its ease of learning and that it is useful now to the earth. In a few years they are of the belief that it will be more useful.

A favorite device of those wishing to evaluate the system is to translate some familiar piece of writing into Basic. The following re-writing of Lincoln's Gettysburg address was included in Lincoln Barnett's "Basic English: A Globalanguage," in the Oct. 18, 1943 *Life*:

"Eighty-seven years back, our fathers gave birth on this land to a new nation, designed to be free and given to the theory that all men are to their Maker equal. Now we are in the middle of a great war among ourselves, testing if that nation, or any nation so designed and given to such a purpose, may long go on. We are come together on a great fighting field of that war. We are come together to put by a part of that field as a last resting place for those who here gave their blood that that nation might go on. It is very right that we do this.

"But, in a deeper sense, it is not for us the living to give this field in their name to history. The true men, living and dead, who saw fighting here have so given it far past our power to do anything more or less. The earth will take little note and keep not long in memory what we say here, but it will ever keep in memory what they did here. It is for us the living, though, to give ourselves up here to the uncompleted work which they have so far so highly undertaken. It is for us to be here given over to the great work still before us—that from the respected dead we may take greater belief in that cause for which they gave the last full measure of belief—that we here make it our high purpose that these dead will not have given their all for nothing— that this nation, under God, will have a new free birth—and that government of all, by all, and for all will not come to end on earth."

There is no doubt that the Basic version of Lincoln's immortal address retains the thought of the original. That it loses much of the great emotional appeal in revision also is obvious. Thus, the question is pertinent as to whether Basic or any other universal language ever could supply more than the simplest needs of travelers who have become separated from their interpreters. Even though thoroughly familiar with Basic, a Frenchman, or a German, or a Portuguese would catch more of the real spirit of the Gettysburg address through a good translation into his own language. Maybe it makes little or no difference whether great poetry or literature ever is translated. The strength of much speaking and writing in politics, economics, and other fields, however, also depends upon emotionalism; and it isn't possible to condemn all emotionalism as evil. Great messages often are presented in great word combinations. Certainly the original of the Gettysburg address is in the simplest of regular English; it was the way Lincoln put his words together, more than the thought they expressed, that has caused two generations of school children actually to enjoy reciting "Four score and seven years ago."

A further, more important question concerning Basic and all other universal languages is this: how long would they remain adequate after being adopted by the entire 2 billion? Language is a cultural product. It changes with a culture, and there is no way to stop its changing except to maintain a static society. That the time to attempt that, if it ever existed, is long since past, all but a negligible minority must agree. Only a cursory study of what has happened to English on the North American continent is sufficient to establish the point that only a comparatively short space of time is required to make it difficult for persons who theoretically speak the same language to understand each other easily. Changes in the written language are slower, so English and Americans can continue to communicate in writing without too much trouble, but the mere fact of the addition of several hundred or thousand (estimated at 5,000 in World War II years) new words annually widens the gulf of understanding. Today even Americans from different parts of the country, sometimes not too far distant from each other, encounter similar difficulty; and it is not all, or primarily, a matter of differences in pronunciation. Whenever a certain Englishman with a Welsh accent spoke, John Foster Dulles, American delegate to the United Nations, used to don earphones and listen to the French translation.

American, of course, is a case without historical parallel because of our polyglot makeup. Hardly had the settlers arrived in 1607 at Jamestown, Va., than they found it necessary to invent new words for new objects and experiences. From that time to this laymen have not waited for teachers and scholars to provide needed new words, carefully worked out from Latin, Greek, or other roots. Although it is possible to trace the origin of some words to outstanding Americans—including some presidents and other statesmen, but mostly novelists, newspaper writers, and radio commentators—tracing a vast majority of Americanisms of three centuries to their sources is an impossible task. The influence of the Indians and of all of the nationalities represented in the colonization of the New World is traceable: skunk, moose, hickory, hominy, persimmon, toboggan, wigwam, squaw, woodchuck, raccoon (Indian); adobe, burro, canyon, corral, coyote, sombrero, mustang, lasso, buckaroo, tomato, tobacco, canoe (Spanish and Mexican); boss, sleigh, snoop (Dutch); prairie, chowder, levee (French). There remain, however, hundreds of thousands of other words explainable only in the light of the circumstances bringing them into being. Specific credit for them can be assigned only with extreme difficulty.

In addition to newly coined or borrowed words there are the new usages of old words, and Americans, from whoever the occupant of the White House happens to be down, have a predilection for such adaptations. The following news item illustrates the point:

New York, Feb. 14—(AP)—President Roosevelt already has become the foremost coiner or popularizer of popular phrases among all American Presidents, according to a study completed by Wilfred J. Funk, lexicographer and publisher.

"With most of his second term ahead of him," Dr. Funk said in an interview Saturday, "the President should set a mark difficult for any successor to surpass. He and his aides have been unprecedentedly adept in crystallizing phrases that are quickly comprehensible, attach themselves to the memory easily and fit into headlines readily."

In his analysis the dictionary publisher listed "New Deal," "The Forgotten Man," "Modern Tories," "Economic Royalists," "Princes of Privilege," "Gold Hoarders," "Democratize Industry," "Off the Record," "Fireside Chat," "The More Abundant Life," "Pump Priming," "Brain Trust," "Quarantine of Nations," "Planned Economy," "Good Neighbor Policy," and the general alphabetizing of the functions of Government.

"An out-cropping of phrases traceable to the New Deal," he said, "include such expressions as 'The 59 Cent Dollar,' 'Soak the Rich,' 'Boondoggling,' 'Alphabet Soup,' and 'Packing the Court.'"

But the President must still take a back seat to Theodore Roosevelt, Dr. Funk said, in the coining or popularizing of expressions that "attract the attention of dictionary makers." Among them he listed "Trust-Busting," "Mollycoddle," "Square Deal," "Frazzle," "Nature-Faking," "Bull Moose," "Pussyfooting" and "Weasel Words."

"The former President Roosevelt invented a word as well as a phrase in his warning not to 'Chinafy' America while he was pleading for preparedness," said Dr. Funk. "Among his other famous expressions were 'The Strenuous Life,' 'Speak Softly but Carry a Big Stick,' 'Predatory Wealth,' 'Undesirable Citizens,' 'My Spear Knows No Brother' and 'We Stand at Armageddon and Battle for the Lord.'"

Dr. Funk cited Woodrow Wilson as "an outstanding phrase maker with his 'Watchful Waiting,' 'Too Proud to Fight' (subsequently revamped into the successful campaign slogan, 'He Kept Us Out of War'), 'Make the World Safe for Democracy,' 'Self-Determination of Nations' and 'The Fourteen Points.'

"Cleveland invented the whimsical phrase 'Innocuous Desuetude' and McKinley's Administration featured 'The Full Dinner Pail,'" said the publisher. "This idea was revived and enlarged years later by Hoover's

'A Chicken in Every Pot,' complemented by 'Two Cars in Every Garage.' This was before he predicted 'Grass will grow in streets.'

"Harding's popularity was enhanced considerably by his phrase 'Back to Normalcy.' Coolidge was a succinct speaker and more famous phrases might have been expected from him. But his best remembered was 'I Do Not Choose to Run.' "

Often phrases have had far-reaching powers to build up or destroy— more than they merited, Dr. Funk observed—but many in his list are meaningless or almost forgotten today, such as "Tippecanoe and Tyler, Too," "Rum, Romanism and Rebellion," and "Burn That Letter."

But one of the oldest in American history, Washington's warning against "Foreign Entanglements," he said, "has seemingly controlled our foreign policy to this day."
—*Christian Science Monitor,* Feb. 15, 1938

In addition to presidents there have been Washington Irving, James Fenimore Cooper, Edgar Allan Poe, Mark Twain, George Ade, Bill Nye, Ring Lardner, H. L. Mencken, Billy Rose, Walter Winchell, *Time, The New Yorker,* and other coiners and adapters.

Greater by far, however, than any other influence upon language growth and development has been sheer necessity as a result of the progress of science and invention and increasing specialization in business and the professions. A slight indication of the extent of such influences was contained in the following news story telling of the appearance of one of twenty volumes of a new dictionary:

Yankee commercial inventiveness, as well as American improvements of the English language, is reflected in the sixth section of the new dictionary of American English, which the University of Chicago is preparing to publish shortly.

The contributions of American business to the language of these United States range all the way from "country store" to "cut-throat" and "derby hat" in the newest installment of the dictionary, which starts with "corn pit" and ends with "dew."

The "country store" in sources studied by the compilers of the dictionary, had a poetic first mention in Freneau's poems (1795), when he wrote, "I, who, at least, have 40 in cash and in a country store might cut a dash."

"Crossroads store," another strictly American combination, crops up a little later in economic evolution, its first written appearance being traced to 1845.

"CROCKERY STORE" APPEARS

The age of specialization makes its appearance, according to the dictionary, with "crockery store" some 18 years later. Massett is credited with first writing the combination in "Drifting About" (1863) when he said, "I went with him to the office at about where Genella's crockery store now stands."

"Department store" shows up still later on the economic word calendar. Harper's magazine is credited with the first use of this strictly American combination in 1893. "Delicatessen" and "delicatessen store" appeared at the same time.

Some early American business words still in the news are "cut rate" (1872), "cutthroat" (1848), "dead-beat" (1881), "dead broke" (1852), "deadhead (1848), "defalcation" (1796), and "demoralize" (1806).

Direct mail advertising is recognized in the popularization of "cracker-jack," a popcorn confection, as an expression denoting something exceptionally fine or splendid and a person unusually smart or skillful. The word first appeared, according to the dictionary, in 1897.

"CURE ALL" DATES TO 1821

"Cure alls," which now occupies much attention of the Federal Trade Commission and business and advertising companies, dates back to 1821 as identifying a medicine or remedy.

Typical of style innovations of a strictly American origin is "derby hat," first identified in 1888 in the Pall Mall Gazette, which noted that "low felt hats—derby hats, as they are generally called in the United States—were universal." Seven years later the Century magazine commented that the girls were wearing "derbys" too, saying: "Among them were several Bluegrass girls in derby hats."

Sir William Craigie, co-editor of the famous Oxford English dictionary; James R. Hulbert, professor of English at the University of Chicago, and a trained staff of researchers are editing the new dictionary. Included are words of strictly American origin, slang and colloquial expressions and mutations of the mother tongue. The dictionary is expected to comprise 20 sections and will be completed in 1942.

—Chicago *Daily News,* Feb. 10, 1939

The fact that the Russians missed the impact of the Industrial Revolution during the nineteenth century is evident in the number of German and French scientific and industrial terms which they have incorporated into their own language.

There have been complaints against the jargons which have become characteristic of almost every phase of American life. They have not all come from patients unable to understand what their physicians try to tell them either. In "I Can't Quite Hear You, Doctor," in the March, 1946 *Harper's,* Joseph A. Brandt related the following experience:

"Yet so impenetrable is the language in which most scientists speak that not only does the layman fail to understand it, but other scientists often are puzzled by it. A zoologist once complained to me that he was at a loss to understand the terms used by a colleague of his, a physical scientist. A few days later I had occasion to bring up this question, obliquely, with the physical scientist himself. I was delighted as well as amused to find that he, too, felt that science was becoming so specialized that it was impossible for him to keep abreast of the other disciplines—and the science he mentioned as having the vocabulary most incomprehensible to him was zoology!"

From his experience as director of four publishing houses, Brandt wrote accusingly: "The higher learning in our country, despite brilliant exceptions, seems to have become a form of self-worship, a series of rites performed by a priesthood which has left its congregation to be served, so far as discernible leadership is concerned, solely by the politician." More plaintive was a businessman, Cyrus Eaton, who reported in the Spring, 1942 *Antioch Review* on his attendance at a meeting of university economists. "With the rest of the laymen," he wrote, "I spent the two days as a spectator on the sidelines of a game of linguistic football, and finally went home with no idea what the score was."

Answering in the Summer, 1942 issue of the same magazine, under the title, "The Professor Talks Back," Robert H. Lowie explained: "In contrast to the simpler primitive peoples, modern civilization rests on a far-reaching division of labor. This has led to spectacular achievements, but also to one lamentable result—a splitting up into many diverse segments of what ought to be a harmonious whole. . . . Naturally the task of understanding should not be made needlessly troublesome by verbal stumbling blocks, but these are trifling obstacles compared to the intricacy of modern life. How many of us understand the principles underlying such objects of daily use as the automobile and the radio? But it is not because the terms 'static,' 'differential,' and 'muffler' elude our comprehensions. It is because the things themselves are extraordinarily hard for any but the mechanically gifted and because few of us have the chance to watch the contrivances in the process of manufacture."

Nevertheless, others wondered with Dr. Frederik C. Redlich, Yale psychiatrist, "whether our system of education fulfills its function of teaching the population certain minimal requirements regarding health and disease," after examining the results of his study of 25 patients to whom 60 medical terms were presented. As revealed in the Winter, 1945 *Yale Journal of Biology and Medicine*, typical answers included: "a bone, way down your back" for spine; "pus that comes out of the spine" for spinal fluid; "blood poisoning, skin wounds cause it," for infection; "disease of the organs, not curable," for organic; and a number of similar "howlers."

Before two persons can discourse with comprehension they must have a common vocabulary. Unless one shares common interests, occupational, professional, recreational, or other, today it is becoming increasingly rare for such to occur. Each sport has its own jargon; devotees of whatever happens to be the vogue in "popular" music at the time are incomprehensible to any others; parents have difficulty knowing what their teen-aged sons and daughters are talking about when they resort to the "latest" which they use on their school mates. In every factory, office, school, club, social group, and family there are pet phrases and expressions understandable only to insiders. To use them fortifies the sense of belonging, the "we" feeling essential to group solidarity. To be ignorant of a group's jargon is a sure mark of the outsider just as their inability to pronounce "shibboleth" correctly was proof to the Gileadites that Ephraimites were trying to slip through their lines.

It is as hopeless as was King Canute's battle with the waves to attempt to check the enrichment of the American language, and the same is true of every other language in the world. A restless, imaginative, energetic people are bound to be inventive in their speech. Even the written English of a half century ago seems somewhat archaic today, and it will not be many more generations before the phraseology of the Declaration of Independence will seem positively primitive. The only hope for a universal language is such easy transportation and means of communication that peoples all over the world are in close touch with each other. The undesirable consequence of such internationalism may be standardization, but the great benefit, it is to be hoped, will be understanding and peace. A common language is more an effect than a cause of such a happy state. It would grow with and help strengthen One World.

Semantics

That the brotherhood of man will not be achieved, with or without world federation, until men learn to think and speak more clearly is the contention of the general semanticists, disciples of Count Alfred Korzybski who wrote *Science and Sanity* (International Non-Aristotelian Library Publishing Company, 1933) and in 1938 founded the Institute of General Semantics. Although some adherents sound like fanatical cultists, making lavish claims to possessing the answer to almost every ill, personal or public, their attacks upon illogical, fuzzy, absolutistic thinking are to be applauded. Regrettably as yet the new gospel has been spread to only a small number of the college educated.

Personal devil of the general semanticists is the ancient Greek philosopher, Aristotle. It seems like gross scapegoating to blame The Old Man (as they call him) for having invented scientific (or unscientific) absolutism. It *is* true that Aristotle was the first great elucidator. What to him and to those who followed him through many centuries was simplification is, in the light of modern knowledge, recognizable as dogmatic. Understandably, in the light of the state of verifiable science in his times, Aristotle stressed likenesses rather than differences. Showing the conscious or unconscious influence of the relativity movement, the general semanticists do the opposite.

Basic premises of the semanticists, according to one of their leaders, Wendell Johnson in *Peoples in Quandaries* (Harper, 1946) are (1) non-identity, (2) non-allness, and (3) self-reflexiveness of language and of the process of abstracting. There is no necessary connection between a word symbol and what it stands for, they insist; no one word can include all the features of a situation any more than a single map can include all the features it represents. Misevaluation comes from thinking that all things which externally appear to be alike are similar. Danger results from accepting the Aristotelian concept that black is black and white is white, with no grays, everything either good or bad, Aryan or non-Aryan, et cetera. The "et cetera" is especially sacred to the semanticists who use it to indicate the possibility of exceptions to virtually every statement even they can make. No two things ever are alike, they preach, and they make liberal use of such enumerations as pencil sub one, pencil sub two, pencil sub three, and so on. Failure to index, they say, leads to false generalizations, to stereotyped thinking. The higher the abstraction the further the retreat from reality. Extensional levels of experience can be verified by sensual observation. For instance, you can stick your finger into the frosting of a cake and take a lick. You could, however, says the semanticist, spend your lifetime in the Kremlin without finding a thing communistic. All you could find would be men, women, and objects to which the label could be applied. There are no scientific sensory tests to determine whether a man is a communist as one can determine whether a particular food is cake.

If it all seems rather difficult, obfuscation rather than clarification of its subject matter, words, the answer is: it *is* difficult. Entire college courses are necessary to rebuild the thinking processes of most students of semantics. The layman can, however, understand this much: the general semanticists expose the fallaciousness of glittering generalities (see pages 123 to 125) and name-calling (see pages 122 to 123). Thus they strike powerful blows against superstition and prejudice and in favor of scientific-mindedness. How extreme their claims can become, however, is illustrated by the following quotation from Johnson:

"Just what would you train a child to do in order to insure that he turn out to be an inefficient, confused and demoralized adult?

"One can answer this question at great length by writing an elaborate handbook and manual of stupidity, or one can answer it quite briefly and to the point, which is what we shall try to do. In order to insure that a child will become a maladjusted adult, he should be trained to confuse the levels of abstraction. So trained, he will indulge persistently in unconscious projection; he will over-generalize as a matter of course; his reactions will tend to be unconditional, stereotyped and undelayed; he will fail frequently to differentiate sufficiently between the past and present, between one situation, person or experience and another, and so will react similarly and thus inappropriately on quite different occasions. Being untrained in evaluation, he will tend to accept whatever is presented to him with sufficient show of authority—the authority of age, precedence, popularity, or financial prestige—and so will be prey to unscrupulous advertisers, self-interested journalists and institutionalized mountebankery of various kinds. He will attempt to solve his problems, of which he will have a great number, not by trying to state them clearly and by taking personal responsibility for obtaining reliable factual answers to his own well-hewn questions—but by trusting in a childish way the pills, platitudes and divers prescriptions of anyone whom he has been trained to regard as an authority. So doing, he will flounder and then confuse himself all the more by laying the blame for his misfortune more or less indiscriminately on everything except his own unconscious identifications. Give a child by such means a misleading map of the terrain of experience, teach him to confuse the map with the territory, and you will not have long to wait for frustration and demoralization to overtake him and make of life an instructive example of how not to administer the human heritage."

To accept the validity of this statement in its entirety would be tantamount to declaring that semantics makes psychiatry superfluous. It is difficult, however, to trace all cases of frustration which reach the mental hygienist's office to the causes which Johnson outlines. Likewise, it is possible to cite examples of those—perhaps a majority of all people—whose mental processes resemble rather closely those which the semanticists deplore, who are by no means frustrated. As a matter of fact, because they are the majority, they are considered the normal ones. That, the semanticists would say, is what's wrong with the world, and maybe that *is* the last word.

Wit and Humor

To relieve tension at crucial wartime cabinet meetings, President Abraham Lincoln frequently preceded or interrupted a discussion of some momentous matter to relate a funny story or read a selection from the writings of Artemus Ward (Charles F. Browne), most popular American humorist of the Civil War period.

The ability to tell and/or appreciate a joke has been a contributing factor to the success of many an influential leader, among the most notable recent examples being Franklin Delano Roosevelt. Aspiring after-dinner speakers are warned not to be "reminded" of humorous anecdotes whose applicability to the subject matter of the occasion is unclear, because the artificiality is bound to be detected. The "natural" good story teller, however, does not encounter much difficulty in becoming the "life" of almost any kind of party, and the witty public speaker holds the attention of his audience, through skillful turning of phrases, by making himself the butt of some of his own sallies, and by "turning the tables" on his hecklers.

People read funny stories, go to see comedies on either stage or screen, and listen to gagmen on the radio when in quest of entertainment. Even when their purpose in attending a lecture, or a political or other meeting is to seek enlightenment, however, they appreciate lightening of the serious by a bit of the humorous. Volumes have been written on why people laugh and on how to acquire the ability to make them do so; and there are numerous theories regarding the psychology of laughter and fun-making. The Freudians generally consider the "comic feeling" as being a sense of superiority to someone else who gets fooled, which implies that all laughter contains an element of hostility. Max Eastman, author of *Enjoyment of Laughter* (Simon, Schuster, 1936) contends that (1) something is funny only when all concerned are "in fun"; (2) when that situation exists there occurs a shift in values, with pleasant things still being pleasant and disagreeable things acquiring a pleasant emotional tone and causing a laugh; and (3) children are most often "in fun" but adults retain the ability in varying degrees.

Whether it is release from social restrictions or taboos or a way to gratify one's vanity, or to obtain vicarious pleasure or something else, laughter helps stimulate the sense-of-belonging or "we" feeling in any group. It is a frustrating experience not to be able to see the point of a joke at which everyone else is roaring. The speaker who succeeds in getting his audience to laugh knows he has established a uniform state of mind upon which he then can "go to work" to achieve a serious purpose. He also has proved himself "a good Joe," especially if he has "told one" on himself, so that his hearers are in a receptive mood toward him personally. Among the best public storytellers in this country have been William Jennings Bryan and William Howard Taft. The former endeared himself by cracks at his own stoutness, heavy appetite, and political defeats. The latter used to chuckle contagiously at his own jokes even before he told them, and the sight of his huge frame rocking started his listeners laughing in advance of his saying a word. A veteran labor organizer relates the anecdote of how Charles Schwab handled a hostile audience of strikers. "Met J. P. Morgan outside a confessional," Schwab said in essence. "The priest had disappeared and when I asked J. P. where he went, he answered, 'Well, if both of us told the truth, he's probably gone for the police.' " The roar which greeted the joke enabled Schwab, then head of the World War I shipping board, to proceed with his serious remarks.

Theodore Roosevelt's nimble wit usually enabled him to get the better of any hecklers. On only one occasion, it is related, did Teddy come off second best. That was when an obviously inebriated member of his audience kept loudly interrupting with, "I'm a Democrat. My father was a Democrat. My grandfather was a Democrat." Finally T. R. took cognizance of the disturbing element to question the logic of the familial political loyalty and concluded by asking his tormentor if his father and grandfather had been jackasses, would he want to be one. "No, in that case, I'd be a Republican," was the silencing reply.

Biographers include such anecdotes in their accounts as revelatory of the characters of their subjects. In addition to those which are verifiable there are also an abundance of apocyphral tales concerning any outstanding personage. Many of these continue to be told even when known to be untrue as regards those to whom originally attached because they are amusing regardless of the principals involved. Wit, which the dictionary says is "the power to perceive quickly and express clearly ideas that are unusual, striking and amusing," also has been called a way of telling the truth when society frowns upon more obvious ways: in other words, a form of circumlocution. Some witticisms have the form and effect of proverbs, as for example many of those of Benjamin Franklin, first real American humorist, under the pseudonym of Poor Richard: "Where there's marriage without love, there will be love without marriage," "God heals and the doctor takes the fee," "If you would keep your secret from an enemy, tell it not to a friend," and many others.

John Randolph's "Thank you" in reply to the man who told him, "I had the honor of passing your house this morning," Dorothy Parker's "How can they tell?" when informed that Calvin Coolidge had died, and innumerable other examples of clever repartee probably always will be understandable and amusing. Others, perhaps even including, "A modern young woman's bathing suit must be believed to be seen," are dated; that is, dependent for their success on their audience's knowledge of current situations which make them seem funny.

Every social group, including the family, has its jokes which are meaningless, or at least not especially amusing, to outsiders. Elaborate footnotes or glossaries are necessary to explain the puns in a Shakespearean play, and a few school boys and girls who laboriously consult them, laugh very hard at the conclusion of their labors. Ward's "High Handed Outrage at Utica" still can cause smiles but it doesn't seem so hilariously funny today as it apparently did to Lincoln and his contemporaries. The same is true of the witticisms and humorous stories of most of the other great humorists of the past, and, incredible as it may seem to those who devote hours listening to them, the same also doubtless will be true a generation hence or sooner as regards the wisecracking of Bob Hope, Fred Allen, Edgar Bergen and other contemporary funnymen.

There is, of course, a great and important difference between *humorists*, such as Ward, George Ade, Bill Nye, Mark Twain, Finley Peter Dunne, Dorothy Parker, Stephen Leacock, and others, and *comedians* of stage, screen and radio who are merely virtuosos in handling lines written for them by others. Much of what is considered their best is traceable to the famous, two centuries' old "Joe Miller's Joke Book." Originally printed in 1738 under the editorship of T. Reed and John Mootley, that fertile source contained 247 jokes; in subsequent editions the number has increased to several thousands. They have attained immortality because they deal with universal topics: husband and wife, mothers-in-law, children, barbers, doctors, women's desire to conceal their ages, city slickers and farmers' daughters, and eternal human weaknesses. In Pericles' Athens, they told this one: "Barber—How will you have your hair cut? Customer—In silence."

In "We Are What We Joke About," in the Sept. 3, 1939 New York *Times Magazine*, the late great Canadian humorist, Stephen Leacock, declared: "Let me hear the jokes of a nation and I will tell you what the people are like, how they are getting on and what is going to happen to them." He then illustrated why he believed that "one might reconstruct the reaction of the history of the United States on its humor during the past 40 or 50 years" with samples of jokes about boarding houses and landladies, automobiles, wartime regulations, disillusionment over the prospects of permanent peace, prohibition, the depression and the New Deal. Leacock wrote:

Has the subject of our humor really changed? No, not in its reality, but only in its latest embodiment. Mankind laughs at its troubles and jests at its oppressors. Children make fun of father, school boys laugh at their teacher, students at their professors and prisoners at their guards and turnkeys. Laughter is the last refuge of sorrow or oppression. Our new oppressions—Industrial Collapse, the War Danger and such—only step into the place of the old ones.

American humor has been called vigorous, exaggerated, satirical, hyperbolic, earthy, more savage than subtle, inclined toward the tall tale, absurd, and obscene. In other words, just what one would expect from a nation with the United States' cultural heritage. Sidney I. Pomerantz in "Newspaper Humor in the War of Independence," in the December, 1944 *Journalism Quarterly*, wrote that although unsophisticated and unpolished, Revolutionary wartime humor helped keep up colonial morale. "In newspapers, broadsides and almanacs," he wrote, "Revolutionary America found the anecdotes, jests, apt sayings, aphorisms, puns, paradoxes, conundrums, parodies in prose and verse, poetical satires and lively songs that lightened their wartime burdens."

It was, however, a sober period. Life was indeed earnest and literature was inclined to be decorous. Franklin, it has been written, was not considered suitable to attempt to compose the Declaration of Independence because of his record and reputation as a humorist. Washington Irving, in the early days of the republic, used the Dutch of a century earlier as the butts of his humor. It really wasn't until the period of Jackson that everyday humor showed the influence of the frontier, as part of the revolt against New England primness which put Old Hickory in the White House. From that day to this there hasn't been a presidential election campaign during which scurrilous jokes, labeled and recognized as such, in addition to others, equally as fallacious but put forward as truth, have not circulated. There have been all kinds about persons in the public eye, ranging from those suitable for polite mixed company to those which men whisper to each other in smoking rooms. Unless they are accepted as true they probably have the effect only of making those agreeing with their points feel good and angering those predisposed to disagree. Like the political cartoons, however, they may skillfully dramatize an argument and thus have a cumulative effect in a particular direction. For instance, the following was typical of the printable anti-Roosevelt jokes: "One friend asked another if he had seen the motion picture *Snow White and the Six Dwarfs*. 'You mean, seven dwarfs, don't you?' was the reply. 'Oh no,' the first declared, 'there were originally seven but Dopey is now in the White House.' "

From the other side, to ridicule what it considered unreasonable scapegoating of the president, his supporters originated jokes such as the following:

"A man awakened on his fiftieth birthday anniversary and was presented by his family with 50 $1 bills. As a present his employer gave him the day off, so he went to the race track and bet his $50 on a horse named 50–50. The animal led until a few feet from the finish when it dropped dead. 'Damn Roosevelt,' said the man as he tore up his tickets."

No American president ever has had what no king at one time could be without: an official court jester. At different times, however, there have been jesters at the court of American public opinion, popular pundits who wielded extraordinary influence with the voting public and whose barbs consequently were feared by those in the seats of the mighty. Three of the greatest have been Charles F. Browne (writing under the name Artemus Ward), Finley Peter Dunne (author of the Mr. Dooley dialogues) and William Penn Adair "Will" Rogers.

Ward's (or Browne's) influence on Abraham Lincoln already has been mentioned. Of Dunne, Lloyd Morris wrote in "Mr. Dooley: a Man of Great Renown," in the March 22, 1948 *New Republic*: "During the period between the Spanish-American war and the First World War Dooley was an active maker of public opinion in the United States. It was the period of a 'quest for social justice,' of muckracking, reform movements, a rising tide of political liberalism. Americans were being confronted by momentous issues: imperialism; the protective tariff; labor's right to organize; control of monopolies and trusts; the corrupt alliance of big business and big politics; and the subordination of human rights to property rights that had resulted from a half-century of industrial expansion."

Modeled after a shanty Irish saloonkeeper in Chicago, Martin Dooley philosophized in Dunne's pieces for the benefit of his friend Hennessy. Still widely quoted are many of his observations such as "No matter whether th' Constitootion follows th' flag or not, th'

Supreme Court follows th' illiction returns," and his statement that he cared not "who makes th' laws iv a nation if I can get out an injunction." It is not difficult to imagine how Theodore Roosevelt liked Mr. Dooley's comments on his book *The Rough Riders*: "If I was him I'd call the book, 'Alone in Cubia.' " When McKinley and Bryan seemed to overdo their quotations from the Founding Fathers, Mr. Dooley quipped: "be hivens, Hinnissey, I want me advice up-to-date, an' whin Mck an' Willum Jennings tells me what George Wash'n'ton an' Thomas Jefferson said, I says to thim: 'gintlemen, they learned their trade befur th' days iv open plumbin',' I says. 'Tell us what is wanted be ye'ersilf or call in a journeyman who's wurrkin' card is dated this cinchry.' "

About the time Dunne was passing from the picture, Rogers was attaining national fame as a deflator of heroes and nonrespecter of dignity wherever found. Few Americans ever were mourned more than was he when he lost his life in 1935 in Alaska while on a round-the-world flight with Wiley Post. By then he had become familiar, not merely to vaudeville and musical comedy audiences but to motion picture fans and newspaper readers of his syndicated daily short piece as well. Rogers' best gags, as listed by Roger Butterfield in "The Legend of Will Rogers" in the July 18, 1949 *Life* were as follows:

"On American Diplomacy: 'The United States never lost a war or won a conference.'

"On War Debts: 'It is much easier for America to whip a nation than it is to collect a dollar from them.'

"On Congress: 'Every time they make a joke it's a law. And every time they make a law it's a joke.'

"On the Democrats: 'I am not a member of any organized party— I am a Democrat.'

"On the Republicans: 'A Republican . . . wants politics to be known as his sideline. He wants to work at it, but he wants people to believe he don't have to.'

"On New Deal Policies: 'What Wallace is trying to do is to teach the farmer corn acreage control and the hog birth control and one is just as hard to make understand it as the other.'

"On Japan: 'The Japanese announced today they are going ahead with shipbuilding. If allowed at the next conference they will have ships. If not allowed, they will have them too. Can't beat logic like that.'

"On Movies: 'Everybody is trying to find out what's the matter with them. If they ever do find out they will ruin the business.'

"On Clothes: 'Every time a woman leaves off something, she looks better, but every time a man leaves off something he looks worse.'

"On Prohibition: 'The South is dry and will vote dry. That is everybody that is sober enough to stagger to the polls will.'

"On Preparedness: 'We are the only Nation in the world that waits till we get into a war before we start getting ready for it.' "

On at least one significant occasion humor helped eliminate the danger of war. George E. Vincent told about it in "A Chuckle Girdles the World," in the July, 1937 *Rotarian* as follows:

"A delightful instance occurred during the excitement caused in 1895 by President Cleveland's bombshell message on the Venezuelan boundary dispute. The Summer before this was issued, Lord Dunraven, an Irish yachtsman, had cut a rather poor figure as a challenger for the America's cup. To be sure, the light breeze had been disappointing; two races had been scarcely more than drifting matches. But Dunraven had been peevish and had made many baseless complaints. Among other charges he insisted that he had lost one race because of the swells from sightseeing excursion boats. His rather poor sportsmanship had been deplored in England as well as in the United States.

"All this was in the public mind when Cleveland's message startled both America and Britain. The papers exploited the affair sensationally. Rumors of impending war spread rapidly. Public feeling reached a high pitch. When the report came that the British Channel Fleet had sailed under sealed orders, the situation suddenly grew tense.

"At this very critical moment, the London Stock Exchange sent to the New York Stock Exchange the following cable:

" 'When the British Fleet sails up New York Harbor, please see that it is not interfered with by excursion steamers.'

"A roar of laughter burst forth on both sides of the Atlantic; absurd fears were swept away; no one any longer took the episode tragically; calm was quickly restored. Laughter proved a valuable antidote to fanaticism and extravagant feeling."

Unfortunately, for every instance in which a joke put an end to ill will, there are scores or hundreds of others in which the opposite effect prevailed. Especially at times of economic distress there seem to be veritable factories producing malicious jokes capitalizing upon and helping to perpetuate racial, nationality, and other stereotypes. Without the stereotype stories stressing the Negro's allegedly thick skull, sexual promiscuity and prowess, and his fondness for chickens and watermelons would be pointless. Likewise, dumb Swede, fighting Irish, tight Scotchman, avaricious Jew, humorless English, and other such jokes would be ineffective without the stereotypes. Although many such stories are circulated merely for their humor, often without those who pass them on realizing they do harm, *deliberately used, the "anti-" joke is an effective weapon in any kind of social conflict.* In "Humor as a Technique in Race Conflict," in the December, 1946 *American Sociological Review,* John H. Burma emphasized the fact, generally unknown to or ignored by smug members of a majority, that those whom they belittle and ridicule, in the company of themselves, "turn the tables" on their oppressors. In fact, Burma stressed, most American Negroes hardly could stand the boorishness of most whites and retain their mental equilibrium unless they could laugh at the absurdities of Jim Crow and take pleasure in every instance in which it rebounds to the displeasure, inconvenience or injury of the white supremacists. Typical anti-white joke recorded by Burma has two colored maids exchanging confidences. "At my place," says one, "I have a terrible time; all day it's 'Yes, Ma'am,' 'Yes, Ma'am,' 'Yes, Ma'am,' " to which the other replies: "Me, too, but with me it's 'No, Sir,' 'No, Sir,' 'No, Sir.' " That, like many other jokes, easily could be told without a racial angle. Maybe that is the way it originated, being adapted to serve a purpose. Certainly such is common practice as regards a great many hoary ones which have amused or shocked millions almost from caveman days to the present.

The Platform

When Abraham Lincoln completed his eight-minute address dedicating the National Cemetery at Gettysburg, Pa., Nov. 19, 1863, the crowd of 20,000, many unaware that the president had finished, gave only perfunctory applause. Back in his platform seat, Mr. Lincoln remarked to Ward Hill Lamon, "Lamon, that speech won't scour," a sentiment which he repeated while on the train returning to Washington and upon his arrival, saying in addition: "It is a flat failure and the people are disappointed," and "That speech fell on an audience like a wet blanket. I am distressed about it. I ought to have prepared it with more care."

Although Edward Everett, who delivered the principal oration, and a few others are said to have recognized immediately the greatness of the 267 words which constitute the immortal Gettysburg address, according to Lamon, most of the president's party shared its deliverer's belief that it had not been a success. Newspapers friendly to Lincoln made at best polite comment; those who disliked him hurled abuse such as the following from the Harrisburg *Patriot and Union*:

The president acted without sense or without restraint in a panorama that was gotten up more for the benefit of his party than for the honor of the dead. . . . We pass over the silly remarks of the president; for the credit of the nation we are willing that the veil of oblivion shall be dropped over them and that they shall no more be repeated or thought of.

In view of what posterity has come to think of the Gettysburg address, the question is pertinent: what constitutes a good speech? Is it to be judged by its immediate effect upon those who hear it, or on those who read it shortly thereafter, or upon succeeding generations? Must it move to tears or shouts or other demonstrative forms or simply be masterly in rhetorical style? Certainly the Gettysburg address, George Washington's Farewell address, and many of the so-called world's great orations which school children used to study, memorize, and deliver more than they do now, have had as much (or more) effect decades or centuries after delivery as at the time.

Today we accept the fact that Demosthenes, Cicero, Mark Antony, Burke, Disraeli, Henry, Webster, Clay, Emerson, and others were great orators, able to sway the minds and affect the actions of those who heard them. Studying their addresses it would seem that organization and word choice must have been determining factors in causing them to be masterful. We do not, however, have recordings of their voices, nor motion pictures of their gestures, so we must depend upon contemporary accounts to evaluate the extent to which those factors were important. The fact that his "Cross of Gold" speech caused his nomination for president by the Democratic National convention in

1896 is prima facie evidence that William Jennings Bryan, then a comparative unknown, deserved the fame the address brought him. Whether the same kind of speech, replete with biblical phrases and borrowings, would have a similar effect today, however, is doubtful, so to postulate universal criteria by which to judge greatness on the platform is well nigh impossible.

As any lecturer of experience knows, a public speech is an event, the total effect being the outcome of the interaction of a number of factors. A speaker's words, for instance, may be identical night after night; likewise, to the fullest extent possible, the same may be true of his gestures and manner of delivery. Nevertheless, the reactions of his various audiences may differ greatly, even when their compositions presumably are similar. Size of the room and the extent to which it is occupied, the acoustics, the hour at which the speaker takes the rostrum, the nature and effect of that part of the program which preceded him, the chairman's introduction of him, the temperature, odors, comfortableness of the seats are among the factors which enter into the total effect. Public speakers can receive too much or too little credit or blame for a successful or unsuccessful meeting.

Most important factor of all in determining whether a public speaker is to "go over" on a particular occasion is the predisposition of his hearers. There are numerous classifications of audiences to be found in the text books on public speaking, mostly in terms of the motivations of those who compose them. Attending a church, political club or other meeting may be hardly more than a ritual, with no intention or desire to receive information beyond that which will fortify preexistent prejudices. On the other hand a subscriber to a forum series may be genuinely seeking an educational experience with an open mind. If the speaker is someone possessing great prestige, some of his listeners will be merely quidnuncs; others are outright hecklers.

There have been innumerable attempts to determine the extent to which public speakers affect public opinion. Most of them have consisted of attitude or opinion tests given before and after a public speech or debate to measure the shifts of opinion. One such was that reported by Howard S. Woodward in an article, "Measurement and Analysis of Audience Opinion," in the February, 1928 *Quarterly Journal of Speech.* He studied 3,540 members of 118 debate audiences with the following results:

Before the Debate		*After the Debate*
1,303	In favor of the motion	1,652
1,162	Undecided	345
1,075	Opposed to the motion	1,543

Of those originally in favor of the motion, 51.9 per cent reported that their opinions were strengthened; 17.5 per cent said their opinions were weakened, while 30.2 per cent said they had undergone no change. Similar results were reported for those originally opposed. The significant results obviously were obtained from those who were undecided at the outset. Of them 40.9 per cent changed to the affirmative, 43.3 per cent changed to the negative, and only 15.8 per cent still were undecided.

A public opinion poll March 3, 1937 on President Roosevelt's proposal to reorganize the Supreme Court showed 41 per cent favorable, 48 per cent unfavorable, and 11 per cent with no opinion. After fireside chats March 4 and 8 on the subject, another poll showed 45 per cent favorable, 41 per cent unfavorable, and 14 per cent undecided.

Other tests have attempted to determine the permanency of the effect of a speech, an extremely difficult matter inasmuch as there are so many other influences operating simultaneously. In 1940, Dr. Allen Edwards studied 150 Northwestern University students, as far as possible equally divided among those favorable, neutral, and unfavorable to the New Deal. Three tests were given: three weeks before the subjects were exposed to a carefully prepared political speech which contained an equal number of facts favorable and unfavorable to the New Deal; immediately after hearing the speech; and three weeks later. Reported Edwards: "The speech resulted in little or no change in the subjects' attitudes toward the New Deal. The favorable group is still favorable, the neutral group is still neutral, and the opposed group is still opposed. There is very little change in attitude even after a period of three weeks.

"That the subject's own attitude is influential in the interpretation of the attitude expressed by the speaker is evidenced by the rating of these factors. The favorable group thought that both speaker and speech were favorable to the New Deal, while the group opposed to the New Deal thought that they were both unfavorable."

Typical of another type of experiment, to test the importance of prestige as well as of argument, was that conducted by a Northwestern University sophomore who made a wire recording of a speech favorable to socialized medicine. Group A was told it was a speech by the surgeon general of the United States, Group B that it was by Eugene Dennis, secretary of the American Communist party, and Group C that it was a Northwestern sophomore whose voice was heard. The conversions among Group A were four times as great as those in either Group B or Group C, or twice as many as Groups B and C together.

From these and scores of other experiments which could be cited, it would seem that generalizations regarding the importance of the platform in the formation of public opinion are difficult if not impossible to make. Basic are the factors which make for credulity, discussed in several earlier chapters. Public speaking is only one way by which the public opinion manipulator reaches his intended "victims."

CHAPTER TWELVE

THE ARTS

The ways in which men seek entertainment and/or cultural enjoyment affect their thoughts and actions in all fields and provide clues as to the public opinion of a time or place.

"If that is art, I'm a Hottentot."

So went part of a telegraphed message in the winter of 1946–47 from President Harry S. Truman to feminine performers for Ringling Brothers and Barnum & Bailey's "greatest show on earth."

"The artist must have stood off from the canvas and thrown paint at it," declared the chief executive in further apology for the Department of State's inclusion of a painting of "a fat semi-nude circus girl" in a collection of 117 pictures by contemporary Americans which was to have been exhibited in several other United Nations countries to keep our former allies up to date as regards post-World War II cultural progress in the United States.

Inspired by the American Artists Professional League, a group of "traditional" artists, the newspapers of William Randolph Hearst vigorously attacked the project, which had opened successfully in Czechoslovakia; and so many congressmen expressed themselves as being scandalized that Secretary of State George Marshall decreed "no more taxpayers' money for modern art." The paintings were sold at public auction for a fraction of the approximately $50,000 which the government had paid for them.

Among those who approved the decision was Thomas Craven, long-time adverse critic of so-called modern art. Having viewed the Department of State's traveling exhibit, in the June issue of '48, he answered "yes" to the symposium question, "Is American Art Degraded?" Characteristically he wrote:

"The effect of the secretary's mandate on the addled custodians of modern art in this country was prolonged and laughable. The neurotic platoons of contemporary painting, the neo-abstractionists, the non-objectivists, and their abortive creations—Lord deliver us!—the mumbling legmen and irresponsible scribblers at the art desks of metropolitan newspapers, the dealers who sold the pictures to the government—all these moaned and wept and threatened. But the secretary wisely paid them no mind.

"It is possible, as some of his critics hinted, that Secretary Marshall is not a connoisseur of painting, but he was wise enough to nail the absurdity of representing American culture by a batch of imitative abstractions and boneless distortions. The pictures, with a few notable exceptions, were either a conventional rehash of cubist patterns born among the wastrels of Paris forty years ago, or the more recent nightmares of surrealism. Not by any conceivable straining at rationalization could they be called a reflection of American culture."

To the unartistic layman the whole business may seem like a tempest in a teapot full of the high-browed and long-haired. Craven's statement, however, suggests a number of factors of extreme pertinence in connection with the study of public opinion, namely: (1) Does art reflect culture? (2) If so, how do you interpret art so as to understand what is being reflected? (3) If not, how explain art? That is, if art is not a reflection of culture, what is it? (4) When rival schools of art exist, which truly reflects the culture? Does each type of art reflect a different aspect of culture? How determine which kind of art reflects what aspect? (5) How, and to what extent, does art not merely reflect but positively influence culture, especially that aspect of it called public opinion? (6) Can that influence be controlled or destroyed, through government or private censorship or by utilization of art for propaganda purposes?

In asking such questions the term "art" should be interpreted not in the narrow sense to mean only easel paintings, murals, and sculpture but broadly to include as well architecture, music, dancing, literature, poetry, drama, motion pictures, radio, and television. All of the questions could be asked individually of each and should be borne in mind during the separate discussions to follow of the different art forms and/or media.

Art and Culture

"Art," wrote Leo Tolstoy, "is the spiritual organ of human life which cannot be destroyed." The literature dealing with the history, interpretation and criticism of art in all its forms abounds with similar statements. Historians, and especially cultural anthropologists, study the art of a period for clues to understanding other aspects of the life and ideas of the times. Available to them, of course, are only the more durable artifacts which have survived throughout decades or centuries; so the possibility, though not the likelihood, exists that the samples were not typical or even popular at the time of their creation. Even though, as was doubtless true, many ancients and medievals, like a great many moderns, became famous posthumously, what they produced *did* "catch on" during either their own or some succeeding generation. Works of art are individual creations, but it is audience response which determines what does and does not endure. *No artist works in a vacuum; no human being can avoid being affected by cultural forces.* So, when it is pointed out that a large number of the world's most creative artists endured hardship, even poverty, and died unappreciated, all that is meant is that the greatest minds have been ahead of their times, aware of new social forces which they attempted to express but which a majority of their fellow men were slower to recognize. To put it another way: many if not most truly great artists have had prophetic vision, which often meant they were not "in tune" with the times during their lifetimes. Rather, they were rebels who helped "point the way."

Regardless of the alacrity with which genius has been recognized, *that the enduring art of a period contains clues to the nature of its culture seems indisputable.* Bertrand Russell began an article, "Man's Diary in Sticks and Stones," in the June, 1937 *Rotarian* as follows:

"Every social system that has existed has had its appropriate type of architecture. Medieval castles make visible the pride of feudal barons; Venetian palaces display the splendors derived from commerce with the East; French chateaux and Queen Anne country seats represent the secure power of a courtly and civilized aristocracy.

"With the French Revolution and the Industrial Revolution there goes a revolution in architecture. Old styles linger where the older forms of power linger: Napoleon adds to the Louvre, but his additions have a florid vulgarity which shows his insecurity. But the typical styles of the Nineteenth Century are two: the factory with its chimneys, and the rows of tiny houses for working class families.

". . . If an age is to be judged by the esthetic quality of its architecture, the last hundred years represent the lowest point yet reached by humanity."

Regarding the same field of interest Albert Mayer wrote in an article, "The Architect and His World," in the Jan. 8, 1936 *Nation*:

"In great periods of architecture the architect found himself in harmony with life at large; he was inspired by the current transcendent faith of his time. And indeed he was an important figure of his time, as the architect should be now. For the abbots and the bishops in the Middle Ages, the court chamberlains in ancient Egypt, rather than the actual craftsmen who carried out the details, were the architects in the modern sense. Great architecture demands first a generally accepted background of life and aspiration of sufficient significance so that the artist and the creator can believe in it with passion and assume with serenity that it exists; and second a position of authority for architecture and the architect commensurate with the importance in a vital civilization and with the extraordinary demands made on him."

No doubt that Russell and Mayer consider architecture at least a reflection of the culture it represents. No doubt either that the world over today the distinctly American creation, the skyscraper, is symbolic of American life as a whole, or, more importantly, of what Americans would like to have the rest of the world believe it is like. Freudians can call the Empire State building a gigantic phallic symbol suggesting puritanic repression; Adlerians can see in it evidence of overcompensation for feelings of insecurity; Veblenites can scoff at the conspicuous display of wealth and waste. Any or all of these and other analyses may be valid. As pointed out several times already in this book, it is impossible, in the light of man's knowledge to date, to state dogmatically that this or that is the true key or yardstick by which to understand all aspects of human behavior. It *is* possible, however, to state that, *no matter how we got that way, what we are is suggested by the art forms which we have either originated or adopted and developed as our own.* In addition to the skyscraper there are musical comedy and jazz music and the kind of dancing which goes with it, all distinctive American art forms.

Because the United States is peopled by descendants of many if not all races and nationalities, from all parts of the earth, it is inevitable that many different types of influence can be detected in all phases of our culture. For the same reasons it is quite understandable that it is only comparatively recently that any distinctly American art forms should have come to exist. After World War II there occurred no such wholesale self-exilism of American artists, writers, and other intellectuals as after World War I when London, Paris, Vienna, and other European cities were overrun with American aesthetes who found it impossible to obtain adequate inspiration or subject matter in their native habitats. James McNeill Whistler, foremost American painter of his time who spent almost a half century abroad until his death in 1903, and Henry James, outstanding novelist who did the same thing until his death in 1916, have no modern counterparts. What was called the "regional" school of American painters was established by post-World War I expatriates who returned home after years of vain search for the artistic holy grail abroad. Notable among them were Grant Wood of Iowa, Thomas Benton of Missouri, and John Steuart Curry of Kansas. All continued to display the effect of their foreign studies but all became convinced that there is sufficient in the American scene to inspire the best in any potentially great native artist and that the present generation needs no longer suffer from a feeling of inferiority or of necessity to imitate, borrow, and steal from the Old World.

This, of course, is far from being tantamount to declaring that the United States has become a nation of art lovers. As a matter of fact the predominant attitude among authorities on matters aesthetic probably isn't far different from that which the sculptor, Gutzon Borglum, expressed to the Committee on Patents of the House of Representatives, as reported in the Appendix to the *Congressional Record* for May 7, 1935:

"Mr. Chairman, dynamically America is yet a tradesman's land without adequate cultural consciousness. Officially she initiates nothing of distinct cultural character or quality. . . . We lack all cultural, far-sighted or courageous conception of what civilization means or the will to listen or to act. . . . Gentlemen, the permanently worthwhile work that has lifted any civilization in the world's history out of the mud, in which most of it was conceived and born, was never initiated by big business, bankers or politics. It is always a product of a few creative, constructive individuals.

"America has a large population of unregistered dreamers of great, of greater and more beautiful lives that might be lived usefully if given a chance, under sound leadership, than all Europe put together. Ours is a population made up of the soul hungry of civilization from everywhere."

Borglum, it will be recalled, was the originator of the ideas to carve the likenesses of Robert E. Lee, Jefferson Davis, "Stonewall" Jackson, and other Confederate leaders in a gigantic frieze on Stone Mountain near Atlanta, and the busts of George Washington, Abraham Lincoln, Thomas Jefferson, and Theodore Roosevelt on Mt. Rushmore in the Black Hills of South Dakota, awe-inspiring evidences of the American love for the "bigger and better" in art as in other things.

Modern Art

To return to modern American art, how is it to be explained, in cultural or any other terms? The simplest explanation is that implied by Russell Lynes in an article, "The Taste-Makers," in the June, 1947 *Harper's*: that the development of photography and changes in building habits have rendered old forms of art obsolete. Wrote Lynes in part:

"The dark view (and perhaps the only tenable one) is that art, as we have been accustomed to think of it—as easel painting, murals and sculpture—quite simply is a vestigial remnant of a once important aspect of western culture. It has been difficult for a long time to justify painting as an essential part of communication or even as a kind of revelation that means much to many people. Our buildings are no longer planned with mural decoration in mind as an integral part of their design. Almost no one has a formal garden into which to put sculpture and few people want it indoors. (What, for example, could you do with the large, handsome Henry Moore wooden reclining figures, seven feet long? There is no place for them but museums.) Most people buy pictures to fill up the dull spaces in their dull houses. Is this the sort of demand that stirs the best talent? Is there any indication that the best talent for visual creation is making pictures and sculpture? Can we be sure that the best artists are not men and women, now anonymous, working in new and exciting media of vision —in the movies, perhaps, or in something still in the laboratory, a new dimension of visual experience as inconceivable to us as the movies were to our grandparents?"

Although the various schools of modernists are by no means in agreement—are, in fact, often violently critical of and hostile to each other—on one point all of them (regionalists, dadaists, cubists, surrealists, abstractionists, impressionists, post-impressionists and any others unintentionally overlooked) were in agreement. That was in accepting President Truman's appraisal of himself as a Hottentot in artistic judgment. When the internationally famous musical composer, Dmitri Shostakovich, was expelled in 1948 from the Moscow Conservatory of Music so that students would not be corrupted by his "formalist influence," the great Russian accepted the Central committee's decree "as stern but fatherly" and indicated that "a worthy reply . . . may be achieved by work—stubborn, creative, joyous work . . . on new compositions which will find a path to the heart of the Soviet people." In a freer atmosphere, however, outraged American modernists struck back at their critics, as they have become accustomed to doing for several decades, especially since the opening of the Museum of Modern Art in 1930.

One of the best counterattacks was that made by one of the most conservative of the rebels against traditionalism, Thomas Hart Benton, whose murals, including a "Frankie and Johnny" scene, in the state capitol at Jefferson City, Mo. made him a storm center in the thirties. In an article, "Art vs. The Mellon Gallery," in the June, 1941 *Common Sense*, Benton commented upon his being fired from a teaching position at the Kansas City Art Institute for suggesting that "a living art might function more effectively in saloons and bawdy-houses than in museums," and explained partly as follows:

"The profession, the critics, the museum boys are ganging up on this new American art. Their lectures and their publications sneer at the art of the 'American scene.' There is plenty the matter with the American scene as it is expressed in art. All of us who paint today need more in the way of mechanical and organizational techniques than we have. Rembrandt still paints better than we do. But this business of making a living American art that will be as good *in its own way* as Rembrandt's is beyond the understanding of critics and museum boys. They have been conditioned to see art as a collection of objects rather than as a living necessity of the spirit of man. They cannot understand that this drive, in its American aspect, *must* eventuate in objects which will be different in kind from the art of the past which they have learned to know and love. Their sneers at a native art, therefore, are directed at what appears to them a presumptuous denial of the values of art. They cannot understand that what the artist of the American scene denies, in his insistence on environmental stimulus, is merely their own highly conditioned and traditional values. What I am now afraid of, because of the power and prestige of the Museums, is that the young and sensitive artist will be caught in his floundering student days and turned away from life and back to imitating the dead or producing attenuations of exotic imports. . . . The museum attitude toward culture implies that art may be bought and that a collection of objects and a mere cataloguing and memorizing of facts about them constitutes a cultural achievement. . . . My objection to museum people is that they are too much like undertakers."

Acceptance of the theses that new art forms are necessary and that resistance to experimentation is wrong still doesn't explain why modern art has taken the direction that it has. Perhaps the "studied nonsense," as it has been called, is just faddism which will die out after not too long a time, as has been predicted. In such case too much attention to it, and to "stream of consciousness" writing, unpunctuated and occult verse, and dissonant music would be superfluous. If such occurs the "revolt against meaning" may be seen to have been merely an echo of jangled nerves in days of depressions and wars. To the historian Arnold Toynbee, however, it is all a symptom of the decay of moral values, and to Rep. George A. Dondero of Michigan, "Modern art is communistic because it is distorted and ugly, because it does not glorify our beautiful country, our cheerful and smiling people and our great material progress. Art which does not portray our beautiful country in plain, simple terms that everyone can understand breeds dissatisfaction. It is therefore opposed to our government, and those who create and promote it are our enemies."

These words were spoken to Emily Genauer who quoted them in

an article, "Still Life with Red Herring," in the September, 1949
Harper's, and then pointed out the paradoxical fact that both Lenin
and Stalin expressed substantially the same opinions as the anti-
Communistic Michigan congressman. Lenin, she wrote, once said:
"I cannot praise the works of expressionism, futurism, cubism and
other isms. . . . Why turn away from the really beautiful? Art must
unite and uplift people in their feelings, thoughts and aspirations,"
while Stalin declared: "Art must forego the higher aesthetics of mod-
ernism. . . . Art . . . has again been invested with the great ideas
of patriotism."

It is in the spirit of the latter quotation that the Soviet Union disciplined Shostakovich and others of its leading musicians, that Hitler
and Goebbels rigidly controlled all forms of artistic expression in
Germany, and that Dondero and others like him advocate the abandonment of the democratic way of allowing any and all creative
artists to compete with each other for popular favor. "Do not let us
deceive ourselves: the common man, such as we produce him in our
civilization, is aesthetically a dead man," wrote Herbert Read in an
article, "The State as Patron," in the Winter, 1947 *University
Observer*. Nevertheless, throughout history, it has been the painters,
sculptors, musicians, novelists, dramatists, and other kinds of artists
who have had to wage battle with the censors and would-be censors,
both public and private, more frequently than is true of any other
element in any culture. Either the various art forms have power to
affect the thoughts and actions of men or hundreds of thousands of
kings, dictators, churchmen and others have suffered tremendously
from a prodigious delusion to the contrary.

Reacting against those who would control thoughts and emotions
has been the entire democratic tradition. A comparatively recent example of how the common man, artistically illiterate though he may
be, behaves when given the opportunity, is related in the following
news account:

Prague (AP)—An overflow Prague music theater audience Thursday
night burst out with a storm of angry protests when a program commentator criticized Bing Crosby as a "greedy American money-seeker,
who sacrifices his art for gold."

The Czech audience, including many bobby-soxers, had stood in long
queues to jam into the little theater to hear a two-hour program of

Crosby recordings. It loosed salvos of shouts and whistling in defense
of Bing.

An hour before the start of the Crosby program, block-long queues
formed in front of the theater. There was a rush for the 200 seats and
every inch of standing room.

When the theater was packed the young folk huddled together in the
lounges and on the steps of two flights of stairs leading to the street,
where they could hear the music over amplifiers.

Before the program started, an unidentified announcer speaking over
the amplifying system declared:

"Now first let us consider this Bing Crosby. He's a typical example of
a man who sacrifices his art to get money. He sings in a way so senti-
mentally sweet it makes you sick (Czech expression unprintable)."

The audience burst out with whistles and boos, but the voice over the
amplifier continued:

"And, politically, this Crosby stands for nothing that could be identified
with the principles of Jefferson or Lincoln."

More indignant boos and cries of "Pfui" from the audience.

A final touch to the noisy evening came when the closing song was
announced—"Irish Lullaby." When it turned out to be a recording by a
Czech singer instead of Crosby there was another noisy outburst.

—Chicago Sun-Times, Oct. 28, 1949

Given a different set of circumstances, however, the same kind of
usually democratic-minded people can join the hue and cry in opposition to free artistic expression. In 1922, for example, Catholic students rioted with knives and stones to destroy a mural in Mexico
City by Diego Rivera who also a few years later scandalized some
Californians by his choice of the tennis player, Helen Wills, as representative of the state's womanhood in a mural for the San Francisco
Stock Exchange and, who still more recently, stirred up a terrific
controversy by including Nicolai Lenin in a fresco in New York's
Radio City on the theme, "Man at the crossroads facing the future
with uncertainty but with hope."

Jacob Epstein, whose sculptured figure of a pregnant woman, in
1931, caused the squeamish to howl, in 1937 heard his two-and-a-half
ton alabaster figure of a dead Jesus in London's Leicester Galleries
called "a disgusting travesty and outrage on Christian ideals." In
1933 New York customs officials caused international laughter by
holding up ten pamphlets of rotogravure reproductions of Michel-
angelo's frescoes on the ceiling of the Vatican's Sistine Chapel, but

three years later Pope Piux XI ordered drapery to be painted on some of the most famous of the nudes.

No group ever complained more loudly than did the Daughters of the American Revolution after appearance of Grant Wood's painting by that name. The same painter's "American Gothic" and "Parson Weems" also are condemned by the extremely ethnocentric and chauvinistic. Early in 1949, after displaced Polish Jews rioted in Berlin to protest the showing of the English motion picture, *Oliver Twist*, the New York Board of Rabbis was instrumental in persuading the distributors not to show the film in the United States. Suit also was brought in New York to ban *Oliver Twist* and *The Merchant of Venice* from the public schools because of the danger that children would get anti-Semitic stereotypes from Dickens' Fagin and from Shakespeare's Shylock. In Trenton, N.J., the National Association for Advancement of Colored People demanded that *Little Black Sambo* be banned.

Objections also have been made to Amos and Andy, radio comedians, and to Stepin Fetchit, motion picture star, because of their tendency to perpetuate a stereotype of the Negro as a lazy, shiftless, illiterate person. The Chinese did not like the Fu Manchu and other films depicting Chinese as cunning, untrustworthy villians. Social workers, psychiatrists, newspapermen, and others have complained of the ways in which Hollywood has portrayed members of their professions.

While he has had to struggle against such pressure (rightly or wrongly applied on behalf of good or bad causes each reader can decide for himself), the artist in America has had little or no counterbalancing help from any department of government. As a matter of fact in the United States there never has developed any kind of patron system, public or private, to compare with those provided by Cheops in ancient Egypt, Pericles in Athens of the fifth century B.C., Augustus, Agrippa, and Hadrian in the heyday of the Roman Empire, and by several of the popes and regal dukes during the Italian Renaissance.

Truman and Marshall were not the first national leaders to refuse assistance to or even recognition for, living artists. At the outset of World War II, Congress refused to appropriate money for a War Department's proposal to send 40 painters to the war fronts, a project which then was partly taken over by the Henry Luce magazines. In the twenties Calvin Coolidge refused a bequest to the White House of 15 paintings by Cezanne by Charles Loeser, a collector. In 1937 the federal government did accept a gift of a National Gallery of Art containing about $19,000,000 worth of masterpieces formerly the possession of Andrew W. Mellon, secretary of the treasury under Presidents Harding, Coolidge, and Hoover. By his gift, the cynical commented, Mellon saved his estate several millions of dollars in inheritance taxes and contributed nothing to the support or encouragement of any living artist. Neither, of course, has the federal government made such a contribution, with the notable exception of the WPA cultural projects—theater, art, music, and writers—during the thirties. Although the work of more than 5,000 WPA artists "was sometimes extravagantly damned by political and aesthetic commentators," to quote the editors of *Harper's* in their discussion of "The Government and the Arts" in the issue of October, 1943, "there have been few prize competitions . . . in which former WPA artists have not placed well; WPA artists have been on every roster of Guggenheim Foundation Fellowship winners from 1935 to 1943; and WPA artists walked off with many fat commissions awarded by the Section of Fine Arts, including the $26,000 San Francisco Post Office mural."

Such success was contrary to what most disseminators of WPA jokes expected. At no time were the cultural projects regarded by Congress with anything but extreme suspicion. After the Theater Project produced Sinclair Lewis' *It Can't Happen Here* and a few other plays with liberal themes, it was discontinued by an irate Congress, many of whose members yelled "Communist." The "red tape" which infuriated so many acquainted with WPA operations was mostly the invention of congressional enemies of the cultural projects who wanted them operated only as relief projects to keep the indigent aesthetes from starvation—and that begrudgingly.

Despite the WPA artists' undeniable record of success, the proposal of George Biddle that there be established a permanent Federal Bureau of Fine Arts got nowhere. Nor have proposals that the federal government emulate the government of Sweden's custom of allotting a certain proportion of the cost of every public building for decoration. In opposition to all such ideas it generally is argued that it is good for genius to be a little bit hungry; that the state as patron would be fickle, probably generally unsympathetic to experimentation; that creating for government is different from attempting to please a private patron—individual or institutional, such as the church—in that the artist never could be as certain of what was expected or wanted of him; that works produced on governmental order must of necessity have broad general appeal, since they are for public display, rather than particularized appeal as in the case of an individual patron. *American artistic creation consequently is a rugged individualistic enterprise*, a point of significance when its effect upon public opinion is under consideration. To succeed in the United States the composer, painter, novelist, playwright, or other artist must please some audience, unless he is content to be "discovered" long after death which seldom happens and the expectation of which probably is not the motivating force to explain the efforts of very many artists of any kind.

Music

With the exception of John L. Lewis, long-time president of the United Mine Workers, no American labor leader ever has been the target for more editorial brickbats than James C. Petrillo, president of the American Federation of Musicians (AFL). "Caesar" (his middle name), "czar," and "dictator" have been among the most frequent appellations applied to him, especially since 1942 when his union began to intensify its efforts to protect its 231,202 members (as of Feb. 1, 1948) against technological unemployment.

"Your union," Rep. Carroll D. Kearns told Petrillo in July, 1947, during one of numerous congressional hearings regarding his tactics, "has interfered with and restricted the inalienable right of the people of the United States to enjoy freedom of religion and education." To explain his point the congressman "cited complaints that the union prevented amateurs from performing over the radio, required churches to pay standby fees for organists, kept orchestra bands and choruses in many schools off the air, and prevented service bands of the armed forces from making records," according to an Associated Press dispatch July 7, 1947, from Washington, D.C. In a formal statement, according to the same source, Kearns said that Petrillo's union had:

Required theater owners throughout the United States to employ stand-by orchestras they did not need, want or use;

Dictated to broadcasters the amount of money they should spend for music;

Engaged in a concerted effort to hold back the technological improvements in radio and television.

To such charges, to which he has become accustomed, Petrillo's defense has not been denial but explanation. On July 30, 1942, he answered an inquiry from James Lawrence Fly, chairman of the Federal Communications Commission, regarding why he forbade the National High School Orchestra to broadcast from Interlochen, Michigan: "This is not a question of being a 'czar' or 'dictator.' It is a question of a large group of men fighting for their very existence."

As Bernard B. Smith implied in "What's Petrillo Up To?" in the December, 1942 *Harper's* and in "Is There a Case for Petrillo?" in the Jan. 15, 1945 *New Republic,* regardless of what anyone may think of the AFM's president, it is a question also for the entire nation, not to be solved by congressional crackdowns such as the Lea (commonly called anti-Petrillo) act of 1946 or Taft-Hartley in 1947. Stated so as to emphasize its broad social implications, that question is this: Does it make any difference if all of the music heard over the radio or on records for use in juke boxes in public places or in the home is produced by 500 or fewer professional musicians, which, it is estimated, is all it would take to supply present needs or, at least, all that would find it possible to earn livings by devoting full time to musical careers?

Opposition by workers to labor saving devices which result in technological unemployment is not new. Neither are most of the made-work tactics that the AFM has used original with it. Because music by its nature is so much a part of the public domain and musicians do not produce anything tangible such as a building or machines, however, any restrictions on musical output have been matters of widespread public outrage. Since almost everyone on occasion whistles, hums, or sings a song and generally is pleased to have a relative or friend able to play a musical instrument, he regards enjoyment of music as a right similar to the rights to breathe the open air, walk in the public streets and sail on the open seas. Overlooked is the fact that producing and playing music also are means of livelihood.

Whether the average music lover's selfish pleasures will be increased if such production and rendition become merely part-time avocations for all but a handful of professionals is a pertinent factor for consideration. Yet these facts seem indisputable:

The introduction of sound motion pictures in 1927 resulted in the discharge of approximately 18,000 theater musicians.

Approximately 500,000 juke boxes, whose rise to popularity dates from the early thirties and which now have become a 200 million dollar annual business, caused the unemployment of at least 8,000 more musicians.

In 1942 a Federal Communications Commission survey revealed that 55.9 per cent of all radio musical time is recorded.

The "star" system whereby "name" bands attain great popularity, has caused the demise of many less known bands and discourages the formation of others.

According to Petrillo in his letter to Fly, "95 per cent of the music in the United States and Canada heard today is canned music. Only 5 per cent is left for the poor professional musician who studied all his life so that he might make a living for his family." AFM members now are paid about 3 million dollars for making "canned" music which, if it had been "live" music instead, would have cost 100 million dollars.

In no other field have those put out of work by labor-saving devices produced the means by which such unemployment has resulted. As Petrillo put it, "The ice man was put out of business because the Frigidaire was installed in the home; but the ice man had nothing to do with the making of the Frigidaire. . . . We make the instrument which puts us out of business. To continue this policy means suicide for the musicians of the United States and Canada."

Impossible to ignore also is the poignant AFM agrument that while professional musicians are being reduced in number and income, others are profiting mightily at their expense. In a completely impartial article, "The American Federation of Musicians and the Recording Ban," in the Spring, 1948 *Public Opinion Quarterly,* Anders S. Lunde pointed out that during 1947 there were 771 recording companies which sold an estimated 350 million records for about 250 million dollars. In 1946 three of the "Big Four" recording companies—RCA-Victor, Decca, and Columbia—"together employed

6,348 musicians at average annual scale earnings of only $166 per man, excluding leaders."

Smith pointed out that WNEW in New York, with an almost uninterrupted program of recordings, grosses over 1 million dollars annually through sale of advertising time. WINX, Washington, D.C., a station with a similar program policy, was built for $50,000 in 1940 and sold four years later for ten times that amount.

To summarize, the problem is not a comparatively simple one of what to do about a dictatorial labor leader or intransigent union. Believe and even do the worst as regards James Caesar Petrillo and still unsolved would be the basic issue: can we do without a sizeable number of professional musicians? If the answer is "yes" it probably is based on the conviction that, although the United States never has produced a composer to compare with the immortals of almost every European nation, radio, motion pictures, and the public schools have made us sufficiently appreciative if not literate so that our musical future is secure.

Certainly few affairs today are complete without music, and Americans are no different from others in responding emotionally to its appeal. They cannot refrain from beating time when a lively march is played any more than can anyone else. Courses in music appreciation today are a part of the curriculum of almost any college or university. In 1904 there were only four college glee clubs in the United States; today virtually every college and high school of any size has both men's and women's glee clubs and, in addition, choruses and often light opera companies too. No American boy feels, as his father did when he was an adolescent, that it is sissy to take music lessons; rather, there is keen competition to belong to school bands and orchestras which make public appearances at football games and other athletic contests and on other important academic occasions.

Americans have learned the commercial use of music also. Singing telegrams and commercials have survived the derision directed at them and the latter now are being used by the United Nations to promote international-mindedness. During the war the value to the morale of factory workers of listening to music while they worked was demonstrated. Mental hospitals are increasingly using music for therapeutic purposes. There is no school today without its alma mater and other songs, and the same is becoming increasingly true of organizations of all kinds. A businessmen's luncheon club meeting without group singing is an anomaly.

What level American musical taste has achieved is for the experts to say. Only a few metropolitan centers support opera companies or symphony orchestras and the "going" is always "tough" even for the largest of them. There are, however, several first-class musical broadcasts which continue year after year with listening audiences large enough to satisfy their sponsors. Slightly jazzed renditions of some of the world's best music also have become popular with the masses of radio listeners and motion picture goers. As is true of the so-called "popular" music—that is, dance music—however, the interest is transient. Old favorites come back after a generation when they are accepted by the youngsters as new rather than old, but of enduring American folk songs there are few or none in the traditional sense. True, Burl Ives and others who have resurrected ditties of the frontier are considered entertaining, and Stephen Foster airs still are appreciated. What is hummed and whistled day in, day out, however, is the latest catchy tune which in six months or a year is considered stale, almost repulsive.

The closest twentieth-century Americans have come to producing songs which endure has been what they erroneously like to call "semi-classical" airs from some of the best musical comedies of the thirties and motion picture musicals of the forties. Earlier in the century one felt a little shamefaced to admit liking their predecessors. Few, however, feel ashamed to have it known that they enjoy some of the best tunes from Jerome Kern's *Show Boat*, Richard Rodgers' *Oklahoma* or Sigmund Romberg's *The Student Prince*, to cite only three typical musical comedies; or from the cinematic successes, *Roberta, The Firefly*, or *The Wizard of Oz*.

"You never know," was, in essence, the answer of Oscar Hammerstein II, one of the leading contemporary lyricists (*Rose Marie, The Desert Song, Oklahoma, Carmen Jones*, etc.), to the question, "What Makes Songs Popular?" to which he directed his attention in the March '48. Elaborating, he wrote:

"What makes popular songs popular? When I write a new song, or hear a new song by someone else, I cannot, with any degree of certainty, predict or measure its probable success. I have met no publisher, performing artist, producer or record manufacturer who can do this. These experts can, of course, make closer guesses than most people, but they are only guesses. The music business constantly passes up winners and backs losers. The gauging of popular values in any one song, then, is a difficult and tricky thing."

For what it was worth, in the light of his admitted uncertainty, Hammerstein gave some advice as follows:

"It seems to me that the most important element in a lyric is subject matter. A song had better be about something fundamental—which is why so many songs are about love. Everyone is interested in the fulfillment or frustration of love. People are also interested in hope: Happy days are in store; blue skies are coming when the clouds disappear. They are interested in yearning for home, a mythical little white house on a green lawn, full of peace and freedom from care. They are interested in children and mothers and patriotism."

Others have described almost the same situation but in disparaging terms: that to succeed the musician must specialize in romance, heartache, and wedding bells to the exclusion of all else. The fact that in the United States only composers of jazz, swing, bebop or whatever the popular "hot" music of the time happens to be called, can make a living also is cited as evidence of low taste or as indication that the ordinary man in "bigger and better" America is frustrated and needs raucous entertainment to help him endure an otherwise drab and frustrating existence.

Much quoted have been the lines from Act I, Scene 1 of Congreve's *The Mourning Bride*: "Music has charms to sooth a savage breast, to soften rocks, or bend a knotted oak." Insufficiently repeated have been the following from Act I, Scene 1 of Shakespeare's *Measure for Measure*: "Though music oft hath such a charm to make bad good, and good provoke to harm."

Aristotle was aware of the evil as well as beneficial potentialities of music when he frowned on flute-playing as bad for public morale because it provides a distraction from an awareness of social responsibility. The Puritans banned all except sober hymns. In *The Magic Mountain* (Modern Library, 1932) Thomas Mann called music treacherous because of its ability to arouse listeners to follow any banner regardless of the cause.

During the first three centuries of the Christian era, music was a potent means of arousing enthusiasm for the young religion. Communicants engaged in the group singing of psalms and improvised their own versions during services. Early in the fourth century, however, the church hierarchy strengthened its own hold by restricting hymn singing to canonical psalmists who had the right to mount the pulpit. This was one of the earliest recorded instances of musical censorship.

The church discouraged all music originating in physical activities. All dance music, work, love, folk, and popular music was declared the devil's work and popular musicians were excommunicated. Even the major scale was outlawed because it was the one in which many popular songs were composed. To replace what it had banned, the church developed its own music which contained no measures, no strong or weak bars, no stimulating accented rhythms which would be too reminiscent of the dance, and no rousing melodic leaps which characterized the Protestant music of a later period. The early church developed the Gregorian chant which was an impersonal sort of an affair intended to lull an audience into a submissive, almost hypnotic mental state.

The fundamental doctrinal differences between Catholicism and Protestantism are reflected in the differences between their musics and in the use of music in religious services. Whereas Catholics still mostly listen, Protestants make much of congregational singing which was reintroduced by Martin Luther. Luther also revived folk songs, street songs, and even Gregorian chants into singable tunes for which he composed religious words. Among his compositions were some thunderous hymns such as *A Mighty Fortress Is Our God*, which still are popular. It has been said that the Reformation was literally "sung into Germany," and to this day music has been a powerful force in maintaining the emotional control of the Christian church over communicants. It is impossible to participate in or even to listen to the singing of *Onward, Christian Soldiers, Ave Maria, Silent Night, Hark, The Herald Angels Sing* or any of a number of other hymns without being moved in spirit.

When Gipsy Smith died, Hughes Rudd consulted files of the Kansas City *Star* regarding coverage of the famous evangelist's visit to Kansas City in 1909. In the Aug. 12, 1947 Kansas City *Times*, Rudd wrote:

Song was one of Smith's favorite methods of "warming-up" the audience. He was a skillful song leader, and continued singing even in his

80s. Each meeting began with a singing period, with Gipsy leading. This advice has been adopted by present-day evangelists as an easy way to get the crowd into the right mood before the exhorting starts.

In one account of the 1909 meetings appeared the following:

Singing hymns on street cars is of nightly occurrence on several of the city lines. The singing begins about 9:30 o'clock when detached portions of the Gipsy Smith audiences board the cars, homeward bound. Hymn after hymn is sung and many persons on the street stop to gaze at the cars as they speed by, leaving a flood of sacred song in their wake. On an Argentine car last night the first hymn was started at Twelfth and Main streets and the last one ended in Argentine. Every stop may reduce the number of singers, but those that are left sing on, and often after the singers have all left the car the conductor sings on.

Cornwell B. Rogers has written a book, *The Spirit of Revolution in 1789* (Princeton University, 1949) subtitled, "A Study of Public Opinion as Revealed in Political Songs and Other Popular Literature at the beginning of the French Revolution," to which "Songs—Colorful Propaganda of the French Revolution," in the Fall, 1947 *Public Opinion Quarterly*, was a preview. Wrote Rogers in the article:

"To a remarkable extent, as the Revolution progressed, songs were used by community and club leaders as an instrument of enlightenment, and from 1793 they were exploited by the national government as a primary agent of propaganda. . . .

"Club meetings, banquets, and reunions of various sorts afforded the patriots—as the Revolutionists customarily called themselves— ample opportunity for singing in unison, a form of expression which they particularly enjoyed. . . . Thus, political songs came to be sung in almost all the theaters and at the opera as well. This practice, at the height of the Revolution, transformed these places of entertainment into centers of great political excitement."

Most successful of the French Revolutionary song hits, of course, was the rousing *Marseillaise*, France's national anthem ever since.

During our own revolution *Yankee Doodle* helped stir lagging spirits and keep marchers in step. Our national anthem, *The Star Spangled Banner*, was composed in the heart of battle during the War of 1812. Abolitionists made great use of B. R. Hanby's plaintive *Darling Nelly Gray* and capitalized upon the effect of a number of the still popular Stephen Foster songs which created sympathy for the

Negro. No war probably ever inspired more lasting melodies than the American Civil War, among the most memorable being the Southern *Dixie* and the Northern *Battle Hymn of the Republic.*

Anticipating Hitler's purge of all compositions by Jewish composers, during World War I any music of German origin was *verboten* in the United States, under penalty of being thought unpatriotic if one played or listened to it. By contrast, during World War II the opening bar of Beethoven's *Fifth Symphony* became a symbol of victory since it consists of three short and a long note, the Morse code for V, symbol for Victory. It was unquestionably the most familiar musical passage in a war which, by contrast with others, especially World War I, was devoid of musical inspiration. Explanation of why such should be so lies in the difference in attitudes of the American people toward the two wars. Whereas World War I was regarded as a holy crusade to save the world for democracy and to end all wars, World War II was thought to be a matter of grim necessity. In World War I it was we who declared war first; in World War II we merely recognized the fact that we had been unexpectedly attacked and had no alternative. Whereas there had been elements openly advocating our entrance into World War II, prior to Pearl Harbor even the most so-called interventionist groups openly sought only greater assistance for the British. The entire atmospheres in which the two wars were fought were different. In 1917 and 1918 there were almost daily bond rallies, parades to accompany national guard units and draftees to railroad stations, Four Minute Men in theaters and at public gatherings of all kinds, knitting clubs, Red Cross work centers, and other opportunities for everyone to participate. The spirit of the times definitely is reflected in such lasting songs as *Over There, We're Going Over, Smiles, Wrap Up Your Troubles, Long Boy* and numerous others.

While some wistfulness was revealed in *There's a Long, Long Trail a Winding, Keep the Home Fires Burning,* and *Smile the While You Bid Me Sad Adieu,* there was not the same nostalgia for prewar "normalcy" which the World War II English songs, *There'll Always Be an England* and *The White Cliffs of Dover,* revealed. Even those songs received no better treatment in the United States than that ordinarily accorded "hits." Popular because of its whimsicality, *Praise the Lord and Pass the Ammunition* amused for a time, but to whip a crowd into any kind of enthusiasm it was necessary to resort to the familiar songs of the various branches of the armed services: *The Marine Hymn, The Caissons Go Rolling Along, The Air Corps Song* and the Navy's *Anchors Aweigh*, made popular by Annapolis bands at football games. Wrote Arthur Berger in "Music in Wartime" in the Feb. 7, 1944 *New Republic*:

"In 1917 concerts were frankly used to arouse patriotic hysteria, heightened by a crusade against foreign music. Anna Case and Schumann-Heinck draped themselves in the flag to sing our anthem; half-hour pleas for recruits and bonds were made in the intermission; 'Patriotic Concert' was a typical rubric adopted for a musical event. Beethoven and Wagner were objects of attack; Kreisler was driven into seclusion because he had formerly served in enemy forces; the conductor Karl Muck, a former friend of the Kaiser, was the victim of audience demonstrations and a prison term on doubtful grounds of espionage."

As previously noted (see pages 277 to 279) one of the ramifications of the greater confidence in victory that the American people had during World War II was considerably greater tolerance toward most minorities, including German-Americans. During the jittery postwar period, however, tolerance reached its lowest point in our entire national history. Red baiters and witch hunters, furthermore, had no monopoly on the quick tempers and irrational thoughts of the period. Thus, whereas during the height of the Sicilian campaign, Toscanini was able to broadcast an all-Verdi program and Ezio Pinza, Italian bass, was able to appear on the American operatic and concert stage without incident, the war over, Kirsten Flagstad had difficulty getting back with the Metropolitan Opera company because her husband supposedly was a collaborator with the Germans during the Norwegian occupation. In San Francisco she was refused use of the War Memorial Opera House for a concert.

Although cleared by the American Denazification board two famous German musicians found it impossible to appear in the United States. They were Walter Gieseking, pianist, and Wilhelm Furtwängler, conductor. The former cancelled a concert tour and returned home when protests became too great. An invitation to the latter to be guest conductor for the Chicago Symphony Orchestra during the 1949–1950 season was withdrawn when a number of top soloists declared they would refuse to appear with the symphony if Furtwängler directed.

The list of protestors was impressive, including Artur Rubenstein, Vladimir Horowitz, Jascha Heifitz, Nathan Milstein, Isaac Stern, and others. As spokesman for the group, Rubenstein said: "Had Furtwängler been firm in his democratic convictions he would have left Germany. He chose to stay and perform, believing he would be on the side of the victors. Now he wants to earn American dollars and American prestige. He does not merit either." And that was that.

In the early days of the republic it usually was attempted at least to compose original political campaign songs. In recent times it has become the practice to adopt a familiar song instead. Thus, *The Sidewalks of New York* was used to further the candidacy of Alfred E. Smith who came from the humble east side of lower Manhattan. Pictures of the governor and his wife dancing to the melody created the "plain folks" effect considered so important in American politics. Franklin Delano Roosevelt's campaign song was *Happy Days Are Here Again* which suggested a fortunate end to the dreadful depression which began with the stock market crash of 1929. In 1936 the Republicans attempted to build up Gov. Alf M. Landon as a "Kansas Coolidge" and as a symbol of the American pioneer spirit by use of Stephen Foster's *Oh Susannah* as a campaign song. *I'm Just Wild About Harry* was a "natural" for Harry S. Truman in 1948. It was "plain folksy" as the bulk of Americans, those against as well as those for him, believed Mr. Truman to be. It also suggested the undeniable fact that the president had fought his way almost single handed to the nomination and, against what almost everyone thought impossible odds, to victory at the polls. The song glorified the man rather than an issue and properly caught the spirit of the campaign which ended in what was universally recognized as a personal rather than a party victory.

Literature

Apocryphal or not—and expert opinion is divided—Abraham Lincoln's alleged greeting of Harriet Beecher Stowe, "So this is the little lady who started this big war," correctly expressed the importance which millions have attached to *Uncle Tom's Cabin* since its appearance in 1851. Almost universally regarded by contemporary experts as mostly "saccharine tomfoolery," the novel nevertheless packed a terrific propagandistic wallop for the Abolitionist cause. As a play it occupied the stage uninterruptedly almost until World War II. Millions of middle-aged Americans who grew up in small or medium-sized towns will recall that its annual presentation was as exciting an occurrence as arrival of the circus or Chautauqua.

Mrs. Stowe, of course, didn't cause the Civil War but her book gave great impetus to the anti-slavery movement, just as a half century later, Upton Sinclair's *The Jungle* was the most potent propaganda piece in the drive for the original Pure Food and Drug Acts. If the discussion were to end with those two books, a strong case would have been made for the power of literature to influence public opinion. In addition there have been hundreds or thousands of other novels and poems which have had more than average effect.

Consider, for example, Charles Dickens whose numerous novels, exposing and satirizing various features of English life, contributed to the success of the Chartist and other reform movements in the middle part of the nineteenth century. *Pickwick Papers* (1836–37) was the first important sympathetic treatment in fiction of the middle and lower classes. *Oliver Twist* (1837–39) exposed the workhouses and other causes of juvenile delinquency; *Nicholas Nickleby* (1838–39) did the same for some of the cheap schools of his day. Those and other Dickens masterpieces helped arouse the social consciousness of Englishmen and started a literary vogue which numerous other writers emulated. Among the other novels of the period which helped focus attention were Benjamin Disraeli's *Sybil* (1845), Elizabeth Gaskell's *Mary Barton*, and Charles Kingsley's *Alton Locke* (1849) and *Yeast* (1849).

In the early years of the twentieth century in the United States, in addition to Ida Tarbell, Lincoln Steffens, and other magazine-writing "muckrackers," there were the novelists, Stephen Crane, Jack London, and Frank Norris, who helped expose governmental and particularly corporate corruption and to create sympathy for the underprivileged. Crane's *Maggie, a Girl of the Streets* (1891) was a forerunner of Theodore Dreiser's *Sister Carrie* (1900), *Jennie Gerhardt* (1911) and, finally, *An American Tragedy* (1925). Norris' *The Octopus* (1901) and *The Pit* (1903) are really close companion pieces of Dreiser's *The Financier* (1912) and *The Titan* (1914).

There is no way to measure even the approximate extent of the influence of these books. Millions, however, read them and the condemnations and attempts at censorship, many of them successful, which each incurred testifies to their importance. Sinclair Lewis' *Main Street* (1920) and *Babbitt* (1922) unquestionably inspired a great deal of introspection on the part of Rotarians, Kiwanians, and other businessmen. John Steinbeck's *Grapes of Wrath* (1939) directed attention to the problem of the dust bowl and the influx of "oakies" into California more forcefully than any formal governmental report; and Erskine Caldwell did the same for the Southern sharecropper with *Tobacco Road* (Scribner's, 1932) and several other novels and plays. Beginning with James T. Farrell's *Studs Lonigan* trilogy (Vanguard, 1935), there have been a number of realistic treatments in fictionized form of how society causes urban delinquency and crime, including Richard Wright's *Native Son* (Harper, 1940), Nelson Algren's *Never Come Morning* (Harper, 1941) and *The Man with the Golden Arm* (Doubleday, 1949) and Willard Motley's *Knock At Any Door* (Appleton-Century-Crofts, 1947). Even though several of these and similar first-rate books appear on best-seller lists, it is argued that their readership is confined to the comparatively better educated. Through them, however, the effects of great literature reach the masses. With a combined membership of 3.5 million, furthermore, the book clubs (oldest and largest of which are the Book-of-the-Month, since 1926, and the Literary Guild, founded in 1927) in 1946 distributed 75 million books, one for every two persons in the United States. With about 50,000 outlets, including drugstores, groceries, and five- and ten-cent stores, publishers of cheap reprints sell about two million books a month. About 40 per cent of them are detective or mystery stories but included among them also are a large number of first-rate novels, often ones made popular by having been made into motion pictures, and some serious nonfiction.

Frank Luther Mott's *Golden Multitudes* (Macmillan, 1947) tells the story of American best sellers of which there were 324 from 1662 to 1945, using the criterion of sales equal to 1 per cent of the population at the time of original publication. Although the formula may be criticized because quite a few of the books reached their heights of popularity later, to be classified as classics rather than as best sellers, the study provides important clues to American thought and action (consequently public opinion) from Michael Wigglesworth's *The Day of Doom* (1662) to Betty MacDonald's *The Egg and I* (J. B. Lippincott, 1945). Prior to 1915, for instance, 87 of the 279 best sellers were religious books. Of the 45 since that time, none is in that category. Whereas the complete list does include quite a bit of what any English teacher would call "trash," the 21 books which Mott says "occupy a kind of best-seller heaven of their own," because they all have had sales of two million or more, are, on the whole, remarkably good. The list follows:

Alice in Wonderland (Carroll)
Ben-Hur (Wallace)
A Christmas Carol (Dickens)
Gone with the Wind (Mitchell)
How to Win Friends and Influence People (Carnegie)
In His Steps (Sheldon)
Ishmael, and its sequel, *Self-Raised* (Southworth)
Ivanhoe (Scott)
The Last of the Mohicans (Cooper)
Little Women (Alcott)

Mother Goose
One World (Willkie)
The Plays of Shakespeare
The Robe (Douglas)
Robinson Crusoe (Defoe)
See Here, Private Hargrove! (Hargrove)
The Story of the Bible (Hurlbut)
Tom Sawyer (Twain)
Treasure Island (Stevenson)
A Tree Grows in Brooklyn (Smith)
Uncle Tom's Cabin (Stowe)

On the other hand, what about the trash? During the same years that Norris, London, and Dreiser were producing socially conscious books, their sales were insignificant by comparison with those of Gene Stratton Porter, Harold Bell Wright, Mrs. Florence Barclay and other producers of potboilers. To the extent that they are accepted as true pictures of American life, the pollyanna (from Eleanor H. Porter's *Pollyanna,* Page, 1913) books may contribute to creation of a false sense of reality and distract attention from the problems with which the more serious works of fiction deal. On the other hand, the potboilers probably are read only for vicarious escapism or innocent pleasure and may have no more effect than any other substitute for daydreaming. Their emphasis is exaggerated, often with absurd plot situations which even their most avid fans recognize as atypical. Reading the light stuff keeps the readers' minds off their own troubles, helps make life more endurable, and thus has a beneficial therapeutic effect.

Detective stories. To satisfy a goodly proportion of the contemporary demand for escape literature, approximately 20 per cent of American novels today are detective stories, which appear at the rate of about five per week. "The most curious fact about the detective story," W. H. Auden wrote in "The Guilty Vicarage" in the May, 1948 *Harper's*, "is that it makes its greatest appeal precisely to those classes of people who are most immune to other forms of daydream literature. The typical detective story addict is a doctor or clergyman or scientist or artist, *i.e.*, a fairly successful professional man with intellectual interests and well read in his own field, who could never stomach the *Saturday Evening Post* or *True Confessions* or movie magazines or comics." That the clientele must be somewhat broader is suggested by the total sales; in 1945 the whodunits of Erle Stanley Gardner alone sold more than six million copies.

On the "Issue of the Day" page of the Sept. 12, 1949 New York *Daily Compass*, Lawrence G. Blochman defended the detective story as "a highly moral form of writing. Evil is always punished, and right and justice always triumph in the end. They have to. If the criminal is not caught, there is no story." Blochman also pointed out that both Hitler's Germany and Mussolini's Italy issued edicts banning and denouncing detective stories as "democratic nonsense" and cited Howard Haycraft, author of *The Art of the Mystery Story* (Simon, Schuster, 1946) as authority for the statement that

All the world's great detective stories have been produced by the democracies—England, France, America and the Scandinavian countries. Moreover, this is not a mere accident. The detective story flourishes in a climate of democracy because, like democratic justice, it is deeply-rooted in fair play and the demand for legal proof. Both of these fundamentals are abhorrent to dictatorships.

"How to" books. During the long depression public libraries reported an increased demand for books giving vocational guidance. Another type of "how to" book is that which allegedly provides a shortcut to knowledge and its popularity often is a clue to widespread frustration. Of the most successful of them, Dale Carnegie's *How To Win Friends and Influence People* (Simon, Schuster, 1937), Sinclair Lewis declared Jan. 13, 1938 in a Northwestern University sponsored lecture, "The Novelist as Prophet":

"This book with three or four million readers has nowhere in it any suggestions that a young man now facing a world which is becoming daily more difficult, a world in which you have got to be better than your father and a lot better than your grandfather—there is no suggestion that a young man should strive for a body trained not to great athletic feats but to endurance, quickness to drainage of long hours of labor. Nowhere does it list the tiniest suggestion that his mind should be trained so that he will not just blankly take everything that comes along. There is nowhere a suggestion that it would have the slightest value for a young man to know anything about economics, history, or anything of the kind. Nowhere is there a suggestion that a man should have more of a chance to success, because he is physically and mentally more purchasable—but simply throughout the book there is a suggestion that you must learn to so approach people that they will think you are better than you are."

Similar criticism could be directed at Walter Pitkin's *Life Begins at Forty* (McGraw-Hill, 1932), Alexis Carrel's *Man the Unknown* (Harper, 1935), Kenneth Goode's *How to Turn People Into Gold* (Harper, 1929), Napoleon Hill's *Think and Grow Rich* (Ralston Society, 1937) and many others. In the same lecture Lewis declared:

"The dozen books I have read are rather alike in four ways: first of all what they desire is surface tricks of manner, valet tricks, slave tricks, pretended courtesy, pretended interest in others, leading up quickly on the other fellow's subject. There is no fundamental integrity; they do not emphasize college fundamental training. The ads say: 'You read our book! You don't need to work. Just read our books and in a few days, weeks or months, you will be that greatest of all things—a rich man!' "

The same urge to obtain something the easy way, in a world so difficult that it seems to stifle initiative, explains the popularity of the many outlines of history and philosophy and science, stories of chemistry, architecture, and other subjects, advice books on how to think, read a book, be a contented bachelor or old maid or acquire the formula for achieving almost any other ambition. Books of this sort "give a lift" merely through creation of confidence that such formulas exist. When such literary quackery is popular it is a sure sign that the need for more psychiatric treatment is widespread.

Historical fiction. Whatever influence historical knowledge has upon contemporary thought and action is determined as much if not more by what men believe happened in the past as by what actually happened. This is so largely because of the extreme difficulty in establishing the truth, and to distortions, conscious and unconscious, in relating and, especially, interpreting it. Men of unquestionable probity have differed considerably, to the confusion of other men.

Considerable attention to the role of historical misinformation was given by this author in his *Hoaxes* (Macmillan, 1940), especially in Chapter 12 in which the following quotation from an article by F. J. C. Hearnshaw in the Aug. 1, 1923 *Fortnightly Review* appeared:

"History has, from early times, been the happy hunting ground of the propagandist. Every kind of zealot has felt that the appeal which he makes to abstract principle will be immeasurably strengthened if he can supplement and reenforce it . . . by a demonstration based on accomplished fact. History is the memory of the human race, but it is a memory artificially created and sustained. It is the historian who determines, by his method of selection and rejection, what facts or legends are to be perpetuated and in what light they are to be regarded."

The effect of myths and legends, with some outstanding examples, was considered in Chapter 6 of this volume. Here we are concerned with how the novelists, poets, and other non-academicians have contributed to popular knowledge and understanding, correct or otherwise, of historical events.

That the beliefs millions have regarding certain historical events and personages have been obtained from novels, poems, and plays rather than from school textbooks is indisputable. Nathaniel Hawthorne's *The Scarlet Letter*, for instance, has been more important than shelves full of solemn tomes on what New England of the second half of the seventeenth century was like. James Fenimore Cooper's *Last of the Mohicans* and Leatherstocking Tales, despite their proved inaccuracies, created a feeling for the pioneer East of early eighteenth century. Bret Harte did the same for the Far West in the Gold Rush days of the middle nineteenth century. O. E. Rolvaag, with *Giants in the Earth* (Harper, 1927) and *Peder Victorious* (Harper, 1929) painted a masterful word picture of Minnesota and South Dakota in the immediate post-Civil War period. Hamlin Garland, Willa Cather, Sherwood Anderson, and many others have used historical material to make literature what W. D. Wallis wrote in *An Introduction to Anthropology* (Harper, 1926) it should be: "the reflection of language in artistic form of the culture of a people and of their ideas, ideals and values."

By contrast with the multitude of first-class works which have increased understanding of the life and times of particular people (Pearl Buck's numerous works are examples of heavy contributions to popular knowledge about a foreign country—in her case, China), there is the literary dross, altogether too much of which the public schools have helped perpetuate in the interest of super-patriotism. Such really feeble stuff as John Greenleaf Whittier's *Barbara Frietchie,* Henry Wadsworth Longfellow's *The Midnight Ride of Paul Revere* and other poems, Parson Locke Weems' *George Washington,* in which he invented the famous cherry tree anecdote, and many of the legendary tidbits with which the McGuffey *Readers* (see pages 206 to 207) were filled, easily come to mind. It is almost uncanny how much historical misinformation is remembered at the expense of historical fact as a result of the freedom that story tellers have exercised in their handling of historical evidence. Rather cynically Ted Robinson wrote in his column in the Cleveland *Plain Dealer,* as reprinted in the Jan. 31, 1947 Kansas City *Star:*

Too Bad

There is no historical proof whatever
That Louis XV
(Or whatever Louis it was)
Ever said *"L'État c'est moi."*
No contemporary heard Caesar say
"Jacta est alea."
The statement that Goethe's last words
Were *"Mehr Licht"*
Has no corroboration.
Everybody knows now
That General Pershing did not say
"Lafayette, nous voila."
So, what about it?
Washington cut down no cherry tree,
Wilhelm Tell shot no apple,
The "Connecticut Blue Laws"
Were invented by a London journalist;
What is the answer?
Here it is, logically deduced:
History did not happen.
The only thing we can count on
Is fiction and poetry—
The rest is phony.

The most important effect of such poetic and fictional license has been on the basic attitudes of Americans, a young people desperately in need of a heritage. Unlike the English and most other peoples we have no internationally or even nationally famous literary shrines. Our chauvinism, however, is fed by pictures and accounts of George Washington crossing the Delaware in a noble standing position, on his knees in the Valley Forge snow, and confessing his youthful mischief-making to his stern but sympathetic father. Similarly we have Abraham Lincoln walking miles after working hours to return some change to a customer, attending a slave auction in New Orleans, supine on the grave of Anne Rutledge, asking the brand of whiskey that General Grant drank, writing a letter to Mrs. Bixby, dashing miles to stop the execution of a young sentry who fell asleep, and doing lots of other things for which no historical proof exists. There is hardly an important figure in the annals of American history of whom anecdotes of questionable veracity have not been related.

Children's books. American parents never have worried overly much over the historical or any other misinformation their children might obtain from either their curricular or extracurricular reading. Each generation of mothers and fathers, however, has been concerned because of the particular kind of "blood and thunder" literature for which American youngsters always have displayed an avidity.

In our grandparents' days it was the dime novels, relating the exploits of Deadwood Dick, Billy the Kid, Wild Bill Hickok, Davy Crockett, Buffalo Bill, and other heroes of the Wild West. Our parents had to sneak Horatio Alger and G. A. Henty books into the house. Today their children squall if deprived of the so-called comic books in which mother and father find little that is funny. Psychologists and educators are by no means in agreement as to whether the concern is justified, but in recent years there have been organized drives, often with Parent-Teacher associations participating, to "clean up" the allegedly worst of the picture books. Some cities even have passed anti-comic book ordinances and in 1949 a bill requiring their inspection and licensing was passed by both houses of the New York legislature but was vetoed by Gov. Thomas E. Dewey. Taking warning from the growing extent of outraged parenthood, many producers of the juvenile escapist literature voluntarily reformed.

In its Report on Recreation for Youth, the National Conference on Prevention and Control of Juvenile Delinquency held in Washington in 1946, pointed out that "the young people of America find greater attraction and invest more time and money in mass entertainment media such as radio, motion pictures, newspaper comic strips, cartoon books and magazines than they do on all forms of organized recreational activities combined. Therefore, the tremendous influence on the thoughts and behavior of our youth as a result of these modern methods of expression cannot be overestimated."

Among the leading journalistic crusaders against comic books has been Sterling North, book reviewer for the New York *Post*, who calls them virtual manuals of crime with "women strapped while sleeping, women thrown to their death from skyscraper windows, men shot in the back with submachine guns, children being tortured, especially named poisons being slipped into drinks—in short, an encyclopedia of every criminal offense mentioned by the law."

In *Love and Death* (Breaking Point, N.Y., 1949) G. Legman, editor of *Neurotica*, wrote:

"The price being only ten cents apiece, and the distribution national, every American child can and does read from ten to a dozen of these pamphlets monthly, an unknown number of times, and then trades them off for others. If there is only one violent picture per page— and there are usually more—this represents a minimum supply, to every child old enough to look at pictures, of three hundred scenes of beating, shooting, strangling, torture and blood per month, or ten a day if he reads each comic book only once. The fortification of this visual violence with precisely similar aural violence over the radio daily, and both together in the movies on Saturday, must also be counted in.

"With rare exceptions, every child in America who was six years old in 1938 has by now absorbed an absolute minimum of 18,000 pictorial beatings, shootings, stranglings, blood-puddles, and torturings-to-death, from comic (ha-ha) books alone, identifying himself— unless he is a complete masochist—with the heroic beater, shooter, strangler, blood-letter, and/or torturer in every case. With repetition like that, you can teach a child anything: that black is white, to stand on his head, eat hair—anything. At the moment it is being used to teach him—and in no quiet professorial tone, but rather in flaming color and superheated dialogue—that violence is heroic, and murder a red-hot thrill.

"The effect, if not the intention, has been to raise up an entire generation of adolescents—twenty million of them—who have felt, thousands upon thousands of times, all the sensations and emotions of committing murder, except pulling the trigger. And toy guns and fireworks, advertised in the back pages of the comics—cap shooters, b-b rifles (with manufacturer's enscrolled Bill of Rights), paralysis pistols, crank'emup tommy guns, six-inch cannon-crackers, and ray-gats emitting a spark a foot and a half long—have supplied that. The Universal Military Training of the mind."

Inasmuch as the comic book industry is comparatively new, dating from 1937 since when it has grown to at least a 72 million dollar business, it is too soon to determine whether the dire predictions of North, Legman, and many others are correct; too soon to gauge the effect upon American public opinion. Already there have been numerous cases of youthful crime in which the children have confessed to having been inspired or taught methods by comic books. On the other hand there was the following item:

Corinth, Miss.—(UP)—An argument in favor of much-criticized comic books turned up here Tuesday.

Annette Lassiter, 13, told how she pulled an 11-year-old playmate from a pond and then saved his life by administering artificial respiration.

"I did it just like I saw it done in comic books," Annette said, telling how she saved Richard Bailey.

The eighth-grade girl said Richard was "all cold and blue" when she grabbed him by the hair and jerked him out of the pond.

She told another playmate to lie down and rolled Richard across the boy's back. "Then I pushed in his sides just below the ribs, and pretty soon water gushed out of his mouth."

"I knew then he was all right," Annette said.

—Chicago *Sun-Times,* June 15, 1949

To Legman there never has been anything like the sadistic comic books, either in dangerous quality or extent of readership. He sees the license that is allowed literary and pictorial presentation of murder to be a substitute for equally frank presentation of sex which is taboo (see pages 402 to 403). Many of the comic strip torture victims are, for the child, father or mother substitutes; in the case of older boys the maiming of women is a sex-substitute act. About all that can be said on the other side, until a few more decades have passed to allow proper evaluation, is that much of the so-called "respectable" reading for children also is violent though not always so bloody and less frequently illustrated gruesomely. Nevertheless, Jack and Jill are injured falling down hill; the likeable Humpty Dumpty is smashed to bits; the bough breaks and baby falls; Little Miss Muffet is frightened; Old Mother Hubbard's dog presumably starves; the Old Woman Who Lived in a Shoe beats her children; Little Polly Flinders is whipped; the anonymous author of Goosey Goosey Gander throws an old man down stairs; pussy gets thrown into the well; the Knave of Hearts is beaten by the King; Punch knocks Judy in the nose, and so on. And in the fairy tales there are giants, witches, dragons, bad kings and queens, and evil people of all kinds. At the 1936 year-end meeting of the American Psychoanalytic Society, Dr. Paul Schilder, New York University psychiatrist, went after Lewis Carroll's *Alice in Wonderland*, insisting that most of the little girl's adventures were "calculated to fill her with anxieties." For instance, he said: "She feels separated from her feet, she is stuffed in and out of small holes, and she never knows from minute to minute whether she will be small or large. . . . There are severe deprivations in the sphere of food and drink. . . . The poem of the Walrus and the Carpenter is of an astonishing cruelty. The Lobster is cooked. Alice herself frightens the birds with tales of devourings. . . . The fear of being cut to pieces comes again and again into the foreground. The head of the Jabberwock is cut off. There is a continuous threat to the integrity of the body in general."

In the literary storm which Dr. Schilder's address stirred up, *Alice* was defended because her readers are more often adult than children. As a matter of fact comic books were popular with the men in the American armed forces during World War II.

Stage and Screen

Henry Phillips Boody, long-time dramatics coach at Ripon College, once declared, "As many great truths have been taught from the stage as from the pulpit." Although the total effect of all preaching undoubtedly is considerably greater than the total effect of all drama, any list of the world's most influential plays would be much longer than any similar list of effective sermons. Aeschylus, Sophocles,

Euripides, other ancient Greeks, Shakespeare, Molière, Ibsen, Shaw, O'Neill, and other great playwrights are read and studied as well as presented and so, directly and indirectly, rival the philosophers in their all-time effect.

During most of our national history theater-going has not been considered sinful by the majority, but the playwright has had to "watch his step" more carefully than even the novelist to avoid the censor's ire. Not merely the distinctively American art (?) form, burlesque, but the legitimate stage as well has undergone periodic "cleanups" with considerable popular approval as well as constant critical scrutiny by a fanatical minority—those particularly squeamish about any display of nudity or frankness in the treatment of problems related to sex.

Almost every important play, including some considered classics, with any kind of sex angle, has run into trouble somewhere at some time. Actual scenes of sexual acts, of course, are completely taboo, and suggestively darkening the lights or lowering the curtain is risky. There are great plays dealing with such social problems as adultery, illegitimacy, homosexuality, perversions, and venereal disease, but theatrical producers and theater-goers have had to fight for them to be shown. Since the contemporary drama public is pitifully small, with college students and graduates disproportionately represented in it, and confined to only a few large cities, whatever widespread effect drama has is becoming more and more indirect and the censorship problem correspondingly minor.

The major factor bringing about the virtual death of vaudeville and the decline of the legitimate stage has been the motion picture which has taken over as the main type of show business in the United States and throughout most of the rest of the world. Although *Hamlet* has been presented, studied, and debated for more than three centuries, more people probably viewed Laurence Olivier's 1948 prize-winning cinematic production of it than have seen it acted on the stage throughout its entire history. With close to 60 million Americans going to almost 90 million movies each week—compared with an average weekly church attendance of 30 million and an average daily school attendance of 27 million—it hardly could be otherwise. Nor could the at least potential importance of motion pictures on public opinion be considered as anything except tremendous.

Of studies of the 1.4 billion dollar motion picture industry, including all phases pertinent to determination of its social effect, there have been many. Among the best volumes in the sizeable library on the subject are Edgar Dale's *Children's Attitudes at Motion Pictures* (Macmillan, 1935) and *Content of Motion Pictures* (Harper, 1935), H. J. Forman's *Our Movie Made Children* (Macmillan, 1930), Leo C. Rosten's *Hollywood: the Movie Colony, the Movie Makers* (Harcourt, Brace, 1941), Gilbert Seldes' *Movies for Millions* (Batesford, 1937) and Herbert Blumer's *Movies and Conduct* (Macmillan, 1933). From them it is determined that from 35 to 40 per cent of those who occupy the 11,400,000 seats in America's 19,000 theaters are below the age of twenty-one years and that attendance steadily declines after one has reached the age of forty-five. Thus, motion pictures are primarily for comparatively young people for whom they are *a*, if not *the*, leading form of entertainment.

"The best pictures are the ones that make money," Dore Schary, head of production for Metro-Goldwyn, stated frankly at a *Life*-sponsored "round table on the movies" as reported, under the editorship of Eric Hodgins, in the June 27, 1949 issue of that magazine. Thus is epitomized the Hollywood defense of much of the criticism to which it incessantly is subjected. It is the familiar alibi offered by newspaper publishers, radio chains and stations, authors, publishers, and distributors of comic books, and all other kinds of low-grade literature, namely: "We are giving the public what it wants."

Disregarding both the validity and the morality of this defense, about which millions of words have been written pro and con, what is the effect of what the public, like it or not, does get? First and most important, it gets entertainment, largely of the escapist variety. It takes only a minimum of mental effort to follow the plot and action of the overwhelming majority of American motion pictures. Rarely is any heavy thinking required of anyone. Consequently, it is possible to arrive in the middle or to sleep through large portions of all but a few of them, without having one's pleasure seriously impaired—something which would be impossible as regards any kind of stage show except vaudeville, burlesque, or musical comedy.

To appeal to the "lowest common denominator," as the movies do, means to avoid the controversial and to simplify or ignore life's problems. To provide the escapism and relaxation which Americans want, Hollywood specializes in creation of a dream world of adventure, love, luxury, and success which its millions of fans vicariously enjoy. Wrote Peter H. Odegard in *The American Public Mind* (Columbia University, 1930):

"The producer must strike, as nearly as possible, the least common denominator of emotion and intelligence. He knows that people everywhere respond to appeals of hunger, sex and ambition. Most men secretly yearn to be Don Juans and John D's, most women long to be composites of Mary Magdalene and the Madonna. The movies provide an emotional outlet for those desires. In the semi-dark of the picture house, the misunderstood husband, the exploited and exhausted worker, the drudge wife, can enter into the romances of the screen, they can commit adultery by proxy, engage in the most thrilling adventures, become Cinderellas or Caesars, and for the time being forget, as utterly as in the dream world, the harsh and dull realities of the workaday world."

Translated into terms pertinent to this study, that means *the movies help people to avoid coming to grips with the important problems of the hour*; in fact, they divert attention from such problems, act as an "opiate of the people," much as did the chariot races and gladiatorial contests of long ago. Outside the theater the average person will admit that life is crueler and justice not so likely to triumph as it does on the screen. That is exactly why he patronizes the movies: to observe life as he wishes it was rather than as it is, a fact which foreign observers of American films comprehend too little. The result is that the motion pictures avoid disturbing sacred myths and legends, including the social ones, and consequently contribute to the perpetuation of them. In its March, 1938 report on "The Movies and Propaganda," the Institute for Propaganda Analysis declared:

"The motion picture dramatist, like the writer of popular fiction, knows the keys to strike to arouse the proper emotions. He secures stock responses by appeals to our interest in sex and sentimentality; violence and excitement; nationalistic symbols; sweetness, optimism and happy endings; wish-fulfilment through reveries and day dreams; popular prejudices. These appeals and interests are combined in popular stereotypes which can play significant parts in conscious or unconscious propaganda. For example:

"1. The successful culmination of a romance will solve most of the dilemmas of the hero and the heroine. . . .

"2. Catch the criminal and you solve the crime problem. . . .

"3. War and the preparation for war are thrilling, heroic and glamorous. . . .

"4. The good life is the acquisitive life, with its emphasis on luxury, fine homes and automobiles, evening dress, swank and suavity. . . .

"5. Certain races, nationalities or minority groups are comical, dull-witted, or possess traits that mark them as greatly different from and inferior to native white Americans. . . ."

Perhaps the most serious charge against the motion picture industry is that whereas it provides vicarious adventure for many, it also increases the frustrations of others. Certainly the average movie-goer's home seems drab by comparison with the settings of most pictures. In Chapter 9 (see pages 324 to 325) examples were given of attempts to make motion picture-inspired dreams come true through imitation of the fads and fashions introduced on the screen. Small boys play Tom Sawyer or Robin Hood and adolescents adopt the mannerisms and speech as well as the dress of their favorite actors and actresses. There is also a sizeable literature on the extent to which the motion pictures cause juvenile delinquency or adult crime. Nobody, however, has even attempted serious proof that increasing the list of unfulfilled desires leads to radicalism or revolutionary discontent.

Rather, the envy of cinematic luxury has resulted in extravagant hero worshipping of Hollywood personalities, the elevating of them, in fact, to positions of popular demigods whose private lives are as much the concern of their fans as their histrionic ability. So intense is this idol worship that even the federal government has not developed a more elaborate system of press agents, publicity men, and public relations counsel to help satisfy the demands of as many newspapermen as are assigned to the national capital. For millions scores of film magazines are the most popular form of reading matter. Never before in the history of the world have so many trivia been reported regarding any group of people as are produced, in a seemingly unending stream, daily in Hollywood. Protest as they may, nobody who has been moderately successful in motion pictures enjoys much privacy; for many, at the height of their popularity, it is impossible to appear in public without protection against autograph seekers and souvenir hunters. So far, furthermore, has the apotheosis gone that a movie star's fans today will forgive him almost any personal foible such as being drunk and disorderly, addicted to dope, or the parent of an illegitimate child. A generation ago, in the silent days, the brilliant career of Roscoe "Fatty" Arbuckle was ruined when he was the cause (even though, as the court decided, accidental) of the death of a young woman at a drunken brawl. Only a similar occurrence today would determine whether the public adulation has developed to the stage that it will tolerate homicide as well as seduction and rape.

When she called it "quits" with her first husband, Shirley Temple weepingly insisted that hers was not a typical Hollywood divorce, thereby indicating the stereotype which has developed regarding the bohemianism of the movie colony. In actual fact, if the automobile magnates of the Detroit area, or any other element in the population for that matter, were watched as carefully as are the actors and actresses in the Los Angeles area, with every item of gossip, including the most unreliable, reported, public opinion regarding them probably wouldn't be much different from the orthodox conceptions of what the standards of morality and conviviality in Hollywood are. For every motion picture star who "elopes" in the manner described in a predated press release, furthermore, there are scores of clients of public relations counsel who are headline-conscious and behave constantly with the potential newsworthiness of what they do in mind.

The sycophancy of the fan is the direct consequence of the "star" system on which Hollywood thrives. More important than title or plot is the actor cast in a leading role. And his worshippers flock to see him act, not the part in the particular picture, but himself. Motion picture advertisers have learned by unhappy experience not to reveal that a widely known actor or actress is to attempt to be versatile in a forthcoming film. One such lesson occurred when it was advertised that the likable Fred MacMurray was to be a "heel" in *Double Indemnity*. Although it was an excellent film and Mr. MacMurray's acting was superb, it was a box office failure. In "Movies in America: After Fifty Years," in the November, 1947 *Atlantic Monthly*, Budd Schulberg wrote:

"Today, if a star can act—or create a living character on the screen —it is only an incidental embellishment of his stature as a member of our contemporary mythology. More often, men and women who came to the screen as actors have had to suspend or freeze their gifts in order to fit into the fixed roles they are playing in the minds, hearts or emotionally immature libidos of the movie fans (short for fanatics). James Cagney, for instance, was an actor before he became the God of Hardboiled Goodness, Soft-boiled Badness and Small-Fry Sex Appeal. Long before Spencer Tracy was deified, he went to the chair in *The Last Mile* and went effectively. But he is a grown-up Eagle Scout now, the Bumbling, Practical, Hard-Headed but Soft-hearted AMERICAN. Why let him play any other part, the producer argues with terrifying logic, when we already have box-office proof that this is the part the public wants him to play."

Whereas old-time drama lovers admired versatility in their Bernhardts, Fiskes, Drews, Booths, Skinners, and Barrymores, it probably would have been fatal for the producers to have attempted to cast anyone except Clark Gable in the role of Rhett Butler in *Gone With the Wind*. The difficulty in finding someone for Scarlett O'Hara in the same picture stemmed largely from the fact that most popular American actresses were typed and the role of Scarlett just didn't fit any of the types. So an unknown English actress had to be imported. Discussing "The Hero" in the Oct. 18, 1943 *New Republic*, Manny Farber wrote:

"The hero in American movies fluctuates between two idealized personalities, whose common bond is an allegiance to Superman. One, the older, is a mixture of Abe Lincoln, Dick the Chimney Sweep and a cowboy, in which goodness and lonesome bravery are the main ingredients. The other is a belligerent, egocentric character who is as malevolent and aggressive as the other is pure of heart and backward; in the gangster-movie days he was called Blackie, now he is called by names like Rick, Joe Rossi and Sam Spade. He is acted mainly by Humphrey Bogart, but also by John Garfield, Alan Ladd, Brian Donlevy and George Raft.

"The older-fashioned hero is a long-bodied, long-armed man whose air is one of troubled silence, and who grew up in the bleaker parts of the country to be shy, honest and not given to excesses. He doesn't seek success, but because he is a physical genius he reaches the hero class and performs there as a good honest man would. He is probably the most likable person to see winning so many rewards, especially when his person is that of Gary Cooper (who had as much to do with shaping this movie personality as anyone else), Jimmy Stewart or Henry Fonda. . . .

"The hero played by Mr. Bogart, which grew out of the gangster film and Dashiell Hammett detective novels . . . is the soured half of the American dream, which believes that if you are good, honest and persevering you will win the kewpie doll. . . . Bogart expresses the hostility and rebellion the existence of which the Cooper tradition ignores. . . . The anti-intellectual, anti-emotional and pro-action life of these heroes is in the historical American patter, and perfectly suited to the movies, where movement and gesture are of so much importance. . . ."

When the numerous forms of censorship and pressure with which motion picture producers must contend are considered, what is remarkable perhaps is that their product is as good as it is rather than the opposite. Not only must Hollywood not violate any of the national taboos, myths and legends, but it must bear in mind the sensibilities of virtually every group of any kind in the country. In "What's Right About the Movies," in the July, 1943 *Harper's*, Sara Colton and Harvey Jones explained how picayunish hawkeyed movie-goers can be. As a result meticulous care must be taken to make the settings 100 per cent perfect, meaning that costumes, furnishings, dialogue, and all other details must be accurate. More important, the reactions that important individuals and groups will have to even the most minute details must be anticipated. For example, Japanese censors disliked *Madame Butterfly* because the heroine's elbow was exposed when she embraced the hero. The National Billiard Association has been known to protest because pool houses are shown as unkempt places; the glass blowers have objected to canned beer being shown, and, vice versa, the canned beer producers have complained that they are discriminated against because the shadows guzzle out of bottles. Among the most vociferous, because they have the facilities with which to make their beefs known, have been newspapermen. A typical outburst was that of Sydney J. Harris in his "Strictly Personal" column in the Oct. 31, 1949 Chicago *Daily News* as follows:

Invited to attend the screening of a newspaper film called "Chicago Deadline," I hastily begged off, pleading a fictitious previous engagement.

The reason being, to-wit, that I am tired of seeing newspaper movies that are laughably inaccurate in the portrayal of the way a paper is put out. Maybe "Chicago Deadline" is authentic, but the chances are against it. Even with the so-called "technical adviser" on the set.

In the score or so of newspaper movies I have been foolish enough to attend, not one even remotely resembled reality, despite the fact that experienced ex-newspapermen often wrote the script. Somehow or other the producer's half-wit nephew always manages to turn the city room into a combination alcoholic ward and a squirrel cage.

I remember hearing, some years ago, about this reporter on the New York Times who went to Hollywood to act as technical director of a city-room drama. He was getting $100 a day, at first took his job quite seriously.

He soon found, however, that the director had his own ideas about the way a newspaper should be run. For instance, he had reporters rushing about madly with galley proofs in their moist little hands.

FARCICAL

When the technical adviser protested that reporters never get to see galley proofs, he was told shortly, "It looks better that way—gives the scene an air of realism."

In another scene, reporters dictated headlines over the telephone, rushed into the shop shouting, "Stop the presses!", sassed back the managing editor, and wore their hats everywhere but in the shower. It was more of a farce than a drama.

After a day or two the technical expert sat by quietly, saying nothing, and when the shooting was finished the director told him that he was the finest technical adviser he had ever had.

His fame quickly spread, and two weeks later he was hired by another studio. Here he smartly kept his mouth shut (at $150 a day) while the same absurdities were being perpetrated. Only once did he offer a suggestion—when he noticed that the lettering on the door reading "Managing Editor" faced into the room. He gently pointed out that the lettering should face the other way.

As the workmen were changing the sign, he heard the director murmur to his assistant, "Where did we find that fellow? He's invaluable!"

By far the most important influence on motion picture production since its organization in 1934 has been the Roman Catholic Legion of Decency which gives ratings to all films. At the time of its origin Mae West pictures were great favorites; the Legion virtually eliminated Mae as a motion picture actress. Joseph Breen who has charge of certifying films for the Motion Picture Producers and Distributors of America, commonly called the Johnston (formerly the Hays) office, is a Catholic, so most movie censorship is censorship at the source. Several states and most cities of any size, however, have their own censors and the net effect is that few pictures are produced which will run counter to any of them. In addition to the American censorship there also is the foreign market to bear in mind. A warning from Nazi Germany was at least partly responsible for the pre-Pearl Harbor shelving of plans to film Sinclair Lewis' *It Can't Happen Here* and Vincent Sheean's *Personal History*, although, in the case of the latter, memory of Catholic opposition to the anti-Franco *Blockade* was a factor.

Orson Welles' *Citizen Kane* survived a terrific lambasting by the Hearst newspapers but Welles and some others connected with the film have suffered from boycott by that segment of the press ever since. *The Birth of a Nation* was not revived in several cities because of organized opposition by Negro groups and others interested in improved race relations. The Grand Army of the Republic's protest against *Gone With the Wind* was less effective, partly because the G.A.R. membership had dwindled to a handful of nonogenarians.

In 1948 the motion picture industry entered its worst period of innocuousness and inanity as a result of the scare thrown into it by the House Un-American Activities committee late in 1947 (see pages 346 to 347). In 1946, and earlier that year, there had appeared a number of pictures with social significance, including *Gentleman's Agreement* and *Crossfire*, which attacked anti-Semitism, and *Best Years of Our Lives*, and there was indication that more of the same were to come. Then, however, the congressional committee, dominated by J. Parnell Thomas of New Jersey and John Rankin of Mississippi, conducted hearings in Hollywood in October and in Washington in December during which the industry was the target for a severe barrage of vitriol, and the famous ten were cited for contempt. At first the producers indicated that they would defy the threats to their independence but almost immediately their courage collapsed and, instead, they joined the witch hunt themselves, presumably to ward off the danger of any governmental censorship. Although no films officially were branded by the Thomas-Rankin group as subversive, at least part of a suspect list prepared by Dr. John R. Lechner for the committee's benefit became known. Those pictures and the reasons for their being regarded as subversive were as follows:

The Best Years of Our Lives, starring Fredric March. It showed a conservative old banker who thought financial values were more important than human values when it came to evaluating GI applications for loans.

Boomerang, which showed corruption in American city government in which an influential real estate operator was one of the villains.

Margie, a flapper-age boy and girl romance, which had a high schoc! debater demand that the Marines get out of Nicaragua. Of course they've been out a long time, but it was once a famous story.

The Strange Love of Martha Ivers, in which an industrialist was the villain.

Medal for Benny, in which John Steinbeck kids a local Chamber of Commerce planning to give a medal to a returning soldier.

The Searching Wind, in which the State Department and politicians are held up to what was regarded as ridicule. This is a Lillian Hellman play.

Watch on the Rhine. Nobody quite knows why this is regarded as subversive. It was anti-Nazi, but again it is a Lillian Hellman play.

North Star, another play by Lillian Hellman showing life in a small Russian village during the war. It apparently was found objectionable on the grounds that it doesn't paint a drab picture of Russia.

Mission to Moscow, which is regarded as out-and-out Russian propaganda and doesn't show Vishinsky as prosecutor of the Moscow trials.

Pride of the Marines. There is a scene in this in which a Jewish marine at the end of the war remarks that while he isn't going home blind as does one of his comrades, he will have to face his own particular problems growing out of anti-Semitism in America.

Inveterate movie goers know that at least during the two years after the hearings it was impossible to prepare a list of any ten films of American origin to compare in quality with that supposed dishonor roll. During that period, however, Hollywood proceeded allegedly to make its production scientific so as to comply with popular demand. The Audience Research, Inc. (George Gallup), and New Entertainment Workshop (Albert E. Sandlinger) methods were described by Ernest Boreman in "The Public Opinion Myth" which appeared in the July, 1947 *Harper's*. The major weakness of these and other pretests of pictures to determine their probable success is that test audiences view only what is presented to them. Masterpieces in any field of art, it correctly is argued, are rare and it is as unfair to judge Hollywood by its worst as it would be to use the same method in judging the quality of literature or any other form of art. Nevertheless, *Hollywood never will improve its product without a free atmosphere in which to experiment.* That it never has had, and, instead of decreasing, the pressures and restrictions are increasing, becoming worse each year than they were the preceding one.

Although they have become an inconsequential and generally boring part of any evening at the theater, newsreels deserve a word or two, primarily because they once were regarded as providing great opportunity for the new gadget to become socially beneficial. Newsreels also are subject to censorship, actual and feared. One of the earliest flagrant examples was the banning of shots of what has become known as the Memorial Day Massacre which occurred in 1937 when ten parading strikers were shot and killed by policemen before the South Chicago Republic Steel Company plant. A senatorial committee, investigating violence in labor disputes, obtained the films and, through friendship with the chairman, Sen. Robert M. LaFollette, Jr. of Wisconsin, Paul Y. Anderson of the St. Louis *Post-Dispatch* viewed them. Anderson revealed what they contained—evidence quite different from that which police and company representatives presented to a coroner's jury—and thereafter the films were shown in many parts of the country; never, however, officially in Chicago or most other parts of Cook County.

Similar situations have been avoided in more recent years primarily by the newsreel people's disinclination to record anything significant. The title of an article by Siegfried Kracauer and Joseph Lyford in the Dec. 13, 1948 *New Republic,* "A Duck Crosses Main Street," suggests the fatuous nature of much newsreel subject matter. As the authors point out, however, the newsreels of 1948 contained plenty of anti-Communist propaganda, speeches of public figures being edited so as to emphasize statements consistent with the administration's foreign policy and its domestic loyalty program.

Perhaps the most effective use of newsreels for political purposes was in California in 1936 when the defeat of Upton Sinclair, Democratic candidate for governor, was accredited to the effectiveness of the motion picture attack. Only discerning movie-goers detected the grease paint on the faces of the army of bums shown dropping off freight trains in Los Angeles, allegedly attracted because of the supposed imminent victory for Sinclair and his EPIC (End Poverty in

California) program. The scenes had been leftovers from a picture, *Wild Boys of the Road*. In other newsreels voters were interviewed regarding their choice of candidates. A shaggy bewhiskered man explained his preference for Sinclair, "Vell, his system worked vell in Russia. Vy can't it work here?" In presidential campaigns the newsreels are careful to give both major parties equal treatment, but in off-election years they are inclined to give priority to bathing beauties, battleships being launched or firing broadsides, forest fires, and rehearsed statements by cabinet members on matters of state. Embarrassing scenes, as the Duke of Windsor tripping over a sound cable with comic effect at his wedding, or King Victor Emmanuel of Italy being lifted onto a horse are self-censored so that the public doesn't even get anything to laugh at in most newsreel programs.

Radio

There is not much to say about the effect upon public opinion of radio that has not already been said about motion pictures. The first broadcasting station, KDKA, began operations Nov. 2, 1920, when about 400,000 Americans owned receiving sets as a hobby. In 1949 there were approximately 2,000 AM stations, 1,000 FM stations, and 100 television stations. Receiving sets were to be found in 94 per cent of all American homes and totaled about 75 million. According to the 1948 annual report of the Federal Communications commission, the average daily listening per family was about four hours.

Thus is provided striking evidence of the American predilection for new mechanical gadgets. More importantly, it reveals the eagerness with which a new means of escapism is taken up. Radio also "gives the public what it wants," and that means, apparently, popular music, gagsters, soap operas, easy quiz shows, and prize contests. The price exacted for such variety is singing commercials and other blatant forms of advertising which, radio bigwigs insist, listeners also like or they wouldn't buy so much of the stuff thereby promoted.

In other words, radio has not lived up to early predictions that it would revolutionize education and politics, for the better of course. It did enable Franklin Delano Roosevelt to counteract some of the bad press he received by means of his fireside chats during which he explained his policies to the American people. During the Munich crisis in the fall of 1938 it "came of age" as a fast reporter of world-shaking news, and throughout World War II it announced news of transcendent importance before the newspapers were able to reach the street. To their great surprise newspaper publishers discovered that radio news increased rather than decreased their sales, so they stopped their two decades-long fight to restrict news broadcasts. Just to play safe, however, they have done their best to rectify their original mistake and have bought out as many stations as possible. In 1949, of 1,066 AM stations, 430 were owned by or affiliated with newspapers as were 290 of 429 FM stations.

Radio has contributed to the standardization of American thought and action. In *The Psychology of Radio* (Peter Smith, 1941), Henry Cantril and Gordon Allport wrote: "When a million or more people hear the same subject matter, the same arguments and appeals, the same music and humor, when their attention is held in the same way and at the same time to the same stimuli, it is psychologically inevitable that they should acquire in some degree common interests, common tastes and common attitudes. In short, it seems to be the nature of radio to encourage people to think and feel alike."

In 1949, 1,066 or 59 per cent of the nation's 1,800 AM commercial stations were affiliated with one of the four major networks, but the influence of the networks is much greater, inasmuch as the proportion of large and powerful stations which are affiliated is well above the average: 78.3 per cent in cities over 250,000; 88 per cent in cities from 50,000 to 250,000 and 85.7 per cent in cities under 50,000. Also 65.8 per cent of all FM metropolitan stations were affiliated. This meant that 55 per cent of the time devoted to commercial programs on large stations originated with networks. The comparable figures for medium and small stations were 49 and 39 per cent respectively, the over-all average being 45 per cent.

Because of the similarity of the radio fare of Americans in all parts of the country, a federal law passed in 1934 requiring stations to make available equal time for rival candidates in any political campaign is considered to be in the public interest. On June 2, 1949, the FCC virtually rescinded a ruling, of eight and a half years' standing, to permit radio stations to editorialize.

The earlier decision had been given Jan. 16, 1941, in the case of the Mayflower Broadcasting Corporation which had applied for the

license assigned to WAAB, then of Boston, now of Worcester, which
was a part of the Yankee Network. Basis for the request was that in
1937 and 1938 WAAB had broadcast editorials backing political candidates and ideas endorsed by the station owner. Although the FCC
denied the application, it ordered WAAB to desist from editorializing.
In part the decision read:

"It is clear that with the limitations in frequencies inherent in the
nature of radio, the public interest can never be served by a dedica-
tion of any broadcast facility to support the partisan ends of the
licensee. Radio can serve as an instrument of democracy only when
devoted to the communication of information and the exchange of
ideas fairly and objectively presented. A truly free radio cannot be
used to support the candidacies of his friends. It cannot be devoted
to the support of the principles he happens to regard most favorably.
In brief, the broadcaster cannot be an advocate."

Fearing for their licenses, which are renewable by the FCC every six
months, stations carefully obeyed the spirit as well as the letter of the
Mayflower decision for several years. There then developed, however,
the popularity of the commercially sponsored commentator who presumably expressed the views, not of the station but of the advertiser
who paid his salary. The result was that during the postwar period
the purpose of the Mayflower ruling—to insure the expression of a
variety of viewpoints over the air—was completely defeated. Liberal
commentators and those critical of the basic tenets of American foreign policy were jobless, and radio listeners received an uncritical,
highly chauvinistic interpretation no matter how they twisted their
dials.

Agitation for repeal of the Mayflower decision began in 1946,
spearheaded by the National Association of Broadcasters which argued
freedom of speech. Said Justin Miller, NAB president: "There is nothing in editorializing which involves clear and present danger to peace,
security, health or welfare. For that reason, editorializing falls clearly
within the meaning of freedom of speech in the First Amendment."
Although in effect a reversal, technically the 1949 decision was merely
a clarification of what constitutes fairness. This was presented in a
13-page report which required editorial interpretation itself. Its mere
vagueness was a virtual "go ahead" signal as it contained plentiful

loopholes which an errant station could use by way of later defense. For instance, the following:

"There can be no one all-embracing formula which licensees can hope to apply to insure the fair and balanced presentation of all public issues. Different issues will inevitably require different techniques of presentation and production. The licensee will, in each instance, be called upon to exercise his best judgment and good sense in determining what subjects should be considered, the particular format of the programs to be devoted to each subject, the different shades of opinion to be presented and the spokesman for each point of view."

From the standpoint of the public, and consequently of public opinion, it makes no difference whether the views expressed by such-and-such a commentator are those of the station to which he is listening or of the particular manufacturer of soap or soup paying for the time. A one-sided presentation is a one-sided presentation regardless of origin or financial backing, and any hope that radio would avoid monopolistic thought control have gone aglimmering. In past years surveys usually have shown greater confidence in radio's handling of news than in newspapers. That radio can take advantage of the new freedom to be unfair that the FCC has offered it and retain that reputation seems doubtful. Three-fourths of the revenue of the four major networks comes from four industries—food, drugs, soap, and tobacco—and the forces that control the advertising dollars of those industries are at best conservative. It is unlikely that editorializers employed directly by networks or stations will be engaged as an antidote to the kind hired by commercial sponsors.

It is not only what the commentators say but, in addition, the way that they say it that is important in its effect. The equivalent on the air of the newspaper streamer headline, sometimes in color, is the breathless style which the newscaster assumes to lend emphasis to what he is saying. Even though he may be reading a text prepared by someone else, the commentator strives for a distinctive manner of delivery to make listeners believe that he is dealing with world-shaking events. Sometimes the effect is achieved by rapid fire delivery with the dramatic pause used for occasional emphasis; or the speaker may sound as though he were about to break into tears or seek a rocket ship to carry him to the moon and away from the world's problems which have become too much for any mortal to stand. There may be the sound of telegraph or typewriter keys or of presses rolling; new items may be introduced by "flashes" or "bulletins" or "extras." All of these tricks are for the purpose of keeping the listener tuned to the particular station and to make him as excited as the commentator pretends to be himself. The effect often is an exaggerated impression on the part of listeners as to the importance of a particular item of news. Since newscasts and commentaries are of short duration, even without attempt at comment or interpretation, there is an inevitable exercise of editorial judgment in the mere selection of items and details to be emphasized or presented at all.

In the February, 1949 *Harper's* an anonymous author who identified himself simply as "One of Them," began an article on "Washington's Armchair Correspondents" with the following anecdote:

"The Senate of the United States was plodding through an earnest debate on the Marshall Plan. The commentator who was sitting next to me high in the press gallery pressed me on the arm. He was a man whose voice is familiar in millions of American homes. For weeks he had been 'revealing' the inside story of the European Recovery Program for his audience.

"He pointed to a white-haired Senator who was speaking on the floor.

" 'Who's that?' he wanted to know.

"It was Senator Arthur Vandenberg."

In the early days of radio, of necessity, news staffs consisted mostly of former newspapermen. Increasingly, however, radio has recruited its talent without regard to previous experience. As a result more and more writers and speakers of radio news never have had journalistic experience outside the radio newsroom. All they know of public affairs and public figures is what they have read in the newspapers or magazines or what comes into the radio offices via Associated Press or United Press which gathers news primarily for newspapers but rewrites it into speakable form for the air waves.

Since the bulk of radio time is devoted, not to news and its interpretation, but to entertainment, the clues as to what the most important aspects of radio's influence on public opinion are must be sought through examination of the soap operas, quiz, and variety shows which receive the high Hooper and other ratings. As stated, similar to motion pictures, radio must seek the "common denominator." That means even stricter observance of the taboos, myths, and legends, avoidance of the controversial, and respect for stereotypes but avoidance of giving undue offense to any strong pressure group.

The Hooper rating—the estimated number of listeners to a particular program—was that obtained by C. E. Hooper, Inc. by means of telephone calls made regularly in 36 cities to radio and television listeners asking what programs they were tuned to at the time. In March, 1950, except for the New York area, Hooper sold out to A. C. Nielsen & Co. of Chicago which for several years used an electronic instrument known as an audiometer, attached to the radio or television set to record every moment of usage, every motion of the dial, day and night.

As reported by Sam Lesner in the March 17, 1950 Chicago *Daily News*, Nielsen planned to install its machines in homes representing "the rich, medium and poor—large, medium and small families in all age, nationality and education levels," and to use a new instrument capable of measuring up to four radios in the same home, or AM, FM and television "whether the three types are combined in a single receiver or arranged in separate sets." Obviously, Nielsen, as was true of Hooper, must deal in statistical totals and averages, unable to gauge intensity of listener interest or effect upon him. Only by inference also is it possible for any such testers to conclude that listeners are being given what they want or merely accepting what they get.

Backbone of all radio is music and, over the years, the total effect probably has been to develop and improve public taste. There are several fine programs of operas and symphonies which have proved popular enough to survive for years. The same is true of a number of forum and quiz programs, notably Town Meeting of the Air, the University of Chicago Round Table, and Information Please. For each high-grade program of this sort, however, there are innumerable imitators of much lower quality. Because a station understandably wants to sell its best time, many of the best educational programs are broadcast during hours of lowest potential listenership. About 5 per cent of the time of commercial stations is devoted to strictly educational programs, and the 46 noncommercial educational stations, chiefly owned by universities and school systems, are low-powered stations with comparatively minor appeal.

By contrast about 20 million women listen to radio serials, usually called soap operas because most of the leading ones are sponsored by soap manufacturers. They are daylight programs which the housewife hears as she goes about her work. In an article, "The Effect of Radio on Public Opinion," in the symposium, *Press, Radio and Film in a Democracy*, edited by Douglas Waples (University of Chicago Press. 1942), Paul F. Lazarsfeld wrote: "Many studies have shown how intensely women listeners take the play to heart; how they wait eagerly from one day to another to learn how things turn out; and how much they are inclined to pattern their own behavior upon the solutions for domestic problems that appear in the serials. This is a unique opportunity for radio to influence public opinion. But actually the soap operas carefully refrain from exercising any such influence. The settings are middle-class, conforming to the environment of the listeners. It is not social forces, but the virtues and vices of the central characters that move the events along."

Soap operas are of the same nature and effect as literary potboilers, except that they are an easier form of recreation. The plots and characters, of course, differ but the formula is pretty much the same. Written to appeal to women they pose such problems as "Can romance begin at 35?" "Can a young girl from a western mining town find happiness as the wife of an English lord?" and "What happens when a wicked stepmother meets a dashing but understanding young psychiatrist?" The serials thrive on suspense which makes the fan eagerly await tomorrow's installment to learn how the problem presented in today's was solved. No great lessons are taught, or even attempted, by the script writers. The shows are intended simply as entertainment, and they did not create the low taste that their listeners display; they simply capitalize upon it.

One of the most serious charges against the soap operas is their tendency to strengthen existent stereotypes. At a conference in July, 1949 on Radio, Television and the Negro People in New York, sponsored by the Committee for the Negro in the Arts, the actor, Canada Lee, charged that "The richness of Negro life, its humor, warmth and humanity and fighting spirit are not considered fit subjects for depiction on the air. Negro actors recently were asked to play the role of cannibals on a television show, to eat a white dummy before the cameras. Of course they refused to take the role. The Negro on the air is depicted in stereotyped fashion as a minstrel or buffoon. He is restricted to characterizations like those played by 'Beulah' and 'Rochester' and 'Amos 'n' Andy.' Where is the story of our lives in terms of the Negro slums in which we must live, insecurity of life and limb, food not available, and jobs not available? The plain fact is that a virtual Iron Curtain against the entire Negro people exists as far as radio is concerned."

What such criticism amounts to is that soap operas have not crusaded against prevailing prejudices and other evils. The same charge can and has been directed against other, in fact all, phases of radio. Thus the total effect of radio has been to strengthen rather than change the status quo which about summarizes the importance of this comparatively new medium in relation to public opinion.

Television

Of the even newer medium, television, the same can be said to date, plus the fact that the quality of entertainment provided during the first few years of full operation fell far short of what it undoubtedly will be necessary to provide in order to induce any fans to abandon old-fashioned radio. Already, however, television has been credited with having put some newsreel theaters out of business, including the first, New York's Embassy Newsreel Theater which opened Nov. 2, 1929 and switched to being an orthodox motion picture house in November, 1949. As already suggested (see page 483) the decline in the quality of newsreels probably is sufficient to explain their fall from popularity even without television's competition.

CHAPTER THIRTEEN

RELIGION AND CHURCHES

*People think differently about political, social and economic
questions because of their religious beliefs, a fact which is
becoming increasingly important as the Catholic population
grows larger in the United States.*

In July, 1949, when Francis Cardinal Spellman of New
York attacked Mrs. Eleanor Roosevelt for her stand on federal aid
to education and the former first lady made reply, most American
newspapers played the story "straight" and refrained from editorial
comment. Thus they deviated no more than the stature of the protag-
onists made necessary from the traditional rule that matters involving
religious controversy are "too hot to handle" in any peace-loving
newsroom.

Long-continued obedience to this journalistic taboo will be in
jeopardy if the trend toward active participation in political affairs by
religious groups continues. Methodist Bishop G. Bromley Oxnam of
New York blamed the shelving of the 1949 federal aid to education
bill by the House of Representatives on Catholic pressure and warned
against formation of an American Catholic political party. Protestants and Other Americans United for Separation of Church and
State had lobbied unsuccessfully for the measure. Other issues about
which religious groups have attempted to influence public and legislative opinion include: prohibition, teaching evolution in the schools,
sterilization of the feebleminded, divorce, dissemination of birth
control information, control of gambling, and public health drives
against venereal diseases. The significant differences of viewpoint between Catholics and Protestants as regards these and numerous other

issues are derived from official church pronouncements and from attitudes conditioned by basic religious beliefs.

Although it is a comparatively recent and generally considered unpleasant phenomenon for religion to be a major factor in consideration of political issues in the United States, exactly the opposite has been true throughout the entire history of almost every other nation in the world. In recent times the battle has been comparatively bloodless but the score card for the centuries doubtless would show that there have been more casualties in the name of religion than in any other cause. *The concept of separation of church and state is a distinctly American one*, stated thus in the first amendment to the federal Constitution: "Congress shall make no law respecting an establishment of religion, or prohibiting the free exercise thereof." State churches exist today in every European nation except Switzerland, and the governments of Anglican Great Britain and Lutheran Sweden, as well as those of Catholic nations provide various degrees of financial support to a favored church and its parochial schools. Since 1870, furthermore, there have been powerful church political parties in all European countries, a situation never duplicated in the United States if one rules out the fanatical and short-lived anti-Masonic and Know-Nothing parties of a century ago.

Major reasons why the separation of church and state idea has worked so well in this country has been its predominantly Protestant character throughout virtually its entire history, not necessarily because it has been Protestant but because of its one-sidedness. In 1790, less than 1 per cent of the population was Catholic. By 1860 the Catholic proportion had increased to 10 per cent. Today it is almost 20 per cent of the total population and about one-third of those with formal religious affiliation. Since most of the Catholic population is concentrated in large cities, the leading political machines have been aware of the "problem" for several decades, and many are Catholic-controlled. Although the total Protesant vote still is considerably larger, it is split into 256 different sects of which the largest, the Methodists, split into 19 bodies, are not more than one-third as numerous as the Catholics. Catholic unity and discipline make the church a powerful political pressure group which even presidents and newspaper publishers do not care to defy.

Despite the first amendment there is no such thing as absolute freedom of religion. Human sacrifices and hex killings, for instance, are murder in the eyes of the law and religious persuasion or revelation is not an adequate defense. Polygamy was made unlawful in 1890 when the U.S. Supreme Court upheld congressional action to that effect and shortly thereafter was outlawed by the Church of Jesus Christ of Latter-day Saints (the Mormons). As long as Roman Catholics were a negligible minority Protestants were unworried and tolerant of the "one true church" concept. Now that the former are strong enough to exercise considerable political pressure, it is not fanatics of the type who belonged to the American Protective Association before the turn of the century nor those who spread vicious canards regarding Alfred E. Smith in 1928 who are in the vanguard of alarmists over the possibility of a Catholic United States. Rather, today it is the usually temperate liberals who are frightened by such books as Paul Blanshard's *American Freedom and Catholic Power* (Beacon, 1949) as to what it would mean if such were to come about. Its centuries' long hold over the economic and political life of Eastern European nations now broken, the Vatican understandably is increasing its efforts to retain and gain strength in other parts of the world, the United States included, perhaps primarily. Already the effects are evident in many hitherto unaffected aspects of American life, and it seems a safe surmise that the long-time journalistic "hush hush" policy is due for modification, if only by the cumulative impact of further incidents similar to that of the Cardinal Spellman-Mrs. Roosevelt correspondence.

The Effect of Religious Belief

It makes a difference in one's thinking on social, moral, economic, political and other matters of public opinion whether he is a Catholic, Protestant, Jew, Mohammedan, Christian Scientist, Mormon, Jehovah's Witness, Buchmanite, agnostic, or atheist. Although not more than one-fourth of approximately 75 million members of approximately 250,000 American churches usually attend services on any particular Sabbath, the effect of religious training in childhood is of lifelong importance. Because of the traditional American desire to avoid religious controversy, religion seldom is an open issue in any political campaign, but as a factor in conditioning a voter's attitudes it is at least as important as the sex, age, economic, and geographical factors which the professional pollsters consider in preparing their samples.

Religious homogeneity makes for social stability within any group. It is perhaps the most basic form of social control, as the essence of any religion is what constitutes proper behavior. "This is the way God wants you to act. He will reward you, either in this life or in a life to come, if you obey his wishes; and He will punish you if you fail to do so," is substantially what any religion says. Conflict results when, in a heterogeneous society, members of one group cannot act in accordance with what they consider God's will to be without infringing upon the freedom of others who interpret the deity's wishes in a different way and behave accordingly. Mere tolerance, furthermore, is not sufficient to resolve some of the difficulties which result. There comes a time, for instance, when it must be decided whether Jehovah's Witnesses shall or shall not salute the flag, and whether conscientious objectors are to be treated as criminals, to be sentenced to penitentiaries, or as exceptions to the selective service laws, allowed to perform whatever civilian duties beneficial to the war effort their consciences permit them to perform.

Because of the preponderance of Protestant votes a free public school system has been maintained in the United States. In the words of Pope Pius IX, however: "Where a Catholic parochial school exists, parents ordinarily violate the general Canon Law of the Church (Canon 1374) if they send their children to public or non-Catholic schools. If they persist in this violation, they sin gravely and cannot be absolved until they make proper adjustment with the Ordinary through the Pastor (Statute 117)." On Jan. 11, 1930, Pope Pius XI issued his famous encyclical, "Of Christian Education of the Young," in which he condemned coeducation, sex education of the young, overmuch physical training and public gymnastic displays by young women, sending children away to school at too early an age, the "new naturalism movement" in education, bad films, and bad radio programs. "Every method of education founded wholly or in part on a denial or forgetfulness of original sin and of grace, and therefore on the sole forces of human nature is false," the encyclical stated. "Such are generally those systems of today under various names, which appeal to the pretended freedom and unconditioned liberty of the child and diminish and also suppress the authority and work of the educator, attributing to the child exclusive privacy or initiative and activity independent of all superior natural and divine laws in working out its own education."

The American compromise has been to permit the existence of entirely separate schools for groups which desire them. Until comparatively recently financial support for Roman Catholic schools has been entirely the responsibility of church members. For several decades, however, there has been an accelerating demand that taxpayers provide some of the services, such as transportation, essential for the maintenance of the private schools. It was because the bill introduced by Rep. Graham A. Barden (Dem. N.C.) specified that only public schools should benefit that Cardinal Spellman and other Catholics opposed it. From the standpoint of the student of public opinion it is important to conjecture whether, if the total Catholic population should pull even with or surpass the non-Catholic population, the existence of two substantially equal school systems would result in two cultures, intermingling on the economic level and partly on the social level but with independent parallel institutions in almost every other phase of life. Or, if such a compromise could not be made to work, would there be bitter conflict? In the papal encyclical also appeared the following:

"Hence the Church is the supreme teacher of men and her right to teach is inherent and inviolable. It follows as a natural consequence that the Church is independent of earthly sovereignty both in origin and the exercise of its educational mission, not only with respect to its specific aim but also with respect to the means necessary to achieve it. The Church, therefore, has the independent right to judge whether any other system or method of education is helpful or harmful to Christian education. And this is so because the Church, being a perfect society, has independent rights on all means to its end, and because every system of teaching, just like any action, has certain relations with the ultimate aim of man, and cannot therefore escape the rules of Divine Law of which the Church is the infallible custodian, interpreter and teacher."

In January, 1949, over 400 Protestant ministers and Jewish rabbis petitioned the New York legislature to legalize euthanasia, popularly called "mercy killings" of the incurably ill. In April, 1949, appeared the new American Catholic catechism prepared by the Confraternity of Christian Doctrine in which it is stated: "The state does not have the right to take the life of a sick person, even at his own request, in order to relieve him of pain."

In another part the catechism declares: "An unborn child has the same right as any other person and may never be directly killed, even to save the life of the mother." This is consistent with the papal viewpoint as reported in the following news story:

By Barrett McGurn
Special to the Sun-Times

Rome—Pope Pius XII told surgeons of 32 countries gathered here that they have a duty to refuse to kill unborn infants even when the mother's life hangs in the balance.

The Pope told the physicians they have a duty not to heed "the understandable anguish of husbandly love" when they are faced with a choice between mother and child.

"The principle is inviolable," the Pope said. "God alone is lord of life and of the integrity of man, his limbs, his organs, and his powers. In a particular way God is the lord of those powers which associate man to God's creative work. Neither parents, husbands, wives nor the patient himself can dispose of any of these matters."

The Pope told the surgeons they have a moral obligation not to sterilize sexual organs unless there are "other reasons" besides the mere desire to avoid conception. He indicated that there is never an excuse for mercy killing.

The Pope compared the killing of the unborn child to "the killing of one innocent in order to save another." He said that it is no more permissible than it is for a doctor to mutilate a man so that he can escape military service in wartime.

—Chicago *Sun-Times,* March 23, 1948

In November, 1949, at the first national congress of the Italian Jurists' Union, Pope Pius XII declared that Catholic judges should not dissolve marriages recognized by the church. As reported by the United Press the Holy Father's viewpoint was as follows:

Castel Gandolfo, Italy—(UP)—Pope Pius XII has told Catholic jurists that they should not dissolve marriages recognized by the church, but Vatican sources said that he left them a loophole.

The Pope laid down the Vatican's view of the moral duty of Catholic justices in a speech to delegates to the first national congress of the Italian jurists' union Sunday.

He said civil divorce decrees lead to the erroneous impression that the affected church marriage has been dissolved, but that this is not the view of the church.

Therefore, he said, Catholic jurists should not issue a divorce decree in a church-recognized marriage "if not for motives of great moment."

Although Catholic justices are morally responsible for the sentences they pass and should not administer unjust or immoral laws, he said, they sometimes must enforce such laws "to impede a much greater evil."

*   *   *

Vatican sources said the Pontiff's pronouncement was not intended to block divorce in countries where it is permitted.

"Many jurists of the Catholic faith, while facing a conflict when called upon to enact a law which their conscience may hold unjust, must in many cases still hold to their duty as magistrates," these sources said.

"The Pope has made it clear that a Catholic jurist who applies a so-regarded unjust law because of circumstances which require him to act as impartial jurist and against his private conscience, would not be giving approval to the law and therefore would not act contrary to church doctrine."

*   *   *

The Pope singled out the duty of Catholic jurists in divorce cases for special emphasis in his speech.

"In particular," the Pope said, "the Catholic jurist cannot pronounce, unless for motives of great moment, a sentence of civil divorce for a matrimony valid before God and the church.

"He must not forget that such a sentence in practice does not touch only civil effects, but in reality leads rather to the erroneous consideration that the present bond is broken and the new is valid and obligatory."

The Roman Catholic Church by historic precedent recognizes only marriages performed within the Catholic Church. It does not recognize divorce in any form.

Sufficient examples have been given to establish the fact that *Catholic thinking differs from Protestant thinking on many important matters which have political ramifications.* In the case of a Catholic what constitutes right thinking and action is unmistakably clear because his church has taken a stand. It is, however, the prerogative of each individual Protestant to make up his own mind as regards any specific issue, even on matters regarding which there have been official pronouncements by some high church body. He is under no compulsion to accept any such edict as binding upon him. He naturally is affected by the judgment of a church leader with prestige but he does

not consider anyone infallible and he does not run the risk of ex-
communication for disobedience. A Protestant counterpart of the
unity of opinion which prevails among Catholics on such matters is to
be found only among some of the smallest sects, or unaffiliated cults.
The adamancy of Jehovah's Witnesses regarding matters patriotic
already has been mentioned. The Dukhobors in western Canada and
the Amish in Pennsylvania and Iowa also are pacifists. The opposition
of Christian Scientists to compulsory vaccination and other public
health measures is familiar. At different times a number of both major
and minor denominations have been engaged in political as well as
moral fights against drinking, smoking, dancing, and scanty attire,
especially for women. Several Southern states, in which fundamentalist
Protestantism is strong, still have laws forbidding the teaching of
evolution in the public schools.

Powerful as is the hold of organized religion, in obtaining obedience,
the church is in competition with other strong influences. For instance,
despite the unmitigated stand of the Roman Catholic church against
artificial means of birth control, the Planned Parenthood clinics in
New York and Chicago report that Catholic women seek information
about contraceptives in the same proportion to the total Catholic population as is true of Protestants and Jews. Young people of all denominations revolt against strictures directed against dress, dancing, card
playing, and other forms of pleasure.

The following two clippings, appearing within two days of each
other, illustrate how different generations interpret the scriptures
differently:

Students from six Lutheran colleges are seeking repeal of a ban on
campus dances.

The students appeared Monday before the synod commission on morals
and social problems at 327 S. LaSalle st.

Marcus Aurelius, 24, of Augustana College, Rock Island, said a poll
showed 75 per cent of the students favor dancing on the campus.

*   *   *

"We don't want to jitterbug or anything like that," Aurelius said. "Most
kids just want to dance—in a dignified sort of way—at the Student Union
building."

He said groups opposing dancing fear church organizations will with-
hold money from the college if rules are relaxed.

Other colleges represented were Upsala, East Orange, N.J.; Gustavus

Adolphus, Northfield, Minn.; Augustana, Sioux Falls, S.D.; Bethany, Lindborg, Kan., and Luther, Wahoo, Neb.

—Chicago *Daily News,* Dec. 13, 1949

Stewartsville, Va.—(UP)—Citizens, indignant because dancing will be permitted in the local high school, plan a mass protest meeting at the school 30 minutes before the "sinful" dancing begins Thursday night.

The Rev. F. A. Brewbaker, pastor of the Beaver Dam Baptist church, called the protest meeting at the urging of his congregation.

"I have read the testimony of many fallen girls," Brewbaker said. "More than 50 per cent of them say that dancing was the first step in their downfall.

"Dancing has a tendency to retard and tear down character."

Teachers who are sponsoring the affair called it a "social" and said it was merely "planned recreation."

H. W. Mack, director of the Bedford County recreation department, said he plans to teach the students folk dancing. Parents and teachers also were invited.

—Chicago *Daily News,* Dec. 15, 1949

There is no evidence that former Boy Scouts, YMCA members, Protestant Sunday school and Catholic parochial school students are more moral, ethical, or law abiding than those who were not subjected to such "character building" influences in childhood. Moralists received a terrific shock with the appearance of *Sexual Behavior in the Human Male* (W. B. Saunders, 1948), containing the results of years of scientific research by Professor Alfred C. Kinsey and associates of Indiana University. Among the startling statements was the following: "It is probably safe to suggest that about half of all married males have intercourse with women other than their wives, at some time while they are married." Indication that factors other than religious teaching are the major determinants of sexual morality is contained in the following from the same book: "A large proportion of the 85 per cent of the population which never goes to college accepts pre-marital intercourse as normal and natural. Most of this group would insist that there is no question of right or wrong involved. . . . With the upper educational level, the question of pre-marital intercourse is largely one of morals."

Inspired in part by the Kinsey findings, in an article, "Cultural Ideology and Heterosexual Reality: A Preface to Sociological Research," in the October, 1949 *American Sociological Review,* Professor Claude C. Bowman of Temple University advocated sociological investigations of "the social causes, conditions and consequences of heterosexual and homosexual activities of all types," with special attention to "sexual myths (which) are legion in the United States and other regions influenced by the same cultural heritage."

If any such research is conducted it will be undertaken in accordance with the accepted sociological concept that morals are cultural products rather than the result of divine revelation, which is the fundamentalist religious viewpoint. For example, consider the point of view of one of the world's leading anthropologists as reported in the Jan. 7, 1950 *Science News Letter*:

"Many kinds of sexual behavior are not even mentioned in Dr. Kinsey's report on the sexual behavior of the human male.

"Dr. Ralph Linton, professor of anthropology at Yale University, reported this to the American Association for the Advancement of Science meeting. If the book had been written about all the males of the world, it would have been a different book.

"In some parts of the world, Dr. Linton said, all individuals accept homosexuality as the normal form of sex expression for persons in certain age groups. In other areas, overt homosexuality seems to be genuinely unknown.

"Dr. Linton spoke at a symposium intended to criticize *Sexual Behavior of the Human Male* as a possible aid to Dr. Kinsey and his associates in writing their forthcoming *Sexual Behavior of the Human Female*. Dr. Kinsey himself suggested this sort of symposium.

"It is safe to say, Dr. Linton also declared, that there is no such thing as normal or natural human sex behavior. He criticized the Kinsey report because, he said, 'one gathers that he (Kinsey) feels that there is such a thing as normal sex behavior.' All our sex practices, he explained, are learned, either by imitation, by trial and error or by instruction. The only thing that is biologically necessary, Dr. Linton declared, is that the sex urge be satisfied.

"The methods by which the sex urge is satisfied, Dr. Linton said, vary greatly from society to society in the human species. However, Dr. Linton went on, the ideals of sexual behavior set up in our culture, whether observed or not, would seem to indicate that some forms have greater social value than others, even though any form of sex behavior which does not involve deprivation or attempted suppression of the sex drive can be made satisfying to the individual. The Kinsey report suggests that our legal regulations should be made more realistic, but it seems certain that we will always have definite patterns of approved and disapproved sex behavior.

" 'What we need,' concluded Dr. Linton, 'is a franker appraisal of the situation and a clearer picture of what sorts of sex behavior are socially desirable. . . .' "

By contrast, in Chapter 1, "Fundamentalism," in the symposium, *Varieties of American Religion*, the Rev. William Bell Riley, Minneapolis Baptist minister, wrote: "The home is a religious institution; the family is the product of some sort of faith. If a tribe could be found that had no religion of any sort it would pretty surely follow that no marriage relation would be regarded and no domestic morality practiced. . . . Irreligion . . . supplants love with lust, parental affection with growing indifference, and the home with a sleeping place where the sexes pig together, where the laws that claim Divine ordination as well as the customs that higher civilization has approved are alike despised. . . . Its [Christianity's] laws are concise and unchangeable. According to Christ, a man shall 'leave father and mother and shall cleave to his wife: and the twain shall be one flesh' (Matthew 19:5). According to Paul, Christ's chief apostle, children must 'obey their parents in the Lord,' 'honoring father and mother.' Fathers are 'not to provoke their children to wrath' but 'bring them up in the nurture and admonition of the Lord' (Ephesians 6:1, 2, 4). According to the same apostle, 'If any provide not for his own, and specially for those of his own house, he hath denied the faith, and is worse than an infidel' (I Timothy 5:8)" [1]

There is no ground for argument with someone who has such a profound faith in revealed truth, except over the correctness of interpretations of some of the more recondite passages in Holy Writ. A considerable amount of the splitting up of denominations to form new sects resulted from irreconcilable differences regarding such matters. In the wake of iconoclastic scientific discoveries, there has been a considerable drift away from a literal interpretation of the Bible. Ecumenical, however, is belief in a divine plan for the universe. Inscrutable as God's will often seems to be, it is faith in the ultimate triumph

---

[1] From *Varieties of American Religion*, Charles S. Braden, ed. Copyright, 1936, by Harper & Brothers.

of justice that buoys up believers in times of adversity. The Christian God of the New Testament is loving and forgiving, promising through his divine Son that "Blessed are the meek: for they shall inherit the earth (Matthew 5:5)." It is vouchsafed for everyone to attain immortality through adherence to the rules of right thinking as ordained by the Almighty and revealed by Him to man through the intermediary of Jesus, prophets, and saints. Through faith in the divinity of Christ and repentance for sin, even upon a deathbed, one can be sure of eternal life.

The concomitant of hope of reward for right conduct is fear of horrible punishment for willful failure to obey the will of God. The Old Testament Jehovah was a wrathful deity whom it was not difficult to imagine abandoning souls to perpetual burning in hell and other tortures which the devil and his retinue might take delight in inflicting. Heaven and hell are believed to be distant places, difficult to locate since astronomers, long before Einstein, caused "up" and "down" to lose the meanings they had when it was believed the Earth is flat and the center of the universe. The tendency in every religion, including the Christian, is for fear of damnation to develop, not only as a result of commission of sin as established by the particular creed, but also because of failure to observe strictly the rituals, sacraments, and sacrifices which church dogma insists are mandatory in order to incur the Lord's favor.

Pertinent to the subject with which this book is concerned—public opinion—it must be asked: what effect does deep religious conviction (of any sort) have upon the way people react to purely secular problems? Because, disregarding the question of how they originated, moral and ethical codes always have had strong religious sanctions, it is not easy to make a clear-cut distinction between what is ecclesiastical and what secular. Judaism and Christianity teach brotherly love, charity, tolerance, fair dealing, forgiveness and other virtuous qualities, and there is no doubt that the extent to which man acts in accordance with such principles is traceable in large part to the influence of church teachings which affect him either firsthand or indirectly. Contrariwise, the extent to which meanness, greed, avarice, sin, immorality and crime exist in a predominantly Christian nation is a measure of the failure of the church in achieving its fundamental purpose. Representing liberal Protestantism in the Braden-edited symposium, the

Rev. Ernest Fremont Tittle, Evanston, Ill. Methodist, wrote: "But what hope is there of producing fine character, or a significant culture, in the environment of a slum? I do not say it cannot be done. It has been done in the case of a few superior individuals. But the odds against its being done are simply terrific, as the proponents of evangelical piety ought clearly to recognize. . . . In order to redeem the lives of individuals you must create a social order in which the potential goodness of human nature has a fair chance to flower."

Throughout his long pastorate Dr. Tittle was under frequent attack for alleged radicalism as his preaching coincided in spirit with his statement of principle. The conflict between the fundamentalist and the liberal viewpoints in all denominations is head-on. In its most extreme form the paramount concern of the old-fashioned religionist is the selfish quest for the salvation of his own soul. Consequently, a considerable amount of his good deeds are done with his own best interests rather than those of their beneficiaries in mind, in the spirit of "he profits most who serves best," as it were. To "buy his way" into heaven he donates his mite or his millions and is strict in observance of his churchly duties. In the elaborate edifices which his generosity helps erect, the less fortunate are importuned to endure their misery with complacency because, "Blessed are ye, when men shall revile you, and persecute you, and shall say all manner of evil against you falsely, for my sake. Rejoice, and be exceeding glad; for great is your reward in heaven: for so persecuted they the prophets which were before you" (Matthew 5:11–12).

There is historical and contemporaneous evidence of the comparative backwardness of countries in which religious beliefs and institutions are static, dogmatic, and superstitious in nature. Take, for example, India, where a religiously sanctioned caste system maintains a few in excessive luxury at the expense of an abject majority. An Indian graduate student in the Medill School of Journalism of Northwestern University explained the operation of the caste system as follows:

"Democracy, as a matter of fact, is contrary to Hindu teachings. Important to Hinduism is the doctrine *Karma,* which takes significance and meaning from the Hindu belief in the transmigration of souls. Simply stated, *Karma* means that the virtuous are rewarded, the wicked punished, not in this life, but in the next. The next life is spent not in some shadowy other world but here on earth.

"A merchant, say, leads a wicked life. He cheats his customers; he sells them mouldy flour. Then in his next life the merchant will be born into a lower caste—as an untouchable, perhaps, or if he was hopelessly wicked, as an animal.

"The untouchable, then, has only himself to blame. Neither state nor society is in any way responsible for his shocking condition. Of course, in this life there is no hope for the untouchable. For society to help him would be for society to go against the will of a divine providence.

"But the untouchable, by performing faithfully the duties of the untouchable, can escape its bonds. Not in this life, you understand, but in the next, when the good untouchable is born into a higher caste. And that, indeed, is the only way a man can escape caste.

"What this boils down to then is this: that the rights and duties of all men are not the same. The untouchable has one set of rights; the politician another. There is none common to both. It is the right of some to govern, of others to be governed."

That religious faith enables many to endure otherwise unendurable hardships is undeniable. To the extent, however, that it diverts attention from solution of mundane problems to pious hope that one will be rewarded and his enemies punished in the life hereafter, it retards what may be called progress. Belief that misfortune in this life is evidence of God's displeasure, and overconsciousness of sin, also lead to frustrations and neuroses, as any practicing psychiatrist knows. Instead of brotherly love, tolerance, and charity, their opposites— bigotry, intolerance, and selfishness—may be the outcome of fanaticism and evangelical fervor. No categorical answer can be given to the query, "What is the effect of religion upon public opinion?" without first inquiring, "What kind of religion?" Obviously, those systems which place emphasis upon ritualistic behavior in and out of holy places, for good or bad, exercise a conservative influence which slows down experimentation, discovery, and adaptation of new ideas and ways of behavior. On the other hand by emphasizing virtuous conduct for its own sake, organized religion can combat evil autocratic forces which develop out of other phases of economic, social and political life.

Journalistically any strong or unusual evidence of faith usually is considered newsworthy. Typical of the kind of story which frequently obtains widespread play in newspapers throughout the country was that which told, in early December, 1949, of a ten-year-old girl who wrote a letter to the Memphis *Commercial-Appeal* asking that readers pray that her right hand not have to be amputated as a result of a bone disease. Many stories, originating from coast to coast, were illustrated by pictures of individuals and groups complying with the request. There have been many similar stories in recent years.

Religion and Custom

In its origins what we today call religion was so interwoven with magic and superstition that it is virtually impossible to separate them in any historical study. According to Lewis Browne in *This Believing World* (Macmillan, 1926) true religion began when man ceased to coerce the elements and began to cajole them. When that was is not clear. Certain it is, however, that every form of belief in anything supernatural grew out of fear on the part of early man who could not understand the true nature of the universe, life and death, changes in the seasons, and other phenomena. His very existence depended upon his ability to control or at least protect himself against the elements and other natural forces.

Myths of the creation, Garden of Eden, and Deluge, similar to those in Genesis, existed at least 1,000 years before the biblical account could have been written, Dr. Samuel N. Kramer, of the University of Pennsylvania concluded after a ten-year study of Sumerian cuneiform tablets found in Iraq, as reported in the April 18, 1943 *Science News Letter*.

A common characteristic of all primitive societies was belief in unseen, supernatural powers. The first stage in the attempt to explain the facts and processes of life and nature was belief in a nebulous and undifferentiated supernatural force (*animatism*). The second stage was *animism,* belief in individual spirits, both good and bad, which controlled men and nature in some ways and consequently had to be placated. It was assumed that all objects possess life: the sun, moon, stars, vegetable and animal life, winds, rainbows, etc.

At first the rites by which to incur the pleasure of these spirits were known to all and were practiced individually. Then, however, medicine men, magicians, and others, supposed to have special powers to obtain spiritual favors, arose, and dealing with the gods became a definite business.

The first gods were tribal only. *Fetichism* was the belief in active spirits embodied in objects, and amulets were worn to avoid harm from them. Tribal fetiches became gods and sacrifices were made before idols of them, prayers were originated to appeal to them, and churches were erected to shelter them. Largely because of the presence of dead persons in dreams, *ancestor worship* developed and appeals were made to the spirits of dead relatives to assist the living. Mourning originated as a device to frighten away unfriendly spirits of the recently deceased.

From early times agriculture was associated with religion; the seasonal festivals with rituals which often were lewd, were considered necessary to assure good planting and harvest conditions. Many myths developed as to the origin of fertility. One, that of Osiris which originated with the ancient Egyptians, was of death, theft of the body, dismemberment, discovery by the goddess Isis, and rebirth. This symbolized the vegetative cycle as did also the Persian myth of Mithras who started fertility by killing a bull whose blood nourished the ground. The spring and fall festivals roughly corresponding to Easter and Christmas were representative of birth and death.

Art and sculpture are believed to have originated in religious painting and idol-making; architecture to have begun with temple-building; poetry with prayer-writing; music with psalm-singing; drama with legend-telling; and dancing with the seasonal festivities. The Egyptians introduced embalming in the belief that correct burial made for immortality; at first only the kings were embalmed because only they were believed to have souls. The Druids considered the mistletoe sacred because it grew between heaven and earth. They had three chief festivals, corresponding to May Day, Midsummer's Night, and Hallowe'en. *Totemism* originated as each tribe was represented by an animal supposed to be friendly; animals also were used to symbolize gods, as the Egyptian sphinxes.

Religion became national as tribes became expansive and imperialistic. Victories were accredited to the friendship of the tribal gods with the result that worship increased, temples were built, taboos became stronger, gifts and sacrifices increased, priestly power grew.

The Greeks had an entire hierarchy of gods representing human virtues as well as objects. The Olympian cult offered little comfort and the Greeks turned to philosophy to make life more reasonable. The Romans resembled the Greeks in religious belief, Jupiter being the principal deity. In 31 B.C. Augustus revived religions of the state and deified himself.

Universal religions developed through the breakdown of nationalism, as when the Hebrews were in exile. In Confucianism and Taoism the emphasis was upon universality of order in the world. Men of ethical or philosophical insight, as the Hebrew prophets, Buddha, Hindu philosophers, Zoroaster, and Mohammed, taught that God has the same relation to all men, not just those of a single tribe or nation. Gradually monotheism replaced polytheism, with the growth of missionary zeal a natural consequence. Christianity differs from the ancient cults in being more ethical. It is, however, indebted to primitive religions for many of its principal holidays. As Browne wrote: "The Roman Perilia in April became the Festival of St. George, and the pagan midsummer orgy in June was converted into the Festival of St. John; the holy day of Diana in August became the Festival of the Assumption of the Virgin; and the Celtic feast of the dead in November was changed into the Festival of All Souls. The 25th of December—the winter solstice according to ancient reckoning—celebrated as the birthday of the sungod of Mithraism, was accepted as the birthday of Christ, and the spring rites in connection with the death and rebirth of the mystery gods were converted into Easter rites of the Crucifixion and Resurrection."

Some writers have contended that the hope and fear which religion inculcates are not necessary for maintenance of a moral code. For instance, in *Earth Is Enough* (Harper, 1933) Baker Brownell contended that in contemporary society social integration is sufficient to justify and enforce morality, defined as man's social balance and sanity. Support and enforcement of the right, he argued, is a social pattern and morals are the rational interpretation of things with a view to the advantage of the social organism. In *Up From Methodism* (Knopf, 1926) Herbert Asbury wrote: "Without religion I thoroughly enjoy the business of living. I am oppressed by no dreadful taboos, and I am without fear; I set myself no standards save those of ordinary self-respect, decent consideration of the rights and privileges of others, and the observances of the laws of the land except Prohibition. To my own satisfaction, at least, I have proved that religion and the Church are not at all necessary to a full and happy life."

Not merely religious leaders but cultural anthropologists as well answer such arguments by declaring that, despite their avowed free-thinking, those who express such sentiments are affected by the religiously-based moral codes of their cultures. Their good behavior results from their acceptance of those codes. There never has been a widespread moral code entirely divorced from religion.

Religion and Science

In the August, 1934 *Harper's,* under the title, "Religious Beliefs of American Scientists," Prof. James H. Leuba, Bryn Mawr psychologist, related the results of several tests of American scientists and college students regarding their attitude "toward the two central beliefs of the Christian religion: a God influenced by worship, and immortality." Only 33 per cent of the scientists believed in God and only 30 per cent believed in immortality. At College A, 31 per cent of the students were believers in God and 39 per cent believed in immortality; in College B, the comparative proportions were only 11 and 18 per cent respectively. Thus, despite the much-publicized declarations of faith by a number of prominent men of science, notably physicists, and despite protestations by liberal churchmen that there is no basic conflict between science and religion, it is sobering evidence to the contrary. Too familiar to require reiteration here is the long history of struggle between iconoclastic scientists and the church. In 1633 the Inquisition condemned Galileo and it was not until 1822 that his books finally were removed from the Index Librorum Prohibitorum. Not only Galileo but virtually every other originator of startling new scientific truth met with vigorous or vicious opposition. Well remembered by the middle-aged is the famous Scopes trial in 1925 at Dayton, Tenn., during which Fundamentalist William Jennings Bryan, special prosecutor, underwent scathing cross examination by agnostic Clarence Darrow, defense attorney. Although the state's anti-evolution teaching law was upheld and the young high school teacher who tested it was convicted, the propaganda victory undoubtedly was won by the modernists. Today, with the negligible exception of a few minor sects, such as the Christian Catholic Apostolic Church of Zion, Ill., organized religion no longer fights against acceptance of the facts of the physical and biological sciences.

Although this is called an Age of Science, the ordinary layman is unaware of the inconsistency of both accepting the latest scientific findings and clinging to completely superstitious beliefs. It is hardly true that faith is greater than scientific proof, but it *is* true that *modern man has no clear-cut philosophy of life based on any certain understanding of both his seen and unseen environment.* His best "out" is to cease thinking too much about either. To him science means new or improved methods of transportation and communication or more and better gadgets to increase his material comfort. To him religion is what he was brought up to believe, what he wants to believe, or what he is afraid to disbelieve. Such mental confusion is a long way from the rational thought that early students of public opinion liked to believe accounted for human attitudes. It also makes it not too difficult to understand the avidity with which a great many persons can be induced to seek the mourners' bench at a revival meeting or to join a new cult. In its comparatively brief history the United States has produced two new major religions, the Church of Jesus Christ of Latter Day Saints (Mormons), and Christian Science. In addition, there have been hundreds of cults, not a few of which later have been exposed as money-making rackets. Revivalism thrives on wars and depressions when unhappiness from fear of death and economic disaster creates an eagerness to discover a "new way out." California, with a weather which caused many who migrated there in the belief they are valetudinarians to recover their health, for a few more years at least, has been the most fertile field for cultism. Aimee Semple McPherson's Four Square Gospel was the most important in recent years and the Mighty I Am Presence of Guy W. Ballard the most scandalous, but there have been literally hundreds of others, all offering salvation and peace of mind at comparatively slight sacrifice.

California also is the American home of the Rosicrucians. A book of prophecies for the coming year is published annually by the AMORC Rosicrucian Brotherhood late each fall for free distribution. That its contention that it is not religious, nor a new form of religion in any sense, should perhaps be taken more seriously than it is by its followers is suggested by a rereading of some of the "previews" of past years. From the 1937 forecast, for instance, comes the following:

"The people of certain sectors of Italy are drunk with the glory of its African victory which has been painted to the populace in colors that will not stand the test of time—say, five years! Its people feel the tingle in their veins of the Roman Conquerors. They believe that their upraised hand is truly a traffic signal to the rest of war-craving Europe to 'stop!' . . . In Germany the first fruits of peace and industry are being enjoyed, even by those carrying the yoke of the machine which took away from them the richness of their former existence. It is truly a land of re-birth and resurrection. . . . What the people of Germany desire more than anything else in this world is Peace, and good father Hitler knows this . . .

"The election this coming fall (1936) will be unique in that the States will be called upon to vote for at least one man whose political platform, for the first time in American history, challenges the soundness of the United States Constitution, the impeccability of the United States Supreme Court, the standardization of our monetary valuation, and the democratic spirit of Congressional administration. All of the fundamentals of the American nation are now challenged for the first time."

Religion and Economics

Historically, the established church, no matter what its character, always has been among the principal props of the prevailing economic and political order. This is, of course, entirely understandable because the church's chief support comes from leaders in the prevailing order. If defeated in its fight against any important change, the church makes the best peace it can and may in time become a leading supporter of the new regime, as is the case today of the Greek Orthodox church in the Soviet Union. The present pope and his predecessor were elected largely upon their records as diplomats. As nuncio to Poland, the future Pius XI completed a concordat with the dictator, General Pilsudski; one of his foremost achievements as pope was a concordat with Mussolini. Pius XII was the first papal secretary of state ever to be elected pope; in 1933, as Cardinal Pacelli, he had negotiated a concordat with Hitler. According to Dr. Paul Hutchinson, editor of *The Christian Century,* who made a round-the-world trip in 1946 for *Life* (see "Does Europe Face Holy War," in the issue of Sept. 23, 1946) to study the role of religion in the postwar world, Europeans did not share the attitude of the American press at the time of the trial in 1949 of Hungarian Joseph Cardinal Mindszenty for treason, espionage, and illegal black market sale of American dollars, or of several other clergymen in eastern European nations. To them it was to be expected that a state should require loyalty from the church. At the same time nobody considered it unnatural for the church to object to the loss of a tremendous amount of land which was confiscated, along with that of other large landowners, and distributed among ownerless peasants. Nor could the church be expected to surrender its long-time control over public school education without a struggle.

In the United States, by contrast with almost every other nation in the world, the salaries of parochial school teachers have not been paid by the state. Churches of all denominations, however, enjoy tax exemption for their real estate holdings, even on land not used for religious purposes. In 1937 it was estimated that church property in New York City alone totalled about 282 million dollars. Typically throughout the nation the Lutherans own about 500 million dollars' worth of property and the Christian Scientists about 65 million dollars' worth. Under the title, "A Priest Warns the Church," the Rev. Peter Whiffin, a Roman Catholic, wrote in the April, 1947 *Forum:* "The very suddenness of the Church's growth to wealth was her undoing. Her clergymen, for the most part used to poverty, all at once found themselves men of money and importance. Business men cultivated their acquaintance, gave them big loans at reduced rates of interest, advised them about investments. Politicians consulted them about appointments and got them all sorts of favors. And soon the poor priests forgot that it was the money of the poor which had made them important, forgot that big business and politics might be smothering the Church with favors only to make it more difficult for her to cry out against them in their exploitation of the masses."

In August, 1948, at Amsterdam, Holland, there was established the World Council of Churches with a nucleus of 154 independent national churches in 44 countries, including virtually all of the major Protestant groups and several Eastern Orthodox, accounting for almost half of the 700 million Christians of the entire world. The following resolution, passed at the first assembly, was of tremendous significance: "The Christian churches should reject the ideologies of both communism and *laissez faire* capitalism, and should seek to draw men away from the false assumption that these extremes are the only alternatives. . . . It is the responsibility of Christians to seek new creative solutions which never allow either justice or freedom to destroy the other. The church should make clear that there are conflicts between Christianity and capitalism." That was a general statement of abstract principle for which hundreds of delegates could vote with impunity. It is a different matter when an individual clergyman speaks up or takes action, even when not directly related to his ecclesiastical duties. In February, 1948, for instance, the Rev. Richard H. Bready, Cumberland, Md., Methodist, was relieved of his appointment after he delivered the invocation at the founding convention of the Progressive party of Maryland. A year after the 1948 election appeared the following item:

Lawrence, Mass., Nov. 22—Rev. Clarence Duffy of New York City, a supporter of Henry Wallace and the Progressive Party, and a foe of the Atlantic Pact and the Marshall Plan, was hit by an egg last night as he was addressing a street rally in behalf of a Protestant minister candidate for mayor.

After a brief interruption, however, Father Duffy completed his remarks before a crowd which police estimated at 2,000. Police said some of the crowd roughed up a man believed to be the egg thrower but no arrest was made.

The speaker was supporting the mayoral candidacy of a Unitarian minister, the Rev. Amos C. B. Murphy, on the eve of the city's nonpartisan primary.

The Chancellor of the Boston Catholic Archdiocese, the Rt. Rev. William J. Furlong, quoted the Vicar General of the New York Archdiocese, the Rt. Rev. Edward R. Gaffney as saying Father Duffy had lost all faculties in the New York Archdiocese because of his "political action."

Church sources said loss of faculties deprives a priest of his right to preach, say mass or administer sacraments and is a punishment commonly referred to as "being silenced."
                                        —New York *Daily Compass,* Nov. 23, 1949

The most outstanding case of its kind in recent years was that involving the Rev. Dr. John Howard Melish, for 45 years rector of the Protestant Episcopal Church of the Holy Trinity in Brooklyn Heights, N.Y. Because Dr. Melish's son and associate rector, the Rev. William Howard Melish, was chairman of the National Council of American-Soviet Friendship, the church's vestry first demanded that the father discharge the son. When he refused the laymen petitioned Bishop James P. DeWolfe of the Long Island diocese to remove the elder Melish. Judge Meier Steinbrink of New York, in April, 1949, upheld the bishop's right to take the action and the House of Deputies of the Episcopal church at its San Francisco convention in October, 1949, also upheld the ouster. Commented the younger Melish: "It is interesting to see that the House of Deputies has called for every effort at getting a rapproachment between the United States and the Soviet Union and is in principle approving the very thing for which we are criticized."

The much-disputed role of Puritanism in shaping the American national character was discussed in Chapter 5. More universal has been the question of the reciprocal influential relationship between Protestantism and capitalism. Whether one caused the other or vice versa, is secondary in importance to the fact that Protestantism certainly was attractive to sixteenth- and seventeenth-century merchant adventurers—the original *laissez-faire* adherents—who sought freedom from restraint in their quest for the newly discovered riches of the New World and, a bit later, in developing the machine civilization made possible by the so-called Industrial Revolution. The original meaning of "liberalism" was freedom from "the immense number of laws and customs that restricted the freedom of movement of laborers, that subjected the market price to prices legally fixed and that hampered freedom of exchange especially with foreign markets," to quote John Dewey in an article, "A Liberal Speaks Out for Liberalism," in the Feb. 23, 1936 New York *Times Magazine,* an epitome of the same authority's views as expressed in *Liberalism and Social Action* (Putnam, 1935). Dewey wrote further: "This mass of restrictions that tended to strangle at birth the new infant industry held over from agrarian feudalism, and were kept in force by the influence of landed interests. Because the restrictive and oppressive conditions were embodied in law and because law was the voice of government in control of human action, government was taken to be the great enemy of liberty; interference with human industry engaged in satisfaction of human needs was taken to be the chief cause why progress was retarded and why a reign of harmony of interests and peace did not exist."

Obviously Protestantism, preaching revolt against authoritarianism, had strong appeal to rugged individualists from that time almost to the present. Today, however, the capitalism which the spirit of free enterprise helped develop has reached the monopolistic stage so that it is challenged the world over to reform. All the oratory eulogizing the pioneer spirit of independence does not contradict the fact that what economic freedom means today to powerful industrialists is freedom to complete the elimination of their few remaining competitors and decide by themselves what their labor and price-fixing policies are to be. One effect upon organized religion was stated by the anonymous author of "Medieval Thinking" in the July, 1928 *Atlantic Monthly* in these words: "In our day the unchurched see little difference between the Protestant and Catholic systems of religion. Both are dogmatic. Both seek to impose their theological conclusions upon the people. The door of religion, therefore, is closed to men of thought and individuality."

Another effect has been the development of a virtual caste system especially among and in Protestant churches. "Have you ever seen a ragged worshipper in one of our well-dressed Protestant congregations?" asked Agnes E. Meyer in "Why Protestants Need to Wake Up," in the Aug. 2, 1949 *Look*. In its report on *Segregation in Washington,* in 1948, the National Committee on Segregation in the Nation's Capital (4901 Ellis Avenue, Chicago 15, Ill.) cited as Case 134: "A devout Catholic from Panama entered a Catholic church in Washington. As he knelt at prayer, a priest approached him and handed him a slip of paper. On the paper was the address of a Negro Catholic church. The priest explained that there were special churches for Negro Catholics, and that he would be welcome there."

In the typical community the most aristocratic Protestant church is the Episcopal followed by the Presbyterian, Methodist and Lutheran. More middle class are the Baptist, Evangelical, and Congregational. The Unitarians are exceedingly small in number but high in intellect, being found almost exclusively in college communities where free-thinking professors constitute their nucleus. Although only 2.5 per cent of the population of New York City is Episcopalian, 57.64 per cent of the weddings considered important enough for mention on the society page of the New York *Times* were performed in Episcopal churches, a study by David L. and Mary A. Hatch of the University of Kentucky revealed. The results are to be found in an article, "Criteria of Social Status As Derived from Marriage Announcements in the New York *Times*," in the August, 1947 *American Sociological Review*. The researchers used as their sample the Sunday society pages during June from 1932 to 1942 inclusive. Further to indicate the caste system centering around religious affiliation, the study showed: ". . . no announcement acknowledged marriage in a Jewish synagogue or gave any indication of association with the Jewish faith." About one-third of New York's populace is Jewish and the *Times* is Jewish owned! "Belonging to a suitable church seems to be somewhat like living in a socially acceptable part of a city or belonging to a distinguished club," the authors concluded. "Theoretically, anyone may join any church, but, in practice, similar social groups may tend to congregate in the same church, with the possible exception of the Catholic church."

Union between different Protestant denominations, strongly advocated from many quarters in recent years, is made difficult as much by the social distinctions which have arisen as by doctrinal differences. Roman Catholicism has profited by this disunity and by the waning value to the American privileged classes of the Protestant ethos as much as by its own prolificacy. In a highly industrialized nation, developed and dominated by *laissez-faire* economics and Protestantism, Roman Catholicism has had greater appeal to the underprivileged who need the comfort and security which it offers in greater abundance. As the American middle class dwindles, Catholicism also offers greater solace for its surviving members suffering the effects of economic bigness with which they are fighting a losing battle.

Pressure-Group Activities

Much of the political activity on the part of religious groups of all kinds has been to impose the particular "shalt nots" of the sponsoring sects upon the general populace. Sabbath and other blue laws, severe penalties against blasphemy and sexual aberrations, anti-evolution laws and prohibition have been mainly puritanic Protestant in origin and support. Ideas of free will and original sin have retarded adoption of criminological and penological theories whereby the law-breaker would be treated as a psychiatric problem rather than as a willful wrongdoer. Similarly public health and medical research have been handicapped by the belief that certain diseases, especially venereal, constitute God's punishment for sin and should not be alleviated. In Chapter 4 of his *The Growth of American Thought* (Harper, 1943) Merle Curti discussed the effect in the early days of the republic of the biblical doctrine that man is created in the image of God, which tended to set humans aside from animals and caused medicine to be insufficiently grounded in animal pathology and physiology. Scientific classification was based on the relationship of various created objects but was hampered by the conviction that God created fixed spheres. In 1768 at Harvard University a disputation on the question of whether American reptiles originated from those preserved by Noah was answered in the affirmative. Epidemics were held to come from an angry God. Mobs prevented autopsies and doctors were suspected, probably often correctly, of robbing graves to obtain cadavers for experimentation. Even today public officials must be careful not to offend religious groups in the disposition of unclaimed and unidentified bodies in their morgues. Many medical schools have difficulty obtaining enough cadavers for teaching purposes because of legal restrictions. In Chicago all advertisements aimed at preventing the spread of venereal disease must be submitted by the Board of Health to the Catholic archdiocese in order to avoid trouble. Attitudes toward laws regulating marriage and divorce, sterilization, sex education, eugenics, birth control, abortion, prostitution, modesty of dress (including bathing suits), and many similar matters are largely determined by church teachings.

In "Religion and Elections," in the Spring, 1944 *Public Opinion Quarterly,* Madge M. McKinney reported on the results of a survey of the 418 changes which occurred in the personnel of the House of Representatives from January, 1935 to November, 1943 and concluded: "A candidate's religious background is more important to the success of his election than is the party he represents." The following quotation from her article includes a summary of her most important findings: "These 418 changes in personnel involved 193 changes in political party but only 81 changes in religion, if we count as a change only a shift from one to another of the three large groups, Protestant, Catholic and Jews, and if we exclude the 42 changes in personnel in which the religion of one Congressman could not be determined. That is, in 295 of the 376 changes in which the religion was known, a Protestant was succeeded by a Protestant, a Catholic by a Catholic and a Jew by a Jew. In short, in practically four out of every five of these changes a Congressman was replaced by a person of the same religious group. In contrast, in only a little more than half of the changes was he replaced by a representative of the same political party."

The tremendous influence of church group-inspired official and unofficial censorship of literature, motion pictures, and other forms of art has been discussed in Chapters 7 and 12. How effective the Legion of Decency has become since its creation in 1934 is suggested in the following newspaper story:

Four out of five current Hollywood screen productions are acceptable to the Legion of Decency of the Catholic Church.

However, there still are too many movies made "for the lunatic fringe" —with foreign studios guiltier than American, the Legion says.

The Legion's only lay officer and chairman of reviewers, Mrs. James F. Looram of New York City, reported on the morality of the postwar movies at a press conference here Thursday.

She is at the Drake Hotel for the triennial convention of the International Federation of Catholic Alumnae, which provides the Legion with trained volunteer reviewers.

Mrs. Looram, a lively brunet grandmother, has been labeled "woman most feared by the movie industry."

The Legion's movie ratings go into every Catholic parish in the United States, and American producers consistently revise pictures labeled "condemned" to avoid box office anemia.

"In the last eight months, of 284 American pictures reviewed, 80 per cent have been rated 'A' and designated as acceptable for a general audience or for adults," Mrs. Looram reported.

"The Legion found 54 American movies 'objectionable,' either largely or in part, and condemned two.

"In the same period, 37 of the 57 foreign films reviewed were rated objectionable, and 16 per cent were condemned. Foreign producers, operating without their own self-regulating code, are inflating the overall number of unacceptable pictures."

Mrs. Looram emphasized that the Legion of Decency not only permits but WANTS "adult" pictures—pictures dealing with the problems of adults "placed in a proper frame of reference."

"The Legion has never objected to sin portrayed on the screen," she said.

"But when sin is shown, producers have a responsibility to show moral compensation, perhaps by retribution or the judgment of some character's conscience."

Even in American-made pictures, she said, there is increasing incidence of brutality, viciousness, and sadistic or unnatural behavior attributable to the fashion of exaggerated realism.

—Chicago *Daily News,* Aug. 26, 1949

In 1937, as *Life* put it in its issue of May 31, 1937, "for the first time, the freedom of the New York stage was seriously threatened. Largely at the instigation of the Catholic church, which had cleaned up the movies with its Legion of Decency, a bill was hastily passed by the Legislature, empowering New York City's Commissioner of Licenses to close any play he deemed 'immoral.' Since most U.S. drama flows from the fountainhead of the New York stage, this measure would have made a political job-holder the supreme censor of the American theater.

"Actors, playwrights, producers and audiences promptly attacked the bill. Petitions were sent to Albany with audience approval. At a climactic meeting of 2,000 theater workers and theatergoers in New York's New Amsterdam Theater May 16, Helen Hayes was cheered when she spoke the lines of the historic Queen she acts in *Victoria Regina:* 'We are not amused.' Three days later Gov. Herbert Lehman vetoed the bill and the U.S. theater was saved again."

In 1948 a series of articles by Paul Blanshard on the Catholic church caused the New York Board of Superintendents, under severe pressure, to ban the *Nation* magazine from public school libraries. Despite the counter-pressure exerted by an Ad Hoc Committee of 107 intellectuals, headed by Archibald MacLeish, former librarian of the Library of Congress, in 1949 the ban was continued for another year and was upheld by Francis T. Spaulding, state commissioner of education. Dr. D. K. Berninghausen of the Cooper Union library, chairman of the Committee on Intellectual Freedom of the American Library Association, expressed the alarm of that group: "The ban on *The Nation* is no isolated case but a specific instance of a national trend toward suppression of ideas."

Although the Catholics alone have 51 newspapers, 81 magazines, and 19 publishing houses in the United States, neither their press nor the Protestant press is so influential as was the case a century ago when, Roland E. Wolseley, professor of journalism at Syracuse University, has estimated, about 75 per cent of the average American's reading matter of all kinds was religious in nature. As a consequence there have developed powerful religious pressure groups to exert influence upon the news and editorial policies of the lay press. Among the best organized and most effective has been the Committee on Publication of the Christian Science Church. As prescribed by Mary Baker Eddy: "This Committee on Publication shall be responsible for correcting or having corrected a false newspaper article which has not been replied to by other Scientists, or which has been forwarded to this Committee for the purpose of having him reply to it. If the correction by the Committee on Publication is not promptly published by the periodical in which it is desirable that this correction shall appear, this Committee shall immediately apply for aid to the Committee on Business."

Wrote Edwin Franden Dakin in *Mrs. Eddy*: "If any city editor ever dared to ignore a communication sent out by the Committee on Publication, the managing editor would shortly receive a telephone call. He would not find the 'committee' talking at the other end of the wire. Rather it would be one of his most valued advertisers. The advertiser would be extremely sorry to have learned that the Unionville *Beagle* was so extremely prejudiced in its news columns. If the managing editor was incredulous, it would be explained that the paper seemed to have a desire to persecute and vilify the religious beliefs of the gentleman who was now speaking. If incredulity was still expressed, the managing editor would be told that he should look at the bottom of column six on page seven of his issue last Monday week; that he would find there a news item which was wholly erroneous, unjustified and an insult to the advertiser who was now expressing complaint. The managing editor would look; would find a stick of type referring to Christian Science as a faith cure; would return to the wire; would try to learn what was the matter. Almost inevitably, before he had hung up, he had promised to print anything the gentleman at the other end wished to have published in correction." [2]

In a "Publishers' Note" to a 1930 edition of *Mrs. Eddy,* Charles Scribner's Sons declared that after the book appeared Aug. 16, 1929, the "enthusiastic reception accorded by non-partisans was accompanied by so virulent a campaign for suppression that if the issue

[2] From *Mrs. Eddy*. Copyright, 1929, by Charles Scribner's Sons.

had been only a commercial one, it might well have seemed the part of practical wisdom to withdraw the book. . . . For many weeks it seemed as if the sale of *Mrs. Eddy* might actually be so reduced that the book could not be kept on the market. Many stores were forced by threats to renounce its sale, and many to conceal it."

The present author has been associated with three daily newspapers which used to reproduce the complete texts of Christian Science lectures which usually consumed at least a full page. Instead of paying advertising rates the local Scientists purchased a large quantity of copies of the edition in which the material appeared.

There is nothing unique about much of the pressure that church groups of all kinds exert on newspapers. It is the same as that practiced by pressure groups of all sorts.

Since 1933 there has existed Religious News Service, often called the Associated Press of religion, set up with funds supplied by the National Conference of Christians and Jews. It serves over 600 member newspapers, magazines, and radio stations which pay as much as $200 monthly for daily mail, wire, and feature services. The annual income is about $125,000 but that leaves a deficit of about $50,000. The avowed purpose of RNS is "to bring accurate religious material to editors and to promote better understanding between the members of different faiths." Catholic cooperation with the sponsoring agency, the National Conference of Christians and Jews, however, is far less than that which comes from Protestants and Jews.

In addition to RNS there is the news service of the National Catholic Welfare Conference set up in 1920 to strengthen the diocesan press. It serves 399 church papers and magazines and some foreign dailies in the Western hemisphere. It refuses to take secular newspapers in this country as clients lest they scoop the weekly diocesan press on church news.

Typical of organized Catholic pressure similar to that exercised by the Christian Scientists is that exerted by the Catholic Laymen's Association of Georgia whose sparkplug until a few years ago was Richard Reid, editor of its house organ, *The Bulletin.* Any editor whose papers print anything considered derogatory, false, or misleading receives a letter from a local Catholic layman. If the editor fails to acknowledge it or declines to publish it or to make correction, the laymen of the area obtain a list of the registered voters to which mailing list goes a letter from the original reader worded somewhat like the following: "You may have noticed an item in the (local paper) on (day) in regard to the (neighboring) Catholic group. We have called our editor's attention to the fact that this was not a Catholic group but (some other) and requested that he make correction in his next issue. As a citizen of this community I know you will be glad to have this information."

In January, 1945, there was organized the Catholic Institute of the Press in New York City, with Niel McNiel, assistant managing editor of the New York *Times,* one of the leading instigators. According to its constitution, "The object of this organization shall be to unite all Catholics regularly employed in the newspaper, magazine, affiliated publishing industries or otherwise engaged in the dissemination of news; to foster fellowship; to inculcate spiritual ideals that the members may become better Catholics and more worthy citizens; and by sustaining the aforesaid to strengthen their own spiritual lives and to further the principles of truth, justice, virtue and religion . . . to support the work of the Catholic Hierarchy, to cooperate with the Catholic Press; to encourage Catholics interested in a career in the newspaper, magazine or affiliated publishing industries, or otherwise engaged in the dissemination of news; and to promote the cause of Catholic literature." Active members in 1949 totaled about 1,200 each paying $5 annual dues. Average attendance at monthly meetings is about 300; annually nearly 100 per cent of the members attend a communion breakfast at the Waldorf-Astoria. There is also an annual weekend "retreat" for spiritual refreshment for men and another for women members. Francis Cardinal Spellman is honorary president and a "spiritual director" is named by the archdiocese to serve the organization as required by the constitution. There are annual awards "to individuals or units contributing most to the advancement of Catholic thought and principles in a literary fashion." Honorary chairman of the awards committee is the archbishop.

There is hardly a phase of American life today in which there has not been organized a separate Catholic organization to parallel the activities of groups presumably organized to include all Americans regardless of race, creed, or national origin. There is a separate Catholic War Veterans organization, a separate Catholic Women's club, separate Catholic Boy Scouts and Girl Scouts, and so forth. In the aggregate it constitutes a culture within a culture, or, as the fast-growing Catholic population approaches that of non-Catholics, a parallel culture. It is the result of the aggressive policies which American Catholic leaders began promulgating after 1928 when the anti-Catholic bigotry engendered by the campaign of Alfred E. Smith convinced them that the former policy of appeasement of their detractors did not work. Although it is popular for groups to open their membership to all "without regard to race, religion, or national origin," the Catholic attitude is elucidated in the following news item:

Vatican City, Feb. 28—(AP)—The Roman Catholic Church has laid down rules under which Catholics may meet with non-Catholics in the interest of Christian unity.

In instructions to Catholic Bishops throughout the world, the Holy Office gave two chief directives:

1. That these meetings, which it described as "desired occasions," be used to spread Catholic doctrine among non-Catholics, and that,

2. Catholics be careful to safeguard their own faith.

The document emphasized that particular vigilance is needed in gatherings of Catholics and non-Catholics "which in these recent times have begun to be organized to promote reunion in faith." Such gatherings present a "desired occasion" to spread Catholic doctrine, but also "easily bring with them grave dangers of indifference," it added.

Such meetings are not prohibited in the absolute sense, but Catholics must have permission of competent church authorities to attend, the instruction said. Bishops are permitted for a period of three years to authorize attendance at local meetings of Catholics with non-Catholics. One of the conditions of such attendance is a report of the meeting to the Holy Office.

—New York *Daily Compass,* March 11, 1950

When, at its 1949 convention, the Congress of Industrial Organizations expelled the United Electrical Radio and Machine Workers of America and the United Farm Equipment and Metal Workers of America, the real victor was the Association of Catholic Trade Unions organized in 1937 in New York City to "bore from within" the organized labor movement, especially the CIO in which left-wing, including communist, interests, had been powerful from the beginning. Each chapter is under the authority of the bishop of the diocese who appoints a chaplain to act as adviser and monthly auditor of financial reports. The chaplain also is ex officio member of all committees and the archbishop is final arbiter of internal disputes. The program is based on two papal encyclicals, the *Rerum Novarum* of Pope Leo XIII, which appeared in 1891, and Pope Pius XI's *Quadragesimo Anno*, issued in 1931. The following passage is from the latter: "Wherever it [is] impossible for Catholics to form Catholic unions . . . they [Catholic workers] seem to have no choice but to enroll themselves in neutral unions. . . . Side by side with those trade unions, there must always be associations which aim at giving their members a thorough religious and moral training that these in turn may impart to the labor unions to which they belong the upright spirit which should direct their entire conduct."

Because of the record of separate Catholic unions' splitting and weakening the labor movement in some European countries, notably pre-Hitler Germany, a number of American Catholic labor leaders at first were not sympathetic toward ACTU. An early convert, however, was James B. Carey, secretary-treasurer of CIO who was appointed in 1949 to head the new International Union of Electrical Workers which immediately began to try to replace the old UE wherever it had contracts.

Another important early convert to ACTU was David McDonald, secretary of the United Steelworkers Union. It took almost a decade to convince Philip Murray, the successor of John L. Lewis to the CIO presidency, to take action against the international unions in which ACTU had found it possible to make the least headway. (See Saul Alinsky, *John L. Lewis, an Unauthorized Biography*, Putnam, 1949.) Murray's surrender left Daniel Tobin, head of the International Brotherhood of Teamsters (AFL) about the only prominent American Catholic labor leader still to regard the ACTU as a menace rather than a help. Leader among the ACTU chaplains almost from the start has been Father Charles Owen Rice of Pittsburgh, a constant attendant and usually a platform figure at all important CIO conventions. Extracts from Father Rice's pamphlet, *How to De-Control Your Union of Communists,* will suggest how he has earned his reputation as a human powerhouse in the American labor movement:

"Remember, if you push something and the union gets it, then you claim credit and claim that you pushed the opposition into going after it. If the union does not get it, yell 'sellout,' 'doublecross,' 'ineffective,' 'stumble bum,' etc. . . . Train your people to yell 'Boo, Sit Down, Back to Moscow,' etc. . . . Teach them to yammer at a meeting like a good infield. . . . It will take time to get the swing, but it will be a joy and delight when it is used.

"After you have been in action for a while, be sure to organize an anti-Communist caucus. Get your groups all together. Before your caucus meets, have your own group well coached as to what you want to do. You want to pick a name for the caucus. Pick one of the following or something similar. 'Rank-and-file,' this name is used all over by anti-Communists. The Communists generally use the name 'Progressive.' You could use 'American Progressive,' 'Independent,' 'Save the Union,' 'Unity,' 'Pro-CIO'!"

In the United Electrical Workers the name adopted was UE Members for Democratic Action. When its efforts to obtain control failed, the ouster movement began, amid, of course, tremendous anti-communist clamor.

At London in December, 1949 the American delegation, representing both AFL and CIO, was successful in obtaining an invitation to Western European Catholic unions to join the new Free World Labor Confederation. Walter Reuther, president of the CIO United Automobile Workers of America, in which ACTU influence is strong, hailed the 46 to 8 vote as "a settlement of this most explosive issue."

Hardly any Protestant equivalent of ACTU exists. According to Jess Cavileer in "Church and Labor Relations," in the Oct. 15, 1944, issue of *Social Action*, publication of the Council for Social Action of the Congregational Christian Churches, the industrial chaplains and morale officers, as they usually were called, in war industries, were ineffective because they were suspected of being stooges of the industries which paid their salaries. The People's Institute of Applied Religion, headed by the dynamic Claude Williams who followed his Tennessee parishioners to Detroit where they went to work in the automobile factories, is too friendly with communists, Cavileer charged, although in the same issue Williams was given space vigorously to deny the accusation. There is a Department of the Church and Economic Life, formerly the Industrial Division of the Federal Council of Churches, and some Protestant institutes, forums, and foundations. None, however, makes any attempts to organize any parallel system of labor unions or to persuade union members to form caucuses or blocs for the purpose of promoting any particular programs within established unions.

During 1949 the Vatican's participation in international politics was open, extensive, and vigorous. Communist governments in eastern European countries, satellites of the Soviet Union, seized the extensive land holdings of the church as part of their agrarian reform programs, ended the centuries' old control of the church over public school education, reduced the support given parochial schools, and in other ways loosened the authority of the church. Fighting back, in July Pope Pius XII called upon Catholics the world over to choose between "Catholicism and Communism, Rome and Moscow." All church members who had any part whatever in the arrest and prosecution of Yugoslav Archbishop Aloysius Stepinac or Hungarian Joseph Cardinal Mindszenty were excommunicated and the same punishment was threatened for all communists and fellow travelers. Within a fortnight, however, the latter edict was modified to exclude Catholics who support communism with votes only, without adopting its alleged anti-Christian doctrines. In August it was decreed that Catholics can marry "militant" communists by special dispensation only. Reading communist literature was forbidden and in November the Holy Office ruled that Catholic sacraments must be refused news vendors who sell communist newspapers "knowingly and freely" and that those forced to sell them should limit sales "as far as possible."

The official Vatican justification of its use of religious weapons in a political fight has been that it is waging a defensive war against godless communism which is bent upon destroying all religion. At the World Council of Churches meeting in July, 1949, at Chichester, England, however, Dr. Joseph Hrmodka, Protestant leader in Czechoslovakia, declared that the conflict, in his country at least, is political rather than religious. He said that the Protestant churches, which have kept out of politics, have not been molested by the communist Czech regime. The Council passed resolutions repudiating communism but also condemning the Catholic church for restricting Protestantism in Spain and Latin America. Shortly thereafter the International Congregational church, meeting at Wellesley, Mass., condemned communism but warned Protestants against joining in a Catholic crusade against it.

Indication of the broadened scope of Vatican political interest was the act of Pius XII one day in February, 1946 when he created 32 new cardinals, only four of them Italians in defiance of tradition that the Sacred College of Cardinals of 70 members be predominantly Italian in composition (exactly 50 per cent when World War II broke out). For the first time there were created Chinese and Australian cardinals, the others being distributed throughout the entire world.

The church also exercises considerable influence in the Department of State and upon the White House. Under its pressure President Franklin Delano Roosevelt appointed a personal representative to the Vatican. In October, 1951 President Harry S. Truman nominated an ambassador but the Senate was unable to consider the matter before adjournment. A storm of Protestant disapproval greeted the proposal.

The Church and War

Since war, as the German military strategist, Clausewitz, said, is just the extension of peacetime diplomacy, the role of organized religion as a peace or war maker is an important consideration. Through its teachings of *brotherly love*—(Matthew 22:39: "And the second [commandment] is like unto it, Thou shalt love thy neighbor as thyself"; Matthew 5:44: "But I say unto you, Love your enemies, bless them that curse you, do good to them that hate you, and pray for them which despitefully use you, and persecute you")—and *pacifism* (Matthew 5:9: "Blessed are the peacemakers: for they shall be called the children of God"; Matthew 5:39: "But I say unto you, That ye resist not evil; but whosoever shall smite thee on thy right cheek, turn to him the other also")—the Christian church preaches peace. Actually it is difficult if not impossible to recall any war in which Christian armies have participated without the blessing and support of the church. World War II comes the closest to being the exception as far as the United States is concerned. Instead of whipping up hysterical hate for the Huns as they did in World War I, the churches accepted the actuality of aggressive assault on our territory in the same attitude of resignation that characterized the majority of the American people. The church, in other words, reflected the national viewpoint and, while it did not oppose the war, it did not promote it as holy as it had a generation earlier. One consequence of the calmer, more businesslike, almost fatalistic way in which Americans waged World War II was more generous treatment for conscientious objectors. Instead of being sent to federal penitentiaries as "slackers" on whom women pinned white feathers, they were allowed to perform pacifistic duties helpful to the war effort.

In the interval between World Wars I and II the church partook of the general disillusionment and preached the futility of force to obtain life's blessings. Typically, in 1931 the famous Harry Emerson Fosdick of New York's Riverside church declared, "I renounce war," and reproached himself for having exploited soldiers before they went "over the top on their murderous and suicidal tasks." Said the former chaplain: "Men cannot have Christ and war at the same time." In the same year 19,372 Protestant clergymen answered a *World Tomorrow* questionnaire with 12,076, or 62 per cent, saying they believed the churches should go on record as refusing to sanction or support any future war and 10,427, or 54 per cent, stating that they were personally prepared to do so. In 1941 the Federal Council of Churches of America resolved against war as did several Protestant denominations separately.

In the early thirties pacifism was rampant on the college campuses of America. A 1933 poll of 70 colleges showed 39 per cent of 22,617 students opposed to participation in any war and 33 per cent more willing to participate only if the United States were invaded. The so-called Oxford oath of pacifism was taken by undergraduates in droves at peace rallies. In 1936 the Veterans of Future Wars were started as a lark at Princeton University but spread across the continent. The avowed objective of the future fighters was to collect immediately a $1,000 bonus with interest compounded annually backward from 1965 and paid at both ends. The salute was an outstretched palm. At Rensselaer Polytechnic Institute there was organized the auxiliary Profiteers of Future Wars, and Vassar College girls originated the Future Gold Star Mothers of America. As a publicity stunt it was a great momentary success, but five years later most of the members of the Future Veterans of America were writing home from Somewhere in the Pacific or Somewhere in France.

To summarize, it is only in times of peace when threat of war is at low ebb that either the church or any other institution dares speak out boldly for a pacifistic point of view.

CHAPTER FOURTEEN

EDUCATION AND SCHOOLS

*American schools tend to turn out conservatives and con-
formists and to discourage heresy in all fields.*

Church and Schools

What is rapidly becoming the nation's No. 1 educational
problem—how to reconcile Catholic and non-Catholic points of view
—has many ramifications, foremost of which is the continued healthy
existence of the free public school system. Quotation already has been
made from Pius XI's encyclical, "Christian Education of Youth"
(see pages 495 to 496). An article headlined, "The Sore Thumb in
the United States," in the July 29, 1945 issue of *Our Sunday Visitor,*
leading Catholic Action weekly, expressed the official Catholic viewpoint in its leading paragraph as follows:

"The sore thumb in our United States, where everything is democratic, is our public school system, which is not democratic. It caters
to a class. It satisfies only those who neither practice nor believe in any
religion. If American parents want their children to have a religious
education, they have to send them to a private school, for the public
schools are set up with the idea in view that an atheistic child should
not be embarrassed (!) by the mention of religion."

The reference might have been to the son of Mrs. Vashti Mc-
Collum who successfully carried her suit to ban the use of Champaign,
Ill., public school classrooms for religious education to the United
States Supreme Court which, by an 8 to 1 decision in March, 1948,
reversed the state courts. It was not only Catholics, however, who de-
plored the decision. At its quadrennial convention in May, 1948, in
Boston, the Methodist church unanimously adopted a resolution,
presented by the Rev. Ernest Fremont Tittle of Evanston, Ill., declar-

ing that religion has a rightful place in the public schools of the country. As a matter of fact what has come to be called the "released time" idea was mostly Protestant in origin, although it has had Catholic support, especially in areas where there are no parochial schools. Professor Frank McKibbon of the Garrett Biblical Institute (Methodist), a long-time leader in the movement, has been frank in admitting its necessity because of the decline of attendance by children at Protestant Sunday schools.

According to a National Education Association survey in December, 1948, the practice of allowing clergymen to come into the schools to hold religious classes or of releasing school children to go to their churches or wherever else such classes are held has spread to 26.8 per cent of the nation's public school systems. This growth has occurred since 1913 when Superintendent William A. Wirt originated the idea in Gary, Ind. The larger the city the more likely it is to adopt the plan, the NEA discovered. In cities of 100,000 population or over the incidence is 45.9 per cent; in cities under 2,500 it is only 17.1 per cent. An earlier survey, announced almost simultaneously with the Supreme Court decision in the McCollum case, is summarized in the following news story:

Washington—(AP)—The National Education Assn. after a survey two years ago reported that nine states and Hawaii permitted religious instruction by church teachers inside public schools during school hours.

The nine are Alabama, Louisiana, North Carolina, Ohio, Oklahoma, Oregon, Texas, Vermont and Virginia. All the other states (except Michigan, Nebraska and Nevada, for which blanks appeared in the survey) replied "no" to this section of the questionnaire.

The survey reported:

"There are few instances of this sort of religious instruction in Alabama and Texas high school credits given for Bible study, but in Texas the course must be taught from the point of view of literature rather than religion.

METHODS DIFFER

"In Alabama teachers are paid by the Protestant churches. In Louisiana Catholic instruction is sometimes conducted in the public schools by church officials.

"Several state departments and attorney generals have ruled against allowing religious instruction in the school building during school hours, even when not under public-school auspices.

"Connecticut reported that it was tried out and discontinued as unsatisfactory."

12 BAN PRACTICE

Most of the states permitted pupils to be excused to attend "week-day church" schools. Fourteen which did not were Arizona, Delaware, the District of Columbia, Iowa, Maryland, Nebraska, New Hampshire, New Mexico, North Carolina, North Dakota, Tennessee, Texas, Washington and Wyoming.

State constitutions, the NEA said, forbade sectarian instruction in public schools in Arizona, California, Colorado, Idaho, Minnesota, Montana, Nebraska, Nevada, New York, South Dakota, Wisconsin and Wyoming.

"No state constitution prohibits Bible-reading in the public schools, and it is a question for judicial interpretation whether Bible-reading is sectarian instruction."

—Chicago *Sun-Times*, March 11, 1948

Catholic opposition to the American public school system is not new. In fact, the Catholic hierarchy never has approved of it. When Robert Dale Owen and other labor leaders, and Horace Mann were campaigning for it early in the nineteenth century, Archbishop Hughes of New York organized a Catholic party of opposition with a platform calling for "public money for Catholic schools." The effort failing, the Catholic parochial school system was begun in 1842. In a little more than a century it has grown to include about 8,000 elementary and 2,000 high schools, 228 seminaries, and 73 Catholic universities and men's colleges. About half of approximately three million Catholic children of school age attend parochial schools for which church members raise about $182,250,000 annually. There is no national head of the Catholic school system, and each school is owned by the hierarchy or some religious order. There are approximately 80,000 teaching nuns, most of whom receive no salary other than maintenance. For the 1947–48 school year there were 180,637 students enrolled in Catholic institutions of higher learning by comparison with 154,572 the preceding year.

Since adoption of the free public school system most Protestant sects have discontinued their schools, virtually the only ones in existence prior to 1825. The only important parochial system today other than the Catholic is that of the Lutherans who operate about 1,200 elementary schools. Although still privately endowed, hundreds of colleges and universities throughout the country which were founded by denominations now are nonsectarian.

In addition to operating their own school system, a right upheld by the United States Supreme Court, Catholics take an interest as great as, if not greater than other citizens in the public school system, with the result that "incidents" have multiplied in recent years. In 1947, for instance, a predominantly Catholic public school board in North College Hill, Ohio, took over the St. Margaret-Mary parochial school, renaming it Grace Avenue school. An annual rent of $6,000 was paid to the archbishop and all eight teaching nuns were placed on the public payroll although they continued to conduct religious classes as previously. When the Protestant superintendent of schools refused to take orders from the board, he was discharged whereupon 28 of the 33 teachers in the city's public high school and a large number of students walked out. After the National Education Association blacklisted the entire system, the school board resigned and the superintendent was restored by court order to his old position.

The same year a group of Protestants started court action to break Catholic control of the public school system in seven New Mexico counties. The agitation began in Dixon where an expensive W.P.A.-built public school was closed down and all children compelled to attend the parochial school which then became tax supported under the name of St. Joseph Public School. The following news story tells the outcome of the statewide action:

Santa Fe, N.M.—(AP)—District Judge E. T. Hensley Saturday barred 143 Catholic teachers from teaching in New Mexico public schools.

The state court's written judgment supplemented a verbal decision from the bench Oct. 7 in the Dixon school case.

Hensley's verbal decision held that employment of members of the Catholic teaching orders in public schools violated the state and national constitutions.

The Dixon case arose from a dispute over alleged teaching of Catholicism in the public schools at Dixon, little Northern New Mexico mountain community.

Harry L. Bigbee of Santa Fe, who brought the suit on behalf of 28 Protestant residents of seven counties, said the effect of the judgment was only to bar specified members of Catholic teaching orders who taught in 25 schools. It did not bar them as a class, he said.

Hensley's judgment means that at least 16 school buildings owned by the Catholic church must be replaced with public schools. This decision comes under a holding that prohibits state or local school boards from acquiring space for public school classes in buildings not under the absolute control of the state.

OTHER JUDGMENTS

Other declaratory judgments were granted prohibiting:

Free state bus transportation for students in parochial schools.

Purchase of textbooks for parochial schools and purchase of books especially for Catholic schools.

Teaching of sectarian doctrine in any tax-supported school.

Holding of public school classes in rooms where religious or sectarian symbols are displayed.

Payment of persons teaching sectarian doctrines.

No decision has been made on appeal of the case.

—Chicago *Sun-Times,* March 13, 1949

In June, 1948, national attention was focused on a referendum vote in North Dakota intended to end a 30-year practice of nuns teaching in public schools. The following news story indicates the outcome and the aftermath:

Bismarck, N.D., July 11—(AP)—Clothed in civilian dress, Catholic nuns may teach in North Dakota public schools next Fall, despite recent passage of a measure intended to stop them.

Two ranking members of the Catholic Church in North Dakota today advised the nuns that the church has no objection to their donning "respectable secular dress" to comply with the state's new law.

About 75 Catholic sisters teach in the state's public schools, predominantly in Catholic communities.

The so-called "anti-garb" act, sponsored by a group of Protestants, including clergymen, prohibits any public school teacher from wearing garb denoting membership in a religious order. The act does not mention Catholic nuns by name, but admittedly is aimed chiefly at them.

The act was approved at the June 29 primary election by a 93,000 to 83,000 vote, with about 300 precincts not reported.

Two Catholic leaders, Bishop Vincent J. Ryan of Bismarck and Auxiliary Bishop Leo Dworschak of Fargo, announced their proposal today at regular services.

A joint statement by the church officials said, in part:

"Some of its sponsors solicited support for this (anti-garb) measure on the claim that it would keep Catholic sisters from teaching. We are informed by competent legal authority that no law can, under the protection of our Constitution, discriminate against any teacher on account of religious membership or belief.

"The withdrawal of the sisters would close some public schools in

North Dakota. An emergency exists in many districts in this state because of the shortage of teachers. Although the sisters are needed elsewhere, in view of the emergency, the sisters will arrange to use in school a respectable secular dress, which in no way indicates the fact that the teacher is a member of or adherent of any religious order or denomination.

"Consequently we announce that in such school districts where the people and the school boards find it necessary and desirable to retain the services of the sisters, the sisters will continue to teach, attired in a manner which is in strict compliance with the law."

Bishop Ryan told newsmen the proposal is not new. He said it had been done in both Canada and Mexico under circumstances similar to those now existing in North Dakota.

—New York *Star,* July 12, 1948

When Dr. George D. Stoddard was named president-elect of the University of Illinois in 1945, Bishop James A. Griffin of the Springfield, Ill., Catholic diocese publicly called for "a profession of faith" from him. Catholic objection was taken to the following passage from one of Dr. Stoddard's books, *Meaning of Intelligence*: "Man-made concepts such as devils, witches, taboos, hell, original sin and divine revelation kept alive in an unending chain of emotionally tinged spoken and printed words, have distorted the intellectual process of millions of persons over the centuries." In reply to the bishop's demand, Dr. Stoddard declared: "In 20 years of professional life I have had no interest in the private beliefs of any person, and I have not known, save incidentally, the church affiliation of any student, colleague or associate. I will follow the same policy at the University of Illinois." The board of trustees upheld the appointment.

The church and Catholic lay bodies have opposed vigorously introduction of sex education in public schools. In 1949 debate centered about showing of a motion picture, *Human Growth*, produced by Eddie Albert for the E. C. Brown Trust for Social Hygiene Education in Portland, Ore. and widely endorsed by medical and educational organizations. In New York State the Catholic Welfare Committee tried unsuccessfully to persuade the commissioner of health to ban its showing. Charles J. Tobin, the committee's secretary, quoted from the part of the encyclical, "The Christian Education of Youth," which condemns naturalism in modern education. Debating the issue in the Dec. 9, 1949, New York *Daily Compass*, Tobin wrote:

Our committee is convinced that no state agency, health or educational, has the right to usurp the prerogatives of parents by disseminating sex education indiscriminately to their children in the classrooms. No teacher in our common schools can impart such information without jeopardizing the religious and moral life of the children. . . . We exhort parents to resist the state and its agencies when an attempt is made to usurp parental rights or to invade the sanctity of the home by disseminating sex knowledge, without morality, to their children in the school.

Incidents such as those cited in news stories included in this chapter are not isolated. Nor is the following:

St. Paul, Minn.—(AP)—Archbishop John Gregory Murray has banned Catholic children from school classrooms where sex education is taught.

Denouncing sex lessons in public or private schools, the archbishop said, in his pastoral letter, sex is a subject "for personal discussion between parent and child, physician and patients or confessor and penitent."

The letter affects 337,200 Catholics in 27 south central Minnesota counties.

—Chicago *Daily News,* Dec. 13, 1949

Properly to report and write such news a newspaperman must have proper perspective in the light of major policies regarding which leading pressure groups have different attitudes. Properly to appreciate the significance of such items, a newspaper reader must possess similar perspective.

Who Controls Education?

For good or evil one charge made by the Catholic Welfare Committee secretary is true: the schools *have* progressively taken over functions of child training that formerly were the prerogative of the home or other institutions. They have done so largely as the result of pressure from interests which often have been powerful enough to obtain legislation to compel the inclusion of their pet subjects or ideas in the curriculum. Despite the widespread distrust of the intellectual, most Americans have a tremendous faith in the value of formal education. Every parent wants his child to go further in school than he did. An applicant's fitness for a job more and more is being determined by his years of schooling; as the specialized nature of the position increases so does the number of diplomas to certify as to one's preparation. Testimonial to the high regard with which a degree is held was the extent to which veterans took advantage of the educational opportunities afford by the GI Bill of Rights. Commencement orators wax eloquent regarding the advantage of staying in school as long as possible. Authors of profound books which view vexatious social ills with alarm invariably suggest in their last chapters that the solution is a matter of education.

If this profound faith in education were not enough to make the schools the happy hunting ground for propagandists and pressure groups of all kinds, the sheer fact that in the average sized community education usually costs about as much as all other governmental functions combined would provide the goad. Anyway, Catholics, communists, psychoanalysts, and educators agree that the early years of life are the most important for habit formation and principals have to be constantly alert to avoid devoting almost full time to promotion of this cause or that, observing special week after special week with essay contests, special programs with speakers and "educational" entertainment, and making available tons and tons of promotional literature from every source imaginable.

In addition to attempting to get one's own propaganda into the schools, it is a great American trait to accuse the other fellow of attempts to do the same thing. The fear of communism is well expressed in the following editorial from the Feb. 21, 1949 Seattle *Post-Intelligencer*:

There should be widespread application, in fact a nation-wide emulation, of the patriotic example provided by the members of the Oklahoma legislature in seeking to assure the state and nation of loyal citizens in the future.

By a vote of 102 to 7, the house of representatives of the Oklahoma state legislature approved a bill requiring all teachers in the schools of the state and all students in state-supported colleges to affirm their loyalty to the United States as a condition of employment or of participation in the activities of the institutions.

Cardinal Spellman warned the country in his magnificent sermon protesting the persecution of Cardinal Mindszenty in Hungary that the American people themselves are in very great and imminent danger from Communism, which thrives upon disloyalty.

Nowhere in the country is the infiltration of Communism being more zealously attempted than in the schools.

Nowhere in the country could it do more harm than in the schools.

Communistic teachers, implanted in the schools of the country, are in a position to poison the minds of young Americans against their country and its institutions, and to poison their souls against the spiritual integrity which is their religious heritage.

Communism in the schools is an infectious disease which could demoralize and destroy the last vestiges of freedom in the United States and leave the American people without a shred of the high moral purpose and lofty human dignity which distinguish their way of life and make it the envy and the marvel of the whole world.

The philosophy of Communism, if taught in our schools and allowed to distort the political and economic and social beliefs of our young men and women, will not only deprive the country of its sovereignty and reduce it to the status of a mere province of Soviet Russia, but will demolish our most vital American concepts of man as master of his own destiny and render our people the mere vassals of a slave state.

That is what Communism accomplished in Hungary, where the people are as desirous of freedom and peace as any other people in the world, but where disloyal minorities were permitted to determine the policies of the country and they betrayed it into the hands of the Communist oppressors.

Communism could do the same thing in America.

It would ruthlessly do that wicked thing in America if it ever had the opportunity.

It is striving endlessly to create the opportunity, especially in the schools of the United States where the boys and girls of today are being prepared to be the men and women of tomorrow and the future citizens of the country—which will be the kind of a country they want it to be, free or slave, according to what they have been taught to believe and want.

Of course the proof of loyalty to America should be a condition of the employment of any teacher in the schools.

Communism should not be taught in the classrooms of the United States any more than thievery and arson and rapine are taught, for it is not only a form of criminality as vicious as any of these but worse than all of them.

Of course the young men and women who are students in the state-supported schools of the country should be encouraged to assert their loyalty to the United States, and earnestly instructed in the meaning and significance and the history and tradition of the institutions of the United States, for only thus can a people worthy of its heritage attain the fruits thereof.

Not only Oklahoma, but all the states of the Union, should assure the loyalty of the schools to America, for only by that means can this free and wholesome way of life we cherish be perpetuated.

An entirely different opinion as to the nature of the threat to the schools was expressed by Dr. Homer P. Rainey, ousted president of the University of Texas, at a Chicago forum in 1946:

"Congressional and other investigating agencies have revealed the presence of numerous organized groups in this country that are trying to get control of education and all other social agencies. Reactionary and pro-fascist groups are organized to suppress liberal thought and liberal leadership wherever they are found. They are sponsoring legislative programs to control labor, social welfare agencies, and education. Also, they are cataloguing and classifying the ministers of this country and making their lists of 'safe' and 'unsafe' ministers available to church-governing boards. Their favorite technique of control is to infiltrate their own men upon all boards and committees that control educational, religious, and social welfare organizations. This form of control is becoming almost universal. Boards of education, college boards of trustees, political boards of regents, church boards, community boards that control Red Cross, Community Chests and other welfare agencies, are all being filled today with corporation lawyers and other representatives of special interest groups."

Dr. Rainey was dismissed Nov. 1, 1944, three weeks after he made a 16-point statement to the university faculty outlining what he considered the reactionary policies of the regents. After one of its characteristically thorough investigations, the American Association of University Professors blacklisted the University of Texas.

Chairman of the Board of Regents which dismissed Dr. Rainey was the head of the legal staff of the Southwestern Bell Telephone Company and representative of a large motion picture monopoly. On the State Board of Education, which controls all Texas public schools, selects texts, and controls 80 million dollars in endowments, was the national president of the Christian-Americans, with headquarters at Houston. That conservatives should be in high positions on school boards also is the rule rather than the exception. Numerous studies have been made of the composition of the boards of education of public school systems. One, which included 967 boards in 104 cities, as reported in the Jan. 20, 1937 *School and Society,* revealed that 75 per cent of school board members are business or professional people, whereas only 4 per cent are from the ranks of labor. Self-perpetuating boards of privately endowed colleges and universities pick wealthy and influential men, partly in anticipation of sizeable gifts or bequests.

Newspapers naturally "go to town" when an incident such as the Rainey dismissal occurs in their bailiwick. In fact, for more than a quarter century the Hearst press has been in the vanguard of forces advocating and promoting almost incessant investigations of curricula, textbooks, and teachers which have led to numerous dismissals, bans of books and magazines, passage of loyalty oaths, and vilification of a veritable "who's who" of scholars and administrators. Otherwise the only news of education which usually is considered fit to print pertains to routine matters regarding expenditures of public money: new buildings or equipment, resignations and new appointments and, of course, most important of all, the athletic programs. With the exception of the New York *Times* and New York *Herald Tribune*, few newspapers have education editors or are concerned with educational, as distinguished from school, news. Nevertheless, to evaluate the effect of education upon public opinion necessitates examination of educational theories and policies and their methods of execution.

Educational Philosophy

In colonial America, even the three *R*'s were taught at mother's knee in the home. The first American high school, the Boston Latin School, was opened in 1635, and was modeled after English Latin schools. It was for boys only, stressed study of the classics, and trained mostly for the ministry. The equivalent of what today is called vocational education was obtained through the apprentice system in the shops. Professional education likewise was obtained by serving apprenticeships. Even today there are some oldsters among practicing physicians and lawyers who got their starts by working and studying in the offices of predecessors. Most of the specialized schools, so common today, as commerce, engineering, journalism, music, art, and speech, are of comparatively recent origin.

The versatile Benjamin Franklin has been called the father of the American secondary school education idea. His Philadelphia academy which shifted its emphasis to history, chronology, morality, politics, and kindred subjects, was widely imitated even as late as 1850. The first high school for girls was opened in 1824 at Worcester, Mass., and the first coeducational high school a few years later at Lowell, Mass.

In 1827 the Latin schools substituted English as the classroom language, and there was no doubt that the old aristocratic conception of education, with its gentleman-scholar goal, was obsolete.

Jeffersonian democracy called for a literate public and for opportunity to obtain a good start in life so as to be able to compete in the rugged individualistic way. Organized labor campaigned vigorously for free public education in the belief that "the equality of man results only from education." The worker wanted his children to have approximately the same background of training as the offspring of the rich so as to be able to hold their own a social notch or two higher than that which the Old Man had been able to attain. A leader was Robert Dale Owen, son of the Scotch socialist, Robert Owen, who originated the New Harmony, Ind. experiment. It was his contact with that adventure in communal living which convinced the younger Owen that adults are too hopelessly wedded to the past to reform; for democratic and ethical ideas to "catch on" they must be taught to children, he concluded.

When the factory system caused the apprentice system to die out, the movement to provide vocational education in the schools developed. So curricula were enriched to include courses in business English, manual training, home economics, shorthand, typing, bookkeeping and machine work of all kinds. Some of the industrial or manual arts, or whatever they are called, high schools which were erected in the twenties, are "sights to be seen," with complete laboratory and shop equipment to prepare youngsters for almost any position in commerce or industry. Thus, an important function formerly performed by either the home—when it was the center of handicraft arts —or the shop, was taken over, by popular request or demand, by the state. In view of the fact that, until the surge of veterans changed the picture, 90 per cent never went beyond high school and only 4.6 per cent of the population were college graduates (according to the 1940 Census), those who denounced high schools for emphasizing their college preparatory courses to the exclusion of all others obviously "had a point."

It is because of the census findings that the median years of formal schooling for 75 million Americans of twenty-five years or above was 8.4 in 1940 that the high school has been called "the college of the people." Much of the pedagogical polemics which seem to the average newspaper reader too recondite and/or erudite to command more than passing attention, grow out of rival ideas as how best to react to the fact that only 25 per cent will complete a high school education and only 50 per cent will continue beyond the eighth grade. Junior high school and junior college ideas are in part attempts to broaden the training of the non-college going populace and to entice more to obtain an additional few years at least of schooling. Many of the new ideas in primary and secondary school education are predicated on the knowledge that unless the student gets such and such training before the tenth grade he may not receive it at all. Likewise, there is an ever broadening conception of what a good elementary education should be considered to be. No longer is there the scholarly advocacy of learning for its own sake, for the purpose of discipline. In schools considered "advanced," children are not compelled to master Latin and Greek, algebra, geometry, and other subjects because they are "good for the mind." Rather, the "mental discipline" concept has given way to theories of how to build character, or how to develop well-adjusted personalities or how to promote public spirited citizenship. Some of the experiments in so-called "progressive" education admittedly were extreme; in the revolt against formal drill and regimented rote learning, whereby every student "took" exactly the same courses as every other, the pedagogical pendulum sometimes swung to the opposite extreme of freedom verging on license. At the time of this writing, the swing is in the reverse direction, out of a recognition that with freedom there must be a sense of responsibility; but there is no agitation among leaders of educational thought for a return to the "learning for its own sake" philosophy. Much of the criticism, favorable and adverse, of educational theories by laymen, including some editorial writers, is based on complete ignorance of the principles involved. Nevertheless, whenever there is a need for retrenchment, as in a period of depression, it is the so-called "frills" that are most likely to be eliminated, including special schools or classes for children with particular problems: feebleminded, crippled, mentally maladjusted, blind, deaf, and exceptionally brilliant, for instance. In their natural tendency to regress in hard times, taxpayers whose schooling consisted of the three R's taught with a hickory stick, resent spending money for "newfangled" notions.

According to the National Educational Policies committee, the goals of secondary school education should be: (1) self-realization (making the most of one's ability); (2) understanding of human relations, including those of the family and community; (3) economic efficiency and (4) civic responsibility. In its July, 1943 issue, *Fortune* editorialized: "We need good citizens, not just a few but many; since high school is the limit of formal education for most prospective citizens we have to determine what sort of high school education we want. What we want—judged in terms of what we seem most to lack—are graduates capable of independent thinking, graduates willing to participate in civic life, graduates with an understanding knowledge of the country and the world.

"If these are our aims we shall know what to decry. We shall decry any form of education which treats the student as an organism that needs to have its reflexes conditioned with a dosage of facts and suggestions. Instead, too much of our schooling aims at having the proper emotions run in students' minds when they hear catchwords and slogans. The participation of the people in their government has no point if they are incapable of independent thinking; if human beings can only react to outside stimuli, if they can only think what they are told to think, then we shall frankly have to admit that democratic ways of life are without sense and should make no pretense of trying to educate children for them."

Since the public school system was intended to operate as a major prop for a republican form of government, the *Fortune* challenge seems a fair one. The quest for an answer involves a delving into the question of the effect of the schools upon American public opinion.

By reducing illiteracy almost to the vanishing point, mass education has exposed a great portion of our population to knowledge hitherto outside its grasp. Because we can read, whole new worlds of opportunity and experience are opened to us and we have a better understanding of what is going on in the world. We are able to compare ourselves and our experiences with other people and their experiences. We can travel mentally to the most remote spot, dream the wildest dreams, test the most bizarre thoughts—all via reading. Knowledge of what others are doing becomes an incentive to improve one's own lot.

Mass education also affords a more uniform base for common living. Promulgation of customs, traditions, ideas and facts of a similar nature give us common meanings for a wide range of things upon which to base our culture. Without such meanings we could make little sense from such actions as obeying a policeman, voting, observing traffic signals, using money or a multitude of other common practices.

All this is on the credit side of the ledger. On the other hand, by becoming the storehouse of knowledge of the past, the schools operate as the medium through which obsolete taboos, myths, legends, and superstitions are perpetuated. The traditional emphasis upon rote learning, through memorization, recitation and examination, is doctrinaire, creates the impression that truth is static, glorifies the *status quo*, and lays the ground for frustration after graduation when the former student begins to learn the "facts" of life. It is, as one of the author's former graduate students in a seminar on public opinion put it, "not education but habit formation."

Any teacher of experience to whom students speak frankly has heard its equivalent often. Scholars have made similar observations and have gone further to examine the reasons for the shortcomings which are so glaring that failure to correct them seems little short of criminal. Earl L. Vance, professor of journalism at Florida State University, in "What Schools Can't Teach," in the Autumn, 1946 *Virginia Quarterly Review* blamed much of the failure of higher education on the boredom which students feel when compelled to pursue courses which they are not convinced are important. Ostensibly to broaden the school's service, the tendency in high school and especially college and university curriculum-making during the past generation has been toward multiplication of the number of courses in all fields so that today it is virtually impossible for a student in search of a general rather than a specialized education to take a single basic course in almost any department and emerge feeling that his desire for an understanding of what that field of inquiry has to contribute to the sum total of knowledge has been satisfied. "Anyone in middle life today can easily remember when many colleges did not have such a thing as a course in education or physical education or home economics," Vance wrote. "Then a single course or two began to appear in these subjects. Today the undergraduate catalogue of a typical medium-sized college lists 72 separate courses in physical education. The same catalogue lists a total of 96 semester hours in education— three-fourths of an entire four-year college program. In home economics the total is 162 semester hours, or enough to require five and one-half years to complete if the student took nothing except home economics."

Vance limited his comment to just three fields. The same criticism holds for the curricula in history, economics, psychology, political science, mathematics, physics, chemistry, biology—any subject that one wishes to consider. Specialization and subdivision have reached such a stage that experts in closely related fields find it difficult to understand or converse with each other. And as far as students in search of a general education are concerned, there is a tremendous elaboration of the trivial. The most dangerous feature in conditioning the student for future life is the lack of correlation between fields. One hour, in high school or college, he studies history; the next hour, English literature; the third hour, civic or current events, and so on. As Vance said, "The effort to teach 'citizenship,' 'literature,' 'science,' and 'economics,' as though they were separate and distinct entities places serious limitations on each. The problems of citizenship become understandable and meaningful only when presented as the interplay of all the forces—social, economic, scientific, literary—of the world as we know it. No one of these can be taught adequately except in relation to all others."

Not only, however, are they taught separately, but in the understandable attempt to broaden the service of the school, the curriculum has become a veritable cafeteria from which the student selects with considerable latitude what he wants to take. To obtain a diploma certifying that he is an educated person he must complete a required number of courses, or obtain a minimum number of credits. So he takes whatever educational diet seems to suit his fancy and may finish his schooling with no coordinated philosophy of life as a whole or of any major segment of it. He has merely spent his time cramming his head full of miscellaneous facts for a long enough period to pass satisfactory examinations so as to obtain passing grades. Because they have no clear-cut purpose—not knowing for what they are preparing whom—the modern liberal arts college curriculum, and the high school college preparatory courses which become necessary so that high school graduates can gain admittance to colleges, are colossal failures. Altogether too many of their products lack the ability to integrate and evaluate data from different sources; their knowledge has been pigeonholed and fragmentary. They simply do not know what the world is all about. And if they have passed through a specialized professional school, such as medicine, engineering, or law, they may be skillful, even brilliant practitioners in their own field, but they are far from well-rounded citizens. They lack perspective regarding the social importance of their own field and an adequate sense of social responsibility in the pursuance of their calling. Their interests are narrow; they are, in fact, positively illiterate outside their own specialties and their middle-aged efforts to learn to appreciate grand opera and modern art and perhaps dabble in amateur photography are no more than a pathetic defense against a deep feeling of inadequacy with which their one-sided education has left them.

School and Community

Cognizant of the cogency of criticism such as that which Vance brilliantly advanced, there have developed among some educators different sorts of "back to" movements, mainly to the so-called humanities, or the classics, or the Great Books. Only a comparatively small group of "progressive" educators promote the idea that to be purposeful education must come to grips head-on with the problems of contemporary life. The principal reason there are not more teachers who speak up for the principle that the best way to seek the truth is through a conflict of ideas is the tremendous pressures, already mentioned, which keep the controversial out of the classroom as much as possible. The Institute for Propaganda Analysis began its May 1, 1939 report on "Propaganda in the Schools" as follows:

"Our public schools are everybody's business. Does the high school text refer to 'Lee's well-trained army'? Into the superintendent's office come the members of the local G.A.R. to complain of 'Southern propaganda!' A Jewish parent doesn't like Shakespeare's *The Merchant of Venice*. Of all the plays that William Shakespeare wrote, they *would* have to pick on that one, he declares. *Uncle Tom's Cabin* displeases the Southern-born. *Little Black Sambo* irks the Negroes. Last week, Jimmy Smith came home from school and told his dad: 'Our teacher says that we all came from monkeys.' On the Sunday following, the fundamentalist church in town resounds again with protest. Once before the fundamentalist teacher was aroused. That was last year when Jimmy's sister Jane announced that 'Washington drank whiskey.' And not only drank it, but made it, too! 'Anyway, that's what *teacher* said.' At the 'every Wednesday luncheon' of the Chamber of Commerce there is talk of 'rooting out these bolshevistic teachers.' Just how it can be done nobody is quite sure; but someone has suggested that all teachers and school executives 'take an oath to uphold the Constitution.' Hard-pressed business men, staggering under the evergrowing tax burden, have been looking around for something to cut from the city budget. 'Why not get rid of the fads and frills in the schools?' they ask. However, the parents' association is against that. Once, the parents, too, were dubious about the so-called fads and frills—music, art, physical education; now they are sold on them, and ready to fight. So fight there will be next fall, when the school board elections roll around."

The Latin schools were spared such controversy because they had clear-cut objectives. So is a clearly avowed vocational school or professional school. Parochial schools are not the storm centers of parental and pressure group activities because their curriculum is decided by the hierarchy and their objective of training for Catholicism is quite clear. It is the public schools and the privately endowed nonsectarian colleges and universities that are the happy hunting ground of the ax grinders. Because they are public every taxpayer feels he has a right to "do something" about them, to demand every possible service. On the one hand the educational system is challenged to come up with the ideas to solve all of life's problems; on the other it is damned and harassed if it attempts bold experiment or if some teacher makes a statement offensive to some vested interest. Certainly the schools did not create whatever confusion there is in contemporary society; they merely reflect it and they are peculiarly hamstrung in their efforts to solve it. The role of the school cannot be considered in isolation from the rest of society. In "Shakespeare's Heavy Rivals," in the March, 1947 *Survey Graphic,* George H. Henry, superintendent of the Dover, Del., Special School District, pointed out the force of factors, other than the school, which play a part in the development of the child, mostly motion pictures, radio, and the press. Wrote Henry:

"While we citizens heap upon the schools more and more responsibilities, these other agencies of education grow more irresponsible in their debasement of taste, their materialism, their false values.

"As the personnel of the teaching profession declines and schools are staffed with substandard teachers, these outside agencies procure high-priced, talented men—scenario writers, blurbists, advertising writers, script men, news analysts, feature writers, headline makers, comic strip artists—who are not under the same restraints as teachers

and need not be as disciplined by truth, logic and integrity. Real education is slow, years in its getting; these Machiavellian schools never let it grow, subtly uprooting it before true values are assimilated beyond destruction. The shabby, thumb-tacked walls of the schools and the inadequate equipment of many teachers are pitted against spectacle, show, sensation, money. . . . Thus, while the schools, inside, have availed themselves of the vast new discoveries of science in teaching youth to read, on the outside youth does not read, and will not read with any degree of effort or critical sense, because he is diverted by another specialized environment that knows every psychological appeal. Our pupils are held captive, and schools, once thought of as liberating influences, cannot cut the bonds. . . . In short, instead of turning our wrath on the schools, as we now do, let us pour it on these powerful outside forces that undermine the school. . . . Youth can no longer be protected from inconsequential, trivial, cheapening, particularistic assaults, which now have an authority—based on impact—outweighing that of the schools."

Most public school teachers do not fit the prim and prissy hatchet-faced stereotype. To endure the kind of life which the average community imposes upon them, however, they must be either failures at any other ways of making a living or saints. Much is made by parochial school critics of the fact that teaching nuns lack contact with the environment from which their pupils come, are unable to read books and magazines of their own choosing or attend public entertainments that the children enjoy. Although the freedom allowed public school teachers is greater, their lives are circumscribed more than those of any other type of public servant. The mayor, alderman, public health officers, and other city employees, including the garbage collectors, can smoke, drink, chew, dance, play cards, and even swear a little in public with relative impunity. Not so the school teacher. He or she is expected to be a model of impeccable behavior, to observe a puritanic moral code usually considerably above that which the boys and girls observe their own parents obeying. Public school teachers, furthermore, are expected to contribute much more to the community than seven or eight hours a day in the classroom or study hall. It is not unusual for Boy Scout leaders, Sunday school superintendents, and choir leaders to request superintendents of schools to bear their needs in mind when hiring new teachers.

Socially the public school teacher rates way below where his intellectual and cultural attainments would rightly place him. He resides in the community but is hardly a part of it; the general attitude toward him often is one of insufferable condescension. Unless he or she is a nephew or niece of a school board member or otherwise has political "pull," he is not a native of the community in which he earns his living as, with the exceptions suggested, there is a general aversion to hiring home town boys and girls. Too many people are able to remember too much of the adolescent mischief in which the local product participated to trust the next generation to its care. On the other hand the teacher is too familiar with the avidity of his fellow townsmen for gossip and scandal mongering to want to live and work there anyway. Quite apart from the fantastically low salaries that teachers receive, in view of their expensive educations and intellectual attainments, it is little wonder that after Pearl Harbor over 40 per cent of America's public school teachers resigned for war jobs. It wasn't entirely patriotism or higher wages; rather, it was grasping at the opportunity to escape from a very disagreeable profession. What red-blooded American young man or young woman is going to put up with roomsful of youngsters defying them to teach them something despite their efforts to avoid learning anything; children and parents who impose a peculiar sort of second-class citizenship upon them and then look down upon them for accepting it; critical and often malicious pressure groups; legislatures with their insulting investigations and loyalty oaths and a pay check which falls far short of being compensation for any one of these and other indignities?

The Schools and Patriotism

If the schools were to even a slight extent the hotbed of radicalism that the Hearst press and some others charge they are, there might be a grain of sense in the harassment to which teachers are subjected and to the alarmist propaganda and infringements upon academic freedom. Actually the schools, including the colleges and universities, are bulwarks of capitalism. Rather than attacking the free enterprise system, from the first grade through the graduate seminar, the schools on the whole teach an uncritical loyalty to it. As already suggested, teachers of potential heretical tendencies either are not attracted to the profession in the first place, or they get out at the earliest oppor-

tunity or they are silenced or fired at the first (or at least second) indication of independence. Such "un-Americanisms" as Ralph Robey, a teacher of banking at Columbia University, uncovered in 1941 while in the employ of the National Association of Manufacturers, are not endured for long. Among those subversive teachings which Robey reported were the following: there are a small number of really large corporations in America; there are trusts and monopolies; there are differences in living standards; vast amounts of money are spent in advertising to break down consumer resistance; the press has enormous power and speaks, in general, for a minority; guarantees of the Bill of Rights are often infringed upon in actual operation; politics are not always clean; and—worst heresy of all— the National Association of Manufacturers has been guilty of subsidizing propaganda against social legislation.

Not all of the ignorance which Americans have regarding other countries is due to iron curtains erected by the inferior foreigners. Hardly any literature except American and English is taught in the schools and almost no history except that of the United States and western Europe which, quiz shows and Gallup polls reveal constantly, few remember. In 1939 the City Council of Cambridge, Mass. voted to purge the schools and public library by banning all printed matter within the city limits in which Lenin or any of its derivatives, including Leningrad, appeared. Hearing the nationwide laughter which resulted, the mayor quietly vetoed the ordinance. Among the most idiotic of the bills introduced into the California state legislature in 1947 by Sen. Jack Tenney were those which provided: (1) no publication of sectarian, partisan or denominational character or other propaganda book or material shall be used or distributed in any school or be made part of any school library, nor shall any sectarian or denominational doctrine or politically controversial subject be taught in any school. No propaganda in any form shall be included in the course of study, and (2) Geography and history shall be taught as independent branches. Instruction in said subjects shall be independent of other subjects and without substitution in any form. No merger or combination of these subjects, or either of them, with any other subject or under any social studies or other program shall be permitted.

Not all, or perhaps not even the most important, conservative pressure on colleges and universities is from outside. The average institution of higher learning in the United States today is itself a Big Business. Many endowments run into seven or eight or more figures and annual budgets are correspondingly high. It is natural that these super-schools should be run in accordance with Big Business principles, with business managers whose salaries rival those of the football coach at the head of sizeable staffs. University presidents no longer are picked for their reputations as great educators. Rather, scholarship now is a disqualifying characteristic as it is a symptom of impracticality, possibly dangerous idealism. Accordingly, the ranks of bankers, lawyers, former governors, and former generals are scoured for prestige-lending big names, even though their owners lack a single day's teaching experience. If faculty members are promoted or appointed from other institutions, they are most likely to be scientists. Despite the careful screening which teachers of the social sciences receive on obtaining any kind of appointment, they are rarely considered trustworthy enough to be elevated to a college presidency.

The Schools and Democracy

One important aspect of the role of public education remains to be examined. This is the extent to which the schools promote or retard the philosophy and practice of democracy. The avoidance of the controversial and infringements upon academic freedom, already mentioned, are not all of the picture. There is also the shameful practice of a majority of institutions of higher learning which maintain a quota system so as to limit the enrollment of Jews, Negroes and members of other minority racial, nationality, and religious groups. The following news article suggests how the brain power of the nation is not to be used to the fullest possible extent as a result:

Do colleges now discriminate against brains?
Educators gathered at the Palmer House in a national conference on discrimination in college admissions Friday were told that they do.
Bias against minorities falls most heavily on the best qualified applicants, according to Prof. Floyd W. Reeves of the department of education at the University of Chicago.
The conference was called by American Council on Education in cooperation with the Anti-Defamation League.
Prof. Reeves summed up what was found in studies of college admissions in New York State and elsewhere.

"The higher the Jewish students rank in their high school classes, the greater the discrimination against them," said Dr. Reeves.

He reported that the same thing was true in the case of youths of Italian origin.

Discrimination was greater against applicants who ranked high in high school classes than against those less well qualified.

*   *   *

The dull well-to-do student has a better chance of getting into the college of his choice than has the bright and studious student of modest means, Dr. Reeves reported on the basis of the New York study.

Youths in the lower half of their high school classes, who belonged to families with incomes of $9,000 a year or more were given the edge, he said.

The youth in the upper fourth of his class had comparatively poor prospects of getting in if his dad earned less than $5,000, said Dr. Reeves.

"It is believed that members of this conference should be wise enough to draw up a statement of what may be done by institutions to correct admission policies," said Dr. A. C. Ivy, vice president of the University of Illinois.

—Chicago *Daily News,* Nov. 4, 1949

A series of United States Supreme Court decisions is putting a crimp into the expensive dual educational system in many Southern states, but it is an inch-by-inch fight, with the forces of prejudice contesting and attempting to circumvent every liberal gain. The education offered Negroes throughout the South is separate all right, but it is far from equal, a quantity of investigators have revealed. Gross inequalities in educational opportunities also exist in other parts of the country. Everett B. Sackett summed up some of the most recent findings in an article, "Has the Nation a Stake in Its Schools?" in the October, 1949 *Survey* as follows:

"As with buying food for a family, the two main factors involved in determining the ease with which a state can support its schools are the number of children to be cared for and the amount of income available. Although the ratio of children to adults does not range so widely among the states as it does among families, there is an important variation. At one extreme is New Jersey with only 166 school-age children per thousand of the population, while at the other end is New Mexico with 283 per thousand.

"The per capita income is over $1,600 in eight states and under $1,000 in ten. As the states with the highest per capita income tend to be those with the lowest proportion of school age children, when the income is changed to a per school child basis the difference becomes far more striking. Seven states have average incomes of more than $12,000 per pupil in average daily attendance in the public schools, while six have incomes of less than $5,000 on this basis. New York, at the head of the list, has an income of $15,739 per pupil in average daily attendance, while at the other extreme of the scale is Mississippi with $3,030.

"For all states, the median percentage of total personal income going for the support of schools below college level is 2.3. This percentage in New York would supply over $360 per pupil while in Mississippi it would supply not quite $70. Mississippi happens to spend exactly this proportion of its income on public schools, while New York spends only 1.8 per cent. Yet these efforts yield in New York an education that costs for current expenses $250 per pupil, and in Mississippi $66.

"The average annual salary for school teachers, including principals and supervisors, in New York is $3,450; in Mississippi it is $1,293. What do these salaries buy in the way of training of teachers in their respective states? In New York, 5 per cent of the teachers have had no college training while 67 per cent have a bachelor's degree or higher. In Mississippi, 23 per cent have had no college training while only 41 per cent have a bachelor's degree or higher. For the nation as a whole, the figures are 3 per cent with no college training and 59 per cent with a degree. . . ."

Thus, in evaluating the effect of the schools on democracy, one outstanding fact is this: the quality and quantity of the offering differs widely as between sections and states and even within states.

Also, as seen, rather than waging war against undemocratic attitudes toward minorities, many schools defy the principle of "all men are created equal" by their segregation and quota systems.

Democracy also—to make a masterpiece of understatement—is not promoted by the fraternity and sorority system, or by the "rah rah" social life on so many campuses. Rather, a veritable caste system, with the inevitable snobbery and injustices that it entails, often exists.

Not only do the schools fail to provide adequate opportunity to learn respect for democracy through its practice on the campus, but they do not inspire the majority of students to participate in off-campus civic or political affairs. Whether the cautious manner in which courses in political science are taught, or the refusal to permit heretical speakers to appear on the campus or undergraduate groups to enjoy much liberty, or some other factor is to blame, the fact remains: *by comparison with the students of other countries, American school boys and girls are politically illiterate and indifferent.* This statement must not be interpreted as meaning that the author believes it would be good for Joe College and Betty Coed to be in the vanguard of political mobs as are their cousins in South America and the Balkans. The American equivalent of street demonstrations is doorbell ringing, petition circulating, attending mass meetings, and stump speaking. Debating is dying out in the colleges not merely because there is a new fad among teachers of speech but also because of lack of audiences. Few American universities have any forum in any way resembling the famed Oxford Union where many of England's future statesmen receive their early training in forensics. The overwhelming majority of American college students just don't give a whoop about social, economic, and political problems, and their conversations regarding them are hardly to be distinguished from those of the completely unschooled. Undergraduate newspapers on the whole are banal with little to suggest they emanate from supposed centers of learning.

Possibly the most important conditioning of all that the American school boy or girl gets is in what constitutes success. Not attainment of culture or the intellectual life; not Christian or any other ethics or charity; not aesthetic enjoyment. Not any of the other qualitative goals which might be expected. Rather, the good old American principle of victory in competition with others. Not only is this fundamental concept taught in history, economics, and other courses; it also is fostered by the course and credit system which is the backbone of the educational setup. A few years ago a professor on Northwestern University's Chicago campus solicited written comments from his students at the end of a course. A revealing one read as follows:

"I don't like the way papers are graded in my class. It makes no difference evidently whether you work on your homework and hand it in on time or if you hand it in one or two weeks late—you still may get a high grade. There is no sense in working (maybe on your only day off) on your homework and handing it in on time and then get the same grade as the fellow who lets it go for a couple of weeks before handing it in."

CHAPTER FIFTEEN

PROFESSIONAL PROPAGANDISTS

*Much that happens nowadays is promoted by experts in court-
ing public favor so that "things" often are not what they seem
on the surface to be to the unsuspecting majority.*

The People's Choices

With the delegates supporting Thomas E. Dewey and
Robert A. Taft apparently hopelessly deadlocked, a claque of several
hundred in the spectators' balcony at the 1940 Republican National
Convention in Philadelphia kept up an incessant rhythmic chant, "We
Want Willkie." Two ballots later the convention stampeded to Willkie
and all over the nation editors, whose morgues were virtually barren
of material on this political unknown, encouraged their readers to
believe that what had happened was a democratic *coup d'état*. Aided
by the inability of the professional politicians to come to a speedy
decision, the non-professionals, the amateurs, the voters, the "peepul,"
as it were, had made their voices heard and the tousle-haired bearlike
farm boy from Indiana became their standard bearer.

Throughout the turbulent campaign, during which Franklin Delano
Roosevelt's defiance of the no-third-term tradition was the principal
issue, the "people's choice" myth was carefully nurtured. Addressing
the convention before its adjournment, the "miracle boy" himself
explained: "It is a moving and appealing and almost overwhelming
thing to be the nominee of a great free convention of this kind. . . .
Forty-eight days ago, and only 48 days ago, I started out to preach
to the American people the doctrine of unity, the doctrine of the
destiny of America, and the fact that I am the nominee of this convention at this time proves conclusively how appealing is this simple
doctrine to the American people."

It was excellent political oratory but, as all insiders knew, completely humbug. Wendell Willkie did not become the Republican party nominee in 1940 because the galleries screamed his name while the roll calls were being taken. His campaign was long and skillfully planned and brilliantly executed. It *was* precedent-breaking but not for the reasons fed to the gullible public. Ordinarily the businessmen and bankers who have controlled the Republican party since shortly after the Civil War, are not themselves candidates for elective offices. Rather, they support professional politicians whom they can trust to represent their interests. In 1940, with the Democrats defying tradition, the real rulers of the Republican party decided it was the propitious time to do likewise. Then, however, they found the party organization which they had supported an obstacle rather than a help, because too many influential leaders and delegates were committed or beholden to orthodox potential candidates. Consequently, this time the business and industrial bigwigs had to circumvent rather than utilize the "usual satisfactory channels."

The exact date of the genesis of the Willkie for President idea is not known. Gen. Hugh S. Johnson, the "Old Iron Pants" who became sour against the New Deal after his stint as head of the National Recovery Administration, is supposed to have made the suggestion more than a year before the convention to Thomas W. Lamont, chairman of J. P. Morgan & Co. After the nomination there was a rush of claimants to having "discovered" the president of Commonwealth and Southern who maneuvered the Tennessee Valley Authority into paying $78,600,000 for a subsidiary, the Tennessee Electric Co.; $23,000,000 more than the government's original offer. Arthur Krock, New York *Times* political columnist, claimed that he had "dropped a hint" as early as February, 1939 and David Lawrence, another columnist, said he had done the same in May, 1939. It was not until Nov. 20, 1939, however, that serious public mention was made of a possible Willkie candidacy. Then it was General Johnson who was responsible, in answer to a question following a lecture at the New York Bond Club. Willkie's "crack" in response to reporters' requests for comment really started the pundits talking: "In view of the speed with which the federal government is taking over my business," the utilities head declared, "I'll probably have to be looking for a new job shortly. General Johnson's is the best offer I've had thus far."

From then on the Willkie campaign snowballed. Between 3,000 and 4,000 speaking invitations poured in from all parts of the country. In February Oren Root, Jr. gave up his law practice to organize Associated Willkie Clubs throughout the country. Almost simultaneously a Willkie Mailing Committee was established. Willkie appeared on *Information Please,* popular radio program; the April issue of *Fortune* printed his political credo, "We the People," and on May 2 the magazine's managing editor, Russell Davenport, resigned to manage Willkie's preconvention campaign. For the *New Republic* Willkie wrote an article in defense of civil liberties. *Life* and *Look* and other magazines which printed series on potential candidates, included Willkie. By mid-June all 18 Scripps-Howard newspapers were "all-out" for Willkie. So was the Philadelphia *Public Ledger* and such widely syndicated columnists as Raymond Clapper, Westbrook Pegler, and General Johnson. So were the Des Moines *Register* and *Tribune* owned by John and Gardner Cowles, who also own *Look.* The week before the convention opened the *Saturday Evening Post* contained an article by Willkie, "Five Minutes to Midnight," and another by General Johnson, "I am Not Nominating Him."

When the convention met the "heat" really began to be poured on. Gov. Harold Stassen of Minnesota, object of GOP awe because of his victory the year before over the Farmer-Labor machine in his state, emerged as floor manager of the Willkie forces. In a near-by hotel Thomas W. Lamont and H. W. Prentis, Jr., president of the National Association of Manufacturers, "kept in touch" until the former was persuaded to leave for fear his presence would do more harm than good. From all over the country delegates began receiving telegrams, telephone calls, and letters from bankers to whom many of them were obligated, prominent industrial and financial men, including Stock Exchange members, Wall Street officers, railroad executives, factory owners, representatives of publishing houses, and Social Registerites. Former Supreme Court Justice William E. Bleakley of Westchester County, chairman of the New York State delegation, received 22,500 messages. Another New York delegate said he got about the same number and approximately 500 of them were of the "or else" variety.

To suggest that it was all the result of spontaneous enthusiasm is, of course, nonsense. The business and industrial leaders who decided upon Willkie sometime between six months and a year in advance of the convention skillfully divided the nation and induced their local equivalents in all of the states to unloose the deluge at the proper moment. The pressure came from exactly the right sources and there was enough of it to impress the professional politicians that not to respond to it would be equivalent to spitting in the eye of the golden goose.

By contrast there was the Democratic National Convention in 1944 in Chicago. There the thousands who turned the Stadium into a state of pandemonium with "We Want Wallace" were ward heelers of the local political machines who were expressing their real sentiments in defiance of their leader, Mayor Edward J. Kelly, who was prominent among the big city bosses who had decided that the vice president should be dropped. Also there were ordinary people who had obtained tickets in one way or another. There certainly was no organized Wallace claque. Nevertheless, the enthusiasm was so contagious that there is no question that if a vote had been taken at the Friday evening session as scheduled, Wallace would have been renominated overwhelmingly. Without anyone ever having heard a motion, much less a vote, the chairman, Senator Jackson of Indiana, declared the session adjourned. The next day there were to have been two sessions, one daytime and the other in the evening, to which there were separate tickets of admission. To avoid the claque's returning, however, there was no adjournment of the afternoon session, and the doors were locked so that holders of evening session tickets could not get in, despite the fact that there were thousands of empty seats. In that atmosphere Harry S. Truman became "the people's choice" for the vice presidential nomination.

The Nature of Public Relations

Although these familiar examples from recent political history have many other obvious implications, they are cited here to illustrate the tremendously important fact that *powerful interest groups are constantly at work to create, convert, or circumvent public opinion for their own ends*. As a matter of fact, counseling individuals, businesses, and groups of all kinds as to how they should behave to be of maximum effectiveness in promoting their own interests rapidly is becoming a major profession in the United States. The carrying out of many of the plans of these brain trusters engages the services of a small army of experts of all sorts: publicity men, advertisers (which means writers, artists, announcers, and so forth), lobbyists, public speakers, salesmen, showmen, photographers, tea drinkers, and others. Press agentry is only a small part of the public opinion making and evading process; for many of the activities undercover, rather than publicity, men are wanted. The all-inclusive term to describe the new "science" of getting one's way in a complex society is "public relations," and those who make good livings at it are "public relations counsel."

Public relations is as difficult to define as it often is to detect. In 1927 one of the greatest, if not the greatest which America produced during the first half of the twentieth century—Edward L. Bernays, nephew of Sigmund Freud—wrote as follows in *Crystallizing Public Opinion* (Boni, Liveright, 1927): "Men in the profession of public relations are as little ready or able to define their work as is the general public . . . [yet] this profession has developed from the status of circus stunts to what is obviously an important position in the conduct of the world's affairs." Two decades later, Rex F. Harlow indicated in an article, "Public Relations at the Crossroads," in the Winter, 1944–45 *Public Opinion Quarterly* that not too much progress had been made toward clarification when he wrote: "Today public relations is a crazy-patchwork of ideas and activities. Everybody is talking about public relations, but nobody seems to know too much about the meaning of the term. Even workers in the field do not agree on where public relations begins and ends, whether it should or should not be a separate activity in a business, or how, when and where it should be applied in an organization."

According to Averell Broughton in *Careers in Public Relations* (Dutton, 1943), "Public relations folk are practical psychologists." As Milton Wright saw it in *Public Relations for Business* (Whittlesey, 1939), "Public relations is simply relations with the public." In "Public Relations: A Profession in Search of Professionals," in the Summer, 1946 *Public Opinion Quarterly,* Stephen E. Fitzgerald wrote, "Public relations is primarily the art of human behavior." In the Aug. 26, 1939 *Editor & Publisher,* in an article titled, "Ad Man Lists 8 Tools for Public Relations," Gerald S. Beskin is quoted as saying, "Public relations is the science of attitude control." Perhaps more cynically but, pragmatically speaking, as accurately, Henry F. Pringle defined public relations as "the voice of great corporations" in "His Master's Voice," in the October, 1936 *American Mercury*. Maybe "Public relations is the organized effort to get your own way" is better in emphasizing the *end sought* whereas the other definitions suggest in general the reasoning back of the means in which public relations practitioners specialize: creating the right state of mind on the part of the right people so that the client achieves his ends.

Regardless of how limited or broad the specific term "public relations" is held to be, the paramount fact is that hardly anything which makes an impression on the public mind, or any significant portion of it, occurs naturally any more. Rather, the behavior which may seem to be spontaneous has been planned carefully, possibly rehearsed. Men and women who count avail themselves of the services of specialists in applied psychology before making a speech, writing an article, joining an organization, making a public appearance, expressing an opinion, donating to a charitable or other cause, extending or accepting a social invitation, announcing an engagement, wedding, impending birth or divorce; and if they disregard or fail to solicit advice in any important situation and get into trouble as a consequence, their counsel, agents, secretaries, ghost writers, and other representatives go into action to get them out of their jams and to suppress or at least minimize the unfavorable publicity resulting therefrom.

As with individuals, so it is also with groups, including businesses. Once unionists had to fight and die for cleaner air, safer machinery, an occasional holiday or day off, and other concessions to make their working life more pleasant. Unions still are fighting for such things or their equivalents, but some employers, under the persuasion of smart personnel men, are anticipating their demands. Not in any attitude of charity or humanitarianism but from enlightened self-interest, in recognition of the value to the paternalistic boss of better morale. No longer, furthermore, does the Vanderbiltian "public be damned" attitude prevail. It has been replaced by the philosophy that "the customer is always right," and deserving of the most lavish courtesy that he can be expected to pay for through higher prices which finance the rest rooms, free telephones, samples, exchange counters, and other indispensable parts of large-scale retail store operations today. What a short while earlier was a luxury in customer service becomes a necessity as it is imitated by competitors and comes to be expected. The artificiality of the whole business, however, is almost as obvious as the breathlessly narrated dialogues contained in some radio commercials featuring testimonials delivered by previously incredulous actor housewives: "I never knew housework could be so easy until I discovered your product." "I could hardly wait for this opportunity to tell every other mother what I have found out," and so forth, ad nauseam.

Public relations, as a profession, though still in its experimental and trial-and-error period, is an inevitable product of a complex industrial society. Publics have multiplied so greatly and are so widespread that expert manipulation is required to reach them. Even in a small community someone has to be obtained to "put across" a Red Cross, Community Chest, or church building fund drive. To "tell your story" and be sure that it is remembered requires continuous effort; the bigger the enterprise the more extensive and expensive the effort needed. As Ivy Ledbetter Lee, the first great American public relations counsel, was supposedly the first to say, and as Bernays and others have repeated, a two-way effort is necessary. That means, the public relations counsel must interpret the public to his client as well as his client to the public. The principal chapter in Lee's success story is that which pertained to his changing the reputation of John D. Rockefeller, Sr., from that of "most hated" to "most loved" American. Because he set the pace for his emulators and successors, Lee's many-times-told tale merits epitome here.

The Rockefeller Story

For more than thirty years prior to the bloody Colorado Fuel and Iron Company strike in 1914, Rockefeller and the companies he controlled, notably Standard Oil, had taken a disdainful attitude toward the storm of criticism which included cartoons by Frederick Opper, magazine articles and books by Henry D. Lloyd, Ida M. Tarbell and others. Standard even "rode out" the anti-monopoly suit which ended happily when Federal Judge Kenesaw Mountain Landis' $29,000,000 fine was set aside on appeal. Then, however, state militia at Ludlow, Colo. killed six strikers and caused the suffocation of two women and 11 children when they set fire to the tents sheltering the strikers' families, and public indignation was high. More sensitive than his father, John D. Rockefeller, Jr. insisted that the policy of cynical aloofness to public opinion had to end. He persuaded his father to employ Lee who, since 1903, had been handling publicity for the Pennsylvania Railroad.

Lee's immediate task was to see that the company's story of the Ludlow strike should become known. He accomplished that purpose by means of a flood of daily news releases to the nation's press. The younger Rockefeller won admiration for his courage in visiting the stricken area and talking to the miners on whom he made an unexpected favorable impression when he said: "This is a red letter day in my life. What you have been told is that those Rockefeller men in New York are the biggest scoundrels that ever lived. They said we took dollars out of this company, oppressed you men and cheated you out of your wages. . . . For 14 years, to my knowledge, the common stockholders haven't gotten one cent out of this company. I just want you to put that in your pipe and smoke it. And see if it tallies with what you've heard about the stockholders oppressing you and trying to get the better of you."

That was a constructive attack. So was the appointment by the Rockefeller Foundation of R. Mackenzie King, former labor minister and later prime minister of Canada, to head an impartial commission to study the mine case. King's commission recommended a liberalization of the company's industrial relations policy which the company adopted. Thus many of the miners' grievances were eliminated. Henceforth they were allowed to hold meetings on company property; to buy at stores of their own choice rather than at company-owned stores; to select their own doctors and to carry complaints to superior officers, even to the president of the company. Lee saw to it that the press was thoroughly informed of each concession.

The negative attack consisted in part of charges against some of the strike leaders which Lee later admitted with regret had been in error. For example Mother Jones was accused of receiving $42 a day for helping to lead the strike while, according to Lee, also being keeper of a bawdy house. F. J. Hayes, who actually received a $4,052.92 annual salary, was accused of getting $32,000. Three months later, after the miners had succumbed to hunger and given up, a news bulletin admitted errors in calculation. At the subsequent investigation of the strike by the Commission on Industrial Relations the following cross examination occurred:

Frank J. Walsh: Mr. Rockefeller told you to be sure to get the truth?

Ivy L. Lee: Certainly.

Q.—Just detail now what steps you took to ascertain the facts before you wrote any of these articles. Give all the steps.

A.—I had no opportunity, Mr. Chairman, to ascertain the facts from my own point of view. It was their story I was to assist in getting before the public.

Q.—And therefore you did not question any fact that was presented to you, any alleged fact, as to its authenticity?

A.—Not when presented by Mr. Wilborn [Jesse F. Wilborn, president of the Colorado Fuel and Iron Company] or any of his committee.

Q.—Did you make any effort to secure the statements of disinterested persons?

A.—I did not.

Commissioner Garretson: Your mission was that of the average publicity agent, was it not, to give the truth as the man you were serving saw it?

A.—That would represent a characterization on your part, Mr. Commissioner. I have tried to tell what happened. As to your characterization, I don't know that I can give an answer.

The strike over, Lee turned his attention to the person and personality of John D. Rockefeller, Sr. It was his task to turn the recluse into a man whom the general public would think of as someone's kindly old grandfather. Through Lee's efforts, for the ensuing 25 years, hardly a week, certainly not a month, passed during which the newspapers and magazines did not print some article concerning the old gentleman. The *Woman's Home Companion* carried an article on "How the Richest Man in the World Observes Christmas," in which the emphasis was upon a simple man who spends the day with his family around him and on the religious man who knows the real meaning of Christmas. *House Beautiful* told its readers about "An American Millionaire's Hobby" (gardening), while *Harper's* unfolded a tale of "Rockefeller at Play." Each article was designed to make the public think of John D. as the elderly man next door.

Typical of the anecdotal pieces on John D. was the following from the Jan. 19, 1931 issue of *Time*:

"As John D. Rockefeller was about to step into his car after a game of golf at Orlando, Fla., the soprano, Amelita Galli-Curci drove up. They were introduced and Rockefeller was seized with great gallantry. He cried, 'Bless you, bless you! I have enjoyed hearing you sing many, many times.'

"From his car he extracted a bouquet of violets and sweetpeas. 'I found these at my plate this morning and they made me think of your voice and here is my picture with an appropriate sentiment. And if you don't mind I would like to read you the daily prayer which we read at breakfast this morning.' " [1]

Hundreds of such stories, illustrating Rockefeller's piety were published from 1914 through 1937, when John D. died at the age of 97; and biographies of the financier-philanthropist are filled with religious verse. Though such stories reeked of the touch of the publicity agent, they were printed as straight news items by editors the country over. And when the public read such news items how could it accuse such a "gentleman" of pursuing greedy practices?

Typical of another type of anecdote was the following from the Jan. 27, 1936 *Time*:

"John D. Rockefeller, 96, was taking his longest automobile ride along Florida's Daytona Beach last fortnight when he spied one Al Garb, a beach photographer who took his picture six years before.

"Ordering the big limousine to stop, Rockefeller peered out. He asked Garb how much money he had made from the previous photograph.

"Al Garb chirped a figure. Cackling with delight, oldster Rockefeller complimented him on his industry, posed for another photo with which Cameraman Garb made more money."

Here was the successful rich man giving encouragement and assistance to a younger man. Lee also encouraged the rags-to-riches story in publicizing his employer, and Standard Oil never has ceased relating the Horatio Alger story of its founder.

[1] This and the following quotes from *Time* magazine are reprinted through the courtesy of *Time*. Copyright, Time, Inc.

Rockefeller also was presented as a friend of children. A typical example is the following from the June 9, 1930 *Time*: "John D. Rockefeller became a tenderfoot boy scout at Lakewood, N.J. Said he: 'I'll get some more of the older boys to join your outfit—boys that will help contribute.'"

The elderly Rockefeller was continually pictured handing out shiny new dimes with the advice: "Save." During his lifetime, it is estimated, he gave away 26,000 dimes, and almost every one was good for a news release.

In the March 30, 1936 *Time* appeared the following:

"One misty morning in 1900 on the Cleveland golf course a stooped-shouldered man of sixty, his bald head shining like a knob of burnished marble, smacked drive after drive off a tee. Seven caddies returned the balls, patted down the little sand tees; scurried down the course as the man kept poling out drives like an automaton. Suddenly from another part of the fairway came a shrill cry of warning. Without hesitation the man dropped his club, scampered into a clump of bushes. Few minutes later there came another cry. The man returned to his work.

"This description of John Davison Rockefeller, Sr. at play 36 years ago was divulged this week. . . . The strange cries which occasionally sounded over the course came from guards posted to warn Mr. Rockefeller of his wife's approach. That this elaborate deception worked was illustrated a few weeks later when Golfer Rockefeller strolled up to the tee where his wife was preparing to swing, casually remarking, 'I think I'll play this morning. It looks as if it might be a nice game.' Mrs. Rockefeller, amazed at the 160-yard drive which her husband thereupon shot down the fairway, cooed, 'John, I might have known it. You do things better and more easily than anyone else.'"

Here we are shown the oil magnate with a sense of humor, and every husband who ever tried to surprise his wife probably compared himself to "Neighbor John." Thereafter golf anecdotes were plentiful. In another part of the same article and in many similar stories, the impression of thrift was created: that Rockefeller had become rich because he managed his money carefully and not because of any predatory business methods:

"Equally hateful of waste, he once drove a brand new ball into the rough, hunted it for ten minutes, finally asked his caddy what his cronies would do in a similar situation. The caddy retorted that they would look for a minute, then drop a new ball.

" 'Huh,' snorted Golfer Rockefeller, 'They must have barrels of money.' "

Still another extract stressed the old man's belief in fair play and dissipated the stereotype of the wicked rich man.

"Rockefeller, a stickler for rules was slightly perturbed one day when his physician teed his ball a full foot in front of the markers. With painstaking care, Rockefeller teed his own ball exactly on a line with the red marker, dryly observing: 'I always play the full course, doctor.' "

Despite the cumulative effect of a quarter century of such publicity it alone could not have effected the miracle which Lee performed. Probably much if not most of the anecdotal material would not even have been printed had there not been the simultaneous campaign to change the Rockefeller reputation through the performance of good deeds. During his lifetime John D., Sr., gave away approximately 530 million dollars. Among other things the money built the Rockefeller Chapel at the University of Chicago, reconstructed several European cathedrals which had been damaged by bombs and shells during World War I, sent public health workers into Greece, Cuba, and other backward countries, provided scholarships and research grants for thousands of scholars, and built the giant Rockefeller Center in New York City.

Early in his career as a philanthropist, Rockefeller declared in an address at the University of Chicago, which benefited handsomely from his largess, "God gave me my money." In the press release containing the statement, Lee explained that what the millionaire meant was that he knew his great fortune was the result of historical accident and therefore felt himself to be a trustee rather than an owner. At another time Rockefeller put it this way: "There is more to life than the accumulation of money. Money is only a trust in one's hands. To use it improperly is a great sin. The best way to prepare for the end of life is to live for others. That is what I am trying to do. Everyone should practice something worth while besides mere money making."

And who can say that the net effect of the work of Ivy Ledbetter Lee, in persuading John D. Rockefeller, Sr. to adopt that point of view was not beneficial to mankind?

The Effect of Wars and Depressions

Lee, aptly called the "father of public relations," concentrated upon publicity. He began operations during a period when Big Business was undergoing terrific attack from the so-called muckrakers and Theodore Roosevelt was wielding his big stick in the direction of the newly created trusts. Business, as Lee saw it, had incurred public distrust in large part because it had not attempted to tell its story. Instead of seeking to utilize the medium of the press, most business leaders refused to be interviewed, frequently locking themselves in hideouts, playing hide-and-seek on shipboard and other places, and even attacking reporters and photographers physically. By demonstrations, including the job he did for the Rockefeller interests, Lee and other pioneers convinced American businessmen that public relations should be an integral part of their operations—which it has been ever since.

Impetus to the developing profession and an opportunity to experiment with new devices was provided by World War I during which many of the postwar leaders in the field received training with the Committee on Public Information, chairmaned by George Creel. In an article, "The Engineering of Public Consent," in the March, 1947 *Annals* of the American Academy of Political and Social Science, Bernays wrote: "During World War I and the immediate post-war years a new profession developed in response to the demand for trained, skillful specialists to advise others on the technique of engineering public consent, a profession providing counsel on public relations." Bernays' "engineering approach" means in essence the application of professional methods of research in accumulating facts and their analysis preliminary to "action based only on thorough knowledge of the situation and on the application of scientific principles and tried practices to the task of getting people to support ideas and programs."

During the decade, 1919 to 1929, the third definable period of public relations, the effort was directed on behalf of business interests toward maintaining public favor and preventing a revival of muckraking. In cruder terms, the emphasis shifted from mere publicity to propaganda. Writing in the January, 1927 *Atlantic,* in an article called "Gnats and Camels," Earnest Elmo Calkins explained, "The technique of this kind of work was greatly improved by the war. It became a public duty to spread propaganda, and an immense amount of talent was available for the purpose. This experience and this talent have since found a profitable field in working for corporations instead of nations, with many new and tried devices at their disposal." In the Nov. 1, 1930 *Editor & Publisher,* John F. Roche quoted Bernays as having declared in a debate with Julian S. Mason, editor of the New York *Post*: "Such propaganda uses the principles of mass psychology relied upon by the United States government and proved effective in the world war."

During the long depression which followed the stock market collapse in late 1929, the combined efforts of the then-existent small army of public relations men were helpless to offset the widespread dislike and distrust of Big Businessmen. It was the all-time low period in popularity for the "money changers" and "economic royalists," and all the criticisms of Franklin Delano Roosevelt and the other New Dealers could not convince the people that their troubles were due to those politicians rather than the bad judgment and bad acting of the upper crust. Books such as *100 Million Guinea Pigs* by Arthur Kallet and F. J. Schlink (Vanguard, 1932) and *Our Master's Voice: Advertising* by James Rorty (John Day, 1934) became best sellers; and Consumers Research and Consumers Union boomed. When approaching war brought back prosperity and ended unemployment there developed a public receptivity for defenses of Big Business, rugged individualism, free enterprise, and the American Way and against governmental bureaucracy, the welfare state, statism, New and Fair dealism.

What the continuous refusal of the voters to rise for its propaganda bait taught Big Business, especially after the surprising Truman victory in 1948 two years after the Republican upsurge of 1946, was that united, coordinated effort was necessary if the United States was to be prevented from joining the world-wide postwar drift to the left. Consequently, the activities of the National Association of Manufacturers, the United States Chamber of Commerce and large trade associations, in the interest of all business and industry, or of large segments of it, in addition to the promotional activities of each company individually for itself, became of increasing importance. In 1938 the N.A.M. is reported to have spent a half million dollars to promote the type of capitalism which it represents. A 15-minute radio skit, "American Family Robinson," in the preparation of which a number of college professors participated, was among the leading efforts. There also were clipsheets for newspapers, "Uncle Abner Says," a cartoon feature, and news releases from the Industrial Press Service.

Indicating the growing alarm and awareness of the need for a united business propaganda front, in 1945 the N.A.M.'s appropriation for public relations was 3 million dollars, six times that of 1938. In 1946 it was 5 million dollars, much of which went for its successful campaign to kill the Office of Price Administration and to lay the groundwork for Taft-Hartley the next year. In April, 1947 the most ambitious combined-effort public relations program of all was announced, as reported in the following news story:

By John K. Weiss

The American public will be exposed to a $100 million advertising campaign over the next 12 months to "sell" the American economic system. The program was announced yesterday by the Advertising Council. The Council, a war-born cooperative of the advertising trade which sprang up with government encouragement to sell the war on the home front, has decided to undertake as its most ambitious program to date a major project of educating the American people about the economic facts of life in a free enterprise system.

Joint Committee Originated Idea.

Idea for this giant "sell America" program originated with a joint committee of two national advertising trade organizations, the Assn. of National Advertisers (ANA) and the American Assn. of Advertising Agencies (AAAA).

The Advertising Council, which describes itself as "a non-profit organization dedicated to the use of advertising in the public service," referred the suggestion to its Public Advisory Committee, a 19-man board which includes representatives of business, labor, education, agriculture and the public.

Members of Board.

Among the members of the board are Dr. James B. Conant, president of Harvard, former Governor Herbert H. Lehman, Paul Hoffman, president of the Studebaker Corp., Eugene Meyer, former head of the World Bank and publisher of the Washington *Post,* Evans Clark, director of the Twentieth Century Fund, Boris Shishkin, economist of the AFL, Kermit Eby, research director of the CIO, and Miss Helen Hall, director of the Henry Street Settlement.

Objectives of Campaign.

The objectives of the campaign, as outlined at a press conference yesterday by Clark, chairman of the Advisory Committee, are two fold:

To show the reasons why, in spite of its shortcomings, the American economic system has given us the highest standard of living and the greatest freedom in the world.

To rally all groups in the nation for a common effort to improve our system through constantly increasing productivity and a wider distribution of its benefits.

Clark emphasized that the formulation of the program had been a difficult and laborious job. Eventually it was delegated to a three-man subcommittee of the Board consisting of Dr. George Shuster, president of Hunter College, Hoffman, and Shishkin. Clark underscored the fact that the 10 points of the program had been unanimously and enthusiastically approved by the entire board.

The reasoning behind the program, according to the Advertising Council's chairman, Charles G. Mortimer, advertising director of General Foods Corp., is to educate an America which is "staggeringly ignorant" of the benefits of the American economic system. In this way, he explained, there will be no danger of encroachment by any foreign ideologies.

Emphasis on Expanding Production.

Most important of the 10 basic points in the program is the emphasis on expanding production. Through technological advance and increased efficiency, the program aims to prove that wages can be raised progressively faster than prices, that hours of labor can be reduced and both income and consumer goods more widely distributed.

The fundamental reasoning behind the campaign rests on the premise that there is no conflict of interest among any of the special interest groups in this country such as labor, management, and agriculture.

The chief shortcoming, according to Clark, is the so-called "boombust" business cycle.

In explaining the role of the Council, Mortimer pointed out that it depends upon voluntary cooperation from advertisers, advertising agencies, and advertising media to carry out its work. He recalled the cooperation received during the war in such campaigns as the salvage of waste fats, sale of War Bonds, and contributions for the Red Cross. He estimated that during the war some $300,000,000 was contributed in advertising space and service.

Expect $100,000,000 Worth of Support.

The Council, he said, operates on a relative shoestring—approximately $250,000 per year. But he added that they expect to get $100,000,000 worth of support for the campaign. He estimated that this would be about 10 per cent of the national advertising budget for the next year.

Mortimer explained that the program was still in skeletal form and depended for implementation on the cooperation of individual firms and organizations. He declined to discuss the effects of any of the 10 points on specific problems (for example, point one as it affects the open shop), says that the program had purposely been left general in order to rally the broadest possible support.

"After all," he said, "the way this is set up, the only people who could oppose our program are totalitarians, either Communists or Fascists."

　　　　　　　　　　　　　　　　　—New York *PM,* April 24, 1947

In addition to those already mentioned, there are the American Meat Institute, the National Association of Real Estate Boards and literally hundreds of other similar organizations which are able to spend into six or seven figures for institutional advertising and other promotional activities. Public relations easily is a billion dollar or more annual industry in the United States today. When it is realized that all of this growth has occurred within a half century, it is all the more breathtaking.

Press Agentry

Extraordinary as his genius to fool people unquestionably was, Phineas T. Barnum was "small potatoes" by comparison with his modern counterparts. Barnum, Harry Reichenbach, and other precursors of contemporary public relations counsel specialized in press agent stunts to obtain immediate results. Their fields of operation were usually restricted to one locality at a time and were limited in terms of days or weeks. They sought free publicity for themselves or their clients in connection with an immediate objective and without regard for the creation of lasting favorable impressions. For example, Barnum once employed a man in evening dress to arrange and rearrange a series of bricks, one to a city block, until he reached the entrance of Barnum's Museum where he quietly purchased a ticket and went inside while the sizeable crowd of quidnuncs his antics had caused to gather watched. Similarly, Reichenbach assisted an obscure restaurant to obtain patronage by placing a bowl of water in the window accompanied by a sign, "only living Brazilian invisible fish in captivity."

Of similar anecdotes concerning both Barnum and Reichenbach there is almost no end. They are related in any of a number of biographies of the great circus man and by Reichenbach in his autobiographical *Phantom Fame* (Simon, Schuster, 1931). This author reiterated quite a few in his *Hoaxes* (Macmillan, 1940) and more involving other pioneer press agents in Chapter 7, "Space Grabbers," of his *Newsroom Problems and Policies* (Macmillan, 1941). Although such stunting has by no means become nonexistent, it is today the prerogative of small timers and amateurs who climb flagpoles, fake kidnappings, pose as royalty down on its luck, or practice other forms of subterfuge to swindle or attain sudden fame. No reputable publicity man or public relations counsel, acting as such, could afford to have his name connected with anything so crude. Modern publicity men, who differ from oldtime press agents in that they operate from fixed offices and seek for their clients recognition that creates more lasting, favorable impressions, are responsible for some outlandish performances but, with rare exceptions, it is all above-board. No city editor, for instance, is fooled as to the motivations of Steve Hannegan when he sends cleverly posed bathing beauty pictures from Miami Beach or scenes from Sun Valley where, as the master publicist puts it, one can enjoy "winter sports in a summer climate." To "crash" the ordinary media of communications nowadays taxes the ingenuity of the publicity man whose best chance almost is to make his yarns or pictures so absurd that they are accepted for their ridiculousness and are captioned as such. In its Aug. 1, 1949 issue, for instance, *Life* devoted a page to "Pickle Propaganda." One picture was captioned, "Steeplejack proudly places pickle on tower's top," and another "Mr. Dill Pickle of Mississippi reclines happily on a rubber boat amid 204,681 soggy pickles." The accompanying article described an orthodox type of modern publicity stunt and suggests the extent to which it serves its purpose. It follows:

"To a world surfeited with special weeks (some of the worst: Large Size Week, Save the Horse Week, Leave Us Alone Week), the emergence of National Pickle Week this summer seemed preposterous. But the National Pickle Packers Association in Chicago, intent on emphasizing the pickle's place on American plates (nine million bushels are sold each year), went ahead with big plans for pickles. They invented liquor-flavored pickles, crowned a Pickle Queen amid flaming pickles in a Chicago night club, and proclaimed as their Man of the Year Mr. Dill Lamar Pickle of Rolling Fork, Miss., who obligingly posed in a vat of pickles. Recently, carried away with the success of Pickle Week (pickle sales were up 22%), the packers painstakingly placed a paper pickle atop a Chicago television tower, proudly hailed it as the Midwest's highest pickle. Then they happily looked forward to spending the summer putting a pickle on every U.S. picnicker's paper plate."

Modern Techniques

The public relations activities which are most important in public opinion formation are much less crude and more subtle. Publicity, as already intimated, is only one technique in the modern counsel's bag of tricks and when it is obtained, for the greatest effectiveness, it is the indirect rather than the direct outcome of the master mind's advice and planning. When stunts are attempted they are on a much more grandiloquent scale, as the much-discussed Light's Golden Jubilee in 1929 when, supposedly to honor Thomas A. Edison, a bevy of notables, including President Hoover, gathered at Dearborn, Mich., and gave the electric light industry a boost. Or an Amelia Earhart is hired to fly solo from Hawaii to California with the Hawaiian sugar interests the beneficiaries from the attendant publicity and, especially, the articles she wrote and the interviews she gave at the flight's conclusion.

Shirts still are stuffed (everyone should read the anonymous "Confessions of a Shirt Stuffer" in the March 3, 1926 *New Republic*) but nobody recently has attempted to match Reichenbach's stunt, to win a $50 bet, of making an unknown famous within a fortnight (by having a famous opera star "discover" the subject singing in a shirt factory). Celebrities still cultivate eccentricities as did Gene Tunney when he took up Shakespeare. And whispers still are for sale to help advertise a product, run down a competitor, break a strike, or put over an idea or helpful rumor. Nevertheless, big-scale public relations, the kind that count most, is much more skillful and its effects much more difficult to detect. The desideratum of the psychologically motivated counsel is to avoid frontal attack and to concentrate, rather, on creation of the conditions out of which the results sought will come as though naturally.

Anything which builds good will for a client is in this category, and that includes boosts to employee morale and service with a smile for customers. Also included are such early Bernays' efforts as promoting Ivory soap-sculpturing contests to increase consumption of the product; a Green Ball to popularize the color for the benefit of Lucky Strikes and successful persuasion of architects to include nooks into which grand pianos would fit in their blueprints for small houses. Even more important is the creation of "front" organizations in which Bernays also was a pioneer. The Sociological Fund enrolled a quantity of progressive-minded people who received, as part of their $4 dues, a ticket to Brieux's *Damaged Goods,* which, because it deals with the problem of venereal disease, was threatened with censorship. After soliciting and receiving letters from a large number of leaders in the music world critical of radio reception, Bernays persuaded Pitts Sanborn, music critic of the New York *World-Telegram,* to publish a symposium and also to accept the chairmanship of the Radio Institute of the Audible Arts. Shortly thereafter Bernays' client, the manufacturers of Philco, announced their new "high fidelity receiving set" as the answer to the much-advertised criticism. Presumably "to disseminate scientific information concerning the latest developments in temperature control as they affect health, leisure, happiness and the economy of the American people," the Temperature Research Foundation actually was organized to promote the sale of Kelvinators.

In the February, 1940 *American Mercury,* in an article called, "Press Agent Tells All," Arthur Lockwood confessed in part as follows:

"One of the first of my nation-wide publicity jobs—now I have a lot—was the onion campaign launched by the Zonite Company. In those days Zonite was advertised for feminine hygiene, and wasn't doing too well. I was called in to promote it as a mouthwash and gargle. Fortunately I was also able to make a tie-up with the National Onion association, which was also undergoing hard times, and promoting the two together was easy. First I got a statement from a Yale professor stating that scientific breath-testing machines had proved that a chlorine solution would cure onion breath in thirty seconds. In Cincinnati two other professors quickly popped up with the statement that the only way to avoid onion breath was to avoid eating onions. At which I organized the Onion Anti-Defamation Committee and demanded a congressional investigation of the motives behind this last statement. (While this controversy raged, Zonite was being advertised as the one mouthwash that killed onion breath.) The Anti-Defamation Committee—headquarters in my hat—worked night and day, holding meetings to discuss the possibility of inventing an odorless onion, advancing legislation making it necessary for everybody to eat onions so that no one would be bothered by them, and writing scalding letters to enemies of the onion—to Walter Winchell, for example, protesting his constant and derogatory references to the noble scallion.

"The papers recounted all these events with great solemnity, and for a long time no one suspected the tie-up with Zonite. Then one day we organized an Onion Parade in New York City, with a dozen trucks, floats, and an Onion King and Queen and their retinue, who waved onions in one had and bottles of Zonite in the other. With this parade the Onion Anti-Defamation Committee showed its hand too plainly, but by that time Zonite sales were up 38 per cent and national onion consumption had trebled. . . ."

The Strategy of Politics

It is not to be wondered at that methods to get one's way that have been tested and proved effective by advertisers and public relations counsel to promote the sale of commercial products should be emulated by individuals and groups interested in the election of candidates for public office or in promulgating political or other ideologies or in favoring or opposing legislation.

The subterfuge employed in promotion of the candidacy of Wendell Willkie, to make his nomination appear to be the result of popular demand, is the rule rather than the exception in politics, certainly when the presidency is at stake. American voters cherish the myth that they select their own chief executives rather than have them hand picked. Consequently, nobody openly runs for the job if he hopes to be elected. In 1944 Willkie learned this lesson although the example is not a good one because by that time the Hoosier had alienated the support of most of his original backers by his support of the foreign policy of the Democratic wartime administration and had gone even further with his dream of postwar global peace as outlined in *One World* (Limited Editions Club, 1944). Harold Stassen is another who campaigned openly for the presidency for about a year and a half and got nowhere. Gen. Douglas MacArthur talked too much and shared the same fate as Admiral George Dewey a half century earlier: as soon as his willingness to run became obvious, his chances declined. Generals John J. Pershing and Dwight D. Eisenhower, on the other hand, kept their mouths shut and had the professional politicians going in circles. Either could have obtained a nomination in the first election after his war service ended had he been so inclined. In Eisenhower's case several pointed public declarations of nonavailability, in the General Sherman tradition, were necessary to quiet strong elements in both the Republican and Democratic ranks.

In 1932 Gov. Franklin D. Roosevelt remained quietly on the job in Albany while James A. Farley handshook his way across the continent and back, never forgetting a face or a name, to line up delegates. The best questioning by reporters could not persuade the governor to indicate he was even cognizant of the efforts being extended in his behalf. That, as Frank Kent explained long ago in his trail-blazing *The Great Game of Politics* (Doubleday, Page, 1923), is the way to do it. If you want to be president, Kent recommended, start about 18 months ahead of time, line up some influential friends and have them front for you. Plant articles by and about you in leading periodicals, get speaking engagements, make whatever promises and deals are necessary behind the scenes to build your delegate strength when the convention meets. Not until you start appointing cabinet members, ambassadors, and administrative heads will the true nature of your support and your pre-election obligations become apparent to the general public, and by that time it will be too late to hurt your chances at the polls.

If it is not the presidency but some lesser office to which you aspire, the process is not much different. You must have influential backing and you must provide those backers with reasons why it is to their best interest to support you. In politics you get only what you go after and you're in competition with other deserving party members for promotion as much as you are with fellow workers in any office or plant. Politics, in other words, as practiced in the United States at least, is a business; Big Business in fact; and you don't become the people's choice merely by thinking and expressing beautiful thoughts. The only exception to this rule of rewarding the wheel-horses when opportunity exists is when chances of victory seem slim. Then party leaders may load the ticket with statesmen as a gamble to wrest the victory from what otherwise would be defeat or possibly to eliminate them as troublemakers within party ranks by giving them their supreme chance at which they then fail. When victory seems certain "outsiders" have little or no chance to get on the ballot as "regulars" scramble for the positions.

All of the foregoing is so commonplace, so well known to anyone with a modicum of acquaintance with things political that it almost seems an apology should be made for its inclusion here. Possibly not so widely recognized is this fact: it is virtually impossible to win recognition for the highest type of disinterestedness in politics. Professional politicians and political editors are so used to hidden motives and doubletalk that they are cynical and cannot bring themselves to believe that nothing is going on behind the scenes even when nothing is. One reason why public-spirited persons who take a fling at politics are loath to repeat the experience is their disgust at discovering that their highest motives are suspect, genuinely suspect, and not just distorted for expediency's sake. Wrote Kent: "From the time a candidate conceives the idea of becoming a candidate until the day he is forced out of politics there is no chance for him to be wholly honest, frank and natural with the voters. From start to finish, he humbugs them—sometimes consciously and deliberately, sometimes unconsciously and reluctantly, humbugging himself along with the rest; sometimes deceiving them only a little and on relatively trivial matters, and sometimes becoming a complete humbug and faker, wholly insincere on the big as well as the small things.

"Political campaigns—most of them—are inherently insincere. It is a game of 'frame-up,' of hidden moves, of concealed and smothered convictions, of fake indignations and forced sympathies, of secret deals and sometimes, sinister alliances, of side-stepping and evasion, of expediency and compromise. Try as he will, even the highest type of man who seeks votes for an elective office cannot wholly escape these things, either before or after his election. Not until he is retired—and permanently—to private life can he completely throw off restraint and become wholly natural. . . . The insincerity of candidates and parties is a natural and inescapable result of such a condition." [2]

As for the individual voter, in dismissing all political oratory as "bunk," as he certainly has sufficient provocation to do, he runs the risk of rejecting what it would be to his best interests to accept and of accepting what may be harmful. Determining where one's best interests lie, of course, is a matter which goes much deeper than any particular election campaign. In the utopian rational society decision would be made on a long-range basis and in the realization that the individual's well being is dependent upon that of society as a whole. Unfortunately, as pointed out many times in this book, most personal decisions are made on the basis of short- rather than long-time considerations which, it might be said, is what is and always has been wrong with the world. Faced with the immediate task of choosing between rival candidates and parties, the voter does well to determine, to the best of his ability, the nature of the interests backing the alternatives. Then he should inquire into the motives of those backers and into the extent to which satisfaction of their selfish interests serves also the public, meaning his own, interests. All of which is expecting altogether too much of the average voter who usually is guided by his pocketbook from election to election and who recognizes a mistake only when the economic house starts falling down on his head.

Although they frequently are as blinded by their personal prejudices and are as cynical and gullible as anyone else, political writers ought to be in better positions to evaluate the meaning or significance of election results. This they can do by analyzing the important support that the successful candidates receive so as to know to whom they will be beholden once they assume their public responsibilities. Like it or not—and there are cogent arguments pro and con—the economic, religious, and social groups from which a public office holder comes are more important in determining what kind of representation is to be expected from him than is the geographical area in which his constituents reside. Most of the duties that an alderman, state senator, or member of Congress performs by virtue of having been elected from a particular bailiwick are of the "errand boy" type, and it is handy for the taxpayer who wants better collection of his

[2] From *Great Game of Politics,* by Frank Kent. Copyright, 1923, by Doubleday & Company, Inc.

garbage, an introduction to the governor, or speedy action on his application for a passport to know to whom to turn; likewise, since each lawmaker presumably represents approximately the same number of voters, the load of such duties is distributed with approximate evenness. When the city council, state legislature, or United States Senate votes, however, every citizen is affected just as much by the vote of a lawmaker from the other end of the city, state, or nation as he is by that of the representative from his own geographical district. Today the differences between men are more social, economic, and religious than they are geographical, so the development of the so-called bloc system in the state legislatures and in Congress is not so unrealistic as its detractors claim. Rather, it is a functional "natural" in our representative form of government. Its success is handicapped by the fact that the majority of states are so gerrymandered that the farm areas have a greatly disproportionate representation which, since it would take their own votes to rectify the situation, is virtually self-perpetuating. Also, because of their greater familiarity with laws and lawmaking, the naturalness of their selection as mouthpieces for interests and their gift of gab, lawyers are chosen from urban areas in numbers way out of proportion to their frequency in the population as a whole. "All out" adoption of the representation-by-interest system would mean selection of law-makers by a quota system so that proportionately there would be as many farmers as there are in the nation (or whatever area is affected) as a whole, as many laborers, ministers, teachers, and so forth. Preparing the categories from which representation should come would be a staggering undertaking. Businessmen are not just businessmen any more, nor are farmers a homogeneous group. Coal and oil men, for instance, oppose each other almost as often as they work together; the same for the railroads, busses, and airplane interests; the same for butter and oleomargarine manufacturers, and so forth. With such a diversification of interests not only the bloc system but also multitudinous pressure groups become virtually indispensable.

Lobbying

So powerful have pressure groups become that the lobbyists who do an important part of their work have been said to constitute an Invisible Government. The plight of the well-meaning member of

Congress was described in the following article from the Jan. 15, 1936 *Christian Science Monitor*:

Down in Washington I have been talking to a congressman who is a friend of mine. I won't tell you who he is, for obvious reasons. He is a Democrat, and, of course, in everything he says you must make allowance for that point of view.

"Well," I asked, "getting ready for the presidential campaign?" He is up for election, too, in 1936.

"Yes." He sighed so heavily that I grinned.

"What's wrong? Fewer Democrats than last time?"

"I wish it were as simple as all that! The question I'm asking myself is, 'When is a Democrat not a Democrat?' and the same thing about the Republicans."

"What do you mean?" He sounded so violent I was interested.

"It's these leagues! Why, I believe every three men or women in the country who have the same opinion, or the same kind of job, or the same peeve, or the same color eyes, say, 'Let's have a league and go into politics!'

"In the old days, you looked around your district and, when it came time to stand for election again, you knew where you were at. There were the rock ribbed party men either for you or against you, and as for the rest, you knew there'd be a couple of good campaign issues, and the local corruption and the local political rows that you understood. But not now: Now there aren't two parties in my district; there are 40 leagues!"

He looked almost offended at my chuckle. Evidently it was no laughing matter to him.

"Look what's happened this week," he went on. "Lots of deputations are here around the beginning of Congress—always are. The first group that came in to see me were some important business men from home— Republicans and Democrats, acting like brothers.

" 'Hello, Charlie,' I said to one of them who always before had been a good old line Democrat; 'getting ready to give me some real support next year?'

"He got red. 'That depends,' he said. 'I'm not here as a Democrat; I'm here as a member of the manufacturers' association.' "

"Well, surely there's nothing new in business trying to influence politics," I argued.

"Of course not. But it used to try to work through the party machinery. Now it brings its own organization to Washington. These fellows talked a lot about the iniquitous NRA, and about business being let alone. Well, I just happened to know, naturally, that nearly every man in the room had gotten some kind of government loan, and were they glad to get them, and did they need them!

"And did they ask me how I felt about anything? No, they just told me how I had to feel if I wanted their support. So when the only question they did ask me was whether I was in favor of rugged individualism, I'm afraid I was a little heated. I said, 'Yes, I was in favor of rugged individualism, but so far as I could see it was a luxury that could only be afforded by successful business men! If a poor congressman indulged in any he wouldn't get elected!' "

Evidently even the memory held "heat" for he went on warmly:
"They had barely gone before another bunch of the boys appeared—a lot of the men from one of our paint factories, here for some paint convention. Most of them were Democrats all right, but there was a spattering of Republicans, too; but they seemed to have forgotten anything that they ever were except members of Father Coughlin's National Union for Social Justice. And were they excited!

"And did they ask me what I thought about anything, or why? Though, as I say, most of them were Democrats and had supposedly elected me to do a little political thinking for them.

"Not much! They told me how I must be against the international bankers and the federal reserve system and how I must be for congressional control of credit and currency!

"Well, now, I don't mind telling you that even senators," he smiled, "don't find these technical questions about money and banking and credit easy." His smile turned to a sort of grin. "I've been in congress for some time now and have heard a good deal of eloquence on these subjects, but I felt so uncertain that this summer I got hold of one of the professors from our state university and had him talk to me about financial theory. Because, you see, I have been worried about these money questions and mighty sorry for all the folks who have been caught up in them, because we've had to do a little 'experimenting' here in Washington.

"Well, here were these boys from the paint shops and a few from a necktie convention, and they knew! They could tell me just what glorious results would take place, for instance, if the federal reserve system were abolished. And if I didn't agree with them, I could just stay out of congress." He snorted.

"And, of course, there was a huge deputation of Townsend planners threatening to fight my reelection if I didn't sign their promissory note on a financial heaven for old folk.

"Then next came the everlasting American Legion lobby, Democrats and Republicans! They told me why I had to vote for the bonus or get out.

"And after them came the League of Nations associations, Democrats and Republicans, and they told me why I had to support 'Geneva'!

"And then came some American Liberty leaguers, Democrats and Republicans, important men in our section, and told me I had to support the Constitution!

"Well, I said I guessed I could promise them that. Then one of them shot at me, 'And do you realize it means exactly what it says?'

"Somehow, I got heated again, for all I could think of was how the particular man who was hectoring me had acted during Prohibition—I almost asked him if, when the Constitution told him not to buy liquor, it meant exactly what it said?"

"But there is an issue in constitutional interpretation, or amendment," I insisted.

"Certainly, a definite, dignified political issue on which there can be honest disagreement between the parties. But why a league meddling with it and acting as if its members were the special guardians of all real Americanism?

"Then groups have been here like the D.A.R.'s, Democrats and Republicans, telling me exactly what was real Americanism and what was wicked foreign propaganda, and threatening me with political death if I showed even faint pink symptoms.

"Then there was the Navy league, Democrats and Republicans, telling me I had to vote for more and bigger ships, and 10 dozen assorted pacifist leagues telling me I had to vote against more ships if I wanted to be reelected!"

Then he rushed on to what he had evidently felt to be the final confusion:

"But, by George," he said. "I had believed I could count on the Communists and Socialists to stay in their own political back yards, because they have always been at daggers drawn, but no sir! This year, didn't some of them come to me together in an organization called the League Against War and Fascism!"

"Well," I tried to console him, "once the party platform gets written, won't most people sort out into parties again?"

The congressman shook his head. "I wish it were as simple as that," he said again. "Whether these leagues get planks into either platform or not, won't make much difference. Win or lose, they'll all keep lobbyists in Washington and will all send resolutions and telegrams and letters. Pressure groups is a good name for them all right! Sometimes I wonder why this bother to elect congressmen at all. Why don't the lobbyists just get together in the capital and fight it among themselves! I'm expecting a league against congressmen soon!"

"Well," I countered, "why don't you start a league against leagues?"

Up to then he had been vehement, but it had really been mostly stage thunder. Now he turned genuinely serious and wistful.

"Do you think these pressure groups are helping us put our political house in order?"

"Do you?"

"Well, I believe they are more than political fads. I think they are a warning symptom of how little most citizens think they can accomplish through the regular party machinery. And it's up to us to correct that."

Like everything else contemporary, pressure groups are giants by comparison with their counterparts of a century or more ago. Nevertheless, they are by no means a new phenomenon. As early as 1787 Manaseh Cutler wheedled four million acres of land from Congress for the new Ohio Company. In the middle part of the nineteenth century the railroads were given 129 million acres of public land, a total area about three times the size of all of New England. Before the Civil War both slaveholders and abolitionists were busy at the polls and in the legislative lobbies. From war's end to 1880 Sam Ward, brother of Julia Ward Howe who wrote "The Battle Hymn of the Republic," won the sobriquet "King of the Lobbies" for his lavish use of wine, women and song to win votes for high tariff supporters and the railroads. In the seventies occurred the biggest scandal involving lobbyists prior to the Teapot Dome affair of the early 1920's. It involved the activities of the Credit Mobilier, a Pennsylvania joint stock company, which was taken over by the directors of the Union Pacific to finance railroad building with federal grants; too many congressmen were discovered to own gift holdings of stock.

Modern lobbyists are as polished by comparison with their predecessors as today's public relations counsel are an improvement over the crude press agents of yesteryear's circuses and road shows. To say that direct bribery has disappeared would be the height of naivete. That more subtle methods of convincing a lawmaker that his best interests coincide with those of the lobbyists are practiced in Washington, if not in all state capitals, however, is certain. Special favors and privileges to self, relatives and friends; stock market and real estate tips; "inside dope" on contracts and job opportunities for constituents; free publicity and, among the most important inducements, promises of campaign contributions generally have been substituted for direct crossings of the palm with silver and even for coercion and blackmail based on skeletons in one's private closet. Even the social lobby—featuring the banquets and cocktail parties in which Sam Ward specialized and the teas and outings popular with legislators' wives and daughters—is not so important now as formerly.

Thriving on the constitutional right to petition, pressure groups are ubiquitous at committee hearings on important matters of legislation.

Chances are that the bills were prepared by one or more of the interested groups and offered to some eager lawmaker to introduce in his own name. To earn their fat salaries (in some cases equal to the $75,000 which the president gets) most lobbyists, however, operate mainly "behind the scenes." If the lawmaker is one of their "boys," all they need do is keep him posted on the desires of his backers; sometimes that can be done indirectly through a political boss. If persuasion seems necessary, the ex-congressmen and ex-government employees and ex-newspapermen, who compose a larger proportion of the footmen for pressure groups, present the arguments. The word from home is by far the most effective type of pressure that can be brought, and a line from a heavy donor or vote controller may outweigh hundreds or thousands of form letters and telegrams from individuals.

In 1924 Frank Kent reported there were 145 "legislative agents" in Washington. In 1929 E. Pendleton Herring, in *Group Representation Before Congress* (Johns Hopkins Press, 1929) said there were 250 "interest groups" there. In 1939 Kenneth Crawford wrote in *The Pressure Boys* (J. Messner, 1939) that he had counted about 6,000. A decade later the number was estimated as between 10,000 and 15,000. In 1941, according to the Temporary National Economic Committee, approximately 400 of the lobbies were permanent, *i.e.,* had year-round offices in Washington. In 1947, as required by the 1946 Lobbying Registration Act, 793 persons and 292 groups registered. Uncounted are the thousands who make occasional efforts, by sending delegations to the national capital or by mail, to influence legislation.

Passage of the 1946 law was the culmination of long agitation. There have been innumerable investigations of lobbying in general and of particular campaigns. They have been conducted by both public and private groups, the former kind being the more important because legislative committees possess the power of subpoena. The investigation of the New York insurance companies, with Charles Evans Hughes as chief investigator, in 1905 was the century's first important such investigation. In the next few years several states passed laws requiring registration or placing other restrictions on lobbyists. In 1913 Congress investigated the lobby which opposed the Underwood Tariff Act and in 1929 it went after Bishop Cannon and the Anti-Saloon League. In 1928 and 1935, however, the House of Representatives failed to duplicate the action of the Senate in passing registration acts. Sentiment for the 1946 law began to gather momentum after the 1936 Senate Lobby committee, headed by Sen. Hugo Black, went into the activities of the utilities lobby which fought a holding company regulation bill. That was the investigation during which William Randolph Hearst unsuccessfully attempted to obtain a court injunction to prevent the committee from subpoenaing copies of Western Union telegrams. Among the messages made public by the committee was the following from Hearst to one of his editors: "Confidential. Why not make several editorials calling for impeachment of Mr. McSwain? [Rep. John McSwain of South Carolina, chairman of the House Military Affairs Committee.] He is the enemy within the gates of congress, the Nation's citadel. He is a Communist in spirit and a traitor in effort. He would leave United States naked to its foreign and domestic enemies. Please make these editorials for morning papers. Also make editorials extolling administration for its preparedness policies which are its main achievement. Suggest advocating duplicating West Point in Middle West and Annapolis on West Coast."

The title of an article by Tris Coffin in the July 14, 1947 *New Republic,* "No Speech Ever Changed a Vote," was quoted from Byron Wilson, for thirty years lobbyist of the National Wool Growers' Association. At times different states have been said to "belong" to this or that lobby, as Pennsylvania to the Pennsylvania Railroad; New York to the New York Central Railroad; and California to the Southern Pacific Railroad. Wrote Stuart Chase in *Democracy Under Pressure* (Twentieth Century Fund, 1945): "Pressure groups have long been 'the despair of patriots.' They have been responsible for some of the darkest days in Washington. Some of them engineered the Hawley-Smoot tariff bill, which raised so high a wall that few imports could scale it, at a time when we were a creditor nation. Others put over the Silver Purchase Act which made it virtually impossible to use our great silver hoard to serve industrial wartime needs. They were responsible for the Chinese Exclusion Act. They killed bill after bill to help the consumers of drugs and foods. They have jammed through bonus grabs, and the totally inadequate tax bill of 1944. They continually pervert, twist and halt the path of progress in the Republic."

Strong as the individual lobbies such as those of the American Legion, American Civil Liberties Union, League of Women Voters, Planned Parenthood Association and others may be, the Big Three are those which promulgate the ideologies of Big Business, Big Labor, and Big Agriculture. The first, as already stated, dates from almost the beginning of the republic, and throughout our national history has been by far the most important. It has had the most money to spend and the greatest number and most powerful organizations—trade associations and others—at work. The labor lobby grew up with the labor unions which means it has existed since the 1890's. Big Labor was the inevitable answer of the working man to the development of Big Business in the form of trusts, holding companies, monopolies, and cartels. Because of its internecine warfare it never has presented a united front, but on such basic matters as the right to organize and bargain collectively and to strike without fear of injunction, AFL, CIO, the railroad brotherhoods, and United Mine Workers are of one mind. The traditional American Federation of Labor strategy, promulgated by Samuel Gompers, was to avoid alignment with any political party nationally but, at the local level, to reward the friends and punish the enemies of labor. AFL endorsements traditionally have been made on exclusive consideration of a congressman's voting record on labor bills. It was not until after the passage of Taft-Hartley, repealing some of the important gains labor had obtained through the National Labor Relations Act of 1933, that the AFL organized its Labor League for Political Education to emulate the CIO's Political Action Committee and engage in doorbell ringing and other practical political activities.

Of important farm pressure groups there are three. The oldest, the National Grange, dates from 1867 when it sprang into existence to lobby for state regulation of the railroads. When it became evident that the Granger laws, as they were called, were inadequate because of the interstate nature of railroad operations, the Grange helped create sentiment for creation of the Interstate Commerce Commission, the first of the so-called bureaucracies. Today the Grange exists mostly as a social rather than political organization and has fewer than one million members. When it takes a stand on political matters, as it frequently does, it usually is a conservative one; and its lobby is not too vigorous.

Youngest farm group is the National Farmers Union whose backbone is about 100,000 small farmers, including sharecroppers. The Union is a gadfly organization, opposed to Big Agriculture, in favor of the Farm Security Administration and measures to assist the little independent farm to compete with the large one. Its efforts are completely dwarfed by those of the American Farm Bureau Federation, the agricultural equivalent of the National Association of Manufacturers and just as conservative. The bureau speaks for the large commercial farmers, among whom are city slickers, including banks, insurance companies and other corporate beings who held mortgages which defaulted in the thirties. The Farm Bureau dates from 1909 when it was organized under the sponsorship of the Chamber of Commerce of Binghamton, N.Y. After passage of the Smith-Lever act in 1914 it qualified as an "interested group of citizens" to receive federal matching funds for extension work. As a result the organization exercises a considerable control over the government's county agent system and has a powerful "in" with the Department of Agriculture in Washington.

In Congress the farm bloc—originated by Senators Kenyon of Iowa, Capper of Kansas and "Cotton Ed" Smith of South Carolina in the early twenties—is more solidified than any other, to a large extent because of the greater ease with which its members can engage in logrolling, *i.e.,* exchange of votes. Cotton, tobacco, and peanut growers of the South, for instance, are not competitors of wool and cattle men of the West so can engage in mutual profitable backscratching with them. Freshmen members of Congress come home for their first vacation fairly gasping at the tremendous influence they learned in short order that the farm bloc and the large farmers' pressure groups exert in Washington.

First step in pressure group activity in the political sphere is to get the right men elected. Second step is to watch the same men after they take office and to obtain their votes, by all of the ways mentioned and others, for the "right" kind of legislation. When there is failure in stopping a "bad" bill, the strategy is twofold. First, challenge the constitutionality of the act and tie up its enforcement as long as possible in the courts. Simultaneously attempt to influence the governmental agencies charged with responsibility for enforcement to interpret the act in the most advantageous manner. If such fails concentrate attention on crippling the measure by amendments, ostensibly intended to strengthen but actually to make operation more difficult. Then, after hamstringing the administrators with an interminable amount of red tape, smear the whole business as bureaucratic and inoperable. Investigate the administrators, charging waste and inefficiency, and, if possible, leftism. Set the loyalty board investigators on the trail of anyone whose Americanism can be made supect even by remote association. Keep all connected with the agency in constant fear that their jobs are in jeopardy or the department's appropriation uncertain to pass by demanding the most outlandish personal favors and service for constituents. Induce someone long connected with the agency to resign and issue a blast through the press, charging anything: such criticisms are news whereas similar complaints by a former employee of a private business concern would be ignored. If the law is being well administered, set up a cry to "take it out of politics," which means, "turn it over to us to run." If all of these common tactics fail, it ought not to be hard to think up some new ones in the same vein. It's been done before. Even though you lose investigation after investigation, some of the mud you throw will stick and you will approach a few inches closer toward your goal of repeal.

As Paul H. Appleby, author of *Big Democracy* (Knopf, 1945) wrote for the Nov. 15, 1948 *Social Action* under the title, "Who Governs America?": "A small public deeply aroused weighs more in political scales than a larger public only mildly dissatisfied." It is consequently the primary purpose of a pressure group to persuade wavering lawmakers that support of their point of view is influential. To offset the special interests there is only the small People's Lobby, Inc., conducted since the early twenties almost as a personal hobby by Benjamin C. March. Barring the development of an aroused public opinion, expressing itself either through that or other public spirited groups, the only hope that the public interest ever will surmount that of the special ones lies in the occurrence of a so-called "act of God." Such occurred in 1938 when the powerful lobby opposing strengthening of the 1906 pure food and drug act was routed by the unexpected deaths of several persons from an elixir sulfanilamide which could not have been placed on the market untested had the proposed new law been in effect. *The Lobbyists* by Karl Schriftgiesser (Little, Brown, 1951) tells of the 1950 congressional investigation.

Government Publicity

On Oct. 12, 1913, Congress passed a law forbidding the employment by the federal government of publicity agents. Nevertheless, in 1948 it was estimated that approximately 30,000 persons were engaged in "educational, informational, and promotional work" for various departments and that 30 million dollars was being spent annually to keep the American people informed of what their government was doing and to answer their questions. The figures, however, are deceptive as included among the 30,000 are the mailing clerks who wrap up seed catalogues to be sent out in response to requests as well as stenographers, clerks, and all others in any way connected with the prodigious effort. The salaries of these civil servants furthermore are merely equal to if not lower than those paid for comparable service in private industry.

Although the "educational, informational, and promotional" activities have kept pace with the developing functions of other phases of the federal government, despite the 1913 law, there never has been a moratorium on congressional criticism of them. Accusations include wastage of paper, postage and taxpayers' funds, corruption of the agencies to serve political ends or to promote the personal ambitions of a public official, inefficiency, hoodwinking of the public, and others in the same vein. So assiduously is the watchdog function performed, furthermore, that the vast majority of the pamphlets, bulletins, reports, and news releases that emanate from any government bureau are notorious for their dullness. Thus charges of using the publicity agencies for the purpose of promoting the policies of whatever administration is in power are avoided, or at least more easily answered. Also, the chances are increased that some really important pronouncements, based perhaps on research for which millions of the public's dollars were spent, will be ignored by editors too bored to search for their significance. The formality of bureaucratic jargon is easy to buffoon but it is inevitable in view of the avidity of critical senators and representatives to condemn any bright word or phrase.

Even during wartime keeping anything that might tend to cause a favorable impression of the party in power out of governmental publications is a matter of major concern to some loud-speaking congressmen. A biography of President Franklin Delano Roosevelt, intended for distribution overseas among the peoples of allied nations, for instance, was criticized adversely. At no time during World War II did the Domestic Operations branch of the Office of War Information have an appropriation more than one-third that of the Overseas branch and its virtual killing by Congress was caused in part by its publication of a brochure, *Negroes and the War* which Sen. Gerald Nye of North Dakota and several Southern senators blamed for causing race riots in some war industry towns.

As was true of public relations for industry, World War I gave impetus to governmental informational activities. Under the vigorous leadership of George Creel, veteran newspaperman, the Committee on Public Information demonstrated what could be done on a nationwide, really a world-wide, scale given the determination and the funds. By comparison with the expenditures made by Elmer Davis' Office of War Information during World War II, the Creel committee spent a pittance: $6,850,000 total expenditures with a return to the treasury of $2,937,447 from expositions and the sale of films and the *Official Bulletin*, a daily chronicle of presidential statements and orders, important speeches, and announcements and casualty lists.

In retrospect it seems clearer than it did at the time that the terrific attacks which Creel underwent from some congressmen and others resulted to a considerable extent because his committee, in addition to engaging in propagandistic activities, also was the official censorship body. Long before Pearl Harbor it was decided that if another war came, that mistake would be rectified. As a consequence, during World War II the Office of War Information was entirely separate from the Office of Censorship, headed by Byron Price, veteran Associated Press editor. Even with its reduced functions, the OWI spent 26 million dollars in 1942, 54 million dollars in 1944 and 39 million dollars in 1945.

It was significant that the word "information" appeared in the official title of each war agency, and that both Creel and Davis steadfastly insisted that they trafficked only in facts without propagandistic intent. Although no authoritative analysis has appeared yet on the work of the OWI, most students of the subject will be surprised if, when one does appear, it does not reveal that Davis came much closer than Creel to achieving that purpose. The similarities in operational setups and management—with the exception noted: the divorce of the censorship from propaganda functions in World War II—probably outweighed the differences, but the tasks that the two agencies had to perform were not alike. World War II was not World War I. The attitudes and opinions of the American people in 1941 were different from those of the preceding generation in 1917 (see pages 000 to 000). Because of the general ignorance regarding world affairs and, especially, propaganda, Creel had an easier job except for the fact that there was considerably more pro-German feeling in the United States when the Kaiser was the enemy than when Hitler had had a decade in which to alienate the respect of all but a handful of Americans.

In his trail-blazing *Propaganda Technique in the World War* (Knopf, 1921), Harold D. Lasswell stated the four objectives of any wartime propaganda machine to be: (1) to mobilize hatred against the enemy; (2) to preserve the friendship of allies; (3) to preserve the friendship and if possible gain the cooperation of neutrals; and (4) to demoralize the enemy. The Creel committee concentrated on Objective No. 1 at home and upon Objective No. 4 abroad. To put it mildly it did nothing to discourage the tremendous number of atrocity stories which flooded the country; its 75,000 Four Minute speakers who gave 755,190 speeches to 314,454,514 listeners in 5,200 communities waxed eloquent about the Hun and the Boche. Woodrow Wilson's 14 points were a constructive propaganda device, but they and his aphorisms ("to make the world safe for democracy," "war to end all wars," and so forth) had different effects on the domestic and foreign audiences. For Americans they helped intensify rather than reduce hatred of the enemy as he obviously was the obstacle in the way of their attainment, a disbeliever in them. Although it cannot possibly be proved, Creel propaganda leaflets, including the Wilson promises and safe-conduct passes, have been credited with shortening World War I by six months or more. By contrast, the Nazis kept on fighting until they had little space in which to stand; the 9½ million safe-conduct leaflets dropped among them during the last ten days of hostilities had an effect upon men who saw their cause doomed, but not to anywhere near the extent that the same sort of thing had a quarter of a century earlier.

Davis was handicapped by the lack of clear-cut war aims to be advertised. There was nothing comparable to the 14 points (the

Atlantic Charter just didn't "take" because of its similarity to the Wilsonian ideals whose failure was so vividly remembered). More than once the Voice of America broadcasters were embarrassed because they did not know what the official American "line" was. Notable example was at the time of the capitulation of Italy when, in desperation, a New York columnist's designation of Victor Emmanuel as "the moronic little king" was used and followed closely by what amounted to an official apology since in the interim we had decided to "do business" for a while with the existent Italian government.

Going about his business in the calm, factual manner which had previously made him one of the nation's most popular news commentators, Elmer Davis was criticized by some for not attempting to arouse the nation to the excitable pitch which had prevailed during World War I. Even had Davis himself wanted to do so, he would have had to overcome White House opposition first, and the effort probably would have been a colossal failure. Creel's hysterical Four Minute Men were a result, not a cause of war fever; World War II was a much grimmer business for every belligerent, including the United States, a nasty job to finish as soon as possible with a minimum of effort. The chiseling on wartime regulations and the "gripings" against government, labor, management, and the military leadership was far in excess of anything which anyone who lived through the first war recalls. So, with Congress insisting upon it anyway, the OWI concentrated its efforts on overseas work where it was of considerable assistance to the underground movements before the second front was opened. Part of the United States postwar unpopularity in nations all over the world derives from the lavish promises of a brave new One World made by our propagandists over the short wave before V-J Day.

World War I had to be sold to a certain proportion of Americans because we entered it by a declaration of war on our own part. World War II did not have to be sold because, with the attack on Pearl Harbor, we had no alternative but to fight. When there occurred an influx of advertising men into the OWI, 15 members of the Publications division, led by Henry F. Pringle, resigned in a group, charging, "The activities of the OWI on the home front are now dominated by high pressure promoters who prefer slick salesmanship to honest promotion." It was charged by some critics that the approach was too much of the "what's in it for me?" variety. If these contentions had validity the reasons probably are to be found in the state of mind already described, and none of the ambitious boys who came and went were able to do much to change it.

The White House and Public Opinion

In war and peacetime alike the most fertile source of news indicating administration policy on important matters is the president's semi-weekly news conference. Restricted by the numerous checks and balances characteristic of the American governmental setup, the chief executive does not speak with the same authority as a dictator. Even when he has a hostile Congress, however, he wields sufficient power through his constitutional control over foreign policy, and through the powers of appointment and veto to make what he has to say about the nation's course prophetic. A recalcitrant subordinate in the Department of State may sabotage a president's policy toward a Latin American country or generals and admirals may discover ways to circumvent his orders concerning discrimination in the armed forces. Nevertheless, as the one public official whom all of the eligible voters have a chance to elect, his words have a powerful effect upon the thinking of the electorate. He can do much to create or influence the basic attitudes that Americans everywhere have regarding major issues. Thus, when he declares that prosperity is just around the corner, he is believed until incontrovertible evidence to the contrary compels disbelief, whereupon the chief executive's every word becomes suspect. When he declares "all that we have to fear is fear itself," and then proceeds dramatically to alter the conditions creating the fear, he wins lasting gratitude and respect from the beneficiaries of his actions which his enemies are impotent to destroy. What these examples mean is that, with the presidential reputation, as with most else, nothing succeeds like success or fails like failure, when the matter is one about the success or failure of which the ordinary citizen is able to judge. Having won confidence on such matters, the chief executive can win popular acceptance for pronouncements regarding foreign policy, about which the ordinary citizen does not feel, or at least does not recognize so readily, the effect upon himself. The president naturally can exercise his discretion as to what diplomatic incidents should be made public and can give his own interpretation of them—a powerful weapon in public opinion formation.

Liberals and Liberalism

Because liberals and liberal organizations are considered newsworthy, which means that the reporter of necessity comes into frequent contact with them, an understanding of what makes them tick, or of what makes them fail to tick, is important. Speaking as a "professional joiner of liberal organizations," the author addressed the Ethical Culture Society of St. Louis Jan. 18, 1948, on "The Plight of American Liberalism." What follows is taken from the portion of that address intended to answer the question regarding liberal organizations: "Why do they enjoy such short life, coming and going interminably by the hundreds or thousands?"

In part, of course, the answer is to be found in the nature of the memberships which are similar, generally overlapping. These liberals are mostly intellectuals—teachers, writers, artists, other professional people. Being intellectuals, they are thinkers—deep thinkers. They think the most beautiful thoughts that are being "thunk" anywhere at any time. Although these thoughts often have a considerable influence on others, they do not as a rule metamorphose themselves into action through the media of their creators. In other words, the thinkers themselves seldom are doers. Not only that. When the ideas are what could be called iconoclastic, they often scare those giving birth to them worse than they do anyone else. That is particularly true when the heat begins to be applied by the opposition and whenever any attempt is made to build up a practical, working program to put any of them into effect. As the late Heywood Broun was fond of remarking, "A liberal is a person who leaves the room when the fighting begins."

To the old-line modern liberal, action may mean no more than a semi-annual mass meeting (possibly featuring a senator or cabinet member with whom he can appear on the platform and be photographed), letters to congressmen, and distribution of tons and tons and tons of literature. He has a lot of fun while it lasts, but—as any regular political leader knows—he has but slight nuisance value.

The entire answer, however, is not to be found in the constitutional inability of most liberals to act as well as brain trust. Even more important are the structural weaknesses in liberal organizations which discourage or make impossible mass action. What I mean can be understood easily by consideration of how most of these groups come into existence. The typical so-called liberal organization gets its start when a small group germinates an idea, formalizes its discussion of that idea, elects officers and rushes to the printers to have a letterhead printed with all the proper names on it. Then there goes out an appeal to the potential rank-and-file to join the great crusade by sending in money contributions.

The structural weakness consists in the fact that paying dues and cheering the leadership at rallies is about all the membership as a whole ever is permitted to do. In other words, the organizations which theoretically are dedicated to the cause of democracy are on the whole the most undemocratic in their setups of any groups to be found anywhere in American life today. Impressed by the stationery and by the important names on it, and by the statement of principles and promises of great things to come, the everyday liberals join up with enthusiasm. If allowed to, they attend a meeting or two at which they make additional contributions. They whoop it up and feel, after an evening in the company of like-minded people, that maybe things aren't so bad as they thought they were after all. The therapeutic effect is very beneficial; it would be a shame to destroy it.

Inevitably, however, there comes disillusionment and/or indifference. The second year, or the third, the recipient of the reminder that his dues are payable finds it easy to shove the dun from one side of his desk to another for weeks or months and finally, in an act of rare boldness, to heave it into the wastebasket.

An overwhelming majority of liberal organizations fail because they do not practice the democracy they preach. No matter how highminded their intentions may be, they are clique originated and clique controlled. As long as the initial exuberance lasts, nobody cares; but people who have no share in policy-making do not continue to maintain interest. There always, of course, are the dissenters who object to the undemocratic control. Until the movement starts to wane, their protests are completely in vain. When anyone is willing to listen to them, it usually is too late.

When that time comes, also, the entrenched directors or officers may be so thoroughly convinced that they and they only have enough knowledge of the inner workings of the organization that it would be suicidal for them to relinquish their leadership. Knowing how many hard hours they have put in, they easily resent any suggestion that the representative base should be broadened, as personal attacks on themselves. They feel hurt in some cases; resentful in others. And they rationalize in orthodox Freudian fashion, thoroughly convinced that it is only the troublemakers and radicals, who have crept into the organization for the sole purpose of boring from within and taking over, who are dissatisfied. If the thing goes on long enough, they may be right, because all of the other members quit or become inactive. It is not generally true, however, of any going concern; and the charges that defenders of the organized liberal *status quo* may make against their detractors may have about as much validity as those of a reactionary manufacturer who "knows" that his workers would be tranquil and content if it weren't for those nasty outsiders who keep stirring things up.

One extremely worrisome fact that we must recognize is this: some of the best red baiters in the United States today are to be found among those who call themselves liberals, organized or unorganized. John Rankin never indicted on flimsier evidence than many of them do constantly. . . .

It is difficult for me to detect much difference between the superiority complex and lack of faith in majority rule—democracy—possessed by many of these letterhead do-nothing liberals and that which characterizes avowed fascists. Consequently, many of these people—and I know and have worked with hundreds of them—often are suspected of maintaining their undemocratic control of liberal organizations for the express purpose of seeing that nothing really important ever is done. . . . Anyone who suggests either that the organizational setup be made more democratic or that the activities become more practical, always is suspected or accused of communism. The most charitable thing that can be said of him is that he has been "taken in" by the reds; and isn't it too bad? . . .

What it all adds up to, of course, is that organizational liberalism in the United States is bankrupt, and the ghosts of Hitler and Goebbels, wherever they are, must be chortling loudly because of the success, in this all-important area, of their familiar diabolical "divide and conquer" techniques. Some consolation may be obtained from the realization that there never has been any powerful united front of liberal organizations in this country. Individual liberals always have been more effective "boring from within" the major political parties, business associations, trade unions, churches, civic clubs, and other orthodox organizations.

What makes the present plight of American liberalism frightening, however, is that the confusion which has proved so fatal to organizational liberalism also affects the individual liberal whoever and wherever he may be. I cannot possibly improve upon the description of the situation which Max Lerner wrote for the 1948 New Year's Day edition of *PM*. Hence, I should like to quote a few paragraphs from Mr. Lerner's piece which was in comment upon the editorial contention of the New York *Herald Tribune* that American liberalism has no body of principles.

The trouble [Mr. Lerner wrote], is that it has two, and the battle between them is so sharp that it gives aid and comfort to the enemies of both. What is that battle? The significant split between liberals today is one of intellectual outlook.

One camp of liberals—or "left wingers"—has its attention fixed on the main current of world revolutionary striving, which still flows through a channel first given shape by the Russians. They are not Communists, and would be incapable of Communist discipline or hardships. Some of them may be fellow travelers, who—like a sunflower—turn by a tropism to the Russian sun. More likely they are not even that, but independent liberals who feel they must put first things first. They may be genuinely troubled, in their more private moments, by the ethical flaws of a totalitarian Russia. But they keep their eyes fixed in a different direction. They see decay and breakdown in the world's economics, rottenness in the world's still feudal social systems, blindness in the conduct of foreign affairs, no real efforts at world peace. They find capitalist and fascist regimes collaborating in order to hem in the Left Wing regimes. They see a hysterical fear of Russia riding mankind.

There is another liberal camp. These liberals have their attention wholly fixed on the ruthlessness by which the Russian ruling group reached and has maintained its power, and on the police states of Eastern Europe that have come up in the wake of that power. They are obsessed with the symbol of the commissar, with the fact of forced labor in Russia. They spend much of their emotional energy speculating on the millions in the prison camps. So fixed are they on this that they give only minor attention to the main social forces in the world at large. The fact that there is a revolutionary energy in the world which must find some sort of expression—that fact they are largely blind to. They are troubled be-

cause American capitalism is making alliances with the most reactionary
regimes in order to fight the Communist influence, but they push this flaw
of American policy into the back of their consciousness.

Thus liberals are caught, like Dante in the midpassage of his life, at
the foot of the Delectable Mountain, with a decent world in view. But
one path that leads to the top is guarded by the leopard of the totalitarian police-state. The other path is guarded by the she-wolf of capitalist
avarice and its social blindness. And each group of liberals is so horror-
struck by one of these animal death's heads that it rushes along the other
path to embrace whatever it finds.

That is, I am convinced, the double-flow of the liberal attitude today.
That is what splits the liberals into two camps, makes it impossible for them
to unite to achieve either an orderly economy or an orderly world. The
weakness, I repeat, is not that the liberals have no principles. The weakness is that they have two sets. The revolutionary liberals want to see
social changes carried through, even at a deadly risk to personality. The
ethical liberals have grown so embittered over Russian police-methods
that they run the danger of preparing their minds for a war that may
destroy the world.[3]

Mr. Lerner, in his short piece, takes it for granted that what makes it
possible for both of the groups he describes to qualify to be called
liberal is understood. It is that they are both for social, economic,
and political reforms generally considered liberal on the domestic
front—such measures as the control or destruction of monopolies, an
end to racial discrimination, governmental aid to assure adequate
housing, educational advantages, public health services; in general,
human rights ahead of property rights, the best interests of the little
fellow as paramount to those of the big guy. Because, however, they
have become so engrossed with their internecine battle on an international ideological front, they are so mutually suspicious of each
other's motives that they no longer can cooperate on the domestic
front. The "plight" with which we should be concerned is not that of
the liberals but of the rest of us because of the stalemate which exists
among those best fitted to champion progressive causes. Although I
am an inveterate internationalist, I wonder if we don't need a little
more isolationism, or America firstism, among American liberals.

American Communism

That they are not America Firsters is the fundamental charge
against American communists. Rather, they are sincerely believed to

[3] Reprinted by permission of Simon and Schuster, publishers.

be agents of an international revolutionary movement and in the event of war between the United States and the Soviet Union would be expected to act as a fifth column. This point of view was given impetus June 4, 1951, by the United States Supreme Court when it upheld the conviction of 11 leading communists for conspiring in a way which apparently represented a "clear and present danger" of violence to the American government.

Granting the worst about native communists, their effect upon American public opinion nevertheless is mostly negative. This is so largely because of their insignificant numbers and because of the extreme unpopularity of their ideas and their tactics. In his dissenting opinion Justice Douglas stated: ". . . in America they are miserable merchants of unwanted ideas; their wares remain unsold. The fact that their ideas are abhorrent does not make them powerful . . ."

Communists who have joined labor unions and liberal organizations in their attempt to win control use tactics which defeat their purpose, for they antagonize and alienate the noncommunists and create dislike, suspicion, and fear. Those persons are either intellectuals in liberal organizations, or working people in labor organizations. The former, as explained, are too much inclined toward purism to tolerate the reds; the latter too concerned with the immediate objectives of more money, fewer hours of work or better working conditions to give a whoop about class struggles or long-range ideologies.

There are intellectual communists who, if they had the chance, could give a good account of themselves in any polemics. Too many rank-and-file reds, however, are of the frustrated crackpot variety. Among them are those of whose allegiance the party never can be certain. It often is as easy for one such to become as fanatically anticommunist as he previously was fanatically procommunist. There also is good money in serving as experts on the foibles of their former comrades.

If the American communists and their Russian and all other foreign friends had to pay for the publicity they receive they would have to spend tremendous sums of money. Not only are the reds accused of most that is considered bad from many different viewpoints in American life, but they also have been given undeserved credit for much which the majority of Americans consider good, including the major liberal gains during the days of the Rooseveltian New Deal. The promiscuous use of the red label has made it meaningless to anyone who takes the time to examine the record.

Radicalism of any kind is the product of unrest, an expression of personal discomfort. Communism does not follow capitalism immediately. It comes only after what amounts to fascism, regardless of what it is called, has been in existence long enough to breed a revolutionary movement. That was true in czarist Russia and in Chiang-Kai-shek China. All of the pressure group activities of American communists will not bring about a strong anticapitalist American movement unless the *status quo* ceases to satisfy a majority of the people.

CHAPTER SIXTEEN

JOURNALISM

In general newspapers and magazines strongly buttress exist-
ing customs and institutions and condition thought conserva-
tively regarding political, economic, and social issues.

Power of the Press

Harry S. Truman had the editorial support of only 16.16 per cent of the daily newspapers in the United States, representing but 13.99 per cent of the total daily circulation. Nevertheless, he received 49.5 per cent of the popular vote and was elected president in November, 1948.

As a consequence, some critics of the American press reiterated the charge they had made after each victory of Franklin Delano Roosevelt in the face of similar overwhelming journalistic opposition: that the newspapers had lost much, if not most or all of their influence over readers.

Actually the four Roosevelt and one Truman victories proved nothing of the sort. Probably the answer to the "She ain't what she usta was" argument is "She never was," meaning that it is doubtful if the press ever possessed the power to sway elections, presidential or otherwise. The recent journalistic failures seem more dramatic because the lineup of support was comparatively more one-sided, but there are plenty of earlier examples of candidates and political machines which seemed actually to thrive on journalistic opposition. Notable among them were the LaFollettes in Wisconsin, New York's Tammany and the Pendergast machine in Kansas City.

What the New Deal and Fair Deal victories indicated is not so much journalistic impotence as the dominating strength of the pocketbook appeal or motivation in causing a voter to make up his mind.

For the majority this means "throwing the rascals out" when times are bad and refraining from "changing horses in midstream" when economic conditions are comparatively good. Neither press, nor radio, nor political orators nor any others can prevail to the contrary. John L. Lewis, despite his powerful hold on his United Mine Workers of America, was unable to deliver their votes to Wendell Willkie in 1940. Even FDR, at the height of his popularity, failed miserably when he attempted to "purge" conservative Democrats in 1938.

Truman's margin of victory, furthermore, was not much: 2,135,336 votes more than Thomas E. Dewey out of a total of 48,680,416 votes cast. Governor Dewey received 45.1 per cent of the popular vote in 1948. In 1944 he got 45.8 per cent and trailed by 2,596,219. With 44.8 per cent of the popular vote, Wendell Willkie was 4,938,962 votes behind in 1940.

Rather than proving the waning influence of the press in matters political, the Republican votes in the five presidential elections from 1932 to 1948 inclusive might be interpreted to establish the exact opposite. That is, were it not for the newspapers, publicizing and supporting its point of view year in and year out, in disregard of the electorate, there might not even be a Republican party any more. Such a conclusion, however, probably would be as much an exaggeration of journalistic strength as many of the claims of journalistic weaknesses in the light of the 1932 to 1948 results are exaggerations in the opposite direction. Without doubt, if they should be deprived of newspaper support, the well-heeled conservative interests would find other media by which to present their case. One can only conjecture how different the course of events in the United States, possibly the entire world, would have been had the American press as a whole given enthusiastic support to Franklin Delano Roosevelt and to New Deal measures.

There is some validity to the defense of the press that, despite its editorial opposition, it helped the Democrats by front-page news attention. Too much weight, however, cannot be given this face-saving argument because (1) during recent campaigns the Republican candidates received much greater news attention from many of the most important newspapers; (2) articles about Democratic candidates or New Deal measures often were slanted unfavorably; (3) headlines and makeup position betrayed pro-Republican and anti-New Deal

Fair Deal bias; (4) pictures, cartoons and other illustrations and features generally had the same effect. More important, when his economic position is relatively good, a voter does not need to consult a newspaper to determine that fact; nor, when the opposite is the case, does he believe a newspaper which attempts to make him believe the contrary.

With slight emendations, the foregoing paragraphs are those with which the writer began an article, "The American Press' Influence on Public Opinion," in the Summer, 1949 *International Journal of Opinion and Attitude Research.* Although it should have been apparent for at least a quarter century preceding 1936 that the press is considerably less than omnipotent in matters electoral, it was not until that year that a majority of newspaper readers were shocked into realization of that fact. In 1940 the Bureau of Applied Social Research of Columbia University studied "those conditions which determine the political behavior of people" in Erie County, Ohio, which was chosen in part because in previous elections "it had deviated very little from the national voting trends." From May to November a sample group was studied to determine the effects of various aspects of the campaign. The results were published as *The People's Choice*, by Paul F. Lazarsfeld, Bernard Berelson and Hazel Gaudet. In Chapter X, "The Conversion Effect," the authors concluded:

"The first thing to say is that some people *were* converted by campaign propaganda but that they were *few indeed*. What we have already learned about the factors involved in vote decisions makes this less than surprising. Clearly, several factors other than short-run communications took precedence in influence. Such factors or conditions actually served to insulate various groups from the conversion influence, thus delimiting its area of application. In combination, they acted as a fine political sieve through which relatively few people passed. As the following summary briefly indicates, a whole set of established behavior patterns operated against conversion and hence made it an uncommon experience.

"*Restriction 1:* Half the people knew in May for which party they would vote and clung to this choice throughout the campaign. They were the least susceptible to conversion.

"*Restriction 2:* Of those who were undecided in May, about half made up their minds after they knew who the nominees were and maintained this decision throughout the campaign. Such partisans, who made their choice conditional on the nominee, were likewise not open to ready conversion.

"*Restriction 3:* The vote decisions of 70 per cent of the people, whether or not they expressed an early vote intention, corresponded to the vote tendencies prevailing among groups with social charactertistics similar to their own. The predispositions of such people were so deeply rooted that they could not be readily converted by the opposition's campaign propaganda.

"*Restriction 4:* The strongly partisan devoted most attention to campaign propaganda. In other words, the people who read and listened most to political communications had the most fixed political views. Thus, in sheer quantity campaign propaganda reached the persons least amenable to conversion.

"*Restriction 5:* The people who read and heard most political communication were exposed to more of their own partisan propaganda. Thus in partisanship too, attention to propaganda led away from conversion.

"In summary, then, the people who did most of the reading and listening not only read and heard most of their own partisan propaganda but were also most resistant to conversion because of their strong predispositions. And the people who were most open to conversion—the ones the campaign managers most wanted to reach—read and listened least. Those inter-related facts represent the bottleneck of conversion." [1]

To return to the thesis of the writer's magazine article: the important influence of a newspaper upon political thought is exercised, not during the six or nine months of a quadrennial presidential campaign, but day by day, year in, year out. The press wields it in its role of leading defender of the social, economic, and political *status quo*. By opposing Truman in 1948 the press was merely acting consistently in view of its more than a half century practice of always backing the most conservative of presidential candidates. Similarly, in congressional elections every two years and in state, county, and municipal elections, most endorsements go to conservative rather than liberal candidates. Although, to this writer's knowledge, no exhaustive study ever has been made to determine the facts, it is probable that the press'

[1] From *The People's Choice.* Copyright, 1944, by Duell, Sloan, and Pearce.

"batting average" of apparent successes would be higher in local than in national elections. At any rate it is indisputable that the same voters who gave FDR large majorities also sent to Congress enough illiberal senators and representatives to hamstring the popular liberal president in putting through much of his New Deal program after the memorable desperate 100 days at the beginning of his term.

If the press is a potent factor in local elections it may result from the fact that on the whole editorial policy regarding local issues is more progressive and consequently more consistent with the desires of voters at the local by comparison with the national level. Since it became Big Business itself shortly before the turn of the century, the press has been unswerving in its conservatism as regards matters of national policy. Rarely if ever has it been an original or even an early supporter of any movement or measure considered, either contemporaneously or in retrospect, to be progressive. Usually, in fact, it has been in violent opposition. Most of the legislation to implement Woodrow Wilson's New Freedom and Franklin Delano Roosevelt's New Deal was passed despite the dire warnings of the press. Other measures undoubtedly failed of passage in some part because of press opposition.

By contrast, there are innumerable examples of the press' championing of the people's causes in exposure of corruption in local government and in promoting worthy civic causes. Possibly such successes in a newspaper's own front (or back) yard are more indicative of its power to influence than are its failures in national elections or in regard to federal legislation. In municipal affairs, however, as stated, the papers generally support liberal proposals by comparison with their conservatism or reaction regarding national issues. When they do not do so, furthermore, they do not go to the extreme of aligning themselves with the "forces of evil" in a community; rather, they remain silent. Any case against a newspaper for shirking its responsibility on the home front must be based on its acts of omission rather than on those of commission. In altogether too many cases publishers in one-newspaper towns are timid about taking sides on controversial matters, as they wish to avoid the risk of offending someone. The net result of all aspects of the strategy in local affairs is public confidence in the newspaper as a defender of virtue and the resulting prestige lends weight to its endorsement of candidates during campaigns. Were the newspaper to champion causes contrary to the public interest in local affairs, because of the closer acquaintance which leaders have with those issues, it probably would be no more successful than it is in its support of conservatism in presidential elections.

A newspaper's direct political influence is greatest upon those who are close to the news itself. Despite the press' poor record in backing winners, politicians generally prize newspaper endorsements and cringe at the thought of editorial attack. As Herbert Blumer pointed out in his address to the 1947 convention of the American Sociological Society (see "Public Opinion and Public Opinion Polling," in *American Sociological Review*, October, 1948), not all persons are of equal importance in the formation of public opinion. Newspapers pay more attention to those in policy-making positions, and they in turn are more impressed by what a powerful newspaper thinks than they are by the mythical man in the street. Regarding that man, Chapter 2 emphasized facts which should be, and generally are, recognized by editors: (1) he pays scant attention to the serious parts of a newspaper and/or (2) he has a short memory for whatever he does read. Nevertheless, though 90 per cent may not read pig iron (newspaper slang for serious news), they do glance at headlines in quest of that which does interest them. And they do look at pictures, cartoons, and comic strips. Thus, they become familiar with and are affected by many of the choicest labels and slogans used to categorize current problems: such headline-fitting phrases, for instance, as "cold war," "iron curtain," "red," "New Deal," and, when the issue is pertinent, "youth control bill," "dictator bill," "slave labor," and the like. The news which these phrases advertise may not be so attractive as that to which attention is directed by "hammer murder," "mad dog killer," "king of swat," and the like, but they are stereotype builders. The nonreader of the articles they present cannot avoid seeing them, if only out of the corner of his eye. He accepts them as accurate and fair definitions of situations and rests content that he has proper opinions regarding the important topics of the day. Surrounded on all sides by a different set of stereotype builders, he would come to different conclusions. Even the complete illiterate, furthermore, is affected indirectly through others who do read them and pass them on.

Determinants of Newspaper Policy

In keeping with the over-all purpose of this book, this chapter is concerned, not with the rightness or wrongness of journalistic ethics and policies but, pragmatically, with the effect of newspaper practices upon readers, *i.e.*, upon public opinion. Brief consideration, however, must be given to some of the principal determinants of newspaper policy for proper understanding of their effect. What, for instance, of the widely held belief that, because advertisers provide 60 per cent or more of a newspaper's revenue, they exercise an active role in helping the editor to make up his mind whether to support or oppose this or that issue, to play down or suppress, exaggerate or distort a particular news story, to smear or heroize a certain public figure and so forth? Such an idea of the role of the advertiser is almost entirely erroneous. Rather, the direct influence of an individual advertiser upon the news and editorial policy of any newspaper is as a successful seeker after free publicity.

The reason for the virtual nonexistence of attempts by advertisers to influence editorial judgment on political matters is lack of necessity. The overwhelming majority of newspapers are conservative not because they are being held in line by their space buyers but because their owners honestly share the same opinions on economic, social, and political matters as do the vast majority of other persons in the same income bracket. If advertiser pressure were needed to keep editors in line, it would be exerted which, perhaps, is the same thing as saying such pressure does exist. Anyway, the end result is the same as evidenced by the fact that liberal publications of all kinds do not receive fat advertising accounts. In recent years the experimental New York *PM* began as an adless newspaper. After six and a half years, when its financial backers warned that they could not continue their support, to get out of the red *PM* desperately tried to save itself by announcing it would accept advertising. Because of the paper's strong liberalism, however, it did not prove attractive to enough business interests to wipe out the deficit; it folded 16 months later and its successor, the *Star*, though it "watered down" the paper's liberalism considerably, lasted only seven months. When the New York *Daily Compass* was started in May, 1949, it found only a few left-wing groups and an occasional bold businessman willing to spend money with it. In 1947 an advertisers' boycott killed the Valley City (N.D.) *Times-Record* because of the strongly liberal editorial policy of the youthful editor, Don Matchan.

The details of a somewhat similar case were contained in a lengthy article in the June 11, 1949 *Publishers' Auxiliary*, the first three paragraphs of which were as follows:

Flora, Ill.—A fight for existence which began almost three months ago was successfully concluded by Charles A. Crowder, publisher of the Flora *Sentinel,* June 3 when he accepted the offer of a loan from the International Brotherhood of Electrical Workers.

Crowder had been under fire since March 18 when he published an editorial favoring recognition of a local electrical workers union by the Flora city council. The union had called a strike against the city-owned light and water system.

A group of Flora businessmen had sought to seize his plant and put him out of business by forming a syndicate. The syndicate brought foreclosure action. . . .

In October, 1949, three Washington, D.C. dailies "played it safe" by refusing an advertisement offered by the National Federation of Independent Business, Inc. which contained an answer to a series of advertisements by means of which the Great Atlantic & Pacific Tea Company was attempting, on a nationwide scale, to create public sentiment in favor of its defense against an anti-monopoly suit brought against it by the Department of Justice. The federation, which claims 140,000 members, planned to insert the advertisements in 500 newspapers and experimented with a test run in eight large dailies, one each in Texas, California, Iowa, and Massachusetts and four in the nation's capital. Although the four papers outside Washington accepted the copy without question, in Washington the *Star, Times-Herald*, and *Post* all refused it. Only the Washington *Daily News* accepted the copy and a representative of that paper explained: "It's perfectly clear why we published Burger's [Washington representative of the National Federation of Independent Business, Inc.] reply and the other three papers refused to do so. The other three get grocery advertising from A & P every week. We don't get any. I have no doubt whatsoever that if we carried A & P ads regularly, we also would have refused Burger's ad."

For anyone interested in investigating similar cases of alleged journalistic venality, there is a small library of literature of exposé, including Upton Sinclair's *The Brass Check* (Author, Pasadena, 1919), Oswald Garrison Villard's *Some Newspapers and Newspapermen* (Knopf, 1923), and *The Disappearing Daily* (Knopf, 1944), William Salisbury's *The Career of a Journalist* (B. W. Dodge, 1908), Silas Bent's *Ballyhoo* (Boni, Liveright, 1927), Harold L. Ickes' *America's House of Lords* (Harcourt, Brace, 1939) and the several books of George Seldes, especially *You Can't Print That* (Garden City, 1929), *Can These Things Be!* (Garden City, 1931), *Freedom of the Press* (Bobbs-Merrill, 1935) and *The People Don't Know* (Gaer, 1949). Seldes' weekly news letter, *In Fact*, which folded in September, 1950, consisted mostly of documented charges of mishandling of news by newspapers. As long as Don Hollenbeck conducted it, the weekly Columbia Broadcasting System program, "CBS Views the Press," was dedicated to the purpose of correcting wrong impressions resulting from newspaper treatment of important events. In their *Your Newspaper* (Macmillan, 1947), nine 1945–46 Nieman fellows are highly critical of the press, and there is hardly an issue of the quarterly *Nieman Reports* which does not contain at least one detailed analysis of a case of journalistic misbehavior. It is significant that all such indictments of the press are for sins committed in the interest of conservatism or reaction, never the reverse.

Freedom of the Press

Because of the prestige of its 13 signers, the least documented of contemporary criticisms of the press caused the biggest uproar among publishers collectively stung by it. That was the report of the Commission on Freedom of the Press, financed by *Time*, Inc., and the Encyclopaedia Britannica. Its principal publication was the compendious *A Free and Responsible Press* (University of Chicago, 1947). The first few paragraphs of Chapter 1, "The Problem and the Principles," should suffice to indicate why the majority of publishers found it decidedly distasteful. Those paragraphs follow:

"The Commission set out to answer the question: Is the freedom of the press in danger? Its answer to that question is: Yes. It concludes that the freedom of the press is in danger for three reasons:

"First, the importance of the press to the people has greatly increased with the development of the press as an instrument of mass communication. At the same time the development of the press as an instrument of mass communication has greatly decreased the proportion of the people who can express their opinions and ideas through the press.

"Second, the few who are able to use the machinery of the press as an instrument of mass communication have not provided a service adequate to the needs of society.

"Third, those who direct the machinery of the press have engaged from time to time in practices which the society condemns and which, if continued, it will inevitably undertake to regulate or control."

When it declares that freedom of the press is in danger the commission means something entirely different than does the American Newspaper Publishers Association when it seeks exemption for its members from a National Recovery Act, National Labor Relations Act, Fair Labor Standards Act, or other laws on the ground that their application to newspapers would violate the freedom of the press clause of the first amendment to the United States Constitution. The ANPA to the contrary, requiring newspapers to obey the anti-trust, child labor, and other laws governing business does not constitute prior restraint upon the right to publish as one pleases, the courts consistently have ruled. Consequently, the American press still is free in the original sense. Furthermore, unless the United States Supreme Court disregards the precedents which it has established in numerous cases, the press will continue to be free legally, able to lambast courts and public officials with virtual impunity, and safe from any attempts at discriminatory taxation, licensing, censorship or other restraints.

As used by the Commission on Freedom of the Press, freedom of the press means, not the right to publish without restraint but the right of the people to know. Properly phrased the pertinent question would be, not "Is the press free?" but "Is freedom of the press working?" An affirmative answer would mean that the expectation of the founding fathers who wrote the clause into the Constitution has been realized. That expectation was that the cause of democracy would be promoted best by permitting any and all to publish as they saw fit. With a profound faith in the ability of the masses to govern themselves, Thomas Jefferson believed that wise decisions were most likely to result if free men were exposed to all possible points of view on all subjects. Freedom of the press, in other words, was intended as a means to an end, not as an end in itself.

Basis of the concern which the Commission and the other critics feel is the indisputable fact that there no longer exists the easy access to a variety of viewpoints which Jefferson and his cohorts imagined would result from compelling government to keep hands off the press. Instead, with few exceptions, the newspapers are substantially alike in their social, economic, and political conservatism. The development of advertising as the chief source of revenue freed the press from subservience to political parties, but the high cost of newspaper operations has not only made essential a wealthy and naturally conservative ownership but also has resulted in a steady decline in the number of competing papers. In 1909, the peak year, there were approximately 2,600 daily newspapers in the United States, one for every 25,000 potential readers. In 1949 there were fewer than 1,800 dailies, one for every 75,000 readers. In only 8 per cent of American cities were there competing dailies; in ten states there were none; in 22 states no competing Sunday newspapers. In the weekly newspaper field 77 per cent of all publishers in 1947 had no local competitors. Through mergers, bankruptcies, and absorption by chains, local daily newspaper monopolies doubled between 1910 and 1940. In cities in which two newspapers still were to be found, usually a morning and afternoon paper, single ownership was becoming the rule rather than the exception, with a radio station often a third property. When Col. Joseph Patterson, publisher of the New York *Daily News*, which has the largest circulation of any American newspaper, died in 1947, probate of his estate of $10,923,366 revealed large holdings of the stock and bonds of the American Telephone & Telegraph Company, Brown-Foreman Distilleries, Chrysler Motors, General Motors, Standard Oil, and duPont. Similar stakes in the future of Big Business are possessed by many if not most other newspaper publishers, helping to explain the sincerity of their Old Dealism.

Newspaper Accuracy

Despite all of the circumstantial evidence, including that which has just been related, it is gross error to conclude that newspaper publishers are deliberately diabolical individuals who use their properties with malice aforethought to spread propaganda favorable to their economic interests. By comparison with any other occupational group one wishes to consider, they are sincere and ethical. They come by their conservatism naturally and honestly, and their indignation at insinuations that the contrary is the case is not feigned. Generalization is difficult, but it is a gross misrepresentation to categorize publishers as a class as conscious hypocrites whose prejudices the lowly reporter must observe in his diurnal reporting and writing of the news. In many if not most cases the exact opposite comes closer to being the truth: the "writing stiffs" through trial and error discover what kind of news publishers like best to read in their own newspapers and do their best to provide it. Since most publishers are smugly sincere, it is the reportorial underling who is more often consciously hypocritical. Happiest and perhaps most likely to succeed is the newsgatherer whose biases coincide with those of his boss. The urge to eat regularly, however, is a strong conditioning factor resulting in the rationalizations whereby what one must do anyway to survive becomes endurable.

Regardless of whether the staff indoctrination has been direct or subtle, most newspapers are put together by underlings with "What will please the old man?" uppermost in mind. Any reporter or desk man hesitates before giving prominent display to the mouthings of a rabid New Dealer if he happens to be working for a stalwart Old Guard Republican, or vice versa. With experience the hired hand comes to see and interpret events in the same way as do his superiors. It's no different than in any other business concern: wherever you work you have to learn to please to keep your job or to win promotion. To help you catch the spirit of the enterprise, there are pep talks, indoctrination courses, house organs and other devices "to build morale," *i.e.*, loyal employees who will do things the way management wants them done.

Under the title, "How Propaganda Finds Its Way Into the Press," in its Oct. 15, 1938, issue, the Chicago *Daily News* presented the following hypothetical case to illustrate how bias can color presentation of the news:

With rival sections of the class press, engaged in bitter recrimination over the publication of propaganda as unbiased news, you are invited this week to sit in and see just how the truth can be poisoned and converted into propaganda that meets the views of the publisher.

A reporter working against deadlines gathers the facts as he sees them and telephones those facts to his city desk. The man on the desk turns the reporter over to a rewriter, and in this article a fictitious labor story will be traced from its inception.

HERE ARE HYPOTHETICAL FACTS

The facts of this hypothetical story follow: The owners of the Blank Foundry at Dash street and Ogburn avenue refused to bargain collectively with their employes.

Three weeks ago a strike was called by the union which was an affiliate of the C.I.O.

Twelve men were picketing the plant.

No disorders of any kind had occurred up to today.

About 3 P.M. a police squad from the Cloud Street Station under the direction of Lt. Thomas Raider arrived at the plant and ordered the pickets to disperse because "you are blocking traffic."

The pickets refused.

The police went after them with swinging clubs. Four of the pickets were injured, two seriously, and taken to the County Hospital. Five other pickets were jailed for disorderly conduct.

Howard Bystander, a salesman, witness of the clash, said the police assaulted the pickets without ordering them to disperse. He also told how a policeman had beaten a picket unmercifully.

The striker in charge of the picket line also insisted the police had not ordered them to disperse.

The police refused to reveal the source of the complaint upon which they said they had acted.

Simple little story, isn't it? Below you'll see how these simple little facts can be twisted to demoniac proportions.

CLASS PRESS

An armed mob of C.I.O. strikers, carrying banners hailing communism, attacked a police squad at the strike-closed plant of the Blank Foundry, Dash street and Ogburn avenue, today and before order was restored four strikers were injured. Five others were jailed.

Police said they had been summoned to the plant on a telephone complaint that the enraged mob were strikers who were blocking traffic and threatening to seize physical control of the foundry.

As they approached, police spokesman said, they were met by a fusillade of rocks; then some of the strikers drew guns.

"I called to the strikers to drop their weapons," said Police Lt. Thomas Raider, who was in charge of the squad. "My call brought more rocks. I again pleaded with the men and when they again replied with rocks, I told the boys to disperse them.

"I'm very sorry we had to hurt four of them, but I think the police did their duty," added Lt. Raider. "After all, the police have no interest in these labor fights other than to see that the laws are enforced."

(SINCE YOU READERS ARE PRIVILEGED TO WITNESS THIS BIT OF FACT POISONING YOU MIGHT TOUCH THE REWRITER ON THE SHOULDER AND ASK HIM WHERE HE GOT ALL THIS STUFF, THAT THE REPORTER DIDN'T TELL HIM ANYTHING LIKE THAT AT ALL.)

Before the police went to the strike scene reports had come to the Cloud Street Station that C.I.O. agitators were fomenting trouble, that the strikers were being trained in army formations and instructed in the use of firearms.

As the rewriter finishes his lead it goes to the city desk. There it's read and passed along to the news editor with the suggestion that it would make a good story to put a line on.

The news editor agrees and marks the copy, "8-col. 96-pt. Gothic with one col. 30-pt. Gothic cap readout." The man in the slot (he's the head of the copy desk) next receives the story. He tosses it to a copyreader who does the editing and writes the heads.

This copyreader goes over the story, then begins playing with words for the eight-column line. He looks up suddenly and gazes contemplatively at the man in the slot, his immediate superior, then a smile flickers as he writes:

C.I.O. Mob Attacks Police

The count is right. Now for the readout:

> RED AGITATORS
> STAND ACCUSED
> OF INCITING MEN

The copyreader hands the story and heads to the slot man. Maybe a sardonic grin flashes as he sees the approval of his boss, but in about 20 minutes the paper's on the street and another crime against the reputable press of the nation has been committed.

UNBIASED

Four striking foundry workers were injured today in a clash at the gates of the Blank Foundry Company, Dash street and Ogburn avenue, when police used their clubs to disperse 12 pickets who were walking on the sidewalks near the foundry gate.

The injured men, all suffering from head contusions, were taken to the County Hospital, where physicians said two of them, William Jones of 23 West Thorn street, and James Howard of 69 West Dash street, may have suffered fractured skulls. The other two in the hospital were Thomas Joyce of 2236 Blank street and David Oval of 6453 Blank avenue.

Arrested and jailed in the Cloud Street Police Station, charged with disorderly conduct, were these four pickets: Carroll Judge and William Guest of 2654 Blank avenue; William James and Thomas Johnson of 6932 Blank street.

An eyewitness of the disorder, Howard Bystander, a salesman employed by the Oil Refining Company of 33 West Jason boulevard, said he protested to a policeman who was clubbing Jones while he lay on the sidewalk, and the policeman later identified as Patrolman Walter Tory, said, "Get the hell out of here or you'll get it, too."

Patrolman Tory termed Mr. Bystander's recital a "lie." In charge of the police squad was Lt. Thomas Raider. His version of the clash ran this way: "We received complaints that these picket guys were obstructing traffic, so we came down here and told them to go home. They wouldn't listen to reason, so we had to touch them up a bit. The police are here to enforce the laws and we're going to do just that, strike or no strike."

Tom Blank, secretary-treasurer of the Foundry Workers Union, a C.I.O. affiliate, who was in charge of the picketing, said after the fight:

"We had 12 pickets walking back and forth. They carried no banners of any kind and none was armed. We called this strike three weeks ago when our demands for collective bargaining were ignored despite the Wagner act.

"For the last week we had been getting warnings to quit picketing or the police would come over here and slug us. We naturally did nothing about the warnings because we were breaking no laws.

"This afternoon the squad car came up and ordered the men away from the plant. They refused and the police began to swing their clubs.

"I'm going to have our lawyers get writs to free the men held in jail and we'll likely file suit for damages against the city, but where politics and crime are bedfellows I fear we haven't much chance of collecting a penny."

This story also goes to the city desk. But on this paper the city desk has been instructed to be fair at all times, so the city editor passes it along to the news editor. He also knows that this publisher demands fairness and decency in the news, so he orders a one-column 30 point chelt. head and places the story on page 15. The head reads:

4 STRIKERS HURT
WHEN COPS SLUG
PLANT PICKETS

CLASS PRESS

Armed with riot guns and strike clubs, an enraged squad of police thugs, acting on orders from their capitalistic overlords, today interrupted the peaceful picketing of the Blank Foundry at Dash street and Ogburn avenue by beating four of the strikers so badly that they were taken to the County Hospital, where physicians indicated two of them would likely die.

If two more lives are sacrificed on the altars of capitalistic greed the

workers of Jonesville said they would petition President Roosevelt to send
in federal troops to patrol the strike zone.

The absurdity of the police assertion that they had been summoned to
the scene because the pickets were obstructing traffic was shown when it
was established that but 12 men were in the line at any time since the
strike was called three weeks ago after the company had repeatedly refused to recognize the existence of the Wagner act which compels collective bargaining.

When questioned as to the identity of the persons who had filed the
complaint, the police were evasive, saying no record had been kept of the
calls.

From sources close to the Cloud Street Police Station, whose officers
did the work of their capitalistic employers, came the information that the
foundry barons paid the police $5,000 to disperse the pickets.

This could not be confirmed for obvious reasons, but the source from
which it came has hitherto been most reliable.

Workers throughout the Jonesville district were incensed over the outrage and preparations were made for a march on the City Hall, where
redress will be demanded of Mayor Sketch.

One of the wounded pickets, William Jones, was beaten unmercifully
by the uniformed city-paid gunmen. He was knocked to the street and
kicked. As he pleaded with the policemen they laughed at him and continued to kick him.

When an onlooker went to his assistance he, too, was slugged; then the
assassins returned to their gory task of pounding Jones as he begged for his
life.

"Please, please, please," he begged, "don't kill me. I have a wife and
children. . . . Please."

As the last word came he was kicked in the mouth. Blood spurted to the
sidewalk. The police laughed. What did they care? Were not the united
forces of capitalism at their beck and call?

After the injured were taken to the hospital and the police had arrested
several pickets, the wives of the injured men appeared at the gates of the
foundry. They were weeping. Clutching their skirts were their children.

It was a pathetic picture.

The head that appeared over this story was this eight-column line:

Police Thugs Slug Pickets

The readout went like this:

COPS EMPLOYED
BY BOSSES TO
KILL WORKERS

There you have the story of how the truth can be twisted to fit the pattern of the publication in which it appears. First you have the violently

anti-labor newspaper; then you have the honest newspaper and third comes the ardent pro-labor publication.

Obviously the second, or unbiased, account is much to be preferred. The bothersome question remains, however: how is the reader to know what is the truth? The contradictory viewpoints of "both sides" are given; which is correct? Suppose there actually is a radical plot to seize or ruin a business property? Or an inhuman murderous design to crush and enslave labor? Can the reader, with only the so-called "objective" facts to go on, determine what the "realities" of the situation are? Jefferson notwithstanding, in our modern complex society, it is extremely difficult to do so, and it is hardly any easier after one has read two or more conflicting slanted accounts. One can test the judgment of a book reviewer, art or drama critic, or sports columnist by reading the book, and viewing the picture, play, or athletic event. He is utterly unable to do the same as regards the vast majority of news items on serious public affairs. Consequently, he is virtually at the mercy of the media of communication to tell him, first of all, what of the billions of occurrences the world over each day it is important for him to know about; how they compare in relative importance with each other, and what point of view he should take toward them. Similarly, the small-town editor is at the mercy of the three press associations (Associated Press, United Press, and International News Service) for determination of what is significant national and international news. Of critical studies of the handling by the American press of certain aspects of foreign news there have been many. Some of the most significant have been in the form of books by former foreign correspondents which include facts, interpretations, and conclusions often quite inconsistent with those which previously appeared in the publications for which the writers formerly reported. Notable recent examples include Leland Stowe's *While Time Remains* (Knopf, 1946), Theodore H. White and Annallee Jacoby's *Thunder Out of China* (William Sloane Associates, 1946), Richard Lauterbach's *Danger From the East* (Harper, 1947), Jack Belden's *China Shakes the World* (Harper, 1949), and George Seldes' *The People Don't Know* (Gaer, 1949).

After World War I Walter Lippmann and Charles Merz made a critical study of the handling of Russian news by the New York *Times,* which was published as a supplement to the *New Republic* for Aug. 4,

1920. The authors concluded: "The news as a whole is dominated by the hopes of the men who composed the news organizations. They began as passionate partisans in a great war in which their own country's future was at stake. Until the armistice they were interested in defeating Germany. They hoped until they could hope no longer that Russia would fight. When they saw she could not fight, they worked for intervention as part of the war against Germany. When the war with Germany was over, the intervention still existed. They found reasons then for continuing the intervention. The German Peril as the reason for intervention ceased with the armistice; the Red Peril almost immediately afterwards supplanted it. The Red Peril in turn gave place to rejoicing over the hopes of the White generals. When these hopes died, the Red Peril reappeared. In the large, the news about Russia is a case of seeing not what was, but what men wished to see. This deduction is more important, in the opinion of the authors, than any other. . . . The chief censor and the chief propagandist were hope and fear in the minds of reporters and editors." In *The Russian Soviet Republic* (Century, 1923), Edward A. Ross, eminent sociologist, summarized as follows: "In the course of a little over two years, the New York *Times* reported the fall of Petrograd six times, announced at least three times more that it was on the verge of capture, burned it to the ground twice, twice declared it in absolute panic, starved it to death constantly, and had it in revolt against the Bolsheviks six times, all without the slightest foundation in fact." The New York *Times*, everyone who studies it invariably explains, is selected because it is generally considered the best or at least almost the best American newspaper.

Reminiscent of the Lippmann-Merz study was the following from an address by Jenkin Lloyd Jones, editor of the Tulsa *Tribune*, before the Iowa Daily Press Association as reported in the January, 1949 *Nieman Reports*: "I wonder if we have not reached the point where we must consider the possible effects of panic in our nation. In the past 18 months the press and the radio of America have been keeping up an incessant war of nerves upon the American people. The traditional calmness of our people is beginning to be shaken. A lot of us are starting to paw the ground and roll our eyes like frightened horses at the smell of smoke from the haymow. This talk of a preventive war and how we ought to atomize Moscow and Leningrad in a sneak attack is not in the American tradition. It is not good old American aggressiveness. It is a symptom of unreasoning fear. . . .

"Our telegraph desks and our editorial writers compound the felony. The wire services, generally speaking, write and edit their news in a manner approved by their large city clients. And the large city newspaper is in competition with its rival for street sales. The emphasis is on the spot development, the new lead, the lead-all bulletin—anything that will make a banner headline to help sell a copy to the man hurrying by on the sidewalk.

"This type of wire reporting is admirable for its speed. It is punchy, terse and interesting. As far as it goes, it is usually accurate. But it often gives a fragmentary and unconnected account of the story behind the spot development. It lends itself to scare headlines. The reader has difficulty in reaching a fair appraisal of its true importance."

Jones suggested another reason why magazine articles and books written by foreign correspondents after they have returned from long assignments abroad are important: written with perspective they relate the events of a period, months or years, as a single, connected story. Daily newspaper accounts are of necessity fragmentary, and even the best efforts of editorial writers and columnists cannot "place" the isolated event with which the day's headlines are concerned in proper focus. Consequently it is the collective impression that a newspaper's handling of the news gives which is more important in its influence upon public opinion than the accuracy of any specific piece of reporting or interpretation.

In an address, "Does Freedom of the Press Work?" March 23, 1949, at the annual Matrix Table banquet sponsored by Theta Sigma Phi at the University of Oklahoma in Norman, Okla., the writer lauded the work of Bert Andrews for his exposé in the New York *Herald Tribune* of the undemocratic operations of the loyalty boards for which he won the 1948 Pulitzer, Sigma Delta Chi, and American Newspaper Guild awards. Then he pointed out:

"How different, however, has been altogether too much of the newspaper handling of loyalty board cases or of charges made by the House Committee on Un-American Activities or of spy hunts and red scares all over the country. . . .

"The first of the contemporary series of spy scares occurred within a month after V-E Day. It was called 'The Case of the Six,' the six being three journalists, a navy officer and two State department employes, all concerned with Far Eastern affairs. One New York newspaper heralded the first news that they were to appear before a federal grand jury with a page one, two-line, 120-point 8 col. streamer, 'Arrest of 6 Reveals Reds Got U.S. Secrets,' and a second New York paper had a comparatively modest one-line streamer, 'Spy Ring Linked to U.S. Reds.' Two months later the grand jury cleared three of the six and all that was charged against the others was indiscretion in aiding newspapermen to obtain exclusive stories based on material from government files, in accordance with a practice which every Washington correspondent knows is prevalent all over the capital. A year later a House Judiciary subcommittee completely cleared all six of revealing highly important secrets. The exonerations were not considered especially newsworthy by the same papers which had screamed so loudly at the beginning of the case.

"In March, 1946, there was the atomic spy ring scare; seven months later the chairman of the Un-American Activities committee had to admit soberly, 'We haven't been able to find any spies. In my opinion there are no spies at Oak Ridge.' That story was given a one-column headline on page 12 of a newspaper which had given the original charge an 8-col, page one, two-line streamer above its flag. In view of the disposition of that case at that time, when another newspaper in July, 1947 had a three-line page one streamer, 'Secret "A" Bomb Files Are Stolen from Oak Ridge,' the exclusive story generally was labeled 'hoatx' by most of its contemporaries. . . ."

In a report on organized violence against two audiences which attended concerts by Paul Robeson on Aug. 28 and Sept. 4, 1949, near Peekskill, N.Y., the American Civil Liberties Union concluded: "The local press bears the main responsibility for inflaming, possibly through sheer irresponsibility, Peekskill residents to a mood of violence." This the Peekskill *Evening Star* did through news stories and editorials prior to the first of the concerts which was planned to be held in Cortlandt, five miles from Peekskill, and which was open to the public only upon payment of an admission fee which ranged from $1.50 to $2.40. Most inflammatory editorial statement, which appeared in the issue of Aug. 23, was the following: "The time for tolerant silence that signifies approval is running out." Nevertheless, referring to the aftermath of the riots, the ACLU reported: "The early mood of jubilation has now almost totally evaporated. The braggart placards 'Wake Up America, Peekskill Did' have disappeared. A deep questioning has set in. This is mainly because the national press almost unanimously condemned Peekskill's actions." Consequently, in one situation was demonstrated the power of the press for both evil and good. A proportion of the same newspapers which condemned the Peekskill hoodlums contributed to the nation-wide unpopularity of Robeson by an incorrect report of his Paris speech, making him seem to say that most American Negroes are unpatriotic.

One reason why the collective effect of the press is uniform and strong is the "gentlemen's agreement" which prevents one newspaper from commenting upon the behavior of other newspapers. This abstemiousness developed with the commercialization of the press and superseded the so-called golden era of personal journalism during which rival editors resorted to almost unlimited vituperation and even came to blows physically. Today no newspaper likes to help publicize another, even with uncomplimentary comments. To a lesser extent the same policy applies as regards magazines, radio, and other media of communication which compete for a share of the same advertiser's dollar. Consequently, it was extremely unusual for *Life* in its Nov. 21, 1949, issue to print the following editorial, "Speaking of News":

"Last week the U.S. public was misled and insulted by a disgraceful abuse of the news. We refer to the latest scare over atomic security, involving charges that during the war years of 1943 and 1944 Henry A. Wallace and the late Harry Hopkins forced other officials to give the Soviet Union atomic information, atomic materials and secret equipment that it should not have received. A house subcommittee has examined the charges and indicated that they were not worthy of belief. Yet the affair persists in the news, with the promise of more investigations, more headlines, more radio alarms, all adding to the huge burden of unease that at best troubles the world nowadays.

"The story behind this episode should give pause to every publisher, news editor and radio executive in the land. It begins with George Racey Jordan, a former Air Force officer who claims to have evidence that there was a nefarious flow of secret equipment and information to the Russians through the Great Falls, Mont. air base, where Jordan was stationed for a time. On Nov. 16, 16 days before the public heard of him, Jordan came to the New York office of *Life* with his story. Our domestic news editor, our science editor and one of our best reporters, a man with long experience in military and security matters, heard the story and carefully examined the 'evidence' offered in support. *Life's* editors and reporter found that Jordan did not substantiate his story. We came to the same conclusion that Congressman Burr P. Harrison of Virginia reached after hearing the charges and counter-evidence in open hearings. Jordan's story was 'inherently incredible.' This is not recounted boastfully. Our point is that no reporter worth his salt and blessed with any discretion in the matter could have taken the charges seriously on the basis of what Jordan told and showed *Life*.

"But Jordan and his charges were taken seriously. Fulton Lewis, Jr., a commentator for the Mutual network, put Jordan on the air and added some charges of his own. This is not surprising. Fulton Lewis, Jr. is just the man to do just that. We wouldn't like to share the responsibility for his radio existence which is borne by the Mutual network, the 314 stations which carry his broadcasts, and the 475 local sponsors who pay him handsome sums.

"The Lewis broadcasts made Jordan and his charges 'news.' A House subcommittee, summoning Jordan to testify, made the news a 'must.' From that point on, Fulton Lewis, Jr. was of no importance. Reporters, editors, radiomen were caught in the toils of their own news processes. To their great discredit a few of those involved continued to pump up the story after its original elements had been disproved. But mostly the press just went along, reporting what was said and what was done—'the news.' Even the more responsible press became a mindless automaton, bereft of discretion and adding willy-nilly to the national alarms.

"Here is a problem for all the press, not excluding *Life*. How to use the mind? How to exercise the duty and power of choice without 'suppressing' or 'distorting' the news? These are hard questions that nobody has completely answered. All concerned in press and radio will do well to ponder the problem, and in particular to reexamine a system which all too often allows no pause for reflection and examination, once an event or an allegation has taken on the compelling quality of 'news.'

"As for Fulton Lewis, Jr., the broadcasters and sponsors who bring him and others of his breed to the millions might get together and have a little talk of their own. They have a lot to answer for."

In its issue of Jan. 9, 1950, *Life* revealed that 351 of 381 letters in comment had been adversely critical of the magazine's viewpoint. By publication time for the issue of Jan. 30, 1950, the score was 52 pro and 428 con. Once formed, listening as well as reading habits are hard to break. Radio commentators and columnists are heroes to many of their followers who resent slurs against their favorites. To confess that one's idol has feet of clay is, of course, tantamount to admitting that one's own judgment has been wrong.

The Press and the "Spirit of the Times"

To accuse the press of having instigated the war agitation and name calling of the post-World War II period would be an act of gross scapegoating. That the newspapers, with few exceptions, aided and abetted the witch hunting, however, cannot be denied. In any social situation in which there is an interaction of forces, it is impossible to discover clearcut causes and effects. In the "whoopee" twenties the press both mirrored and encouraged the public clamor for "bigger and better" thrills by exaggerated coverage of homecomings for returning heroes (Charles Lindbergh, Gertrude Ederle, Admiral Byrd, etc.); of receptions for visiting celebrities (Queen Marie of Rumania was the most widely press-agented); of competitive skyscraper buildings (notably the Empire State versus Chrysler Building story); of grandiloquent and more grandiloquent world fairs, and of all the other extravaganzas of the era of speculative Coolidge prosperity. On their own the newspapers press agented a series of "crimes of the century" —Loeb-Leopold, Hall-Mills, Snyder-Gray, Hauptmann—and "battles of the century"—Dempsey vs Carpentier, Dempsey vs Tunney, Sharkey vs Schmeling. The hysterical journalism of the twenties was "in tune with the times."

In the sober thirties the press responded to the universal demand for explanation. After the depression hit, bewildered victims at first turned to editorial pages, but these dull anachronisms proved unsatisfactory. So did interviews with and articles by nonjournalistic experts, including academic brain trusters. The answer was found in the new cult of the columnist. Ended was the anonymity characteristic of corporate journalism since the turn of the century. The newly famous by-liners helped satisfy the normal quest for personal leadership in times of distress. Once their value in meeting psychological needs was apparent, the columnists multiplied like mushrooms. They continued as a fixture as war and postwar jitters kept alive a necessary interest in alleged "inside dope." They and their radio commentator counterparts pontificate very lucratively although anyone who bothered to keep a box score on the runs, hits and errors of their prophetic analyses soon would realize that they have little or no greater knowledge or perception than the overwhelming majority of their readers. Any writer who develops an attractive style, however, will be read by enough people to provide him with a comfortable living. The best columns are highly quotable and there is prestige value in being able to pose as a persistent reader of any of them. Furthermore, anyone who reads a column regularly can enjoy the self-delusion of being well informed. Naturally readers pick their columnists as they do their radio commentators; that is, they prefer those with whom they most often agree. Shortly after the end of World War II an important development was the dropping of all but the most conservative columnists or the intimidation of erstwhile liberals to cause them either to deal in platitudes or to turncoat. A similar purge quickly cleared the air of all but conservative radio commentators, so the reader or listener in search of a prophet had little choice. In *Your Newspaper* the 1945–46 Nieman fellows wrote: "In practice the columnists with very few exceptions are just about as conservative or as liberal as the papers which employ or publish them. One has only to study the columns when some crucial issue arises, such as the 1946 coal and railroad strike and the accompanying hysteria for anti-labor legislation, to see how similar a tune most of the columnists sing. Columnists know that their freedom has limits; if they disagree with their paper's editorial policies too often or too widely, they are apt to find their columns being dropped. A good case in point is Thomas Stokes, the Scripps-Howard columnist who has been much too liberal for Roy Howard and some of Howard's editors. Howard's New York *World-Telegram* in one ten-week period in 1946 killed 18 of Stokes' columns —columns which were critical of Republicans, regretted the scuttling of Wilson Wyatt's housing program, reported big businessmen's attempts to get rid of trust-buster Wendell Berge, warned of the revival of German cartels by American industrialists, urged that a common meeting ground be found with Russia, spoke well of Franklin Roosevelt and his son James. Stokes' columns were so often suppressed that he asked to be relieved of his contract with the chain so that he might sell the column to individual papers that wanted it. But Scripps-Howard refused; it reserved the right to kill his columns when it didn't like them and at the same time prevent its competitors from getting Stokes." [2]

Crime news. Although the Uniform Crime Reports of the Federal Bureau of Investigation (which contains the best statistics available on lawbreaking in the United States) showed no appreciable falling off of crimes of violence, while the nation was at war crime news occupied much less space than is customary in peacetime. It just got crowded out by the bloody reports from battlefronts and capitals which naturally were of greater concern to readers than murders and rapes in which the number of victims was infinitesimal by comparison with the casualties of war. Once the wholesale slaughter was over, however, the stranglers and poisoners and trigger-happy again received the journalistic attention to which they had become accustomed in prewar days. Let two similar crimes occur in the same vicinity and it frequently was interpreted as signifying a "wave" and each new perpetrator of whatever type of offense happened to attract the editorial eye became the community's "newest" or "latest" problem. It does criminologists no good to point to the statistics which invariably show that crimes do not occur in waves; only news interest does that. Belief to the contrary, the result of newspaper sensationalism in regard to one or a series of offenses has led to more than one shakeup in law enforcement agencies, creation of new courts or branches of courts, additional ordinances, statutes and laws.

While on the subject of crime news it must be stated that in one important respect there has been great improvement. As much or more space still is devoted to such news, and accounts contain as many scandalous details as ever. The privacy of innocent persons still is invaded unnecessarily, and judges and potential jurors still are prejudiced by newspaper accounts. Nevertheless, no longer do most newspapers inflame the populace to lynching madness. During the summer of 1947 the writer happened by when the notorious William Heirens was re-enacting his murder of Suzanne Degnan on Chicago's

[2] From *Your Newspaper.* Copyright, 1947, by The Macmillan Co.

north side. A huge crowd silently followed and watched sullenly. It was interested and resentful, but there was no danger of violence. Why? Because, despite the printing of much rumor as fact, wholesale pretrial of the case, and overplaying of the sensational, Chicago newspapers had abandoned preachment of the Mosaic law of vengeance. Instead, their editors had become influenced sufficiently by psychiatry to cause them to emphasize the certainty that there must be something wrong with a person who would commit such horrible acts. Thus, a tremendously important lesson had been learned. Today reporters go to psychiatrists for help, not, as a few years ago, to phrenologists and other quacks (see pages 239 to 241). In reporting a heinous offense, they usually raise the question, "What in his life history is responsible?" The editorial finger is pointed at parents, teachers, juvenile authorities, and the community as a whole. Many, probably most, of the explanations and suggested solutions still are ridiculous; but there has developed a laudable attempt to have the right attitude and approach. The journalistic understanding still is crude; the press, for instance, has changed the meaning of "moron" from "high-grade mental defective" to "sexual pervert," and it has fallacious ideas about the antisocial tendencies of the feebleminded. However, abandonment of the belief in force and punishment as the only correctives is a sizeable step in the right direction. In this respect, of course, the press also is "in tune with the times" as World War II gave great impetus to public interest in psychiatry, if for no other reason than the dramatic incident of Gen. George Patton's slapping a neurotic soldier. The efforts of the National Society for Mental Hygiene, since its founding by Clifford Beers in 1909, also have played a part as the 48 affiliated state societies have as one of their chief aims "working on" the press to increase its enlightenment.

Albert Deutsch, outstanding newspaper columnist, magazine writer, and book author who specializes in mental health topics, directed attention to a contemporary journalistic practice in the Dec. 8, 1948 New York *PM* as follows:

The campaign against child delinquency erupts now and then into a "One Cause, One Cure" fad that captures the popular imagination, sends many of us chasing another scapegoat and winds up by leaving us all exhausted, more confused than ever and not a little ashamed. Right now the child-delinquency scapegoat happens to be comic books. . . . I am certain that if every last comic book in America were destroyed tomorrow, the child crime problem still would be with us.

Deutsch was directing his barbs at some newspapers which were making it a practice to inquire about the comic book reading habits of every child who got his name in the newspapers for some misbehavior. At other times it is broken homes that are supposed to be the "one cause" although Chicago Area Project studies reveal that children of divorced or separated parents are no more prone to lawbreaking than others. In good times miscreant children are said to have too much money provided by overindulgent parents; in bad times they are motivated to crime, it also is explained, because of a lack of spending money. Social scientists still are seeking the proper answer but are less prone than newspapers to ride hobbies.

Science news. About the same can be said of the newspapers' handling of science as of their treatment of news of crime: it is better from the standpoint of the scientists. The change also has occurred because of influences outside the newspapers themselves. Over the years the press has been no more ahead of the times in this field than in any others, and less than a generation ago science news was played only for its sensationalism. Scientists were reluctant to talk to reporters, trusting neither their intelligence nor their intentions. Too often they observed their serious reports garbled or exaggerated, often by newsroom humorists who liked to speculate as to whether their interviewees really believed their great grandmothers were apes or were planning to spend their next holiday on the moon or Mars. The reporter who once asked Dr. Robert A. Millikan what cosmic rays are "good for" typified what, until comparatively recently, most scientists understandably thought most newspapermen were like.

Newspapers did not start taking science seriously until the general public started to take it seriously. As long as the religiously fundamental seemed to be in a sizeable majority, the press as a whole treated the subject of evolution about as gingerly as it now treats something like the Cardinal Spellman-Mrs. Eleanor Roosevelt exchange of pleasantries. When, however, the automobile and, especially, the radio made a new generation of school children gadget-conscious, popular interest in science became widespread. Magazines glamorizing science grew in popularity and editors' kids increasingly embarrassed their dads with questions which the middle-aged could not even understand, much less answer. Airplanes are airplanes to most non-World War II veterans, but it was a rare fourth grader who couldn't identify flying craft by type, name, and number, sometimes merely by their sound. And then came radar and television and the atomic and hydrogen bombs. As a result superlative reverence replaced gross irreverence. For a while after Hiroshima almost every high school science laboratory assistant was considered somewhat of an authority on matters atomic, and no scientific claim, no matter how crackpot, went unnoticed. At mid-century the press' understanding of pure science still was erratic, but the journalistic intentions were good. What was lacking was enough science writers with the ability to capitalize upon the potential reader interest.

The Press and the Mores

The ignorance, timidity or whatever it is that causes the press to be a little or quite a bit behind the times, rarely if ever ahead of them, in matters criminological and scientific, is characteristic of its conservatism in most or all other fields. The traditional political conservatism of the press has been mentioned, and in numerous references to the press in preceding chapters what is perhaps its most important social effect was implied if not directly stated. That is its effective exercise of the role of upholder of the mores. As a review of several earlier chapters, especially Chapter 7, "Taboos; Superstitions," will make clear, the press obeys and perpetuates most of the twentieth-century taboos, superstitions, myths and legends, traditions, and moral precepts. Never does it offend public taste if it can avoid doing so. The great caution it exercises is shown by the fact that it is only within a decade that gruesome pictures of automobile accidents have become customary; and this innovation was preceded by a dramatic descriptive article in a popular magazine ("And Sudden Death," by J. C. Furnas, *Reader's Digest,* August, 1935) which broke the literary ice. About the same time the press began to assist the surgeon general in his campaign to break down the taboos which prevented attacking venereal diseases as a medical rather than as a strictly moral problem. Led by the McCormick papers, the Chicago *Daily Tribune* and the New York *Daily News,* the press started using the words "venereal disease," "syphilis," and "gonorrhea." It was ready to draw back fast if public reaction was adverse, but it continued when it "got away" with it. Today papers even say "rape" for what only a short while ago was "statutory offense" or "criminal attack."

Primitive taboos persist as modern superstitions and are much more widespread than commonly recognized. As was pointed out in Chapter 7, fortune telling, astrology, numerology, and similar pseudosciences are huge businesses. Newspapers aid and abet rather than discourage them and thus contribute to perpetuation of states of mind inimical to all forms of human progress. Most papers of any size carry daily horoscopes for the benefit of the gullible. Editors have an avidity for stories of supposed modern miracles or visions. They play up supposed examples of the efficacy of prayer and feature freakish examples of religious sites or symbols untouched by fires or storms. When a prominent person meets an accidental death, especially in an air crash, a stock reportorial question is whether he had a premonition.

The Newspaper as Entertainment

In "The Threat to American Newspapers" in the June 30, 1945 *Saturday Review of Literature,* R. E. Wolseley directed attention to a danger which he considered more important than "the usual bogies: television, facsimile, frequency modulation radio and another financial depression," and explained: "This danger to the life of our newspaper is the non-news material. Under the present trend the post-war newspapers may be converted into daily or weekly magazines with newspaper format. Charm columns, comics, cartoons, short stories, puzzles, and scores of other typical magazine ingredients which now shove news into the background may before long shove news out of the paper altogether."

Examining a small New England daily, Wolseley found that only 189 of a total of 1,320 inches of space "available for all kinds of copy, included advertising," was given to news. Even if the example is extreme, the trend is unmistakable, as any city editor crying for room in which to relate what is happening in his community knows. Only a handful of newspapers with limited and specialized circulations, notable among which are the New York *Times* and the *Christian Science Monitor,* have resisted the temptation to broaden subscriber appeal by a quantity of non-news material. Newspapers still correctly insist that their principal excuse for being is to report news, but the loyalty of many subscribers is held by the pictorial serials (erroneously called comic strips), short stories, advice to the lovelorn columns, health columns, gossip columns, "how to" columns, crossword puzzles, and other entertainment features. Much of this copy is instructional and, through utilization of the service usually offered of obtaining personal answers to letters or booklet information on how to prepare for motherhood, rear a family, cook, sew or garden, readers who otherwise might remain ignorant of such matters are enlightened. The chief function of such voluminous space fillers, however, is to provide entertainment and opportunities for escapism from the unpleasant realities of what otherwise might be a humdrum existence. Thus, in this respect, the press supplements or competes with a quantity of "thrill" magazines and cheap fiction, low-grade motion pictures, and slapstick radio programs. The therapeutic value of such vicarious adventure-seeking was considered in the section on cheap literature (see pages 464 to 465). Of importance in consideration of the effect upon public opinion of the newspaper's performance as chronicler of the news is this fact: much of the contents of the strictly news columns is presented in such a way as to produce the same effect as the non-news entertainment material. That is, it provides not "the truth that shall set men free" but a hopped-up picture of what life is like. Take, for instance, the following news story which obtained nationwide play:

Omaha, Neb.—(UP)—The girl from Michigan and the boy across the aisle, strangers when they boarded a cross-country train Monday, met on Wednesday and are now man and wife.

"I knew from the moment I saw her I was going to trap her somehow," said Marine Cpl. Floyd Simonis, 23, of Milwaukee.

"I had already made up my mind to say yes if he asked me to marry him," said Mary Ella Taunt, 19, of Flint, Mich. "Well, he asked me."

"TALKED WITH EYES"

"We did most of the talking with our eyes," said Simonis. "Across the aisle."

Both boarded the train at San Francisco, taking opposite aisle seats.

"I was bashful," explained Simonis. It was two days before, with considerable urging by Joe Burns, 45, a merchant seaman from Brooklyn, he got up courage to cross the aisle.

SETTLED IN 2 HRS.

In two hours, it was all settled.

"When he told me he loved me and asked me to marry him when

we got to Chicago," Miss Taunt said, "I told him I couldn't wait that long."

They got off the train at Omaha Friday night and dashed to the courthouse for a license. County Clerk Joe Belitz wouldn't issue one because Miss Taunt was only 19 and didn't have her parents' consent.

The couple thumbed a ride across the Missouri River to Council Bluffs, Iowa, where the age of consent is 18.

They were married by Frank Larsen, justice of the peace.

After a night in Omaha, the couple entrained for Flint to see Mary Ella's parents. They will visit his mother at Milwaukee later.

In Flint, the bride's father, J. C. Taunt, an insurance agent, said the news was a "shock and a complete surprise."

"What's done is done," he said. "We're just hoping that he's a good guy. We think a lot of our daughter."

—Chicago *Sun-Times,* Feb. 20, 1949

Considered as an isolated news story the foregoing provides pleasant, amusing, even thrilling diversion from the serious happenings of the day. It not only allows readers a brief chance to take their minds off their own troubles or those of the rest of the world, but it also enables those in psychological need of it to share vicariously in a romantic experience.

That is typical of what may be said about this particular story. What, however, about the cumulative effect of similar stories—stories which also give a glamorized picture of society—day after day, month after month? Statesmen and others interested in international good will frequently complain because of the impression that American motion pictures and news sent abroad make upon foreigners. Advocates of the government-sponsored Voice of America radio broadcast and of government-operated world-wide news services contend that the commercial news agencies must traffic mostly in sensationalism at the expense of more serious information regarding American life. It is easy to understand how denizens of other countries obtain a warped opinion of the United States from viewing our movies or reading only of our lynchings, gang warfares and silly activities. But what about the effect upon Americans of the same kind of journalistic diet? If the psychiatrists are correct in condemning the hurly burly of contemporary American life as conducive to frustrations and mental disorders, how is frenetic journalism to be evaluated?

On the one hand it can be contended that the escapism it makes possible is a preventive of neuroses; on the other, that by making life seem so exciting to so many, it intensifies the feelings of inferiority of those whose lots seem drab and uninteresting by comparison. In either case the chances of public opinion formation on the basis of a realistic conception of public affairs are reduced when what, in journalistic circles, is called the "human interest" appeal, is overemphasized. Reading of the more serious parts of the newspaper becomes less likely or such news also is sensationalized to enable it to compete for interest with the more trivial. Just as the radio commentator who intersperses his comments with sounds suggesting telegraph machines or who is almost breathless no matter what he has to report, newspapers create an exaggerated impression of events with large, perhaps colored, headlines, overdrawn and detailed accounts, and plentiful use of descriptive adjectives.

For most American newspapers during the summer of 1949 the romance of Ingrid Bergman and Roberto Rossellini was front-page news. In February, 1950, when a son was born to them before Ingrid had been able to obtain a divorce from Dr. Peter Lindstrom, it would have taken the dropping of a hydrogen bomb or the commission of hara-kiri by President Truman to have robbed the unconventional couple of its place in the streamer headlines. By contrast, a prominent Swedish editor explained to Dean Kenneth E. Olson of the Medill School of Journalism of Northwestern University in August, 1949: "We carried the story of her making this *Stromboli* picture some time ago and anything that concerns Ingrid's movie career is news. But this unfortunate affair, that's her private affair—it's not news and we don't use it."

In defense of the lavish treatment accorded Ingrid's indiscretion in the American press, some argued that it is good to publicize sin as a warning for others. Editorially however, *Editor & Publisher* in its Feb. 11, 1950, issue complained that the American press hardly had succeeded in making sin unattractive. The first paragraph of its comment, which was entitled "Nauseated!" was as follows: "After reading the newspapers during the last week we have the distinct impression that for a woman to have a child by one man while she is still legally married to another is the most romantic and glamorous thing in the world." Seven of eight persons answered in the negative the question, "Do you think Ingrid Bergman should be refused re-entry into this country?" asked by Dottie Justin in her "Inquiring Reporter" column in the Feb. 7, 1950 Miami Beach *Morning Mail*. Typical comments were: "I think that the press is making a mountain out of a molehill and persecuting Miss Bergman just because she is a celebrity," "The publicity Miss Bergman is getting is unfair and unkind," "I'm for Miss Bergman one hundred per cent and I admire her spirit and guts in telling the world that she's in love," "She hasn't done anything that thousands of Americans don't do all the time," "I'm terribly sorry for Miss Bergman," and "I think it's a darn shame that Ingrid Bergman happens to be in the limelight and has to face this adverse criticism."

Some persons of influence prefer to operate "behind the scenes" and shun publicity. Most entertainers, politicians, business and civic leaders, however, realize that they need the limelight to remain important. Even unfavorable publicity is better than none at all. The most effective treatment consequently that a newspaper can give someone whom it dislikes is to ignore him. That is what the Chicago *Daily Tribune* did for years to former Mayor William Hale Thompson. Instead of his name, the expression "a former mayor" was used whenever essential to a story.

Comic Strips

One of the most venerable of the non-news type of entertainment features is the so-called comic strip. Once they appeared only in supplements known as "funny papers" which were published only on Sundays. They were read by youngsters sprawled on a rug or by adults who grumbled at "having" to read them aloud to the children. Today, four out of every five newspaper readers, or almost 70 million persons, read them. The huge syndicates that handle them claim that next to the front page news, it's the comics that sell papers. Sixty per cent of the income of the vast Hearst empire is attributed to comics owned by Hearst's King Features syndicate.

The effect that comic books have upon the reading habits and consequently the attitudes of children was discussed in Chapter 12 (see pages 469 to 472). In its February, 1950, issue *Parents' Magazine* published the results of research by a Committee on Evaluation of Comic Books in Cincinnati, in the form of an article, "Cincinnati Rates the Comic Books," by Jesse L. Murrell. The "box score" for 555 comic books studied was: 165 no objection; 154 some objection; 167 objectionable, and 69 very objectionable. According to Jane

McMaster in "Comic Ratings Bring Comment About Taboos," in the Feb. 11, 1950 *Editor & Publisher:* "About 97 of the comic magazines featured newspaper comic characters, the majority of these consisting of reprints of newspaper strips. A breakdown of the 97 is: 34 without objection; 31 with some objection; 26 objectionable, and six very objectionable. This gave a total of 67 per cent of comic books featuring newspaper characters deemed suitable for children—or about 10 per cent cleaner than the average run of comic books surveyed." The standards used by the Cincinnati group in its evaluation were grouped under the headings, "cultural area," "moral area," and "morbid emotionality." The criteria under the first classification, typical of those for the other two, were as follows: *No objection*—good art work, printing and color arrangement; good diction; the over-all effect pleasing; any situation that does not offend good taste from the viewpoint of art or mechanics; *some objection*—poor art work, printing and color arrangement; mechanical setup injurious to children's eyes; print too small; art work too crowded; poor grammar, underworld slang; undermining in any way traditional American folkways; *objectionable*—propaganda against or belittling traditional American institutions; obscenity, vulgarity, profanity or the language of the underworld; prejudice against class, race, creed or nationality; divorce treated humorously or as glamorous; sympathy with crime and the criminal as against law and justice; criminals and criminal acts made attractive; *very objectionable*—an exaggerated degree of any of the above-mentioned acts or scenes.

In a letter to Peter E. Fitzsimmons, advertising director of the United Feature Syndicate, in reply to an inquiry inspired by the report, the Rev. Mr. Murrell gave an "A" rating to Fritzi Ritz Comics but said of some of the others: "In the case of Sparkler Comics, Tarzan gets a low rating because of the fact that animals are after him and attacking him. . . . There's a frightening experience which the child goes through which may crop out in dreams or in later life. . . . Concerning the Captain and the Kids, our reviewers thought the dialect in this story rated 'some objection.' "

Miss McMaster quoted Harold Straubing, comics editor of the New York *Herald Tribune* Syndicate, as saying: "It's a terrible thing if pressure groups out of ignorance push comic books back even as much as ten years because they are so valuable as a means of communication and learning . . . nobody bothers to investigate the person who is criticizing; when it comes to the comics, every Carrie Nation who waves a hatchet makes everybody tremble." Several syndicate officials emphasized the force of taboos which keep comic strips in line. For instance, Ward Greene, editor and general manager of King Features Syndicate, said: "Cagney can push a grapefruit in a woman's face in the movies, but it couldn't happen in the comics. Though Maggie has landed a lot of crockery on Jiggs' head, he has not struck her once." Summarized Miss McMaster: "While syndicates are responsive to legitimate criticism, they say they frequently receive far fetched complaints. Sometimes, they even act on these. A pig named 'Luther' in a King strip was displeasing to a lot of Lutherans. When a scientist in 'Little Annie Rooney' advocated a knowledge of the stars and nature, complaints came in saying that praising science was praising Communism. A rejuvenation machine in one strip brought in a reader reprimand that the only place where one can be rejuvenated is in Heaven. A garden of plenty in 'Uncle Remus' seemed somehow, to some readers, communistic."

The October, 1950 *Parents' Magazine* revealed that "comic books are being improved according to findings by the Committee on Evaluation of Comic Books in Cincinnati." Whereas in February 57.47 per cent of these magazines were suitable for children and young people, 69 per cent made that rating in the follow-up review.

When Joe Palooka enlisted in the army in 1939 and became the first comic strip character to don a uniform, President Roosevelt paid homage to the importance of comic strips by personally thanking the artist, Ham Fisher. A Sunday speech by Flip Corkin in "Terry and the Pirates" inspired newspaper editorials and was read into the *Congressional Record*. The United States Treasury commandeered the help of the comics for the sale of war bonds. Drives for the Red Cross and United Service Organizations and for scrap collections were boosted by comic strip characters.

Evidence of the cultural influence of comic strips is not difficult to uncover. Sadie Hawkins Day, a sort of annual leap-year day, first celebrated in Li'l Abner's village of Dogpatch, has become an institution on the campuses of many colleges, in high schools and towns. Blondie has given the nation the mountainous Dagwood sandwich. "Bringing Up Father" inspired Dinty Moore restaurants specializing in corned beef and cabbage, and hamburger stands have been christened for Popeye's ever hungry Wimpy. American slang has been enriched with a long list of expressions which originated with comic characters: hot dog, thanks for the buggy ride, baloney, banana oil, horsefeathers, hotsy totsy, sweet mamma, heeby jeebies, jeep, and schmoo, to mention some of the most popular. Polly and her Pals, Winnie Winkle, Tillie the Toiler, Dixie Dugan, Brenda Starr, and others have helped set feminine styles by portraying the latest and smartest to every town and crossroads. The glamor girls of the future who decorate the Flash Gordon strip have popularized the upswept hairdo, bare midriff playsuits, and wedgies.

Not so harmless is the occasional influence of the comics on the young. One boy had to have 16 stitches taken in his mouth after he tried to bite off the top of a can of spinach as Popeye does. Another fell 30 feet on his head while trying to fly like Superman. Adults, however, often take the comics as seriously as the kids. For instance, when Blondie was expecting, Artist Chic Young offered $50 for a name and received 400,000 suggestions along with copious advice on how to rear babies. Dick Tracy, wounded, was showered with notes of sympathy and even got an offer of a blood transfusion. When Little Orphan Annie lost her dog, Artist Harold Grey received this telegram: "Please do all you can to help Annie find Sandy. We are interested." It was signed Henry Ford.

So real do comic characters become to many readers that rarely does an artist take what would be the easiest way to get rid of one no longer useful to him; that is, by having him die. It took years for thousands to forgive Sidney Smith, creator of "The Gumps," for allowing Mary Gold to succumb to an illness, and it was a long time before anyone else dared to do anything of the same sort again. Then, Smitty's father was brought back to life after a long period in which he presumably was dead. When Milton Caniff killed off Raven Sherman, students at Loyola University in Chicago held funeral services for the mythical character.

For the record, the first colored comic appeared Sunday, Nov. 18, 1894 in the New York *World*. It was by Richard F. Outcault and consisted of a six-box series of funny pictures entitled "The Origin of the Species." It was the predecessor of "The Yellow Kid" which Outcault shortly thereafter began drawing for Hearst. Meanwhile the

Katzenjammer Kids was created for another New York paper. All of these, and other early strips—Buster Brown, Little Nemo, Foxy Grandpa, Happy Hooligan and others—lived up to their name. That is, they tried at least to be funny. Most of them, furthermore, told a complete story in a single installment. Although the characters remained the same and their experiences were in keeping with their personalities, it was not until a generation later that the trend toward straight serialized storytelling—the continuity strip—began. Chief credit for giving it impetus goes to Frank King whose "Gasoline Alley" turned into a pictorial chronicle of the life of Skeezix, first introduced as a foundling on bachelor Uncle Walt's doorstep on Valentine's Day, 1921. Whereas most comic strip characters, even today, remain the same age year after year, Skeezix has matured with the passage of time, has served in the war, married, and become a father himself. When his second child was born May 15, 1949, the Chicago *Daily Tribune* announced it in a serious page-one article.

Intentional or accidental omission of a single day's episode of a popular comic strip brings more inquiries and complaints to a newspaper than would overlooking almost any potential news item or commission of any kind of journalistic sin. During a printers' strike in New York the late Mayor Fiorello LaGuardia read the comic strips over the radio. Seldom do the strips, with the notorious exception of Little Orphan Annie, attempt to propagandize. In September, 1947, however, the Pittsburgh *Press* omitted "Li'l Abner" for a week, resulting in more than 700 letters to Al Capp, cartoonist. In an open letter to Edward T. Leech, the *Press'* editor, Capp protested as follows:

"Mr. Leech has the right not to read 'Li'l Abner' himself. But if Mr. Leech really believes in freedom of the press—if his attitude isn't phony—instead of constantly beefing and griping about the story in print—instead of mutilating it and censoring it—he ought to turn 'Li'l Abner' loose so that some other Pittsburgh paper can print it and you people can get a chance to read it."

The paper's viewpoint was expressed Sept. 18, 1947 in an editorial entitled, "Li'l Abner vs The Editor," as follows:

The variety of problems which can arise on a newspaper is almost endless.

For instance, answering questions about what happened to this week's installment of Li'l Abner.

Our explanation that it was omitted because it was objectionable seems to have whetted the curiosity of a good many readers. Some even objected that Li'l Abner is being denied freedom of speech and press.

Well, there's nothing secret or mysterious—so perhaps a fuller explanation is in order.

This week's installment revolved around a burlesque of the U.S. Senate. The central figure is Senator Phogbound of Dogpatch—illiterate, corrupt and moronic.

The trouble was that the artist didn't stop with Senator Phogbound but made all his senatorial associates of the same type. The Senate is pictured as an assortment of boobs and undesirables.

In order to get Phogbound's vote against a bill to broadcast Senate proceedings ("You realize what monkeys we'll sound like if the folks back home can actually hear us on the air") Phogbound's senatorial associates want to know his "price" for voting with them.

Finally Senator Phogbound is bribed with a two-million-dollar appropriation for a university to be named for him. He salves his conscience with the thought that "that's a high price—but it isn't my money—it's just taxpayers' money."

The week's continuity ends with the Dogpatch senator returning home to present the university to his constituents. In addition to the burlesque of Congress, the continuity also contained a double-meaning statement so obvious that we considered it vulgar.

Practically all children read comics.

We don't think it is good editing or sound citizenship to picture the Senate as an assemblage of freaks and crooks.

There already are too many efforts to weaken faith in American institutions.

A comic artist's product is sold on the basis that it is interesting, comical or entertaining—and in good taste. We thought this week's Li'l Abner episode in bad taste.

Therefore the various responsible editorial executives, after discussing the matter, decided to give Li'l Abner the air till he gets back to a point more in keeping with the qualities for which the feature was purchased.

Among the most important effects of the comic strips is their perpetuation of familiar stereotypes. Their characters are mostly social types, commonest among them being the Jew, Negro, English lord, newly rich, orphan, cripple, scheming widow, nosy boardinghouse keeper, interfering mother-in-law, rich uncle, soldier of fortune, kidnapper, spy, and philosophic child of about ten years of age. The

Negro is always the shuffle-footed Uncle Tom, the Chinese always has a long pigtail and speaks pidgin English, and the Englishman invariably is a dignified appearing nobleman who doesn't quite understand what's going on around him. Since the comics are among the first pictures that a young child sees, during his most impressionable years, the lasting effect of this form of journalistic "art" is properly a matter of concern.

Cartoons

Even though they no longer are primarily humorous, comic strips are intended to provide entertainment. Their characters and plots are fictional and they avoid the controversial issues of real life. By contrast cartoons are pictorial editorials published with the timely purpose of influencing readers' opinions regarding the contents of the news columns. Their characters are recognizable, usually labeled caricatures of real persons in the news and/or symbols representing individuals, groups (including nations), issues, and ideas. Usually they satirize, ridicule or in some other way attack something; seldom do they praise or exalt except for the purpose of belittling someone or something else. Hence, they thrive only in a atmosphere of political freedom and flourish best in times of intense controversy. In the United States no person or institution is immune from attack by cartoonists, not even the president or the Supreme Court, although reverence is accorded the traditional American institutions in which publishers believe. Appearing regularly on either the editorial or front page, sometimes on both, political cartoons have a readership considerably higher than formal editorials and serious articles on public affairs. They are quicker to read and easier to understand as they reduce a subject to the simplest and fewest details. The symbols are either familiar ones in the public domain—such as Uncle Sam, John Bull, the Russian bear, Democratic donkey, Republican elephant, et cetera—or are carefully labeled to assist understanding.

No calibrating machine has been invented to record the extent or intensity of the effect of cartoons any more than it is possible to measure exactly the impact of any other factor in the determination of public opinion. Nevertheless, there is enough empirical evidence to establish the fact of the historical and contemporary importance of this form of graphic journalism. Although caricatures (distorted representations of an individual) are known to have existed as early as the fourteenth century B.C., cartooning as we know it today got its start in the seventeenth century A.D. following the invention of printing. It flourished first in art-conscious and politically free Holland and spread to other parts of the continent and to England.

Generally believed to have been the first American cartoon, certainly one of the first to be of influence, was "Join or die" by Benjamin Franklin in the May 9, 1754 issue of his *Pennsylvania Gazette*. It used a dissected snake to signify the lack of unity between the American colonies and was widely reprinted and copied to aid the fight for independence. With the end of the Era of Good Feeling in the early 1820's political debate became more acrimonious and so did the cartoons used as weapons in the fight. By Civil War days the political cartoon was a fixture in the popular magazines, and the first great American cartoonist, still considered by many to be unsurpassed by any who have succeeded him, appeared. He was Thomas Nast, most of whose work appeared in *Harper's Weekly*. Of him Abraham Lincoln said, "He is our best recruiting sergeant," and Gen. U. S. Grant remarked, "Two things elected me: the sword of Sheridan and the pencil of Thomas Nast."

It was Nast who originated the symbols of the elephant for the Republican party, the donkey to represent the Democratic party, and the Tammany tiger. The first was born Nov. 7, 1874 in a drawing entitled "The Third Term Panic." It showed the animals of the forest, representing various papers, states, and issues, being frightened by a donkey in a lion's skin crying "Caesarism." The elephant, labeled "Republican vote," was on the verge of falling into a pit protected only by broken planks, some of them labeled "inflation," "repudiation" and "reform" with dark "chaos" beneath. A fox, its face resembling that of Samuel J. Tilden, represented the Democratic party, although four years earlier, Jan. 15, 1870, Nast had used a donkey to represent the "Copperhead Press" kicking a dead lion labeled former Secretary of War Edwin M. Stanton. In that cartoon obviously the donkey stood for Democratic sentiment rather than the party itself.

The success for which Nast is chiefly remembered was in connection with the exposure of the notorious Tweed ring which controlled Tammany Hall, the New York City Democratic organization and consequently the city government. Nast's "The Tammany Tiger Loose," which appeared Nov. 7, 1871 in *Harper's Weekly,* two days before election day, has been called "the most impressive political picture ever produced in this country." It showed the vicious tiger in a Roman arena devouring the remains of civic virtue while Boss William Marcy Tweed presided as Nero surrounded by Peter Barr Sweeny, Richard T. Connolly, A. Oakey Hall and other members of the plunderbund. It was the *coup de grâce* to Tammany. Nast had withstood attempts to bribe him to desist and Tweed had declared of his work: "Let's stop those damned pictures. I don't care so much what the papers write about me—my constituents can't read; but, damn it, they can see pictures." His corruption exposed, Tweed fled to Spain where an illiterate Spaniard recognized him from a Nast cartoon and turned him over to authorities for extradition to the United States.

Nast and his predecessor and contemporary cartoonists drew mainly for magazines. During the presidential campaign of 1884 Walt McDougall composed the first series of political cartoons for a daily newspaper, the New York *World,* dedicated to the defeat of James G. Blaine. Most famous was "Belshazzar's Feast" which showed the Republican nominee dining lavishly with most of the leading big financiers of the day: Gould, Fish, Vanderbilt, and others. Since then virtually every campaign has produced memorable additions to the gallery of great American cartoons. Homer Davenport in the New York *Evening Mail* showed William McKinley as the tool of the capitalists and pictured Republican Boss Mark Hanna dressed in clothing decorated with dollar signs.

Use of the "Remember the Maine" theme by several cartoonists helped stir up sentiment for the Spanish-American War. They supplemented the atrocity stories and line drawings which Joseph Pulitzer's *World* and William Randolph Hearst's *Journal* ran in a competitive warmongering campaign generally considered to have been among the strongest influences causing the war (see *Public Opinion and the Spanish-American War,* by Marcus M. Wilkerson, Louisiana State University, 1932). In 1902 for the Washington *Post,* Clifford K. Berryman created the now-familiar teddy bear in a cartoon depicting the refusal of Theodore Roosevelt on a hunting trip to shoot a tiny bear that had been dragged to his camp. For the New York *World*

Rollin Kirby invented the caricature of the prohibitionist, with stovepipe hat, long chin, closed umbrella, and coal black clothes. Congress
came to be depicted as an old man with whiskers as the result of
caricatures of "Uncle Joe" Cannon, longtime despotic speaker of the
House of Representatives. Tool of many a modern cartoonist is the
forlorn little mustached man with clothes too big for him labeled John
Q. Public or Taxpayer or in some other way to indicate it is the average reader who is meant. Bewhiskered leering Bolsheviks, often with
smoldering bombs protruding from their pockets; long-haired, heavy
spectacled, mortar-board-capped brain trusters; cigar-smoking political bosses, and other stereotyped cartoon symbols are familiar to
even casual newspaper readers. More than word descriptions, they
help those who look at them to get a quick impression of the artist's
viewpoint or, to use the sociologists' term, his definition of a situation,
which he hopes others will accept. That there is at least widespread
exposure to this type of editorializing is revealed by results of the
continuing readership surveys of the Advertising Research Foundation. On Oct. 10, 1946, for instance, 63 per cent of all readers of the
Cleveland *Press* read the inside editorial cartoon although only 36 per
cent perused the leading news story on the first page. A check
of the Washington *Post* for Sept. 25, 1947 similarly showed that
44 per cent read the cartoon and only 26 per cent the leading news
story.

Political cartoons are not the only type of importance in public
opinion formation. Possibly they are no more effective in causing
voters to make up their minds than are any other parts of a newspaper. In addition there are the human interest cartoons, of the type
made famous by Clare A. Briggs with his "When a Feller Needs a
Friend," "Days of Real Sport" and similar series of boyhood and
small town life; by Gaar Williams with his "Among Folks in History"
and "My Secret Ambition" series; by H. T. Webster's "Life's Darkest
Moment," "The Timid Soul" (Caspar Milquetoast), "Bridge," "The
Unseen Audience," "The Thrill That Comes Once in a Lifetime,"
and "How to Torture Your Wife"; by Gluyas Williams' "Out Our
Way" and by others of the same sort. Some saccharine and nos-
talgic, others whimsical or satirical, they are stereotype builders
and perpetuators. They deal with human foibles, with the inconsistencies of everyday life. Just about every type to be found in American

society is lampooned or extended sympathy because of the frustrations which it has to battle to overcome. Most of these cartoons are intended to produce a smile or laugh, occasionally a tear; instead of the balloons containing conversation such as those used in most comic strips, a majority of the modern single boxed human interest cartoons rely upon one-line captions for their gag effects. The difference between a human interest cartoon and an illustrated joke, of which newspapers and magazines use plenty, often is one of degree rather than kind. The jokester may have no other purpose than humor to be worthy of being called a human interest cartoonist. Some depth of understanding and motivation are necessary. The illustrated joke might be called the lowbrow's cartoon. At one extreme there is complete absence of subtlety. At the other extreme, appealing to the most sophisticated, there are the more biting cartoons in the inimitable *New Yorker* magazine which, since the early twenties have had a big influence on the work of those who draw for less highbrow magazines and newspapers. Although toned down and directed at different targets than are most *New Yorker* cartoons, they follow that magazine's lead away from the old tradition of American humor—tall tales and outlandish fables. Making fun of the policies, slogans, and smugness of Big Business and taking jibes at upper-middle-class club women, the *New Yorker* has created streotypes of the fat, suburban club woman, the elderly D.A.R. member, and the capitalist who sports a large white mustache and appraises chorus girls. Rather than exploit sex, *New Yorker* cartoonists, chiefly Peter Arno, poke fun at it.

For the Nov. 13, 1949 *This Week*, syndicated weekend newspaper magazine supplement, Leslie Lieber wrote "Cartoonists' Dream World," which, despite a tendency toward hyperbole, made cogent comment on the influence of this type of graphic art.

Have you ever read a dispatch in the newspapers about missionaries being boiled in a pot? Did you ever hear of a woman throwing a rolling pin at her husband? Is it customary for girls in your neighborhood to prop ladders against their bedroom windows before eloping? Have you ever stood neck deep in water in your cellar, waiting for the plumber? Do you often attend banquets at which a girl jumps out of a cake?

Your answer is no? Well, so is mine. And that's very peculiar because there's an influential group in the United States—the fellows who draw magazine cartoons—who evidently believe things like the above happen all the time.

The suspicion that cartoonists may be living in a cockeyed dream-world dawned on me in full force just the other day. Out of a clear sky my nephew asked why he had never seen anybody at his school wearing a dunce cap.

Henry's remark caught me off guard. Like millions of other Americans, I had always laughed my head off at cartoons, no questions asked. "Better check with your teachers," I answered testily. "If your school doesn't have any dunce caps, why, it's a pretty poorly equipped institution."

But the boy's skepticism had dented my faith in all the time-honored cartoonist themes. The situation warranted a full-scale investigation. The first suspicious character to come under scrutiny was that hardy perennial, the boiled missionary.

WHAT'S COOKING? NOT MISSIONARIES

One of my informants on this ticklish topic was Dr. Elmer Fridell, distinguished foreign secretary of the American Baptist Foreign Mission Society. "I've traveled far and wide in the African Congo," he told me after recovering from his initial shock at such a question, "and as far as I know, nobody has ever cooked a missionary. Furthermore, the cartoon people err when they insist on stewing us in iron kettles. Tribes on the cannibal level haven't developed the kettle."

One century-old case of minced missionary was reported, however, by a specialist in the Pacific area, the Reverend Wynn C. Fairfield, secretary of the Foreign Missions Conference of North America. He and Kenneth S. Latourette, professor of Missions and Oriental History at Yale University, issued me a joint report revealing that two missionaries were killed—and probably eaten—by the Batak tribes of Sumatra back in 1834. To this day descendants of the guilty tribesmen recite a special prayer asking forgiveness for their indigestible sin before entering their churches.

Dr. Fairfield said that God had forgiven them, and he wished the cartoonists would do likewise.

The question about dunce caps caused quite a flurry at the New York City Board of Education. I found myself being switched unpopularly from person to person as if there were a hot potato inside the telephone receiver. Officials put their hands over the mouthpiece as they held harried consultations. Finally Mark A. McClosky, director of community education, nabbed the phone.

"What's this about dunce caps?" he wanted to know. "There are no dunce caps, absolutely none. Of course we do have plenty of dunces. But our school system makes no budgetary provision for dunce caps."

THAT BRITISH MONOCLE

Somebody along the way had suggested that the dunce-cap habit once flourished in England. The British delegation to the UN was somewhat flustered upon receiving our query on this subject. Nobody there admitted to ever having worn or seen one; the dunce cap was completely disowned as an adjunct to the Crown.

While we were still on Empire territory, we asked the press attache about another cartoon fable: the monocle which the artists always use to identify a Britisher.

"Monocles are as passe as the gout," he said. "Austen Chamberlain was the last great public figure who wore one. The monocle has outlived its day as the trademark of the Englishman."

Next on my list for investigation was the role of the rolling pin in the American home. Cartoon tradition has touted it as the weapon *par excellence* for bashing husbands' skulls.

Our question on the pantry brickbat ambushed Judge Doris Byrne, of New York's busy Home-Term Court, in the judicial sanctity of her chambers. "The rolling pin is one of the few objects which wives in this city do not throw at their husbands," she said. "I can cite lots of pots, pans, dishes, chairs and, of course, half-empty bottles if that'll help."

Lieutenant James Walsh, a detective with 18 years experience in a precinct riddled with family squabbles, says rolling pins lead a blameless existence. "It beats me what crazy things they do pitch at each other though," he mused. "Woman the other night threw a dog at her husband."

At the police station we checked on another crime habit of cartoonists: robbers wear black masks. Veteran detectives just laughed.

The assistant warden at Sing Sing put the kibosh on still another ancient cartoon myth: "Our modern laws of penology forbid tying prisoners to a ball-and-chain," he said. "And tell the cartoonists to take criminals out of those zebra-striped suits, too. That garb hasn't been worn since the turn of the century."

As an acid test of the old refrain that goats dote on tin cans, I journeyed out to a farm to place five delicacies in front of a hungry nanny personally and record the results.

The goodies consisted of an empty tin can, a copy of "The New Yorker" magazine, a plastic ash tray, one spool of blue typewriter ribbon, and a small portion of prepared Goat Chow, a prosaic fodder consisting of corn, alfalfa, meal, oats, grains and molasses.

With one quick movement, the goat blasted the cartoonists' notion to smithereens. She nose-dived straight into the goat feed and didn't look up until the last morsel had been guzzled. Then she went to sleep.

NO STEAM SHOVELS

On the way back from the goat project, I stopped off at the Bronx Zoo to find out whether ostriches hide their heads in the sand. "Ostriches live mostly on grassy plains," declared Lee S. Crandall, general curator. "For them to dig a foxhole to hide their heads, they'd need steam shovels for beaks. When an ostrich wants to conceal himself, he lies down and stretches his neck out flat. All you see then is the mound formed by his body."

A little higher in the animal kingdom comes the dog. In cartoons, dogs always wag their tails and come running when addressed as "Fido." Charles Woodford, license clerk at the ASPCA, took a sample census of dog tags down there and found that Fido "was as dead as the dodo." Nowadays it's usually Fala or Skippy.

The faces of several Indians clouded over with a warpath look when I sauntered up and said "Ugh." It seems they're sick of being saddled with a word that has absolutely no meaning in any of their dialects. Harry Tschopik, assistant curator of ethnology at the American Museum of Natural History, said he had combed the Red Man's rhetoric from coast to coast without finding the slightest justification for the word.

A SAD ADMISSION

But Miss Rosebud Yellow-Robe, a Sioux squaw with a college degree who directs the Indian Village at Jones Beach, L.I., admitted sadly that many of her people had been forced to incorporate some "ughs" into their conversations in order to convince tourists that they're the real McThunder-Cloud.

Even the cartoonist's journalistic cousin, the newspaper reporter, wishes the pen-flourishers would mend their ways. He wishes the boys would stop drawing him with a battered hat parked on the back of his cranium. I braved the wrath of three harried city editors one night by calling them in the middle of Manhattan's deadline hubbub.

Result of the spot-check: of 175 hardened newshawks surveyed in their native habitat not one was wearing a battered hat. "All the hats here are on racks," shouted one city editor over the din. Another growled, "Try the Associated Press. Used to be two screwballs over there that never took their hats off. They saw 'Front Page' and never got over it."

The A.P. doesn't own up to them any more. And a spokesman for the Columbia University School of Journalism denied that seniors had to type 40 words a minute—with their hats on—before getting their degrees.

Next we delved into the weird romantic habits of some of the cartoons' Romeos. For instance, a man proposing to a girl in magazine sketches always gets down on his knees. We checked the popularity of this method with an NBC radio program called "Honeymoon in New York." Two thousand husbands have been interviewed on how they popped the question. The knee, their testimony proves, is extinct as an adjunct to wedlock.

Kissing booths where you can buy bliss for a buck at carnivals are another myth. According to the Outdoor Department at "Billboard," pulse of the show business, there are no professionally puckered lips in any of the 300-odd fairs operating in the U.S.

Hardly a summer goes by without its quota of gags about svelte maidens who feign drowning in order to meet muscular life guards. I checked with

Mike Borotkin, supervisor of 220 life guards at Rockaway Beach, the largest controlled sand playland in the world. "In twenty years," he says, "I've never heard a wolf call substituted for a cry for help. And if there was any, it never ended in wedding bells. That's for sure."

As for that other character who lives between the four walls of a cartoon, the barrel-appareled gambler, a visit to the "Daily Racing Form" brought this response from a tackwise editor: "All I got to say is you can't put clothes through a pari-mutuel window. Lots of people do lose everything except their clothes. But even they go home on a train. They've got sense enough to buy round-trip tickets."

NO K.P.

Another example of odd behavior by cartoon heroes is their habit of washing the restaurant dishes when they can't pay the bill. I pulled the no-money alibi in three eateries.

"The owners' reaction was calm, unruffled and considerate. No dishrag glint crept into their eyes. In fact, an offer to go on K.P. duty was brushed aside. They simply requested my name and address, putting me on my honor. Call the police? It's too much trouble.

"We just take the beating with a smile," was the consensus. They all smiled even more when I came back later to pay the checks.

So much for the petty foibles and fables of the cartoonists. It's doubtful whether our comic friends will ever recognize the world in its true light. But really, now that we know, who cares if they don't?

Go ahead, cartoonist, boil some more missionaries.[3]

Magazines

Development of the political cartoon is not the only "scoop" that American magazines can claim to have scored over American newspapers. National advertising, now the most important source of income for radio and for many newspapers, originated in nationally circulated magazines. It is difficult to think of a nineteenth-century writer of any importance whose work, including the serialization of some of the greatest novels, did not appear first in some magazine, and the same is true to only a slightly less extent today. Future presidents, former presidents and other statesmen and politicians have written more frequently for magazines than for newspapers. Magazine campaigns and often single articles have had profound effects upon public officials and consequently upon political history. Fads have

[3] Reprinted from *This Week* Magazine. Copyright, 1949, by the United Newspapers Magazine Corporation.

been created, fashions have been dictated and ideas regarding architecture, interior decorating, health and medical care, manners, and social, economic and political problems of every sort have been affected by magazines. Because of the great variety of reading matter that a multitude of magazines always has provided, there has been enlightenment and entertainment for all types of Americans. No complaint of sameness such as is often heard against the nation's newspapers ever has been valid against magazines. Whatever his interest or taste the reader always has been able to find a magazine catering to it; usually today he can choose between a number of competitors. As a result the United States, throughout almost its entire history, has been known as a nation of magazine readers by contrast with most European countries in which book reading traditionally has been more popular.

The versatile Benjamin Franklin, first in so many other things, was only three days late Feb. 16, 1741 with *General Magazine* to have earned the additional title of first American magazine editor and publisher. It lasted through six issues whereas *American Magazine, or a Monthly View of the Political State of the British Colonies,* which Andrew Bradford hastened to publish Feb. 13, 1741, upon obtaining a secret tip regarding Franklin's plans, lasted for only three issues. The weekly newspaper, *Pennsylvania Gazette,* which Franklin purchased in 1729 when it was a year old from Samuel Keimer, survives to this day as the *Saturday Evening Post,* which it was renamed in 1821. How many scores of thousands or more of other magazines have completed their life spans in the interim it would be a fantastic undertaking to attempt to determine. At latest count there were about 7,000 periodicals other than newspapers being published in the United States, with about 3,500,000,000 copies of those properly classified as magazines being distributed annually.

Suggesting the broader scope, appeal and influence that magazines from the beginning have had by comparison with any single American newspaper, James Playsted Wood wrote in *Magazines in the United States* (Ronald, 1949): "Obviously Franklin was editing his magazine not for Philadelphia or for Pennsylvania, but for the Colonies as a whole. Unformed as they were, and of short duration, the first American magazines were not merely local in content and appeal. They showed from the first the magazine trend toward coverage of all the

Colonies that developed a century and a half later into the nation-wide coverage of the national magazine." [4]

Just to list the names of some of the early American magazine editors is to suggest the importance of the medium: Thomas Paine, Noah Webster, Isaiah Thomas, Matthew Carey, and Joseph Dennie. Contributors included almost every statesman and writer whose name comes to mind as having lived during the period. The novels of Charles Brockden Browne, the United States' first man of letters, were first serialized in *Columbia Magazine*. The Yale poets, John Trumbull, Joel Barlow, and Timothy Dwight, were introduced through Webster's *American Magazine*. Throughout almost all of the nineteenth century it was through magazine serialization rather than book publication that the vast majority of American novelists and short story writers reached their publics; the roster of those who served as steady contributors and/or editors could be a veritable Who's Who of American Men of Letters of the century. Writing styles consequently were set by the magazines. More familiar to contemporary readers of how important such examples may be are recent cases such as Henry L. Mencken's *American Mercury,* which was the model of every campus editor and author during the late 1920's and early 1930's; *Time,* which started college sophomores and even newspaper and other mature writers inverting their sentences, resurrecting archaic words and expressions, telescoping and coining modern words, especially titles; and the *New Yorker* whose profiles have revolutionized biographical writing within the past generation, whose reprints filled more than 100 books and of which Henry F. Pringle wrote in an article, "Ross of the New Yorker," in the March '48, "Not merely does it set fashions; it creates and changes ideas."

Citing their tremendous circulation (at that time 4,090,659 for the *Ladies' Home Journal*; 3,586,231 for the *Woman's Home Companion*; 2,623,202 for *Woman's Day*; and 3,523,350 for *McCall's*), Elizabeth Bancroft Schlesinger said of "The Women's Magazines," in the March 11, 1946 *New Republic:* "Such a reading public would give pause to publishers who felt a sense of social responsibility and were able to shed their advertiser and reader fears." Instead, even in war years, these magazines specialize in "the smartest fashions, new

---

[4] James Playsted Wood, *Magazines in the United States.* Copyright, 1949, by the Ronald Press Company.

recipes prepared and the cult of making their readers beautiful." And in so doing they have been a powerful social force. Of the famous *Godey's Lady's Book,* during the period (1837–1877) it was edited by Mrs. Sarah Josepha Hall, Boston feminist, Wood wrote: "It affected the manners, morals, tastes, fashions in clothes, homes and diet of generations of American readers. It did much to form the American woman's idea of what she was like, how she should act and how she should insist that she be treated." Generally avoiding politics and intellectual subjects, Mrs. Hall, among other things, introduced the unknown Harriet Beecher Stowe, advocated education and physical exercises for women, and campaigned for Thanksgiving Day until President Lincoln proclaimed the first such holiday Oct. 20, 1864.

In 1889 Cyrus H. K. Curtis installed Edward W. Bok as editor of the six-year-old *Ladies' Home Journal* which rapidly replaced the moribund *Godey's Lady's Book* (it succumbed in 1898) as feminine America's most popular magazine. Although Bok did not change the basic pattern as far as contents were concerned, his was one of the most courageous editorships, until 1930, in the annals of American magazine history. In 1906, for instance, he lost approximately 75,000 subscribers and a quantity of advertising by being almost three decades ahead of the times with editorial attacks on venereal disease control methods. Under Bok the *Ladies' Home Journal* was constantly campaigning for or against something. Among the most important enterprises were those intended to promote simpler and more practical house building, to elevate taste in interior decoration, and to clean up and beautify cities. To accomplish these ends Bok ran several nationwide contests, printed numerous series of articles, heavily illustrated, and made available complete sets of plans, specifications, and estimates. Of him the leading architect of the times, Stanford White, declared: "I firmly believe that Edward Bok has more completely influenced American domestic architecture for the better than any other man in this generation." Although women accepted much personal advice which Bok gave them in a column, "Side Talks to Girls," using the pseudonym of Ruth Ashmore, they refused to turn from Parisian to American dress models or to abandon the wearing of aigrettes despite vigorous campaigns on his part.

As is true of newspapers, a magazine's deepest influence comes from the cumulative effect of its basic editorial policies. The trend of American public opinion—what topics were most interesting or worrisome, what needs existed to be satisfied—probably could be written by thorough study of the rise and fall of magazines. Of specific crusading victories there also is a long list. The smashing of the Tweed Ring which had robbed New York City of more than 200 million dollars, largely as a result of the articles and Nast cartoons in *Harper's Weekly,* has been mentioned. In 1861 *Leslie's* won a three-year fight when the New York State legislature forbade sale of "swill milk" after at least two New York City official investigations had resulted in whitewashes and a grand jury had been asked (unsuccessfully) to indict Frank Leslie for criminal libel. In 1869 creation of the Massachusetts Railroad Commission followed publication in that year's July issue of *North American Review* of an article, "Chapter of Erie," by Charles Francis Adams who was appointed one of the first state commissioners and later became chairman.

The period from 1902 to 1906 was the Era of the Muckrakers during which numerous cities, states, and the federal government were inspired, if not compelled, to investigate, clean house and legislate as the result of the exposé of corruption by a small band of brilliant magazine writers. Foremost among these were a quartet who wrote for *McClure's Magazine.* Together with the books which grew out of their magazine series, they were: Ida M. Tarbell, *History of the Standard Oil Company;* Ray Stannard Baker, *The Railroads on Trial;* Lincoln Steffens, *The Shame of the Cities* and *Enemies of the Public;* and Burton J. Hendrick, *The Story of Life Insurance.* It was the last-named which led to the famous Armstrong investigation in New York and made Charles Evans Hughes a national figure. During the same period Upton Sinclair wrote *The Jungle* for a socialist magazine and contributed to creation of sentiment for passage of the first Food and Drug Act. *Everybody's* and *Cosmopolitan* and, to a lesser extent, *Collier's,* also contributed to the muckraking literature of the period.

Although the intense campaigning of that period never has been duplicated, there have been many individual magazine articles which have been effective in one way or another, examples being Ellin Mackay's article on New York cabarets in the Nov. 26, 1925 *New Yorker;* Alfred E. Smith's "Catholic and Patriot; Reply to C. C. Marshall" in the May, 1927 *Atlantic Monthly;* J. C. Furnas' "And Sudden

Death," in the August, 1935 *Reader's Digest;* Milton Mayer's contribution to the "Jews in America" series in the March 28, 1942 *Saturday Evening Post;* and Henry L. Stimson's "Why We Used the Bomb," in the February, 1947 *Harper's.*

With few exceptions, even during the muckraker period, American magazines have been as staunch defenders of the *status quo* as American newspapers. There always has been at least one mass circulation magazine specializing in success stories in the Horatio Alger tradition. Since Cyrus H. K. Curtis bought it for $1,000 in 1899 and installed George Horace Lorimer, a Boston *Post* reporter, as editor, the *Saturday Evening Post* has been what Will Rogers called it: "America's greatest nickelodeon." Appealing to intelligent businessmen, it has been a potent defender of American capitalism and culture and has a conservatively estimated weekly readership of 10,000,000. Commented Wood: "The *Post* operated from the first to reinforce the conservatism, the middle-class sanity, of the economically and morally controlling class in the American community. To do this, it avoided the esoteric, the sensational and, usually, the adversely critical. It stressed American nationalism, American business, material success, the economic viewpoint; assumed accepted morals and mores without question and built from there. It provided information on every subject of conceivable interest to its readers, information obtained and capably presented by unexcelled reporters. It printed inspirational biographies and the best entertainment fiction of its kind, broadening the horizons of its readers' experience and at the same time providing the factual reports and sensible interpretations which enabled them to form their judgments on subjects of national concern."

By contrast liberal and left-wing magazines never have fared so well. The weekly *Nation* and *New Republic* have continued to exist through subsidies only. Whereas as recently as a generation ago there were at least a dozen intellectual magazines of comparable standing, only *Harper's* and the *Atlantic Monthly,* both considerably popularized by comparison with the old days, survive. For the sophisticates there is only the *New Yorker,* the only one of those mentioned which attracts any considerable amount of advertising, unquestionably due to the fact that its ribbing is gentle, its cartoons superb and its contents carefully edited to eliminate anything which could be suspected of radical content. In the so-called "little" magazines, though they have dwindled greatly in number, struggling unknown writers, especially poets, still find a medium by means of which to establish themselves; and in the specialized professional journals scholars and specialists are able to impress their colleagues with their wisdom. Although all varieties of what might be called "highbrow" magazines have picayunish circulations by comparison with the giants published by the Curtis and Crowell-Collier companies, they nevertheless have great indirect effect as they are read by school teachers, clergymen, social workers, and other molders of public opinion.

To survive, mass circulation magazines must "keep up with the times." The *Literary Digest,* once required reading in thousands of schools, offices and homes, didn't do so and it failed. When the depression inspired the masses of Americans to start seeking the answers as to what caused their misfortune, the *Digest* formula of uninspired and uninterpreted reprinting of editorial comment in which readers had lost confidence no longer was a formula which clicked. After the polling debacle of 1936 there was not much left to do but bury and forget the once proud publication. To take its place there already, since March 3, 1923, was *Time* and its imitators which did more than just round up opinion. In the belief, which proved correct, that many newspaper readers were dissatisfied with merely surface reporting of the news, Henry Luce gave them news plus explanation plus interpretation plus breezy defiance of stuffy rhetorical writing rules. News weeklies have the advantage over newspapers in that they can consider as a single story a series of events which the dailies must report piecemeal day after day. Consequently, they can view the news with greater perspective and can summarize the happenings of a seven-day period. Their appeal is to the inhabitant of a fast-moving, complex world who wants to keep up with what is going on but who needs someone to do the job for him of ferreting out what is important and of giving him an inkling as to what it all means. To quote Wood again: "All of the modern news magazine weeklies, as has been pointed out, arose in response to the twentieth-century American's need for more, more complete, and more timely knowledge of current happenings across the United States and outside of it, in a world where the flux of history has increased rapidly and even terribly. In part they owe their success to the skill with which they have met the reader's nervous impatience, his desire to gulp the news—arranged, predigested, and served in capsule form—as he runs. In meeting these needs and desires, by keeping public opinion well and fully informed, the weekly news magazines have added greatly to the public usefulness of all of the country's national magazines."

The same social need which accounted for the success of the news weeklies also resulted in *Reader's Digest,* founded in 1922, and a quantity of similar digest magazines. Through reading them, the harried American is encouraged to believe that he can, in the shortest possible time, find out all that it is necessary to know about most everything and thus avoid the frustration which otherwise would overcome him. To declare that the *Reader's Digest's* influence has been as conservative as that of the *Saturday Evening Post* would be a masterpiece of understatement. Several studies have shown that not more than 40 per cent of the magazine's contents are *bona fide* digests and, more importantly, have pointed out the extent to which the *Digest* influences the editorial policies of scores of other magazines in which it "plants" articles for later apparent reprint. More important still, DeWitt Wallace and his editors do a clever job of editing to create the impression that they present a well-balanced picture of current affairs. Several scholarly analyses have proved this not to be so. Perhaps the most important of such studies was that prepared in 1943 by the Committee on Newspapers and Magazines of the National Council of Teachers of English. So successfully did the *Digest* bring pressure to bear that the executive committee of the teachers' group did not permit the committee, headed by Helen Rand Miller, to present its report to the 1944 convention in Columbus, Ohio, although Mrs. Miller's group had undertaken its survey a year earlier upon specific assignment from the executive committee. This, despite the fact that the report contained only factual material without conclusions or recommendations.

Not so cautious have been many prominent members of the medical profession in comment upon one important feature of the *Digest*. In the July 31, 1946 Chicago *Daily News* Sydney J. Harris summarized from a layman's standpoint the prevailing view in his "Strictly Personal" column as follows:

What surprises me is that people are still taking sick and dying. But I am counting on *Reader's Digest* to stop all that nonsense any month now. I have been reading that cheerful little magazine for a year now (someone with a practically invisible I.Q. gave it to me for a gift), and it seems incredible that folks go right on kicking the bucket with all those wonderful new medical discoveries around.

Every month, as soon as I get my palsied paws on *Reader's Digest,* I turn feverishly to the Miracle Drug Article. You know, of course, that there is a miracle drug guaranteed with each article. Why, it's an old standby, just like the Table of Contents.

According to the enthusiastic authors of these pieces, all man's mortal ills will soon be at an end. You just rub on a smudge of special powder and your cancer disappears. One shot of some mysterious liquid and a man of 70 begins running around again looking for concubines. Just like that.

Flat feet, baldness, eczema, halitosis, caries and Parkinson's disease— all of these succumb, month after month, to the miracle drugs. Tuberculosis is no worse than a slight summer cold as long as you carry around a copy of *Reader's Digest.* The thing is better than Dr. Kickapoo's Indian Snake Oil.

Of course, the doctors don't agree, but that's a minor matter. Everybody knows how fussy and old-maidish medical men can be. If 50 per cent of the cases treated with a new drug recover, the doctors figure that 50 per cent might have recovered anyway. But not our drug-happy Digesters— they are hard at work in the Miracle Department every minute of the day.

And if some of the cures turn out to be of greater harm than benefit to patients who try the stuff themselves by way of home treatment—well, you can't please everybody in the magazine racket. And it's so nutritious for the circulation department, if I may ring a sordid note.

By Christmas, according to my calculations, everybody in the Continental United States will have a life expectancy of 150, will grow a third set of teeth, and will start playing leap-frog with the grandchildren. This isn't precisely the way the American Medical Association looks at it, but an editor has a right to draw inferences, hasn't he?

I hear, though, that a little trouble is brewing. You see, the medical researchers aren't developing new miracle drugs fast enough for *Reader's Digest,* which requires a minimum of one a month. So the word is being passed around that the *Digest* itself is planning to build a laboratory of its own, to take up the slack. Nothing like controlling the source of your supply, especially in the miracle field, which is apt to be shaky.

Once the magazine starts working on its own home-made wonder drugs, we may confidently expect bigger and better things for the human race, on the 25th of each month. Babies may be born with a full set of clothes and a year's supply of safety pins. And when the project really gets rolling, the magazine may give away a brand-new gall bladder with every subscription renewal. Sort of makes you breathless, doesn't it?

And this is one column of mine that isn't going to be reprinted in you-know-where.

To summarize, most of the points made regarding the influence of newspapers upon public opinion could be repeated as pertaining also to magazines. Present-day mass circulation magazines represent some of the greatest accumulations of wealth in the United States, and their contents contain little which would cause readers to question the rightness of any aspects of the economic system which enables them to become so prosperous. Whereas the newspaper is discarded quickly, the magazine remains around the subscriber's home for a week or a month or longer, gathering rather than losing prestige with age. Bound volumes of old magazines are a fertile source of material for students and researchers who give them a higher reliability rating than they do newspapers. Factually many magazines unquestionably deserve this confidence as they employ expensive research departments to check and recheck manuscripts. It is in their selectivity of material and in its slanting that magazines influence the thinking of readers, which means millions of Americans, an overwhelming majority of them, for good or for evil.

Advertising

Although the $1,019,707,000 which Americans spent during 1947 for subscriptions to 10,282 newspapers and 4,610 magazines, for which *Printers' Ink* collected data ($599,925,600 for the former and $419,782,000 for the latter) seems a staggering sum, it comprised only 35 per cent of the total income of these publications. The rest was derived from the sale of advertising space. With few exceptions—*Reader's Digest* being the most notable today—newspapers and magazines would cease to exist without advertising revenue; or they would be reduced to a comparatively few in number or to much smaller sizes.

Consequently, if for no other reason than its having provided the income to keep alive and cause the expansion of communications media, advertising has had a prodigious influence upon public opinion. Even more fundamentally, without advertising it is inconceivable that the capitalistic economy ever could have developed to anywhere near its present status. Scientific invention, of course, created the machine which made possible mass production, but it has been advertising that has made possible the mass distribution of the goods which factories have been able to produce in such quantity. Advertising has been called correctly the maidservant of industry, and it is impossible to separate consideration of it from that of the private capitalistic enterprise system as a whole. Much of the discussion, which has commanded the attention of thousands of authors of books and articles, concerning the effect—beneficial or baneful—of advertising, is really a debate on the merits of the capitalistic system as a whole. Wrote Neil H. Borden in *The Economic Effect of Advertising:*

"Advertising's outstanding contribution to consumer welfare comes from its part in promoting a dynamic, expanding economy. Advertising's chief task from a social standpoint is that of encouraging the development of new products. It offers a means whereby the enterpriser may hope to build a profitable demand for his new and differentiated merchandise which will justify investment. From growing investment has come the increasing flow of income which has raised man's material welfare to a level unknown in previous centuries.

"In a static economy there is little need of advertising. Only that minimum is necessary which will provide information regarding sources of merchandise required to facilitate exchange between buyers and sellers who are separated from each other. Clearly in a static economy it would be advisable to keep informational costs at a minimum, just as it would be wise to keep all costs at a minimum.

"In a dynamic economy, however, advertising plays a different role. It is an integral part of a business system in which entrepreneurs are striving constantly to find new products and new product differentiations which consumers will want. Without opportunity to profit relatively quickly from the new products which they develop, entrepreneurs would not be inclined either to search for them or to risk investment in putting them on the market. Advertising and aggressive selling provide tools which give prospect of profitable demand. . . .

"For much of this new merchandise advertising and other forms of aggressive selling play the significant role of aiding the expansion of demand and the responsiveness of demand to price reductions upon which widespread enjoyment of the products among the populace depends. Widespread usage is made possible by low prices, which in turn require low costs. For many industries low costs of production depend upon large-scale operations which are not possible until there is a large volume of sales not only for industries, but also for individual producers. Advertising may make increased sales possible not only through shifting demand schedules but also through increasing the elasticity of demand for products. Thereby it provides business concerns with the opportunity to increase dollar sales volume through price reductions and makes it worth their while to do so as production costs decrease. In past years in industry after industry the economies which have come from large-scale operations and technological development have been passed along in lower prices." [5]

Although factual, Borden's statement is by implication both a defense of advertising and eulogistic of it. Eliminating those who accept the thesis that advertising is what it is because it is an essential part of capitalism and who want none of either, a majority of those who have a less roseate view of the institution contend that the "price" which the public must pay for advertising's admitted blessings is unnecessarily high. Typical statement from advertising's critics is the following from *Our Master's Voice, Advertising* by James Rorty:

"Competitive business is war. Advertising is a means by which one business competes against another business in the same field, or against all business for a larger share of the consumer's dollar. The World War lasted four years. The depression has lasted four years. You would expect that advertising would become ethically worse under the increasing stress of competition, and precisely that trend has been clearly observable. But . . . ethical value judgments are inapplicable under the circumstances. Good advertising is advertising which promotes the sale of a maximum of goods or services at a maximum profit for minimum expense. Bad advertising is advertising that doesn't sell or costs too much.

"Judged by these criteria, and they are the only permanently operative criteria, good advertising is testimonial advertising, mendacious advertising, fear-and-emulation advertising, tabloid balloon-technique advertising, effective advertising which enables the advertiser to pay dividends to the widows and orphans who have invested their all in the stocks of the company. It is precisely this kind of advertising that has increased and flourished during the depression— this kind and another kind, namely, price-advertising, which advertising men . . . view with alarm." [6]

Economic waste through artificial stimulation of demand; encour-

[5] From *The Economic Effect of Advertising*. Copyright, 1941, by Richard D. Irwin.
[6] From *Our Master's Voice, Advertising*. Copyright, 1934, by John Day.

agement of excessive consumption practices; useless competition in luxuries; promotion of harmful products (chiefly food and drugs); awakening of cupidity, greed, and attention on a desire for material goods at the expense of aesthetically and morally higher standards; and offenses against the privacy, decency, and sanctity of the home, have been charged by hosts of critics from Thorstein Veblen to Stuart Chase. And they have been as vigorously denied or counteracted by the arguments of a larger host of defenders of advertising. To attempt to pick the winner of the argument as to whether the good effects of advertising outweigh the evil is beyond the scope of this study. To determine the effect, important or unimportant, it is necessary to consider some of the by-products of its admitted function of making possible large-scale production and distribution, *i.e.*, keeping the capitalistic system going.

In the first place, for good or evil, *advertising has promoted cultural homogeneity*, or, to use a synonym with a slightly less complimentary connotation, national standardization. From coast to coast, that is, people now eat the same breakfast foods and canned beans, wear the same style clothing, see the same motion pictures, desire the same kind of luxuries. On the one hand it is correctly contended that this has meant a considerable raising of the minimum standard of living; on the other it is deplored as destructive of individuality, robbing millions of their ability to exercise free judgment. Colston E. Warne, president of the Consumers Union of the United States and a long-time critic of advertising, told the First District, Advertising Federation of America, July 1, 1949, at Poland Spring, Me. (as reported in the July 9, 1949 *Editor & Publisher*):

"It is requested, demanded, shouted, yelled and screamed that we should smoke cigarettes, that we must smoke cigarettes. Ordinary standards of value and choice crumble under the onslaught. We are reviled to secure romance through cosmetics, deodorants, soap, garters and toothpaste. Many of us respond as best we can, often not knowing quite why. You urge us to drink and we drink, alkalize and we alkalize, travel and we travel. We buy your cars, enjoy the vicarious thrills of the movies and crowd your shops. The way of life of the nation is set by advertising. Dodge it we cannot. Pleasant towns are adapted to a 'coca cola civilization' and assume their place in a characterless procession of green-bordered billboards and neon signs.

Agile specialists in human frailty goad us on toward a commercialized uniformity, toward movement, toward ostentation, toward pecuniary emulation."

That the attempt to attain the easier and more pleasant life which the advertisements say is possible, has, in large measure, led Americans to set their goals of personal achievement higher than is true of any other peoples is indisputable. Through advertising in newspapers, magazines and circulars, on billboards, calendars and blotters, over the radio and in other forms, Americans know of the existence of better gadgets and more pleasant ways of doing things. Their desires unquestionably are multiplied many times. In the opinion of the Warnes, also increased in direct proportion are the potential frustrations as a result of inability to satisfy these desires. It is unfair, however, to make advertising the scapegoat for the shortcomings of contemporary society. Advertising may seem to be the direct cause of some herd thinking, but it is itself an effect, a natural consequence of the speed and complexity indigenous to the Industrial Revolution and its aftermath.

Lacking contact with reality the reader of advertisements certainly would obtain a warped conception of life as it really is lived in these United States. Instead, he would conclude that the nation is populated only by beautiful women, all under thirty years of age, and handsome men, all smiling and apparently gloriously happy, with clothes which fit perfectly, gadgets which eliminate drudgery both at work and at home and possessing the know-how to eliminate any illnesses or impending misfortunes before they become serious. Wrote Thomas Whiteside in "Seduction, Incorporated," in the Jan. 20, 1947 *New Republic*:

"By looking at our perfume ads, a stranger from afar would certainly realize that ours is an exotic country, peopled by uniformly beautiful, well dressed and cultured women who dedicate themselves exclusively to the friendliest understanding with the opposite sex. He would note with some surprise that few men appear in this world, and that when they do, they fail conspicuously to take full advantage of the opportunities offered them. For the women in the perfume ads seldom establish rapport except with violinists. Other skilled groups seem much more elusive. Thus, most of these attractive women wait around alone in a state of tense expectancy and frequently may be seen leaning against Corinthian pillars on the porch of some fine old Southern mansion, with tropical leaves to right and left and a lake, presumably private, in the background. An improbable reason for their solitude may be some unfortunate functional disturbance, for their heads are invariably tilted upwards at an angle of 45 degrees, which to outsiders is not normal. Whatever the reason, sheer beauty is not enough, and perfume has to be resorted to."

More generally, Agnes Rogers wrote in answer to her question, "Is It Anyone We Know?" in the June, 1946 *Harper's*:

"According to the advertisements which liberally adorn and, to a large extent, support the numerous newspapers and magazines of the United States, the typical American woman is young, beautiful, well dressed, beloved and very, very happy. Statistics, or a look at your friends, do not bear out this radiant picture, but the picture remains, and with good reason. The men who plan and produce the ads are a highly intelligent and skilled lot and they are, after all, in business. The women they present are what American women like to think they are, or could be; otherwise the products wouldn't sell . . . the census reports tell us what occupations American women are engaged in. The advertisements reveal which of these occupations American women approve of."

Elaborating, Miss Rogers pointed out that the advertisements never depict factory workers, domestic servants, shop girls, teachers, waitresses, elevator operators, beauty parlor operators or seamstresses— at least not glamorously; but they do eulogize nurses, professional models, office workers and, especially, housewives. Of the office worker, she wrote: "She is about twenty years old, rather small, brunette, and dressed well but modestly in a neat suit or shirtwaist type of dress. Her hair is perfect, her complexion flawless, her stocking seams straight, her blouse immaculate. A very lovely girl and definitely wholesome. She is very happy indeed. And why shouldn't she be? Doesn't her boss provide the finest and newest office equipment? What more could a worker want when typewriters, carbon paper, water cooler—even the paper towels in the washrooms—are of the finest quality? No wonder she smiles all day long. No dissatisfaction over salary, hours, or overtime mars the cheerful efficiency of advertisement office life, where all the girls are the same age and all are equally contented."

And of the housewife: "The housewife smiles even more than the office worker. After all, there are more things in a house than in an office. All that household equipment, all those new sheets, towels, soaps, lotions, waxes, polishing agents, her own clothes—every item in the inventory gives her rapturous pleasure whenever she uses it. And if this weren't enough, there are countless brands of food, each one of which sends her into ecstasies as she sees the pleasure—and health—they bring to the members of her family."

In "The Inconography of Advertising Art," in the June, 1938 *Harper's*, Paul Parker declared, "Advertising is, in fact, itself a religious art," meaning that it is stereotype building, reverence inspiring in depicting perfect models to be emulated. All anyone has to do to dispel the myths created by advertising art is to look about him, but the sound appeal is: you can be like this if you buy our product. No group ever has exceeded those engaged in the advertising profession in skillful application of all of the appeals which psychology has proved possible. Copy writers lucratively capitalize upon fear of social ostracism (B.O., halitosis); fear of bad health (pink toothbrush, gingivitis); the desire to be superior ("They laughed when I spoke to the waiter in French," "Men of Distinction"); the desire to "keep up with the Joneses"; the desire to be like successful persons (use products to which motion picture actresses, baseball players, and other accredit their success) and so forth. Advertising art is excellent in its composition, symmetry, use of color, balance, proportion, and rhythm. Advertising copy is persuasive through expert use of suggestion, prestige, repetition, emphasis, and direct address.

To convince readers that theirs is the way to success, power, happiness, self-improvement and avoidance of their opposites, advertisers pound home trade and brand names, and popularize slogans and other symbols. According to the February, 1936 *Reader's Digest*, Beatrice Lillie responded to a *Vanity Fair* canvass of New Year's resolutions: "for 1936 I am resolved to: get over on the alkaline side; keep kool; get a lift; refuse substitutes; start the day right; look for the date on the can; taste the difference; lose that fat; be kind to my throat; see my dentist twice a year; get rid of that tired feeling; ask the man who owns one; guard the danger line; see my grocer tomorrow; tune in again next week, same time, same station."

In 1888 George Eastman invented a portable camera and within a decade made "Kodak" synonymous with camera. Similarly people said "Victrola" instead of "talking machine," "B.V.D." for "union suit" and "Jello" for "gelatine," to cite only a few typical examples. Among the earliest of the advertising slogans, of the type suggested by Miss Lillie's resolutions, to become almost universally known was Procter & Gamble's "99 44/100% pure" for Ivory soap. Among the long-standing popular trade marks are the two bearded Smith Brothers (cough drops), Old Dutch Cleanser, and the Gold Dust Twins. More recently there have been Chessie, the Baltimore & Ohio's peregrinating kitten and Borden's Elsie the Cow to join the advertising menagerie begun with Victor's fox terrier straining to hear his master's voice. Radio commercials have made almost interminable the number of slogans, ditties, and tunes associated with particular products. Frankly called "uglies" by the profession and roundly cursed by most listeners, these singing messages nevertheless make the indelible impression that their perpetrators intend. In no other field of life's activity has the power of repetition been proved more effectively than in that of advertising. Even in wartime, when production is curtailed, the trade name must be kept alive. To consider it so well known that it will be remembered without reminders has been proved to be folly, notably in the cases of some products which once were best sellers: Pear's soap, Rubifoam and Sozodont dentifrices; Force and Egg-O-See breakfast foods and others, for instance. In 1759 Dr. Samuel Johnson declared, "The trade of advertising is now so near to perfection that it is not easy to propose any improvement." Could he return today the good doctor probably would need not one but several of the best-advertised stimulants to revive him after being told that in 1947 about $25 per capita was spent on advertising in the United States, or a total of more than 2 billion dollars. Exclusive of those employed by advertisers themselves and by the media in which their messages appear, more than 25,000 persons were engaged full-time in the trade, as he called it. They were, of course, in advertising agencies, now a Big Business, experts in handling the accounts of advertisers and thriving on commissions, usually 15 per cent, from the lucky publications.

As far as is known the first advertisement appeared in Thebes about 300 B.C. when a slaveowner distributed papyrus offers of reward for a runaway's return. In early Greece and Rome advertising generally was limited to dignified handbills or posters giving the names and addresses of doctors and lawyers, whose professional ethics forbid their use of the medium in modern times. The first attempt at newspapering in the American colonies, the Boston *News Letter* in 1704, had advertisements offering rewards for the capture of a thief of some wearing apparel and for the recovery of some stolen anvils. In 1720 patent medicine advertisements appeared in Andrew Bradford's *Weekly Mercury*. Both here and abroad until the second half of the nineteenth century most advertising was simple and dignified, consisting mainly of notices and announcements. Then it rapidly began to become what it is today, its accelerated growth being part of the great industrial expansion of the period.

A comparatively recent development, given impetus by the institutional and public service advertising during World War II, is the use of advertising to sell, not purchasable commodities, but political, social, and economic ideas. Whenever a major bill is being considered today by Congress, Washington, D. C. newspapers in particular profit handsomely from the full-page messages of the United States Chamber of Commerce, National Association of Manufacturers, American Federation of Labor, and other lobbying groups. According to the *Guild Reporter* for June 11, 1948, during 1947 the Washington *Post* had 256,500 lines or 105 full pages of such "public relations" messages. Since the *Post*, known as the "breakfast table companion" of statesmen, charges about $1,050 a page, the total revenue was tremendous. Since New Deal days it has become increasingly common to reprint, as paid advertisements, editorials, speeches, and public statements which already have appeared in news columns, often in the same papers in which they originated. During strikes management and labor both buy space to tell their sides of the story. In 1950 the Great Atlantic & Pacific Tea Company spent millions to broadcast its answer to the charges of the federal government in its anti-trust suit (see page 607). Because of the huge cost nationwide use of periodical advertising for the advocacy of ideas is possible only for the moneyed interests. If the trend continues the total effect of newspapers and magazines upon public opinion undoubtedly will be more conservative than at present. As a consequence, there probably may be expected a return to pamphleteering by poorer-heeled interests, a trend already indicated in the rise in number and popularity of newsletters, often mimeographed or produced by means of other cheaper techniques. In 1948 and 1949 a long printers' strike in Chicago compelled the four daily newspapers to experiment with the varitype and offset processes, resulting in a remarkable demonstration of the possibilities of restoring to minority groups the opportunity to make their voices heard. Thus, mechanical invention, which for a long time has seemed to have defeated or at least placed great financial obstacles in the way of attainment of the Founding Fathers' dream, may itself restore the balance.

HOW IMPORTANT IS PUBLIC OPINION?

Neither original nor unusual was the penultimate sentence of an editorial in the Aug. 2, 1949 Chicago *Sun-Times*: "In the long run it is public opinion which counts." Identical or similar language is part of the lexicon of editorial writers everywhere, and the same is true of political orators, preachers, teachers, and many others. Even Abraham Lincoln once declared: "It is true that you may fool all the people some of the time; you can even fool some of the people all the time; but you can't fool all of the people all the time," according to Alexander K. McClure in *Lincoln's Yarns and Stories* (Chicago, 1904).

If public opinion—meaning the will of the majority—is king, supreme, not to be ignored, certain to avenge itself if deceived, or anywhere close to being as powerful as its eulogists contend, its potency derives as much from belief—by persons who it is important should feel that way—in the veracity of the encomiums as in the actuality of its force. That is, as long as public opinion is believed to be mighty, by that very fact it *is* mighty. Through fear of its power lawmakers may vote contrary to their personal convictions and through hope of currying its favor aspirants for leadership in public affairs may speak and act in ways they believe to be popular.

For this reason to distinguish between the force of *real* public opinion and the *myth* of public opinion is difficult, and it becomes increasingly so as public relations counsel, propagandists, lobbyists, advertisers, and other so-called "molders" of public opinion multiply in numbers and in ability to utilize the media of mass communications. It is the objective of these technicians to convince whoever it is who counts in the particular instance that reward and/or punishment lies in this or that direction. One orthodox method of doing so is to create as big a noise as possible so as to make it seem that a vocal minority really is a majority, and not merely a numerical majority but an intensely interested one which never forgets and which acts upon its memories. Rarely do these special pleaders confess that it is their own interests, or those of clients, which they are promulgating. Rather, they attempt to create the impression that they speak for many others, often for the "peepul" as a whole.

When someone succumbs to such efforts he succumbs, not to public opinion but to the myth of public opinion. Not all apparent succumbing, however, is of that sort. Rather, there may be surrender to the tempters in the belief that one is defying public opinion, in which case he is either willing to pay the price or hopes in some way to be able to "get away with it." Just as in instances in which one behaves in the belief that he is acting in accordance with public opinion, it may be the myth rather than the real thing that one defies or ignores. It's a great relief, of course, to discover that fact and a temptation to be careless on future occasions.

Happy is he who can operate as though public opinion—either real or mythical—is nonexistent. It behooves the champion of a cause likely to "stir up a hornet's nest" if widely publicized in advance to operate quietly, even clandestinely, to "slip it through" while his potential opponents are unaware of what is happening. What those who declare, "In the long run it is public opinion which counts" mean is that such underhandedness is bound to be exposed, or that its evil effects will arouse so many that there will be rectification of error. Such presumably occurred in the case of prohibition and in the cases of many other unpopular laws. Familiarity with the business and political worlds, however, gives cause for plenty of skepticism as to whether any appreciable amount of "behind-the-scenes" skulduggery ever is uncovered. Every day decisions and actions affecting the welfare of others are taken with few the wiser. If, as a consequence, any appreciable number note a turn for the worse in their fortunes, there results what is known as an "aroused" public opinion. But there is no certainty, in many cases not even much of a probability, that the result will be tracing the evil to its source, placing the blame where it belongs. Clamor for remedy of an intolerable situation there will be, but it may result in a palliative only or in diversion of attention. Faced with a threat, real or imaginary, to life or economic security (to cite only two outstanding incitements) people will insist that those in responsible positions do something. Public opinion is not so wise, however, that the "something" always will be the best possible under the circumstances. That is, if public opinion were held to be omnipotent, it still would be far from omniscient.

Many of the questions frequently raised regarding public opinion seem to be ones in semantics. For example, "Is it possible for public opinion to exist except in a democracy?" Implied as a definition of democracy is a social situation in which there is uninhibited access to information and divergent opinions. By way of approaching an answer, imagine at least two types of undemocratic situations: one in which the people are content and the other in which they are discontented. In the former an absolute monarch or dictator or ruling class not only dams or pollutes the fountainheads of knowledge but also suppresses expressions of opposition or anything calculated to weaken authority. Does the dissatisfaction that the downtrodden underdogs feel but dare not express, their inarticulate opposition to specific actions of their oppressors, constitute public opinion? If not, what is it? Finding the correct answer, in semantic, philosophical, sociological, or other terms, is not so important as recognition of the fact that under such circumstances public opinion is not an effective force. *To be influential public opinion must as a first requisite be capable of expression.*

And now what of the situation in the popular dictatorship, as, for example, Hitler's Germany? Was the whooping and hollering at the Nuremberg rallies an expression of public opinion? Indisputable is the fact that the Nazis indoctrinated the German people by means of the most efficient propaganda machine ever operated by a government, with a tight censorship protecting the victims from competing ideas. No important instances ever have been cited by scholars who have examined the phenomenon, of Hitler's having modified a course of action out of consideration for public opinion. If he ever went slow it was merely to give Dr. Goebbels time to prepare the public mind. As a result of the masterful job that his propaganda ministry performed, the *Fuehrer* could declare, without danger of contradiction, that he had the backing of public opinion. It was not public opinion, however, in the democratic sense and it was hardly more important in determining public policy than the unvocal public opinion (or whatever it is) in the unpopular dictatorship. There was expression of public opinion all right but it was a public opinion artificially created, not the kind which editorial writers say counts "in the long run."

Even in democratic America much of what passes as public opinion is the result of propagandistic activities and thus hardly more a determinant of thought and behavior than in the dictatorships. As the preceding chapter pointed out there is far from a free flow of unadulterated information here. Even if there were, as most of the earlier chapters should have made clear, *public opinion is the result of many, many factors in addition to possession of the absolute truth about any matter.* And so it is popular to scoff at public opinion as being more emotional than rational and either to discount or deplore it therefore. Disregarding the fallacy of attempting to create a dichotomy of rational versus emotional, it should be freely admitted that public opinion is the latter. Rooted in prejudices, taboos, superstitions, myths, legends and other elements in the mores, it could be nothing else. In defense it can be contended that in the long run (that phrase again) emotions are enough. His rumbling belly is all the "information" a hungry man needs to conclude that something is wrong somewhere. For a while, hoodwinked or ignorant, he may muddle around with scapegoats and wrong experiments. Eventually, however, in a democracy, changes necessary to alleviate his condition will occur, directly or indirectly as a result of his emotionalism. It doesn't make much difference whether the hungry man yelling for bread is expressing an opinion, an attitude or an emotion. When he supports or rejects a specific proposal intended to improve his lot, he is, by definition, expressing an opinion. That opinion, however, is an end result or at least a by-product of more fundamental social forces. What is true of personal opinion also is true of public opinion; it is more a result than a cause. One might say, in fact, that it is a symptom of factors which—to speak directly to the point with which this postscript is concerned—are more important sociologically. Whatever power public opinion as an end product has is derived from the elements in the mores that determine what it is, which is another way of saying that *what really is important is not public opinion at all but the mores, morals and popular sentiments.*

We call it public opinion when people take sides on this or that specific matter. Suppose, however, that instead of the particular proposal which has been made to correct a bad situation, some other is put into effect and achieves the desired result. Presumably public opinion has scored a victory if it compelled action of any kind even though it was different from that which it supported. Suppose, however, the situation complained of is corrected in an entirely different way, deliberately, accidentally, or naturally. For instance, if people are demanding a government dole and new private industries suddenly start up to provide jobs for the unemployed, or war breaks out to bring about the same result, or pestilence reduces the potential working force so that nobody remains idle. In all likelihood any such occurrence would bring an end to the agitation for the dole; public opinion on the matter would cease to exist or would change so that the opponents would outnumber the proponents whose influence would wane.

This hypothetical case illustrates the power of events to influence other events. In such instances public opinion is almost a superfluous by-product as far as consideration of what is and is not important is concerned. Certainly such was the case when the Japanese attacked Pearl Harbor; there was no alternative but to recognize the existence of a state of war, so deeply rooted in the culture was belief that any nation should defend itself when attacked by another. Only a negligible number of pacifists were of a contrary belief. So opinion which previously had been divided as to the wisdom of entering the war became united when an event made only one course of action possible, given the basic beliefs of the nation. Belief in that instance proved stronger than opinion as is almost always the case. Even though dying of hunger a person with a strong belief that stealing is sinful will not steal. Another whose belief is not so strong may decide that the extenuating circumstance of his famished condition justifies theft but under no circumstance would he murder to obtain food. Thus, as long as deep-seated beliefs exist they act as stronger determinants of action than opinions in the same field of interest. Rather, they determine what opinions are to be. To say that it is public opinion which enforces the moral code is to emphasize an immediate cause in a chain of cause and effect. The strongest attitudes of which opinions are the verbalizations are those rooted in beliefs.

Before Pearl Harbor a majority of Americans hoped that the Allies would win and wanted the United States to aid in every way possible, short of actual warfare. Test of the existence of this attitude came each time President Roosevelt took a new step to provide such aid, as swapping 50 obsolete destroyers for a chain of Atlantic bases, sending an expeditionary force to Iceland, convoying ships carrying lend-lease material a good part of the way across the Atlantic, allowing damaged British vessels to enter American ports for repairs, and so forth. Doubtless if the President had submitted each proposal for congressional and public debate there would have been long delay and possibly frustration as a large number of factors came into play, including the desire of FDR's political opponents to oppose him as a matter of strategy if not principle. President Roosevelt's actions were highhanded, no doubt, but he got away with them because he had correctly gauged, not public opinion but public attitudes or sentiments.

In many if not most cases involving government, even in a democracy, the role of public opinion is restricted to approval or disapproval of a *fait accompli*. By approving FDR's measures to assist the British, the American public strengthened the Allied cause. Even though each proposal had been passed by Congress after protracted consideration, that strength would have been weakened. It may seem paradoxical that most of the presidents whom we regard as having been the strongest exponents of democracy also took important actions first and obtained public approval afterward. That certainly was the case when Jefferson negotiated the Louisiana Purchase, when Lincoln issued the Emancipation Proclamation, and when Theodore Roosevelt seized the Panama Canal Zone. In all these instances it was the public attitude that was important, not public opinion.

In many other instances, when the usual procedure of congressional consideration is followed, the will of the people is disregarded rather than obeyed. It is impossible, of course, to say with any certainty that a particular election result means that the people have proclaimed a mandate that this be done or that undone. Different voters support the same candidate or party for a variety of reasons. It is, however, incredible that an overwhelming majority of voters should prefer a particular candidate or party while opposing the platform in toto. Nevertheless, there is not much positive correlation between promise and performance no matter what election or congress one studies. For whatever they are worth, public opinion polls often show the public way ahead of Congress in its support of certain measures. In such cases public opinion is unable, except slowly, to overcome the power of special interest groups with a stake in the *status quo*.

When reforms are a long time coming sociologists speak of cultural lag. However, regardless of how far behind schedule it may be, progress, or at least change, *does* occur. How much of it is the result of public opinion? Once again, it depends upon how deeply you want to go in your quest for original causes. True, no new idea is of maximum effect until there is widespread conversion to it, but ideas do not originate in vacuums. Determinism, defined by the *Thorndike Century Senior Dictionary* as "doctrine that human actions are the necessary results of antecedent causes," is not synonymous with fatalism, which, according to the same source, is "1. belief that fate controls everything that happens. 2. submission to everything that happens as inevitable." History is too full of "ifs" to believe in inevitability: "If Giuseppe Zangara had succeeded in his attempt to assassinate President-elect Franklin Delano Roosevelt in March, 1933," "If FDR had lived," and so forth. Every new discovery, invention, or phenomenon of any kind nevertheless does have important, widespread repercussions. Every current idea, custom, or practice (our habits and attitudes) is the result of some past experiences of our cultural group. Nothing "just happens" in group behavior any more than in individual behavior. When we talk about public opinion we usually are talking about the next-to-the-last step in a chain of influence leading up to some specific item of group behavior.

So important are the ramifications of major events that to some historians individual man is hardly more than an impotent chip floating on the ever-present wave of the future. Possessing hindsight it is easy to interpret a train of sequences as having been inevitable. What has happened has happened and is usually explainable. Many of the chapters in history books make wars and revolutions, the rise and fall of empires, the blossoming and decline of civilizations seem to have occurred in accordance with inexorable laws. At any time, however, something conceivably could have happened to alter the course of events. Viewed historically such phenomena may be considered as part of an inevitable chain of events. You can't win in opposition to anyone who adamantly holds to that point of view, which really is rooted in fatalism, not determinism.

Just as insight is the highest form of intelligence in the individual, so it is also among groups. To predict where one is going it is necessary to understand where one has been. Those we call prophets are ones

who have been able correctly to appraise a developing situation and
to predict where it will lead. To be exact, those to whom in retrospect
we give the title prophet were ones who forecast disaster unless their
advice was taken and who failed to persuade enough others to their
viewpoint. Had he succeeded in winning his point the prophet would
be revered as a reformer instead. Whether he succeeds or fails in
selling his prescription, and even if his diagnosis proves to be wrong,
he who thinks in terms of historical trends recognizes what is called
public opinion to be largely a result rather than a cause of other social
forces. Used broadly to include all current thought in a culture, it is, of
course, a tremendous force—the greatest there is in determining
human action. Given a narrow connotation to refer only to specific
issues which can be expressed by a pollster's questions, public opinion
is of comparative insignificance.

INDEX

[673]